D0116330

Public Administration
in Developed Democracies

PUBLIC ADMINISTRATION AND PUBLIC POLICY

A Comprehensive Publication Program

Executive Editor

JACK RABIN
Graduate Program in
Public Affairs and
Human Services
Administration
Rider College
Lawrenceville, New Jersey

Public Administration in Developed Democracies

A Comparative Study

edited by

Donald C. Rowat

Department of Political Science
Carleton University
Ottawa, Ontario, Canada

MARCEL DEKKER, Inc.   **New York and Basel**

Library of Congress Cataloging-in-Publication Data

Public administration in developed democracies / edited by Donald C.
  Rowat.
    p. cm. -- (Public administration and public policy : 32)
    Includes index.
    ISBN 0-8247-7807-3
    1. Public administration. 2. Comparative government. I. Rowat,
Donald Cameron. II. Series.
JF 1351.P818 1987
351--dc 19   87-27449

Copyright © 1988 by MARCEL DEKKER, INC.   All Rights Reserved

Neither this book nor any part may be reproduced or transmitted in any form
or by any means, electronic or mechanical, including photocopying, micro-
filming, and recording, or by any information storage and retrieval system,
without permission in writing from the publisher.

MARCEL DEKKER, INC.
270 Madison Avenue, New York, New York 10016

Current printing (last digit):
10 9 8 7 6 5 4 3 2 1

PRINTED IN THE UNITED STATES OF AMERICA

Preface

A peculiarity of the comparative literature on public administration has been its concentration on the developing countries. This book is the first comprehensive survey of public administration in the developed democracies. Although there are several comparative books on various specialized aspects of public administration that cover varying numbers of the Western democracies, none of them attempts to cover all the main aspects of public administration in all these countries.

Besides covering the four democracies that are often the only ones considered in comparative courses—Britain, France, West Germany, and the United States—the book also includes the three other big democracies, Italy, Japan, and Spain, and 13 other countries. Any decision about which countries to include among the developed democracies is, of course, an arbitrary one. I decided to include the 20 that are the most highly developed on the basis of national income per capita, because the concept "developed" is usually thought of in economic terms, and national income has the advantage of being an objective measure. This resulted, for example, in Ireland and Israel being included, while Portugal and South Africa (whose status as a democracy is in any case doubtful) were excluded. Even though Iceland and Luxembourg had per capita national incomes much higher than those of Ireland and Israel, they were not included because of their relatively tiny populations. Hence, among the medium-sized and small democracies, the following countries were included: Australia, Austria, Belgium, Canada, Ireland, Israel, New Zealand, Netherlands, the Nordic countries, and Switzerland.

It is remarkable that most of our countries are in Europe, except for Australia, Canada, New Zealand, and the United States, which inherited British parliamentary traditions, and Israel and Japan. It is also noteworthy that among our 20 countries there are six federations—three in Europe (Australia, Switzerland and Western Germany), two in North America (Canada and the U.S.), and Australia. Although there are about 16 countries in the world that have federal constitutions, it can be argued that, with the possible exception of India, our six are the only true or genuine federations in the sense that they are politically decentralized. Public administration in these six countries has special characteristics arising from the fact that they are federations in which the state governments have separate administrative systems. Because of the necessary brevity of the essays, the authors for these countries were unable to include much on public administration at the state level. However, one would be fairly safe in assuming that it is much the same as at the federal level.

The book has been divided into parts that group together countries with a common historical inheritance, on the assumption that their bureaucracies are likely to have some common characteristics that distinguish them from the others. These groups are: the developed Commonwealth countries, the Nordic democracies, and the other countries in Western Europe. The countries in two of these groups—the Nordic and the other European countries—are also closely related geographically. For each of these three groups of countries I was fortunate enough to be able to find an author willing to write a comparative essay on the whole group. The only countries that did not fit this group pattern were Israel, Japan, and the U.S., which have been placed in a separate group at the end. Within each group the countries have been arranged in order of their importance as measured by size of population.

The book concludes with a chapter by Professors Aberbach and Rockman on the difficulties of trying to make cross-national comparisons in public administration, and with a comparative chapter of my own. In this chapter I try to sum up some of the recent common trends revealed by the chapters in the book and the implications of these trends for the power of bureaucracy and its influence on policy-making in the developed democracies.

A book of this nature, which requires the international collaboration of scholars from many countries, is necessarily a long time in the making. It involved first finding an eminent specialist on each country who was capable of analyzing the essential characteristics of its administrative system in a short space, and then trying to get 24 authors to finish their chapters within a reasonable period of time. Because some of the chapters had been drafted long before the book was complete, all the authors were later asked to update their chapters to the end of 1986.

So that the chapters would be reasonably comprehensive, uniform, and comparable in content, it was thought that they should all cover the main topics ordinarily dealt with in courses on public administration. Hence the authors were asked to organize their material under the following headings: the history and environment of their country's administrative system, including the constitutional and political framework; the structure and management of the system, including central government organization, nondepartmental agencies, and decentralized organization; public service personnel, including ranks, recruitment, promotion, pay, unions, and political rights; top civil servants, including their role in policy-making and budgeting and their education, social background and degree of politicization; and administrative accountability, including the role of the legislature, the control of expenditure, and whether there is an ombudsman or a law on public access to documents. I am happy to say that nearly all the authors were able to deal with the topics listed. One important topic on which several of them had little to say was public service unions, but I have been able to include some comparative statistical information on this important topic in my concluding chapter.

I should like to thank all the authors for their willingness to undertake these chapters without compensation, simply to meet the need for making a comprehensive survey of this kind available, and without even the assurance of knowing whether or when the work would be published. I should also like to thank them for their willing submission to the editor's whip regarding deadlines and proposed editorial revisions, most of which, I am happy to say, they found acceptable.

Literature in English on the administrative systems of countries whose language is not English is scarce. For this reason I have added at the ends of the essays on these countries a list of references in English. I especially thank the authors of these chapters for agreeing to provide them in English, and for their willingness to accept the editor's suggestions for turning some of their expressions into more readable English. I have tried wherever possible to have the authors use the same English terms for the same things, in order to avoid confusion (although I recognize that sometimes the "thing" is not the same, and using the same term sometimes hides important differences).

I am sure that all the authors are happy that this book has at last seen the light of day, and I hope that it will make a significant contribution to their own comparative knowledge as well as to that of the other readers of the book.

Donald C. Rowat

Contents

Contributors

Joel D. Aberbach   Professor of Political Science, Department of Political Science, and Program Director, Institute for Social Science Research, University of California - Los Angeles, Los Angeles, California; and Professor of Political Science and Public Policy, Department of Political Science, and Research Scientist, Institute of Public Policy Studies, The University of Michigan, Ann Arbor, Michigan

Thomas J. Barrington   Director* and Vice President, Institute of Public Administration, Dublin, Ireland

Miguel Beltrán   Professor of Sociology, Department of Sociology, Autonomous University of Madrid, Madrid, Spain

Peter Bogason   Associate Professor, Institute of Political Studies, University of Copenhagen, Copenhagen, Denmark

Jaap Breunese   Senior Organization Advisor, Ministry of Home Affairs, The Hague, The Netherlands

Sabino Cassese   Professor, Department of Political Science, Institute of Public Law, University of Rome, Rome, Italy

Ross Curnow†   Senior Lecturer, Department of Government and Public Administration, University of Sydney, Sydney, Australia

Audrey D. Doerr   Executive Director, Policy and Constitution Branch, Department of Indian Affairs and Northern Development, Hull, Quebec, Canada

Yehezkel Dror   Professor of Political Science and Wolfson Professor of Public Administration, and Director for Security Studies, Department of Political Science and Davies Institute of International Relations, The Hebrew University of Jerusalem, Jerusalem, Israel

---

Current affiliations:
*Retired.
†Project Director, History of Government Administration in New South Wales Project, University of Sydney/Premier's Department, Sydney, Australia

Ferrel Heady   Professor Emeritus, Public Administration and Political Science, Division of Public Administration, The University of New Mexico, Albuquerque, New Mexico

Kurt Holmgren   Judge Emeritus, Supreme Administrative Court of Sweden, Stockholm, lecturer, Faculty of Law, University of Uppsala, Uppsala, and Faculty of Law, University of Stockholm, Stockholm, Sweden

Ulrich Klöti   Professor of Political Science, Research Center for Political Science, University of Zurich, Zurich, Switzerland

Jan Kooiman   Professor of Public Administration, Rotterdam School of Management, Erasmus University, Rotterdam, The Netherlands

Lennart Lundquist*   Professor, Institute of Political Studies, University of Copenhagen, Copenhagen, Denmark

Don MacDonald   Management Consultant, Oslo, Norway

Yves Mény   Professor, Department of Government, University of Paris II, Paris, France

André Molitor   Professor Emeritus, Faculty of Political, Economic, and Social Sciences, Catholic University of Louvain, Louvain-la-Neuve, Belgium

Bert A. Rockman   Professor of Political Science and Research Professor, University Center for International Studies, University of Pittsburgh, Pittsburgh, Pennsylvania

Donald C. Rowat   Professor, Department of Political Science, Carleton University, Ottawa, Ontario, Canada

Heinz Schäffer   Professor, Institute of Constitutional and Administrative Law, University of Salzburg, Salzburg, Austria

Heinrich Siedentopf   Dean, Post Graduate School of Administrative Sciences—Speyer, Speyer, Federal Republic of Germany

Brian Smith   Reader in Public Administration, School of Humanities and Social Sciences, University of Bath, Bath, England

V. Subramaniam   Professor of Political Science, Department of Political Science, Carleton University, Ottawa, Ontario, Canada

Ku Tashiro[†]   Special Assistant to the President, International University of Japan, Tokyo, Japan

Ian Thynne   Senior Lecturer, Faculty of Law, National University of Singapore, Kent Ridge, Singapore

Juha Vartola   Professor of Public Administration, Department of Administrative Sciences, University of Tampere, Tampere, Finland

Roger L. Wettenhall   College Fellow in Administrative Studies, Canberra College of Advanced Education, Canberra, Australia

---

Current affiliations:
*Professor, Department of Political Science, University of Lund, Lund, Sweden
[†]Special Assistant to the Chairman, Board of Trustees, International University of Japan, Tokyo, Japan

Public Administration
in Developed Democracies

I
COMMONWEALTH COUNTRIES

1

New Zealand

IAN THYNNE
Faculty of Law, National University of Singapore, Kent Ridge, Singapore

New Zealand is a small country, both geographically and in terms of population. It is 26.9 million hectares in size and has fewer than 3.4 million people. Maoris, the indigenous population, number 300,000. A large proportion of the rest of the population are Europeans of British descent, Great Britain having colonized the country and commenced the establishment of European settlements early in the 19th century (1).

SOCIAL AND POLITICAL CONTEXT

Social Influences

The factors which condition the evolution of societies and the structure and operation of their governmental systems are inevitably numerous and diverse. This is no less so in respect of New Zealand than it is elsewhere. Nevertheless, for present purposes it is appropriate to single out but two such factors, an egalitarian ethos and a pragmatic tendency, which have found expression in important aspects of the country's political and administrative development.

Lipson writes of egalitarianism being regarded in New Zealand as "the core of the democratic doctrine" in the sense that where "something good is to be had . . . the New Zealander will argue, let it be spread as widely as is possible" (2). Similarly, Ausabel comments that "from the standpoint of the New Zealander, all people, irrespective of their station in life, are intrinsically valuable and important" and, as a result, "it is imperative that everyone has the same legal and political rights and enjoys equal opportunities for advancement" (3). These sentiments, while not preventing the emergence of definite forms of inequality based on age, sex and race, have clearly lent support to the maintenance of a strong central government capable of ensuring country-wide uniformity in the administration of public programs and services. An implication of this is that, as a Task Force on Economic and Social Planning recognized in 1976, any meaningful decentralization of governmental decision-making "will require considerable effort and ingenuity to devise guidelines which will permit some regions to achieve higher standards in certain fields, without at the same time permitting others to provide markedly inferior service" (4).

The other notable influence, that of pragmatism, has its roots in the country's early history; for, as Lipson remarks, it was "a condition which confronted the colonists, not a theory" and so the advancement of the society was largely to become "an empirical response to the newness of the environment" rather than something guided by consciously prescribed principles (5). The practical person quickly took pride of place in the community and has continued to be regarded with a certain awe. There was, moreover, a ready acceptance of the state's having to assume responsibility for the provision of most required services and for the achievement of other objectives of community significance. The adoption and implementation of several innovative policies and programs earned the country the reputation of a "social laboratory" in which governments of the day were able to experiment in their meeting of community interests and demands. As Milne records, however, this laboratory view of developments was relevant only for some 16 years of Liberal Party rule from 1891 and for the period 1935 to 1939 under the Labour Government (6). Initiatives in other periods have seldom been as remarkable, nor molded by a clearly discernible social philosophy.

Political Framework

Established and regulated by a flexible "unwritten" constitution, the governmental system in New Zealand is unitary, monarchical and parliamentary in form. The national Parliament, which possesses supreme legislative authority, is composed of a single chamber with ninety-five members elected by simple majority vote from ninety-one European and four Maori electorates. The Queen as head of state is vested with the executive authority of the country and is represented locally by an appointed Governor-General. The effective head of the executive government is the Prime Minister who presides over a Cabinet, all members of which (including the Prime Minister) are drawn from Parliament to which they are individually and collectively responsible. The permanent body of appointed officials directly subject to ministerial control is organized into departments which are integrated under the umbrella of Cabinet into a unified public service. The actions and behavior of officials are governed by the conventions of loyalty, political neutrality, and anonymity; also, the personnel policies and conditions of service employment are provided for in laws administered by a politically independent personnel authority.

The governmental system in operation has long been marked by political stability, with essentially a two-party contest for electoral success at regular, three-yearly intervals (7). The National Party, which was defeated in the election on 14 July 1984, had governed for all but six years (1957-60 and 1972-75) since 1949. The Labour Party held power during the periods noted in brackets and came to office again after the 1984 election. The Nationals advocate free enterprise, while the Labour Party espouses social democratic ideals; but both parties for some years have been committed to the maintenance of a mixed economy with considerable state involvement (8).

ORGANIZATIONAL ARRANGEMENTS

The State Services and Public Service

The *State Services Act 1962* defines the state services as comprising "all instruments of the Crown in respect of the Government of New Zealand, whether Departments, corporations, agencies, or other instruments," whereas the public service is defined more narrowly as comprising only those departments and other bodies to which the personnel provisions of the Act apply. As at 31 March 1986 the public service had a staff of 88,507 (9). The figure for the state services, including the public service, was in excess of 280,000. The exact figure is not recorded; however, available figures for 1984 show a total of 277,462 for the public service, railways corporation, post office, education and hospital services, armed forces, police, and other bodies financed by government funds (10). This figure, which excluded the staff employed in government corporations and companies not financed by government funds, represented approximately 20 percent of the total labor force in the country.

The central personnel authority for the public service is the State Services Commission which, under the *State Services Act 1962*, is also responsible for: reviewing and reporting to the Government on departmental structures, the allocation of departmental functions, and the efficiency and economy of departmental operations; approving and reviewing staff establishments; prescribing and assisting in the offering of staff training programs; determining the physical working conditions of staff; and providing departments with management consultancy services. In addition, the commission can at the direction or request of the Government undertake reviews and provide certain services in relation to other parts of the state services. These responsibilities clearly make the commission a more widely focused and potentially more powerful body than are its counterparts in Britain and Canada and to a lesser extent in Australia.

Ministerial Departments

The departmental form of organization is a feature of central government administration in New Zealand which dates from the introduction of responsible government in 1856. Departments as administrative devices subject to immediate ministerial direction have been used to perform a considerable number and variety of functions. Often, however, the desire of successive governments to respond quickly to the community's needs has led to the establishment of departments, with little thought being given to the overall development of a logically structured administrative system. Consequently, the responsibilities of various departments created over the years have not been as clearly defined and contained as they could have been, and the system generally has remained inadequately adapted to the demands of ministerial responsibility and control.

Following periods of dramatic growth in state activity in the 1890's and early 1900's and again in the late 1930's, moves were made to consolidate departmental arrangements through the amalgamation and restructuring of several departments (11). Subsequently, other important changes have been made. The most significant (in 1985–86) have involved the reorganization of departments and related agencies dealing with forestry, land, environment, energy, mining, post and telecommunication, transport, and trade matters, and the "hiving-off" of certain responsibilities in these areas to newly created corporations and commissions (12). Nevertheless, the departmental system as a whole continues to accord with the least advanced of the four "modes of ministerialization" which Wettenhall has identified through an analysis covering 13 governmental jurisdictions, for there are still "more departments than ministers; departmental and portfolio titles do not necessarily correspond; and ministers, lacking strong secretariat services, stand face-to-face with each of their multiplicity of agencies" (13). Thus, thirty-three departments are the responsibility of twenty ministers who each have between two and four portfolios. The allocation of portfolios is such that a few departments are subject to the control of more than one minister.

While the head offices of all departments are located in Wellington (the capital), many of the functions of departments are performed through a complex network of district offices. In establishing their district administrative structures, the departments with recognized field interests have concentrated on the meeting of their own special administrative and technical needs, with the result that there is considerable diversity in the number and size of districts and a lack of effective means of achieving inter-departmental communication and co-ordination at the district level. This emphasis on functional specialization is consistent with the requirements of individual ministerial accountability and control and of intra-departmental efficiency, but it has often been at the expense of the type of locally co-ordinated activity more easily secured through a territorially integrated, district commissioner system of field administration.

Where certain changes have been made to the district administrative arrangements they have been specific to individual departments rather than service-wide. One such change of an experimental kind involved the replacement (in 1981) of the Auckland and Wellington district offices of the Department of Maori Affairs with "kokiri" (community administration) units, which the State Services Commission has described as being "mobile task forces permanently deployed amongst the department's clientele, where they might be better placed to respond positively and quickly to the changing initiatives of the local communities" (14). The success of these units is being monitored by the commission with a view to their possible creation in other areas served by the department and also in other departments where circumstances justify their introduction.

Non-Departmental Agencies

While departments have constituted the main element of the central government's administrative machinery, extensive use has also been made of non-departmental (or quasi-governmental) agencies in the form of government boards, commissions, councils, corporations, companies and the like. Mascarenhas (15) records that these agencies, some 480 of which exist, are of several types:

1. Agencies set up to administer government services and to make discretionary payments out of public funds, e.g. National Roads Board, hospital boards.
2. Agencies that receive funds to spend at their discretion for the promotion of certain activities, e.g. Arts Council, University Grants Committee.
3. Agencies set up to regulate public activities such as licensing and rate fixing, e.g. Air Services Licensing Authority, Broadcasting Tribunal.
4. Agencies that regulate the operation of private enterprise in order to protect the public interest, e.g. Commerce Commission.
5. Advisory bodies set up to advise the government and . . . to enlist participation of interests.
6. Agencies responsible for the production of goods and services, like the Housing Corporation, Air New Zealand, etc.

Questions have often been raised about the autonomy, efficiency, financial costs, accountability and control of these types of agencies, as they have in Australia, Britain, Canada and elsewhere (16). The Government is particularly concerned to increase the managerial flexibility and financial viability of those agencies (including departments) which have commercial functions, while also providing effectively for their accountability and control. The State Services Commission (17) has argued in this regard that:

> The underlying principles must . . . involve the clear separation of commercial and non-commercial functions; the need to run the former as successful businesses; for these to have appropriate performance objectives; with both adequate flexibility and accountability for managers in the use of resources; the removal of special advantages and disadvantages to ensure a competitively neutral and fully contestable trading environment; and organizational forms, including boards of directors, appropriate to these objectives.

A Bill introduced into Parliament in late 1986 provides for these principles to be applied to the creation (or reform) and operation of all state-owned enterprises listed in the legislation.

One of the most recently established non-departmental agencies (but of a non-commercial kind) is the Parliamentary Service Commission, which replaces the old Legislative Department. The commission is chaired by the Speaker of Parliament and comprises the Leader of the House, the Leader of the Opposition (or a nominee), and four other members drawn from the Government and Opposition. Officers of the commission are employed under the *State Services Act 1962*, rather than under arrangements controlled by the Prime Minister as were the staff of the former department.

Increasingly, an effort is being made to have women appointed to various boards and committees in government. A "women's appointment file" is maintained by a unit which was originally created within the State Services Commission to service the Advisory Committee on Women's Affairs and to advise the commission on matters affecting women employed in the public sector. This unit is now part of the Ministry of Women's Affairs, which was established in 1985 (18).

PERSONNEL POLICIES AND THE HIGHER PUBLIC SERVICE

Recruitment, Classification, Promotion and Retirement

During the first 56 years of responsible government in New Zealand the public service operated virtually devoid of any established personnel policies. A *Civil Service Act* of 1866 provided for cadets to be appointed to the service only on passing a qualifying examination, and a *Civil Service Reform Act* of 1886 made this examination competitive. Nevertheless, patronage could still be exercised in appointments and promotions; also, staff were frequently classified differently from one department to another (19). Consequently, it was not until the *Public Service Act 1912* came into effect (in 1913) that the employment of staff became regulated on a service-wide basis and controlled by an appointed, politically independent public service commissioner.

As the (McCarthy) Royal Commission of Inquiry into the State Services noted in its report in 1962, the system of recruitment adopted in 1913 was based on an assumption "that most career officers would enter the Service straight from school, working their way up from the bottom, and that this was desirable" (20). Almost three-quarters of a century later this assumption still applies in that, although the holders of professional and technical qualifications have been recruited, and while growing numbers of persons with non-specialist degrees and diplomas have been attracted to the service, the largest group of annual recruits continues to be secondary school leavers.

In addition to the main recruitment arrangements, there has also been provision for the appointment of outsiders to permanent positions above the base grades. Originally, the Public Service Commissioner could appoint an outsider to a vacant position in a department only where he was satisfied that no available person already in the service was appropriately qualified and able to perform the duties of that position. Since 1946, however, the requirements in this respect have been noticeably less restrictive. The Public Service Commission, which operated from 1946 to 1962, had only to satisfy itself that the qualified outsider was "in a great degree more suitable and capable" than any serving officer available and fit for appointment, and the present State Services Commission has only to be satisfied that the outsider has "clearly more merit" than any qualified and available officer (21). Nevertheless, only a small number of outsiders has been appointed, especially to the more senior positions. Indeed, the career service and the entitlements of existing staff have been protected to an extent that surely has not always been in the best interests of the service, government and community.

Between 1913 and the late 1960's staff recruited to the service were usually assigned to one of two divisions—professional or clerical—above which was an administrative division comprising only permanent heads and a few other senior officers. This divisional system was subsequently replaced by a system which is based on specific occupations and associated tasks and such that staff are classified into and graded within some 140 occupational classes or groups of classes. The adoption of this system was stimulated by recommendations of the McCarthy Commission and, in practice, it has been described by the Task Force on Economic and Social Planning as representing a "real advance" on the previous divisional structure (22).

During the change from the divisional to the occupational system of classification and grading extensive negotiations were necessary between the State Services Commission and the Public Service Association over pay rates and other conditions of employment. The determinations then and since concerning pay and related conditions have been governed by the principle of "fair relativity" with circumstances in the private sector and, although negotiations have not been devoid of conflict, the commission has commented that the service "enjoys a good record of harmony on the industrial scene when compared to public services overseas and indeed to the private sector," and that "major disruptions experienced in some other advanced western democracies as a consequence of industrial action by Public Service employees are . . . alien to . . . this country" (23). The machinery designed to ensure this situation includes the *State Services Conditions of Employment Act 1977* which provides for occupational class reviews, pay research, employer–employee negotiations and the settlement of disputes, with the commission being the pay-fixing authority other than in respect of top level salaries which are determined by a Higher Salaries Commission.

So far as promotions in the service have been concerned, the fitness and seniority of staff were once required under the *Public Service Act 1912* essentially to be given equal emphasis. In 1927, however, the Act was amended to specify that whenever two or more officers applied for a position preference was to be given to the one who was "the most efficient and suitable for appointment" (24). Likewise, the *State Services Act 1962* provides for promotions on the basis of merit, with the factors to be considered in determining merit being stated quite explicitly. Seniority since 1927 has been of significance only where two or more applicants for a position have been of equal merit.

At the time of writing only one woman had ever been appointed to the permanent headship of a department; also, at 31 March 1986 there were only two women among the 134 officers in the administrative and senior management occupational classes, and only 398 women (compared to 5,039 men) were earning annual salaries of $35,000 or more (25). The reasons why women have not succeeded to senior positions in the service lie partly in the sex-based salary differentials which were only removed from the service's salary scales in 1963.

Subsequently, and especially since 1975, the employment opportunities for women and also for Maoris, Pacific Islanders, and persons with an intellectual or physical handicap have received close attention from the State Services Commission. Measures adopted by the commission include: the introduction of provisions which "give preference to re-employment of those who resign and are absent from work for up to 4 years to care for a young child"; the development of a scheme under which qualified school leavers from the Maori and Pacific Island communities can be employed as "special trainees" and later "absorbed into the executive/clerical mainstream of the Service"; the enforcement of a requirement that government buildings be designed, or redesigned, so as "to provide for disabled employees . . . by way of ramps, level access, and special facilities"; the modification, for example, of "typing examinations and telephone switchboards . . . to open employment to blind typists and telephone operators"; and the recruitment of, and imparting of various work skills to, a limited number of persons who are intellectually or physically handicapped "to the extent that they would have difficulty in obtaining ordinary full-time employment" (26). These and other developments culminated in 1983 in the establishment within the commission of a unit specifically responsible for promoting and monitoring programs and activities designed to facilitate equal employment opportunities in departments and non-departmental agencies.

Finally, until the 1960's the provisions governing retirement from the service were that staff were obliged to retire either at the age of 65, irrespective of their length of service, or on the completion of 40 years' service. In 1964 the compulsory retirement age of 65 was lowered to 60. Staff who commenced their service careers prior to that date, however, are able to continue to the completion of 40 years' service or age 65, whichever is the earlier.

Permanent Head Appointments

With a few exceptions, appointments to positions of permanent departmental head between 1913 and 1962 were made by the Public Service Commission(ers) pursuant to the promotion provisions mentioned above. When making an appointment the commission(ers) were not required to consult the relevant minister or the Prime Minister, but apparently the practice of their doing so was well established. Thus, Campbell (a chairman of the commission in the 1940's and 50's) has commented (27) that consultations with ministers were "sensible and necessary" and that, as far as he was concerned, there was

nothing improper, nothing inconsistent with non-political control, certainly nothing new, about this. Public Service Commissioners since the New Zealand

Act came into force in 1913 have informally discussed with Ministers their proposed appointments to such positions—that is not to say that appointments are or would be made on improper political, religious, or personal grounds. It is a courtesy due to the Minister, and the system would hardly work otherwise.

The McCarthy Commission, on the other hand, was troubled that power and responsibility in this respect tended not to be matched, for there was evidence that the commission(ers) were "not prepared on certain occasions to proceed with the appointment of a candidate unacceptable to the Government" (28). A different, more open procedure was therefore devised and recommended; but, although the Government acknowledged the need for change, the proposed procedure was not endorsed.

The new system subsequently adopted and presently operative provides for permanent heads, plus a number of other senior officers, to be appointed by the State Services Commission specially augmented to consist of the commission chairman, one other member of the commission, and "three permanent heads appointed by the Minister from a panel of 12 permanent heads, elected every 2 years by a meeting of permanent heads of the Public Service" (29). The commission in this augmented form is able to determine its own procedure and to inform itself in any manner it deems appropriate; also, its decisions are final, except where a disappointed candidate later successfully appeals against a decision to the Public Service Appeal Board. Appeals are restricted to decisions in favor of candidates from outside the service and the appointments made are tenured, subject to provisions of the *State Services Act 1962* governing transfers, discipline, redundancies and dismissals. These arrangements, which act to protect the career service and its political independence, differ markedly from the procedures in Britain, Canada and Australia where the responsibility for the making of the top departmental appointments rests with the respective governments.

Permanent Heads 1913–80

Given these personnel policies, it is pertinent to refer to available data on the social, educational and career backgrounds of the 247 officials who secured appointments to permanent head positions between 1 April 1913 and 31 December 1980. An analysis of these matters allows conclusions to be reached about the openness and representativeness of this important group of senior positions. It also provides a basis for speculation as to the personal qualities the officials have brought to the discharge of their various responsibilities.

Set out in Table 1 are occupational percentages for the fathers of the New Zealand permanent heads and also of higher officials in nine other countries. It needs to be noted that the officials included in other than the New Zealand study were the occupants of a range of senior positions and not just the most senior. Also, before specific comparisons could be drawn from the table, it would be necessary to calculate for each country the ratios of occupational representation based on the percentages presented and the occupational distributions of the total male workforce. The general conclusion, however, is that the occupational representativeness of senior officials has been more a feature of the New Zealand public service than it has been of the national bureaucracies of the other countries for which data are provided. This is particularly so in the case of skilled and unskilled workers on the one hand, and of governmental and business employees on the other. The only country for which both the skilled and unskilled worker percentages began to match those for New Zealand is Australia, which has had a similar history of egalitarian influences and a similar tradition largely of recruiting public service staff with no higher than secondary school qualifications.

Differences of the type shown in Table 1 are also found when the New Zealand data are compared with corresponding data from a study of permanent secretaries in the British civil service during the years 1900 to 1963; a study of deputy ministers and the equivalent in the Canadian service in 1953; and a study of higher officials in Britain, France, Germany, Italy, the Netherlands, and the United States in the period 1970 to 1974 (30). The findings of these studies and the data presented in Table 1 throw light on the extent to which the principle of equity has been served in public service appointments. Their implications for the community responsiveness of bureaucratic decision-making, however, are much less clear and will remain so until more is known about the relative effects of social origins, organizational socialization and upward mobility on officials' attitudes and patterns of behavior.

Unlike in the British civil service, for example, the preparation for permanent headship in the New Zealand service has frequently not included the attainment of a university degree. This is indicated by the data presented in Table 2. But as the data also indicate, a lot of the New Zealand permanent heads whose backgrounds are analyzed came to office with professional certificates or diplomas and so were not as poorly educated as the lack of a degree might initially suggest.

As to the subject areas studied by the permanent heads, it is clear from Table 2 that considerable importance has been attached to the possession of knowledge and skills in accountancy, law, engineering, surveying and the like. This marked professional and technical orientation supports a comment by Robertson about permanent heads having been educated more as "doers" than as "thinkers" (31). Moreover, it has set many of the permanent heads apart from their British counterparts, a considerable percentage of whom have been graduates in arts and the humanities. Official acknowledgment of the value of a liberal arts education for employment in the New Zealand service has really only been forthcoming since the late 1960's. Until then it had been limited to the support that was given to a select number of officers to study full-time for a diploma in public administration at the Victoria University of Wellington.

Further, when the career data provided in Table 2 are examined, it is found that many New Zealand permanent heads (unlike permanent secretaries in Britain) have been appointed to administer departments in which they had served for 20 years or more and often for their entire careers. This finding, coupled with the professional and technical emphasis identified above, illustrates the extent to which functional specialists have been favored as permanent head appointees.

Since the main issues in the specialist-generalist debate have been well canvassed in other discussions, they need not be raised. Suffice it to doubt whether functional specialists of the type noted have so frequently been the best candidates for permanent headships, and also to say that one of the great challenges facing the State Services Commission concerns the recognition and development of administrative talent in officers with widely varying educational backgrounds and career experiences.

Table 1 Comparison of the Occupational Distributions of the Fathers of Higher Public Servants in Ten Countries (per cent).

Country	Shopkeepers, Businessmen, etc.	Governmental (Incl. Army) Employees	Business Employees	Professionals	Skilled Workers	Unskilled Workers	Agricultural Workers and Farmers
New Zealand							
(1913–80)	11.3	(——13.8——)		15.4	23.8	22.9	12.9
(1953–62)	10.5	(——13.2——)		18.4	21.1	15.8	21.1
Australia							
(1961)	(————————62.0————————)				16.0	12.0	10.0
Britain							
(1949–52)	17.8	27.0	13.3	30.4	8.7	1.5	1.3
U.S.A.							
(1959)	20.0	?	24.0	20.0	17.0	4.0	15.0
France							
(1945–51)	11.4	50.2 (41.8)	8.3	23.1	3.3	—	3.6
Denmark							
(1945)	19.5	25.1	4.3	38.3	—	4.3	8.5

Turkey (1960)	16.0	45.5	—	29.0	1.0	8.5
India (1947–56)						
(a) IAS	12.0	50.6	4.5	29.2	—	4.7
(b) A/cs Services	7.5	46.7	5.2	28.2	4.2	8.6
Brazil (1968)	13.0	21.4	29.5	25.9	1.4	7.7
Peru (1964)	14.5	48.0	10.7	12.6	1.2	12.6

Sources:

New Zealand–Ian Thynne, *An Analysis of the Social Backgrounds, Educational Qualifications and Career Patterns of Permanent Heads in the New Zealand Public Service 1913–73* (Victoria University of Wellington: Unpublished PhD. Thesis, 1978), ch. 4. The main data included in this study were subsequently updated to 31 December 1980.

Australia–S. Encel, *Equality and Authority: A Study of Class, Status and Power in Australia* (Melbourne: Cheshire, 1970), 278.

Britain, U.S.A., France, Denmark, Turkey and India–V. Subramaniam, "Representative Bureaucracy: A Reassessment," *American Political Science Review* 61 (1967), 1016. Subramaniam's sources were: his own research on India; R. K. Kelsall, *Higher Civil Servants in Britain* (London: Routledge and Kegan Paul, 1955), 150–51; W. Lloyd Warner, et al., *The American Federal Executive* (New Haven: Yale University Press, 1963), 321; T. B. Bottomore, "Le Mobilité Sociale dans la Haute Administration Francaise," *Cahiers Internationaux Sociologie* 12 (no year recorded), 169; Henry Stjernquist, "Centraladminis-trationens Embedsmaend 1848–1946," *Centraladministrationen 1848–1948* (Copenhagen: Ministerialforeningen, 1948); and C. H. Dodd, "The Social and Educational Background of Turkish Officials," *Middle Eastern Studies* 1 (no year recorded), 271.

Brazil and Peru–Paulo Roberto Motta, "Social Background of Brazilian Higher Public Officials: A Comparative Research Note," Department of Admin-istrative Studies for Overseas Visiting Fellows, University of Manchester, Research Series 5 (1975), 12. Motta's sources were: his own research on Brazil; and Jack W. Hopkins, *The Government Executive of Modern Peru* (Gainesville: University of Florida Press, 1967), 72–73.

Table 2   Comparison of Aspects of the Educational and Career Backgrounds of Permanent Heads in New Zealand and Britain (per cent and mean).

Aspect of Educational and Career Background	New Zealand (1913–80)	Britain (1900–63)
Highest qualification:		
Secondary school or equivalent	25.1	29.0
Professional certificate or diploma	37.1	–
Degree	37.8	71.0
Area of tertiary specialization:		
Arts, commerce, social science	40.9 (Mainly accountancy)	57.5 (Mainly arts and humanities)
Law	10.8	13.4
Engineering, surveying, land valuation	17.0	–
Medicine, science	11.6	2.7
No. of departments served in prior to appointment as permanent head:		
0 (appointed from outside the public service)	0.8	3.2
1 (department headed)	51.4	} 43.0
1 (not department headed)	4.6	
2	21.2	} 40.3
3	12.0	
4 or more	10.0	13.4
No. of years pre appointment service in department headed:		
0	17.4	Mean no. of years:*
1–9	13.9	(1900–19) 14.8
10–19	13.5	(1920–44) 15.7**
20 or more	55.2	(1945–63) 13.9**
	Mean no. of years: 20.3	

Sources:

New Zealand—Thynne, *op. cit.*, chs. 5, 6 and subsequent research; and Britain—John S. Harris and Thomas V. Garcia, "The Permanent Secretaries: Britain's Top Administrators," *Public Administration Review* 26 (March 1966), 34–36, 38–39.

*Percentage distributions were not provided by Harris and Garcia.

**It would seem from the analysis by Harris and Garcia that this figure includes the number of years the permanent secretaries actually served in their positions. A lesser figure for pre appointment service alone, however, could not be accurately determined from the data provided.

OFFICIALS AND THE POLICY PROCESS

Factors Affecting Involvement

The questions of who influence and really determine the content and form of public policies can be as complex and difficult to answer in New Zealand as they are in other parliamentary democracies. Often many people will contribute to the development of a policy and have differing reasons and opportunities for doing so. Nevertheless, at various stages in the process the involvement of senior departmental officials is usually significant and is affected by several factors. These factors extend beyond the personal attributes, interaction, and work experiences of officials and ministers, and beyond the changing political implications of the issues requiring consideration by the Government (32).

A change of government has an obvious effect on officials and their policy work, if only until the new government's electoral promises and main policy initiatives have been acted on and effective working relationships with ministers established. The departmental-ministerial adjustments following the Labour Party's taking office in July 1984 were relatively smooth, and it can only be assumed that Labour ministers are receiving the same loyal and professional support from officials as that enjoyed by the previous National Party ministers. Indeed, in a letter to the State Services Commission in early 1985 the Prime Minister stated that "the support and advice . . . received [after the election] and since has convinced me that the New Zealand Public Service serves the Government of the day with political neutrality and with great distinction" (33).

Since policy deliberations and the parliamentary scrutiny of legislation and administrative action are now so often conducted through committees of Cabinet, government caucus and Parliament, the attendance of limited numbers of senior officials at committee sessions has become a regular occurrence. This and related matters prompted the Chairman of the State Services Commission (in 1983) to prepare and distribute throughout the service a management leaflet setting out the constitutional relationship between officials and their ministers and the obligations of officials especially when assisting caucus and parliamentary committees. The chairman stressed that whenever officials appear before a caucus committee they "are serving the minister"; consequently, such appearances "should only be with the knowledge and approval of the minister" and policies "should not be attacked," though "a constructive contribution to policy development, or to the review of policy, is helpful" (34). In the case of select committees of Parliament, on the other hand, the chairman (35) argued that:

> Officials attending . . . are there as servants of the minister; but they should also remember that they are there as officers assisting the committee. Furthermore, . . . [they are] dealing with both the Government and the Opposition, and often the minister will not be present. Without diminishing the public servant's loyalty to the minister, officials must remember that they must not . . . either directly or by silence, mislead the committee and must not conceal information even if it tends to weaken the case for a government proposal or provision. Arguments for and against a proposal must be stated, although there may be occasions when the official should tell the committee that the information it seeks would be more appropriately sought from the minister (for example, when questions relate to policies still under consideration, or to classified information of a particularly sensitive kind, or to matters that are politically sensitive).

The chairman added that "much the same type of considerations exist when public servants appear before the Public Expenditure Committee" (36). The means, however, of reconciling any conflicts of loyalty to a minister and obligation to a committee were not addressed.

Another notable aspect of the policy process is the use which has been made of committees of officials, as mechanisms for facilitating communication and the co-ordination of policy advice across departmental boundaries and for enabling their members—permanent heads—to appreciate more readily the significance of perspectives and needs of departments other than their own. With the change of government in mid-1984, the use of these committees was suspended while a review was conducted of their membership and roles. Since then some new committees have been formed. One, an Officials Co-ordinating Committee, has responsibilities in the general area of economic policy and reports on an ad hoc basis to the Cabinet Policy Committee.

On assuming office in late 1975, the then National Party Prime Minister separated the Prime Minister's Department from the Ministry of Foreign Affairs (with which it had always been connected) and established within it a small advisory group comprising staff whom he appointed both from within and from outside the public service. This departmental and associated advisory arrangement has been retained by the present Labour Prime Minister; but under neither government have other ministers been able to form their own teams of personal advisors of the type found in Britain, Canada and Australia.

Resource Management and Planning

Adopted in the 1970's, the existing system of program budgeting has been outlined by Boag (37) as including:

> first, a three year forecast of the cost of existing policies, formerly by a Committee of Officials on Public Expenditure (COPE) and latterly by a Forecast Review Committee comprising officials from the Treasury, [State Services] Commission and an operating department; second, "existing policy" reviews carried out on a more or less regular annual basis through the Cabinet Committee on Expenditure and approved by Cabinet; and third, annual reviews of ministers' "new policy" proposals through the CCEx [Cabinet Committee on Expenditure] . . . These lead to the main expenditure Estimates, the preparation of financing measures, . . . the tabling of the Budget in Parliament by the Minister of Finance, parliamentary scrutiny, and final approval.

After the change of government in 1984, the Cabinet Committee on Expenditure and the other functional committees of Cabinet were replaced by a Cabinet Policy Committee and five sector committees, each of which is responsible for expenditure in its particular area of concern. Also, departments are now required to detail in their annual estimates of expenditure, not just the personnel, financial and other resources necessary for programs to be implemented, but also the specific targets which programs are expected to meet and against which performances can be assessed by Cabinet and Parliament. This requirement, as an element of corporate planning, has extended substantially the initiatives which departments began to take in the specification of their objectives in the late 1970's.

In April 1976 the Government decided that the total number of full-time equivalent staff in the public service would be frozen at the ceiling level which applied on 28 February of that year (ceilings as a means of controlling staff numbers having been introduced in 1967). An accompanying decision was that departments would be required to reduce their individual ceilings by 0.125 per cent per month so that the annual total of 1.5 per cent could be reallocated inter-departmentally in response to special demands and changing policy priorities (38). The imposed ceilings and the reduction-reallocation arrangements (commonly referred to as the "sinking lid") sought to curb growth in the size of the service, while generally allowing flexibility in the use of staff resources. In March 1985, however, the "sinking lid" approach to staffing control was abandoned and replaced by a system of allocating staff resources on the basis of departmental proposals examined within the budgetary process (39).

Under the *State Services Act 1962*, responsibility for the efficient and economical administration of departments and for the conduct of reviews thereof rests with permanent heads and the State Services Commission, respectively; and under the *Public Finance Act 1977*, responsibility for ascertaining whether funds appropriated by Parliament have been expended not only as approved, but also effectively and efficiently in accordance with relevant policies, resides in the Controller and Auditor-General. These responsibilities are intended to be complementary; thus, the latter Act prescribes that when proceeding with an effectiveness and efficiency evaluation the Controller and Auditor-General shall pay due regard to the commission's related responsibilities. Moreover, where permanent heads undertake reviews of the policies, functions and procedures of their departments, as they are required to by regulation 64 of the Public Service Regulations 1964, the reports subsequently prepared and presented to their ministers must also be sent to the commission.

Given the serious financial situation, especially since the mid-1970's, regular reviews have become essential as a means of identifying where and how more could be done more efficiently and economically. The reviews conducted—including machinery of government studies, management and operational audits, management systems analyses, and "ministerial reviews" which are departmentally based and involve ministers and permanent heads directly—are reported often to have led to beneficial changes in departmental structures, the distribution of functions, management practices, and administrative procedures (40). But clearly there is still much to be accomplished, particularly in the areas of performance measurement, evaluation, and adjustment.

Management improvement is also being sought through greater concentration on the training and development of senior officers, with many officers attending senior management courses, with select groups participating in programs and seminars on special topics, and with others going to the private sector and to the federal and state public services in Australia under staff exchange schemes. In addition, for those in finance positions a series of financial management courses has been organized as part of a wider response to major financial management and control deficiencies highlighted by the Controller and Auditor-General in a report to Parliament in 1978 (41).

Finally, brief mention is necessary of the New Zealand Planning Council (which was established in 1977) and of the now defunct Commission for the Future (which was created in 1976). These two agencies were included by Dror in a study of "think tanks" which he defines as being "policy research, design and analysis organizations . . . as . . . distinct from policy analysis units engaging in decision improvement and management within governments on one hand; and from 'institutes for advanced study,' devoted mainly to the production of pure knowledge, on the other" (42). The commission was short-lived and had only a limited opportunity to make its mark. The planning council remains and has generated considerable discussion and awareness within government and the community of planning perspectives and of various options for the future development of the country. The council comprises the Minister of National Development, the Secretary to the Treasury, and six other members appointed by the Governor-General on the recommendation of the minister.

THE OMBUDSMEN AND OFFICIAL INFORMATION

Ombudsmen

In October 1962 New Zealand became the first English-speaking country to appoint an ombudsman. Since that time several other countries have followed suit, often drawing on New Zealand's experience and similarly wishing to establish an accessible and effective means of redressing administrative grievances. The need for such means and for legislation promoting access to official information has arisen partly because of defects in the traditional mechanisms of administrative scrutiny and control.

There presently are two ombudsmen in New Zealand (one being designated Chief Ombudsman) and provision exists for others to be appointed. This change in number was introduced under the *Ombudsmen Act 1975* which replaced the *Parliamentary Commissioner (Ombudsman) Act 1962* and which added the administrative organizations of the country's numerous local government authorities to the ombudsmen's established jurisdiction over central government departments and specified non-departmental agencies.

The ombudsmen are officers of Parliament and are appointed by the Governor-General on a resolution of Parliament for terms of five years. Their jurisdiction relates to matters of administration, exclusive of ministerial decisions and the decisions of elected councils or boards, but not of the advice given to ministers, councils or boards. They are authorized to conduct investigations on their own motion, on receipt of a special reference from the Prime Minister or from a committee of Parliament, and on the basis of written complaints from members of the public—with some 1,500 to 2,000 complaints being received annually (43). On completion of an investigation, they are unable to demand compliance with any recommendations made to a department, agency or local body. Their persuasive armory, however, is significant and includes the right (which has seldom had to be exercised) to raise a matter with the Prime Minister and thereafter to bring it to the attention of Parliament.

Official Information

On 1 July 1983 the principle of open government in New Zealand acquired a more positive meaning than it had ever had before. The *Official Information Act 1982*, which came into force on that date, repealed the *Official Secrets Act 1951* and established in respect of the work of some 170 departments and non-departmental agencies a legal presumption in favor of the disclosure of official information other than where non-disclosure is justified in accordance with specified criteria. The spirit of the Act therefore is quite clear, and no doubt the *Directory of Official Information* (compiled pursuant to provisions of the Act) is proving to be a useful guide to persons who wish to gain access to various documents. The Act itself, however, is complex and the exemption criteria are stated in broad terms. Consequently, it is not surprising that the ombudsmen, being the review authorities under the Act, have had to respond to a sizable number of access-related requests for investigation and review (44).

Obviously, a few years will need to pass before the political, administrative and community impact of the Act can be thoroughly evaluated. By the end of March 1984, however, the State Services Commission was able to record that "the resource implications have been much less than some had forecast and it appears likely that few, if any, additional resources will be required" (45). In reports for 1984–85 and 1985–86, the issue of resources was not even raised by the commission—thus indicating its insignificance as compared to the situation in Australia, for example, where freedom of information legislation has been operative at the national level at a considerable financial cost since late 1982.

Under the New Zealand Act provision is made for the State Services Commission to advise and assist departments and other agencies in the meeting of the Act's requirements. There is also an independent Information Authority which is responsible for reviewing the ambit and operation of the Act, with particular emphasis on the manner in which information is obtained and supplied. This authority has a limited life, as the Act provides for it to be dissolved on 30 June 1988.

CONCLUDING COMMENTS

New Zealand's adoption of a Westminster system of responsible parliamentary government naturally has meant that the structures and processes of administration examined in this chapter have much in common with the arrangements in Britain, Canada and Australia. This will be quite apparent if the above discussion is read in conjunction with the following chapters. On the other hand, it will be equally apparent that each of the systems considered has had its own distinctive history and characteristics. New Zealand, for instance, led the English-speaking world in the establishment of an office of ombudsman but, subsequently, it has chosen not to complement this office with other elaborate mechanisms of administrative review of the kind developed in Australia in the 1970's. Moreover, the social representativeness of New Zealand's top public service officials is particularly noteworthy; yet, surprisingly, the egalitarian influence which is evident in this finding has only recently been reflected in moves to enhance the employment opportunities within the service for women, ethnic minorities and the handicapped and, in this respect, the experience has simply paralleled developments in Australia and Canada.

Over the last few years in New Zealand there has been a lot of talk about the need for administrative reform and the possible means of achieving it (46). An important response of the Government with respect to the commercial aspects of state activity was referred to earlier in the discussion; but subsequent to the completion of this chapter, the reorganization of the public sector has been pursued much more extensively and with more vigor than was then anticipated. Indeed, the country's administrative system is now being radically transformed; so, in the near future, the new order of personnel policies, management practices and techniques, and the structures and responsibilities of departments and non-departmental agencies in the form of statutory boards and limited liability companies will stand in marked contrast to the order described above (47).

REFERENCES

1. Department of Statistics, *New Zealand Official Yearbook 1985* (Wellington: Government Printer, 1985), 5, 67, 69, 95.
2. Leslie Lipson, *The Politics of Equality* (Chicago: University of Chicago Press, 1948), 8.
3. David P. Ausabel, *The Fern and the Tiki* (New York: Holt, Rinehart and Winston, 1965), 27.
4. *New Zealand at the Turning Point*, Report of the Task Force on Economic and Social Planning (Wellington: Government Printer, 1976), 152–53.
5. *Op. cit.*, 148–49.
6. R. S. Milne, *Political Parties in New Zealand* (London: Oxford University Press, 1966), 8.
7. See Hyam Gold (ed.), *New Zealand Politics in Perspective* (Wellington: Longman Paul, 1985).
8. *New Zealand at the Turning Point, op. cit.*, 269.
9. *Report of the State Services Commission* (Appendix to the Journals of the House of Representatives (AJHR), G.3, 1986), 27.
10. Department of Statistics, *op. cit.*, 957.
11. See R. J. Polaschek, *Government Administration in New Zealand* (Wellington: New Zealand Institute of Public Administration [NZIPA]/London: Oxford University Press, 1958), chs. 1, 2.
12. *Report of the State Services Commission, op. cit.*, 7–9.
13. R. L. Wettenhall, "Modes of Ministerialisation Part I: Towards a Typology–The Australian Experience" and "Modes of Ministerialisation II: From Colony to State in the Twentieth Century," *Public Administration* 54 (Spring, Winter 1976), 1–20, 425–51 (at 437).
14. *Report of the State Services Commission* (AJHR, G. 3, 1982), 14. For an assessment of the units, see I. P. Puketapu, "Reform From Within?" in C. Burns (ed.), *The Path to Reform* (Wellington: NZIPA/Government Printer, 1982), 40–61.
15. R. C. Mascarenhas, "Quasi-Governmental Bodies in New Zealand," *Public Sector* 7 (June 1984), 2. Also on non-departmental agencies, see R. C. Mascarenhas, *Public Enterprise in New Zealand* (Wellington: NZIPA, 1982); and D. R. Hutton, *The Role of Statutory Boards in N.Z. Public Administration* (Wellington: NZIPA, 1980).
16. On significant events concerning two of these agencies, see *Report of the Royal Commission to Inquire into the Crash on Mount Erebus, Antarctica of a DC10 Aircraft Operated by Air New Zealand Limited* (Wellington: Government Printer, 1981); and *Report of the Commission of Inquiry into the Marginal Lands Board Loan Affair* (Wellington: Government Printer, 1980).
17. *Report of the State Services Commission* (AJHR, G.3, 1986), 5. Also see the State Services Commission, *New Directions* 4 (Nov. 1986).
18. *Reports of the State Services Commission* (AJHR, G.3, 1982, 1984, 1985), 16–17, 21, 11–12.
19. See Lipson, *op. cit.*, 150–63, 422–32; and Polaschek, *op. cit.*, 93–111.
20. *The State Services in New Zealand*, Report of the (McCarthy) Royal Commission of Inquiry (Wellington: Government Printer, 1962), 223.
21. *Public Service Amendment Act 1946*, s. 12 and the *State Services Act 1962*, s. 26.

2^   *Op. cit.*, 262. The old structure also comprised an educational division and a general
       division in addition to the professional, clerical and administrative divisions.

23.   *Report of the State Services Commission* (AJHR, G.3, 1982), 7. On public service
       union activity, see the three discussions entitled "The Changing Face of State
       Unionism," *Public Sector* 2 (Spring 1979), 2–5.

24.   *Public Service Amendment Act 1927*, s. 8.

25.   *Report of the State Services Commission* (AJHR, G.3, 1986), 28, 30, 32. The em-
       ployment of women in the service is discussed by Barbara Holt, "Sex and the Public
       Service," *Public Sector* 2 (Summer 1979), 5–6; and Thomas B. Smith, *The New
       Zealand Bureaucrat* (Wellington: Cheshire, 1974), ch. 13.

26.   *Report of the State Services Commission* (AJHR, G.3, 1981), 4–6.

27.   R. M. Campbell, "Public Service Commission in Operation," *New Zealand Journal
       of Public Administration* 12 (Sept. 1949), 41, 51.

28.   *Op. cit.*, 264.

29.   *State Services Act 1962*, s. 29.

30.   See John S. Harris and Thomas V. Garcia, "The Permanent Secretaries: Britain's
       Top Administrators," *Public Administration Review* 26 (March 1966), 32–33; John
       Porter, "Higher Public Servants and the Bureaucratic Elite in Canada," *Canadian
       Journal of Economics and Political Science* 24 (Nov. 1958), 494; and Joel D.
       Aberbach, *et al., Bureaucrats and Politicians in Western Democracies* (Cambridge:
       Harvard University Press, 1981), 55, 62–65.

31.   J. F. Robertson, "Efficiency and Economy in the New Zealand Public Service,"
       New Zealand Journal of Public Administration 28 (Sept. 1965), 92.

32.   See R. M. Alley (ed.), *State Servants and the Public in the 1980s* (Wellington:
       NZIPA, 1980); T. M. Berthold (ed.), *The Accountability of the Executive*
       (Wellington: NZIPA, 1981); B. V. J. Galvin, "Some Reflections on the Operation
       of the Executive," *New Zealand Political Studies Association Newsletter* 7 (Aug.
       1982), 8–34; Aynsley J. Kellow, "The Policy Roles of Bureaucrats and Politicians
       in New Zealand," *Politics* 19 (Nov. 1984), 43–53; J. F. Robertson, "Changes in the
       Machinery of Government and Their Effects on Senior Officials," *Public Administra-
       tion* (N.Z.) 40 (March 1978), 31–49; and Smith, *op. cit.*, ch. 11.

33.   As quoted in the *Report of the State Services Commission* (AJHR, G.3, 1985), 7.

34.   M. C. Probine, "The Public Service and Ministers," *Public Sector* 6 (Dec. 1983), 22
       (reprinted from the State Services Commission, *Management Leaflet* 6 [June 1983]).

35.   *Ibid.*

36.   *Ibid.* For comments on the chairman's remarks, see J. L. Roberts, "The Public
       Service and Ministers," *Public Sector* 6 (Dec. 1983), 25–28.

37.   P. W. Boag, "Responses to Overload: A New Zealand Perspective," *Australian
       Journal of Public Administration* 43 (March 1984), 63.

38.   *Ibid.*, 63–64; and *Report of the State Services Commission* (AJHR, G. 3, 1977), 18.

39.   *Report of the State Services Commission* (AJHR, G. 3, 1985), 9–10.

40.   E.g., see Boag, *op. cit.*, 64–65, 67–68; and *Reports of the State Services Commission*
       (AJHR, G.3, 1980, 1983, 1984, 1985, 1986), 4–6, 4–8, 7–9, 10–15, 4–10.

41.   *Report of the Controller and Auditor-General on Financial Management and Control
       in Administrative Government Departments* (AJHR, B. 1, 1978).

42.   Yehezkel Dror, "Required Breakthroughs in Think Tanks," *Policy Sciences* 16
       (Feb. 1983), 199–200. For further details on the two agencies, see the *New Zealand
       Planning Act 1977* and the *New Zealand Planning Act 1982*.

43.   Statistical summaries of the complaints received and responded to are provided in
       the ombudsmen's annual reports to Parliament—see, e.g., *Report of the Ombudsmen*
       (AJHR, A.3, 1986), 21–22. On the work and impact of the ombudsmen, see L. B.

Hill, *The Model Ombudsman* (Princeton: Princeton University Press, 1976); and the series of articles in the *Victoria University of Wellington Law Review* 12 (Sept. 1982).

44. See, e.g., *Report of the Ombudsmen, ibid.*, 8, 22–24.

45. *Report of the State Services Commission* (AJHR, G.3, 1984), 20. Assessments of the Act and its initial effects are provided in R. J. Gregory (ed.), *The Official Information Act: A Beginning* (Wellington: NZIPA, 1984).

46. This perceived need for reform has been the central theme of three of the recent annual conventions of the NZIPA—see Alley, *op. cit.*; Berthold, *op. cit.*; and Burns, *op. cit.*

47. For recent, detailed discussions of these and related reforms (which are becoming increasingly more extensive), see: Geoffrey Palmer, *Unbridled Power: An Interpretation of New Zealand's Constitution and Government*, 2nd ed. (Auckland: Oxford University Press, 1987), ch. 6; John Roberts, *Politicians, Public Servants and Public Enterprise* (Wellington: Victoria University Press, 1987), especially chs. 6 and 7; John Roberts, "Ministers, The Cabinet and Public Servants" in Jonathan Boston and Martin Holland (eds.), *The Fourth Labour Government: Radical Politics in New Zealand* (Auckland: Oxford University Press, 1987), ch. 6; and Robert Gregory, "The Reorganisation of the Public Sector: The Quest For Efficiency," in *ibid.*, ch. 7.

2

Australia

ROGER L. WETTENHALL
Canberra College of Advanced Education, Canberra, Australia

ROSS CURNOW
University of Sydney, Sydney, Australia

HISTORY AND ENVIRONMENT OF ADMINISTRATIVE SYSTEM

Derivative and Indigenous Influences

Australians are often told that their system of government and public administration
is modeled on that of the two major Anglo-Saxon powers, with Britain having contributed the basic pattern of responsible parliamentary government and America the
federal structure. Although there is much force in this conventional argument, it does
not allow for the considerable indigenous innovation and experimentation which has
taken place. The derivative and innovative strands have intermingled over the years
to produce a pattern which, in the later 20th century, exhibits a number of distinctive
features while still remaining firmly embedded within the governmental sub-culture of
Western parliamentary democracies (1).

Federation

The Commonwealth of Australia came into being in 1901 when the British colony-
states of New South Wales, Victoria, Queensland, South Australia, Western Australia
and Tasmania joined to devolve certain clearly defined governmental powers to a
seventh government and parliament to be chosen directly by their several electorates
voting together. Sections of the state public services now moved to the new Commonwealth service, but the state systems remained to handle all but the functions specified
for transfer. The six state constitutions also remained in force; the seventh (Commonwealth) constitution was enacted by the British parliament but, contrary to the
Canadian situation, it provided for internal Australian amendment by a referendum
process. A High Court was established to decide disputes on constitutional matters
and to act as a court of appeal from state courts—although appeal to the Privy
Council in London was not eliminated, and has been only slowly restricted over the
intervening years.

Drafted much later than the state constitutions, the machinery-of-government sections of the Commonwealth constitution were based on a much clearer appreciation

of the Westminster prescriptions for responsible parliamentary government. The parliament-executive government-public service links are therefore more clearly defined. But this constitution also borrowed from the United States and Canada in formulating the federal relationships, and from Switzerland for methods of amendment. Like Canada, Australia mixes federation with Westminster-style responsible government, and the combination is not without tension (2).

Post-Federation Developments

The last main ingredient of the Australian constitutional system was installed in 1911, when two separately administered internal territories (Northern Territory and Australian Capital Territory) were transferred to the Commonwealth by the states of South Australia and New South Wales respectively. Today they complement a number of external territories in near Pacific and Indian Ocean waters and on the Antarctic mainland. In 1978 many of the attributes of state-level self-government were given to the Northern Territory, adding an eighth to the Australian family of major governments.

Over the years since federation there has been spectacular growth in Commonwealth and state governments alike, reflected in the embracing of many new functions at both levels, a trebling or quadrupling in the number of ministers and departments (with a smaller increase in the number of MPs generally), and dramatic expansion in the sizes of the public services. The several Australian governments have also become great users of the device of the statutory authority, first restored to favor in its public enterprise (or government-in-business) application in the reform of the Victorian railway enterprise in 1883: these statutory authorities employ roughly three-quarters of all

Table 1   Australian Public Sector Employment (as at 30 June 1982—in '000s).

Jurisdiction	Public Service	Other (mostly in statutory authorities)	Total
A. Commonwealth	151.0	251.1	402.1
B. States & Territory:			
New South Wales	76.3	263.3	339.6
Victoria	35.8	233.3	269.1
Queensland	49.8	107.6	157.4
Western Australia	15.0	92.4	107.4
South Australia	14.6	84.3	98.9
Tasmania	6.7	30.1	36.8
Northern Territory	9.8	4.4	14.2
Sub-totals	208.0	815.4	1023.4
C. Local government (aggregate only)	—	—	133.4
Totals	359.0	1066.5	1558.9

Source: Ref. (9).

Australian public sector personnel. Public sector employment in Australia constituted some 24.4 per cent of the total workforce of 6,378,700 in mid-1982: Table 1 gives some idea of the major components of this employment.

There has been a gradual but fairly steady accretion of power to the Common-wealth, both because the financial center of gravity has moved in that direction and because of a number of centralizing High Court decisions. But "states' rights" remain an important value and often a popular electoral catchcry, and *formal* amendments to the constitution have been few. In their absence, there has been a significant effort to construct intergovernmental co-ordinating and linking devices: now many hundreds of ministerial and official councils and committees, some of them with statutory power, exist to lubricate the workings of the federal system.

STRUCTURE AND MANAGEMENT

Central Government Organization

Almost inevitably, students wishing to view Australian public administration from an international-comparative perspective concern themselves mainly with Commonwealth (or national) administration, and this centralist focus is observed for most of the present chapter. Readers are, however, reminded that the state administrative systems have historical priority, and that together they employ the bulk of the nation's public-sector personnel.

In Australia, as in other parliamentary countries, ministers are chosen from among the parliamentary leadership of the majority party or coalition in the legislature and collectively form "the government of the day." For most of the Commonwealth's history they have also formed the cabinet, although the recent tendency—following British custom—has been to limit cabinet membership to an inner group of ministers. Almost invariably the majority party leader is commissioned by the Governor-General to form a government. In Labor governments the ministers are elected by the "caucus" (i.e. the whole parliamentary membership of the party), whereas non-Labor prime ministers choose their own ministry. In the second Hawke Government appointed in December 1984, there were 27 ministers in all, 17 forming the cabinet. Departmental titles correspond to portfolio titles, and a one-to-one ratio between ministers and departments is generally observed. In the 1984 government one minister administered two closely related departments; otherwise each minister administered a single department (4).

The Westminster conventions of collective and individual responsibility of ministers are generally followed, with the usual qualifications encountered in all Westminster systems today, and perhaps a few special ones related mostly to the politics of coalition-building (i.e. some concessions have to be made where significant policy differences exist between the coalition partners) and the development of administrative-law accountability (to be discussed below). Decisions of government requiring formal legal expression are ratified by the Executive Council of ministers presided over by the Governor-General.

While the Governor-General's functions are seen mostly as formal and ceremonial, the events of November 1975 (when the incumbent Governor-General terminated the commission of a duly elected government which failed to gain parliamentary approval for its budget) show that that office holds significant discretionary powers capable of being exercised in times of political crisis. There is inevitable argument about the extent of these powers, bound up with questions about the role of the Senate (or upper house), in which the smaller states have equal representation with the larger— for it was the Senate which denied the 1975 government its budget. Other current debate centers on the question whether the constitution prohibits the appointment of two ministers to a single department; up till now, governments have generally assumed that it does.

The departments are staffed under the provisions of the Public Service Act, which has traditionally divided personnel authority between a Public Service Board originally established to develop and protect the merit system of non-political appointments and promotions, and the secretaries of departments (analogous to British permanent secretaries and Canadian deputy ministers). The Board is itself a statutory authority formally free from ministerial direction; however (subject to recent changes to be noted below) its powers were expanded over the years to include the fixing of departmental establishments and classifications, the determination of wages and conditions of employment and (from time to time) the administration of government-imposed staff ceiling schemes, and in such areas which are often politically sensitive it has not been able to operate with the autonomy originally intended. Its role has nevertheless been a vital one in establishing compatibility of employment standards across the functionally disparate departments. Other co-ordinating instruments are the Treasury and the Department of Finance, which handle the policy and operational sides respectively of each Commonwealth budget, the Department of Administrative Services which similarly co-ordinates in areas such as property management, and the Auditor-General, a statutory official traditionally regarded as the "watchdog of parliament."

Statutory Authorities

The Auditor-General and Public Service Commissioner (forerunner of today's Board) were probably the earliest autonomous agencies to be set up under the Commonwealth jurisdiction. Their form—that of the statutory authority empowered by the legislature to perform public functions outside the areas of direct ministerial control, and usually itself reporting to parliament on its work—has, however, been copied again and again by successive parliaments. Today there are between 250 and 300 such authorities at the national level alone. They range from huge managerial corporations running major public enterprises (banks, airlines, shipping services, railways, posts, telecommunications, broadcasting and television, etc.), through executive bodies undertaking closely defined tasks (such as conducting elections, determining taxation assessments and organizing the nations' bicentennial celebrations scheduled for 1988), commodity boards (for all the main areas of primary production) and regulatory bodies (e.g. for the broadcasting and insurance industries), to tribunals and review boards re-assessing decisions made in other parts of the administrative system. Though statutory classification of these authorities is (compared with the Canadian situation) immature, much effort has been devoted since the mid–1970s to exploring and codifying this hitherto largely uncharted area of Commonwealth administration (5).

Some of these authorities are staffed, along with the departments, under the provisions of the Public Service Act; but many, including the larger commercially oriented bodies, constitute entirely separate employment "services." Many of them have the legal personality of bodies corporate, but not all. Some are profitable by commercial standards, and return dividend, interest and/or taxation payments to the central revenue fund; some, from their earnings, contribute heavily to their own capital development; others are funded partly or entirely from the central revenue fund.

Decentralized Organization and State Administration

Here it is useful to employ the categories used by A. W. Macmahon in his classic US/ Indian study *Delegation and Autonomy* (6). As indicated in Figure 1, the cabinet/ departmental organization stands at the centralization pole of the centralization-decentralization spectrum for the Commonwealth. Since World War II the central departments have increasingly been establishing their own networks of field offices in all the major centers of population, these offices occupying ever more obviously the "administrative deconcentration" ground just to the right of that pole. Further to the right, the "statutory devolution" ground is, in its functional division, heavily occupied by the statutory authorities which have already been described. In its territorial division, however, this ground is occupied only by the Northern Territory with its own post-1978 government conferred by act of the Commonwealth parliament. Otherwise there are no effective lower-level governments (like local/municipal governments) within the Commonwealth's jurisdiction, the Australian Capital Territory having so far always been directly administered by central departments and associated statutory bodies.

The six Australian state governments, with their own separate constitutions entrenched by provisions of the Commonwealth constitution, occupy ground near the pole of decentralization. For each of them, of course (and for the NT government), it is possible to visualize another such spectrum, identifying and locating relevant cabinets, ministers and central departments; field offices of departments; functional statutory authorities; and territorial local/municipal governments. The states too make vast use of the field office method of minimal decentralization; and even vaster use of statutory authorities (a recent survey located more than 9,000 of them in Victoria alone) (7). And there were, as from mid–1986, some 835 general-purpose local governments distributed among the seven systems as follows:

Victoria	210
New South Wales	175
Western Australia	139
Queensland	134
South Australia	124
Tasmania	46
Northern Territory	7

In New South Wales there were also some 50-odd specified-purpose "county councils" superimposed on the local government map (8).

One consequence of this pattern of decentralization is that regions away from the capitals have become crowded with administrative agencies and officials representing a great variety of organizations answering to all three levels of government, Commonwealth, state and local. A sense of regional identity is for this reason difficult to achieve, and there are few opportunities or rewards for people seeking to serve integrated *regional* public interests. The Australian federation has not achieved the

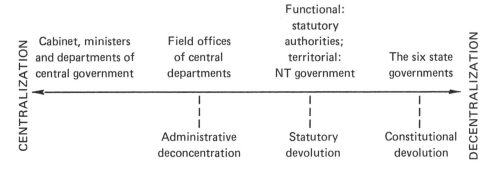

Figure 1   The Macmahon Spectrum—Australian Commonwealth.

apparent simplicity of the West German system, where greater attention to the rationality of decentralization has led the federal government to delegate the performance of many of its functions to the states, and the states the performance of many of theirs to community-level governments.

It remains here to note that, in one important respect, the apparatus of *central* government in the Australian states differs markedly from that of the Commonwealth. When self-government came (mostly in the 1850s), none of the states adjusted its departmental machinery to ensure that each minister would have just one department (or one portfolio) to administer. In consequence there are in each state many more departments and portfolios than ministers, often titles of ministers and departments do not coincide, and few ministers are provided with co-ordinating public service secretariats to match their own responsibility-spans. Many other stylistic differences flow also from the essential historical fact that, in the states, pre-existing administrative systems endured with little change when the relevant political systems underwent virtually total transformation. The states have long seemed to have focused their organizational energies primarily on developing the technical, operational, and service-delivery sides of government; nevertheless they have done much since the early 1970s to improve their policy structures to enable them better to match Commonwealth capability in this area.

PUBLIC SERVICE PERSONNEL

The Traditional Divisional Structure

From the early 1920s the Commonwealth public service was divided clearly and simply into four "divisions." The *first* comprised permanent heads of departments and a few other high officers with permanent head powers (usually in large statutory authorities staffed under the Public Service Act). The *second* encompassed senior policy-advising and executive personnel, mostly working in departmental head offices but sometimes also heading state-branch offices of Commonwealth departments. The *third* contained the great bulk of clerical and professional staff. And the *fourth* included large groups of operative personnel engaged, for example, in manipulative, keyboard, technical and general assisting work. The numbers of full-time staff in the four divisions were reported in 1983-1984 to be: 1st, 31; 2nd, 1,489; 3rd, 76,674;

4th, 87,805. This public service staff complement was also distributed among permanent, temporary and exempt categories ("exempts" were staff engaged directly by departments and exempted from some provisions of the Public Service Act) in the following proportions: permanent, 136,794; temporary, 7,842; exempt, 21,363 (9).

The four divisions were distinguished primarily by levels of responsibility, salary levels and means of recruitment. Salary levels have been set in proportion to degree of managerial and policy-making responsibility, with those of departmental secretaries standing in the early 1980s at about five times the rates for unskilled or semi-skilled fourth division officers such as clerical assistants, laborers and cleaners. Until the 1960s, bulk recruitment from outside the service occurred only at the base grades of the fourth and third divisions, usually with elementary English and arithmetic testing in the first case and a minimum qualification of success in the secondary school leaving examination required in the second. An internal "third division examination" set at about the same level provided an opportunity for some fourth division officers to move upwards. The normal means of filling second and first division positions—and all positions above the base grade in the other divisions—was by promotion from within. First division appointments were made by the government rather than the Public Service Board and there were occasional examples of outsiders being brought in for political or other reasons at that level. There was a special dispensation allowing veterans of the first and second world wars to enter the third division at lower than normal standard, and it frequently happened that positions above the base grade in that division requiring technical or specialist qualifications had to be filled by "lateral recruitment" from outside for want of suitable promotees from within.

Until the "quiet revolution" of the 1960s, this was one of the two main ways in which the service gained some university graduates; the other was *via* the time-honored Australian process of part-time higher education by which officers already in the service gained degrees or diplomas by evening study at local universities. The changes of the 1960s, which mostly happened during Sir Frederick Wheeler's chairmanship of the Public Service Board, saw special schemes introduced to attract university graduates to general clerical and administrative employment, the opening up of such employment to women recruits, and a breaking down of formal barriers which had kept the service closed for so long to other than those who had entered *via* the base recruitment to the fourth and third divisions. These changes, which led to a substantial enhancement in the quality of the personnel resources available to government, served as a prelude to other significant reforms to come during the 1970s and 1980s.

Industrial Relations

Industrial relations is one of the more interesting and lively areas of Australian public administration. The characteristic solution to industrial disputation, in both the private and public sectors, has been arbitration—a solution which some observers see as confirmation of the Australian penchant for creating bureaucracies to deal with social problems. [The arbitration system has been described as an "organ of syndical satisfaction" (10).] Thus convoluted institutional arrangements exist to handle industrial matters in the public sector: central personnel agencies; Commonwealth and state arbitration authorities embracing both public and private sectors, particularly staff in statutory corporations; separate public service arbitrators for certain categories of government employees and so on. Whether the central personnel agencies are subject to the authority of the government in industrial matters has, on occasions, been a contentious issue.

The origins of public service unions go back to 1885, when the Public Service Association of South Australia was formed. The 1880s also saw the emergence of postal and teachers' unions, and it has been argued that "government staff associations led the way in organizing white-collar workers" (11). Government employment is thus highly unionized and, although once thought of as relatively conservative bodies, public service unions (including professional associations) have become increasingly militant since the 1960s. Strikes and work-bans no longer cause surprise and political campaigns are waged by declaring support for or opposition to a particular party or candidate. In most cases, support is for the Labor Party.

The Commonwealth and most state public services have service-wide unions covering administrative and clerical officers (notably, in the Commonwealth case, the Administrative and Clerical Officers' Association or ACOA), along with various professional associations. The Australian Postal and Telecommunications Union, covering statutory authority officers and employees, is about the same size as ACOA (approximately 50,000 members). The states too have sizeable unions, such as those composed of teachers and railway workers.

In 1976 the Royal Commission on Australian Government Administration was critical of the number of unions covering Commonwealth employees—over 70 in all—more than half of which were "outside" unions embracing private sector employees as well as public servants. Complaints about the number of unions are common in critiques of industrial relations in Australia, as often strikes in both the public and private sectors are over demarcation issues (12). Several inquiries have also recommended greater worker participation or "industrial democracy." This did not necessarily mean through the existing union structure, although there were already in place some consultative or representative mechanisms such as union representation on disciplinary and/or appeal boards and a "Joint Council" in the Commonwealth public service. (None is as elaborate as the British Whitley Council system.) Up to 1985 limited progress had been made with democratic forms of self-government in administration, but some states are implementing a policy of having an elected staff representative on the boards of statutory bodies.

Public servants have also been allowed relative freedom to engage in partisan political activity. There are few restrictions on accepting elective office in local government but if elected to state or federal parliament a public servant must resign. Although this policy can cause difficulties for senior officers who want to engage in highly visible partisan activity, such cases have been rare. The desirability of public servants commenting publicly on government policy and administration and disclosing official information has excited more controversy than public servants standing for parliament. Although some of the restrictions on public comment have now been removed, the expectation is that public servants will be discreet. By and large they are; "whistle blowing" in Australia is by the "leak" rather than by "going public."

The question of "leaks" raises the issue of the norms of official behavior, and their enforcement. While the conduct of public servants has long been circumscribed by public service acts and regulations and by crimes acts, until recently there was no "code of ethics" formalizing many of the conventions and precedents recognized within the public service. However, partly as a consequence of certain conflict-of-interest cases in the 1970s, both the Commonwealth and Victorian governments encouraged their public service boards to produce sets of guidelines on official conduct and a Commonwealth parliamentary committee also reported on the subject (13). Given that the early 1980s have seen some well-publicized lapses from the high standards of behavior expected of officials, particularly in the area of judicial administration, the topic of administrative (and political) ethics may soon come into fashion.

THE BUREAUCRACY AND POLICY-MAKING

Strands of Administrative Reform

A Committee of Inquiry on Public Service Recruitment which reported in 1959 provided the guidelines for the "quiet" reforms of the '60s which have already been described. However, confidence continued to decline in the ability of traditional Westminster values to ensure efficient, economical, responsible and accountable administration, and in this context the Royal Commission on Australian Government Administration produced a wide-ranging report in 1976. Among the reform strategies espoused were budget and planning reform, accountable management, authority decentralization and more lateral recruitment. Some changes followed, but the crisis of confidence in the administration continued, marked by the reports of several other inquiry committees in the later '70s and early '80s. While all stressed the need to strengthen the capacity of ministers to control, mostly they seemed—like contemporary public inquiry activity in comparable systems—to be pursuing "managerialist" solutions which sat awkwardly against the values of public service, public interest and public participation supposedly enshrined in the liberal democratic state (14).

Among other system developments of the 1970s were the provision of a Legislative Research Service within the Department of the Parliamentary Library, which enabled MPs—particularly Opposition MPs—to gain substantial research assistance from the public payroll for the first time, the expansion of ministerial offices to furnish policy advice to ministers independent of advice from their departments, and an invigoration of the parliamentary committee system, in which the Senate took most of the initiatives. This group of reforms was designed to equip politicians to play a more effective role in government according to Westminster precepts. And yet another set of reforms seemed often to be running against that goal, and to be importing a European-continental legalistic approach to accountability.

Thus, also since the mid-'70s, the so-called New Administrative Law has seen the introduction of an ombudsman, an administrative appeals tribunal, a much expanded administrative jurisdiction in a new Federal Court, and freedom of information legislation. The legal profession has espoused and largely implemented these reforms. Other concerned groups have seemingly acquiesced—because of the general crisis of confidence in the traditional system—in this major shift in the avenues of accountability away from elected representatives of the people (ministers and MPs generally) towards non-elected judges and judge-like persons. It is a moot point whether the cause of accountability is helped or hindered by these developments (15).

The Hawke Labor Government elected to office in March 1983 was the first federal government ever to "arrive" with a clearly thought-out policy of administrative reform. While still in opposition, the party established a Task Force on Government Administration which developed recommendations in the areas of cabinet organization, cabinet-caucus relations, the public service, statutory (or public) authorities, parliamentary procedure and relations between Labor in government and trade unions and business. The resulting report entitled *Labor and Quality of Government* was published a month before the March 1983 election, and it served as a blueprint to guide the new cabinet and ministers in tackling the task of reform as they saw it. By December 1983 they were able to publish a White Paper on *Reforming the Australian Public Service* which carried part of the more general reform program forward. Several of its proposals were given quick statutory effect, notably those reforming the methods of appointing departmental secretaries (previously termed "permanent heads") and the "senior executive service" constituting the next level of the hierarchy; transferring some establishment control functions from the Public Service Board to the Department of Finance and departmental managements; reforming promotion procedures and establishing new grievance machinery; and furthering implementation of equal employment opportunity and industrial democracy programs. Ministers now have more discretion to bring sympathizers into the senior service, leading to criticism that it is being politicized in the American fashion; it has to be said, nonetheless, that companion reform documents prepared under Liberal Party guidance have been moving in the same direction, so that the changes have a bi-partisan quality about them. In order to encourage mobility between different types of occupations, the formal barriers between the four divisions of the public service have also been removed. A companion White Paper on *Budget Reform* was issued in 1984; two other "policy papers" seeking to establish guidelines for the use of statutory authorities have appeared during 1986 (16).

The Policy-Making and Budget Systems

It should come as no surprise that senior ranks of the public services are heavily involved in policy-making. The introduction of responsible government did not prevent individual administrators, throughout the second half of the 19th century, from shaping public policy to their preferred ends and being identified with particular policies. As the ideology of the Westminster system took root, public servants were urged by reformist writers of the day to act as executors and implementors of policy rather than as formulators, in line with the then fashionable politics/administration dichotomy (17). By the 1940s, however, perceptive studies of the administrator's actual role had begun to appear (18), and the wisdom of today accepts the legitimacy of a political component (although ill-defined) in the work of senior public servants (19). Recent changes to the senior levels of the public services reflect this ideology.

These changes, along with other reforms already noted, have been aimed at making the policy-making process more rational, responsible and responsive. This is being sought first, by a "technocratically" rational process in which cabinet and its sub-committees, or ministers alone, together with senior administrators set objectives and determine priorities for implementation by the bureaucracy. The stress is on the factoring of goals, performance standards, accountable management and so on, with techniques such as program budgeting seen as a valuable aid in achieving efficient allocation of resources and co-ordination of policy. Nevertheless the familiar budget procedure by and large remains: a budget agency reviews and consolidates estimates into a preliminary budget for submission to cabinet and/or its sub-committees.

State public services have embraced this new philosophy with varying degrees of zeal, and the Commonwealth's discussion paper on budget reform encapsulates the present trends. It recommends a ministerial strategy review of policies and priorities to set the "broad framework" for the budget; oversight of expenditure by Cabinet's Expenditure Review Committee; integration of human resource and financial budgeting; an increasing emphasis on program budgeting; "an improved information base for parliamentary and public scrutiny of the budget and expenditure programs;" and so on (20).

Responsibility and responsiveness are said to be increased by some of the other major changes to the policy-making process during the past two decades. Parliamentary committees have grown dramatically in number to embrace not only the "financial scrutiny" category (such as public accounts and expenditure review), but also specific policy areas with various standing and *ad hoc* committees. Parliament now has more than a formal claim to be added to the more familiar institutional framework of public policy-making in Australia, namely cabinet, the bureaucracy and pressure groups.

The reforms in the bureaucracy itself are also important to the policy-making process. The history of administrative reform in Australia until about the 1960s could be characterized as the steady development of the career service. While this had produced a reliable and honest public bureaucracy, virtually free from political patronage and nepotism, critics maintained that its shortcomings were serious; as a predominantly WASP male enclave it discriminated against women and minority groups, and either imposed its own values on policy or at least limited the options presented to ministers. Two of the proposed reforms were aimed directly at making this bureaucracy more responsive and responsible. The first was to open up the recruitment and promotion processes by various means, the most popular being the introduction of equal employment opportunity, affirmative action, lateral recruitment, and, where it still existed, the abolition of seniority as a factor in promotion. The other was to introduce a degree of "politicization" into the system, in the sense of more ministerial appointments at senior levels of departments and provision of a limited number of non-departmental ministerial advisers.

Top Public Servants: Education and Social Background

These reforms are beginning to alter the face of bureaucracy. By the middle of this century senior officers were predominantly upwardly mobile males (a survey conducted in 1956 found that about 20-25 per cent were of working class origins), many of whom had acquired tertiary qualifications on a part-time basis (21). Although contemporary data are scattered, the composite picture of the senior ranks of the public service is, in the mid-1980s, one of increasing representation of women and "ethnics." Lateral entry is no longer confined to the professionally qualified, and mobility within and between public service departments and statutory bodies is increasing, as is movement among the nation's several public services.

Of course the public services are changing at differential rates. However a recent study shows that senior members of the Commonwealth public service are more representative than most other elites, as are their Canadian counterparts. Neither class, region nor educational institution has a lien on public office in Australia, although Commonwealth public servants are now clearly better educated than all other groups with the exception of the academics. In terms of opinions and ideologies they frequently approach the mean, giving some support to the stereotype of "gray" public servants, at least in terms of outlook (22).

A recent survey of appointments to senior positions in the New South Wales public service has demonstrated that quite marked changes have occurred in the departments, with the proportion of females appointed increasing from 0 per cent in 1977 to 10 per cent in 1980 and that of "outsiders" from 7.3 per cent in 1977 to 38.5 per cent in 1980 (23). A similar increase in lateral recruitment was found in the state of Victoria following an inquiry into its public service. It should be noted, however, that the majority of lateral appointees came from other parts of the public sector rather than the private sector (24).

In terms of education, the figures for both states are comparable—approximately 50 per cent of senior public servants have university degrees. In the Commonwealth public service, educational standards have been steadily rising. About 87 per cent of those in what is now called the Senior Executive Service have degrees; 18 per cent have higher degrees. Overall, in terms of reputation, the Commonwealth public service has ranked above the state services but the gap is now narrowing (25).

Nor could it be argued—at least at the federal level—that the ministerial staff under the last three Prime Ministers have been any more "representative" than the public service elite. Indeed, given the different political complexions of these ministries, the backgrounds of the advisers have been surprisingly similar—mostly male, relatively young, highly educated and from prestigious private schools, with about half coming from inside and half from outside the public service. Ministerial staff structures are now institutionalized, and relationships with the public service appear less fractious than previously. The 80-odd current senior advisers (or "minders" as they are now popularly called), most of whom have previously worked in advisory and party positions, place a high priority on advising their ministers on policy and claim to make an important contribution to the policy process (26).

Degree of "Politicization"

The situation varies between the several public services, ranging from Queensland where such policy advisers are virtually absent, to Victoria where there appears to have been most enthusiasm for politicization by a combination of advisers and short-term or contract appointments. Turning to the statutory authorities, the boards and commissions of the many non-departmental agencies in all jurisdictions have offered scope for political patronage.

Nonetheless, in comparative terms—relative to, say, the United States—the degree of politicization in Australia to date has been minimal. There has been some re-shuffling of permanent heads/departmental secretaries following changes of government, but not wholesale movement, and for good reason. Even if political partisanship seems to have been a factor in some senior appointments, the individuals concerned have also possessed plausible qualifications and experience (with the occasional exception). Then too a number of "a-political" or non-partisan appointments have been made, where the reputed administrative ability and political impartiality of an applicant have been the deciding factors. The moves towards politicization are still in their infancy, with their impact as yet uncertain. What concerns many public servants is the possibility that the range of positions subject to political patronage will be extended to cover those below the most senior levels, and that political party affiliation could become at best a necessary, and at worst a sufficient, condition of appointment (27).

Whether greater politicization will result in more efficient and effective policies is problematic; there may be an inevitability about certain outcomes irrespective of the reforms in structure, process and personnel. In times of economic stringency, for example, cutbacks may occur irrespective of particular structural arrangements. [There is some irony in the fact that the state of Victoria, which has progressed furthest in re-vamping its policy process, also has the most luxuriant bureaucratic growth (28)]. What can be said with some confidence is that governments are now taking a much keener interest in the policy-making process.

Generalists and Specialists

Unlike some other countries with a British heritage, Australia has never been dominated by a generalist ideology, in either the sense of education or the structuring of administrative roles. Indeed professionals have often been to the fore, and not only in the "guild" departments (such as Public Works or its equivalents) which were vital to the governments' active role in development. Not only were many permanent headships reserved for such professionals but, once within the service, they could generally move within it, their superior educational qualifications giving them many advantages. In some states (although not the Commonwealth), the public service structures still clearly separate administrators from professionals.

To the extent that any one field of study is currently pre-eminent in government administration it is economics. Approximately one quarter of all university graduates employed in the Commonwealth public service have majored in this discipline (29). Such specialization, if part of an Arts degree, has some affinity with a generalist education, although many with Economics or Commerce degrees are of the "professional" or econometric mold. If the present penchant for rational policy-making endures, the proportion of economics graduates is unlikely to decline—although the new administrative law is providing increased opportunities for graduates in law.

ADMINISTRATIVE ACCOUNTABILITY

Does Parliament Still Scrutinize?

The most striking development in Australian public administration during the past two decades has probably been the growth of administrative scrutiny. The several inquiries into Commonwealth administration which have already been noted were matched by others in four states (30). As we have also seen, the more familiar parliamentary and internal public service review mechanisms were strengthened. The rationale—or in some cases, the rationalization—behind such scrutiny has been the issue of accountability, and the concern that public agencies and administrators are no longer responsible to ministers or to parliament.

Ironically, while parliamentary scrutiny of the administration has increased in both scope and intensity, it was the alleged failure of parliament's traditional roles of control of the executive and citizens' redress which was used as one of the major justifications for the administrative law reforms. While the familiar portrait of the parliamentarian as an intermediary or advocate for the citizen in dispute with the public bureaucracy is still accurate, general oversight of governmental administration is now more effectively handled through committees such as public accounts, expenditure review and public bodies review. Some spirited questioning of public servants has occurred, and new rules of the game are being worked out to determine what areas are the preserve of ministerial policy, whether parliamentary committees have the power to conduct their own efficiency audits, and so on.

The development of the committee system is all the more interesting as conventional wisdom held that the tight party discipline which prevails in Australia would prevent the effective working of such a system—not only would a committee divide on party lines, but the executive would find its functioning all too embarrassing. However the enthusiasm for committees shown by the Senate has now infected many of the state parliaments. Too much should not be made of this: Australian parliamentary committees are insignificant in comparison with those of the U.S. Congress, and critics claim that only the tip of the bureaucratic iceberg can be exposed to them, given their limited resources.

The New Administrative Law

The New Administrative Law had its origins at the Commonwealth level in the Kerr committee, appointed in 1968 to examine the field of administrative law as it applied to the Commonwealth, following a proposal to establish a new Commonwealth superior court to relieve the High Court of much of its work. This Committee recommended far-reaching reforms for the review of administrative decisions, including internal and external reviews of complaints on the merits, judicial review, greater access to governmental information, and provision of reasons for decisions. Two further committees examined the nature and extent of administrative discretions and prerogative writ procedures respectively (31). Overseas experience was influential; Swedish (and other European) precedent was freely admitted. In the case of the ombudsman, the Australian version was clearly filtered through New Zealand's Anglo-Saxonization of the device in the 1960s.

From these inquiries has emerged a set of institutions which together embody the administrative law package. The most familiar of these is the ombudsman (now also present in each of the states), whose main task is informally to investigate complaints of defective administration. While relationships between ombudsmen and governments and their agencies have, on the whole, been amicable, some lively exchanges have taken place on issues such as the extent of an ombudsman's power and jurisdiction (in the states, local government and police have been contentious issues), what constitutes "administration" as distinct from "policy", and the like. From the citizen's point of view, the ombudsman has become an alternative to the local MP as the favored means of redress.

Most innovative is the Commonwealth's Administrative Appeals Tribunal (AAT), a body which reviews on the merits across a wide range of discretionary decisions, sometimes on appeal from other more specialized tribunals. Its full-time members are either Federal Court judges or lawyers; its part-time members, called upon as required, have expertise in specific areas. The Tribunal in most cases has power to set aside an administrative decision already made and to substitute its own decision. The number of applications it received annually for review increased from 49 in 1976–77 to 652 in 1980–81, and then almost quadrupled to over 2500 in 1985–86, including 286 cases under the Freedom of Information Act (32). The percentage of decisions appealed against which have been altered in some way, either by the original decision-maker after review or by the AAT itself, has averaged over 40 per annum, a significant figure. There is provision for further appeal to the Federal Court of Australia from a decision of the Tribunal on a question of law.

The operation of the Tribunal raises some important questions in a Westminster system of government. The most contentious issue is the *de facto* power of the AAT to review decisions of ministers. The practice evolved by the Tribunal has been enunciated as follows (33):

> When the Tribunal is reviewing the exercise of a discretionary power reposed in a Minister, and the Minister has adopted a general policy, the Tribunal will ordinarily apply that policy in reviewing the decision, unless the policy is unlawful or unless its application tends to produce an unjust decision in the circumstances of the particular case. Where the policy would ordinarily be applied, an argument against the policy itself or against its application in the particular case will be considered, but cogent reasons will have to be shown against its application, especially if the policy is shown to have been exposed to parliamentary scrutiny.

However, little weight has been given to ministerial policy if the Tribunal has considered it too hard or rigid. Although the AAT does on occasions adopt informal procedures, there seems to be a trend towards court-like formal hearings, with representation by counsel and an adversarial rather than inquisitorial stance. Not all administrators and lawyers have welcomed this development.

Many specialized review tribunals (such as Taxation Boards of Review and appeals tribunals in the field of social policy) pre-dated AAT. Whether the work of these bodies was to be absorbed by AAT, or whether, if they were to remain, a further appeal was to be allowed to AAT, were issues of recent debate. In other words, the question was whether there was to be a hierarchy of review tribunals to replace what some regarded as an untidy patchwork. Recent decisions suggest that the "rational" school will triumph; the Taxation Boards of Review, for instance, are now the Taxation Appeals Division of AAT.

The Administrative Decisions (Judicial Review) Act of 1980 is concerned with another aspect of administrative law, namely the lawfulness of administrative action. It simplified the procedure for invoking review, and confers jurisdication on the Federal Court of Australia. Unlike AAT, the Federal Court may not substitute its own view of the merits of a decision for that of the original decision-maker. One section of the Act requires that any individual adversely affected by an administrative decision should be given reasons for that decision. In personnel matters at least there have been questions raised about the cost-effectiveness of this requirement (34).

Another reform which is generally seen as a part of the New Administrative Law is freedom of information legislation. This has had a short but checkered history. The federal Act, which came into operation in December 1982, has been criticized on the grounds that the exemptions which deny access to documents are too numerous and give too much discretion to ministers. There is, however, a right of appeal to AAT from such decisions.

The federal government has not been overwhelmed with requests—a total of 4,159 were determined in the first seven months of the operation of the Act, of which 62 per cent were granted in full, 25 per cent in part, and 13 per cent were refused (35). Most requests were to check the accuracy of personal data on file. Even if not the panacea for the ills of democratic government, as some of its enthusiastic supporters had implied (36), the legislation has nevertheless forced public bodies to put their record systems in order, particularly their procedural manuals, policy directives and the like. The Act has also proved of some use to journalists and academics. The principle of freedom of information has been taken up by most of the states, and two already had their own Acts in operation by the time of writing (mid–1985).

The final component in this package of reforms is the Administrative Review Council, an advisory body which has general oversight of the processes of administrative review. Composed of individuals with diverse backgrounds (including *ex officio* the AAT president, federal ombudsman and chairman of the Law Reform Commission), it is the government's main source of external advice in the field.

At the state level the ombudsman and freedom of information laws are the major manifestations of the New Administrative Law. Limited enthusiasm to date has been shown for the equivalent of an AAT (Victoria being the exception), but other specialized tribunals have appeared such as Anti-Discrimination Boards and Equal Employment Opportunity Tribunals. Each has had an effect on the operation of state government administration, particularly in the area of personnel policy, and some tribunals have become involved in costly and drawn-out legal wrangles.

Internal Review Processes

The pursuit of accountability is not merely by the "external" review of decisions. Long-standing internal mechanisms still function, supplemented by new initiatives. Efficiency and performance reviews or audits are carried out by various bodies—the auditors-general, public service boards or departments of heads of government—with mixed success. Sometimes this can be a competitive business: in the state of New South Wales, for example, the Public Accounts Committee of the legislature, external consultants, the Auditor-General, Public Service Board and Premier's Department are all involved in the review process. Of course, treasuries and finance departments continue their traditional roles in relation to expenditure review, as do the auditors-general.

There are a number of general issues which arise out of the galloping pace of reform in the areas of administrative law and scrutiny. Some have already been touched on. To what extent is it desirable that an appointed quasi-judicial tribunal should over-rule an elected minister on the merits of a decision? Is the "continental" flavor of administrative law and the "judicialization" of the policy process ill-suited to the Anglo-Saxon, Westminster milieu? Of prime importance, what are the costs and benefits of the reforms—for example, are we in danger of creating a second bureaucracy to check on our existing administration? Are there more scrutineers that operatives? To what extent do the new requirements interfere with the effective and efficient delivery of services, and so on? To its credit, the Administrative Review Council is now sponsoring research on the cost/benefit issue, as more dissenting voices question the desirability of the innovations of the past two decades (37).

Public Administration and the Public

The early 1970s saw some experimentation with citizen participation in administration, partly as a result of the spread of the "access" ethic. Most of this was in the areas of social and urban and regional affairs. Not all innovations have survived from this period, but many mundane yet significant improvements at the shop-front level do remain: the simplification of forms and the establishment of departmental field offices and government information offices are of importance to the proverbial ordinary citizen. While commercial "brokers" who act as negotiators between the public bureaucracy and citizen are evident in fields such as taxation or customs, in social welfare this role, where necessary, has been taken up by voluntary organizations. Then too, many agencies have their advisory committees in one guise or another; some allow for the direct or *de facto* representation of interest groups, which in turn raises questions about disproportionate influence.

Accountability and responsibility are thus much more fragmented in Australian public administration in the 1980s than in previous times. Paradoxically, this creation of a variety of scrutinizing bodies and processes ostensibly to ensure the responsibility of administration may result in filleting responsibility so small that it slips through the interstices of the institutional and process nets.

ANALYZING THE CHANGES (38)

More or Less Bureaucratization?

Max Weber's writings on administration—which of course cover much more than the concept of bureaucracy (39)—offer what is probably the most comprehensive framework for analyzing the trends already outlined. There are grounds for arguing that Australia is moving towards an even greater degree of bureaucratization. On the one hand, there is the emphasis on greater use of rational techniques—rational, that is, in the Weberian sense of formal rationality. Program budgets, efficiency audits, corporate plans, cost-benefit analysis, accountable management and the like have given administration a technocratic flavor, reinforced by the extensive use of "managerialist" terminology which has been gaining ground in Australia in part because of considerable interest Australian investigators have taken in post-Glassco developments in Canada. On the other, the lush growth of institutions is highly Weberian when it is recalled that many of these bodies are scrutinizing agencies: the escape from existing bureaucratic authority is only by the creation of other bureaucratic authorities. Australian public administration as a whole has become more byzantine.

However, there are also grounds for arguing that "patrimonial regression," or at least debureaucratization, is occurring. Personal and program loyalties are said to count more than the *sine ira ac studio* (40) stance of professional bureaucrats, and politicization and patron/client relationships have become lively issues with career public servants. There is no suggestion that grossly incompetent individuals are being appointed or that entire services are being politicized. Nonetheless, it would seem that legal-rational authority is being loosened up in some of the more senior levels of the public service, and that practices more akin to Weber's patrimonialism are returning.

Weberian precepts also help us see the two sides of the questions of equal employment opportunity and affirmative action—issues which arouse intense passions. For some, policies in this area amount to the imposition of *de facto* quotas, that is, appointment and promotion may now be on the basis of ascription rather than achievement. For others, such policies and programs represent the belated fulfillment of the ideals of the career service (41).

The traditional, if not the occasional charismatic, elements emerging in the Australian system should cause no surprise. After all, the fully fledged bureaucratic form of administration is historically a very recent creation, and there are many examples of a relatively bureaucractized system regressing to a less "rational" one. For instance, feudalism interrupted the transition from the bureaucracy of Imperial Rome to the bureaucracy of 20th century Europe.

The Australian administrative system demonstrates to the full the complexities of managing the modern national state (42), particularly a federation. The system must try to cope with the contrary pressures towards more and less central direction (co-ordination), more and less autonomy for line departments and "fringe" authorities, more representation (but on what terms?) of the diverse groups within the community, more economy and efficiency on the one hand and more social equity and democracy on the other (43)–all of which "puzzles" are incapable of solution in an absolute sense. This is the inevitable predicament of modern administration, and the Australian system is coping with it in a way which is blending traditional elements both derived and locally crafted with more radical strands of development which are also both derived and locally crafted.

REFERENCES

1. This theme is developed further in R. L. Wettenhall, "Administrative History: An Australian Perspective," *Cahiers de l'histoire de l'administration* (IIAS, Brussels) 1 (1984), 1–9. Readers seeking more detailed treatment of Australian public administration generally are advised to consult R. N. Spann, *Government Administration in Australia* (Sydney: Allen and Unwin, 1979); R. N. Spann and G. R. Curnow (eds.), *Public Policy and Administration in Australia: A Reader* (Sydney: Wiley, 1975); L. F. Crisp, *Australian National Government*, 4th ed. (Melbourne: Longmans, 1978); G. R. Curnow and R. L. Wettenhall (eds.), *Understanding Public Administration* (Sydney: Allen and Unwin, 1981); K. W. Wiltshire, *An Introduction to Australian Public Administration*, revised (Sydney: Allen and Unwin, forthcoming); and the *Australian Journal of Public Administration* (originally just *Public Administration*), published quarterly in Sydney since 1937.

2. G. S. Reid, "Responsible Government and Ministerial Responsibility", in Curnow and Wettenhall, *op. cit.*, 317.

3. The "Public Service" in each case is made up of persons employed under the relevant Public Service Act, and the figures are taken from the 1981–1982 Annual Reports of the several Public Service Boards. Considerable difficulties are encountered in securing accurate data about other public sector employment, due amongst other things to the diversity of the field and to variable treatment of part-time employment. The figures here must be regarded as approximate only, and are based on statistical collections originally prepared with the assistance of Mr. T. O'Shaughnessy, for inclusion in P. R. Hay, J. Halligan, J. Warhurst and B. Costar (eds.), *Essays on Victorian Politics* (Warrnambool: Warrnambool Institute Press, 1985). June 1982 is the latest date possible at time of writing for collection of comparable figures over the whole public sector.

4. The best guide to these arrangements is the official *Commonwealth Government Directory* (Canberra: Aust. Govt. Publishing Service [AGPS], published most years).

5. The major documentation is to be found in a series of reports issued by the Senate Standing Committee on Finance and Government Operations under the chairmanship of Senator Peter Rae during the period 1979–1983. See also Roger Wettenhall,

"Statutory Authorities", in Alexander Kouzmin, J. R. Nethercote and Roger Wetten-hall (eds.), *Australian Commonwealth Administration 1983*: *Essays in Review* and in Nethercote, Kouzmin and Wettenhall (eds.), *Australian Commonwealth Administration 1984*: *Essays in Review* (Canberra: Canberra College of Advanced Education and ACT Division, Royal Australian Institute of Public Administration, 1984 and 1986), 105–166 and 74–147.

6. A. W. Macmahon, *Delegation and Autonomy* (Bombay: Asia Publishing House, 1961), Ch. 2.

7. Victorian Parliament, Public Bodies Review Committee, *First to Eighth Reports* (Melbourne: Victorian Government Printer, 1980–1983).

8. On the local government systems, see J. Power, R. Wettenhall and J. Halligan (eds.), *Local Government Systems of Australia* (Canberra: AGPS for Advisory Council on Inter-government Relations, 1981).

9. Public Service Board, *Statistical Yearbook 1983–84* (Canberra: AGPS, 1984), 4. The difference between the total figure and that shown in Table 1 represents the growth in the service since 1982.

10. J. D. B. Miller, *Australian Government and Politics*, 2nd ed. (London: Duckworth, 1959), 131.

11. R. N. Spann, *op. cit.*, 375.

12. An evaluation of these critiques is provided by Howard Gill and Vivien Griffin, "The Fetish of Order: Reform in Australian Union Structure," *Journal of Industrial Relations* (Sydney) 23 (September 1981), 363–382.

13. A short history of this topic is contained in Colin A. Hughes, "Administrative Ethics," in Curnow and Wettenhall, *op. cit.*, 192–201.

14. The major reports, with names of chairmen in parenthesis, were: Committee of Inquiry into Public Service Recruitment (Boyer), *Report* (Canberra: Govt. Printer, 1959); Royal Commission on Australian Government Administration (Coombs), *Report and Appendices* (Canberra: AGPS, 1976); Joint Committee of Public Accounts (Connolly), *The Selection and Development of Senior Managers in the Commonwealth Public Service* (Canberra: AGPS, 1982); Review of Commonwealth Administration (Reid), *Report* (Canberra: AGPS, 1983). For a general discussion of such inquiries, including state inquiries, see R. F. I. Smith and Patrick Weller (eds.), *Public Service Inquiries in Australia* (Brisbane: University of Queensland Press, 1978).

15. Probably the first substantial critique was that of G. S. Reid: "The Changing Political Framework", *Quadrant* XXIV (Jan.–Feb., 1980), 11–14.

16. *Reforming the Australian Public Service, Budget Reform, Reform of Commonwealth Primary Industry Statutory Marketing Authorities* and *Statutory Authorities and Government Business Enterprises*: *Proposed Policy Guidelines* (Canberra: AGPS, 1983, 1984, 1986 and 1986). Also *Labor and Quality of Government* (Canberra: Federal Parliamentary Labor Party, 1983) and *Facing Facts*: *Report of the Committee of Review* (Canberra: Liberal Party of Australia, 1983). For a review of these developments, see J. R. Nethercote, "Public Service Reform: Its Course and Nature", in Kouzmin, Nethercote and Wettenhall, *op. cit.*, 16–42.

17. See, for example, F. A. Bland, *Shadows and Realities of Government* (Sydney: Workers Educational Association of NSW, 1923), Ch. 1.

18. Such as P. W. E. Curtin, "Politics and Administration," *Public Administration* (Sydney) VII (December 1948), 188–200, and VIII (March 1949), 10–18.

19. This view is enunciated in both the Coombs Report, *op. cit.*, and in Review of NSW Government Administration (Wilenski), *Directions for Change* and *Unfinished Agenda* (Sydney: NSW Govt. Printer, 1977 and 1982).

20. As in note 16.
21. Quoted in R. N. Spann, *op. cit.*, 334.
22. John Higley *et al., Elites in Australia* (London: Routledge & Kegan Paul, 1979), 81.
23. This has been taken from Barry Moore, "Top Administrators in New South Wales," *Australian Journal of Public Administration* XL (December 1981), 35.
24. Martin Painter and Penelope Sears, "The Impact of Recent Changes to Recruitment Practices in the Victorian Public Service," *Australian Journal of Public Administration* XLI (December 1982), 387–395.
25. Public Service Board, *Statistical Yearbook 1982-83* (Canberra: AGPS, 1983), 123.
26. See James Walter, "Ministerial Staff under Hawke," *Australian Journal of Public Administration* XLIII (September 1984), 203–219; *The Ministers' Minders: Personal Advisers in National Government* (Melbourne: OUP, 1986).
27. The importance of these issues was underlined when the Royal Australian Institute of Public Administration devoted its 1985 National Conference to the theme: See Ross Curnow and Barbara Page (eds.), *The Career Service: Crisis or Consolidation?* (forthcoming).
28. Jean Holmes, "Administrative Chronicle: Victoria," *Australian Journal of Public Administration* XLIII (June 1984), 135.
29. A. Petridis, "Economics Degrees and the Australian Public Service: A Note," *Australian Journal of Public Administration* XL (September 1981), 246–253. See also V. Subramaniam, "Specialists in British and Australian Government: A Study in Contrast," *Public Administration* (London) 41 (Winter 1963), 357–393.
30. For a discussion of these inquiries as they related to departmental structures of the several public services, see Roger Wettenhall, *Organising Government: The Uses of Ministries and Departments* (Sydney: Croom Helm, 1986), Chs. 6-7.
31. The three Committees were: Commonwealth Administrative Review Committee (Kerr), *Report* (Canberra: AGPS, 1971); Committee on Administrative Discretions (Bland), *Interim Report* and *Final Report* (Canberra: AGPS, both 1973); Committee on Prerogative Writ Procedures (Ellicott), *Report* (Canberra: AGPS, 1973).
32. These figures are based on a table in J. H. Howard, "Perspectives on 'Overloaded Government'," *Australian Journal of Public Administration* XLIII (December 1984), 374, and recent Annual Reports of the Administrative Review Council.
33. *Re Drake (No. 2)* (1979) 2 ALD 634 at p. 645, quoted by The Hon. Mr. Justice Brennan, "Administrative Law: The Australian Experience," in E. N. Scott (ed.), *International Perspectives in Public Administration* (Proceedings of the IASIA Round Table in Canberra: Canberra College of Advanced Education and IASIA, 1981), 80.
34. R. C. Davey, "The New Administrative Law: A Comment on Cost," *Australian Journal of Public Administration* XLII (June 1983), 261–265.
35. Attorney-General's Department, *Freedom of Information Act 1982, Annual Report to 30 June 1983* (Canberra: AGPS, 1983).
36. For example, John McMillan, "Who Owns Government Information?" *Australian Journal of Public Administration* XXXVIII (March 1979), 42–50.
37. For example, Brian Jinks, "The 'New Administrative Law': Some Assumptions and Questions", *Australian Journal of Public Administration* XLI (September 1982), 209–218.
38. Some of this final section is based upon material in G. R. Curnow, "Recent Developments in Australian State Government Administration," Paper presented to the New Zealand Institute of Public Administration Annual Conference, Christchurch, September 1984.
39. Many of these are contained in Max Weber, *Economy and Society*, edited by Guenther Roth and Claus Wittich (New York: Bedminster Press, 1968), 3 volumes.

40. *Ibid.,* ("without hatred or passion").
41. See, for example, the debate in the *Australian Journal of Public Administration* XLI (September 1982), 300–306; and XLII (June 1983), 266–273.
42. The literature on administrative reform is suggestive with its dichotomized variables of exogenous *vs.* endogenous change; incrementalism *vs.* innovation; comprehensiveness *vs.* narrowness; balance-oriented *vs.* shock-oriented and so on: Arne F. Leemans (ed.), *The Management of Change in Government* (The Hague: Nijhoff, 1976), Part I.
43. See discussion in P. Wilenski, "Administrative Reform Commissions and Administrative Reform: The Australian Experience," in E. N. Scott, *op. cit.*, esp. at 92–98. Wilenski, who was appointed Chairman of the Commonwealth Public Service Board in 1983, has been a leading "change agent": for his collected papers, see Peter Wilenski, *Public Power and Public Administration* (Sydney: Hale and Iremonger, 1986).

3

Canada

AUDREY D. DOERR
Department of Indian Affairs and Northern Development, Hull, Quebec, Canada

In Canada, governments have played a central role in the country's economic and social development. Nation-building has been promoted and supported by public sector activities and undertakings which have been used to forge links and to balance regional economic disparities across a sparsely-populated, yet vast, geographic area. When political solutions have been difficult to achieve, administrative expedients have often been developed to maintain national cohesion and unity (1).

THE ENVIRONMENT

The environment of the Canadian public service is influenced by many factors: the size of the country, its regional diversities, its two official languages, a federal system, and parliamentary institutions and conventions. Canada is the second largest country in the world but it has a small population of about 25 million people concentrated in a narrow band several hundred miles wide along its southern border. There is no shortage of governmental institutions to serve this population. The federal government centered in Ottawa has approximately two-thirds of its public service staff located outside the national capital. Each of the ten provinces has a separate public service and, in addition, each has authority for municipal government institutions within its boundaries. Although processes of urbanization have concentrated people in a few large cities, there are thousands of smaller municipal governments across the country as a whole. North of the 60th parallel, there are two territorial governments which are the responsibility of the federal government.

The expansion of federal and provincial activities in the 20th century has meant the development of parallel bureaucracies at the federal and provincial levels. Thus provincial governments have departments that complement those of the federal government. Examples include departments of health, communications, environment, economic development, transportation, consumer and corporate affairs, employment and labor. As a consequence, a great deal of time and effort is devoted to federal-provincial coordination of policies and programs by public officials. Despite occasions when politicians may desire to act unilaterally, the degree of interdependence that has been built into the fiscal and administrative infrastructures of government undertakings in major program areas can be expected to require continued co-operation and collaboration (2).

Another key feature of the constitutional provisions which affect public administration is the parliamentary system of government. Canada's Parliament is bicameral. It includes an elected House of Commons consisting of 282 members and an appointed Senate of 110 members. The Governor-General performs the function of a constitutional monarch. The customs and conventions of selecting an executive and the relationship between the executive and the legislature are central to the operations of the public service.

Although responsible government was firmly established before Confederation, sections 9 to 16 of the *Constitution Act, 1867* set out the executive authority as being vested in the Crown. By custom, the power of the Crown is exercised by Cabinet. Members of Cabinet are normally selected from among elected members of the majority party in Parliament. The principle that executive power flows from the Crown but is held accountable by Parliament is the foundation of the system and provides the basis for the collective and individual responsibility of ministers.

Collective responsibility of ministers is based on custom and convention. Collectively, ministers are responsible to each other and as a group to the House of Commons, the elected legislative chamber. The collective exercise of power requires consensual decision-making and solidarity in Cabinet ranks. The role of the Prime Minister is central in ensuring the effective exercise of ministerial responsibility through the exercise of certain prerogative powers of the Crown. For example, The Prime Minister appoints and removes ministers and senior personnel in the public service and government agencies. It is the Prime Minister who initiates the creation or reorganization of departments and agencies and who is responsible for assigning ministerial responsibilities. As chairman of the Cabinet, he must act as chief policy co-ordinator and in conjunction with ministers such as the Minister of Finance and President of the Treasury Board provide for the overall management of government activities including the public service.

The individual responsibility of ministers is based in the constitution; its legal expression is in statutory enactment. Constitutionally, all initiatives for the raising or spending of money must be sponsored by an elected minister of the Crown. Ministers are responsible for the direction and management of their departments but day-to-day administration is considered the responsibility of the senior official, the deputy minister or agency head.

Historically, Parliament has been involved in directing the public service to the extent that it must approve legislation authorizing the creation of new departments and agencies and approve appropriations for them including public service salaries. Through statutes such as the *Financial Administration Act*, the legislature has delegated responsibilities to the executive, for example, to be responsible for financial management and personnel management practices in the public service including acting as employer for purposes of collective bargaining. In turn, Parliament holds the executive accountable for the management and operations of government.

The representative needs of cabinet-making have resulted in larger Canadian cabinets than what administrative requirements alone would warrant. In 1867 the Canadian cabinet included 14 ministers; by 1984 the number had grown to 39. One of the first acts of Prime Minister Trudeau's successor in 1984 was to reduce the size of the

Cabinet to 29 members. Nevertheless, the need for representation *and* visibility of political and policy concerns afforded by Cabinet structure was demonstrated again following the defeat of the Liberal government in the general election of September 1984. When the Progressive Conservative party led by Prime Minister Mulroney came to power, the Cabinet that was formed comprised some 40 members. In comparison, provincial cabinets, on average, consist of about 20 members.

Finally, it can be argued that the environmental factors that have had the strongest influence on the management *of* government in Canada pertain, in large measure, to the inheritance of British institutions and conventions, but influences affecting management *in* government have been derived primarily from American ideas and management practices. The influence of scientific management principles on personnel policy and administrative systems, for example, has early historical roots and persists to the present day (3).

In recent years, "systems theory" as applied to policy, organizational and financial management provides another example of an American management approach that has been used extensively in Canada. In the policy realm, elaborate systems designs have often guided the structuring of central planning operations and co-ordinative processes within ministerial portfolios. Efforts to achieve economy and efficiency of operations through rationally designed systems of organization have been reflected in the development and application of financial management techniques such as Planning, Programming, Budgeting Systems, operations research and related planning techniques and methods.

In fact, the application and adaptation of American ideas and administrative practices to the Canadian public service, bounded as it is by the operations of a parliamentary system in a federal state, have often been considered the distinguishing feature of the Canadian system (4). The manner in which these influences have blended together have resulted, in turn, in distinct forms and practices suitable to the Canadian situation. In particular, Canadian practice built upon British parliamentary tradition infused with American methods has emphasized pragmatic approaches and solutions to administrative problems. The following discussion will highlight how these influences have shaped the administrative system.

THE ADMINISTRATIVE SYSTEM

The size and scope of governmental activities have expanded substantially in the last several decades. In terms of government expenditures alone, the size of the federal budget has risen from approximately 11.3 billion dollars in 1967–68 to 103.6 billion dollars in 1985–86. Despite measures to restrain expenditures, federal deficits have continued to increase and have contributed in no small way to government costs. The size of the federal public service has fluctuated over the same period. For example, in 1968, 200,329 individuals were reported to be employed under the Public Service Employment Act. A peak of 283,169 was reached in 1977; by 1985, the number reported was 223,173. However, these figures do not include those public sector employees who work for government enterprises, armed forces, post office and Royal Canadian Mounted Police, and others not appointed through the Public Service Commission. In 1985, this number was reported to be 364,965 for a total of 588,138 public sector employees of the federal government (5).

Changes in the machinery of government in recent decades have reflected the growing complexity and concentration of state activities. Few areas of government structure and management have been left untouched as new systems and methods have been tried to improve the quality of decision-making and administrative effectiveness.

Structure and Management of the Public Service

As noted earlier, the individual and collective responsibilities of ministers have an overriding influence on the structure and design of the Canadian public service. Individual ministerial responsibilities for policies and programs are supported by line departments and agencies organized primarily on a purpose or clientele basis (6). Examples include the departments of transport, agriculture, national defense and veterans affairs. The exercise of collective responsibilities by the Prime Minister and colleagues such as the Minister of Finance and President of the Treasury Board is supported by central policy agencies such as the Privy Council Office and Department of Finance and by central service organizations such as the departments of public works and supply and services.

Major changes in the organization of departments and, more particularly, in central agencies were most pronounced after 1968, although some reorganization had been implemented a few years earlier. The *Government Organizational Acts* of 1966, 1969, 1970, 1978 and 1982 established several new government departments and reorganized others. The structures which emerged related directly to the public policy agenda of government. For example, among the organizations were departments of environment, regional economic expansion, energy, mines and resources, communications, urban affairs, and science and technology (7).

If the period was one in which major changes were made in the organization of departmental activities, it was also a period characterized by the enhancement of units supporting the central decision-making and management system of government. Some writers have attributed these developments in part to the personal philosophy and style of Prime Minister Trudeau (8). However, the preoccupation with strengthening central coordination and control was reflected in practices elsewhere (9). It could perhaps be said that there has been greater experimentation in the Canadian context.

The emphasis on collegial decision-making in this period led to the development of a number of central co-ordinative systems. The first system focussed on strengthening the political and policy support to the Prime Minister. In 1968, the Prime Minister's Office and the Privy Council Office were the two key organizations that served the head of government. The former comprised political staff responsible for managing the Prime Minister's schedule, dealing with the partisan side of the Prime Minister's responsibilities and, on occasion, intervening with ministers on major policy issues. Although this Office was reorganized a number of times during the 70's and early 80's, its primary role has remained that of a political unit. The Office has never integrated its activities with the Cabinet committee policy process; it has only become involved on particular issues.

On the other hand, the Privy Council Office, which is staffed by public servants and is often referred to as the Prime Minister's department, was expanded through the establishment of secretariats to support the Cabinet committee system. In particular, the Cabinet Committee on Priorities and Planning, the central policy committee of Cabinet which is chaired by the Prime Minister, has been supported by the Privy

Council Office secretariats. Other Cabinet committees such as economic policy, social policy and government operations are chaired by different ministers but have also been served by secretariats in the Office. These units report, through the Secretary to the Cabinet and Clerk of the Privy Council, a deputy minister, to the Prime Minister and keep him informed on all matters coming before the committees.

In 1974, the Federal-Provincial Relations Office, which had been a division within the Privy Council Office, was elevated in status with the creation of an Office of the Secretary to the Cabinet for Federal-Provincial Relations. In addition to serving as a secretariat to the Cabinet committee on federal-provincial relations, this Office also provides liaison with federal departments and provincial governments on policy and related matters of federal-provincial concern. Other types of duties have also become associated with it. For example, support to the Prime Minister on matters respecting constitutional reform have been located in this agency.

The second system of central agency co-ordination centered on financial and personnel management activities. In 1962, the Royal Commission on Government Organization had recommended the creation of a separate agency, the Treasury Board Secretariat and a new ministerial portfolio, President of the Treasury Board, who would also be the chairman of the Treasury Board. The Board is a Cabinet committee which dates back to 1967 and is the only Cabinet committee that has a statutory base. Prior to the adoption of this recommendation in 1967, secretariat services had been provided to the committee by a small unit in the Department of Finance and the Minister of Finance had been chairman of the Board.

The primary purpose of this reorganization was to distinguish the internal management and resource allocation activities to be performed by the Board from the macroeconomic policy responsibilities of the Department of Finance. Thus, the Secretariat was set up to support the Treasury Board in respect of its responsibilities for the expenditure budget and for management in the public service. The introduction of Planning, Program Budgeting Systems in 1966, the introduction of collective bargaining in 1967 and the passage of the *Official Languages Act* in 1969 added new functions to the Secretariat, which assumed responsibility for the implementation of these measures.

The preoccupation with maintaining central control over administrative systems was demonstrated in 1978 when, following several highly critical reports on management standards and practices in the public service issued by the Auditor General, part of the Government's response was to divide the staff of the Treasury Board Secretariat and create an Office of the Comptroller General. The secretariat has continued to be responsible for resource allocation matters including review and control; the Comptroller-General's responsibilities focus on the development of management procedures and standards and the evaluation of the efficiency and effectiveness of government programs. Like the Secretary of the Treasury Board, the Comptroller General has deputy ministerial rank.

The third system of central agency co-ordination was the sectoral policy agencies. In 1970 the Ministry of State for Urban Affairs and the Ministry of State for Science and Technology were created as policy secretariats with no direct program responsibilities. Their success in influencing the development and implementation of policies in these sectors was limited and the Ministries were ultimately wound up (10).

The so-called second generation of Ministries of State emerged in 1978 and 1979 and accompanied reforms in the planning and expenditure system within the public

service. In addition to being policy secretariats like the earlier ministries, the Ministry
of State for Economic Development and the Ministry of State for Social Development
served Cabinet committees responsible for allocating funds within the respective policy
sectors. Thus, they had the formal authority to review policy and program activities
of the departments that made applications to the Committees. The lack of program
responsibilities of the Ministries did not detract from their ability to influence departments' policies and programs since this was achieved through their hierarchical position-
ing between ministers and their departments on the one hand and the Cabinet decision-
making structure on the other. In effect, the Ministries tried to combine the features
of the committee secretariats in the Privy Council Office and the program review
activities of the Treasury Board Secretariat within a particular policy sector.

In some respects, the evolution that occurred in this machinery of government
reflected an attempt to marry the needs of individual and collective responsibilities
of ministers with sophisticated policy and management structures. The emphasis on
central co-ordination and interdependence of issues, nevertheless, has made it more
difficult to maintain lines of departmental responsibility. In 1962, the Royal Commission on Government Organization had brought forward a set of recommendations
directed to promoting efficiency, economy and improved service "in the despatch of
public business" (11). In proposing a system of checks and balances between the
needs of central administration and the departments, the Commission had argued that
departments should have a maximum degree of control over financial, personnel and
material management to allow managers to manage. Ostensibly these proposals of the
Commission were implemented but they were offset by the innovations and changes in
Cabinet committee processes and by the introduction and implementation of new
management policies such as PPBS, bilingualism and collective bargaining. Every new
policy or administrative reform that was introduced was accompanied by the establishment of a central agency unit to initiate or monitor the change. In the areas of administrative reform, in particular, the saturation psychosis generated by these central
initiatives actively inhibited the departments from managging with a degree of
autonomy (12).

A Royal Commission on Financial Management and Accountability reported in
1979, but some of the Commission's recommendations were overtaken by the implementation of the Planning and Expenditure Management System which had been
developed before the Commission's work was completed. The central feature of
PEMS was the Fiscal Plan which attempted to integrate policy and expenditure issues
in much the same fashion that the Commission proposed. The planning framework
was one in which activities were co-ordinated and managed within defined policy sectors and established resource limits. A key feature of the Fiscal Plan was the establishment of expenditure limits for the government as a whole and within particular policy
sectors (13). The policy sectors determined the broad organizational framework within
which particular policy and program activities were grouped. Tne resource envelopes
were designated within five policy sectors. The funding allocated to each envelope
was determined in part by the relative priority of each policy sector. Decisions respecting priorities, programs and expenditures were thus ultimately meshed within the confines of individual envelopes.

The issues of accountability of government, combined with a growing political commitment to policies of restraint, enhanced the role of the Department of Finance in

central economic and financial planning and focused the activities of management in government on the efficiency and effectiveness of expenditure decisions. Despite this, the overlay of decision-making processes at the center and the elaboration of bureaucratic support structures that were intended to facilitate these processes lengthened the decision process and often appeared to subvert it. The PEMS process and the role played by the two Ministries of State responsible for two key policy sectors came under heavy criticism from many ministers. The Ministries were abruptly abandoned in June 1984 when the government of Prime Minister Turner replaced that of Prime Minister Trudeau. The rationale for the action was to implement changes that would streamline the decision-making process of Cabinet and enhance the role of individual ministers and their departments in that process (14). These decisions were not reversed when the Progressive Conservative government took office in September 1984.

It may be said that the year 1984 marked a watershed in the development of elaborate, complex machinery to co-ordinate the activities of government. Following the general election in September, the new Progressive Conservative government continued to streamline policy and financial planning processes. Greater emphasis was placed on allowing ministers to exercise their individual responsibilities without having to be subjected to formalized processes of co-ordination. Cabinet committees continued much as they had previously but the role of central agency offices in relation to reviewing and monitoring ministerial initiatives was diminished and with it their influence. The level of activity of interdepartmental committees also dropped appreciably. While it is too early to make any conclusive assessment, the present operation of the central machinery of government is much less formal and bureaucratized than it had been in the previous decade and a half. Furthermore, with down-sizing the public service as a major political objective, there have been few initiatives involving the creation of new organizations and structures generally, and no major innovations in central roles and responsibilities.

The Case of Non-Departmental Bodies

Concern with accountability of and in government has also extended from departments and agencies under direct ministerial control to non-departmental bodies such as Crown corporations and regulatory commissions. Non-departmental bodies are organizations designed to perform certain functions of government that are deemed to require varying degrees of independence from the political control of ministers and the administrative controls applied to the public service. Unlike departments, the authority to carry out the functions of these organizations is vested in the individuals or boards that head the organizations rather than in ministers. However, as agents of the Crown, these bodies must be accountable in some measure to the executive and, ultimately through ministers, to Parliament. The degree of independence enjoyed by a Crown agency or conversely the degree of control exercised by the government over it, has been a function of the status of the organization as defined in the *Financial Administration Act* (15).

Traditionally, non-departmental bodies have been construed as operational arms of government. Their policy objectives are set in legislation. In recent years in Canada, non-departmental bodies have been characterized as one type of policy instrument which governments may choose to achieve particular objectives (16). For example, the selection of a non-departmental body rather than some other type of policy instrument, such as regulatory policy or a simple statement of intent, establishes a particular organizational framework within which policy issues will be defined. As a consequence, governments have become increasingly preoccupied with ways and means of exercising control over them and ensuring their accountability to ministers.

When the Royal Commission on Financial Management and Accountability addressed these issues, it focussed first on the need to identify and classify these bodies, the presumption being that a sound classification regime preceded the establishment of systems of control (17). Its findings revealed a lack of precision in the classification of these bodies and, in some cases, the lack of a clear rationale for their creation. The Commission identified several broad categories of Crown agencies and attempted to develop accountability regimes for each. The Government's interest in reform in this area, however, has concentrated on two types of Crown agencies, the Crown corporation and the regulatory commission.

The number and variety of Crown corporations are great. In 1979 Treasury Board officials reported to the Royal Commission that there were 426 of these organizations. Only 54 were officially listed in the schedules of the *Financial Administration Act* (18). It was also found that, in certain instances, parent companies were able to create subsidiaries the activities of which were removed from direct scrutiny by the executive and Parliament.

As a result of internal study, the Government had begun planning legislative reform with respect to Crown corporations as early as 1977. A bill was introduced in 1979 but failed to pass before Parliament was prorogued for the 1980 general election. During the period, pressure for legislative reform was maintained by the Auditor General. For example, in his 1982 annual report, he referred to the several hundred Crown-owned companies of the federal government as a sub-government. Little was known about their activities but, in his view, often they had not pursued the purposes for which they were created.

Finally, in June 1984, Bill C-24, "An Act to amend the *Financial Administration Act* in relation to Crown corporations and to amend other acts in consequence thereof" was passed by the House of Commons (19). The bill set out a range of accountability and control measures that would be applied to all corporations listed in the Act. In particular, provisions were included to allow the Governor in Council, on the recommendation of the appropriate Minister, to give a directive to any parent Crown corporation "if the Governor in Council is of the opinion that it is in the public interest to do so" (20). Although considerable detail was spelled out on how the directives would be prepared and implemented, there were no provisions identifying on which matters the Governor in Council could give instructions to the corporations. The bill also contained detailed requirements for the formulation, submission and review of corporate plans and budgets, financial accounting and audit systems. However, the schedule to this Act listed only 62 corporations. The extent to which it applies to these Crown agencies is thus limited.

A problem that can be expected to linger in the aftermath of this legislative reform is the one of political choice of these types of organizations as policy instruments. The privatization of public enterprises has been an issue in some of the provinces of Canada, in the United States and in Great Britain. The Mulroney administration includes a minister responsible for privatization who is engaged in attempting to sell selected public corporations. To sell off public companies, however, requires willing buyers and, in some economic sectors, these may not be readily available.

A second main type of non-departmental bodies which has generated considerable interest in government is regulatory commissions. Like Crown corporations, these bodies also have power vested in an individual or board rather than a minister. Members who serve on these commissions may be full-time or part-time. Expertise in the particular field being regualted is the primary qualification for appointment although the composition of the boards of these organizations also reflects the representation of regional interests (21).

The traditional justification for the establishment of this type of organization has been the need for impartiality in the making of regulatory decisions, especially in economic sectors (22). Activities such as granting licenses, setting prices and standards of service and supervising activities in a particular industry or sector often involve the adjudication of individual rights in the market place. Such decisions are presumed to require protection from direct political pressures or interference for they will determine which individuals and groups will receive the benefit and/or pay the price of undertaking the activity.

A common problem that has often been identified with the operation of these bodies is that they become captives of the industry or groups they purport to regulate. In Canada, the evidence on this issue is mixed. One study, for example, has shown that the participation of former public servants on the boards of these commissions has ensured the maintenance of government policy goals in their operation (23). In cases where the commissions have appeared to serve the interests of the industry, it has been attributed to a relative lack of expertise on the commission in comparison to the industry.

Another problem which has arisen with respect to regulatory commissions relates to policy formulation. Although the statutes creating these bodies are expected to contain clear statements of policy objectives, they are usually set out in general, rather than precise terms. As a result, through the consideration of cases brought before them, commissions can determine policy direction in the field being regulated. Difficulties can arise when the government wishes to change the direction of existing policy or implement new policy.

For example, attempts to promote deregulation in the transportation and communications sectors have occasionally led to direct clashes between politicians and heads of commissions. In these instances, policy decisions have been imposed on commissions by the Cabinet. Ministerial desires to strengthen their influence on policy matters have, as in the case of Crown corporations, centered on the need and use of directives to these bodies as well through the apointment (and replacement) of the heads of the agencies.

In conclusion, the primary use of non-departmental organizations has had a pragmatic basis in that either governmental activities could be carried on more expeditiously by a semi-autonomous body or the nature of the activity required impartiality and hence independence. However, as non-departmental bodies have come to be perceived as public policy instruments, greater attention has been paid to them, especially given their numbers. Although improved accountability systems may be desirable for these bodies, it should be kept in mind that overconcern with policy directives and administrative controls can diminish the usefulness of these organizations derived from their independence from those controls. The degree of flexibility afforded government by using non-departmental forms to achieve public purposes can be offset by a preoccupation with developing systems that ensure they are performing those purposes.

PUBLIC PERSONNEL MANAGEMENT

The early history of personnel management in the federal public service has been characterized as a steady but gradual removal of the vestiges of political patronage in the recruitment and staffing of positions (24). The first legislative step was taken in 1868 with the passage of a Civil Service Act establishing a system of simple, voluntary pass examinations to be administered by a board of deputy ministers. An amending act of 1908 provided for the establishment of a non-partisan, independent Civil Service Commission. Subsequent reforms of 1918 more firmly established the merit principle as the basis of recruitment and selection through the use of competitive examinations and through their application to civil servants outside Ottawa. In addition, the Commission was charged with the responsibility of organizing and classifying the entire civil service. Although the authority of the Civil Service Commission in relation to Treasury Board and deputy ministers on personnel matters ebbed and flowed over the ensuing decades, it came to be an arm of management as well as a central staffing agency before its role was changed in 1967 (25).

Promotion of merit as the fundamental principle for staffing the public service has been and continues to be the foundation of the Commission's philosophy. The establishment of a merit system based on a merit principle has required flexibility to accommodate rights of employees, operational requirements of departments and the demands of the public interest. For example, the introduction of collective bargaining established a new set of employer-employee relations in the public service. The passage of the *Official Languages Act* resulted in bilingualism becoming an element of merit in the staffing of positions. Concern with underrepresentation of particular groups such as women, natives and handicapped persons has resulted in special recruitment programs. Furthermore, departmental needs for particular types of expertise to undertake specialized or high priority tasks have affected staffing practices. Some of the effects of these developments are discussed below.

Collective Bargaining

The introduction of collective bargaining in the federal public service in 1967 represented a major change in employer-employee relations. The concept of civil servant was replaced by that of public servant with the attendant rights to belong to public service unions, to bargain collectively and to strike under certain circumstances. The processes of classification and certification cut across departmental lines and thus strengthened the notion of a unified public service within the myriad of departments and agencies covered by the legislation.

There were several legislative measures that were passed to put the new system in place. First, amendments to the *Financial Administration Act* designated the Treasury Board as the employer for purposes of collective bargaining. Previous responsibilities of the Civil Service Commission for personnel planning, pay classification and training policy were transferred to the Treasury Board. Secondly, a new *Public Service Employment Act* was passed establishing the Public Service Commission as the central, independent staffing agency without any direct management responsibilities. Finally, the *Public Service Staff Relations Act* was enacted to provide for the machinery of collective bargaining. The authority to certify bargaining units and to administer dispute settlements through either arbitration or conciliation processes were vested with the Public Service Staff Relations Board.

An elaborate process of certification of occupational groups within six main occupational categories was undertaken. In 1983 seventy groups were identified as representing the population covered by collective bargaining. The executive, or management category as it is currently called, was, of course, excluded from collective bargaining. Other exclusions including those of a managerial or confidential capacity were also provided for in the legislation. The groups eligible for bargaining are represented in negotiations by bargaining agents from the professional and employee organizations.

In 1985 the distribution of employees within the main occupational categories was as follows (26):

Category	Total
Management*	4,400
Scientific and Professional	23,220
Administrative and Foreign Service	57,978
Technical	27,184
Administrative Support	68,437
Operational	41,813
	223,173

Affirmative Action

The concept of representative bureaucracy is, at best, a very difficult one to define (27). A literal definition would imply that the public service provides a mirror reflection of society in terms of individuals and groups or, more broadly defined, the values of those groups. Based on the assumption that representativity in some ways ensures responsiveness to societal needs, governments have, in one way or another, attempted to develop policies that support the "public interest" on these matters. The approach of the government of Canada and, more particularly, the Public Service Commission has been to focus on institutional and attitudinal barriers to equal opportunity and to remove discriminatory practices with respect to particular groups (28).

The government's policy on bilingualism as an element of merit in the staffing of the public service encompassed the need to improve the representation of francophones. The Treasury Board Secretariat began a service-wide undertaking to designate language requirements for public service positions and initiated language training programs in French and English. Special recruitment programs were put in place to increase francophone participation in all categories.

More recently, specific affirmative action programs have been initiated to assist public service careers of women, native people and the handicapped. Following several pilot projects, the President of the Treasury Board announced in June 1983 a number of precise methods and timetables by which departments would be required to increase the numbers of women, natives and handicapped. In particular, numerical goals were established for women in the Management Category. And yet, the Government's policy has not been to establish quotas. The main objective has been to

---

*Non-bargainable category.

achieve an "equitable representation" of qualified individuals from all groups. As stated in the 1983 Report of the Public Service Commission, the commitment is to "the development of a distinctly Canadian approach to the identification and elimination of discriminatory practices in the workplace" (29).

For the public service as a whole, francophones accounted for 27.8 per cent of total employees in 1985; women accounted for 41.6 per cent. Based on 1981 census statistics, the percentage of francophones with respect to the total population of the country is about 27 per cent; in the case of women it is about 52 per cent. The participation rates of native peoples and handicapped persons in the public service are, at the present time, statistically insignificant.

The following table sets out the participation rates of francophones and females in the public service by occupational category. It is interesting to note that, after more than a decade since the *Official Languages Act* was passed, the distribution of francophones by category is not far off the national percentage. In the case of women, the gender gap is evident in all categories (30):

Category	% Francophone	% Female
Management	20.3	7.8
Scientific and Professional	22.0	24.1
Administrative and Foreign Service	29.8	36.6
Technical	20.7	13.1
Administrative Support	33.1	82.7
Operational	24.9	12.9
% of total employees	27.8	41.6

Career Blockage

The impact of the operational needs of departments on the merit system has had some interesting effects on the composition of the public service. Although the Public Service Commission is the central staffing agency, staffing authority for all positions below those in the Management Category can be delegated to departments. Furthermore, deputies have statutory authority for management of their departments and, in practical terms, determine the types of expertise required to fulfill the department's mandate.

The organizational and management changes undertaken during the 1970s resulted in an emphasis being placed on creativity and innovation rather than experience or seniority as the basis of appointment and promotion of individuals. As a result, a large number of new university and college graduates were recruited into the public service and often promoted rapidly in particular fields, especially policy areas. As noted earlier, the expansion of the public service reached its peak in 1977, although the period of expansionary organizational reform had passed by that time. Moreover, declining economic conditions from the mid-seventies led to restraint measures being implemented within governments. The resulting slowdown, not only in new recruits entering the public service but also in individuals leaving the public service as opportunities have diminished in the private sector, has created the phenomenon of career blockage for individuals in particular categories.

In 1981, a study was published by the Institute for Research on Public Policy entitled "Nowhere to Go." In examining the problem of blocked populations, the study found that this problem tends to be concentrated in senior levels of professional groups and management ranks (31). Proposals were made for use of lateral transfers, increased period of time in jobs, increased levels of classification and early retirement. All of these strategies have, in fact, been employed. For example, executive classification levels were increased from 4 to 5 and a new group called Senior Management (SM) was introduced to net in those individuals who had reached the top of their classification levels in the professional categories in 1981.

The fact that 59.6 per cent of the total number of public service employees in 1983 were between the ages of 25 and 44 indicates that the problem of blocked careers may be one part of a larger issue. Demographic trends in organizations can be expected to reflect demographic patterns in society more closely than representation of particular groups. However, over time, blockage of certain populations reinforced by the lack of mobility upward or outward can work to the disadvantage of younger individuals who cannot gain entry or, if employed, cannot expect advancement, and of currently underrepresented groups such as women or natives. In the latter case, the existing resource pools will not be replenished and individuals from those groups will not be available when openings are. These conditions become more critical when measures to down-size the public service are undertaken. The objective of the current government is to reduce the ranks of the federal public service by 15,000 during its term of office. Although normal attrition will assist in achieving these objectives day-off schemes and surplus employees are part of the current personnel environment.

Collective agreements and the convention of job security, for example, have not guaranteed permanence of employment. Recent reorganizations of government departments and the dismantling of others have been accompanied by job reassignments and even lay-offs. Should further down-sizing of government operations occur, there is likely to be a heightened potential for conflict between the public interest writ broadly and the interests of individual public servants concerned about employment "rights."

PUBLIC SERVANTS AND POLICY-MAKING

The tradition of political neutrality and public service has been a central concept of Canadian parliamentary practice and has been closely linked to the principle of ministerial responsibility. The idea that advice to a minister is provided in confidence, that decisions are political ones and that continuity in government is ensured by a neutral public service have been the essential components of this concept (32). With the advent of an activist role for government and an emphasis on co-ordination and interdependence in the development of policy, however, the traidtional concept of neutrality has undergone a reformulation.

With respect to partisan activities, the rules have been and remain quite clear. Public servants are prohibited from direct political activity in partisan matters by virtue of Section 32 of the *Public Service Employment Act*. Specifically, the provision forbids deputy heads and employees "to work for or on behalf or against" a candidate or political party in any federal, provincial or territorial election. More detailed guidelines regarding the nature of prohibited activities have been provided by the Public Service Commission (33). The political rights that federal public servants do enjoy are the right to vote, to make financial contributions to political parties, to stand for nomination and to run in a federal, provincial or territorial election subject to prior approval by the Public Service Commission, and to attend meetings of a political party.

While public servants are prohibited by law from associating with partisan issues, the fact that they are expected to support the policies and programs of the party in power can lead to a close association and identification of those policies and programs with senior levels in the bureaucracy especially when a government is in power for a number of years. In particular, deputy ministers have played a role in policy-making from time to time which has created a major challenge to the notion of political neutrality and anonymity in the traditional sense.

Deputy ministers are the senior officials in charge of departments and agencies who are appointed by the Prime Minister (technically the Governor in Council) "at pleasure" and, thus, do not have the type of tenure enjoyed by other public servants employed under the *Public Service Employment Act*. Normally, they are career public servants who are appointed from within the public service rather than from outside. Theoretically, they can be removed from office when a change of government occurs, but, in practice, this has happened only rarely at the federal level and then usually in cases where the personal and, occasionally, political relationship between minister and deputy in a former regime has been perceived to be too close. Furthermore, there is no established practice or custom for senior officials to automatically submit letters of resignation at the time of a change of government. Practices at the provincial level differ in that frequently there are major changes in sneior personnel when governments change, reflecting perhaps a closer and even partisan relationship between ministers and senior officials at that level of government.

The evolution of a career service for deputies in the federal government dates back to the 1930s and the recruitment of a number of senior academics to key top posts. Each of these individuals recruited a number of competent subordinates, often from the universities, who by the 1940s and 1950s became what has been styled the Ottawa mandarinate. The influence of these individuals on post-war reconstruction policies has been well documented and to some extent mythologized (34). In any event, by the 1960s, the golden age had declined and other forces were to shape the role played by public servants in the policy process.

Deputy ministers have acted as senior policy advisers to ministers as well as chief administrative officers in charge of their departments. It has been widely accepted that a minister should not be expected to be involved in purely administrative matters respecting this department. For the most part, the deputy has authority in these areas, received on delegation either through the *Financial Administration Act*, the *Public Service Employment Act* or on direction from the Prime Minister. At the same time, deputies are expected to be involved in both policy and administrative matters respecting their departments. As pressures on ministers' time have increased and as the scope of activities of departments has expanded, deputies have come to play a larger and more visible role in the formulation and development of government policy. The essential nature of the relationship between the minister and his deputy has, nevertheless, invariably been described as a partnership (35). The minister provides the political judgment and direction; the deputy head provides the professional advice and expertise.

The emphasis placed on the coordination of activities and the interdependence of issues has also required a high degree of interaction among senior officials and their subordinates in the development of policy. In operating within these processes, senior officials have often had to play the part of policy advocates. They have had to persuade central agency officials, for example, of the importance and effectiveness of their departments' proposals compared with those of other departments. They have to defend their ministers' proposals from criticism by senior officials in other departments and agencies. Perhaps one of the best examples of the degree of influence that senior officials could exercise over the approval of policy proposals of departments and agencies was evident with respect to the processes generated by the Ministries of State prior to their disbandment.

In the routing of departmental submissions to the Cabinet committees through the former Ministries of State and other committee secretariats, Mirror Committees of deputies chaired by the Secretary of the respective Ministry of State were established and met weekly to discuss policy initiatives submitted by departments to the respective policy sector committees (36). This co-ordinative exercise was to ensure that ministers would not be caught off guard by proposals emanating from the various departments. The Committees also acted as buffers between departments and the political level of decision-making but were also seen as means of undermining ministerial responsibility.

With the dismantling of the Ministries, the Mirror Committees have also disappeared and further streamlining of the political decision-making process may yet occur. Nevertheless, while contemporary concerns with politicization of the public service have some credence, the bureaucratization of the political decision-making process also had a bearing on the role of senior officials and their subordinates in policy-making. The elaboration of systems and structures around the Cabinet and Cabinet committee system resulted in a high degree of involvement of officials in all stages of policy formulation and approval. It was one thing for a deputy minister and his professional staff to develop and formulate policy options for a minister to consider and choose from; it was another for a deputy and his staff to solicit the collaboration of other departments in the development of policies and to solicit the support of central agency officials in formulating the proposals in a manner considered suitable for ministerial consideration.

In some cases, ministers tried to ensure that their proposals are not just bureaucratic products by looking to political staffs in the development and formulation of policy. Since 1984 a higher profile has been given to ministerial staff. Each minister has a Chief of Staff responsible for managing political activities and co-ordinating policy matters with the respective departments. The result has been an upgrading of the functions rather than an increase in staff of ministerial offices.

However, the highly technical nature of most subjects requires the input of professional expertise often available only within the bureaucracy. The need to reconcile the individual and collective responsibilities of ministers requires some means of co-ordination and integration of activities with the government structure. Given the complexity and scope of government activities, this issue can be expected to be a recurring one that will concentrate on the need to improve the responsiveness of public service staff to both political and technical needs of political decision-making.

ADMINISTRATIVE ACCOUNTABILITY

The principles of ministerial responsibility provide the broad framework within which public servants are held accountable. The main means by which Parliament supervises the activities of the administration are the surveillance of government activities during daily Question Period, during debate on major government measures, and in standing and special committees of the House. Available to assist members in obtaining information are the Standing Order for the Notice of Motion for Production of Papers and the new access to information law.

Given the responsibilities of public servants and their expertise on policies and programs, it is unrealistic to expect ministers to be the sole providers of information on government activities. It is an established practice in Canada for public servants to appear before standing committees of the House of Commons to explain and provide information on programs when the committees examine departmental estimates, and to explain technical features of new legislation or legislative amendments. Equally, it is the practice of public servants to provide detailed information on the expenditures of their departments before the Public Accounts Committee of the House. However, it is not the practice nor the expectation that senior officials become engaged in debate on policies with elected officials.

In 1979, the Royal Commission on Financial Management and Accountability had recommended improving administrative accountability to Parliament through strengthening the role played by House committees. In particular, it proposed that a deputy minister, as chief administrative officer of his department "account for his performance of specific delegated or assigned duties before the Public Accounts Committee," that standing committees study the impact of government programs and that Government submit its proposed Fiscal Plan to a special standing committee for scrutiny (37). While there has been reform to improve the operations of parliamentary committees generally, efforts to create a more direct link of accountability of public servants to Parliament have not been made. Nevertheless, public servants are susceptible to public criticism in the House and there have been occasions when Ministers have denied responsibility for actions of officials on matters related to their departments' operations.

For the most part, the accountability link between parliamentarians and public servants on policy and program matters is informational in nature and is maintained through formal channels. However, there are other means whereby Parliament can exert control and exact accountability for administrative action especially with respect to delegated authority. There are, for example, special agents of Parliament that serve an ombudsman function in ensuring that acts of officials comply with legislative provisions and standards and that rights of individuals are not violated. To date, the federal Parliament has not adopted a general ombudsman office to investigate complaints from the public against administrative actions of government, although all of the provinces save Prince Edward Island have instituted such an office (38). The key agencies that do exist at the federal level are the following.

The most venerable and prestigious watchdog of Parliament is the Auditor General's Office, which was originally established in 1878 by the "Act to Provide for the Auditing of the Public Accounts." The Auditor General is appointed by the Governor in Council "during good behaviour" for a ten-year term. In addition to his investigatory powers in auditing departments' expenditures, his main instrument of control is the annual report which is submitted to Parliament and, more particularly, to the Public

Accounts Committee. The report is used to expose practices in the financial management of programs in the government which the Auditor General considers unsatisfactory or unacceptable. In this regard, the Auditor General can exert strong pressure on departments to improve administrative practices.

In 1977, legislation was passed creating a separate act for the Office and expanding the mandate to include value for money auditing. Thus, in addition to reviewing the economy and efficiency of programs, the Auditor General may now pronounce upon their effectiveness (39). Other reforms, including the introduction of the comprehensive audit, have resulted in considerable expansion of the Office and its activities. In particular, the practice in recent years has been to target specific areas of government activity for detailed scrutiny as in the case of recent reports that have focused on Crown corporations.

A second key watchdog of Parliament is the Official Languages Commissioner who holds office "during good behaviour" for a term of seven years. The Commissioner's responsibilities are to exercise the authority of the Office to ensure that both official languages have equal status and equal rights and privileges as to their use in all of the institutions of Parliament and the Government of Canada. To that end, the Commissioner may conduct investigations on his own initiative or in response to some complaint made to him. Like the Auditor General, the main tool of the Commissioner is that of publicity provided through the submission of an annual report to Parliament. This report may include recommendations for any proposed changes in the Act that may be considered desirable as well as for ways in which the policies of the government are being applied in the departments and agencies covered by the Act. The Official Languages Commissioner tables his report for consideration by a standing committee of the House.

A third main area in which an ombudsman function is found relates to human rights legislation. In 1977, the Canadian Human Rights Commission was established to deal with complaints of discriminatory practices in any federal department or agency or any other institution or undertaking covered by federal legislative jurisdiction. Grounds for complaints against discrimination are broad and include: race, national or ethnic origin, color, religion, sex, marital status, conviction for which a pardon has been granted, and certain matters respecting employment such as physical handicaps. The application of the Commission's authority is of particular concern to recruitment and staffing activities in the federal public service.

Finally, a recent development in the area of freedom of information has witnessed the creation of an ombudsman function under the Canadian Access to Information Act and the Privacy Act, proclaimed on July 1, 1983. Of the two, it is the Access to Information Act which impacts most directly on the release of information. Essentially, the Act provides the public with a right to information in federal records subject to a number of mandatory and discretionary exemptions in the Act. The legislation also provides for means of redress in the event information is withheld, including the provision for an Information Commissioner who acts as an ombudsman. This person has access to the information which has been withheld and can make recommendations for its release.

The number of exemptions under the Act includes approximately thirty-seven types of records which may or, in some cases, must be withheld from access, along with a schedule of thirty-three provisions in other statutes prohibiting the disclosure of government information. The scope of exemptions has been criticized by academics and journalist alike, but the counter argument made is that the potential user has a more precise idea of what may be available than under the American legislation. It has only nine broad exemptive grounds for withholding information, which have required judicial interpretation to clarify them.

The Information Commissioner has broad powers of investigation and can gain access to documents which are subject to the Act to make a finding whether information in dispute ought to be released. The Commissioner can also act as mediator between a complainant and the government. In the event a case is appealed to the Federal Court, the Commissioner can act as the advocate of the complainant.

With the exception of the Office of the Auditor General, the offices discussed above are of relatively recent origin. The formalization of procedures and requirements for scrutinizing administrative action in these areas may be viewed as a growing tendency towards establishing the objective responsibilities of administrators (40). By developing a more formal institutional framework in which administrative action is held to account, the requirements become more precise and, hence, attempt to ensure more predictable behavior. Nevertheless, they also contribute to a more impersonal and sometimes adversarial environment in which public servants conduct their work.

Some writers have stressed the need for equal if not greater attention to be paid to the elements of subjective responsibility, that is the values of public service that are inter-directed and motivate administrators to behave according to ethical and moral standards (41). Parliament has concerned itself with conflict of interest guidelines to ensure that the public interest is not compromised by the pursuit of personal interests, especially financial ones. But the positive values of service to the public are often left unarticulated.

CONCLUSIONS

The role of public service in the modern state is multi-faceted. As government activities have expanded, public service responsibilities have moved beyond the mere execution of political decisions. They include an active role in the formulation and development of policies and programs. This brings with it the exercise of power and influence over a broad range of matters affecting the interests of major sectors, groups and individuals in society. It is not surprising, therefore, that accountability has become such a pervasive theme in all aspects of public sector management.

In Canada, recent years have seen rapid changes and shifts in the political agenda of governments. These changes have impacted most notably on the structures and design of the machinery of government and of internal management systems. At the same time, efforts to maintain the essential character of the public service have also been evident. Political control of the administrative apparatus requires that the principles of ministerial responsibility determine the parameters of public service action. The need to maintain a responsive bureaucracy that is not entangled in processes and legal procedures that result in delay and inaction continues as a major concern in an age of growing institutional complexity.

In comparing the federal administration in Canada with provincial counterparts, there is a tendency to describe provincial administrations as less complex structures with less complicated decision-making processes. The relative size of provincial governments in comparison with the federal government may be a main factor here, but the point that is often missed lies more in the limited degree of differentiation of functions and activities at the provincial level than in the complexity of tasks. The operations of the federal public service reflect a growing specialization and structuring of activities and processes at all levels—political through technical. The problems that arise, therefore, are ones that invariably relate to means and methods of ensuring co-ordination across a range of diverse organizational structures and perspectives.

The challenge of future years is likely to focus on the limits of growth, especially in periods of continued recession. This will require further adaptation in public service functions and management to ensure that maximum levels of efficiency and effective-ness can be achieved. But perhaps even more important will be the changes that will be necessary to ensure that the human resources employed in the public sector are managed in a way that will not only promote producitivity in the economic sense but also provide for the continuing quality of public service that Canadian public administra-tion has been noted for in the past.

REFERENCES

1. Donald Smiley, (ed.), *The Rowell Sirois Report, Book I* (Toronto: McClelland and Stewart, 1963), pp. 204–212.
2. An excellent case study of this feature is Donald J. Savoie's *Federal-Provincial Collaboration: The Canada–New Brunswick General Development Agreement* (Montreal: McGill-Queen's University Press, 1981).
3. This point is particularly evident in the area of personnel management. See, J. E. Hodgetts, *et. al., The Biography of an Institution, The Civil Service Commission of Canada, 1908–1967* (Montreal: McGill-Queen's University Press, 1972).
4. J. E. Hodgetts, "Implicit Values in the Administration of Public Affairs," *Canadian Public Administration*, Vol. 25, no. 4 (Winter, 1982), p. 472.
5. Canada, Public Service Commission, *Annual Report, 1985* (Ottawa: Supply and Services, 1986), pp. 54–55.
6. An examination of the application of organizational principles to departmental development may be found in J. E. Hodgetts, *The Canadian Public Service, 1867–1970* (Toronto: University of Toronto Press, 1973).
7. There are several main references on the subject of departmental reorganization during this period. See, in particular, G. Bruce Doern and Peter Aucoin, eds., *Canadian Public Policy* (Toronto: Macmillan, 1979) and Richard W. Phidd and G. Bruce Doern, *The Politics and Management of Canadian Economic Policy* (Toronto: Macmillan, 1978).
8. See Colin Campbell, *Governments under Stress* (Toronto: University of Toronto Press, 1983), pp. 77–104.
9. *Ibid.* Campbell's work is a comparative study of executive structures in Canada, United States and Great Britain. While he attributes personal influence as being central to the particular design of the machinery, clearly the purpose and motivation behind developments in these three cases was to strengthen the steering capacity of governments.
10. The Ministry of State for Urban Affairs was officially abolished in March 1979. The dismantling of Science and Technology has been more incremental. The function of science adviser to the government remains and the organization was changed in 1982.

11. Canada. Royal Commission on Government Organization, *Report* (Ottawa: Queen's Printer, 1965), Vol. I, p. 19.

12. H. L. Laframboise, "Administrative Reform in the Federal Public Service: Signs of a Saturation Psychosis," *Canadian Public Administration*, Vol. 14, no. 3 (Fall, 1971), pp. 303–25.

13. This feature of expenditure limits is treated in detail in an article by Aaron Wildavsky, "From Chaos Comes Opportunity: The Movement toward Spending Limits in American and Canadian Budgetting," *Canadian Public Administration*, Vol. 26, no. 2 (Summer, 1983), pp. 163–81.

14. Office of the Prime Minister, Press Release and Statement, June 30, 1984, mimeo.

15. Schedules to the Act have identified 4 groupings known as A, B, C, and D. Schedule A includes organizations which are departments reporting directly to ministers; schedules B, C, and D include all Crown corporations. The fewest controls have applied to Schedule D corporations, known as proprietary corporations.

16. A key reference here is Allan Tupper and G. Bruce Doern, eds. *Public Corporations and Public Policy in Canada* (Montreal: Institute for Research on Public Policy, 1981).

17. This theme in the Report finds fuller expression in an article by a former member of the Commission staff. See, John W. Langford, "The Identification and Classification of Federal Public Corporations: A Preface to Regime Building," *Canadian Public Administration*, Vol. 23, no. i (Spring 1980), pp. 76–104.

18. Royal Commission on Financial Management and Accountability, *Final Report*, p. 277.

19. *Statutes of Canada*, Second Session, Thirty-second Parliament, 32–34 Elizabeth II, 1983–84, June 28, 1984.

20. *Ibid.* sec. 95.

21. See Caroline Andrew and Rejean Pelletier, "The Regulators," in G. Bruce Doern, ed., *The Regulatory Process in Canada* (Toronto: MacMillan, 1978), pp. 147–164.

22. See Economic Council of Canada, *Responsible Regulation*, Interim Report (Ottawa: Supply and Services, 1979).

23. Andrew and Pelletier, pp. 161–63.

24. The seminal study of the historial evolution of personnel management and its administration is the work by J. E. Hodgetts, *et. al.*, *The Biography of an Institution*, 1972.

25. *Ibid.*, especially chapters 4 to 7.

26. Public Service Commission, *Annual Report, 1985*. Statistics were extracted from Table 10, pp. 64–5.

27. See Kenneth Kernaghan, "Representative Bureaucracy: The Canadian Perspective," *Canadian Public Administration*, Vol. 21, no. 4 (Winter, 1978), pp. 489–512.

28. *Report of the Special Committee on the Review of Personnel Management and the Merit Principle* (Ottawa: Supply and Services, 1979), especially chs. 5 to 7.

29. Public Service Commission, *Annual Report, 1983*, p. 16.

30. *Annual Report, 1985*. Statistics were extracted from Tables 10 and 11, pp. 64–5.

31. Nicole S. Morgan, *Nowhere to Go? Possible Consequences of the Demographic Imbalance of Decision-Making Groups of the Federal Public Service* (Montreal: Institute for Research on Public Policy, 1981).

32. See Kenneth Kernaghan, "Politics, Policy and Public Servants: Political Neutrality Revisited," *Canadian Public Administration*, Vol. 19, no. 3 (Fall 1976), pp. 432–56. Recent commentary on this subject may be found in J. E. Hodgetts, "The Deputies' Dilemma," *Policy Options*, May 1983, pp. 14–17; and, Gordon Robertson, "The Deputies' Anonymous Duty," *Policy Options*, July 1983, pp. 11–13.

33. Public Service Commission, "Message from the Commissioners of the Public Service of Canada to Federal Employees," February, 1984, mimeo.

34. An historical account has been provided by J. L. Granatstein, *The Ottawa Men, The Civil Service Mandarins 1935-1957* (Toronto: Oxford University Press, 1982).

35. Articles which set out the essential features of this relationship include: Rt. Hon. Lord Bridges, "The Relationships between Ministers and the Permanent Departmental Head," *Canadian Public Administration*, Vol. 7, no. 3 (Fall 1964), pp. 295–308; and A. W. Johnson, "The Role of the Deputy Minister," *Canadian Public Administration*, Vol. 4, no. 4 (Winter 1961), pp. 363–73.

36. See Richard Van Loon, "Ottawa's Expenditure Process: Four Systems in Search of Co-ordination," in G. Bruce Doern, ed., *How Ottawa Spends* (Toronto: James Lorimer & Co., 1983), pp. 93–120, especially pp. 111–4.

37. Royal Commission on Financial Management and Accountability, *Final Report*, 1979, pp. 585–6.

38. For a report on the Canadian review of these bodies, see Government of Canada, *Report of the Committee on the Concept of the Ombudsman* (Ottawa: Government of Canada, 1977) and for current comment on developments in Canada and elsewhere see, Donald Rowat, "A Public Complaints Commission," *Policy Options*, March/April 1982, pp. 33–36.

39. For an assessment of recent changes, see Sharon Sutherland, "The Office of the Auditor General of Canada: Watching the Watchdog," in G. Bruce Doern, *How Ottawa Spends Your Tax Dollars* (Toronto: James Lorimer & Co., 1981), pp. 184–231.

40. The distinction between objective and subjective responsibility of administrators is examined by Kenneth Kernaghan, "Responsible Public Bureaucracy," in Kernaghan, ed. *Public Administration in Canada* (Toronto: Methuen, 1982) 4th ed., pp. 289–306.

41. *Ibid.* and H. L. Laframboise, "Conscience and Conformity: The Uncomfortable Bedfellows of Accountability," *Canadian Public Administration*, Vol. 26, no. 3 (Fall 1983), pp. 325–43.

4

The United Kingdom

BRIAN SMITH
University of Bath, Bath, England

HISTORY AND ENVIRONMENT

In the United Kingdom administrative institutions and processes are shaped by the development of liberal democratic ideology within the changing conditions of contemporary politics. The origins of the bureaucracy's constitutional relationships with other political institutions lie in the eighteeneth century when the permanency of the Civil Service emerged to meet contemporary political needs (1). In the nineteenth century a system of recruitment based on open competition gradually replaced patronage. The expansion of state activities in the twentieth century produced problems for the organization of central administration, especially as an increasing number of officials with professional, scientific and technical qualifications were recruited. Since the 1960s the personnel of central administration have, along with some other institutions, been made the scapegoat for the country's economic malaise. In the 1960s the civil service was accused of being insufficiently professional. Currently it is accused of being unnecessarily large.

Constitutional and Political Framework

The constitutional framework of public administration in the United Kingdom is that of a liberal democracy. The administration is deemed to perform a neutral role in providing policy advice to ministers and in implementing policies sanctioned by Parliament. Politicians with executive responsibilities are held accountable for the actions of their executive agencies. Administrators, particularly the civil servants who staff central government departments, are expected to serve the political heads of their organizations with equal loyalty, regardless of which political party currently forms the government. Civil servants are recruited on the basis of merit rather than patronage in order to guarantee political neutrality and efficient administration. Quite severe restrictions are placed on officials as regards political activities. In return for their neutrality, civil servants are protected by anonymity to the extent that secrecy and confidentiality prevent Parliament and the public from identifying which officials were instrumental in developing a particular public policy. Such rules and conventions flow logically from the basic presuppositions of representative and responsible government, whatever "language" is used to describe the role of Parliament in the constitution (2).

This constitutional model of the administrative system has been found unrealistic by political scientists who have stressed the political power which senior officials are able to wield from a knowledgeable and secure position within the permanent bureaucracy. Ministers often seem to be in alliance with their civil servants in resisting parliamentary and public scrutiny. The power of the bureaucracy sustains the power of the executive in relation to the legislature. As functional representation has grown in significance at the expense of territorial representation, the administration has become the focus of political pressure from groups which, in many instances, are the clients of individual departments. This is the main revision to the classical liberal theory of responsible government, and the role of public administration within it, to come out of the pluralist interpretation of democracy. Yet another interpretation of the role of bureaucracy in the political system of the U.K. is offered by those who detect corporatist tendencies in the contemporary state (3).

The agenda for the student of public administration is thus set by whatever interpretation is placed upon the role of the state in contemporary society. However, in the U.K. the agenda is still to a large extent dominated by liberal democratic presuppositions about the constitution. Some measure of accommodation has been provided for the perspective of organizational sociology, but alternative theories of the state have yet to differentiate and specify the administrative component in any detail (4).

Recent Developments

What is distinctive about the condition in which public administration currently finds itself is the hostility that the Thatcher Government has demonstrated to both central administration and local authorities. The size of the civil service is being reduced. "Efficiency" is to be increased mainly by reducing the tasks performed. The Thatcher Government has viewed the civil service as a political opponent. It was perceived as being attached to Keynsian economics and consensus politics, neither of which form part of the Thatcher Government's program. A concerted attack on the Civil Service's pay and promotion system has been successfully mounted (5). Morale has slumped in the face of repeated public criticism of the service, and the impartial loyalty of civil servants to the government of the day is under increasing strain.

At local government level a series of unprecedented actions have been taken against local authorities, particularly those which tend to be controlled by the major opposition, the Labour Party. Some of these policies raise important constitutional issues, and include restricting the level at which local authorities can levy their own taxes in the face of cuts in central grants, and the abolition of the Labour-controlled metropolitan counties and their replacement by appointees of the central government. Tighter government control over non-departmental bodies has also been announced. This will entail ministers and their departments ensuring that the policies and objectives of these bodies are brought into line with those of the relevant central department and are performed as cost-effectively as possible.

The anti-state policies of the Thatcher government have also had a considerable impact on the publicly owned sector of the U.K. economy and therefore on the administrative institutions of public enterprise. "Privatization" has meant breaking

public monopolies in the bus, gas, postal and telecommunication industries; and dena-
tionalization has involved selling publicly-owned assets to the private sector (6).

STRUCTURE AND MANAGEMENT

Central Government Organization

The executive organizations of central government can be roughly divided into two
broad categories. There are the central departments and ministries of state, headed by
ministers of the Crown; and "quangos"—executive agencies separated by statute from
ministries and exercising powers within a narrowly defined sphere of public policy,
adjudicatory bodies, and a complex network of permanent and temporary advisory
committees of differing status but with no executive powers.

The pattern of ministerial departments is a changing one, with new ones being set
up and existing ones terminated by abolition or merger. Reorganization usually follows
general elections. Between 1960 and 1979 twenty-eight new departments were created,
and thirty-one were dismantled. These changes were concentrated in election years.
The five election years of the period 1960–81 accounted for sixty-one per cent of the
new creations and fifty-six per cent of the abolitions (7).

Explaining the "continuous process of creation, fission, fusion and transfer" (8) is
no easy task. Some regard it as the organizational consequence of cabinet reshuffles.
The departmental structure is modified to suit the needs of the Prime Minister in
deploying senior members of the majority party. More systematic research suggest
that departmental changes are made to underline new policy directions; to improve
administrative efficiency; to create a reforming image; to make the deployment of
ministerial talent by the P.M. easier; to adapt to changes in the wider political environment; and to provide for the administration of new governmental functions. Whichever motive applies in any particular case, there are no theoretical principles to structure the location of central government tasks and functions within Whitehall. Changes
to the pattern are made *ad hoc* to meet the political exigencies of the moment (9).

There are approximately 500 public agencies with executive tasks, apart from the
central ministries, including the nationalized industries and health authorities. Such
agencies are generally headed by boards appointed by the minister with ultimate
responsibility for the special functions delegated by Parliament to the quasi-independent
body. In addition there are numerous adjudicatory and advisory bodies at different
levels which push the total to around 1,600. The current Conservative government has
tried, without much success, to reduce the number of "quangos" and to improve their
efficiency. Considerable opposition to the use of this type of agency comes from different parts of the political spectrum. Their use appears to those on the Right as an
extension of state powers and to those on the Left as a denial of democratic accountability and ministerial responsibility. Moreover, all parts of the political spectrum
have at times expressed unease at the powers of patronage that ministers enjoy.

The creation of special-purpose agencies is usually justified by reference to the
need either to depoliticize or debureaucratize administration. In the former case it is
argued that the nature of the task to be performed requires its management to be at
arms length from political "interference" and partisan control. Public broadcasting or
public sponsorship of the arts are cases in point. More commonly the second justification is given: that the methods of decision-making in the central departments are

inappropriate to the tasks to be performed. These tasks must therefore be "hived off" to bodies which can, say, operate more like a business concern.

"Quangos" raise a number of issues of principle which are fundamental to the system of administration in the U.K. First, there is the issue of patronage. Should the quango be regarded as an occasion for an unhealthy extension of ministerial patronage, or an opportunity to bring in outsiders for public service and participation? Secondly, there is the question of efficiency. Unfortunately, it is virtually impossible to know whether quangos perform better than ministerial departments, partly because there is so little opportunity for comparison, and partly because we do not know what weighting to give some of the presumed benefits of this type of organization, such as political impartiality. Thirdly, there is the question of accountability. Quasi-autonomous status is no guarantee against ministerial intervention, but it does restrict parliamentary scrutiny. Are the costs in terms of restricted democratic control by Parliament outweighed by the benefits which quango status brings? And finally, there is the problem of administrative complexity which *ad hoc* administration creates. Again it is a question of weighing intangibles: the public frustration brought about by an incomprehensible system of administration versus the independence and expertise (real or imagined?) of a special-purpose, appointed agency (10).

New Management Techniques

Since the early days of output budgeting there has been a succession of attempts to improve management efficiency in government departments: "a melancholy history of techniques based on private sector practice which have been hailed as the answer to long-standing problems but which have sunk without trace" (11). These have all been variations on a theme—that of specifying objectives, allocating responsibilities, planning the use of resources, and monitoring performance. The latest examples are MINIS—a management information system for ministers—and the financial management initiative.

MINIS aims to provide management information in a way that strengthens management control. What perhaps distinguishes MINIS from its predecessors is its association with cuts in public expenditure. Unlike earlier management techniques, MINIS fits tasks to the resources available, attempts to counter the tendency of departments to grow, and makes it clear to managers how cuts will take effect. However, like its predecessors (PPBS, accountable management, program analysis and review, and management by objectives) MINIS is designed to locate responsibility for specified budgets, to cost operations in such a way as to make it possible to evaluate performance, and to suggest alternative policy options. Indeed, after MINIS was introduced into the Department of the Environment (DoE) a number of officials from other departments argued that they already had MINIS is some other guise. Nevertheless, it is claimed that MINIS represents a more "rigorous" approach to current information systems (12).

MINIS has raised the same doubts as well as enthusiasm around Whitehall as its predecessors. Is it appropriate for all departments, no matter what their tasks? Is it cost-effective itself? Is it appropriate for government ministries to emulate the private sector to such an extent? Could the publication of so much information cause embarrassment to individual ministers or officials? Will the indicators of its success be the size of cost reductions and the number of staff shed?

MINIS has to a certain extent been generalized in the "financial management initiative" (FMI) proclaimed by the government in May 1982 and described in a White Paper (Cmnd. 9058) in September 1983. This policy again revived the old Fulton idea of delegating financial responsibility to "cost centres", and accompanied other reviews of management processes in the civil service: staff appraisal and reporting, management development, personnel work, and the role of post-entry professional qualifications in career development. FMI has clearer organizational consequences than MINIS. The authority of senior line managers in change of "organizational blocks" for the planning, management and control of the resources assigned to them is strengthened. Delegation down the line will be increased. Cash, manpower and objectives will be divided into "block budgets." Lines of responsibility will be clarified. Parallel hierarchies of specialists and generalists will be integrated into single organizational units (another Fulton idea).

Once again we are confronted by old wine in new bottles—old ideas in the case of the civil service, and established practices in the case of other parts of the public sector, especially the health service and local government. And once again the familiar doubts are being expressed. These center on the classic division in the work of senior officials between policy advice to ministers and the management of large organizations. FMI also has serious implications for ministerial responsibility in its delegation of authority to officials. Finally, by increasing the power of career officials and making it easier to judge the success or failure of their decisions, there is a risk that the topmost ranks of the civil service could become politicized (13).

Decentralized Organization

Most central departments that need to decentralize their operations do so by creating a regional organization which divides England into eleven or twelve territorial units. Central administration in Scotland and Wales is the responsibility of either the Secretaries of State for those regions and their departments, or the Scottish and Welsh regional offices of the other ministries. Many decentralized structures descend to the area level.

As there is no generally accepted conception of a region, least of all in central government, there has been a proliferation of regional patterns, with each department dividing the country more with regard to its own administrative needs than to interdepartmental co-ordination or spatial unity. Only Scotland and Wales have "fixed" boundaries that all departments and other central or regional agencies respect.

Scotland, Wales and Northern Ireland are the only regions with area-based ministries or Offices under the direction of Secretaries of State who sit in Cabinet. This system replaced one of devolution in the case of Northern Ireland in 1972, though there is still greater decentralization to the province than in the case of Scotland and Wales. Having a minister of Cabinet status in charge of central administration for these two regions gives them an advantage in that they are part of the decision-making process at the center in a way that the English regions are not.

The level of authority delegated to regional and sub-regional offices of central departments varies considerably. Some regional officials administer standardized rules, while others have discretion in applying departmental policy to individual cases, albeit within financial limits in some cases. Regional organizations also perform a wide variety of tasks: providing goods or services; supervising lower-level field offices; and the oversight of other parts of the machinery of government such as local authorities.

Such variations reflect the different circumstances which have led to decentralization to field offices of central departments. The administrative convenience of an intermediate level in the hierarchy, or ease of access to client groups, are two such factors. Another is central government's tutelage of subordinate institutions. As far as the other agencies of central government are concerned, such as regional health and water authorities, economies of scale point to a regional pattern of operations. There may also be vested interests which maintain a regional level of administration (14).

The decentralized structure of central administration in the U.K. can therefore be characterized as fragmented, lacking any kind of co-ordinating mechanism at regional or local levels, such as the prefectoral forms of control found in many other European states. The arrangements for Scotland, Wales and Northern Ireland produce territorial Cabinet ministers (departmental organization on the basis of area), not administrative coordinators. But the most striking feature of administrative decentralization in the U.K. is the way in which pressures for regional government have all but died away in the last few years, even in the "nations" of Scotland and Wales.

Public Corporations

The public corporation is the most distinctive institution which has been devised in the U.K. for the ownership and management of public assets. The most important public corporations are the nationalized industries, employing some seven per cent of the labor force and accounting for about ten per cent of total output. However, the corporation is also used as a form of public ownership for non-industrial assets, as for example in the case of public broadcasting, new towns, the Bank of England and the Welsh Development Agency. Such corporations are legal entities set up and empowered by statute but under varying degrees of ministerial control. There has been relatively little consideration given to alternative forms of organization for managing publicly owned enterprises.

There have however been changes in some of the key features of public corporations in the last decade. The governing boards of some corporations have come to include civil servants. Employees have been involved in decision-making at both board and plant levels. Consumer representation has been strengthened in some nationalized industries by the appointment of representatives of consumers to managing boards.

The political accountability of the public corporations has always been a contentious issue in the U.K. Their accountability to Parliament was made more problematic in 1979 when the Select Committee on Nationalized Industries was abolished and the job of scrutiny fragmented to the select committees charged with the oversight of sponsoring departments.

The statutory framework of ministerial control has not changed significantly since the second world war. Ministers still remain responsible for appointments to boards, matters affecting the national interest, and approval of plans for capital expenditure and borrowing. However, statutory provisions have left room for additional areas of ministerial influence to develop, notably over capital investment and the fixing of prices and wages.

Organizationally some nationalized industries have undergone considerable and sometimes frequent change. Such changes have reflected varying ideas about the functions of boards and senior executives and the levels and forms of decentralization felt desirable. Different public corporations have moved in different directions under the impact of changing ideas (15).

PUBLIC SERVICE PERSONNEL

Classes of Personnel

Approximately 7½ million people work in the public sector, or some 30 per cent of all employment. These may be broadly divided between central government, local government and the public corporations. "Central" government includes the civil service, the armed forces and the National Health Service, and accounts for just over 31 per cent of public employment, or 2.3 million employees. "Local" government includes teachers, the police and other professional groups employed by local authorities such as social workers. These constitute nearly 41 per cent of public sector manpower, or 3 million employees. The public corporations include the nationalized industries and over 40 other bodies such as Regional Water Authorities, Passenger Transport Executives and New Town Development Corporations. They employ nearly 2.1 million, or 28 per cent of public sector employment (16).

These are very broad categories which conceal many different career structures, rates of remuneration and other aspects of personnel management, which vary between occupational groups in different parts of the public sector. Space prevents a full treatment of all such categories. Since this volume is mainly concerned with central administration, some detail of civil service structure is given, followed by a brief discussion of recruitment and pay.

There are some 528,000 non-industrial civil servants divided into three main groups: administrative, scientific and professional/technological. Personnel from each of these are found in all departments. In addition there are some 500 departmental classes of civil servant such as tax inspectors, prison officers and immigration officers. Specialists and generalists can compete for the so-called "open structure" of the three top levels in the departmental hierarchy: permanent secretary, deputy secretary and under secretary. This was in response to the recommendations of the Fulton Committee in 1968 which criticized the lack of professionalism among generalist administrators, the subordination of specialists to generalists (see below), and the barriers between classes of staff which frustrated efficient staff deployment. The recommendations for reform made by Fulton have only been implemented to a limited extent, not least because the civil service was able to control and manage the details of the changes that were accepted. And some of the innovations based on Fulton, such as the creation of a Civil Service Department responsible for recruitment, training and managerial efficiency, have been reversed by successive governments. The CSD, for example, was dismantled in 1981. The idea of a single, unified grading structure has also been abandoned.

The Management of the Civil Service

British civil servants are recruited through a system of open competition organized by the Civil Service Commission. Recruitment procedures are designed to be free of bias, but a disproportionate number of entrants to the higher civil service come from middle class backgrounds and have been to public schools and "Oxbridge" (Oxford or

Cambridge). Some would argue that this reflects "self-selection" by those within the service seeking people similar to themselves from outside, thereby perpetuating an outdated elitism. Others argue that the educational system is discriminatory, sifting out people from a different class background before they can acquire the qualifications needed by a merit system of appointment; and discouraging non-Oxbridge graduates from applying. The controversy lingers on since, despite Fulton, entrants to the higher civil service continue to be drawn from a narrow social and educational stratum.

Until recently civil service salaries had been decided on the basis of a formula devised by the Tomlin Royal Commission of 1929–31 and amended by the Priestley Royal Commission of 1953–55. Essentially this leaves pay to be determined by "fair comparison" with relevant occupations, rather than market forces. Clearly this requires an independent arbitrator to establish which comparisons are fair. A Civil Service Pay Research Unit was established for this purpose. However, the Thatcher Government decided to treat civil servants (and other public servants) as if they were employees negotiating their wages in the private sector and within the context of supply and demand. In 1980 the civil service pay arrangement was abandoned, and the recommendations of the Unit were ignored. Civil Servants were in effect told to take what was an offer or go elsewhere. Not surprisingly, civil servants have responded to being treated like industrial employees in the private sector by behaving like them and employing the sanction of strike action (17).

The 21-week strike of 1981, though won by the government, led to the setting up of a committee under Sir John Megaw to devise a new civil service pay system. It recommended that civil service pay should match "broadly" levels of remuneration in comparable private sector jobs. Information on pay trends would be analyzed by an independent board (18).

The management of the civil service is now the responsibility of a unit within the Cabinet Office—the Management and Personnel Office (MPO). Since the Fulton Report there had been a Civil Service Department which symbolized the need to co-ordinate recruitment, training, management services, manpower planning and remuneration. This had an unhappy history and failed to assert itself among the "common service" departments at the center. Above all else, the Treasury resented losing control over manpower, pay, superannuation and allowances. Within the context of the Thatcher Government's policy of reduced public expenditure it was perhaps inevitable that the CSD would be dismantled, with its financial responsibilities returning to the Treasury and its personnel functions going to a new unit within an established central organization. The CSD could not survive being regarded by Mrs. Thatcher as "an agency which would defend the position and rights of civil servants instead of shaping the machinery of government on the lines she preferred" (19). The new arrangement leaves the MPO responsible for promoting efficiency and new management systems throughout the departments of central government, without controlling manpower.

Public Service Unions

Approximately half of the twenty largest trade unions in the U.K. represent workers almost all of whom are in the public sector. The remainder also have members who work in different parts of the machinery of government. The main public sector unions have over 3 million members, almost a quarter of total trade union membership. Some 83 per cent of all public sector employees are estimated to be members of a trade union. It is common to find a multiplicity of trade unions representing employees in any one part of the public sector. For example, there are 43 unions and staff associations representing people employed in the National Health Service (20). Some unions represent relatively small groups of specialist public servants, such as tax inspectors or the professional civil servant grades.

In the non-industrial civil service collective bargaining over terms and conditions of employment is conducted within the National Whitley Council. "Whitleyism," named after the chairman of a committee on industrial relations which reported after the first world war, has spread to many parts of the public sector. The civil servant's employer, the Crown, is represented by the "Official Side" consisting of the Head of the Home Civil Service, senior Treasury officials and Permanent Secretaries from the main departments. Other parts of the public sector have devised their own machinery for collective bargaining. There are, however, three groups for whom it is thought appropriate to have independent pay review bodies to advise the Prime Minister on pay and allowances: the armed services, NHS doctors and dentists, and the top ranks of the judiciary, civil service and military.

Because of the difficulty in reconciling industrial action with public service, until quite recently it had been widely accepted that public sector pay should be settled by fair comparisons with jobs in the private sector rather than by market forces and industrial sanctions. Pay comparability, as we have seen, has come under increasing pressure in recent years as government policy to reduce public spending has been enforced. The argument that it is difficult to find jobs in the private sector comparable to some public sector work has been augmented by the economic philosophy that public sector pay should be determined by the forces of supply and demand in the labor market. Industrial relations in the public sector have undoubtedly suffered as a result. Some public service unions have become more politicized as the jobs and pay of their members have been threatened, and have taken a stance on a number of public policy issues such as the quality of social services, the issue of unemployment generally, and the distribution of wealth. Public sector trade unions often behave as pressure groups in defense of the services in which their members are employed.

Political Rights of Civil Servants

The political activities of civil servants are governed by the principle of political impartiality. Political activities were classified by the Masterman Committee in 1949 in the light of this fundamental principle. "Political activity" refers to adoption as a parliamentary or local authority candidate, co-option to a local authority committee, holding party office at local or national levels, canvassing at national or local levels on behalf of candidates or parties, speaking in public on matters of national political controversy, or expressing views on such matters in letters to the press or in publications.

The civil service is divided into three groups for the purpose of enforcing rules about political activities. First, there is the "politically free" group, which includes all industrial civil servants and minor non-industrial grades. These are free to engage in the political activities identified by the Masterman report. Next there is an "intermediate group" of typists, clerical grades and grades in other classes parallel to the clerical and executive grades, but not including people in executive grades. These are entitled to engage in most of the stated political activities, subject to departmental permission and conditions. Finally, the "politically restricted" group contains all other civil servants, who are debarred from engaging in political activities at the national level and need departmental permission to engage in them at the local level. It can be seen that political activities are tightly controlled for even junior and middle managerial and specialist levels.

When permission is given to engage in political activities, officials are required to obey a "code of discretion" which prohibits personal attacks on, or embarassment to, ministers. There is no right of reinstatement of civil servants in the intermediate or restricted groups who resign to seek election to Parliament, and even those in the "free" group are reinstated only if specified conditions have been met.

Even when governments have acknowledged the need for greater openness, as in the early 1970s, this did not imply a license to civil servants to discuss with unauthorized persons government policies and decisions in the process of formulation, or the participation of civil servants in the public discussion of politically controversial topics. The exposition of government policy is the responsibility of ministers. Any contribution to knowledge made by a civil servant on the basis of specialist expertise must not prejudice national security, create the possibility of embarrassing the government, or bring the impartiality of the service into question. Civil servants who wish to take part in outside activities which involve drawing on official information or experience (lectures, seminars, conferences, articles in learned journals, etc.) must obtain departmental permission and must not disclose classified or confidential information, or discuss matters of political controversy or relations between civil servants and ministers. They are also prohibited from commenting on individuals or organizations in terms which their department would regard as objectionable, and from participating in outside activities in a way which could conflict with the interests of the department or bring its good name, and that of the civil service generally, into disrepute. Against rules such as these "open government" has little chance of survival.

Educational and Social Background

Recent reforms have failed to widen the social and educational background of higher civil servants (21). A bias towards graduates in the arts and humanities in the system of recruitment to the higher civil service sustains a bias towards candidates with a privileged social and educational background. The Fulton reforms had no impact on the "unrepresentative" nature of the civil service in the U.K. Subsequent changes in recruitment methods have been half hearted (22). Given these and other biases in recruitment the higher civil service is likely to be even more elitist in 20 or 30 years because of a strengthened bias in recent recruitment practices (23).

It is difficult to predict what the consequences would be of a civil service that was made, through some kind of positive discrimination, more representative of society. The power of socialization within departments is probably great enough to offset any attitudes imported from outside, though this would obviously change over a long period if a concerted effort were made to widen the social basis of recruitment. And there is no guarantee that bureaucrats with working class backgrounds will be more favorably disposed towards the interests of that class, especially after experiencing embourgeoisement, than other types of recruit. Such positive discrimination would be strongly opposed, on the ground that it would risk lowering the standard of entry. However, recent experience indicates that the principle of recruitment on merit, as currently interpreted, does not remove social bias from the system.

Problems of Politicization

The current government's attempts to withhold information from Parliament about the sinking of the Argentine cruiser, the *Belgrano*, during the Falklands conflict, is the latest in a sequence of events which have strained the loyalty of civil servants. Secret documents have been leaked to the press by civil servants who disapprove of government decisions.

Problems of conscience for civil servants clearly raise important political and constitutional issues. In theory, civil servants are required to carry out the wishes of their ministers, in the knowledge that ministers will be held accountable for any wrongdoings. A neutral and loyal civil service can only be guaranteed if governments and policies, not civil servants, are changed by the democratic process. The orthodox interpretation of a civil servant's relationship with ministers was summed up (24) by a permanent secretary recently as follows:

> the civil servant advises in the light of his own conception of the national interest, but subordinates his views to those of his minister and carries out with loyalty and enthusiasm the policies and decisions of his Minister whatever his private opinions of them.

Resignation is the only legitimate course open to civil servants who experience a crisis of conscience while in government service.

Against this, however, it is argued that ministerial responsibility is a dead principle and that civil servants have a higher loyalty than that to the government of the day—a loyalty to Parliament and the public interest. Senior civil servants have also spoken of their duty to reflect the "common ground" in politics. From time to time senior officials have proposed a code of conduct which would establish values over and above that of loyalty to the current minister, values which a civil servant could use as a yardstick with which to measure the legitimacy of what ministers were requiring of him. Thus a civil servant might reasonably be required to implement current ministerial policy, but yet still be able to resist any dishonest act or government deceit designed to mislead Parliament or the public. Civil servants could become a significant part of the defence against abuse of power, an intention of the U.S. Civil Service Reform Act of 1978.

This line between the enthusiastic implementation of ministerial policy by civil servants and their public rejection of ministerial methods which violate their conscience may be a fine one to draw. A code of conduct which allowed civil servants to develop their own conception of the public interest could have serious consequences for the content of government policy as well as the conduct of government business. If civil servants begin to impose their view of professional ethics, moral principles, the good of the country and the legitimate scope of governmental authority, to whom will they be answerable in a system of representative and responsible government? Much of the problem could be removed if there were a Freedom of Information Act, and repeal of the Official Secrets Act, to make it easier for Parliament and the public to scrutinize the political executive. Civil servants would then be freed from pressures to "leak" information and so betray the trust which, it is held, the Crown places in them.

Specialists and Generalists

The number of specialisms within the civil service has increased as state intervention has grown. This expanding role for specialists—scientists, technologists, economists, lawyers, statisticians, computer specialists and the like—has taken place within an administrative tradition which asserts the dominance of the generalist (25). Unlike the civil services of most western democracies, greater authority is given to those in the administrative grades, for whom a good standard of education regardless of subject is thought appropriate for their tasks. A training in public administration is not regarded as relevant to an administrative career. The skills required by an administrator are taught after entry. People with professional qualifications are recruited into specialist groups whose work requires the skills of a professional, a scientist or a technologist. Tension between the two categories of officials has developed. From time to time, and notably with the report of the Fulton Committee in 1968, strong criticism is leveled at the administrative structures and processes which perpetuate a relationship suspected of being bad for both efficiency and the morale of substantial numbers of highly qualified, professional staff.

Resistance to change has come from within the generalist ranks of the civil service and has been strengthened by the reluctance of successive governments to pursue the matter with any vigor. The generalists have argued (from a position of power within the civil service) that it is precisely their own professionalism—in the workings of the political environment of central administration—which justifies the greater authority they tend to enjoy within departmental structures. Despite the abandonment of an exclusively administrative "class" some ten years ago, the most senior posts within a department are monopolized by administrators, not specialists. While it is true that specialists have to perform more managerial tasks within their specialist groups as they become more senior, they are discriminated against in the filling of senior managerial and policy positions within the department. The complex processes of parliamentary government and politics require skills and techniques which only generalists possess. The generalist's understanding of the politics of Whitehall as well as Westminster—interdepartmental politics and the world of interest group negotiations—further strengthens the generalist's claim to senior managerial and policy making posts within central departments.

The organizational consequences of this are that policy-making is carried out in hierarchies which are usually separate from those in which specialist advice is managed. The generalists act as the "interpreters and gate-keepers" of specialist information flowing to ministers (26). Some attempts have been made to create more integrated structures in which management positions are not regarded as the prerogative of any particular group or class of civil servant, yet generalists still tend to be given responsibility for ministerial, parliamentary and financial business.

It is important to recognize that this is ultimately a political rather than a managerial issue. The debate about whether specialists do in fact have access to the most senior positions and whether they prefer to practice their science or profession rather than become managers, has obscured the political need within the British system of government for a generalist intermediary between minister and department to co-ordinate departmental tasks within a policy framework that consists not only of ministerial objectives but also the immediate political environment of party, parliament and pressure groups. Co-ordination within and between departments is facilitated by this "common society of generalists" (27). This arrangement contrasts starkly with the civil services of North America, where administrators are more likely to be professional managers than intellectual amateurs; and with continental European states, where the lawyer reigns supreme.

THE BUREAUCRACY AND POLICY-MAKING

Policy-Making and Budgeting Systems

Most central departments have set up planning units to assist senior officials and ministers in their role as policy-makers (28). The precise responsibilities of such units vary from department to department. They also vary in the extent to which they have direct access to the minister, are separated from day to day management, and are engaged in long-term planning. The following are typical duties:

planning the annual budget
co-ordinating the department's research program
policy analysis and review of effectiveness
co-ordination of other departmental policy analysis by research units, economics
    and statistics branches, policy groups, project teams and operating divisions
identifying policy issues for special attention
medium-term planning
monitoring implementation processes
preparation of briefings for ministers.

The 1960s and 70s saw a number of changes made to departmental planning and budgeting processes in central government, all designed to strengthen the rationality of policy-making. These included systems analysis, PPBS, corporate planning, management by objectives and program analysis and review (PAR). The most ambitious of these was PAR, since it was intended not only to systematize and extend policy evaluation within departments, but also to provide the Cabinet, Treasury, Public Expenditure Survey Committee and Central Policy Review Staff (a Cabinet-level planning unit) with a central controlling and co-ordinating system. Each PAR was supposed to take a key program and analyze its goals, resources and alternative ways of achieving those goals (29).

The history of PAR reveals a good deal about the effect of the political environment on any attempt at more synoptic planning in government. First, a changing political and economic climate characterized by expenditure cuts created pressures for cost reductions rather than output maximization. PAR was unsuited for this, and was soon replaced by the "Rayner scrutinies," the cost-cutting exercises initiated by the Prime Minister's senior advisor on "efficiency." These scrutinies have been far more concerned with cutting costs than with analyzing the consequences for administrative performance or outcomes.

Secondly, like many other evaluative processes in government, PAR suffered from a lack of understanding as to how it was supposed to operate or what its methodology was: how to ensure that really analytical questions were asked; how to ensure implementation; how to ensure the analytical capacity to carry out this type of analysis. Thirdly, such analytical processes are expensive. Time and personnel have to be found and this is often done on a temporary, ad hoc basis. Fourthly, organizational resistance is quickly generated when analysis constitutes a threat to vested interests.

Nevertheless a number of improvements in the analytical capability of departments can be attributed to PAR. There are now more specialist analysts. More policy analysis and review are being undertaken (MINIS, Rayner scrutinies, FMI, etc.). But these approaches to planning and budgeting are dominated by the ideological preoccupations of the government of the day.

The Role of Top Civil Servants

It is now a commonplace of political analysis to say that top officials are involved in the making of policy and thus have a political role. In the U.K. there has been considerable debate on the issue of whether civil servants have come to dominate policy-making or at least exercise a good deal more influence than other actors in the policy-making process, including ministers.

It is argued that the civil servants' permanency, experience and expertise give them a monopoly of knowledge relevant to policy-making with which ministers cannot hope to compete. Government departments are, in any case, just too large for ministers to control, even if they did not have functions to perform outside their departments. Consequently civil servants must select the information going to ministers. In this way, it is feared, civil servants guide the policy choices which are ultimately made in the minister's name. Problems are identified and policy options are selected by civil servants before presentation for ministerial choice. Even when a policy choice has been made, implementation does not necessarily follow automatically. Administrative discretion may alter policies significantly, as may inertia and deliberate obstruction.

Ministers of both parties have in the past complained of civil service influence and obstructionism. The argument that ministers often only have themselves to blame for allowing officials to dominate them does not entirely undermine the proposition that civil servants rule. However, many ministers claim to have got their way when in office. Personality, ideology and circumstance are all important in the relationship between ministers and their officials. Nevertheless it is clear that the constitutional description of the senior official's role is inadequate, and that civil servants do far more than advise ministers (30).

ADMINISTRATIVE ACCOUNTABILITY

The Role of Parliament

Party discipline in the House of Commons is part of the foundation of executive dominance in the political system of the United Kingdom. It severely restricts Parliament's competence in the scrutiny of administration and in enforcing ministerial responsibility. It is rare, though not unknown, for ministers to resign as a result of serious administrative error, and it appears to be increasingly difficult for Parliament, even through its select committees, to extract the information that it needs to perform the task of scrutiny successfully.

Parliament's arsenal of weapons to enforce administrative accountability appears impressive at first sight. They undoubtedly have a deterrent effect, but the balance of power lies in favor of ministers. Question Time keeps departments alert to the possibility of embarrassing revelations, but it has to serve other political purposes than the scrutiny of administration. Select Committees—of which there are now fourteen, each corresponding to a central department, with a fifteenth, the Public Accounts Committee, following up the reports of the Comtroller and Auditor General—have achieved some important objectives in recent years. Government policy and departmental management have been influenced. Valuable information has been extracted and publicized. Yet it is still possible for ministers and civil servants to withhold information if they feel that publicity would be damaging to the government. And such committees can only hope to cover a small proportion of departmental administration. Debates in the whole House offer extremely limited opportunities for Parliamentary scrutiny of administrative processes. Two new committees were set up in 1973 to scrutinize delegated legislation, but these have worked more to the advantage of the executive than to Parliament, by enabling the Government to remove more statutory instruments from scrutiny and decision by the whole House of Commons (31).

When considering the balance of power between Parliament and the executive in the matter of administrative accountability it is important to remember that Parliament does not confront the executive as a unified bloc. Ministers are drawn from Parliament and have the backing of their party supporters who are generally less inclined to support a strengthening of Parliamentary control when their leaders are in office than when in opposition. From time to time members of the majority party can exert considerable influence by the threat of abstention or even of voting with the opposition, as in the recent case of student grants. But such rebellions, important though they are, represent Parliamentary control of policy rather than of administrative processes.

The Control of Expenditure

The cycle of expenditure control suffers from a number of defects which are difficult to correct, given the prevailing structure and operation of government. First, the Public Expenditure White Papers do not provide revenue projections, so it is not possible for Parliament to judge how expenditure plans relate to taxation policy. Secondly, the Treasury does not include its medium-term economic survey with the expenditure plans, so that public expenditure is unrelated to the economic resources available. This is evidence that Treasury control has moved away from planning expenditure in the light of resources available, towards short-term projections of monetary costs. Thirdly, the volume of expenditure is so large (almost half of GNP) that parliamentary scrutiny, let alone control, is virtually impossible given that only three days are available to debate the Estimates and that much of this time is used for purposes other than purely financial control. The select committees make only a marginal contribution to the role of financial scrutiny. Fourthly, the Public Accounts Committee can only cover a small proportion of the expenditure which falls within its jurisdiction, and its jurisdiction covers only about half of total government expenditure. The National Audit Act of 1983 widened the scope of the Comptroller and Auditor General to a limited extent, but left the nationalized industries outside the system of parliamentary financial control (32).

Courts and Ombudsmen

Although the courts of the United Kingdom have no power to question the validity of statute law, they are competent to review executive action. The prerogative writs of *certiorari, mandamus* and *prohibition* can be sought to quash, direct or prohibit the actions of public agencies. A remedy may also be sought by an aggrieved individual in the form of an application to the courts for a *declaration* that the proposed act of a minister or official would be beyond his legal powers. So, though there is no constitutional limitation on legislative power, there is a system of judicial review of the executive.

Judicial review operates through the interpretation of statutes: whether a ministerial action is enpowered by statute; whether a common law right, threatened by executive action, has been abrogated by statute (for example, a right to natural justice or *habeas corpus*). Such review is somewhat unpredictable in its results. This is because public law in the U.K. is no more than the application to relations between the state and the citizen of principles that apply to relations between citizens themselves. The U.K. has no *conseil d'état*, no constitutional court and no body of administrative law. As Lord Scarman put it: "Technically, the problems are seen merely as the construction of a statute, the application of a common law rule, or the exercise of a judicial discretion. We lack the machinery to develop a co-ordinated system of public law" Judges therefore often have to choose between leaving ministerial discretion unqualified or exercising judicial discretion without the guidance of general principles. The choice will always in part be determined by the political values of the judge, thereby undermining a judicial impartiality which is in any case more an ideological assertion than a political reality.

Administrative tribunals are an alternative to the courts as a means for the redress of grievances. These have been set up in many areas of public administration to offer quick, cheap and informal adjudication between the individual and the authorities. Such tribunals are supposed to be open, fair and impartial. Great variability can be found in the first quality, and it has been a constant source of debate as to how fair and impartial tribunals can be when their members and officers are appointed by the minister responsible for the department against which the appeal is lodged. However, monitoring by the Council on Tribunals, an advisory body created in 1958, goes a long way towards ensuring that these quasi-judicial extensions of the administrative process conform to the rules of natural justice.

Under an act of 1967 Britain's "ombudsman," the Parliamentary Commissioner for Administration (PCA), investigates complaints from the public against maladministration. There are few reforms which have attracted as much critical comment for their inadequacy to meet perceived needs, in this case for the redress of citizens' grievances against the state, as the Act of 1967. The impartiality of the office has been questioned because the majority of successive Commissioners and their staff have been seconded from the civil service. Under the Act citizens have been denied direct access to the PCA, having to seek an investigation into their complaint through a Member of Parliament. The jurisdiction of the Commissioner was so narrow that separate ombudsmen, with their own procedures and limitations, had to be created for National Health Service hospitals and local government. Nevertheless the ombudsman institution in Britain can reasonably be called a "qualified success" (33).

Public Administration and the Public

The dominant trend in British public administration during the last ten years has been towards tighter central political control and away from participation by, or consultation with, sections of the public. The axe taken to Britain's quangos has fallen most heavily on those with purely advisory functions, set up as instruments of consultation and liaison with groups representing different social and economic interests.

Participation, so much a vogue in the early 1970s, has virtually disappeared from the British political scene except in its electoral form. The current Conservative government is more likely to seek the "participation" of the business sector than service users in the provision of public services, through various forms of privatization. Whereas in the 1970s there were many schemes to involve the public in the management of public services aimed at community development, this is now more likely to be left to the dictate of market forces. It is interesting to speculate why the issue of participation is no longer on the political agenda in the U.K. Disillusionment with the experiments of the late 1960s and 1970s undoubtedly has something to do with this.

The public have increasingly to be seen as the recipients of state action rather than as participants in processes of service design and delivery. A government with a large majority in parliament is unlikely to be interested in other, more direct, forms of administrative accountability than the conventional processes of representative government. Moves to get legislation through Parliament on access to information have so far been successfully resisted. This has only partially been compensated for by the deliberate leakage of information to the media by civil servants, a practice which has strengthened the distrust of the service felt by the Thatcherite wing of the Conservative Party (34).

The present government has become noted for its secrecy and for withholding information from the public and Parliament. Much was made of the publication of MINIS information (see above), but a wide circulation is unlikely when one department's MINIS report costs over £140. There is a great deal of skepticism about the power of Parliament to extract accurate or reliable information from the administration. Concern is growing at the capacity which public authorities are gaining from information technology to invade privacy and manipulate confidential personal information in a way that threatens the individual's interests and liberties (35). The Official Secrets Act and judicial interpretations of it give ministers power to define a very wide range of activities involving the release of information as offenses against the law.

Different sections of the public still have recourse to conventional indirect linkages with the bureaucracy—through MPs, local councillors, pressure groups, the mass media and, in some areas of public policy, public inquiries and consultative committees. It is unlikely that we will see much experimentation in the near future with alternative modes of public involvement in the management and control of public services. On the contrary: government at the local level is being increasingly subjected to centralized bureaucratic and ministerial control, and will continue to be until there is a change of government at the center.

CONCLUSION

Some of the key controversies in public administration within the U.K. may be highlighted by comparisons with some other western democracies. Foremost on the agenda at the time of writing is the central administration's obsession with secrecy and the potentially unlimited coverage of the Official Secrets Act. The almost total anonymity of central government officials that this entails contrasts with the greater public visibility of civil servants in France and the U.S.A. Anonymity and political neutrality go hand in hand, and the restrictions on the political activities of U.K. civil servants contrast starkly with the French, Italian and West German civil servant's freedom to stand for parliament, engage in other kinds of political activity and move relatively freely between the worlds of representative, partisan politics and professional administration.

The dominance of the generalist administrator in policy-making and departmental management may be contrasted with the access which technocrats in France have to posts at the highest administrative levels and with the predominantly legal backgrounds of higher civil servants in West Germany. The culture and traditions of the British civil service help shape the organizational structure of central administration in the U.K. which may be contrasted with the impact which the different methods of managing the civil services of France and West Germany have on the structure of central departments and special-purpose commissions.

The absence in Britain of a representative of government and state at the local or provincial level, such as the French and Italian prefects, produces further contrasts not only in the structure of civil services but also in the relations between different levels of government. Such co-ordinating and perhaps centralizing mechanisms reveal fundamentally different conceptions of the state as between the U.K. and her European neighbors, as does the fragmentation of the public services in the U.K. compared with the integration of public servants into a single unified civil service as found in West Germany and, albeit stratified and segmented, in France.

Comparisons and contrasts in terms of institutions and processes—civil services, administrative justice, functional and territorial decentralization, control and accountability, the organization of work within and between departments of state, and so on—are relatively easy to make. It is much more difficult to identify and compare the underlying historical, social and political forces—political cultures, perceptions of the state, constitutional forms and other environmental factors—which shape the structure and practice of public administration. Such comparison is an underdeveloped area of academic inquiry.

REFERENCES

1. Henry Parris, *Constitutional Bureaucracy* (London: Allen & Unwin, 1969), Ch. 1.
2. A. H. Birch, *Representative and Responsible Government. An Essay on the British Constitution* (London: Allen & Unwin, 1964), 165–67.
3. A. Lawson, *Corporatism and Welfare, Social Policy and State Intervention in Britain* (London: Heinemann, 1982).
4. But see P. Dunleavy, "Is there a radical approach to public administration?," *Public Administration*, vol. 60, no. 2, 1982.
5. G. K. Fry, "The development of the Thatcher Government's 'Grand Strategy' for the Civil Service: a public policy perspective," *Public Administration*, vol. 62, no. 3, 1984.
6. J. R. Greenwood and D. J. Wilson, *Public Administration in Britain* (London: Allen & Unwin, 1984), 178.
7. C. Pollitt, "The CSD: a normal death?", *Public Administration*, vol. 60, no. 1, 1982.
8. A. H. Hanson and M. Walles, *Governing Britain. A Guide Book to Political Institutions* (London: Fontana Collins, 1975), 121.
9. Pollitt, *op. cit.*
10. N. Johnson, "Quangos and the structure of government," *Public Administration*, vol. 57, no. 4, 1979.
11. A. Likierman, "Management Information for Ministers: The MINIS system in the Department of the Environment," *Public Administration*, vol. 62, no. 2, 1982, p. 129.
12. *Ibid.*, p. 135.

13. J. M. Lee, "Editorial: financial management and career service," *Public Administration*, vol. 62, no. 1, 1984.

14. B. W. Hogwood and M. Keating, *Regional Government in England* (Oxford: The Clarendon Press, 1982).

15. D. Steel, "Organizational change in the nationalised industries," paper presented to the Annual Conference of the Public Administration Committee, University of York, 1978.

16. D. Farnham and M. McVicar, *Public Administration in the United Kingdom: An Introduction* (London: Cassell, 1982), 225.

17. G. K. Fry, "Compromise with the market: the Megaw report on civil service pay, 1982," *Public Administration*, vol. 61, no. 1, 1983.

18. *Ibid.*

19. J. M. Lee, "Editorial: epitaph for the CSD," *Public Administration*, vol. 60, no. 1, 1982, p. 8.

20. Farnham and McVicar, *op. cit.*, 236–37.

21. Expenditure Committee, *The Civil Service*, Eleventh Report and Volumes of Evidence, 1976–77, vol. I–III, HC 535 (London: HMSO, 1977); Brown and Steel, *op. cit.*, 77; P. Kellner and Lord Crowther-Hunt, *The Civil Servants: An Inquiry into Britain's Ruling Class* (London: Macdonald, 1980), Ch. 6.

22. Greenwood and Wilson, *op. cit.*, 103–7.

23. R. C. Chapman, "Civil Service recruitment: bias against external candidates," *Public Administration*, vol. 60, no. 1, 1982.

24. Quoted in R. Norton-Taylor, "In search of a civil service code of conduct," *The Guardian*, 12 October 1984.

25. D. Judge, "Specialists and generalists in British central government: a political debate," *Public Administration*, vol. 59, no. 1, 1981.

26. G. Drewry, "Lawyers in the UK civil service," *Public Administration*, vol. 59, no. 1, 1981.

27. Judge, *op. cit.*

28. J. Macdonald and G. K. Fry, "Policy Planning Units—ten years on," *Public Administration*, vol. 58, no. 4, 1980.

29. A. Gray and W. Jenkins, "Policy analysis in British central government: the experience of PAR," *Public Administration*, vol. 60, no. 4, 1982, p. 435.

30. Greenwood and Wilson, *op. cit.*, 77–84; Kellner and Crowther-Hunt, *op. cit.*, 220–37; B. C. Smith, *Policy Making in British Government* (Oxford: Martin Robertson, 1976), 108; B. Heady, *British Cabinet Ministers* (London: Allen & Unwin, 1974), 131–35; H. Young and A. Sloman, *No, Minister* (London: BBC Publications, 1982); P. Norton, *The Constitution in Flux* (Oxford: Martin Robertson, 1982).

31. P. Byrne, "Parliamentary control of delegated legislation," *Parliamentary Affairs*, vol. 29, no. 4, 1976.

32. See J. Garrett, *Managing the Civil Service* (London: Heinemann, 1980); E. L. Normanton, "Reform in the field of public accountability and audit: a progress report," *Political Quarterly*, vol. 51, 1980; A. Robinsin, "The House of Commons and public expenditure," in S. A. Walkland and M. Ryle (eds.), *The Commons Tody* (London: Fontana Collins, 1981); J. Stancer, "The Public Accounts Committee," *Public Administration Bulletin*, no. 37, December 1981; M. R. Garner, "Auditing the efficiency of nationalized industries: enter the Monopolies and Mergers Commission," *Public Administration*, vol. 60, no. 4, 1982.

33. W. B. Gwyn, "The ombudsman in Britain: a qualified success in government reform," *Public Administration*, vol. 60, no. 3, 1982.

34. G. Peele, "Government at the centre," in H. Drucker (ed.), *Developments in British Politics* (London: MacMillan, 1984).
35. A Data Protection Bill to control personal information held in computer systems has been introduced. In enacted, it will provide some safeguards for personal information in official files.

5

A Socio-Historical Overview

V. SUBRAMANIAM
Carleton University, Ottawa, Ontario, Canada

Much administrative change, reorganization and reform has taken place in all the four Anglo-Saxon Commonwealth countries in the post-war period as is made clear in the foregoing chapters. To put all that in perspective, we must remember that an unprecedented degree of administrative change has occurred all over the world in the post-war period for obvious reasons. In the first place, the disappearance of colonial rule has forced the imperial metropolitan regimes, including the British, to readjust and reform and the newly independent countries to refashion and refurbish their own new administrative structures, with great enthusiasm and faith in administration as the magic key to economic and general development. Secondly, the great changes in the world economy following massive technological changes have generated equally massive changes in administration, management and policy making. Thirdly, the wave of mutual imitation triggered off by faster information dispersal produced further changes particularly in the Commonwealth, now laid open to the winds of change. The administrative developments in the Anglo-Saxon Commonwealth thus flow partly out of a universal momentum for change and partly from specific local factors operating in the Commonwealth itself. But in this chapter we will have to assume the universal factors simply as the general background for our more detailed analysis of the specific factors, which provide one of the best examples of the interactions of economy, society and bureaucracy on a formerly compact and conservative political culture. Our thesis will be developed along the following lines.

1. We will begin with a brief discussion of the special socio-historical features of the delayed development of administration in Britain from the late 17th century—such as the gentleman-amateur ethos, in contrast to the emergence of bureaucracy under absolute monarchy in France and Prussia—and the 19th century British achievement of "constitutional bureaucracy" through working out a system of an elitist civil service within an elitist democracy.
2. We will then look briefly at the Anglo-Saxon colonies taking over some structural elements of this system such as the Ministerial department, as part of the "emigrant culture" and bypassing other elitist elements not suitable to their egalitarian, pragmatic culture.

3. Against the background of the massive socio-economic and technological changes
   since the second world war, we will discuss how the administrative systems of
   Britain and the other white Commonwealth countries have developed common
   features through complementary and converging changes in their socio-economic
   systems and the effects of two-party dominance.

EARLY BRITISH ADMINISTRATION

The basic forces that shaped British administrative institutions in the eighteenth and
nineteenth centuries have been researched in some detail, but their convolutions are
still worth highlighting to understand better their special features in Britain and her
colonies. The dominance of the landed aristocracy and squirearchy, from the Glorious
Revolution of 1688 until the late 19th century and their consummate shaping of the
tentacular gentleman-amateur ethic and its later entrenchment through the public
schools have been discussed by several authors including this writer, as also its overwhelming influence in shaping the reformed British administrative structures in the
late 19th century (1). In analyzing this period, different authors have overemphasized
different socio-political factors: for example, Ernest Barker has stressed the mutual
influences and affinities between France, Germany and Britain, while Martin Albrow
has highlighted the suspicion of continental bureaucracy by the British ruling class (2).

A brief balanced account of this British evolution is necessary to understand the
development of British administration then and now. The Glorious Revolution started
the development of the gentleman-amateur ethos by the landed aristocrats, the chief
element of which was an emphasis on decentralized democratic handling of political
affairs and a de-emphasizing of administration. This was in stark contrast to the continental ethos evolved mainly by Louis XIV of France with his stress on centralized
administration and a gradual downgrading of the aristocracy. The reason was that
Britain had largely achieved under Tudor despotism what Louis XIV sought to achieve
in his time—namely, the end of feudalism and the evolution of a national polity. As
the Tudors did it so much earlier with poorer communications and less commercial
development, they could not, and did not, build up as strong a centralized bureaucracy
as could have been achieved in later centuries. After the period of the Stuarts and of
Cromwell, a more national and enlightened landed aristocracy had come back to the
political arena and during the crucial century and a half after 1688, they shaped the
elements of the British political and administrative system.

Part of their ethos was what any compact elite with strong peer group feelings and
willingness to admit a small number of outsiders would have evolved anywhere else in
the World—as the Samurai did in Japan; and another part of it was the product of
British historical givens, namely, increasing wealth through an Industrial Revolution
and increasing power through colonial expansion. The ethos has been generally called
the ethos of the gentleman-amateur and has been described in snatches by contemporary observers such as Emerson, Tocqueville and later by the author of *The English*:
Are They Human? while attempts at a more rounded picture were made by Bagehot,
and later by historians and social scientists such as Karl Mannheim in the recent
decades. Let us look at some aspects of this ethos.

The gentleman served the country voluntarily without remuneration. This led to
the extensive use of the country squire in local administration as a voluntary

administrator in various capacities, till elected local government bodies replaced him. Even there, the peer group ideal came into its own in the form of committees.

Voluntary administration involved a distaste for hierarchical centralized bureaucracy and the ruling elite of Britain kept it down to a minimum for as long as possible. Thus a sort of aura grew round the idea of decentralization. The emotional under-tones of this term "decentralization" in English, are best illustrated by contrasting it with the strong commendation attached to its opposite, namely, centralization in French—witness the eulogistic panel on centralization on the walls of Napoleon's tomb at the Invalides. Such decentralization was possible in Britain not only because feudal separatism was long since dead but also because government was not called upon to do as much as in France or Germany: the Industrial Revolution in Britain was carried out almost entirely by individual inventors and entrepreneurs demanding little state intervention and voluntary associations looked after several social problems without calling for government help.

Successful decentralized and voluntaristic administration requires good leadership qualities in its practitioners in the field. Throughout the best part of the 18th cen-tury, the responsibility for leadership training was left to the gentlemen's families themselves, and it was not till the 19th century that the Public Schools took over the function of training gentlemen on a regular formal basis.

The training and education were essentially aimed at molding character and improv-ing one's general judgement. The inclinations of the landed aristocracy and squire-archy in this direction were legitimized by the writings of John Locke (3). This was responsible for placing the generalist in administration well above the specialist and for a heavy reliance on practical judgement as against bookish logic.

To sum up: the British gentleman-amateur ethic was thus essentially decentralist, voluntary-service oriented, peer group based and so against importing the hierarchical, disciplined, bureaucratic institutions of France and Prussia, fashioned as instruments of their absolute monarchies. Such aversion, as we have noted, was functional for reasons the British themselves were scarcely aware of. The continental bureaucracies were shaped and used initially as instruments for defeudalizing and integrating the nation, achieved much earlier in Britain by the Tudors. The hierarchy, ridigity and discipline of continental bureaucracies were thus totally unnecessary if not counterproductive in Britain. But criticisms were voiced not in these cold, honest socio-historical terms but in the name of liberty by British liberal intellectuals and the landed aristocrats, and against oppression through an instrument of state by the dominant capitalist class by Marx and his followers (4). Neither of these critics acknowledged each other's criti-cism of the common "villain." This ironical situation became less and less tenable as British society changed through industrialization, urbanization and the acquisition of a large empire, all demanding more organization, regulation and administration than the squirearchy could provide in the country and the ad hoc boards could in London. The popular and simplistic official version tells a tale of engineered reform by deter-mined reformers against a background of administrative inefficiency caricatured by novelists such as Dickens.

The real, complex story includes the fortunate concatenation of at least four factors. In the first place, some useful continental ideas of cameralism, controls and structures were recast perhaps unconsciously into a more liberal democratic mold by Jeremy Bentham and his colleagues in their writings, and thus made more acceptable.

Secondly, some of their basic ideas, such as recruitment by competitive examination, were tested and found workable in India. Thirdly, there were dynamic entrepreneurial top administrators such as Sir Charles Trevelyan and Sir Robert Morant who made changes with firmness and determination (5). Lastly, the limited scope of British democracy in a deferential society, compared to Jacksonian America, made possible such smooth social engineering. The final administrative system that emerged by the 1870s was highly elitist, informed by the gentleman-amateur ethic, fitting perfectly into the middle class democracy of the times. It was a system run by a generally educated middle class elitist club, suspicious of the specialist, subject to strict but smooth peer-group control by the Treasury, and working in closest collaboration with Ministers with a similar background to sustain the former's responsibility to Parliament. It was essentially concerned with central administration without spreading its tentacles (unlike the French system) into the country where the country squire was being smoothly replaced by elected local government bodies.

The British ruling class ultimately accepted the need for bureaucracy after half a century or reviling it. This was no real paradox in the light of our brief socio-historical explanation. They had achieved the initial purpose of national integration as conceived by Louis XIV and the great Electors of Prussia, two centuries earlier, and they took in bureaucracy only when it was reshaped ideologically (by Bentham) and practically (by top civil servants and politicians) to fit into middle class democracy. More interestingly, the social and economic changes which the continental bureaucracies brought about on their initiative were already happening in Britain through private initiative, industrailization, voluntary organizations and popular movements. It other words, bureaucracy came late to Britain in time to sustain the results of modernizing socio-economic changes which in Europe, were set in motion by it (6). In essence, the initial achievement and entrenchment of elitist parliamentary democracy by the gentleman aristocrats over a century and a half ensured that the ultimate shape of the administrative system was governed by their ethos in contrast to the reverse process in Western Europe, where bureaucracy, already well established was being taken over by an inexperienced new democracy.

THE ANGLO-SAXON COLONIES

The Anglo-Saxon colonies of Canada, Australia and New Zealand were being settled largely by British emigrants during this period of the evolution and entrenchment of the gentleman-amateur ethic in Britain. By the middle of the 19th century they were establishing "Responsible Governments" just about the time the British ruling elite was coming to terms with bureaucracy and shaping the new structures of democratic British administration. This timing led to several common features based on the British heritage, and several differences between Britain and the Dominions, based on the colonial context (7). The first of these may be described as the dialectic between the "emigrant culture" representing an attachment to some democratic elements of the British socio-political tradition, and an "emigrant's culture," representing an aversion to some other "aristocratic" elements of the same tradition and a commitment to face new realities (8). In the case of Australia and New Zealand, the latter expressed itself in terms of a strong egalitarian ethos, and in the case of all the Anglo-Saxon colonies the challenge to explore and exploit the resources of the new harsh environment generated a strong base of pragmatism (9). At the same time, the emigration of dissenting elements strengthened the elitist elements of British administration.

To spell out the consequent resemblances and differences: the British achievement of the mid-nineteenth century was a workable compromise of the gentleman-amateur ethic and limited parliamentary democracy with a Weberian type of bureaucracy. It established the modern ministerial department—with the minister presiding over and controlling a Weberian bureaucratically structured department fully answerable to Parliament for all its actions—together with the doctrines of Ministerial Responsibility and the Rule of Law. At the same time, the administrative structures and processes incorporated the aristocratic elements in the gentleman-amateur ethic—in establishing an elitist administrative class based on exclusive Oxbridge education with a strong peer group ethos to help the minister—along with the glorification of the generalist and strong control by the Treasury. The Anglo-Saxon colonies took over the former (i.e.) democratic parliamentary control of administration along with the ministerial department as part of their package of responsible Government—but rejected or diluted considerably the elitist elements of British administration. Their acceptance of the former flowed from two historical factors. After the loss of America, there developed considerable mutual understanding between the mother country and the colonies and "responsible government" for each colony meant automatically the replication of the British Parliamentary system including its administrative adjunct, the ministerial department. Secondly, there was some mutual interaction between Britain and the colonies in the evolution of these very administrative forms in the last century thus generating parallel structures (10).

At the same time, local compulsions, and the emigrant's culture led to some dilution or bypassing of the British elitist ethos. Thus Australia and New Zealand developed a strong anti-elitist egalitarian ethos, leading to the rejection of the institution of the administrative class, the entrenching of public service recruitment at school leaving age, and promotion to the upper rungs by seniority, while Canada, less committed to the egalitarian ethos, nevertheless did not entrench elitism (11). All three of them faced the basic problems of settlement, survival and resource exploitation in an unknown challenging environment. Hence there was a premium on specialists and professionals in administration and no particular need for the gentleman-amateur (12). Secondly, such resource exploitation was not sustained through private enterprise in the colonies as the Industrial Revolution was in Britain; hence the early and continuing commitment (through corporations) to public enterprise in contrast to the developing British aversion to non-ministerial structures in the last century (13). Thirdly, this commitment to public enterprise also reduced the sacredness of Treasury control, and particularly in Australia, where independent public service boards took total control of personnel administration, Treasury control was purely functional and rarely sacralized as in Britain (14). To sum up, it was a picture of common structures on the one hand based on the parliamentary system and its administrative controls and several differences on the other hand, based on emigrants' culture and local challenges in exploiting resources. In the postwar period, the former have continued, perhaps even strengthened themselves through two-party dominance, while the differences have become less significant with convergent and complementary socio-economic changes in Britain and the Dominions.

CONVERGING CHANGES

The post war period has been a time of massive politico-economic changes the world over for several reasons we cannot discuss here in detail (15). The "world village" took shape with faster transport and a faster flow of information, and led to the spread of several administrative institutions from their home bases. The fast development of technology generated concomitant changes in management and administration and not only in the use of the computer and mathematical tools. The increased interdependence of national economies, and the emergence of common markets and regional reconomic arrangements following the general commitment to Keynesian economics increased the area of public enterprise and, together with the spread of the welfare state, public administration has become essentially public economic management. All these factors operate with different force all over the world—but their effects are felt in the Anglo-Saxon Commonwealth in a special way because the dissolution of the British Empire forced one set of readjustments on Britain, while her entry into the European Economic Community forced another set of readjustments on the Dominions as well as Britain.

We are, of course, concerned with particular developments in the four Commonwealth countries even while bearing in mind the universal factors. The first of these is the increasing influence of the governmental bureaucracy in policy making in all of them. This is also a universal tendency based on factors such as the enormous increase in the scope of governmental administration and the increasing dependence of elected politicians on the bureaucracy to cope up with it, on the one hand, and the increasing discipline of organized political parties in vesting power and trust in their political executives to run the administration, on the other (16). Both trends are much stronger in the four Anglo-Saxon Commonwealth countries mainly because of the combination of the two party dominant system with parliamentary cabinet government. In contrast to European multiparty systems, two major parties have occupied the political arena for decades in all these four countries with a third party being either squeezed out or replaced as in Britain, or being reduced to an alliance status as the Country Party in Australia or the New Democratic Party in Canada. This had built up a certain tradition of policy continuity—of a centrist nature without too much veering to the Right or Left—in spite of ideological differences between the parties. The background of this continuity consists of a concatenation of factors. It is partly "brokerage politics," the two parties appealing to the same organized groups, thereby effecting similar compromises and evolving similar platforms. Once this process is established the bureaucracy takes over as the guardian of the continuity of such a centrist policy. Secondly, the Anglo-Saxon commitment to stable government, exemplified by phrases like "Her Majesty's Loyal Opposition" and declarations like "The Queen's government must be carried on," also aligns a two party system towards the middleground and bureaucratic guardianship thereof. Thirdly, the two-party and parliamentary systems have an enormous mutual reinforcement effect. The American presidential system with two parties still leaves a lot of power with the Congress over the bureaucracy, while European multiparty parliaments can still create and operate various controls over bureaucracy. But a parliamentary two-party system tends to legitimize bureaucratic power under various euphemisms, as shown by actual experience.

Empirical studies of the Prime Minister, Cabinet, and top bureaucracy in all these four countries clearly suggest an overall pattern implied in the catchy phrase "Prime

Ministerial bureaucracy." An "ideal type" of this would include a strong prime minister (with a somewhat glamorous public image), a hierarchical cabinet, well-organized cabinet committees, and strong secretarial services and top bureaucrats with a tendency to identify themselves with individual ministers or the political executive as a whole. Most of the features of this ideal type seem to have prevailed during most of the post-war period in Canada, Britain and Australia.

Evidence before Royal Commissions of the senior bureaucrats in Canada, of the new Second Division in Australia and the Administrative class as well as the "High Flyers" in Britain clearly indicates that they attach overwhelming importance to their "function" of policy advice to the Minister, regarding all else as secondary (17). Secondly, much has been said and written about the dominance of the Prime Minister over the whole cabinet in Britain under Churchill, MacMillan, Wilson and Thatcher; in Canada under Trudeau, and in Australia under Menzies and Frazer. These accounts also indicate some direct communication of the higher civil service with the Prime Minister, bypassing other ministers. This Prime Ministerial dominance is buttressed in part by the development of a separate Prime Minister's office, which liaises with the Cabinet Secretariat and the secretariats of various cabinet committees from a vantage point. The Cabinet committees themselves, by bringing in more system, order and pattern in the work of the cabinet as a whole, together with the formalization of procedure through the secretariats, bring not only more control and power to the political executive but pyramidize it in favor of the Prime Minister and the top bureaucrats. Simultaneously with these developments the top bureaucrats have been encouraged in the post-war decades to do the political groundwork for their ministers and the cabinet as a whole, by meeting interest groups, private and public corporation executives and other involved ministers and their civil service counterparts. This complementary process of the bureaucratization of the political executive and the politicization of the top bureaucracy has far-reaching psychological consequences not fully acknowledged yet.

The foregoing generalized "ideal type" based on common socio-political factors has several local variations—which can only be assessed empirically. The preceding chapters discuss these details but take for granted the overall context of parliamentary democracy with a two-party dominant system (18). We may note however that the various efforts on the part of the political executive to control the top bureaucracy and *vice versa* are actually in-house rivalries that do not improve the power situation of parliament or the wider grass-root party organizations. Indeed, the tragi-comedy of the parliamentary system with two-party dominance is that it sees the problem mainly in terms of these in-house rivalries between the political executive and the top bureaucracy—and thus partly legitimizes such rivalries.

A bird's eye view of administrative developments in this area supports this description. Thus in Canada, the Trudeau era witnessed the "rationalization of policy making" with mathematical tools—and a consequent increase in bureaucratic inputs therein (19). At the same time, Trudeau's vaunted attempts to limit bureaucratic inputs—by strengthening the cabinet committee system and thus making it more difficult and less meaningful for the top bureaucrat to "capture" a single minister—have not produced the expected result. During the same period, much importance was given to the very high degree of formalization of policy coordination through four organs, namely the Privy Council office, Prime Minister's office, Treasury Board and the Federal-Provincial Relations office, and to the rise of the "Superbureaucrats" of these agencies. More recent accounts suggest that these central co-ordinating agencies have less power, but one suspects that any such weakening is marginal.

Similar "rationalizations" were instituted in Australia, New Zealand and Britain in regard to policy and management through various management tools, thus augmenting the input of the bureaucracy, but in all these countries there is also a counter move-ment to contain the power of the top bureaucracy *vis-a-vis* the political executive (20). This includes several measures, two of which are widely used. One of them is cur-tailing governments' commitments and the size of the civil service by "privatization"—selling off public enterprises to the private sector and letting out on contract some "non-sovereign" functions. Thatcher's Britain has gone further than the rest in this direction with Mulroney's Canada a distant second. Another measure is the use of political intermediaries between the Minister and the top bureaucrat, usually called Chiefs of Staff. This institution has taken shape in all these four countries under different names. The Chief of Staff is not a member of Parliament like a Parliamentary Secre-tary but needs the same political background and skills—nor a civil servant either but much like a member of the French, ministerial cabinet. It is too early to evaluate this institution and its effectiveness in terms of political control of bureaucracy.

So much for the basic resemblance in terms of increasing bureaucratic power in the context of cabinet government and two-party dominance. The second factor leading to the emergence of common features in the post-war era derives from the socio-economic developments converging from opposite directions in Britain and the Dominions—reducing the differences based on British elitism and the egalitarianism and pragmatism of the Anglo-Saxon Dominions. Thus in Britain, the whole apparatus of administrative control based on Ministerial Responsibility and the Rule of Law and the generalist-dominated elitist personnel administration, were fashioned, as we have described, during a period of limited democracy and enormous confidence in the gentleman ethic in the late 19th century. These were proving increasingly less func-tional in this century with the evolution of mass democracy but were sustained by sheer inertia and sufferance on the part of its victims, the specialists (21). The second world war weakened the British Empire and British domestic economy. The post-war period witnessed the dismantling of empire the rise of the British Labour party to power—and later a partial disentanglement from the old white Commonwealth, with Britain's entry into the European Economic Community. These changes forced the British politico-administrative elite to start looking inward and readjusting to the new domestic realities of mass democracy in a non-imperial context. At the same time, the simplistic 19th century egalitarian assumptions in Australia, and to a lesser extent in New Zealand, were all being fast eroded by changes in their economic and educational systems demanding more sophisticated and even elitist administrative readjustments. The resultant changes have the appearance of mutual learning and a converging onto some similar structures and processes. We may mention these briefly.

In the first place, the recruitment of young school leavers and the bypassing of graduates could no more be defended on egalitarian principles in Australia with the fast increasing availability of university education, nor by rustic pragmatism in a com-plex economy, with a fast growing managerial sector in private enterprise and a need for sophisticated multivalued choice in public administration. Thus step by step, the graduate intake into the Australian federal public service was increased slowly from the late thirties and faster from the fifties onwards so that the present Second Division is not so different from the traditional British Administrative class in regard to university education or policy advising skills (22). More interestingly, its socio-economic origins are gradually becoming similar to the old British Administrative class though there is still less exclusiveness (in terms of an Oxbridge education and public schooling) in Australia (23). There is also a similar convergence in the institutional arrangements for personnel. Thus the Establishment side of the British Treasury which made it so powerful by the combination of finance and personnel for a century, was finally hived off to a civil service department, loosening its institutional ties with personnel somewhat. By contrast, in Australia, both in the federal service and the New South Wales Public Service the independent public service boards, which were more powerful than the Treasury till well into the 1960's, have now become much weaker and more glaringly so in the State of New South Wales, while both the Federal and New South Wales Treasury Departments have assimilated more powers, thus getting a little closer to the British position (24). In the Canadian federal administration also, the recent trend towards greater powers for central co-ordination as against departmental autonomy in management, following the momentum of the Lambert Commission, has augmented the powers of the Treasury Board (and the Privy Council office). One must add that the Public Service Commission in Canada similarly had much power and prestige but in the post-war period it has delegated most of its initiative to the departments and the Treasury Board (keeping mostly some appellate powers)—which again adds to the Treasury's importance (25).

Another personnel area in which the mother country and the white dominions have come closer is in regard to the relative power and position of the professional or specialist civil servant *vis-a-vis* the generalist (26). The British tradition of placing the latter on top was based on the basic assumptions of the gentleman ethic and the historical development of British industry, commerce and technology mainly through private initiative without government help which made it less necessary for government to use specialists. This situation was changing gradually between the two world wars and it changed much faster in the period after the 1940's. The elevation of the Labour Party to power enlarged the share of public enterprise through large scale nationalization. Also, the nature of the post-war world economy forced each nation to act as one compact competing economic unit. These factors and the continuous economic decline of Britain attributed by several critics to an outmoded generalist administration led to the recommendations of the Fulton Committee in favor of considering specialists for an equitable share in higher administration and policy formation along with generalists. During the same post-war years, the economies of the old Commonwealth countries had outgrown their pure resource-exploitation base, becoming more demanding in terms of more balanced multivalued policy making. This was more obvious in the case of Australia—for several reasons, such as Britain's entry into the European Economic Community forcing Australia to seek other trading partners and the exposure of her national economy to international forces. The major policy decisions were no longer simplistic yes or no choices about natural or human resources, based on specialist criteria, but complex multivalued choices demanding sophisticated generalist skills from generalist policy advisors. The emphasis thus shifted from recruiting pure specialists to training specialists for policy advice and encouraging generalists. This new trend became more visible in Australia with Prime Minister Whitlam's efforts to secure Arab development capital and with the resource boom controversy in the final years of the Frazer cabinet (27). Similarly in Canada, resource exploitation (and later free trade) involved central-provincial relations and demanded more negotiating than specialist skills in policy making (28). To sum up, just as post-Fulton Britain is gradually ending the segregation of the specialist and involving him in the policy process, the old Commonwealth countries are recognizing the importance of generalist skills in policy making in the context of multi-valued choice.

The large socio-economic changes of the post-war period have also increased the importance of public enterprises variously called public corporations or crown corporations in all Commonwealth countries. Here again, there has been a converging movement. Late 19th century Britain, with its laissez-faire policy had little interest in public enterprise—and in governmental organization it followed Benthamite logic by gradually replacing boards with ministerial departments. This process was legitimized and strongly recommended by Beatrice Webb in her report on the Poor Law Board in 1908, and again in the Haldane Report in 1918 (29). The public corporation was treated as a deviation till 1945, when Atlee's Labour government nationalized several industries and created public corporations to run them in preference to ministerial departments. By contrast, the Australian colonies and New Zealand used the corporate form extensively in the latter part of the 19th century for building the economic infrastructures and have continued that process ever since. Canada too used public corporations, at an early date, and went for them in a big way during the second world war and thereafter. Of course, the public corporation in some form or other has now become a universal administrative instrument posing a universal problem in terms of the difficulties of financial accountability and policy control. In the Commonwealth, the two-party dominated parliamentary system, with cabinet government, seems to have intensified this problem of control and accountability so much that it has occupied the center of attention in Canada in the last decade and constitutes a major issue in Australia, Britain and New Zealand. Mutual comparisons, however, have not led to any mutual learning in this regard.

In the broad area of democratic control of administration and mechanisms for handling citizens' grievances or increasing citizen participation there has been much experimentation, borrowing and mutual learning but mainly from outside the Commonwealth, for obvious historical reasons. British doctrines and instruments of control such as Ministerial Responsibility and the Rule of Law were evolved in the context of a limited democracy, accepting bureaucratic structures on their own terms in the mid-19th century. They persisted without reform mainly because of the smugness of the ruling elite about their adequacy long past their period of usefulness (30). By contrast, when West European countries changed from absolute monarchies to democracies, they inherited established bureaucracies and had no illusions about the overwhelming power of bureaucracy *vis-a-vis* the citizen. Hence, they built up grass roots remedies like the ombudsman and administrative courts. Post-war Britain, shorn of imperial pretensions and faced with class-conscious labor, gradually saw the usefulness of West European remedies, as did the other Commonwealth countries. The non-legalist ombudsman offered few legal hurdles and could be fitted smoothly into the Anglo-Saxon framework, but a system of administrative law could not be so directly incorporated, though some streamlining of administrative law and tribunals has taken place in all these countries.

The administrative evolution of the Anglo-Saxon Commonwealth over two centuries may be regarded as the strophe and antistrophe of a sonnet. The major development in the last century was the creation of "constitutional bureaucracy" within a parliamentary system with an elitist ethos at home and a contrasting egalitarian pragmatic ethos in an emigrant setting. The major development of the post-war era is the convergence of these two administrative ethoses towards a midpoint and a common willingness to look around for administrative answers outside the Commonwealth.

REFERENCES

1. V. Subramaniam, *Transplanted Indo-British Administration*, Ashish Publishing House, New Delhi, 1977. Chapters 5 and 10.

2. Ernest Barker, *The Development of Public Services in Western Europe*. Archon Books, Hamden CT, 1966; Martin Albrow, *Bureaucracy*, Pall Mall Press, London, 1970.

3. John Locke, *An Essay Concerning Human Understanding*, Cleveland, Meridian, 1964.

4. For Liberal criticisms see Martin Albrow, *op. cit.* pp. 21–26, and for Marxist criticisms pp. 68–72. But Albrow does not highlight the paradox that Marx and Mill (J. S.) attack the same institution for opposite reasons.

5. For details about the contribution of various men to the final British compromise between bureaucracy and limited democracy see Henry Parris, *Constitutional Bureaucracy*, Allen and Unwin, London, 1969, *passim* and in particular chapters III, IV and V.

6. John Armstrong, *The European Administrative Elite*, Princeton University Press, 1973. Armstrong lumps together all West European administrative elites, as social engineers initiating economic development. The British development, however, was substantially engineered by private enterprise though the higher civil servants, and politicians helped in consolidating it.

7. V. Subramaniam, *Transplanted Indo-British Administration*, chapter 1. See also V. Subramaniam, "British Administrative Institutions: Paradoxes of Acceptance, Adaptation and Rejection," *The Round Table*, London (1983), pp. 306–316.

8. V. Subramaniam, *Transplanted Indo-British Administration*, chapter 3, "Emigrant Culture and Emigrants' Culture."

9. V. Subramaniam, "The Relative Status of Specialists and Generalists—An attempt at Comparative Historical Explanation," *Public Administration*, London (Autumn, 1968).

10. For example, some elements of the Ministerial Department were generated by Lord Sydenham as Governor-General of Canada, about the same time it was taking shape in Britain, leading to some mutual exchange of ideas. See J. E. Hodgetts, *Pioneer Public Service: An Administrative History of the United Canadas 1841–67*, university of Toronto Press, Toronto, 1955, chap. III. For the Australian parallel evolution, see R. L. Wettenhall, "The Ministerial Department," *Australian Journal of Public Administration*, Sydney, vol. xxxii, no. 3. These sources are summarized and discussed critically in V. Seymour Wilson, *Canadian Public Policy and Administration*, McGraw Hill Ryerson, Toronto, 1980, chapter ten.

11. The Canadian political tradition, as Alan Cairns points out, was originally conservative—inasmuch as it was based on an explicit rejection of the American Revolution. But a country based on successive waves of immigration and a need to grapple with resource exploration had to develop rugged pragmatism and some basic egalitarianism along with it.

12. V. Subramaniam, "Specialists and Generalists in British and Australian Government Services: A Study in Contrast," *Public Administration*, London (Winter 1963).

13. F. M. G. Willson, "Ministries and Boards: Some Aspects of Administrative Development since 1832," *Public Administration*, London (Spring 1955).

14. On the independence of Public Service Boards in Australia, see the following: G. E. Caiden, *Career Service*, Melbourne U.P., Melbourne, 1965; and B. N. Moore, *Administrative Style*, Ph.D. Thesis, Sydney University, 1986.

15. For a general discussion of worldwide tendencies, see V. Subramaniam, "Administration in the Eighties: Major Trends and Changes," *Indian Journal of Public Administration*, New Delhi, vol. XXVI, no. 3.

16. The argument about two party dominance is elaborated in detail in V. Subramamiam, "The Higher Bureaucracy and Policy Making in the Anglo Saxon Commonwealth: The Psycho-social Syndrome of Two-party Parliamentarism," *International Review of Administrative Sciences*, Brussels, No. 3 (1985).

17. Evidence before every Royal Commission in Britain from Tomlin to Fulton, emphasized policy advising as central, as did evidence before the Royal Commission on the Second Division in Australia in 1972–3, and before the Glassco (1962) and Lambert (1978) Commissions in Canada.

18. The authors evidently assume the parliamentary system, party discipline, cabinet government with its committees, central co-ordination, etc., all as a "natural" part of the respective administrative systems of each country they deal with. It is only when one looks at Anglo Saxon countries as a whole as against the American presidential system or West European multiparty systems that their socio-political interrelationships become clear.

19. There has been no single concerted critical account of the "rationalizations" of the Trudeau era and their overall consequences. G. Bruce Doern, "Recent changes in the philosophy of policy making in Canada," *Canadian Journal of Political Science*, Vol. 4 (June 1971), pp. 243–264, is the most detailed account of Trudeau "rationalizations," soon after they were introduced, but does not cover Trudeau "era" down to '83 with all its variations. Audrey Doerr's chapter on Canada in this book discusses this briefly and there is some more discussion in Audrey Doerr, *The Machinery of Government in Canada*, Methuen, Toronto, 1981. There is further material from several sources in Robert F. Adie and Paul G. Thomas, *Canadian Public Administration*, Prentice-Hall, Scarborough, Ont. 1982, Chapter Four. "The Theory and Practice of Public Policy Making in Canada." There are of course several specific studies of policy making in specific areas like energy and all of them highlight bureaucratic inputs.

20. For an optimistic account of the counter-movement see Donald C. Rowat, "Bureaucracy and Policy Making in Developed Democracies: The Decline of Bureaucratic Influence," *International Review of Administrative Sciences*, Brussels, no. 3 (1985).

21. The topmost professional civil servants (bar the doctors) were paid about half the top salary of the Administrative Class in Britain. Yet they did not complain loudly during the interwar period. It was only when the Labour party came to power that various neglected and suppressed groups began to voice their grievance loudly in Britain.

22. All recent studies of the social background and education of the Second Division in Australia show that in terms of the proportion of Ph.D.'s it is even better than the British Administrative class. For details consult the issues of *Australian Journal of Public Administration*, Sydney, 1970 onwards.

23. Recent social background studies including one in 1966 and another in 1980 by this author again show that the socio-economic origins of the new Second Division are clearly middle class.

24. On the downgrading of the New South Wales Public Service Board and the augmentation of the powers of Ministers and the Treasury, see B. N. Moore, *Administrative Style*, Ph.D. Thesis, Sydney University, 1986. See also Peter Wilenski's reports which led to these changes: Peter Wilenski, *Directions for Change*, Government Printer, Sydney, 1977 and 1982.

25. See Chapter 3 on Canada by Audrey Doerr. For more details see Audrey Doerr, *The Machinery of Government in Canada*, Methuen, Toronto, 1981, chap. 2, and Robert F. Adie and Paul G. Thomas, *Canadian Public Administration*, Prentice-Hall, Scarborough, 1982, chapters Four and Five.

26. The following argument is based on theories of multivalued choice. For a brief account of the theories in a public policy context see V. Subramaniam, *The Science of Public Policy Making* (mimeo), University of New South Wales, Sydney, 1981, chapter 5.

27. Compared to the earlier unquestioning exploitation of resources as basic to survival, the question of Australia's "resource boom" in 1980–81 was simply talked out of existence when discussions made it clear that the cost of exploitation would outweigh possible benefits in terms of conflicting values. It was a clear case of multivalued choice.

28. The Canadian debate about energy policy (and later free trade), clearly showed technical considerations to be quite secondary to balancing conflicting values. This becomes clearer in Canada because each value is more openly advocated by a pressure group and when the provinces constitute these advocates, multivalued choice is more evident.

29. Lord Bridges, "Haldane and the Machinery of Government," *Public Administration*, London (Autumn 1957). There are of course differing views on Webb's influence on Lord Haldane in this regard.

30. V. Subramaniam, "The Fulton Report—A Social Background Analysis," *Administration*, Dublin (1970).

II
THE NORDIC DEMOCRACIES

6

Norway

DON MAC DONALD
Management Consultant, Oslo, Norway

In its origin the Norwegian public service closely resembles the German *Beamtenstand*. The service today may be looked on as a Beamtenstand which has been accommodated to a parliamentary democracy.

GEOGRAPHIC, HISTORICAL AND SOCIAL CONTEXT

Country and People

Norway is a long (1.750 km), narrow, mountainous (three per cent arable) country on the periphery of Europe, extending far beyond the Arctic circle, and with long and cold winters. As such, pre-industrial Norway was an extremely poor country, with a thin population, largely farmers and fishermen, and with limited contact with the rest of Europe. Even today the population is only four million, equal to 13 people per square kilometer. The population is culturally, ethnically and linguistically homogeneous (1).

Historical Background

1814 marks the beginning of modern Norwegian history. Up to then Norway had in effect been a province of Denmark. In 1814, with the ending of the Napoleonic wars, Norway was allocated to Sweden by the victors. The Norwegians opposed this, and in the course of some hectic months they formed a constituent assembly, formulated a constitution for the country and attempted to found an independent kingdom with a Danish prince as regent. They failed in this—but managed to retain their constitution during the union with Sweden.

The constitution was strongly influenced by American and French models, was based on the sovereignty of the people and the inalienable rights of the individual, and included in its provisions the separation of powers, in an executive, a legislature and a judiciary. Its acceptance by the Swedish king, Karl Johan (the previous French Marshall Bernadotte), may be assumed to be due to his confident expectation of being able to annul its provisions over time. He did not, however, succeed in this.

The Norwegian population at this time can be roughly divided into four groups: independent farmers and their tenants; fishermen (who of course overlapped with farmers); a small urban element which included a commercial patriciate based on exports; and one other group. This other group, of crucial importance for the country's future development, consisted of the so-called *embedsmenn*—tenured, mainly higher-ranking public officials (2).

This *embedsstand* was almost wholly analogous to the German *Beamtenstand*. Members were university educated, the administrators normally in law (3). While their numbers were very few indeed—with their families they accounted for 0.7 per cent of the population (Seip, 1974:64)—they were the country's undisputed intellectual, social and administrative elite. Their security of tenure was incorporated in the constitution, in the formulation of which they played a central role. Then, as today, they were appointed to their posts (*embeder*) by the King in council, i.e. the government. The public service included lower-ranking employees also, but all of the rank of bureau chief and over were embedsmenn.

Their dominant position was not surprising. They were an educated elite in a country without competing elites, cosmopolitans in a culture of local communities. They represented the state and thereby authority. Additionally, like their fellows in Germany, while capable of an insufferable arrogance, they were also, undeniably, the bearers of a powerful norm of service. Finally, they were not a closed corporation. While the sons of embedsmenn had definite advantages, and while some embedsmenn dynasties did, in fact, arise, it was nonetheless possible for a farmer's intelligent son, who took a good honors degree, to make a career in the public service.

The embedsmenn remained Norway's most influential group until the introduction of parliamentarism in 1884, so that Norway in the period from 1814 to 1884 has been called the embedsmenn's state. The king's council—the government—consisted almost exclusively of embedsmenn, with ministerial posts to a degree being the highest rank in an *administrative* career. Appointments to ministerial posts were at first undertaken by the king; later, as the ministers became stronger, the government came close to becoming a self-perpetuating corporation. In addition, a large percentage of the members of parliament (the *Storting*) during this period were embedsmenn: in the period 1814-30, 47 per cent; in 1833-48, 40 percent; in 1851-69, 32 per cent; and in 1871-91, 26 per cent (Eckhoff, 1966:20).

During this period the embedsstand at first defended, later extended, Norwegian interests in relation to the Swedish king; they initiated, led and to a degree administered Norway's initial industrialization (4); and they opposed stubbornly the growing power of the Norwegian legislature.

In 1884, increasing rivalry between legislature and executive ended in victory for parliament. From now on the government was responsible to the Storting, so that the embedsmenn's state had come to an end. By now, too, Norway's industrialization was picking up speed, and economic liberalism was a dominant ideology, hostile to the administrative state and its bearers. Further, the first political parties were established in 1884, signaling the ultimate replacement of the independent parliamentary member by the party and its leadership (who formed the government) as the dominant actor in politics.

The 50 or so years after 1884 marked the nadir of power and influence for the public service. The ruling doctrine was liberalism, and society was not yet complex enough to necessitate a large and active public sector irrespective of party ideology. During this period, however, the working class in Norway worked its way up to political power, thus guaranteeing a renaissance for the public sector. This renaissance was realized after 1945, so that the years characterized by economic liberalism could be claimed to be an interval between two "normal" periods of state-dominance, as opposed to the English or American experience.

From 1945 to about 1975 the so-called administrative state again became a dominant factor in Norwegian development. The period was characterized by economic growth and the development of the welfare state, within the framework of a corporative society, with a high level of aggregate activity ensured by Keynesian means. In this period, however, the embedsmenn, while important, were by no means the dominant elite they once had been. The role of the public sector, its aims and priorities, were determined at the political level, with the function of the embedsstand being confined to the administrative. From about 1975 the international economic crisis began to affect Norway also. The corporative economy, including the public sector, began to experience increasing difficulties, and the national consensus began to weaken.

Obviously, this history and these roles form part of the embedsmann sub-culture (5) and, indeed, of the national political culture today, in the same way as, say, the English civil service still incorporates a reflection of the sober, middle-class, Victorian values of Northcote and Trevelyan (6). It serves as a background for the description below of the present-day public service, which is dealt with at the individual, organizational and societal level.

PUBLIC SERVICE PERSONNEL

Demographic Characteristics

Some demographic characteristics of the Norwegian public servant are given in Table 1 below. The characteristic departmental staff member is male, of middle or upper-middle class, university educated, and grew up in a town in South-East Norway. He is not at all representative of the population as a whole, and has a good deal more in common with ministers of state than with members of the Storting. Nor is he a passive bureaucrat: in the period 1977–1981, 44 per cent of members of parliament were public employees by profession (8). While the public employee, with some very minor exceptions, has the same formal political rights as other citizens, the figure above confirms that he in practice certainly has greater political access.

Recruitment and Promotion

All vacant positions in the public service are advertised so that anyone can apply (though in practice recruitment to higher positions is largely internal). Each department recruits its own personnel. Lower-ranking employees (first secretary, consultant and first consultant) are appointed by the minister on the basis of nominations made by a staff employment committee. Embedsmenn (bureau chiefs, under-directors, division heads and departmental councillors) are appointed by the King in council (the government) on the nomination of the minister of the department concerned, after his having heard the recommendations of the other embedsmenn in the department.

Table 1   Norway: Departmental Employees (DE) (1976) Compared with Members of
Parliament (MoP) (1973–76), Ministers of State (MoS) (1965–76), and the General
Population (GP). Per cent figures.

	DE	MoP	MoS	GP
Employment of head of family				
Self-employed	18	18	22	6
Employee, private sector	14	9	11	} 3
Employee, public sector	35	18	22	
Farmer/fisherman	13	34	28	19
Skilled/unskilled worker	13	19	15	62
Other employment	7	4	2	0
Region where grew up				
South-east Norway	67	39	47	45
South and West Norway	22	36	29	30
Trøndelag and North Norway	11	26	24	24
Municipality where grew up				
Oslo	34	8	19	5
Other towns	34	27	28	17
Rural municipalities	33	65	53	77
Sex				
Men	85	85	84	50
Women	15	15	16	50
Age				
Under 40	34	10	11	47
40–54	39	57	66	28
55 and older	27	33	24	26
University level education	87	34	64	12
Field of study:				
law	38	5	23	
economics	11	5	13	
business studies	7	1)	1)	

Source: Maktutredningen (7). NOU 1982:3, tables 3.6 and 3.7. 1) = under 1%.

There are no clear, formal, written criteria to guide the process, but rather an implicit agreement among those concerned that appointment should be on merit, which again is associated with formal professional qualifications, seniority and ability in the candidate's previous post (9). The degree to which these rather vague criteria have in fact been followed has been the subject of debate, most intensely following the two main shifts of political power in modern Norwegian history, after 1884 and when the Labour (social democratic) party came to power in the thirties, but also, though more sporadically, at other times.

In practice, appointment by merit does seem to have been the normal procedure. Thus, Labour was the dominant party during most of the period since 1945, but membership of the party among departmental embedsmenn in the seventies is believed to be less than in the population as a whole (10). This is partly due to the attitudes and efforts of the embedsmenn themselves, but reflects also a strong norm in the political culture as a whole.

Recruitment to lower-ranking positions is almost wholly the responsibility of the administrative staff, so that they effectively control the body of persons from which the majority of embedsmenn will later be drawn. As indicated above, however, the appointment of embedsmenn incorporates a political element, since the minister concerned participates in the process of choice, makes the final recommendation as to who should be appointed, and may be expected to favor persons of like mind. To the extent it occurs, though, such political choice is made among qualified candidates.

In the 1970s demands were made that other (additional) criteria should be applied, in order to attain a more representative public service, in particular that women be favored, since they are now grossly underrepresented at higher staff levels. While these demands have received political support, results have been meager.

Socialization, Norms and Role Perception

Once employed, the public servant must be socialized. Analysis has shown that while "Social background is important (in deciding) who comes into the departments, . . . (it) has little effect on the values, attitudes and viewpoints they have (in their capacity) as public servants" (11), so that the process of socialization is of some importance. The method used is normal acculturation, through which the new candidates absorb departmental views and values in the course of training and the daily routine. The process is not free of problems. In the period 1970–74 almost half the newly-employed resigned (12). Once the acculturation watershed is crossed, however, resignations are few, so that the service is a lifetime career, which in fact offers fairly good prospects. In the period 1970–74, 90 per cent of the intake took place at the secretary or consultant level. Of those leaving or retiring in the seventies, 81 per cent had been in the service for 20 years or more. The result is a cohesive group, with cohesion in the individual department strengthened by the fact that transfer between departments is limited, though greater than transfer to or from the private sector.

The present-day embedsmann's basic norms are those of loyalty, neutrality and professional independence (13). Historically, they have developed in the sequence neutrality (representing the classical, rule-oriented administration), professional independence (reflecting the rise of specialists in the latter half of the 19th century), and loyalty (representing a necessary adaptation to party political government). These norms are not, of course, mutually congruent, but coexist rather in a state of tension.

Table 2   Norway: Role Perception in the Departments by Rank, 1976. Per cent figures.

Role	Division head	Bureau chief/ Underdirector	Consultant	Total
Judge	54	44	30	37
Researcher	44	43	36	40
Negotiator/mediator	89	65	40	54
Company manager	81	51	15	35
Bookkeeper	5	10	15	12
Publicist/journalist	50	39	44	43
Teacher	39	33	24	29
Social worker/guardian	20	16	13	14
Party politician	9	7	5	6
Interest group representative	26	13	13	14
Number of answers	(80)	(286)	(390)	(750)
Unanswered	(2)	(6)	(20)	(28)

Based on a questionnaire sent 1,200 public servants—784 answers. Question: Below are listed a number of professions. We would like to know, for each of these, if they in your opinion have anything in common with the position you have today.
Source: Maktutredningen, NOU 1982:3, table 3.9.

Table 3   Norway: Methods of Problem-Solving in the Departments. (Percentage who consider the method mentioned to be important)

Method	Total percentage
Obtain more knowledge and information	82
Strengthen the public service (more money, staff)	51
Reorganization of public service	34
Improve international co-operation	31
Radical changes in the international society (economic and political)	12
Radical political, economic, social change in Norway	12
Transfer functions to the private sector	4
Number of answers	(761)
Not answered	(23)

Question: When we consider the most important problems in your area of responsibility, how do you look on the following means of dealing with these problems?
Source: Maktutredningen, NOU 1982:3, table 3.9.

Their embeddedness in the political culture inhibits any one or two of them from dominating, and they form the frame of reference for a number of sub-norms, such as the avoidance of public criticism of government policy in one's own field, discretion in one's personal political activity, and the like.

An implicit norm which has existed for a very long time is that of service, an inheritance from the embedsmannsstat. A norm which has made itself felt since 1945, and increased in importance with the growth of the corporative society, is that of consultation, the administrative analog of political pluralism.

The role perception of public servants is given in Table 2. The emphasis laid on the negotiator role here indicates a change in emphasis from rule-based decision-making (the role of judge), or the role of expert (researcher), to behavior suited to the corporative society. This is in accord with views on methods of problem-solving in Table 3.

THE ORGANIZATIONAL LEVEL

Organizational Structure

The basic organizational structure in the Norwegian public service is the Weberian bureaucracy, specialized, rule-based and hierarchic, an administrative tool very lacking in flexibility.

Efforts have been made to lessen difficulties here by incorporating greater flexibility in the organization. Specialization has been modified through arrangements for coordination of which committees have been the most important. Thus, in 1951 there were 378 permanent and 125 temporary committees, while the corresponding figures in 1976 were 912 and 229. Rule-based decision-making has been modified by permitting the use of discretion. And hierarchical decision-making has been modified through delegation—to lower departmental levels, to external agencies such as directorates, and to regional and local levels of state administration. While these modifications have been of value, the basic Weberian structure sets limits to how far it is possible to go. More extensive alteration would require a change in the political-administrative relationship in the direction of lessened political control over administrative decisions, as well as in Norwegian political culture as a whole, since this at present has very strong norms relating to equal treatment of (formally) equal cases, rule-based decision making, and the like.

The individual units are small, as Table 4 shows. While this is not surprising, it inevitably leads to capacity limitations, encourages the use of external sources of information, and contributes thereby to development of the corporative pattern.

As administrative structures the departments are characterized by specialization and fragmentation (see Table 4). There are few persons per division, supervisory and control capacity is limited, and means of co-ordination are limited. The departments form the highest level of the state administrative apparatus. Some indication of the relative importance of the rest of the administrative structure is given by Table 5.

The growth in the state administration excluding the departments—organizations such as the Telecommunications Directorate, the Water Resources and Electricity Board and the Central Bureau of Statistics—is due partly to the transfer of functions from the departments, partly to the establishment of new organizations, but mostly to a general growth in existing organizations. These external organizations have

Table 4   Norway: Departmental Growth, 1900–1977.

Budget year	Number of departments	Number of divisions	Number of bureaus	Number of employees
1901–02	8	15	51	357
1920–21	10	25	85	666
1939–40	10	31	105	765
1945–46	10	47	172	2103
1955–56	15	63	203	2141
1960	15	64	204	1965
1970	15	77	231	2212
1977	15	81	304	2730

Source: Hernes, 1978:146.

increased the fragmentation of the public service, and the difficulties of coordinating public policy.

While the rule-based hierarchic structure was suitable to the stable conditions of the 19th century, and could be accepted as late as the 1930s, it has been a far from ideal organization structure since 1945. Complex and changing conditions, and the *active* role of the state, have demanded new administrative tools, including the capacity for mutual adjustment (Thompson, 1967:56). Modifications in specialization, rule-based decision making and hierarchic steering are mentioned above. In the late sixties and

Table 5   Norway: Employment in State Administration, Different Levels, 1947–77.

	1947		1957		1967		1977	
	No.	%	No.	%	No.	%	No.	%
The departments	2159	11	2010	10	2049	8	2730	9
State auditors/ombudsmen	368	2	394	2	481	2	426	1
State administration excluding departments	3558	19	4217	21	6306	26	8636	28
State administration at local level	12918	68	13796	68	15748	64	19421	62
N = 100%	19003		20417		24584		31213	

Source: Maktutredningen, NOU 1982:3, table 3.11.

early seventies, program budgetting was emphasized, to improve planning and governmental control of the system. It was, however, de-emphasized in the period after 1975, since it failed to meet expectations, in Norway as elsewhere. At present administrative data processing is probably the most important management technique being developed. It was initially used for extensive, routine functions such as wages and salaries, accounting generally, dealing with income tax returns, customs duties, and the like. More recently it is being introduced in connection with the daily administrative work, being used for word processing, creation and use of data bases, filing systems and so on. The use of administrative data processing, as this is being developed, may be expected to increase the information-processing capacity of the public service, and thus to lessen the disadvantages of the Weberian organizational structure.

Political-Administrative Relationships

Relationships between the public administrative structure and the political leadership will naturally vary, not least in accordance with characteristics of the ministers concerned—including their experience, their administrative capacities and personal qualities, and their demands on the embedsmenn. With this proviso, it can, however, be said that relationships generally are good. On an average, 30 per cent of departmental employees meet the political leadership of their own department once a week, varying from 80 per cent for departmental councillors and division heads to 9 per cent for consultants (14). Further, most of the public servants are satisfied with their access to the political leadership, and express few difficulties in deciding which matters should be taken up with the minister, or how the minister may be expected to want the matter dealt with. The ministers share this view, so that the political-administrative relationship is normally characterized by coordination and trust. This state of affairs indicates *inter alia* that the public servants actively attempt to adjust to the requirements of the minister, and are successful in this (15).

The question of to what degree the embedsmenn play a political role or decide public policy, cannot be answered precisely. As mentioned above, and further developed below, Norway is a corporative society, where policy-making norms presuppose participation by interest group organizations as well as the political-administrative system. The standard procedure when dealing with a problem is to establish a commission, consisting of representatives of affected interests, including public servants, to investigate all sides of the problem, as the initial step and basis for all further action. An important aim in this process is consensus. Furthermore, the minister for whom the embedsmann works will himself or herself commonly be a representative of the sector concerned, and thereby very frequently share the aims and goals of the departmental employees. The embedsmann himself is normally a highly qualified and experienced participant in the decision-making process as a whole—but at the same time one who accepts loyalty to the minister as an important determinant of his own behavior. Generalizations regarding who decides what, and to what degree the function of the embedsmann is political rather than administrative, become virtually impossible under these circumstances.

THE SOCIETAL LEVEL

A Corporative Society

After 1945 a corporative society (16) developed in Norway, industrialized, egalitarian and culturally homogeneous. A high degree of consensus prevailed between the participants—government, political parties, parliament, the public service, unions, industry and other organized interests. Developments from 1945 to the present can be expressed in terms of the course of a paradigm (Kuhn, 1970), moving through four phases: those of institutionalization, normal science (i.e. standard operating procedures—SOPs), anomalies and crisis. The paradigm concerned, which has served as the basis for policy coordination on the basis of shared values, is structured round economic growth and social welfare, with Keynesian macro-economic methods as a central tool.

The institutionalization phase lasted until the early fifties, and marked the incorporation of the paradigm and relevant actors' adjustment to its requirements. This period was characterized by disagreement on both goals and the means of realizing these, so that the locus of decision-making was political. The role of the public service was thereby lessened, and the corporative decision-making arena characterized by disagreement.

The normal science phase, characterized by a national consensus on goals and means, lasted until near the end of the sixties. In this phase the critical questions were technical, concerning how best to apply accepted means for the attainment of accepted ends, so that the locus of decision-making tended to move from the political to the administrative level. In this period also, with actors adapted to each other, the corporative societal structure tended towards a multi-organization, with relative rank a function of congruence with dominant values. Thus the Ministry of Finance had a dominating position, ministries such as those of Industry or Transport and Communications ranked high, while e.g. the Ministry of Social Welfare ranked low. The importance allocated the norm of consultation in this phase is understandable. It could very reasonably be claimed that under these conditions, instead of the public service becoming politicized, what actually happened was that the rest of the corporative society became bureaucratized.

The anomalies phase, during the end of the sixties and early in the seventies, was one of growing social protest over neglected values, such as the environment, resources and the ecology generally. In this phase the administrative components of the corporative society experienced difficulties, because their accustomed procedures (SOPs) had difficulty in incorporating the new priorities, so that decision-making again became a political matter. However, since the dominating political parties themselves shared the priorities of the establishment of which they were part, they too had difficulty in incorporating the new premises, so that an appreciable element of grass-root action made itself felt (17), with the political parties incorporating the grass-root premises as best they could and over time.

The crisis phase may be said to have begun with the oil shock in 1973. It was characterized by increasing difficulties in applying accustomed procedures (SOPs), by a weakening of the corporative (multi-organizational) structure, and by increasing disagreement leading to the locus of decision-making again becoming political. This is the phase in which the consultative state ceased to consult (see Olsen, 1978:134).

The Role of the Public Service

In the corporative decision-making structure the public service has formed a central element and played a key role. Its importance is indicated by Tables 6 and 7 below.

As the tables make clear, the departments have more contact with organized interest groups than any other part of the public sector, as well as being rated of importance by most of the interest groups. The reason for this is that the public service forms a linkage between the public and private sectors (between "industry and politics"); it consists of a concentration of information and thereby of premises for decision-making, for both public and private sectors; and for the private sector it controls a flow of resources.

Administrative Accountability

Formal procedures to ensure administrative accountability exist. Budgets are normally specified in detail (though the amount of detail has lessened over time) and the state auditors' control of accounts ensure they are followed; but this control is not a matter of central political interest. The ombudsman for the public service serves a useful purpose in investigating administrative practice on behalf of the public and if necessary requiring corrections; but it happens that departments are slow and even negligent in replying to his queries, or in undertaking corrections. Court cases on behalf of the public are infrequent. There is a law to ensure public access to documents; but

Table 6 Norway: Contact Patterns of Interest Group Leaders, 1976. Monthly contact with different authorities/groups, for secretariat employees (SE) and elected officers (EO). Per cent figures.

Authority/group	SE	EO
Department	45	8
Directorates	32	
Regional and local administration	26	10
Storting and its organs	3	1
Individual members of the Storting	10	5
Political parties	8	6
Other organizations (those not having members or associated)	65	28
International non-state organizations	21	4
Sister organizations in other countries	26	4
Central board in own organization	73	—
Individual members	94	83
Local associations of members	75	56
Associated national organizations	50	33

Source: Maktutredningen, *op. cit.*, table 4.2.

Table 7   Norway: Evaluations of Different Agencies' Importance, by Public Servants and by Elected Officers and Employees in Organizations in Economic Life. Percentage stating the agency concerned is very or quite important.

Agency	Employees in departments	Elected in organizations	Employees in organizations
Departments[a]	59	85	91
Government (cabinet)	75	75	85
Storting	68	70	80
Public committees	46	66	72
Regional and local public admin.	33	41	41
Opposition parties	16	29	27
Organizations in economic life[a]	49	49	47
Other organizations	16	not asked	not asked
Research and educational institutions	24	54	44
Mass media	18	53	54
Private companies	13	37	31

Source: Maktutredningen, op. cit., table 4.8.
[a]Own organization excluded.

complaints that departments have declared secret material which should be public are not unknown. Thus the formal procedures exist, but crusading zeal in their application is not at all common.

Among possible reasons for this state of affairs, two may be mentioned. The one is that scandals in fact have been very few in the public service, so that the pressure of demand for strict accountability, strictly applied, is limited. The other reason is the corporative decision-making structure. Within this structure the public service, broadly speaking, is not looked on with suspicion as an organization with its own aims, separate from those of other participants. Norms of persuasion, negotiation and compromise are felt to apply, rather than those of orders, commands and control (18). Such a frame of reference is not conducive to emphasis on accountability.

A Fragmented Corporative Structure

While the Norwegian societal decision-making structure is corporative, it is not a unitary corporative structure, but rather divided into loosely-coupled components. Research in the seventies has analyzed the public sector as a segmented structure (see Olsen, 1978:122 et seq.), consisting, as the name indicates, of a number of segments or separate decision-making (policy-making) areas, each with its associated departments, goals, procedures and interest and client groups, so that public policy as a whole consists of a number of only partially coordinated sector policies. This result is very much a consequence of the individual department, aided by its associated interest groups, being capable of defending its own policy area from external influence, while itself having great difficulty in influencing others.

CONCLUDING REMARKS

It is not difficult to point to problematic aspects of the Norwegian public service. It is not a representative bureaucracy, which may quite possibly be a weakness. Public access to records is far less than e.g. in the U.S. This quite definitely is a weakness. Criticism is made of bureaucratic treatment of the public, of red-tape, and so on. The division of functions between national, regional and local levels is a matter of debate, as it the desirability and extent of privatization.

From a comparative perspective, however, it must be acknowledged that the Norwegian public service has very few serious or dramatic problems. The population is very small, society is egalitarian and homogeneous, and national income is among the world's highest (partly because of the North Sea oil). Problems deriving from size and consequent complexity, from great differences in wealth, from class or ethnic conflict, from cultural and sub-cultural difference, and so on, are necessarily limited. While there is no consensus on the matter, a list of some of the most important problems might be as follows:

1. In several sectors, of which agriculture is possibly the most striking, identification with client group interests has gone very far. The fragmented corporative structure has in other words led to sectoral interests being given very high priority.
2. Difficulties have been experienced in developing suitable responses to problems which overlap several sectors. Transsectoral policy has tended to consist of a number of individual, poorly coordinated sectoral policies.
3. The administrative unit in the public sector is the bureaucratic organization. This is an unsuitable administrative tool for an increasing number of the problems being dealt with (19).
4. A final, debatable problem may be mentioned. The public service, considered as an administrative tool, presupposes a dividing line between the political and the administrative, between decision-making and the application of decisions, as well as a dividing line between public and private sectors. The historical roots and justifications for these presuppositions are very obvious, but their empirical relevance today is becoming increasingly questionable.

REFERENCES

1. The Lapps form the main ethnic minority, numbering today perhaps 20,000 and resident mainly in the far North. This group has not had any influence on public policy; they have rather been the objects of attempts to force them to adapt to the majority culture.
2. An "embede" is a tenured office or post in the public service, so that "embedsmenn" are tenured office holders or officials, and the "embedsstand" is the estate of office holders. I have used the designation "embedsmann" in this chapter, to emphasize the difference between the Norwegian office-holder and what one normally, at least in an Anglo-Saxon context, tends to associate with "civil servant."
3. In 1814 the lawyer-administrators accounted for only about one third of the embedsmenn, the clergy and officers also accounting for about one third each. In the course of the country's development the proportion of the latter lessened, and they are ignored in the following.

4. Despite being based on a laissez faire ideology, this early industrialization was dominated by the state (Seip, 1968:22–71), because the embedsstand was the main source of administrators, as the state was of capital.
5. Compare Stinchcombe, 1965.
6. See, for example, Pollock's characterization of the Treasury (Pollock, 1982:150–159).
7. Where only page numbers are given in the following, the source is Maktutredningen, NOU 1982:3.
8. Page 48.
9. Pages 45–46.
10. Page 48.
11. Page 53.
12. Page 49.
13. See Jacobsen, Knut Dahl, 1960:231–248.
14. Page 55, table 3.10.
15. Page 76. Compare also Mayntz and Scharpf (1975), concerning the corresponding process in the German federal bureaucracy.
16. This has variously been described as a mixed economy, an administrative state, and a "negotiated economy and mixed (public) administration" (Hernes, 1978).
17. The most striking instance of this is the Norwegian referendum on joining the EEC in 1972 when, despite almost the entire establishment being for membership, a tremendously active grassroots movement led to a majority voting against membership.
18. See page 78 *et seq.*
19. Compare the rigidity of the mechanistic departmental structure with, for example, organic structures increasingly common in the private sector.

REFERENCES IN ENGLISH

Bernt, Jan F., "Norway," in Donald C. Rowat, ed., *International Handbook on Local Government Reorganization* (Westport: Greenwood Press, 1980), 142–149.

Eckhoff, Torstein, and Knut Dahl Jacobsen, *Rationality and Responsibility in Administrative and Judicial Decision-Making.* Copenhagen: Munksgaard, 1960.

Frihagen, A., "Norway," in Donald C. Rowat, ed., *Administrative Secrecy in Developed Countries* (N.Y.: Columbia Univ. Press, 1979), 106–126.

Higley, John, K. E. Brofoss, and K. Groholt, "Top Civil Servants and the National Budget in Norway," in Mattei Dogan, ed., *The Mandarins of Western Europe* (N.Y.: Halsted, 1975), 252–74.

Kvavik, Robert B., *Interest Groups in Norwegian Politics.* Oslo: Universitetsforlaget, 1978.

Olsen, Johan P., *Organized Democracy: Political Institutions in a Welfare State–The Case of Norway.* Bergen: Universitetsforlaget, 1983.

7

Finland

JUHA VARTOLA
University of Tampere, Tampere, Finland

HISTORICAL BACKGROUND

Political Development

Finland was for over five hundred years part of Sweden, although there were many interesting special features in the internal administration of the "eastern province." One can speak of Finland's own administrative history beginning only with the year 1809, when Finland under the Tsar of Russia received the status of an autonomous Grand Duchy. Finland was granted its own Diet, based on the four Estates, its own Senate, and its own administrative machinery (1).

The development of the administrative machinery of Finland largely conforms to the pattern according to which the public bureaucracies came into being in the countries of Western Europe. As have all countries, Finland also has a number of special characteristic features which in the course of centuries have shaped its political life. Among these special features have been the following (2):

1. The Self-Government Principle of the Nordic Countries

The roots of Finland's political modes of organizing date back to the local units of self-government which developed spontaneously and independently in the prehistoric period. The important thing was that Finland, linked to the realm of Sweden, obtained an almost equal position, that the people were not subjected to serfdom, and that the continental system of feudalism was not put into effect in Finland. The tradition of popular self-government was preserved and developed as a kind of democracy of free peasants, both in ecclesiastical and temporal local administration and in the application of law. After 1809, when Finland had been annexed to Russia, the traditional administrative structure of the province began to develop towards a unified State. From around the middle of the century onwards, a national awareness of the Constitution and a State rapidly strengthened under the influence of Western cultural ideals, and the idea of independence came to life. The party system, which came into being at the end of the century, also strengthened this development. In 1906 Finland obtained its own unicameral Parliament (*Eduskunta*), and universal suffrage (at the same time, the women obtained the right to vote). After vigorous efforts at Russification, and the so-called "years of oppression," Finland finally won its independence in 1917.

2. Lutheranism

The influence of religion and the church upon politics and administration has never been as strong in the Lutheran countries as in the Catholic countries. However, the Lutheranism of Sweden-Finland became a State religion as early as the 16th century, when it was rooted by rigorous measures. The institutionalized practicing of the Lutheran religion may have aimed as much at securing public morals and the religious legitimacy of the administrative system as at caring for the individual salvation of people. During the period of autonomy (1809–1917) the Church avoided conflict with the Greek Orthodox rulers of Russia by flexibly shifting the object of its doctrine of the necessity of honoring the powers that be from the King of Sweden to the Tsar of Russia. Especially its tremendous emphasis on the honoring of the authorities has been the factor by which the Lutheran Church has in its own way upheld the legitimacy of the wielders of State power.

3. Capitalism

Private ownership as the form of economic organization in Finland as in other Western countries dates back to the distant past. The capitalist market-ideology came to the fore in Finland towards the end of the nineteenth century along with rapid industrialization and the elimination of the mercantilist restrictions on business life. With the establishment of the party system, all the parties except the socialist party were ideologically on the side of the free market. As during the period of autonomy, the civil servants were few in number but largely drawn from the upper class. The development of the administrative machinery was dominated by the promoting of business activity and satisfying the needs of capitalism emerging within it.

4. Nationalism

The vigorous development of a feeling of nationalism during the 19th century was also an important tension factor in the shaping of the administrative machinery. Nationalism in Finland was especially controversial since the Finnish-speaking "common people" were ruled primarily by an aristocratic Swedish-speaking upper-class bureaucracy, in a situation in which the country was a part of the vast Russian Empire. The emerging ideal of Fennicism thus envisaged two enemies: the Russian rulers and the Swedish-speaking bureaucrats. Thus the objective of gaining independence had many elements within it. There was the desire on the one hand to defend Finland's own administration against the dominating power and oppression of the Russians. On the other hand, the emerging ideal of Fennicism demanded that Finnish be the language of the bureaucracy, and in general also that the predominance of the Swedish-language culture be displaced.

5. Legalism

The changing of the political status of Finland from that of a Swedish province to an autonomous Grand Duchy brought to Finland its own central administration, and thus a bureaucratic machinery which increased both in size and in influence, but which during the first half of the century had no political representative institution of any sort to serve as a supplementing force and as a counter-weight. During this "golden age of a civil servant Estate and of officialdom" the significant roles in society were the official posts of the administration, the university and the church. In this State, the burghers and the free peasants were actually not at all subjects in the sense of themselves acting, but rather were only objects, and their "activity" was focused on engaging in their own occupations (3). The top-level administration was committed to the patriarchal-bureaucratic administrative style and viewed itself as knowing the needs of the people. It maintained the facade of social harmony, and wanted to keep the masses of the people separate from politics. The system was vigorously directed from above, and it emphasized attitudes of subjection. The Diet, which was rarely convened, did not even at a later stage attain the status of being a democratic counter-weight to the bureaucracy, and the ideology of legality adopted in the struggle on behalf of autonomy did not tend to strengthen the element of popular sovereignty in the exercise of power but rather contributed to the stability of the administrative legalism, which was rigidly formalistic (4).

Independence and the New Politico-Administrative System

The background of the attainment of independence by Finland included the period of the "policy of oppression," when Russia endeavored to take away from Finland the rights which had been granted a century earlier, the general development of the idea of the nation-state, and finally, specifically within Finland, the movement of conscious striving for independence. Other factors contributing to Finland becoming independent included the impact of the First World War on Russia, and the Russian Revolution. The year 1917, when Finland became independent, was a culmination of development up to that point. In 1918 Finland entered a civil war in which the opposing sides were the "Whites" and the "Reds," the whites consisting of elements in the society favoring independence as such, the reds—largely from the industrial and agricultural proletariat—favoring far-reaching social reforms. The civil war was the culmination of a long-continuing conflict among a number of opposing interests.

The immediate background of the way in which Finland became independent had a significant effect upon the contents of the *Form of Government Act* [Constitution Act], which was ratified in 1919. The political system of the newly independent State of Finland strongly favored the executive power. The general organizing principle of the politico-administrative system was in accord with the doctrine of the separation of powers. Nevertheless, it was at the same time explicitly both parliamentary and presidential in principle. Finland had obtained a system of parliamentary elections with universal suffrage as early as 1906. However, during the enacting of the *Form of Government Act*, with the civil war fresh in memory, the most decisive question was the relative strengths of the Parliament (the upper classes feared that the socialists would win a majority in it) and the Executive (the conservatives desired to have a monarchy). The final result was a compromise—a system which is formally parliamentary, but in which the position of the President is very strong.

MAIN FEATURES OF THE ADMINISTRATIVE STRUCTURE

The Central Administration

Finland has a parliamentary, democratic system of government, based upon the tripartite division of powers. The parliament of Finland, because of its legislative and budget powers, is the most essential organ of State power. Nevertheless, the parliament does not intervene in the administration of the State, since the President of the Republic is formally the most important organ of the executive power. Actually, the administration of the country is directed by the Council of State, which is composed of the sitting government, that is the ministers, and by the ministries (13) directed by the ministers. In addition the central administration in Finland includes the central administrative boards, numbering 22, and about 80 comparable units of central administration having research, service, or business functions.

The President of the Republic

The President of the Republic is elected every six years in indirect elections. If in the voting of the Electors (301) any of the candidates receives more than one-half of the votes cast, he is elected. If need be, a second and a third balloting are carried out. If in the third balloting—between the two candidates who received the highest numbers of votes in the second balloting—the votes are tied, the decision is to be by lot.

In matters relating to legislating, the President has the power to take the initiative for the enacting of a new law, and for the amending or repealing of a law which is in force. In addition, he has a right to veto laws passed by the Parliament and, in his name, issues presidential statutory orders (decrees) which regulate in greater detail matters prescribed in laws. The President can also call the Parliament into extraordinary session, and dissolve the Parliament. He also has a competency to order new elections.

As regards actual administration, the important functions of the President include the following: the President decides regarding Finland's relations with foreign powers, acts in time of peace as the Supreme Commander of the Armed Forces, can grant exemptions and pardons, and supervises the administration of the State (for example by requesting information from heads of government agencies and setting on foot inspections within such agencies, although this last has hardly ever been done).

The high political status of the President is indicated by the fact that the President appoints the Prime Minister as well as the other members of the Council of State. Thus, in practice, the ministers must enjoy not only the confidence of the Parliament but also the confidence of the President of the Republic. The President's extensive powers of appointment are significant not only for the practice of administration but also for the setting of lines of policy. He appoints not only the leading civil servants of the ministries and the central boards but also the governors of the provinces and the professors of the universities and—since there is a system of established religion in Finland—the Archbishop and the bishops.

The powers of the President of Finland are thus very great, and the Republic of Finland has always been viewed as being among the countries which have a strong presidential system. Nevertheless the situation of the actual exercise of power by the presidents has varied greatly. The manner in which the powers of the President have been used has been much affected by the personality and the real political influence of the successive presidents, and their desire to exercise power. As regards the directing of internal policy, Finland has been a standard Western-style democracy in which the parliament and the government are answerable. On the other hand, in foreign policy Finland has always been clearly President-centered since the second world war, and there has been a truly personal directing of foreign policy by the President.

The Council of State and the Ministries

The Council of State is headed by the Prime Minister and it is he who generally proposes the composition of the government. The so-called "night-school" session of the Council of State is an unofficial conference. In it decisions are not made officially, but it is nevertheless very important, since many matters which are later decided upon officially in the general sitting have already been unofficially settled beforehand in the "night-school."

In the general sittings the government makes decisions and prepares matters. The Council of State has a quorum at the general sitting if at least five ministers are present.

The presentment of the President is a meeting of the Council of State in which matters are formally presented to the President and the President makes decisions. In so-called "cabinet-matters" (for example concerning military orders) the decisions of the President are made outside the Council of State.

The Chancellor of Justice is also part of the Council of State, but he has a special position. He does not participate in legislating and he does not belong to any actual organs of the government. His role is to observe and keep an eye on the activities of the organs of the State, and to check whether the laws are being upheld and the civil servants are carrying out their duties—and this role extends to the highest levels of the administration.

The Chancellor of Justice is present both at the sittings of the Council of State and at the presentments to the President. Likewise, he inspects the statements of the Council of State and the records of the presentments to the President. He acts as a general prosecutor and he is the chief of all the public prosecutors of Finland. The President of the Republic appoints him to his post. According to the Constitution Act, the Chancellor of Justice is to be "outstanding in his knowledge of the circumstances in the country related to justice and law."

The main functions of the Council of State are:

making proposals to the parliament
putting into effect the decisions of the parliament
putting into effect the decisions of the President
directing the administration

The ministers have responsibilities of two sorts. First, they have the standard responsibility to parliament for the expediency of their measures. Second, they have also a legal responsibility for the legality of their acts as sovereign directors of their ministries.

Normally, there is only one minister at the head of each of the ministries, but ministries with a wide range of functions such as the Ministry of Social Affairs and Health and the Ministry of Education, as a rule have two ministers. Each ministry has an administrative director (secretary general). The administrative director has such duties as taking care of the internal functioning of the ministry, presenting the most important personnel matters, and presenting matters concerning the budget.

All of the ministries are divided into departments and bureaus. In practice it is the department heads who are the chiefs in the different areas of functioning, directing their own sectors from above downwards as well as seeing to it that matters within their own sectors are brought to the attention of the minister so as to be brought to the attention of the government. The average number of the personnel within each ministry is about 250 persons. There are, on the average, five departments within each of the ministries, and each department, on the average, has two bureaus, each headed by a bureau chief. Although each minister has the power to decide any matter within the decision-making power of any of his subordinates, this is done extremely rarely in practice. Although the Finnish administrative system does not favor official delegating of matters, delegating actually does occur to a large extent.

The Central Boards

A "central board" is an administrative authority under the Council of State, its function being to take care of a branch of administration and its activity in principle covering the whole country. In accordance with this definition, each central board functions under the direction of some ministry, although in practice the board may be relatively independent. A certain rigidity in the boundaries of the areas of jurisdiction is characteristic of Finland's state administration; the division of functions and decision-making powers among the governmental authorities is in accordance with fixed general norms. In addition, there is a strong continuing tradition of the independence of the central boards, running back to the period of Russian rule. Making the guidance function between the ministries and the central boards more effective has been a prominent objective in the development of administration.

Within the central administration of the State there are altogether over a hundred agencies and institutions and the differences among them are very great. It has been the custom to distinguish and classify them roughly according to their function as: institutions carrying on administrative functions, institutions the activities of which are analogous to business activities, and investigative institutions engaged in delimited special tasks. As regards their overall organization, most of them are either administrative agencies or institutions, business enterprises of the State, or corporate entities having a public character. In terms of the consequences or the product of their functioning, another tri-partite division has been made into administrative, productive and informational.

Provincial and District Administration

According to Article 50 of the Constitution Act, Finland is divided for the purposes of general administration into provinces, administrative districts, and municipalities. The municipality has self-government.

The development of the provinces into administrative units of the State began over 400 years ago, during the period of Swedish rule. With the increasing of the population and the extending of the administration, there has been a transition toward ever-smaller regional units, and this has resulted in a continuing growth of the number of provinces. At present the country is divided into twelve provinces.

The provincial government, directed by the Governor of the Province, is the general authority in the province, under the Council of State and more specifically under the Ministry for Internal Affairs. According to the general definition of the function of the provincial government, it "shall be concerned with the state and needs of the province, and shall in all respects endeavor to foster the development of the province and the best interests of its population." Probably the basic functions which go furthest back are: taking care, as the highest police authority of the province, of the maintenance of general order and security, and the direction of the police; collecting the revenues of the State; and the functions of the highest executive authority putting into effect decisions and judgments. But, in addition to these functions, it has been charged with an ever-increasing number of the economic, social, and cultural functions of the welfare state. Another dimension of its functions is the direction and supervision of self-governing communities and the local authorities of the State.

The significance of the provincial level in the system of public administration has slowly been on the increase. They are expected to engage in wide-ranging activities on their own initiative, in cooperation with other regional entities. Accordingly, the role of the Governor of the Province has changed from that of the representative of State power to that of being concerned with looking to the interests of the province and its population. At this intermediate level there has been a trend toward piling up functions and powers and this has led to functional differentiation and structural compartmentalization. (The transferring of the tax-levying function to special authorities has been an exceptional example of a development in the opposite direction.) There has long been discussion of a more comprehensive reorganization of this intermediate level administration, but it has proved difficult to find an acceptable model.

Outside the administration by the provincial government are important functions of district administration, such as labor administration, labor protection, taxation, and water administration. For these functions there are many different authorities, which are directly under a ministry or central board, and their areas may not coincide with the area of the province.

Municipal Self-Administration

In analogy to the State, the municipality is a territorial self-administering community organized as an entity which has precisely determined borders and an obligatory membership of persons who are registered as belonging to it. The division of the entire area of the nation into municipalities is indeed a basic territorial division, and most of the other administrative divisions are based upon it. The Council of State decides regarding any change in the division of the country into municipalities. In 1985 there were altogether about 450 municipalities in Finland.

THE CIVIL SERVICE

The Status of Civil Servants

The State is the largest single employer in the country, and the comparative significance of the public sector in the labor market, compared to that of the private sector, has been continuously increasing. The persons in the service of the State are classifiable into a number of groups according to their legal status. The main body of the civil service is made up of permanent holders of a post or position—a good half of all of them—who enjoy the full rights of civil servants.

The general development of the society and the growth of the public sector have been reflected also in the civil service, and in ways other than mere growth. The changes which have been considered the most important are: (1) the differentiation of functions, (2) the increased practice of political appointment to posts, (3) the adoption of collective bargaining regarding the terms of civil servant posts, and (4) the participation of employees in the internal management of government bureaus (government-bureau democracy).

The raising of the level of the requirements has resulted in both a general raising of the level of training and a differentiating of functions. The share of civil servants in the central administration with an academic education rose in the period 1950–75 from 27 per cent to 43 per cent. Structural compartmentalization has caused a need to increase expertise in various fields by taking in an ever-increasing number of specialized persons. It has traditionally been required for appointees to high administrative posts to have training in law, and in 1987 about 60 per cent of these posts were still occupied by lawyers (5). However, the basis of training has been gradually widened to include, for example, the attainment of degrees in the social sciences. In central administration the personnel with specialized education are perhaps concentrated most in staff-level functions, such as preparatory work and planning, which does not include actual decision-making. During the last twenty-year period the number of posts in research and planning has multiplied (6).

Since the sixties there has been much talk in Finland about the politicization of administration. What is in question, however, is not a completely new feature of the political system; there had been politics in the appointment of the civil service earlier too. What has occurred is a political and social structural change in the higher civil service, a change which is a very understandable reflection of a corresponding change in the political leadership of the country. As regards those authorities in which appointments are with tenure, this change is occurring with a time-lag.

Undeniably, party politics has increased within the administration both of the State and of the municipalities, particularly from the 1960s. Politicization of administration is ordinarily linked with the recruiting of civil servants, and it is manifest in an increase of appointments in which an essential basis of selection has been party affiliation. In this connection there has been much imprecise talk also of "representative bureaucracy," and political appointments have been defended by referring to the need for politically guiding the administration under changed circumstances.

In 1983 there were in the service of public administration altogether some 544,000 persons, of whom 212,000 were in the service of the State. A little over one-half of these, about 135,000 were actual State civil servants having a stipulated basic salary. The overall development is presented in Table 1.

In the Finnish system the civil servants have, in principle, all the standard political rights. Thus, with a few separately defined exceptions, they can be elected as representatives to parliament and as members of municipal councils. Similarly, they have the right to strike, although the government can limit this right to strike in areas "vital for the society."

The Senior Civil Servants

In Finland, as in other developed countries, the power of the senior civil servants is significant in many ways. The average life-span of the successive governments during the whole period of independence has been very short, one year on the average. Even though in very recent years this average life-span has been clearly on the increase, the position of the permanent civil service has been of particular importance.

Table 1 Finland: The Personnel of the State and the Permanent Labor Force in the Municipal Sector, 1970–83 (in thousands).

	1970	1976	1980	1983	Increase 1983/70 in thousands of persons
Employed work-force in national economy	2126	2163	2203	2320	264
State	169	190	199	212	43
Municipalities and federations of municipalities	166	229	305	332	166
The State and the municipal sector in total	335	419	504	544	209
Share of State and municipal sector of employed work-force, %	16	19	23	23	–

During the period of autonomy during the 19th century, the senior civil servants of the State were drawn in large part from the aristocracy, and in general the civil servants were drawn from the upper classes. During the period of independence the social background of the civil servants has evened out.

Nevertheless there is still an "over-representation" of the highest social strata in the social background of the senior civil servants. To be sure, the situation varies to some extent in different fields of administration. For example, in the administration of foreign affairs the civil service is recruited still rather notably from among the descendants of senior civil servants, while in such fields of administration as labor and social affairs the civil servants have more frequently come from a working-class background.

There have been very few women among the senior civil servants. Thus, among the 352 highest civil servants in the country there are currently only 15 women, although women make up over 40 per cent of all persons in the service of public administration. It is characteristic of the system in Finland that all of the senior civil servants have academic degrees.

ADMINISTRATIVE ACCOUNTABILITY

The Political Supervision of Administration

The Parliament

As in other countries with a similar political system it is possible in Finland to distinguish five types of supervision of the administration: political, legal, financial, administrative proper (meaning from within the administration), and a supervision conducted in various forms by the citizens. Since the internal supervision of administration is extensive and complicated, and since its structure is more or less the same in all bureaucratic organizations, it will not be dealt with here. The other systems for the supervision of administration are presented here in concise form.

The Parliament of Finland has the right and duty to engage in continuous super-vision of the official actions of the government, regarding both their legality and their expediency. Parliament can make the members of the Council of State and the Chancellor of Justice *answer legally* for their official actions; thus it can decide to raise a charge against them in the special High Court of Impeachment. The Constitu-tional Law Committee of Parliament has the specific task of continuously controlling legality in conjunction with the preparation of matters for decision.

The *political or parliamentary responsibility* of a ministry and its individual mem-bers, which includes responsibility for the expediency of measures, can be implemented in many ways. *Questions and interpellations* in parliament are especially suitable for this purpose. Any representative can present a simple question to a minister. Ques-tions are of two types, written and oral.

The interpellations are above all a weapon in the arsenal of the opposition, by which it puts pressure on the government, criticizes its general policy and individual measures, and endeavors to oust it from power. It nevertheless should be noted that during the whole period of independence, up to 1980, only four governments have fallen as a result of votes of lack of confidence resulting from an interpellation.

In a number of ways the parliament engages in direct inspection of the administra-tion. It elects for four years at a time a "person known for being eminent in his knowledge of the law" as the *Ombudsman of the Parliament* to supervise the upholding of the laws in the courts and other authorities and to investigate complaints from the public. He, like the Chancellor Justice, gives a report to the parliament annually. In the main, the position of the Ombudsman is similar to that of the Chancellor of Jus-tice as a guardian of the rights of the individual.

Parties and Interest Groups

Listed in order of size, the political parties represented in the parliament are the Social Democratic Party of Finland, the National Coalition, the Center Party, the Finnish People's Democratic Union (within the frame of which the Finnish Communist Party functions), the Finnish Rural Party, the Swedish People's Party, the Christian Union, the Constitutionalist Rightist Party, and the Greens. The nonsocialists have for a long time had a clear majority.

Supervision of administration by the parties is primarily through the parliament; in the municipalities it is through the municipal councils. The politicization of administra-tion in Finland has nevertheless advanced rather far. Thus politicization can also be regarded as a form of political supervision of the administration. It has for a long time been very difficult for civil servants who are not committed politically to advance to leading posts in administration.

Also, as a consequence of the corporatization of administration, interest-groups have actually taken on political significance. The interest-groups nevertheless do not nor-mally focus on Government policy and thus generally on the planning and supervision in administration—an exception being economic policy—but rather on those sectors in which they represent their interests. The most clearly political role is played by the central organizations of the workers, the employers, agricultural producers, and indus-try; to these organizations the government naturally listens regularly.

The interest-groups are usually represented in various committees, the development of the number of committees being shown in the following table (7):

	Temporary	Permanent	Total
1960	254	74	328
1970	253	273	526
1980	90	342	433
1982	105	343	448

In 1982 committees had a total of about 5,000 members. The clear growth in the number of continuing committees indicates the increasing significance of interest-groups in the preparatory work of the central administration.

The Finland of the 1980s is being characterized more and more frequently as "consensus-Finland." The country is living in a state of equilibrium. The welfare society has been built to the degree that the resources allow. The economic development, in terms of international comparisons, has been relatively good. There have been no great social or political conflicts. In the prevailing stable situation the leading government parties and the most influential interest-groups are living in "peaceful co-existence." In terms of administration, the implication of the stable situation is that long-pending projects for the reform of administration are at a standstill. During the whole period of independence not one single large-scale reform of the structures of administration has been implemented, although the reform of intermediate level administration has been pending. Presumably, the slight decrease in legitimacy of the politico-administrative system, together with the excessive centralization of decision-making in administration will tend to strengthen the development of decentralization, which has already begun in Finland as in other western countries having a similar pattern of development. The strengthening of local self-government, the move toward grass-roots democracy, and in general the endeavor to bring administration closer to the citizens will certainly change the relations of politics and administration.

Supervision of Legality

In the supervision of the legality of administration, the Chancellor of Justice and the Parliamentary Ombudsman are most important. Since they have been described earlier, the supervision of the legality of administration will be sketched here only with reference to the machinery of the administrative application of law.

This machinery is rather complicated. Appeals against the decisions of administrative authorities are handled by the administrative authorities themselves, by general courts, and by specific administrative courts. The development has nevertheless been proceeding away from internal control of the administrative machinery toward more effective control by courts. At the highest instance, the application of administrative law is for the most part in the hands of courts which have been established specifically for this purpose, whereas at the lower instances the handling of appeals is divided among administrative authorities, special courts, and general courts.

The Supreme Administrative Court is the highest organ for appeal under administrative law. The jurisdiction of the Supreme Administrative Court is general in character; all appeals involving administrative law in matters not specifically reserved for investigation by other authorities can be submitted to it for decision at the highest instance. Appeals against decisions of the Council of State, of ministries, of national boards and of other higher administrative authorities are addressed to the Supreme Administrative Court unless, on the basis of specific provisions, they go to some other authority. Specifically, tax complaints provide a great deal of work both for this court and for lower authorities in the application of law. At least half the members of the Supreme Administrative Court are required to have qualifications for the post of a judge. The court usually works in sections, and a sitting of the court must have at least five members.

At the lower levels, the modes of appeal are considerably more complicated in administrative matters than in the general application of law. The 1950 Act on Appeal Procedure classifies administrative authorities referred to in the Act into three categories: (1) the Council of State and its ministries; (2) the higher administrative authorities, including the national boards, the provincial governments, the chapters of dioceses, and other authorities directly under the Council of State; and (3) lower administrative authorities. The principal rule, to which there are many exceptions, is that a complaint, or appeal, is made from the decision of a lower administrative authority to that superior authority to which it is subordinate.

The national boards and the provincial courts play a central role in the lower-level application of administrative law. An Act issued in 1955 established courts for the provincial governments; the function of these courts is to handle and settle appeals and complaints in matters having an administrative-legal character and belonging in general to the jurisdiction of the provincial governments, as well as to handle other matters assigned to them in several specific laws.

Financial Supervision

There are two major types of financial inspection: Parliamentary inspection and administrative inspection. Parliamentary inspection is based on the right of the parliament to supervise the activities of the government and the administration under it. Administrative inspection is further divided into two parts, internal inspection by the authorities themselves, and inspection by the State Auditors' Office.

As are all control systems which have developed and expanded in the course of history, the system of financial control in Finland is too complicated to be described in this small space (8).

The basic problem of the financial control system in Finland, as in other western countries, is that the supervision focuses too much on purely technical questions. The system in Finland functions rather satisfactorily as regards the correctness of the accounts, upholding the norms for the management of State finances and compliance with the budget. On the other hand, determining whether the administration has been "economical" in terms of cost-benefit or cost-efficiency has had considerably less attention. In addition, assessments of the effectiveness of social measures are entirely lacking in the *official* control system, although research does produce such assessments in different fields. Systematic policy assessment is only at the planning stage.

ADMINISTRATION AND SOCIETY: CONCLUDING COMMENTS

On the Development of Administration in Finland (9)

Ever since the administrative machinery of independent Finland was organized in the 1920s, the basic structures of public administration in the country have remained relatively unchanged. Overall, the development was rather slow and stable, at least until the mid-sixties. Then, the changed political situation, economic growth, and a systematic effort to build a welfare society set in motion a rapid and far-reaching change, which included the following developmental features:

the functions of the State and the municipalities increased rather rapidly

the increase in the number of functions implied an increasing intervention of the government into an increasing number of social relations

the number of administrative organizations and suborganizations increased rapidly

the size of the civil service increased very considerably

the administration itself had more recourse to plans and planners, to experts and expertise, to science and scientists, to technology and technocrats—and became more international-minded and more politicized

the influence of interest-groups on preparatory work and planning in public administration increased—and at the same time the importance of the executive branch increased

in the public, collective, and market-based system of governing there was an increase of mutual dependence and mutual commitment—while simultaneously the relative significance and power of the political parties increased

there was a move within administration towards a new type of personnel policy and personnel administration, through shifting to participation systems, rapidly strengthening personnel training, and renovating styles of leadership

in administrative technology there was an ever greater use of automatic data processing

The changes listed above were nevertheless only a part of all the changes that occurred within public administration, changes which to a very great extent were a logical consequence of the dynamic renovation of Finnish society. The structural changes of the 1960s, which were followed at a rapid pace by the social reforms made at the end of the decade and at the beginning of the 1970s, occasioned quite substantial changes in administration. However, it is important to observe that this change concerned primarily procedure and administrative practice—and was not institutional or structural.

A problem in the developing of the welfare state was that a revision of administration did not take place at the same time. Consequently, the old bureaucratic structures and ways of functioning were preserved and indeed—with the new functions—have spread in the society. Thus the society has become bureaucratized. When, especially at the turn of the 1960s and 1970s, the State expanded its sphere of functions, it kept the power of decision firmly at the level of the central administration. A consequence of this was a narrowing of the decision-power of the municipalities. To be sure, a great number of new functions were given to them by special legislation. And the State financed these new functions to a great extent. But, at the same time, the State wanted to determine how these functions were to be performed, and hence wanted to supervise their performance in great detail.

During the 1970s attempts were made, by establishing many committees, to reform the administration. However, the state's local-level administration was not reformed. Reform at the provincial level has been pending for about a hundred years. Nevertheless, it still resembles the provincial administration which originated in the 17th century, and reforms have been postponed year after year. Also, no essential reforms have been made in the central administration. Although the administrative organizations of the State and the municipalities have been developed through training, planning, and new data processing systems, this development has always occurred within the framework of the same old basic bureaucratic structures.

The Present Situation

Efforts in other developed countries to improve the quality of administration have been observed closely in Finland. In terms of international comparison, the managerial, planning, and accounting systems are functioning adequately in Finland. Steady economic growth and stable societal development without conflict have guaranteed a relatively high standard of living. Administrative services in health care, schooling, social security and so on have generally reached a relatively high level by international standards. The level of training of the civil service, and its capability, are also at a relatively high level, although a number of recent corruption cases have aroused a great deal of public discussion. At the same time, there are problems in the present situation. Among the most important of these are:

1. The legitimacy of the politico-administrative system has weakened. The citizens have an indifferent attitude toward politics and administration, less respect for them, and less trust than previously in the administration being neutral.
2. The building of the welfare state greatly increased the centralization of the decision-making power in administration. As a consequence, there are now clear tendencies toward decentralization, which is indispensable if administration is to be brought closer to the citizens.
3. The expensiveness of the administrative machinery has produced in Finland, as elsewhere, pressure toward privatization. For the time being, privatization measures have hardly been embarked upon, but it appears that the cost of administration will in the future compel cuts of the sort which other western countries have already made.
4. Relatively bureaucratic administration directed from above has proved to be not close enough to the citizenry. Reorganizing administration to increase the opportunities of the citizenry to participate in administration is an extensive and difficult project, considering the variety of the different administrative sectors, but it is nevertheless indispensable if the objectives of dismantling bureaucratic structures and abolishing bureaucratic attitudes are to be attained.

REFERENCES

1. Rasila, Viljo, *Suomen uusimman ajan historia* (Helsinki: Tammi 1971), 14-17.
2. Nousiainen, Jaakko, Suomen poliittinen järjestelmä (Juva: WSOY, 1980), 18-22. (*This book, The Political System of Finland, has been the main source throughout*

the article, together with Juha Vartola, *Administrative Change, Strategies of Development and Current Problems in the Central Administration of the State of Finland*) (University of Tampere, Department of Administrative Sciences, Division of Public Administration, Research Reports 3/1978 A).

3. Palonen, Kari, *Aatevirtauksia Suomessa Snellmanista nykyaikaan* (Helsinki, 1975).
4. Paasivirta, Juhani, *Suomi ja Eurooppa* (Helsinki, 1978).
5. Vartola, Juha, Ministeriöiden rakenteesta. Tampereen yliopisto. Hallintotieteiden laitos, Julkishallinnon julkaisusarja 3/1977 A. Vartola, Juha, Valtionhallinnon kehittämisperiaatteista. Tampereen yliopisto. Hallintotieteiden laitos, Julkishallinnon julkaisusarja 1/1978.
6. Lundquist, Lennart, and Krister Ståhlberg (eds.), *Byråkrater i Norden. Meddelanden från stiftelsen för Åbo Akademi forskningsinstitut* Nr 83 (Åbo, 1983). Ståhlberg, Krister, "De statligt anställda i Finland," 80–129, in Lundquist/Ståhlberg.
7. Tuori, Kaarlo, "Valtionhallinnon sivuelinorganisaatiosta 1," Suomalaisen Lakimiesyhdistyksen A-sarja Nr 159. (Vammala, 1982), 382–389.
8. See Ahonen, Pertti, *Public Policy Evaluation as Discourse* (Helsinki: Finnish Political Science Association, 1983), 100–103.
9. Vartola, Juha, "Valtionhallinnon rakenteellisen muutoksen ongelmasta," *Acta Universitatis Tamperensis*, Ser. A, Vol. 103 (Tampere, 1979). Vartola, Juha, "From Careless Nonchalance Towards Responsiveness," in Leo Klinkers, (ed.), *Life in Public Administration* (Amsterdam: Kobra, 1985).

REFERENCES IN ENGLISH

Ahonen, Pertti, *Public Policy Evaluation as Discourse.* Helsinki: Finnish Political Science Association, 1983.

Brunn, Otto, *The Administration of the City of Helsinki.* Helsinki, 1950.

Harisalo, R., and P. Ronkko, "Proposals for Finland," and "Finland", in Donald C. Rowat, ed., *International Handbook on Local Government Reorganization* (Westport, Conn.: Greenwood Press, 1980), 150–157 and 302–307.

Heiskanen, Ilkka, and Sirkka Sinkkonen, *From Legalism to Information Technology and Politicization: The Development of Public Administration in Finland.* University of Helsinki, Department of Political Science, Research Reports 31/1974.

Hidén, Michael, *The Ombudsman in Finland: The First Fifty Years.* Berkeley: Institute of Governmental Studies, 1973.

Kastari, Paavo, "Finland's Guardians of the Law: the Chancellor of Justice and the Ombudsman," in Donald C. Rowat, ed., *The Ombudsman* (London: Allen & Unwin, 2nd 1968), 58–74.

Kastari, Paavo, "The Constitutional Protection of Fundamental Rights in Finland," *Tulane Law Rev.* XXX, IV, 696.

Modeen, T., "Finland," in Donald C. Rowat, ed., *Administrative Secrecy in Developed Countries* (N.Y.: Columbia Univ. Press, 1979), 51–75.

Modeen, Tore, ed., *Recruiting for High Offices in the Central Administration.* University of Tampere, Department of Administrative Sciences, Number 2/1983 A, prepared for the International Institute of Administrative Sciences.

Nousianen, Jaakko, *The Finnish Political System.* Cambridge, Mass.: Harvard Univ. Press, 1971, Ch. 9.

Rowat, Donald C., "Finland's Defenders of the Law," *Canadian Public Admin.* IV, 3 (Sept. 1961) and IV, 4 (Dec. 1961), 316–325 and 412–415; revised as Ch. 2 of Rowat's *The Ombudsman Plan* (Lanham, Md.: Univ. Press of America, 2nd 1985).

Vartola, Juha, *Administrative Change, Strategies of Development and Current Problems in the Central Administration of the State of Finland.* University of Tampere, Department of Administrative Sciences, Division of Public Administration, Research Reports 3/1978 A.

Vartola, Juha, "From Careless Nonchalance Towards Responsiveness," in Leo Klinkers, ed., *Life in Public Administration* (Amsterdam: Kobra, 1985).

8

Denmark

PETER BOGASON
University of Copenhagen, Copenhagen, Denmark

HISTORY AND FORMAL PRINCIPLES

Ministerial System and Cabinet Responsibility

The modern Danish administrative system is rooted in the changes of the political system leading to the Constitution of June 5, 1849, which at that time was the most liberal constitution among the European monarchies.

The Constitution put an end to nearly 200 years of absolute monarchy, instituting a separation of powers between a parliament, the executive (the king) and the courts. As in most European countries around the year 1800, the King's administration was until 1849 headed by a number of commissions (*kollegier*) of senior civil servants which decided by voting, if necessary. The responsibility for implementing the king's policies rested with the commission but, as one might expect, some individuals could become quite powerful, especially the commission chairmen who could bring matters before the king for his decision.

The new administration broke away from the commission system (1). The administration was split up among ministers who became personally responsible for all decisions taken by their administration. This principle of responsibility had its roots in France (Napoleon Bonaparte), was carried to several German states and to Russia, and it was introduced in Norway in 1814 after the separation from Denmark. After the new system was adopted in Denmark, although commonly desired and accepted, it had many troubles outside the walls of the departments. During the first years, most ministers were former top civil servants, but gradually other segments of the population in the top levels of society got a share of governmental power.

The rest of the 19th century saw a continuous battle between the cabinet ministers and the parliament to whom they were responsible. After a period when parliament was not even convened, and the government was financed by provisional bills of finance, the cabinet in 1901 conceded to the principle that it was responsible to the majority of the parliament, not the king. Cabinet responsibility (parliamentarism) was not written into the Constitution until 1953.

The changes of 1901 also soon meant that most ministers had a previous political career, but for certain positions most incumbents also have been professionally engaged within the field.

The number of ministers was kept at seven until 1894, but by 1984 had increased to twenty-one. Their fields of administration vary considerably in terms of organization and size of personnel. The basic organizing principle requires matters related substantially to one another to be directed by one minister. Reorganizations under a new minister have occurred when certain sub-fields have grown sufficiently (in absolute terms or in terms of political interest) such as social affairs, labor, housing, environment, and energy.

Constitutional and Political Framework

The parliamentary framework in Denmark is rather similar to most democratic monarchies. The role of the king is formal in signing laws and naming ministers. Elections must be held every four years, but parliament can be dissolved if the prime minister decides so. Difficulties in forming majority governments after the second world war have pushed most governments into comprehensive compromises and recently even into defeats without resigning—the rationale being that if the government considers the policy problem as "minor," defeats are acceptable, whereas "major" questions (like the bill of finance) must be carried through without major changes from other parties. Most ministers are members of parliament. If not they normally seek election for the next term.

The cabinet meets once a week, and in spite of the formal personal responsibility of each minister, all major decisions like the preparation of parliamentary bills, policy statements and appointments of top civil servants are presented in this forum. A minister needs this back-up from the cabinet. For certain policy problems crossing the organizational boundaries of the ministeries, cabinet committees are set up, staffed by senior civil servants.

A Big and Decentralized Public Sector

Denmark is a fairly small country with 5 million inhabitants and no significant minorities. By international standards, the modern Danish public sector is big, in 1982 paying out 61 per cent of the national product, while taxes only constituted 44 per cent of the GNP. More than one fourth of the labor force had public employment.

Though this chapter discusses mainly the central administration, it should be stressed that local governments play a very significant role in the day-to-day administration of public services. For instance, 70 per cent of all public employees earn their salary in local government jobs. In 1982, while the state spent 45 per cent of the whole public budget, counties spent 11 per cent and the muncipalities 44 per cent. At the same time, the state received 73 per cent of all public revenues, while counties received only 7 per cent and the muncipalities only 20 per cent. Accordingly, the state finances a significant proportion of local government budgets by grants and reimbursements.

Within several sectors, notably education, social welfare and assistance, health, housing and environment, the major role of the central administration is to formulate general policies, to be adapted and implemented by local government. Policies reserved for the state are foreign affairs, defense, industry, higher education, and law enforcement. Labor, transport and housing are shared responsibilities.

ORGANIZATION AND MANAGEMENT STYLE

Departments and Directorates

Because of the personal responsibility of the minister, the organizational principles of central government are formally very much centered upon him as a person. Basically, two types of organizations are found: departments and directorates (2).

Departments are the top organizations of ministries, responsible for policy preparation and evaluation, planning and budgeting for the department itself, and for its subordinate and attached bodies. Most of the 21 ministries have one department responsible in these terms for the whole ministry, but the ministries of Foreign Affairs, Finance, Public Works, and Taxes have two or more departments divided by policy fields. Departments report directly to the minister and all decisions are formally taken by him or on his behalf. If a ministry is organized with only one department, the minister has his office there, close to the permanent secretary who acts as his advisor in all administrative matters.

A directorate is subordinate to a department on the basis of a formal delegation of decision-making powers from the minister to the directorate, which is headed by a director. The purpose of the delegation is to take away all routine decisions and/or decisions demanding highly specialized knowledge from the minister, whose personal energy should be used on principles of policy rather than routine questions. Typical tasks of a directorate would be to decide on applications for specific permissions, to process complaints about subordinate organizations, to prepare decisions (e.g. regulatory) within its policy field, to inspect that rules and procedures are followed by citizens and/or organizations and to evaluate the adequacy of public intervention within its policy field. Empirical research has found that the actual division of labor between departments and directorates is not so clear as the principles indicate (3).

Complaints about the decisions of a directorate must be filed with the department which will then prepare a decision for the minister. In principle all contacts between a minister and one of his directorates should go through the department, but in actual fact most directors can go to their minister when they wish.

To sum up, then, a main principle of Danish central administration is that of organizing so that most routine decisions are kept away from the minister and his secretariat, the department. In the 1960s and 70s, several ministries have been reorganized according to this principle, and all new ministries are divided into department and directorates. In 1984 four ministries had no directorates, and ten had them for all routine functions. The remaining 7 ministries had a number of directorates but had not reorganized so that all routine tasks were handled by such organizations.

Commissions and Boards

The administrative reforms of 1849 led to extinction of nearly all administrative decision-making by commissions deciding by voting. Only the top administration of medical doctors was headed by a commission. After half a century, however, a growing need for involvement of expertise and points of view from interests outside the administration was recognized, and several commissions were set up. They grew rapidly during both world wars, and again in the 1960s and the 1970s. In 1975, 667 central administration commissions existed—including advisory bodies—of which 41 per cent concerned regulation, 53 per cent public services, and 7 per cent coordination functions (4). Many of these commissions only have minor or *ad hoc* tasks and eighty per cent of them have secretarial assistance from the central administration, often on a part time-basis. Some important commissions have their own Directorate which in budgetary and staff terms is part of a ministry.

Commissions typically have two purposes. First, a commission may involve expertise and interests that are not present in the professional administration. The commission thus acts as a sort of link between the public and the private sectors. A second reason for creating a commission is based on a wish to reduce the influence of a minister on administrative matters.

Certain commissions have administrative roles that are simply lifted out of party politics because of their status as independent commissions. Typically, this is the case for the administration of a number of money incentives for industrial, cultural and scientific purposes. The minister can only influence such commissions via their budget or by appointing members and maybe by having one direct representative on the commission. In addition, a channel of some potential may exist if the staff of the commission's secretariat is recruited from the department. Other independent commissions are those that function as boards of appeal, e.g. in environmental regulation. In 1975, there were less than twenty of such boards of appeal.

Public Corporations

Compared with other Nordic countries, Denmark have very few public corporations. The railroads, mail and telecommunications are run as departments of the Ministry of Public Works. They have a special budgetary status. Until 1985 they had very few ties set by parliament on the use of their budget. From 1985, parliament's main instrument of influence is to make them produce a profit decided by parliament.

One important public corporation is the state oil company which is organized as a private joint stock company with the state as the only shareholder. The board and chairman are named by the Minister of Energy. The state also has venture capital in a few private companies. In most cases, the rationale was to save a fairly high number of jobs, the companies being unable to go on without new capital. The state also runs a trade company for Greenland, organized as a directorate under the Ministry for Greenland.

Decentralized Organization

In the 1970s, a comprehensive administrative reform was carried out in order to sort out the tasks of the state and local government, the principal aim being that as many daily services as possible should be run by county councils and muncipalities. The number of towns and parishes was reduced by 80 per cent to 275 muncipalities, and the number of county councils was reduced from 25 to 14. Some of the old parishes were virtually powerless. The new, consolidated local governments were able—financially and in terms of staff—to take an active role in public service delivery.

The state keeps regional and/or local offices in the fields of labor, state taxes and duties, police, forestry and civil defense. Furthermore, the Ministry of the Interior has regional offices for certain aspects of family law, headed by prefects who are also heads of the muncipality supervision boards. Previously, the prefects were also heads of the county councils, but the reforms of 1970 put an end to that.

Planning Reforms and Modernization

Various reforms have aimed at increasing the management potential of the central administration, in particular the minister. The reforms decentralizing day-to-day services to directorates and local government were intended to reduce the number of individual cases that could be taken to the minister for decision. In turn, his time was to be devoted to setting up general policies within the field, to budgeting and to the evaluation of the results of public activities.

In particular, a number of planning reforms have been implemented. In many sectors, planning and implementation takes place in local government, but most central departments are involved by issuing planning manuals and advising on new types of policy programs, where desired. In general, local plans are not to be approved by the minister, but often procedures exist to call in a plan, if it is found lacking in certain aspects. A budgetary and accounting reform in the late 70s has enabled the Ministry of Finance to set up a four-year budget for the whole public sector, subdivided within policy fields to enhance the evaluation of total public involvement, regardless of administrative level. This reform has been followed by several policy initiatives to include local government in the national fiscal policies. In sum, then, the central government has increasingly got control over macro-aspects of policies while leaving the details to other levels of administration.

Most of these reforms have been made under a social democratic minority government. In 1982, a bourgeois coalition minority government took over, and it has initiated compaigns for deregulation and more financial responsibility.

PUBLIC SERVICE PERSONNEL

Generalists and Specialists

Basically, two groups of personnel are found in Danish central administration: staff actively engaged in decision-making by drafting decisions in whole or part (mainly university graduates), and the supporting staff. The University graduates are part of a career pattern that may lead to the highest offices while the supporting staff have limited prospects of promotion. We shall not discuss the supporting staff.

A basic line of distinction is one between generalists and specialists. In actual administrative practice, the dividing line is based on education. Those who hold a university degree from the social sciences, i.e. economics, law, political science and related subjects, would fill a position for a generalist. Engineers, planners, biologists and those trained by their own organization—the armed forces, mail, customs and railroads—would normally hold specialists' positions. Apart from the last mentioned examples, both types graduated from universities or comparable institutions. The main difference is that the specialists are employed in positions where they use and develop professional knowledge, on the verge of applied science, whereas the generalists have positions that presuppose general administrative skills—budgeting, interpretation of rules, organizational matters, personnel administration, preparation of bills for parliament etc. By theoretical standards, the distinction between generalists and specialists is blurred, but administrators seem to have a common-sense perception of what positions are for what type of administrator.

Pay, Positions, Recruitment

In 1980 the central administration had 6050 positions excluding support staff, of which 4 per cent were top officials, 14 per cent were chief of section, and 82 per cent were junior officers (5). Women held about 20 per cent of these positions, but proportionally fewer top positions, partly due to the fact that women did not enter the university-trained category in any great number until the early 1970s. The 1980 support staff numbered about 6000, making the total central administration personnel about 12,000. Total state employment in 1980 was about 186,000; local government had about 420,000 (full-time equivalent).

The career positions for the civil servants are roughly at three levels: junior officer, chief of section and finally a top position as a director, deputy director, head of division or permanent secretary. The 1986 salaries for juniors ranged between Dkr 170.000 and 260.000 according to a seniority scale from one to fifteen years. Chief of section and positions above this have status as permanent employees (*tjenestemænd*) with a pension paid by the state. The pensions of those who do not get this status are based on monthly installments to a pension fund, paid by the employer (two thirds) and the employee (one third). In 1986 the salaries of the top officials ranged from Dkr 370.000 to 500.000, and a chief of section got about Dkr 310.000.

The relative proportion of generalists and specialists among junior officers is not known. Among the generalists, law graduates dominated those recruited in 1965 (80 per cent); the rest were economists. By 1979 the pattern had changed: law graduates took 45 per cent of the vacancies, economists 30 per cent and other social sciences took 25 per cent. This may reflect an interest in recruiting more of those not trained in law, but one should also take into account that in 1965 political science and sociology were in their infancy at Danish universities, so there were few to recruit. Therefore, it is not so surprising that in 1977 law graduates had 75 per cent of the top positions held by generalists. Of all top positions in 1977, generalists held 69 per cent, specialists held 18 per cent, while 13 per cent had no higher education or "education unknown" (6). Over time, the generalists have increased their share of the top positions, from about half to 70 per cent, and the increase was dominated by economists and other social scientists.

As part of the reforms in the 1970s, it was recommended that during their first ten years of employment, generalists should hold three different positions, and one of these should preferably be in another ministry or in local government. That recommendation was not adopted by all ministries until 1986. The career pattern until the late 1970s was quite narrow. Of the top positions in 1977, 70 per cent of the generalists had their whole career in the same ministry, 23 per cent had been in two ministries, five per cent in three ministries and two per cent came from outside the ministries. The specialists had a broader career pattern: 23 per cent did not come from a ministry, but still, 58 per cent had never been employed in another ministry.

Entry procedures into public services vary among the departments. From 1985, only the number of chief positions is determined by the budget. Junior positions are only limited by the size of the budget plus a ceiling on total working hours. The ministries that have set up the above-mentioned training system hire junior officers once or twice a year, and the selection will take place on the basis of university grades and previous job experience, plus personal qualities as revealed at interviews by chiefs of sections and personnel representatives. Those selected will get a position in a section of the department or one of the directorates (if such exist) for a couple of years and then go on to another position in other sections of the ministry. Selection for higher office (chief of section, etc.) is made on the basis of merits, as perceived by superiors and by a selection committee where personnel representatives have seats. Such promotions are always made on the basis of formal applications for a vacancy or a new higher position. No formal examination system exists; merits are judged on the basis of performance in one's previous career.

In ministries where such a formalized on-the-job-training and career placement system did not exist, recruitment procedures varied, and frequently hiring was controlled by the chief of section. With the new system, hiring procedures are more centralized, the departments becoming more influential.

Age at the time of promotion varies among ministries. Depending on age at the time of graduation, a new chief of section would be in the late thirties or early forties after 10–15 years as a junior officer. A top civil servant would typically be in the mid-forties or early fifties at the time of promotion. A civil servant must go on pension at the age of seventy, so some may hold a top position for twenty-five years or more. In order to encourage change in top positions, some senior officials are offered a special, high salaried position as consultant or the like if they appear to wear out in their present position. In the 1970s, there was a tendency to formally limiting employment in top positions to five or seven years, but it has never become a principle in employment policy.

Political appointees are next to non-existent. No political undersecretaries are found. Now and then, it is alleged that this permanent secretary or that director was appointed on the basis of political merits, but that is an exception to the rule. And even in such cases, the administrative merits of the incumbent can hardly be disputed.

Rights of Civil Servants

The right of voting, seeking election, speech, print and organization are guaranteed by the constitution. Civil servants can express their political opinion freely, orally or in print, and they may organize in any political party or union. At the same time, however, there is a principle of secrecy in the bureaucracy on the part of the employees, meaning that they cannot freely tell about what is going on in their agency. But they have a right to express their opinion publicly on such matters, as long as they do not disclose details that are not yet released.

From the point of view of civil servants, then, the problem is to strike a balance between the right to express oneself and the principle not to disclose matters that are in the process of being prepared for a political decision. Here, quite strong disagreement is found between legal experts, some taking the point of view that one must protect the political decision-making process so that undue pressure cannot affect the process, and others holding the freedom of expression sacred. In most cases, of course, a practical balance is found, but in the opinion of some people, this balance favors secrecy rather than information, the civil servants putting themselves under voluntary censorship from their supervisors.

Salaries are bargained by unions every second year. As the salaries are fixed within classes, memberships in unions are not required, but felt to be desirable. Most junior servants are unionized, but as they get senior, the percentage decreases, partly due to a less felt need for collective bargaining, partly due to ideological stances. For higher positions, the result of bargaining is put into a bill to be passed by parliament. For the junior level, the result is an agreement between the Minister of Finance and the unions, most of which cooperate in an "umbrella organization" for university graduates. Therefore, the salaries of each level are very homogeneous.

The permanent civil servants are not permitted to strike. These are not only top civil servants. Certain clerks, police officers, military officers and those responsible for communication—mailmen, transport workers—plus some others are permanent, so if dismissed, they must get three years' pay and a pension (unless they were dismissed because of a felony).

Although civil servants are free to seek election to parliament, it is not customary for those with high office to do so. Junior officers elected to parliament will get leave of absence for part of their annual working hours, and it is not likely that they will get a position that is close to the minister or a policy-making section of the ministry regardless of which party they belong to.

THE BUREAUCRACY AND POLICY-MAKING

The Budgeting and Policy-Making System

According to the budgetary process, the government proposes the annual budget in August, the parliament then goes through the bill, changing it where priorities differ and thus in detail, if necessary, sets the scope and level of government activity for the following financial year (same as calendar year). The bill is voted into an Act before December 31st. Before the presentation of the budget, each ministry sends its proposal to the Ministry of Finance which then goes through the proposals, changing figures where necessary, in consultation with the ministry.

Some administrators complain that 80 per cent of the time in the budgetary process is used for discussing nitty-gritty details of 20 per cent of the budget. Thus, 80 per cent of the budget passes without any priority being set. It is a fact that in 1981, 59 per cent of the state budget could not be changed without changes in existing laws, and was therefore left without any in-depth discussion. This proportion had increased from 47 per cent in 1970. In spite of various attempts from the Ministry of Finance to restrict the growth of the rest of the budget (ideally to zero per cent), it grew by four per cent per annum in the period 1977–81. The growth came during the so-called budget campaign in May–June where the proposals were discussed between the ministries and the Ministry of Finance. Thus, piecemeal engineering proved to be a rather effective way of increasing a budget (7).

The budgetary system was accused of being too rigid in detailing the number of personnel and in the gross appropriation system leaving little room for changing priorities in certain services within the fiscal year. In 1984 measures were taken to reduce that rigidity and at the same time to stop the piecemeal growth. The 1985 budget introduced a new system of budgetary ceilings for each ministry. The former budgets were gross budgets, detailing all types of expenditure. All incomes and savings had to be turned over to the Ministry of Finance and therefore could not benefit the agency itself. The new budget is a net budget, permitting each ministry to finance activities by own income (charges) and to transfer savings in one function to other purposes in the ministry. Furthermore, a ministry is now permitted to change priorities between types of expenditure and to save for the following fiscal year. As to personnel, all chief positions must still be approved while junior positions are only limited by a total number of working hours and total number of jobs. The agency is free to choose between junior classes and clerks, etc. These reforms aim at increased economic management efficiency.

As a result of the reforms of the 1960s and 1970s, legislation has changed much from detailed law to enabling law, and consequently, the ministries have needed more potential for planning their own affairs, and, in cases where the tasks have been decentralized to local government, to take care of general policy planning. In addition, public intervention in the economy and society has increased, and consequently, the need for coordination among public agencies. Accordingly, the importance of the judgments and initiatives of civil servants has increased.

In the 1970s, most ministries built up information systems and a planning staff with the aim of being able to plan the activities and policies for the ministry and local government taking care of the decentralized administration of the ministry. Researchers do not agree on how much the working procedures of the central administration have in fact changed as a result of the planning systems. Certainly, the ministries have not succeeded in planning understood as having more control over future development within the policy field. But in terms of information quality, ability to link policy changes to budgets, and preparedness in policy overview and evaluation, there is hardly any doubt that the capabilities of the ministries have increased very much as a result of the planning reforms. In addition, much more insight has been gained regarding local government policies. The Ministry of Finance has been leading in attempts to integrate the whole public sector in budgetary terms. As a result, the bases for producing information have been made uniform: the same forecasts for population and economic growth (and many technical bases) are being used by most public agencies in their planning documents.

There has been no desire, however, to push this technical planning system too far, and some limits to the degree of coordination have been recognized in the discussions of future planning systems between ministries (and local government organizations). It was realized that detailing information very far did not help administration and policy-making as long as the politicians were exogenous to the system. The work with the systems, therefore, was reoriented towards enhancing the involvement of politicians in policy-making, first of all in local governments.

There is a long-standing tradition for the bureaucracy to work in close consultation with interest organizations when preparing and implementing political decisions. In the preparation phases, drafts for bills are sent to the affected organizations for comments, and if necessary, meetings are scheduled. In case of an enabling law, such organizations are also consulted before administrative regulations detailing the law are released (8). This is in particular the case in intergovernmental relations, where the two major interest organizations of local government—the Association of Municipalities and the Association of County Councils play an important role.

Regarding private business, an important fact is that many commissions have been set up with members from the private sector who thus get a responsibility in administering law and regulations. This helps in calling attention to responsibility in consultation procedures: the associations are becoming very well aware of administrative problems.

If agreement is reached between a ministry and the interest organizations, e.g. in drafting a bill, it is unlikely that the parliament would change the basic features of their agreement.

The Role of Top Civil Servants

It is extremely difficult to get detailed knowledge about the influence patterns in administrative decision-making. But one can conclude a few things about the relations between a minister and his advisors, the top officials.

Top officials can influence most aspects of decisions to be taken. They have a natural authority in their agency, they have many years' experience within the policy field, often they have detailed knowledge, and they can have other officers go into detail with problems they want explored. The minister, on the other hand, has mostly only short experience in the ministry, and he is normally an amateur within the policy field. Though he may have policy experience from parliamentary committees and as a spokesman for the party, he has only the resources of one person against—in extreme cases—several hundred employees. And there are many ways that a bureaucracy can prevent a minister from having his way, primarily by delaying things.

The permanent secretaries of the most important departments coordinate their work and administrative policies by lunch meetings every now and then. Furthermore, they are always representing their minister in subcommittees of cabinet committees.

Given that most top civil servants were graduated from universities, one cannot be surprised to learn that they come from the better-off segments of society: in 1977, 31 per cent of their fathers had been salaried employees, 11 per cent had been farmers, and 20 per cent had their own firm, while only 29 per cent had been in mid- to lower-income occupations (9).

ADMINISTRATIVE ACCOUNTABILITY

Role of Parliament

The parliament can vote no confidence in a minister, who will then have to resign. If the vote concerns the prime minister, the whole cabinet must resign—or hold an election. A number of less drastic means of control exist, however.

In the open parliamentary sessions, a minister may be asked to put forward a policy statement or a review of actions taken. This statement is then subject to debate, and in extreme cases, a proposal of no confidence may be put forward by a member. Normally, however, the parties supporting the Government will counter by another proposal, indicating corrective steps to be taken, or simply stating that parliament has taken note of the minister's statement.

When the parliament is in session, ministers answer written questions once a week. Normally, the answers are brief and only the member putting forward a question can discuss it with the minister. No further steps can be taken.

The permanent committees of the parliament provide excellent forums for in-depth control of a minister. All bills must go through a committee, and most committees use such an occasion for discussing all paragraphs by formulating written questions to the minister. These are then answered in writing by the minister, i.e. by his department. Such questions also provide occasions for investigating administrative practice within the policy field. In addition, the committee can ask the minister to be present (normally accompanied by a senior civil servant) for a non-public hearing of certain aspects. On the basis of questions and hearings, the committee will then send back the bill to the floor, with or without proposals for amendments.

In addition, however, the committee may, as part of its running obligations, discuss and evaluate the administration of a policy field, and put questions to the minister or invite him for a hearing. Over time, then, members of a committee will get a fairly detailed knowledge of the policy field, a knowledge that may help in the public floor debates. The press increasingly reports that ministers are being taken to a committee, but details are not known because committee meetings are not open to the public. Written questions and answers are, however, normally accessible to the press.

The permanent committees are undoubtedly strong instruments of control, where members of parliament, the minister and his top civil servants can discuss problems of administration without having to commit themselves before the public. Of course, control may go both ways in that the committees are becoming dependent on the information they get from the central administration; by being selective in providing this information, the administration may be able to influence the perspectives of committee members in the policy field.

Control of Expenditure

When the proposed budget has been voted into a law, the amounts stated are turned into appropriations for the next fiscal year. Until 1985 a number of specifications had to be followed closely, and changes had to be approved by the budget committee of the parliament. This committee also appropriates money for unforeseen costs during the year. These appropriations are then put into an amended budget which will be voted after the fiscal year has ended. The approval of the committee is a political guarantee that the amended budget will be passed by parliament.

Five members of parliament are named auditors, and they go through the accounts of the ministries in order to criticize the use of appropriated money—in some cases the legality of procedures, in other cases the suitability of the actions taken. Their work is preparatory to the approval of the state accounts in parliament.

Of course, the time of these five auditors (with little staff) is limited. The Department of Auditing for which the Minister of the Economy is responsible audits and criticizes the accounts of the ministries in detail. The audit concerns the legality and appropriateness of actions taken, of the procedures followed and of the treatment of cash flows, etc. In addition, state agencies are controlled by *in situ* checks of the administration of public expenditure.

The Ombudsman

Unlike most West European countries, Denmark has no administrative courts. The ordinary courts can treat matters of dispute between a citizen and the administration in cases where the decisions are rule-bound. If there is a large degree of discretion in the decision, the courts will tend not to accept litigation. Denmark does, however, have the ombudsman institution which was created in 1955.

The ombudsman is appointed by the parliament and reports to the parliament once a year. In his daily affairs, however, he is independent of the parliament. Any citizen can complain to the ombudsman, provided that a final decision has been taken by the administration. He cannot change a decision, but he can propose a change, and in cases of fault he can mandate the state attorney to initiate prosecution, or he can mandate an agency to discipline the civil servants involved. The ombudsman can also initiate an investigation himself. The office of the ombudsman is highly respected. His recommendations are usually accepted and are seldom, if ever disputed in public. The importance of the ombudsman lies, of course partly in the access of the public to an impartial agency. In addition, the cases that have been decided since 1955 constitute a set of norms for administrative behavior that no administrator can neglect.

Administration and the Public

Since 1971, the general public has had access to administrative files. The access does not include personal matters (except own), nor pending cases, foreign and military affairs, certain planning documents and documents related to the correspondence between ministers and the parliament. Working documents that are not of importance for the decision taken are not accessible.

Generally, there has been a significant change in the attitudes towards informing the public. A state agency has been set up to promote public information, including a campaign to make administrators write more clearly. Increasing numbers of agencies are publishing annual reports and other information material. As a part of its "modernization program" the government has initiated a campaign to secure better treatment of clients. An Act on general administrative procedures was passed by parliament in 1986. The Act regulates disqualification of administrators and local government councillors in matters where their personal interest might be involved. Furthermore, it regulates a party's access to documents related to the case, and the hearing of the party. Finally, rules of complaint and rules on statement of grounds for a decision are detailed to secure that anybody who is dissatisfied with an administrative decision would know the reasons for that decision and would have information about possibilities of complaint—if any exist apart from litigation. To a certain degree, this Act is just a conglomerate of previous rules, but it is more comprehensive in scope and includes local government.

CONCLUSION

A main problem for the Danish central administration has been that of managing a growing public sector without overburdening the political head of the administration, the minister. A solution seen in many other countries has been to expand the top management by politically appointed assistant secretaries. Such constructions have neither attracted political nor administrative support in Denmark. Instead, many tasks have been decentralized by enabling laws to local governments and some new tasks have been given to state commissions. Furthermore, many ministries have set up directorates for routine or very specialized administrative purposes.

An important task for the central administration has been, therefore, to develop new instruments of information and control. New planning techniques and planning procedures have, in connection with budgetary reforms, increased the quality of policy information. This process may have been eased by a diversification of the university-trained personnel where the hiring practices of the 1970s and 1980s have increased the relative proportion of those trained in other social sciences than law. Thus, Denmark is on its way from the German, lawyer-based style of administration towards a policy-program administration based on enabling laws. Consequently, the parliament has strengthened its procedures of review by stressing the need for policy reports and other information to the permanent parliamentary committees.

The planning movement notwithstanding, regulations are still of great importance as administrative instruments, and the 1980s have seen attempts at deregulation, less rigid planning requirements, more flexible budgets and fewer controls of number of personnel below top positions.

The Danish central administration has a long tradition of close cooperation with interest organizations. This is reflected by hearing procedures for bills under preparation and for administrative circulars and advisory instructions. Moreover, most commissions have representatives from the business organizations affected. Even in commissions of appeal, the organizations may have seats or can influence the naming of members. This, of course, helps to create a common understanding among administrators and organization representatives.

Compared with many continental European countries, the Danish administration is open for public access to documents, and the ombudsman institution is a safety valve for complaints that are not treated responsively by the bureaucracy. Cases of fraud and abuse are extremely rare, and due to the legal tradition in administrative procedures, the central administration is highly accountable. A change of minister is not likely to change the policies and practices of a ministry overnight: there are no politically appointed civil servants and most of the incumbents of the top positions have a long career in the central administration behind them.

The stability in career patterns has not led to roadblocks against innovation, however. Danish central administrators have been able to carry through a large number of reforms in the 1960s and 70s. At the same time, public employment has grown to a number that has created worry among most political parties, and the administrative policy for the remaining part of the 1980s seems to be to stop the growth and even turn it into a decline.

REFERENCES

1. Harald Jørgensen: "Oversigt over Ministerialsystemets indførelse og udvikling i Danmark gennem 100 aar" (An overview of the introduction and development of the Minister government principle in Denmark through 100 years) In Ministerialforeningen: *Centraladministrationen 1848–1948.* (The Central Administration 1848–1948). Copenhagen: Nyt Nordisk Forlag 1948.

2. Poul Meyer: *Offentlig forvaltning* (Public Administration). Copenhagen: CEC Gad 1979.
3. Jørgen Grønnegaard Christensen: "Den administrative ledelsesfunktion i central-administrationen" (The Management function in the Central Administration). *Nordisk Administrativt Tidsskrift* 1982: 4.
4. Ole P. Kristensen: "Centraladministrationen og de særlige forvaltningsorganer i Danmark efter 1945" (The Central Administration and the special administrative agencies in Denmark after 1945). *Nordisk Administrativt Tidsskrift* 1979:1:69–98.
5. Jørgen Grønnegaard Christensen: "Ministrene og lederuddannelsen" (The Ministers and the education of leaders) in *Debat om den offentlige lederuddannelse* (Debate on the education of public leaders). Copenhagen: Danmarks Forvaltningshøjskole 1984.
6. Jørgen Grønnegaard Christensen: "Karrieremønstre i dansk centraladministration" (Career patterns in Danish Central Administration) in: Lennart Lundquist and Krister Ståhlberg: *Byråkrater i Norden* (Bureaucrats in the Nordic Countries). Åbo Akademi 1983.
7. *Hovedpunkter i budgetreformen* (Main elements of the budgetary reform). Copenhagen: Finansministeriet, Budgetdepartementet 1984.
8. Jørgen Grønnegaard Christensen: *Centraladministrationen: organisation og politisk placering* (The Central Administration: organization and relations to politics). Copenhagen: Samfundsvidenskabeligt Forlag 1980.
9. See note 8. Nine per cent do not fit into these categories.

ACKNOWLEDGMENT

Comments on an earlier draft by Jørgen Grønnegaard Christensen, Lennart Lundquist, and the editor are gratefully acknowledged.

REFERENCES IN ENGLISH

Christensen, Bent, "Free Speech for Public Employees in Denmark," *Scandinavian Studies in Law* (1982), 39–75.
Holm, N. Eilscou, "Denmark," in Donald C. Rowat, ed., *Administrative Secrecy in Developed Countries* (N.Y.: Columbia Univ. Press, 1979), 76–105.
Krarup, Ole, "Judicial Review of Administrative Action in Denmark," *Int. Rev. of Ad. Sciences* 33 (1967), 9–16.
Miller, K. E., *Politics in Denmark*. Boston: Houghton Mifflin, 1968. Ch. 6.

9

Sweden

KURT HOLMGREN
Supreme Administrative Court, Stockholm; University of Uppsala, Uppsala; and University of Stockholm, Stockholm, Sweden

Sweden is a relatively large country geographically (five-sixths the area of France) though not particularly densely populated, having 8,300,000 inhabitants. At present, one and a half million Swedes are employed in the public sector; 30 per cent of these by the state and the remainder by the municipalities and countries.

A public administration first came into existence under King Gustaf I Vasa during the 1500s, partly under German influence. This administration was consolidated during the 1600s, when Sweden, through its participation in the Thirty Years' War under Gustaf II Adolf, became a great power, a status which it retained until about 1720. At that time Sweden was reduced to approximately its present area, with the exception of Finland, which, having been colonized from Sweden during the Middle Ages, was a part of Sweden until 1809.

It was under Gustaf II Adolf—during the earlier part of the 1600s—that a more stable administration developed through so-called collegiates working under members of the council of the realm, a group of immediate advisers to the King. The administration expanded further during the latter part of the 1600s, at which time the system of central agencies and boards for various spheres of state activity—under the ministries but relatively independent in relation to them—developed. In 1809 Sweden received a new constitution, which in essential respects remained in force until the 1974 constitution currently in force. During the period 1809 to 1974, Sweden was generally described as a constitutional monarchy. Though the country is still a kingdom, the monarchy now has essentially a representative function, while the Parliament (*Riksdag*) and the Government have the decision-making power.

The Parliament is composed of 349 members. In 1986, five political parties were represented: the Social Democratic Party with 159 seats, the Communist Party with 19 seats, and three non-socialist parties—the Conservative Party, the Liberal Party, and the Center Party—with the remainder of the seats.

Of importance in considering contemporary Swedish administration is that the Social Democratic Party has since the end of World War II had a predominant position in the Government of the country—either alone or in coalition with some non-socialist party. Between 1976 and 1982 the country was governed by various non-socialist party constellations, but since 1982 the Social Democrats have reassumed the position of governing party.

THE GOVERNMENT AND THE MINISTRIES

In 1986, the Government of Sweden was composed of twenty ministers, while the number of ministries was twelve. Each member of the Government, except the prime minister, is responsible for specific spheres of activity. In six of the ministries there are two or three ministers who are responsible for the activity of the ministry in accordance with a strict division of responsibility. The ministries in Sweden constitute relatively small units, comprising together approximately 2,000 persons. A system of such small ministries is rendered possible by the fact that in principle only the more important decisions are taken in the ministries. Most decisions on implementation are taken in subordinate central agencies and boards and in regional county administrations.

With regard to the recruitment of civil servants to the ministries and central agencies and boards, significant changes have occurred during the past half century. The previous predominance of lawyers no longer exists, and at present quite a number of those employed are economists and people with education in the social field. In addition, the ministries have a large number of persons with a purely political background, called "political experts." The question of personnel recruitment is discussed further below.

The proposals which the Government wishes to submit to the Parliament are formulated in the ministries; within the framework of parliamentary decisions, the ordinances and regulations, which are to guide the work of public authorities and put the decisions of the Parliament into effect, are then issued by the ministries.

With respect to the work in the ministries, the system of *commissions and committees of inquiry* should in particular be noted. In almost all countries governments rely on the method of appointing a commission or committee with its own secretariat to solve difficult political or administrative problems which demand a lot of time. In Sweden this organizational form has become more comprehensive and of more practical importance than in most other places. It is the great variety of commissions and committees alongside the ministries which—together with the central agencies and boards—makes it possible to maintain the ministries as small units, as previously mentioned.

The preparation of government matters is only very briefly dealt with in the Swedish constitution. In Chapter 7:2 it is stated: "In preparation of government matters the authorities concerned shall be consulted with a view to obtaining the necessary information and opinions." Nothing is stated about preparation through commissions or committees—despite the fact that this form of preparation is so important. Commissions are appointed for the preparation of a number of different matters. The reasons for establishing commissions vary. A matter may be so comprehensive and complicated or so special that it is not appropriate to prepare it within the relevant ministry or agency. However, even the need to investigate more limited matters may be sufficient cause to appoint a commission or call in an outside inquirer. Not infrequently there are political motives behind the establishment of a commission of inquiry, for example the desire to let the opposition participate in the preparation of politically controversial questions; it may also be felt important to provide interest organizations with possibilities for influencing the proposals of an inquiry at an early stage.

The number of commissions active at any given time has varied during the post-war period; for a long time the number was about 300 but has now declined to about 200. The commissions are generally composed of a chairperson and a varying number of members and experts. A secretariat, normally with a full-time secretary, is connected to each commission. Engaging the right secretary is often a precondition for a successful inquiry.

Civil servants constitute the predominant group for all positions on commissions of inquiry, not only as secretaries and experts but also as chairpersons and members. The chairpersons are often drawn from within the higher level of the public administration, and it has become increasingly common for the ministries to place higher-level civil servants in various positions on the commissions.

Traditionally commissions of inquiry in Sweden generally work very thoroughly, and consequently their work sometimes takes a long time, in some cases a remarkably long time. The commission on constitutional reform appointed in 1954, which was active for nine years, is often cited as an example. A few commissions have, however, worked for a significantly longer period of time than that. A study of the inquiries which were concluded during the period 1968 to 1973 shows that one-third of the inquiries were completed within one year. The same study found the average length of time for an inquiry to be three years.

CENTRAL AGENCIES AND BOARDS

It has previously been mentioned that an interesting characteristic of the Swedish public administration is that the ministries—in comparison with the situation in most other countries—comprise rather small units with essentially staff functions, while a very large number of important decisions in the administration, not only matters of implementation, are entrusted to subordinate, but nonetheless independent, organs. The most important of these are called central agencies and boards, eighty to ninety in number; other units of this kind are called committees, institutes, councils, etc., amounting to about 200 in number.

It should be emphasized that the continuous expansion of the public administration in many western European countries has forced governments to entrust specific central tasks to organs independent of the Government, but the only country in Europe other than Sweden in which there is a general system of independent agencies is Finland. The advantage with the Swedish system is obviously that the ministers and their political collaborators can devote attention primarily to more important matters and do not need to take—at least not formally—responsibility for thousands of implementation decisions. A drawback with the Swedish system, as is sometimes pointed out, is that central agencies can at times display a propensity toward executing important tasks of the state in another spirit than that intended by the Government; in most cases it nonetheless appears to have been possible to correct such tendencies.

Certain agencies are represented only on the central level, such as the National Patent and Registration Office. Others may in addition have a regional and even a local organization. This is the case with the Labor Market Administration, for example, which, in addition to the National Labor Market Board in Stockholm, has county employment boards in every country. The latter are moreover in charge of the labor exchange offices and district representatives which comprise the local outposts in the organization. An agency which organizationally operates on the central and regional levels but not on the local level is the National Housing Board with its county housing boards. The local service in matters of housing loans has instead been enjoined upon the so-called intermediary organs in the municipalities, i.e. as a rule the municipal boards.

Some agencies are called government enterprises. The term is related to the nature of their activity: they produce and sell goods and services. Examples are the State Railways, the National Power Administration, and the Swedish National Industries Corporation. Several of these also have a regional organization.

Closely related to government agencies in terms of tasks are government-owned business companies. They assume a juridically special position, however, since their activity is not regulated by public law but by private law; formally they are therefore not administrative authorities. That business activity is entrusted to organs in the form of companies is not only justified in terms of the fact that there is greater leeway in a company than in a ministry or an agency for setting salaries at levels that can attract engineers and economists having salary demands above the normal standard for state salaries.

REGIONAL AND LOCAL PUBLIC ADMINISTRATION

The vast area of the territory of the Swedish state (the distance from the most northerly city to the most southerly being as great as between Calais and Palermo) necessitates a comprehensive and widely ramified regional and local state administration.

Regional State Administration

The regional state administration is divided into a number of different organs. The most important have the *county* as their geographic area of activity. But there is also a large segment of administration based on other regional divisions: the district organization of government enterprises does not accord with the boundaries of the counties. The State Railway is, for example, regionally organized into 18 districts and the Post Office Administration into 32. In both of these cases there is, in addition, a widely ramified local administration. In certain cases the regional organization does not cover the entire county. This is the case with the National Board of Fisheries, for example, with its coastal districts and fresh-water districts, and the local administrations of the National Power Administration.

Among the county organs the most important is the *County Administration Board*, the head of which, the County Governor, is appointed by the Government. Other members are elected by the regional legislature, the County Council. The County Administrative Board operates within a very broad sphere of activity and has a variety of different tasks, from weapon licensing, and licenses for the sale of alcoholic beverages, to municipal control, and a variety of other control functions—also major planning decisions for the county as a whole. Alongside of the County Administrative

Board is a number of county boards, lay organs with specialized tasks, and so-called county experts. An example of these is the County Housing Board, all of the members of which are appointed by the Government. The County Housing Board administers the main portion of state loans and subsidies to housing within its area. Another example is the County Agricultural Board, composed of the county council manager and eight other members, of which half are appointed by the Government and half by the County Council. The board is in charge of state measures for the promotion of agriculture. The County Forestry Board, the County Employment Board, and the County Education Board can be cited as further examples.

County Councils and Municipalities

County councils exist in twenty-three of the twenty-four counties and constitute regional parliaments of a kind. The exception is the island of Gotland in the Baltic Sea, which comprises a single municipality and where the municipality is responsible for the tasks which are otherwise within the sphere of the county councils. Two major cities—Goteborg by the North Sea, and Malmo in southern Sweden across from Copenhagen, the capital of Denmark—are also outside of the county council organization. The primary tasks of the county councils involve health care and hospitals within the country. They are also responsible for dental care and the care of the mentally retarded.

Although these regional units have important functions, the municipalities (primary local government units) undoubtedly have more important tasks. For a long time Sweden had over 2,000 municipalities, which generally originated as ecclesiastical units, but amalgamation reforms have resulted in a reduction of the number of municipalities to 284. These amalgamations were undertaken in order to create municipalities which would be large enough to assume responsibility for important local tasks demanding a relatively large economic base. The intention behind the most recent reform was that every municipality should have at least 8,000 inhabitants.

The municipalities have through legislation been entrusted with important responsibilities in the fields of education, social welfare, health care, and fire prevention. Furthermore, they are to assume a general responsibility for the interests of the inhabitants of the municipality. What the municipalities can do within this general field is not stipulated by law; this unspecified description of competence has led to municipal initiatives in new areas often being appealed, with the result that administrative courts frequently set aside such decisions. The setting aside of decisions of this kind has occurred particularly in cases in which municipalities have been tempted to become involved in business activities.

The activities of the municipalities, which have for a long time been quite comprehensive, are presently showing signs of further expansion; a general view is that if the public administration continues to grow, it will be necessary to entrust some tasks hitherto within the domain of the state to the municipalities and its organs. A drawback frequently mentioned when the question of entrusting the municipalities with public tasks comes up is the risk of differences in practice within similar policy areas from municipality to municipality.

Municipalities as well as county councils levy taxes. Especially the municipal taxes are often fairly high and form an important part of the total tax burden.

PERSONNEL

Recruitment to higher posts in the public administration is in all countries and particularly in western European states (with mixed economies) an important question. This subject has been of significance even in the past, but during the 1900s it has become of even greater importance—in Sweden particularly due to the great expansion of the public administration during the time after World War II. This expansion has been even more pronounced during the most recent decades due to the increase of public activity in the economic and social fields. From 1968 to 1980 the number of persons employed by the state or by local government increased from 830,000 to 1,400,000, i.e. an increase of 74 per cent. The greater part of this increase is attributable to the municipalities; in the purely state sector the increase has been limited to 24 per cent.

Considering the growth of the public administration, it is natural that recruitment to public service has become an interesting topic in the political debate. One thing which has in particular given rise to concern is the difficulty for the public sector in drawing—in competition with the private sector, in which there is more leeway for setting salaries—a reasonable percentage of the best people to the highest posts; this concerns particularly engineers and economists, but the problem also arises with regard to lawyers and people in the social field.

In Sweden the Government and Parliament have—particularly in times of Social Democratic majorities—maintained a salary level for their higher civil servants which in no way corresponds to the private sector. This has led to difficulties in recruitment, not least of all in relation to engineers and economists. In addition to difficulties in recruitment, there has also been a movement of qualified employees leaving state employment in recent years. Officials in the tax system and in the administrative courts constitute recent examples of this. In connection with the administrative courts, it can be noted that about 80 to 90 per cent of the rapporteurs in the administrative appellate court in Stockholm—the intermediate instance in the geographical area of the capital—have in recent years left for better-paying jobs in business after four to five years of service. It is also noteworthy that in Sweden, which has a very substantial defense organization, a rather significant number of officers have in recent years been attracted to better-paying positions in the private sector.

Sweden is among those countries in which the higher-level civil servants are recruited to a significant degree from among lawyers. Particularly in the case of the ministries, qualified people have been drawn from the courts to higher ministerial posts—something that is also characteristic of France. This has generally occurred by first engaging younger civil servants on leave of absence from the courts on a temporary basis for inquiries, etc., in the ministries, and then, if they have displayed general competence and a practical disposition, appointing them to various top posts. This can be exemplified by the fact that in 1957 (under a Social Democratic government) twenty-eight of thirty-four top posts in the ministries were occupied by lawyers, among which sixteen were judges on leave from their court positions. A large number of these lawyers have afterwards gone from the ministries to independent top posts—e.g. as county governors and general directors of central agencies.

With regard to the recruitment of lawyers, a significant change has occurred in recent decades, as a result primarily of the expansion of public activity to increasingly include technical, economic, and social spheres of activity. It is illuminating that of approximately 60 top posts in the ministries at the beginning of 1985, barely one-third were occupied by lawyers.

The number of women in the ministries has increased substantially in recent years. Of the ministers, five are women, and about twenty of the top posts are held by women.

A question often posed concerns the extent to which more typical civil servants—i.e. those not recruited on political grounds—exercise influence over Government policy. This question is difficult to answer in general terms. However, it can be said that the ministers—not infrequently people with limited educational background—are often knowledgeable about only certain key political issues, while they are forced to make decisions on important matters not related to political party ideology about which they lack sufficient knowledge. In such cases—in Sweden as in other countries—the opinion of the civil servant acting as rapporteur on a particular matter is usually of great importance.

Another question concerning public administration current in Sweden and many other countries is the *politicization of the administration*—the extent to which political considerations are of importance in appointments to higher and lower posts. Before an attempt is made to answer this question, it should be emphasized that attempts at obtaining facts relevant to this question meet with great difficulties, well illustrated by the comment of the Danish administration expert, Poul Anderson; he found it charac- teristic of political appointments that political considerations are always denied. Irrespective of this complication, there is reason to emphasize that the following pre- sentation only concerns higher-level civil servants, i.e. those holding higher positions in the ministries (under-secretaries, permanent secretaries, chief legal officers, and minis- terial advisors), general directors and other high-ranking officers in central organs, and county governors. Clearly, political considerations play a part in appointments below this level as well, but the propensity towards favoring politically merited persons with appointments to less important posts is weaker than in relation to top posts in Sweden.

In relation to the ministries it should be mentioned that the positions of under- secretary, when they were created at the end of World War I, were considered political offices through which the minister would obtain a close collaborator who shared his political opinions and was familiar with the area of work in question. Other chief posts in the ministries—permanent secretaries, chief legal officers, etc.—seem to be appointed to a much lesser extent on the basis of political views.

The heads of central agencies and similar administrative organs constitute a category within which political appointments have in particular increased in recent years; of about ninety posts of this kind, 30 to 35 per cent are held by persons who can be assumed to have been appointed on the basis of political merits. There is, however, reason to emphasize that the political element in appointments does not mean that the persons concerned are not capable of dealing with the new duties; the political world of Sweden fortunately comprises many persons who unite a taste for politics with admin- istrative competence. Now and again the appointment of a politician to a leading post is justified by the fact that a reform is to be implemented in a given area and that the relevant top post should be held by a person who has a positive attitude toward the spirit of the reform.

The group of civil servants for whom political appointments are most common is county governors. Of twenty-four county governors, there are at present only a few for whom political qualifications cannot be assumed to have played a decisive role.

Among ambassadors, general consuls, and other top posts outside of the country, political appointments have also occurred, though to a lesser extent: there are approximately ten persons within this group (of about ninety in all) for whom political considerations can be assumed to have entered into their appointments. It is worth mentioning that the low frequency of political appointments within the Foreign Office sector depends at least in part on very strong objections to political appointments by the personnel organizations of the foreign service.

One area in which political appointments have thus far been rather rare is the court system. Only a modest number of ex-ministers, under-secretaries, or parliamentarians can be found who can be assumed to have been appointed at least partly on the basis of political merits.

The political parties have performed mutual favors for each other at the top level of the state administration. Until 1976, when the Social Democrats were still in power, it was not uncommon for even non-socialist politicians, who were in need of a retirement post, to be appointed to high positions. Likewise, the non-socialist governments, which were in power during the period 1976 to 1982, showed a clear tendency to take care of a number of Social Democrats who wished to leave the political scene. The fact that all of the parties (with the exception, perhaps, of the Communist Party) benefit from political appointments has been one reason that none of the political groups has wished to openly criticize the system as being illegal or inappropriate. Although many political appointments imply a clear departure from the rule in the Swedish constitution, stipulating that substantive grounds such as merit and competence are to be decisive in appointments, the tendency toward politicization has not given rise to much criticism in public debate, not even among lawyers or political scientists.

Sweden is a country in which the citizens cooperate to a great extent through membership in associations and organizations of various kinds. Of great significance in this respect are those organizations which have the task of representing the wage interests of their members in relation to employers, including state and local government authorities. In the state sphere there are three main organizations: the State Employee Section (TCO-S) of the Central Organization of Salaried Employees (TCO), the State Employees Union (SF), and the Swedish Confederation of Professional Associations and National Confederation of Civil Servants (SACO/SR).

TCO is the largest organization and includes both higher level and lower level civil servants, although primarily public employees in comparatively lower positions. Within TCO there are about twenty unions, of which the largest is the Federation of Civil Servants (ST), with about 120,000 members in 1982.

SF is a union which is affiliated with the Confederation of Swedish Trade Unions (LO), the central labor organization. This union has about 200,000 members, of which the vast majority are either active in state service or are pensioners. Most of the members of the union are employed at the large government enterprises—the Post Office Administration, the National Telecommunications Administration, and the State Railways.

The central organization SACO/SR has the lowest membership of the three predominant organizations within the state labor market; it includes, however, a large percentage of the higher civil servants. Affiliated with this confederation are twenty-six unions with a total membership of about 250,000. Of these, more than 100,000 were employed by the state or by local government in 1982.

With regard to employees within local government, there are also three main organizations, which correspond to those in the state sphere.

APPEALS AND CONTROLS

Swedish public administration is characterized by wide-ranging possibilities for individuals, businesses, organizations, etc., to appeal administrative decisions. In principle, everyone has the right to take a case all the way to the highest instance (to go to the King) to win a remedy if dissatisfied with an administrative decision. In many cases appeals are made to the next highest authority—an agency or other responsible authority—but in matters of a juridical nature, of which taxation cases constitute the largest category, appeals are taken to the administrative courts. In the first instance there is a county court in every country; from there appeals can be made to the appellate courts and then to the Supreme Administrative Court. With regard to the Supreme Administrative Court, however, the right to appeal is generally limited to cases which are of interest as precedents.

As a control organ and authority for the protection of the citizens against abuse of authority on the part of the administration, Sweden has for over a century and a half had the institution of the ombudsman, which has in recent years been imitated in both European countries and in other parts of the world. One can to turn to an ombudsman and request examination of all sorts of administrative matters which are felt to be questionable. Furthermore, an ombudsman can initiate investigations into administrative conditions which, on the basis of newspaper accounts, for example, are found worthy of investigation. Approximately 3000 complaints are received annually by the four Swedish ombudsmen, who specialize in different spheres of activity. The fact that about 80 per cent of the complaints received are not considered to be well founded speaks well for the quality of the Swedish administration. The institution of the ombudsman has proved to be of particular value in recent decades, during which time the regulation of Swedish society has been expanded to a great extent and dissatisfaction with regulations of various kinds have been able to be expressed in the form of letters to the ombudsman. The institution has in this case been a type of safety valve for dissatisfaction with different changes. Both the activity of the ombudsmen and other institutions of control have revealed very few cases of corruption and the like within the administration. Almost without exception, qualified jurists from the courts are elected to the positions of ombudsman.

Another institution of significance for control of the public administration, which was introduced early in Sweden but which has been imitated in other countries only recently, is the rule that the citizens have the right of access to public documents of various kinds. The first legislation on this subject was introduced as early as 1776. This right is part of the constitution and applies, generally speaking, to all public activity, as long as explicit exceptions have not been made in the so-called Secrecy Act.

GENERAL CONCLUSIONS

In general, it can be said that the Swedish public administration is of high quality and functions rather well. The competence of the civil servants is as a rule good. It should also be underlined that the public service almost completely lacks the elements of corruption—economic and political—which are sometimes found even in a number of Western democratic countries. The legal rights of the individual are generally well provided for, e.g., through a law on administration practice and a vast number of other administrative regulations. The regulatory system does, though, display a propensity toward sluggishness at times, and in order to counteract this, efforts have been undertaken in recent years to increase the efficiency of public activity, among other ways, by simplifying the regulatory system.

There are also other shortcomings in the Swedish administration which should not be ignored. The tendency toward economic equalization, which has characterized public life in Sweden since the end of World War II, has involved the fixing of salaries for higher civil servants at a fairly modest level. This has led many qualified persons in various categories—particularly engineers and economists, but even lawyers—to seek positions in the private sector rather than enter state service. The trend toward politicization of appointments to higher positions previously discussed has a similar effect; younger persons, who feel that they have the qualifications for higher positions but do not hold opportune political views, tend to avoid state service.

BIBLIOGRAPHY

Anderson, Stanley V., "Public Access to Government Files in Sweden," *Am. Jour. Compar. Law* 3 (1973), 419–473.

Aberbach, Joel D., *et al., Bureaucrats and Politicians in Western Democracies.* Cambridge: Harvard University Press, 1981.

Andren, Nils, *Modern Swedish Government.* Stockholm: Almquist & Wicksell, 2nd ed. 1968, Ch. 7.

Anton, Thomas J., *Administered Politics*: *Elite Political Culture in Sweden.* The Hague and Boston: Martinus Nijhoff, 1980.

Anton, Thomas J., *et al.*, "Bureaucrats in Politics: A Profile of the Swedish Administrative Elite," *Canadian Public Administration* XVI, 4 (1973).

Board, Joseph B., *The Government and Politics of Sweden.* Boston: Houghton Mifflin, 1970, Ch. 6.

Carlson, Bo, *Trade Unions in Sweden.* Stockholm: Tiden, 1969.

Castles, Frank G., "The Political Functions of Organized Groups: The Swedish Case," *Political Studies* 21, 1 (March 1973), 33.

Gustafsson, Agne, *Local Government in Sweden.* Stockholm: Kommundepartementet, 1978.

Gustafsson, Gunnel, *Local Government Reform in Sweden.* Umea: Gleerup, 1980.

Hancock, M. Donald, *Sweden: The Politics of Postindustrial Change.* Hinsdale, Ill.: Dryden, 1972.

Krarup, Ole, "Judicial Control of Administrative Powers," *Scandinavian Studies in Law* 15 (1971), 144–162.

Meijer, Hans, "Bureaucracy and Policy Formation in Sweden," *Scandinavian Political Studies* 69, 4, 103–116.

Modeen, Tore, ed., *Recruiting for High Offices in the Central Administration.* Tampere: University of Tampere, 1983.

Premfors, Rune, "Sweden," in *Efficiency and Effectiveness in the Civil Service* (London: House of Commons, Treasury and Civil Service Committee, 8 March 1982).

Richardson, Jeremy John, ed., *Policy Styles in Western Europe.* London and Winchester, Mass.: Allen & Unwin, 1982.

Stromberg, Lars, and Jorgen Westerstahl, *The New Swedish Communes.* Stockholm: Liber, 1984.

Verney, Douglas V., *Public Enterprise in Sweden.* Liverpool: Liverpool University Press, 1959.

Vinde, Pierre, and G. Petri, *Swedish Government Administration.* Stockholm: Bokforlaget Prisma, 2nd ed., 1978.

10

A Comparative Overview

LENNART LUNDQUIST*
University of Copenhagen, Copenhagen, Denmark

INFLUENCES OF HISTORY AND ENVIRONMENT

The five Nordic countries all have small populations (in millions: Denmark 5.1, Finland 4.8, Iceland 0.2, Norway 4.1 and Sweden 8.3), but some have a large area (in 1.000 km^2: Denmark 43, Finland 337, Iceland 103, Norway 325 and Sweden 450). With the exception of Denmark they are all sparsely populated.

The Nordic countries are highly urbanized. Finland has the biggest share of people employed in agriculture and forestry (about 15 per cent) and Sweden the smallest (about 6 per cent). They are advanced, industrialized, western countries with a big public sector. About 25 per cent of the labor force are public employees and about 60 per cent of the GNP consists of public expenditures. Generally, there are no language cleavages, except that Finland has a Swedish-speaking minority of seven per cent. The islands of Greenland and the Faroes (Denmark) and Aland (Finland) have achieved a substantial autonomy in relation to the central authorities.

Historically, the Nordic countries are closely connected. Norway and Denmark were united from 1390 to 1814. Eventually, the Danish influence in constitutional matters grew stronger within the union, although Norway had a certain autonomy. In 1814, Norway was forced into forming a union with Sweden. Before the union was a fact, a constituent assembly created its own Norwegian constitution, and the Swedish constitutional influence on Norway was negligible. The union was dissolved in 1905.

Finland was a Swedish province up to 1809, when it was conquered by the Russians and made a Russian Grand Duchy. Up until the time of its independency in connection with the Russian revolution of 1917, Finland had a certain legislative, judicial and administrative autonomy, which was based on the Swedish constitution of 1772.

Iceland was for a long time a Danish colony. It became a separate state in union with Denmark in 1918. In 1944 Iceland was proclaimed an independent republic.

Today there is a close communication between the five Nordic countries and they have a formal organ of cooperation in the Nordic Council (a consultative body of the Nordic parliaments and governments). There is a permanent organized cooperation in the tourist and recreation sectors and in matters relating to commerce, industry and

---
Current affiliation: University of Lund, Lund, Sweden

the environment. There is also a common labor market, which means that citizens of one Nordic country are free to work and reside in another on the same economic and social terms as the native population. Nordic citizens do not need passports when traveling in the area (Gustafsson 1983). The countries cooperate in several areas of legislation in order to get a common system of law and there is a mutual influence even in areas which lack formal cooperation. Even private actors cooperate across the borders of the Nordic countries. In the relations between Finland and Sweden the big interest organizations play a vital role (Karvonen 1981).

In some respects the Nordic countries differ in their international situation. Denmark, Iceland and Norway are members of the Common Market and NATO. Finland and Sweden are neutral countries, and Finland has a friendship agreement with the Soviet Union.

Denmark, Norway and Sweden are parliamentary democracies. Finland and Iceland have a mixture of parliamentary and presidential systems. The parliaments have multiparty systems traditionally containing five parties (communists, social democrats, liberals, farmers and conservatives). Since the beginning of the 70's the party systems have been enlarged with new parties: in Denmark, Finland and Norway there are "protest parties" among the new ones. Voter participation in general elections is very high (80-90 per cent).

Formally, Denmark, Norway and Sweden are monarchies, while Iceland and Finland are republics. However, the actual center of public power in Denmark, Iceland, Norway and Sweden is the parliament and the cabinet. The cabinets are normally formed from a party coalition. In Finland the president has a substantial power (responsibility for foreign affairs, the right to make rules for implementation and organization of the public administration, and the right to appoint the highest civil servants). It has been said that next to the French president, the Finnish president is the most powerful in Europe.

Minister rule means that an individual minister may decide on behalf of the cabinet in his sphere of competence. In Sweden minister rule is very unusual and occurs only in minor cases. Instead the decisions are made by the cabinet as a whole. In Finland and Norway the most important decisions are made by the cabinet, but the responsible minister decides in quite a few cases. In Denmark and Iceland government decisions are as a rule made by the minister involved (Petersson 1984).

The Nordic societies are characterized by a high degree of interest group organization. It has been said both of Denmark and Sweden that they are the most thoroughly organized societies in the world. This characteristic concerns all sectors of societal life. Especially powerful are the big organizations dealing with the labor market, which in Denmark and Sweden contain about 90 per cent of all employers and employees. The interest organizations are tightly woven into the state apparatus. As a matter of fact there are no clear-cut borders between public and private sectors.

STRUCTURE AND MANAGEMENT OF THE SYSTEMS

The Nordic countries have two different designs of central administration: an East-Nordic (with Sweden as the most typical case) and a West-Nordic (with Denmark as a model). The remaining systems are mixtures of these designs. Finland is closer to Sweden and Iceland and Norway are closer to Denmark. The pattern may be explained historically.

In the Swedish central administration, there is a division between the small state departments, which are the staff organization of the cabinet for planning and preparing government policies, and the central administrative boards, which are the main implementors of current public policy. The central administrative boards are directly subordinated to the cabinet, not to individual ministers. Thus, there is no minister administration (that is, individual ministers making, in principle, all administrative decisions).

The central administrative boards have, furthermore, a considerable autonomy vis-à-vis the cabinet, which cannot intervene in cases concerning the rights of individuals. However, the cabinet may direct the boards (and other administrative units) on all general matters, such as planning, investigations, organizing and appointments. Although there is no hierarchical relationship between a state department and the central administrative boards in its policy area, they often have reason to cooperate, e.g. in the budgetary process (SOU 1983:39).

Finland has developed a modified version of the Swedish model. The ministries are relatively bigger than the Swedish departments and the Finnish central administrative boards are formally subordinated to the ministries, though in fact they may be substantially independent.

Of special interest is the composition of the governing bodies of the central administrative boards. In Sweden almost every unit and in Finland about a third have such a governing body. It is composed of the director and his deputy and a number of members from outside the staff of the central administrative board in question. In Sweden in 1979, the total membership of all boards consisted of 24 per cent politicians, 15 per cent from the unit itself, 20 per cent from department and other administrative units, 31 per cent interest group representatives, 9 per cent experts and 1 per cent others (SOU 1983:39, Ståhlberg 1976).

The Danish central administration follows the general European pattern. It is dominated by ministries, each one headed by a minister. The minister may decide on all matters in his ministry, and he is parliamentarily responsible for all administrative decisions. Thus Denmark has a system of minister administration. Within the ministry there are two kinds of organization. The top unit is the department, working on policy preparation and evaluation, planning and budgeting. The other unit is the directorate, to which in principle is delegated all routine decisions and implementation tasks. However, this distribution of functions between departments and directorates is sometimes blurred (Christensen 1980).

Norway has departments containing departmental divisions and directorates. Even if the directorates are subordinated to the minister, there are a number of directorates which in fact have a substantial autonomy.

Both designs of central administration contain other administrative units (permanent or temporary) with various functions and organizational forms (boards, commissions, committees and so on). As a rule these units are smaller than the ministries, directorates and central administrative boards.

After the second world war a convergence between the two Nordic main designs has been noticed. Increasingly, administration in Denmark and Norway takes place outside the departments. The ambition has been to relieve the departments of routine decisions. In Swedish discussions, the traditional autonomy of the central administrative boards is seriously questioned (cf SOU 1983:39). In all of the countries, special units are formed for special tasks.

The central authorities are represented at the regional and local levels. There are generally two main forms: the functional system, which means that each central unit has an organization of its own at the regional and local levels, and the prefect system, where the regional state administration is organized in one unit. The Nordic countries have a mixture of these two forms, which are related to the two Nordic main designs of central administration.

In Finland and Sweden, the county administrative board is directly subordinated to the central government. Its tasks are very important, especially in Finland where the county administrative board is the highest police authority as well as responsible for the maintenance of general order and security. Furthermore, it collects the state revenues, and it effects an increasing number of the social, economic and cultural functions of the welfare state. The governor of the county increasingly plays the role of the county's representative in relation to the central authorities. Although the Finnish and Swedish county administrative boards are very important, there are regional units acting independently of the boards. These units are directly subordinated to the ministries or the central administrative boards.

Denmark and Norway have a regional prefect organization too, but it is far less important than the Finnish and Swedish county administrative board. One of its important tasks is supervision of the municipalities. The regional state administration is instead dominated by units directly subordinated to various ministries and departments. In all Nordic countries, there are developed systems of local self-government which have extensive powers of initiative and action and which become more and more important as implementors of public policy. No less than 60–70 per cent of all public employees work for self-government organizations at the regional and local levels.

Since the second world war, there have been far-reaching amalgamations of the municipalities in Denmark and Sweden. Today Denmark has 275 municipalities, Finland 461, Iceland 224, Norway 454 and Sweden 284. The municipalities have two kinds of tasks. One is self-government in its own right, and the other is implementation of policies decreed by the state. To the latter kind belong the two most important (and costly) tasks: social welfare and primary and secondary education. The municipalities have the right to levy taxes and they also get contributions from the state. To an increasing degree, public expenditures concern the municipalities.

The bigger Nordic countries, with exception of Finland, also have important self-government organizations at the regional level. The numbers of units are: Denmark 14, Norway 19 and Sweden 23. This regional organization is not hierarchically related to the municipalities but works in different issue areas. The most important tasks are health, medical care and roads in Denmark and Norway, and health and medical care in Sweden. In Iceland the regional self-government is of little importance (Petersson 1984).

The self-government organizations at both levels are headed by councils elected in general elections. The councils elect members to committees in various issue areas. Each organization has at its disposal a professional bureaucracy, which has grown very fast during the last three decades.

In Finland certain tasks are carried out by cooperation between municipalities at a regional or local level. In 1980, there were 390 federations of municipalities, of which more than 50 per cent were for health and medical care (Ståhlberg 1983). The importance of federations is clear from the fact that they employ more than a third of the total labor force of the local self-government.

The business activities of the Nordic states are performed in two main organizational forms. Sometimes a public business activity is organized as an ordinary administrative unit, e.g. a directorate or a central administrative board. Sometimes the form chosen is a public corporation which has much the same characteristics as a private corporation, with the state functioning as "owner" at the annual meeting of shareholders.

The use of these two kinds of organization varies among the Nordic countries. Thus, railroads, mail and telecommunication are organized as ordinary administrative units. Public corporations are common in Sweden, where 167 enterprises are organized as public corporations. Together with the seven enterprises organized as central administrative boards, these corporations own or have shares in 1049 corporations (SOU 1983:39). Denmark, at the other extreme, has only a few public corporations. Local governments have business activities correspondingly organized. During the post-war period there was considerable expansion of the public administrative systems. This rate of expansion decreased during the period of more conscious cut-back policy in the late 70's. The expansion at the central level has been expressed in continuous differentiation of functions. This differentiation has demanded specialized units (advisory, investigating, planning, consultative, policy-preparing, implementing, reviewing, and so on). The specialization has demanded units for coordination. Also, the increased intervention in the private sector has caused the need of units for contact and cooperation between public and private interests.

This development has been organized in different ways. The number of directorates and central administrative boards has increased very much, but still more significant is the increase in temporary and permanent units for special tasks more or less independent from the old units. Between 1951 and 1976, the number of such units increased from 503 to 1141 in Norway (Egeberg 1981), and between 1960 and 1974 from 328 to 565 in Finland (Ståhlberg 1976, cf. Fivelsdal 1979).

Another characteristic has been the continuous subdivision within the existing authorities. The number of levels has increased from two or three to four or five. A lot of internal temporary units have been formed for special tasks. For instance the Swedish central administrative board for education had more than 200 project groups in the middle of the 70's (Tarschys 1978, Ståhlberg 1983).

The main expansion, however, has been in the self-government administration. The Finnish figures for public employees present an excellent illustration. Indexes for the period 1972-79 were: the state 107, the municipalities 130, and federations of municipalities 175 (Ståhlberg 1983a). Norwegian local government activity (measured in annual working hours) has doubled in the last fifteen years (Laegreid-Roness 1983).

The big and growing public sector is problematic seen from the point of view of political steering. The parliament and the government are not able to steer our modern dynamic society by precise rules. Instead, there is a tendency to use framework steering, a steering by goals and general directions. The task of filling the frames has been delegated to the public administration. This development has been seen as a substantial shift of power from politicians to civil servants: more and more public decisions are actually made by the bureaucracy.

One indication of this shift of power is that interest groups increasingly direct their activities towards the public administration. These activities take many forms. Sometimes interest organizations have formal representation in administrative units.

One-third of the members on the Swedish administrative boards represent interest organizations. Very often the "new" units in the central administrations have interest representation.

Even more common are various informal arrangements. Implementation of public policies on all administrative levels is sometimes negotiated between the actors in more or less permanent networks. At the regional and local levels, such networks may contain state civil servants and representatives from municipalities, interest organizations and business enterprises (Hjern–Lundmark 1979).

PUBLIC SERVICE PERSONNEL

The only formal basis of recruitment and promotion in the Nordic countries is merits such as "skill and length of service." The actual pattern generally follow Olsen's description of the Norwegian system of recruitment and promotion: "Initial recruitment is based primarily on university exams. At the executive level promotions primarily follow internal seniority. At higher levels performance is important, together with the superior's knowledge of and evaluation of personal style, i.e. ability to cooperate, loyalty and decisiveness" (Olsen 1983:128).

One interesting exception from this general rule may be mentioned. When the Swedish labor market authority (a central administrative board) was formed after the war, the recruitment of its employees was more or less delegated to the big labor market unions. The basis of recruitment was not formal exams but experience of union work (Rothstein 1979).

Are there any political appointments (where party considerations predominate)? Formally this kind of appointment does not exist, but in reality there are some modifications. However, the differences between the Nordic countries are very big on this point. In Denmark political appointments are next to non-existent (cf. Christensen 1980). In Norway the norms against political appointments are very strong, but some key positions in the central administration are occupied by persons from the governing parties (Laegreid–Olsen 1978). Sweden resembles Norway: some positions in the state departments are politically ear-marked. At the shift of cabinet in 1976, about 50 department employees (a little more than 1 per cent) were regarded as political appointees. There has always been a tendency to place former politicians, regardless of party affiliation, in higher administrative positions, e.g. as county governors.

Finland differs in a striking manner from the other countries on the question of political appointments. More and more, appointing authorities make overall political considerations when recruiting and promoting people, which is why party affiliation and party merit become important. All the big parties get their share of the administrative positions. Civil servants who are not politically committed have difficulties in advancing to leading positions. The reverse of the coin is that civil servants are to an increasing degree involved in the organizations of the political parties. The bureaucracy is politicized and the parties are bureaucratized (Djupsund 1977).

Inter-ministerial mobility is low. Of the top civil servants in the Danish central administration, 70 per cent of the generalists and 58 per cent of the specialists have served in only one ministry (Christensen 1983). In Norway only 7 per cent of the civil servants moved from one ministry to another between 1970 and 1974. On the other hand, mobility is considerably greater in the higher echelons. Of the top civil servants in Norway, 45 per cent were recruited from other public administration units (Olsen 1983).

Generally, the system of recruitment and promotion is decentralized to the administrative units in question. Only top civil servants are appointed by the cabinet. In Finland civil servants are appointed by the president to the highest positions, and other top and middle civil servants are appointed by the cabinet.

Nordic public employees are organized in unions to a very high degree (in Finland the figure is 90 per cent). Public service unions had been formed already in the 19th century. The normal pattern today is that public employees are organized in several unions together with employees of the private sector. There are especially two areas in which public servant unions play an important role. The first is in negotiations concerning salaries and other working conditions. The second is in the system of co-determination described later.

At the beginning of the 20th century, the state dominated the relations between the state and its employees. In the period before the second world war, the situation changed to a system of substantial mutuality in practice. After the war the negotiations between the state and its employees resulted in formal agreements. Later the means of conflict used in the private sector, the strike, was permitted even in the public sector, namely in Norway (1958), Sweden (1965) and Finland (1970). In Denmark, though most civil servants have the right to strike, top civil servants do not (Keränen 1983).

In the 1970s a debate on the question of co-determination started in the Nordic countries. Various arrangements have been discussed in order to form a viable system of co-determination for the employees in the private as well as the public sector. Since 1977 Sweden has had an extensive law on co-determination, which regulates the relations between employers and employees, both private and public. The employer has two duties. The first, and most important, is to initiate negotiations with his employees if important changes are about to be made. Even the unions, which define what is important, have the right to initiate such negotiations. The negotiations are part of the preparation of the decision, which the employer still has to make. The second duty of the employer is to inform his employees continuously about his activities (Lundell 1983). Co-determination in the public sector has brought about a discussion of the relation between organizational co-determination and political democracy. The situation is particularly delicate at the self-government level.

Public servants in the Nordic countries have the same political rights as other citizens, and they use them to a very high degree. The general Nordic pattern follows Olsen's description of the situation in Norway: "On the average, civil servants engage more in political parties, interest organizations and other political activities than does the rest of the population" (Olsen 1983).

THE BUREAUCRACY AND POLICY-MAKING

The importance of the participation of interest groups in the administrative process has already been mentioned. Another characteristic of the total political process is a high degree of segmentation. Actors in various issue areas are more or less independent of each other. This state of affairs is possibly strengthened by the civil servants' lack of mobility between administrative units.

On the one hand, segmentation has been looked upon as something positive: it makes specialization possible. On the other hand segmentation has been seen as a source of bad coordination. Olsen has tried to explain why the special situation in the Nordic countries makes this segmentation possible and perhaps necessary: "The smaller and more homogeneous the society, the easier it is to develop a consensual policy-making style and to use anticipated reactions as a major form of coordination. The more efficiently coordination through anticipated reactions works, the easier it is to exploit the benefits of specialization and segmentation" (Olsen 1983:117).

The bigness of the administrative systems makes it impossible to make all decisions at the cabinet level. "There are many bargaining tables and many policy-making arenas." Civil servants are involved in the policy-making process in several capacities: "taking initiatives in their own field, making formal choices, and affecting interpretations of how programs and policies are working in practice." No doubt top civil servants in Norway, as in other Nordic countries, "are key participants in public policy-making processes" acting "within institutionalized networks of organized public and private interests" (Olsen 1983:145).

The formal regulation of administrative procedures is summarized in one law in Finland, Norway and Sweden. In Denmark such a law is being prepared. There is a general correspondence between the administrative laws of the Nordic countries.

The different designs of the Nordic administrative systems make comparisons of the characteristics of top civil servants difficult. Available data have been collected for different purposes and investigations do not often use the same categories.

Education is probably the most important civil service characteristic in the homogeneous Nordic societies. In at least one major Norwegian analysis the conclusion is that one's educational specialization is the only characteristic possible to trace in explaining the different attitudes of civil servants (Laegreid–Olsen 1978). The similarities in the educational background of the civil servants in the Nordic countries are striking. As in most European countries, almost every Nordic top civil servant has a university degree (about 90 per cent). Most frequent is a degree in law (40–50 per cent), which is more usual in Finland and Denmark than in Norway and Sweden. During the last decades degrees in one of the social sciences have become more frequent among generalists (Lundquist-Ståhlberg 1983, Mellbourn 1979, Leagreid–Olsen 1978).

As a consequence of the social exclusiveness of university education, the social class background of top civil servants diverges very much from that of the total population. Different principles of division in various investigations make comparisons difficult. We have a division into three classes (upper, middle and lower) for Sweden (41, 43, and 15 per cent, respectively) and Finland (30.5, 59, and 10.5 per cent, respectively). From other divisions we may conclude that the Danish top civil servants have a higher social background than their colleagues in the other Nordic countries. Finland's top civil servants have the lowest social background, and Norway and Sweden are somewhere in between (Lundquist-Ståhlberg 1983, Christoffersson 1983).

There are very few women among top civil servants. Finland, Denmark and Sweden have 4–5 per cent. Norway deviates from this pattern, as about 10 per cent of its top civil servants are women.

ADMINISTRATIVE RESPONSIBILITY

The Nordic parliaments may influence public administration through their legislative and economic powers. In cases of minister administration, the minister has a parliamentary responsibility for the administrative decisions. If the parliament votes no confidence, the minister has to resign. The parliaments also have the competence to review administrative decisions and expenditures.

The increased use of framework legislation and budgets makes it very difficult to review the implementation. Parliamentary reviews take place in two forms. Firstly, all the parliaments have an ombudsman, whose primary task is to protect the individual from abuse of bureaucratic power. Secondly, the parliaments elect accountants who review the economic conditions of the public administration.

The parliaments elect an ombudsman (in Sweden four). The ombudsman acts independently of the parliament, to which he reports annually. Anybody can complain to the ombudsman, and he can himself initiate investigations. His means of sanction is public objections to the erring authority. Sweden was the first country in the world to introduce an ombudsman, which was done in the constitution of 1809. The institution of ombudsman was introduced in Finland 1919, in Denmark 1955, and in Norway 1962. With the Nordic ombudsman as a prototype, the institution has spread throughout the world.

The governments in Finland and Sweden have a counterpart to the parliament's ombudsman, namely the chancellor of justice, introduced already in the Swedish constitution of 1719. In the area of review he has the same competence as the ombudsman, and he reports annually to the government.

Both the parliament and the government in the Nordic countries have an audit organization. The best possibilities of parliamentary economic review are offered by the Norwegian system by which the parliament's accountants have a special public authority at their disposal (Debes 1978). In the other countries, the opposite numbers of this authority are subordinated to the government and work independently of the parliamentary accountants, but they sometimes cooperate (Meyer 1979). The objective of these audits is to improve the organization and the efficiency of administrative processes. The routine process of administrative review means that superiors review subordinates. Citizens may appeal to the authority superior to the one that made the decision. Furthermore, it is often possible to appeal to other instances and the total systems of review are very complicated (cf. e.g. Lundquist 1976).

The systems of review follow the two main Nordic administrative designs. Finland and Sweden have a system of administrative courts with a Supreme Administrative Court on the highest level. Denmark and Norway haven't any administrative courts of this kind. Instead, the ordinary courts have the power to review the lawfulness of administrative decisions. Some exceptions from this pattern may occur. In some cases in Denmark and Norway, e.g. in the area of social services, complaints are made to a specialized unit. In Finland (and only indirectly in Sweden) the ordinary courts have some competence to review administrative decisions (Petersson 1984).

Each of the Nordic countries has a special unit (a central administrative board or a department) that works on the rationalization of administrative organizations and processes. In every Nordic country there is a law that provides a right of access to public documents. The law is especially important for and used by mass media. In Finland and Sweden this law has very old traditions; it appeared in the Swedish law on freedom of the press in 1766. Denmark and Norway introduced a corresponding law in 1970. The principle of such a law is that the necessary exceptions from the rule of publicity should be restricted to a minimum. However, secrecy is still often a characteristic of the administrative process. The law seems to function better in Sweden and Finland, with their old traditions, than in Denmark and Norway.

CONCLUSION

The current problems of the Nordic administrative systems are about the same as those of other Western democracies. The still dominating bureaucratic organizational form is not always fitted to the demands of the welfare state. The size and complexity of modern society make coordination difficult. The economic crisis has brought further complications.

However, some changes have occurred. Within the old administration, new categories of civil servants have been recruited. New administrative units have been established outside the ministries and the central administrative boards. Local self-government on various levels has developed its own big administrations to handle an increasing proportion of public tasks.

Generally there has been a shift in power from legislative to executive bodies. One indication of this shift of power is the interest organizations' choice of influence targets. Now they mainly direct their activities towards the public administration. Also, representatives from the interest organizations are formally integrated in the public administration. Probably more important are the informal networks formed by interest organizations and public and other private units in the making and implementation of public policies.

The shift of power and the corporativization of the political process have to a considerable degree blotted out the borderline between the public and the private sector. The development has been discussed as a democratic dilemma: the electoral channel from citizens to politicians becomes of secondary importance.

Sometimes the Nordic countries have functioned as "constitutional innovators." A modern example is the development of new employment conditions for civil servants. In all Nordic countries civil servants today have almost the same position in relation to the state as private employees have to their employers. This innovative ability has been particularly pronounced in Sweden. Three internationally remarkable cases may be mentioned: the laws on access to public documents (1766), the ombudsman (1809), and co-determination in the private and public sector (1977).

The international interest in the Nordic countries has mainly been directed towards some important issue areas in the development of the welfare state, particularly labor market policy and social politics. But even the style of the Nordic political systems has been the subject of international attention. Often this style is described in terms of "consensual democracy" and "compromise politics."

In connection with this "consensus thesis," the Nordic democracies are described as "open societies": they have a considerable social equality and political freedom, they have close relations between ruler and ruled, and they implement "the principle of the goldfish bowl." The latter means that the citizens are well informed about public affairs, i.e. due to their free access to public documents.

The question is why the Nordic countries have been able to solve their problems and conflicts in a peaceful way and why democratic institutions are functioning comparatively well. One answer is that the countries are small and homogeneous. They are, of course, not monolithic; there are cleavages of various kinds.

In another international discussion, Sweden has been designated a New Totalitarian State. Sweden is, the critics indicate, a society in which the state intervenes in all spheres of human activity and where the individual has very little freedom. It is not very easy to combine this statement with the conception of the consensus state. It might be possible to find some tendencies in the actual system that coincide with the totalitarian model. However, in a comparative perspective, the Nordic democracies stand out as consensual systems.

REFERENCES

Christensen, Jørgen Grønnegård (1980): *Centraladministrationen: organisation og politisk placering*, Copenhagen: Samfundsvidenskabeligt Forlag.

Christensen, Jørgen Grønnegård (1983): Karrieremønstre i dansk centraladministration, in: Lundquist–Ståhlberg (1983) pp. 55–79.

Christoffersson, Ulf (1983): De statligt anställda i Sverige, in: Lundquist–Ståhlberg (1983) pp. 154–177.

Debes, Jan (1978): *Statsadministrasjonen*, Oslo: NKS–Forlaget.

Djupsund, Göran (1977): *Förvaltning, intressegrupper och partier*, Åbo: Meddelanden från statsvetenskapliga fakulteten vid Åbo Akademi serie A:117.

Egeberg, Morten (1981): *Stat og organisasjoner*, Bergen: Universitetsforlaget.

Fivelsdal, Egil–Torben Beck Jørgensen–Paul Daugaard Jensen (1979): *Interesseorganisationer og centraladministration*, Copenhagen: Nyt fra Samfundsvidenskaberne.

Gustafsson, Agne (1983): *Local Government in Sweden*, Stockholm: The Swedish Institute.

Hjern, Benny–Kjell Lundmark (1979): Blandekonomi och postweberiansk förvaltningsteori, in: *Statsvetenskaplig Tidskrift* vol. 61 pp. 257–66.

Karvonen, Lauri (1981): *"Med vårt västra grannland som förebild"*, Åbo: Meddelanden från stiftelsens för Åbo Akademi Forskningsinstitut nr 62.

Keränen, Marja (1983): Tjänstemännens förhandlingsrätt och dess utveckling i de nordiska länderna, in: Lundquist–Ståhlberg (1983) pp. 191–209.

Laegreid, Per–Johan P. Olsen (1978): *Byråkrati og beslutninger*, Bergen: Universitetsforlaget.

Laegreid, Per–Paul Roness (1983): De statligt anställda i Norge, in: Lundquist–Ståhlberg (1983) pp. 128–153.

Lundell, Bengt (1983): Medinflytande för de offentligt anställda i i Sverige, in: Lundquist–Ståhlberg (1983) pp. 210–224.

Lundquist, Lennart (1976): *Förvaltningen i det politiska systemet*, Lund: Studentlitteratur, 2nd ed.

Lundquist, Lennart–Krister Ståhlberg (1983): *Byråkrater i Norden*, Åbo: Meddelanden från stiftelsens för Åbo Akademi forskningsinstitut nr 83.

Mellbourn, Anders (1979): *Byråkratins ansikten*, Stockholm: Liber Förlag.

Meyer, Poul (1979): *Offentlig forvaltning*, Copenhagen: Gads Forlag 3rd ed.

Olsen, Johan P. (1983): *Organized Democracy*, Bergen: Universitetsforlaget.

Petersson, Olof (1984): *Folkstyrelse och statsmakt i Norden*, Uppsala: Diskurs.

Rothstein, Bo (1979): AMS som socialdemokratisk reformbyråkrati, in *Arkiv* nr 18 pp. 56–76.

SOU 1983:39—Politisk styrning—administrativ självständighet.

Ståhlberg, Krister (1976): *Utvecklingsdrag inom den offentliga förvaltningen under åren 1960-75*, Helsinki: Research Reports, Institute of Political Science, University of Helsinki.

Ståhlberg, Krister (1983a): De statligt anställda i Finland, in: Lundquist—Ståhlberg (1983) pp. 80-127.

Ståhlberg, Krister (1983): *Självstyrd eller dräng*: Åbo: Meddelanden från stiftelsens för Åbo Akademi forskningsinstitut nr 89.

Tarschys, Daniel (1978): *Den offentliga revolutionen*, Stockholm: Liber Förlag.

REFERENCES IN ENGLISH

Allardt, E., *et al., Nordic Democracy*. Copenhagen: Det danske selskab, 1981. See Gustaf Petren on Nordic admin., 163-182.

Arneson, Ben A., *The Democratic Monarchies of Scandinavia*. N.Y.: Van Nostrand, 1939.

Elder, Neil, Alastair H. Thomas, and David Arter. *The Consensual Democracies?* Oxford: Martin Robertson, 1982.

Lauwerys, J. A., ed., *Scandinavian Democracy*. Copenhagen: Danish Institute, 1958.

Meyer, Poul, "The Development of Public Administration in Scandinavian Countries since 1945," *Int. Rev. Ad. Sci.* 26 (1960), 135-146.

Small States in Comparative Perspective: *Essays in Honour of Erik Allardt*: Norwegian University Press/OUP, 1985.

III
WESTERN EUROPE

11
Ireland

THOMAS J. BARRINGTON
Institute of Public Administration, Dublin, Ireland

HISTORY AND ENVIRONMENT

Any system of administration is, I suppose, the product of the interaction between its origins and the character of the people whom it serves and who staff it. Certainly, one can readily make the point that the Irish administration reflects very well the strengths and weaknesses of the people of Ireland themselves. Unlike some other administrations, it is staffed, not from an economic or hereditary elite, but from the children of the small farmers, the small shopkeepers and other groups, petty bourgeois and other, who have set the tone of the Irish State since it achieved Independence (1).

In 1922 Independence was secured by about two-thirds of the population inhabiting about three-quarters of the island of Ireland, namely, some three million of the 4.5 million inhabitants of the island: we are, in terms of people, a small State—next to Luxembourg the smallest numerically of the members of the European Community. Administratively this smallness presents ready opportunity for communication across organizational boundaries, opportunities accentuated by a high degree of informality and dislike of status-seeking, advantages we do not always fully exploit. Moreover, it is not always easy to get clearcut decisions where every course of action would adversely affect somebody's brother-in-law. This smallness, coupled with the homogeneity of both parliamentarians and administrators in relation to the population, makes it exceptionally difficult for politicans and public servants to get away from the practical sense of the common people. This makes for pragmatic day-to-day management and leaves little room either in politics or in administration for ideology. But for this a price has to be paid, as we shall see.

At Independence 50 per cent of the population was engaged in agriculture; in 1983 the proportion was 17 per cent. These figures are typical of substantially underdeveloped and developing countries. (The developed country may have only 3 or 4 per cent of its population so engaged.) In 1983 the gross domestic product per head measured in terms of purchasing power was two-thirds of the average for the European Community as a whole. We are not only small but, in European terms at least, relatively poor.

If one thinks of Ireland in 1922 in terms of what we would now describe as a typical under-developed, ex-colonial country achieving independence, one can say that it started off with, by comparison with those countries that achieved independence after World War II, quite remarkable advantages.

In the first place it inherited a very strong parliamentary, democratic tradition; secondly, a pretty complete system of public administration; thirdly, a well developed legal system; and, fourthly, a well developed secondary education system, crucial to the staffing of at least the middle ranges—the executive or practical grades—of modern government. On the whole, the Irish public service normally has had no difficulty in recruiting many of the very best people—in terms of intelligence and commitment—in the whole country. Because, for various reasons, there remained at that time no Irish ruling class, this recruitment enabled the public service to be, to quite a remarkable extent, fairly representative of the society as a whole. The price we paid for this was, in a peasant and petty bourgeois society, an extra dose of peasant and petty bourgeois conservatism.

Moreover, as the country is about 95 per cent Roman Catholic, the public service could not help but reflect special features of Irish Roman Catholicism. In consequence it was—and still is behind the laughter, the drinking, and the apparent irreverence—austere in its approach to life, exceptionally honest and remarkably unintellectual.

Origins

Irish public administration dates from the end of the 12th century, but the real foundations of modern Irish government were laid in the 19th century under the United Kingdom of Britain and Ireland.

Ireland lost its separate parliament in 1800 and some parts of its administration, but as the 19th century wore on and the United Kingdom (U.K.) government became involved in ideas of positive government, a number of Irish ministries and "boards" came into being, and branches of U.K. ministries—such as the Post Office—played an active part in various forms of development, political, infrastructural, economic and, because of the great poverty of Ireland, social. Also environmental and social problems led to the development of local government in the latter part of the 19th century. By the end of the century a local government system, closely modeled on that recently devised for England and Wales, had been established (2). Oddly, it was in relation to central government that the biggest differences manifested themselves. Here we had Irish ministries, branches of U.K. ministries, and a great variety of "boards," some with ministerial participation, some not, in the attempt—given the perennial political restlessness—to associate Irish "worthies" with the administrative process (3). The great mass of the Irish people, for reasons of religion and property, had been excluded from membership and representation by the 18th century Irish parliament but, as these impediments were steadily eroded during the 19th century, the pressure to restore a separate Irish parliament (and administration) became severe. In the process the Irish people showed themselves to have a special affinity for democratic politics. The great peasant movement in the early part of the century, led by Daniel O'Connell, was to be the inspiration of European christian democracy and, later in the century, the masterly use of party discipline by Parnell in the U.K. parliament was to set a headline for later party managers.

On Independence the new state inherited a British style of political and administrative system—a parliament substantially modeled on the British one, a legal system based on the British system of common law, a typically British-style civil service and a British system of local government. In sixty years of Independence there was been some modification of these systems by the importation of American ideas and, in more recent times, some European ones, plus some indigenous adaptation. Nonetheless, both in parliamentary and administrative institutions, considered as institutions, and as compared with the British model, there has been much stagnation.

Members of the Irish government after Independence were revolutionaries but conservative ones, determined to show their capacity to govern. But they faced formidable problems: the partition to a moderately autonomous part of the U.K. of six of the country's 32 counties; a civil war waged by former companions-in-arms dissatisfied with the settlement made with the British; a large, well established public service transferred to them whose loyalty to the new State was doubted—groundlessly as it proved; the post-war slump and post-revolutionary destruction; and a lively consciousness of smallness, poverty and the consequential need to restrict the activities of the State. The new rulers were determined to be fully in charge of what had been so hard won and they saw as the route to this a vigorous policy of centralization. They also aimed, at first, to limit the range of government, but as infrastructural, economic and social problems increasingly pressed for attention, and as private enterprise proved so weak, government was forced willy nilly to extend its role. So were born the two dominant features of Irish administration—its intense centralization and its central role in national development.

Constitution

We have had since 1922 a written constitution. After much amendment from 1922 we had a new constitution in 1937, which much weakened the remaining constitutional links with Britain—the last was swept away in 1949. The Constitution (*Bunreacht*) of 1937, in particular, has brought a special flavor into Irish administration (4). It provides for a relatively clear division of the legislative, executive and judicial functions of government, except that the system of cabinet government as a committee of the parliament—with all the ambiguities inherent in that—has been carried over from Britain. The Constitution incorporates two significant American conceptions, namely that of what might be called a Bill of Rights entrenched in the Constitution, and a Supreme Court concerned to apply these principles and to interpret the Constitution in accordance with the evolving situation. In this way the Irish Constitution, like that of the United States, has received significant development, perhaps beyond the conception of those who originally drafted it. In the area of human rights in particular the leadership given by the courts contrasts strongly with the sluggish performance of the governmental system. The effect has been the attempt to create in Ireland a government of laws and not of men and to subject the laws themselves to the control of some general principles.

This has been a gradual, erratic process and there have been a number of setbacks. There has not been universal agreement as to what principles precisely should govern law making. The main effect, so far as is relevant here, is that on the administrative system itself. A striking feature of the Irish administration, which it shares with the British one, is that very few lawyers are employed in it so that many administrators have little sympathy for, do not fully understand or are confused by the active, creative role of the courts.

Ireland has played an active part in the United Nations and its associated bodies, in the Council of Europe and, now, in the European Community, and governmental discretion and domestic law are governed in some degree by the conventions adopted by these bodies, by membership of the European Community, and interpretation by the European Court of Justice of constitutional and legal implications of the Treaty of Rome.

A small matter of nomenclature. Constitutionally, the *name* of the State is "Ireland" which is also the name of the island as a whole. However, when one wishes, in matters of comparison, to distinguish it from Northern Ireland one uses the *description* "The Republic of Ireland."

Parliament

A further factor influencing the administration is the kind of parliamentary system that we operate. There is in Ireland, as we have seen, a very strong parliamentary and democratic tradition, developed in the 19th century. The trouble is that, until very recently indeed, the parliament we inherited from the British has remained stuck in a 19th century groove, one that failed to adjust itself to the demands of modern government (5). Our parliament (*Oireachtas*) has been extraordinarily ill-equipped in methods of keeping parliamentarians well informed of the complexities of the system over which they are expected to preside. It suffers from limited staff and accommodation, an embryonic committee system, few research facilities, and an inadequate library system, constraints that only slowly now are being eased. Hence, the general tasks of parliamentary oversight have been discharged only by exceptional members of the parliament, and the bulk of the parliamentarians, still locked in local, special, particular problems, are not well equipped to think in national, general or broad administrative terms. As against the ordinary member of parliament, so handicapped, ministers tend to be extremely powerful, partly because they have had a virtual monopoly of the sources of information on matters of general importance and partly because many of them tend in our system to have long experience of office.

There are two houses of the parliament—the *Dail*, directly elected by proportional representation in multi-seat (3–5 member) geographical constituencies on the basis of the single, transferable vote, and the *Seanad* (Senate) largely indirectly elected and with little power. One effect of multi-member constituencies is intense rivalry between elected representatives in what they call "servicing" constituents, a rivalry perhaps more intense *within* political parties than between them. This results in an enormous flow of representations to official bodies.

STRUCTURE

In Ireland the expression "public service" comprises the defense, security, teaching and various administrative services, employing about 30 per cent of the total of those at work. But, for the purpose of this chapter the "public service" is confined to the three branches of the administrative services, about three-quarters of the public service as a whole—the civil service, the local and regional (chiefly health) services, and the services of the parastatal bodies, which we call state-sponsored bodies (6). The chart (Fig. 1) attempts to set out how these administrative services constitute the executive system of Irish government.

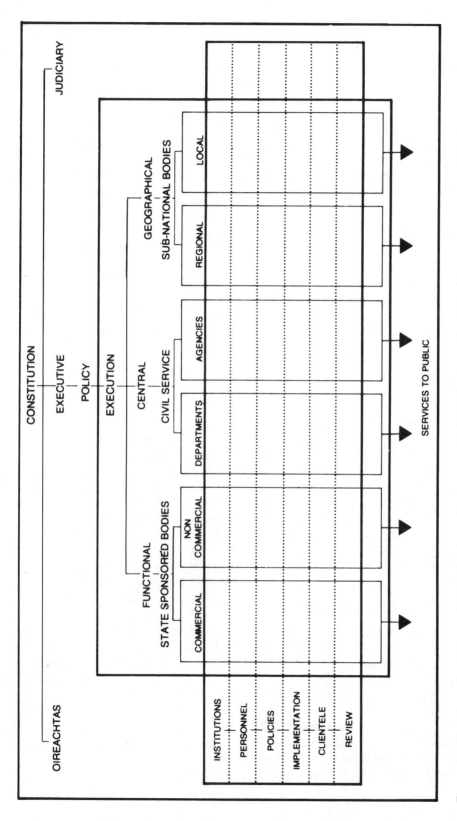

Figure 1   The Executive System of Irish Government. *Source*: T. J. Barrington: *The Irish Administrative System* (1980), p. 26.

Within the executive system the first task of central government is to settle overall policy. The preparation of much of this policy and the actual execution of the policies adopted is done in the three administrative branches. In terms of aggregate employment the functional and geographical branches are broadly equal in size, each comprising about 40 per cent of the whole; the civil service is about half the size of either of the others (7). If one reads the chart horizontally one finds in the functional areas of government what we call the state-sponsored bodies—commercial (i.e., public enterprises) and non-commercial (mainly promotional). Then there are the two main kinds of central government executive bodies; and finally, the two main kinds of geographical or areal bodies—the regional and local structures.

Now let us look at the system of executive institutions analytically, as stages in a process. This is attempted in the vertical breakdown of the chart. One can say that the administrative process takes off from the success of the political process in achieving some firm ground on which there is a consensus, so that an *institution*, an organizational structure, can be established to achieve the agreed ends. The institution is staffed by *personnel*, who come up with proposals for *policies*. These, when they have received political approval, are *implemented*. The policies impinge on the public (or *clientele*) either to their satisfaction or dissatisfaction, or, more usually, a mixture of both. Feedback of various dissatisfactions leads to a *review* of some sort. This stage, once reached, closes the system and enables it to adjust to change.

INSTITUTIONS

Civil Service

The most important administrative institution, because of its position at the center of the governmental process, is the civil service (8). It can be seen as consisting of departments and agencies. The total size of the civil service in 1984 was about 43,000. Civil servants are under tight political control and formal accountability to parliament.

There were in 1984 seventeen government ministries, or departments as they are called, each answerable to one of the fifteen full *ministers*, the maximum permitted by the Constitution, who constitute the Government. The departments vary in size from about 5,000 staff (Agriculture) to about 100 (Gaeltacht, concerned with the development of the scattered Irish-speaking areas).

The Ministers and Secretaries Act, 1924, and corresponding legislation in relation to local government, aimed to centralize all the administration of state services firmly under the control of ministers who would be answerable to parliament for the discharge of their responsibilities.

The method adopted was to constitute the *minister*—not the ministry or department— as the legal entity, so that virtually every act of the department, to be legally done, must be done by the minister himself. In this way he could be held clearly accountable to parliament and the electorate. This had some chance of working in the conditions of 1924 when Irish government was small business and most of it could flow over the desks of ministers; but, as the business of government grew, the "corporation sole" concept became less and less workable. Nonetheless, although the 1924 Act has been amended many times, this feature of it has not been altered. In the attempt to work the unworkable, great masses of detail get sucked up to the desks of the most senior civil servants, who could be relied upon to know the mind of the minister. The result has been the besetting sin of the Irish civil service—the passionate concern for detail and the corresponding weakness in policy formulation. This was the analysis of the Devlin Report of 1969 (9), which—noting that the rise in the state-sponsored bodies showed ad hoc responses to the problem of separating policy and execution—urged that the problem be tackled head on. But this advice has been, if not rejected, then largely ignored.

The problems are made worse by the bent of the parliamentarians towards specific issues. On the one hand, is the huge flow of representations on individual cases, leading amongst other things to the virtual collapse of the parliamentary question system from overload. On the other hand is the lack of concern to establish systems to cope with *classes* of problems and grievances voiced by citizens, and the very slow evolution of a committee system.

There seems to be an inability both in the political and the administrative systems to grasp the needs for distinguishing between effective democratic control, on the one hand, and either detailed interference or total disinterest on the other. As the size and range of the administration increase, this problem becomes more and more exacerbated, relieved occasionally by the setting up, outside the civil service and outside direct ministerial control, of state-sponsored bodies. A failure to respond effectively to the implications of substantially increased size of and pressures on government, and the dearth of policies to deal with mounting problems, have contributed to the steady decline in the quality of Irish government and administration since the late 1960s and to the present discontents. It is no accident that, since 1969, the electorate has, at each of the five opportunities that offered to 1986, dismissed the government.

Even in 1924 some exceptions were made from the otherwise all-embracing ministerial system. These exceptions, the agencies, included the Revenue Commissioners, in charge of all central taxation and now, with some 7,000 staff, the largest organization within the civil service; the Office of Public Works; and (slightly later) the Civil Service Commission. These agencies, while remaining within the civil service and its general rules and reporting in general terms to ministers, are corporations in their own right and, at the executive level, operate according to their own discretion. In recent years there has been a tendency to add to their number—though often under a single head with a statutory range of discretion: a Director of Prosecutions, a Director of Consumer Affairs, etc. There are about forty of these agencies, most very small.

Functional Bodies

One of the aims of the Act of 1924 was to wipe out the large number of administrative agencies that operated under nominated "boards" that existed at Independence and incorporate them in ministries. However, as the state began, hesitantly, to be concerned with the development of a backward society, this soon conflicted with the rigidities of a highly centralized civil service system. So, the ink was scarcely dry on the 1924 Act when new bodies—which we now call state-sponsored bodies (10)—were established outside the civil service. Some of these, like the Electricity Supply Board and the Agricultural Credit Corporation could be classed as "commercial," or, in more general terms, public enterprises. Others, "non-commercial" state-sponsored bodies, were established as time wore on, each for a specific function but collectively over almost the full range of government. For all the state-sponsored bodies the model was the business firm. There are now about 100 of these (their number steadily grows) employing about 95,000, or 40 per cent of the public service.

Despite the 1924 Act, there was widespread acceptance, as each body came to be established, of the "inappropriateness" of civil service procedures for discharging specific functions. But the logic of this clash between centralization and pragmatism has not been faced. Whatever the lack of consistency, the state-sponsored bodies were set up with a high degree of autonomy in relation to day-to-day operations, recruitment and, until the seventies, pay. On the whole they proved to be a remarkably successful feature of Irish public administration; but in recent years some of them have shared in the general decline in the quality of Irish government.

The commercial state-sponsored bodies number just over one-third of the state-sponsored bodies as a whole and represent about 90 per cent of those employed in this sector. They are similar to public enterprises in other counties and mainly operate in the communications, energy, finance and transport fields. They tend to be heavy consumers of capital and recent disappointing returns have been a source of some anxiety, as we shall see. In 1984 they were added to when Posts and Telecommunications were taken out of the civil service (reducing it by nearly half) and were set up as two commercial state-sponsored bodies. There is a joint committee of the two houses of Parliament which scrutinizes the reports, accounts, and results of most commercial state-sponsored bodies and reports on general issues that arise.

In November, 1984, the committee was examining the wholly owned Irish Shipping Ltd., when the company's board requested the High Court to appoint a provisional liquidator because of very heavy losses in the years to March 1984, and huge expected losses, from disastrous long-term chartering. The committee were unable to probe whether there had been major errors of judgement at management level, effective board control and adequate supervision by the relevant government departments, because those concerned would not give evidence to it (11).

The non-commercial state-sponsored bodies are concerned normally with one function, but between them cover much of the range of modern government—chiefly the functions of research, regulation, ancillary health services, and promotion. Their most distinctive function is promotion. Under this heading come the formidable Industrial Development Authority, Coras Trachtala (the export promotion board), Bord Failte (the tourist promotion board), the Shannon Free Airport Development Company, and others. These agencies are formed by or under statute or are incorporated under the general Companies Acts. They are modeled on private business organizations but are financed directly by government, which appoints their boards and approves their programs. Especially since the 1950s they have become a most distinctive form of Irish administration—basically single-purpose bodies with a high level of autonomy (as contrasted with the typically multi-purpose, tightly controlled government departments) and with, usually, some participation through their board members from the private sector on which they impinge. Their staffs are not normally civil servants, although they enjoy comparable conditions of employment. Some of them, notably the Industrial Development Authority, were "hived off" from their parent departments; but most were constituted *ad hoc.*

Geographical Bodies

Given the centralizing ethos of Irish government—if it proves impossible to centralize *all* functions under ministers let at least the functions be administered centrally and separately—it is surprising that geographical and moderately multi-purpose local authorities have survived. But it is not surprising that they are in poor shape and, with one notable exception, sadly neglected (12).

At Independence a large number of mainly small rural local government bodies was inherited, with councils directly elected on a property franchise and having varying relationships with the central authority. Central control was immediately standardized at its most extreme form and all the small rural authorities were rapidly swept away. A number of small urban authorities remained but with functions that steadily diminished. The main thrust was to strengthen the 31 county and county borough authorities and a small number of other urban authorities of some size. As part of the policy of strengthening the capabilities of these bodies, there was the remarkable Irish innovation in 1926 of the Local Appointments Commission, the successful attempt to apply a civil service commission system of recruitment to the most important appointments under local authorities. From 1929 to 1942 there was imported gradually from the United States a version of city and county management that was extended to all directly elected authorities, now with full adult suffrage. The result was the development of a remarkable administrative instrument with significant potential for development. However, after World War II interest in a vigorous system of local government flagged. Steadily local government lost functions, morale and much of such autonomy as it had enjoyed. Over the past decade, during which things got steadily worse, there have been repeated, unfulfilled promises of reform.

This decline in local government is in striking contrast to what is happening in other European countries; to the fact that in Ireland we are going through the greatest period of urbanization in our history; and to the steady rise throughout Ireland of local self-consciousness and local organizations seeking a role in relation to the activities of official institutions. With these developments the political and administrative systems, failing and congested as they are, have been unable to come to terms.

This gloomy picture was lightened for a while by a fashion for regional structures. We have seen that a striking feature of Irish administrative history has been the series of *ad hoc* responses to individual problems, well illustrated in the uncoordinated growth of regional structures throughout the country, each special to the designs of its creator. A "region" in this sense means a grouping, almost always for a specific purpose, of three or four counties with, usually, a different grouping for each purpose. A regional body usually operates under a board of indirectly elected local representatives, nominated officials and some others. Regional bodies have diverse origins—in one instance (tourism) decentralization from a central body, and in another to achieve some form of mainly infrastructural regional coordination; but by far the most important regional boards, the health boards, represented a step towards centralization of a service that had constituted about half the activities of the county authorities. After the late 1970s the interest in regionalism died.

PERSONNEL

The Irish civil service, being an offshoot of the British, replicates its staff structures with its administrative, executive and clerical classes and, within those, a comparable grading system. Rather similar class and grading systems now exist in the functional and geographical bodies, imported from the civil service partly through central controls over pay and partly through the efforts of public service unions—which are very strong and have in membership a very high proportion of public servants, except those at the very top. From the beginning, the higher classes and grades were reasonably permeable from below. For example, the majority of those in civil service administrative classes have been promoted from the executive class. More rigid, especially in the civil service, has been the separation between, on the one hand, the administrative and executive classes and, on the other, the professional and technical classes, each with its own hierarchy. In those departments where engineers, architects, veterinarians, agriculturalists, etc., are employed, there is the well known "dual structure," a source of some frustration to professional men who feel themselves subordinated to administrators with limited technical background; and also a source of some duplication of effort and, consequently, waste. Occasional efforts have been made to ease this problem but with little success. Even within a single profession there is seldom any concession to the idea of a "corps;" so, for example, although engineers are employed in many departments, their promotional outlets are not only within their profession but are usually confined to the department in which they serve. However, since 1984 professional officers may now compete for vacancies in the two top tiers of civil service administrative posts as part of the new promotion systems introduced in that year.

Recruitment to all branches of the public service is almost invariably by open competition. For the civil service for all grades this is conducted by the Civil Service Commission. For the higher administrative and all professional posts in the local government service and health service this is conducted by a sister organization, the Local Appointments Commission. For the more junior posts recruitment is by the individual local authorities and health boards. Each state-sponsored body recruits its own personnel. For long the public service, because of the shortage of jobs in the country as a whole, enjoyed very considerable advantages in recruitment; but in more recent times, until the onset of the present recession, it had difficulty in filling its jobs.

Mobility as between public bodies is possible in that various pension schemes are linked but it has been very limited—except for the local and health services where virtually all senior posts are filled through the Local Appointments Commission after public advertisement. A number of the state-sponsored bodies have tended, in recent times, to fill their top jobs after public advertisement. Hitherto, in the civil service promotion to higher posts had been almost wholly within each department, but the 1984 decision to fill all the top two tiers of the most senior posts, and half to one-third of the next two tiers, through competition within the civil service as a whole is a major step towards the evolution of more dynamic personnel policies for the public service.

Retirement for most members of the public service is optional at 60 and compulsory of 65. Until recently most public servants served to 65, so that, by comparison with many other countries, Irish senior officials tended to be old, so reinforcing the general tendency towards conservatism. This has been changing, partly because of a combination of steeply progressive income tax and inflation-proofing of pensions.

The broad approach to public service pay and conditions is that they should reflect reasonable levels of remuneration in the community, but the State should not itself be a leader. Attempts have been made, as a counter to inflation, to use the public service as a headline for moderating pay rises generally but, given the strength of trade unions in Ireland and especially in the public service, with indifferent success. Important here are the elaborate negotiating procedures culminating in arbitration for nearly all office staffs. These procedures and other industrial relations machinery the unions have been able to use to considerable effect. Governments have not, when the chips were down, felt sufficiently strongly about pay policy as an ingredient of incomes restraint to attempt to put procedures and machinery in abeyance.

Part of the machinery is a committee to review the pay of the most senior officers of the State—ministers, judiciary, chief executives and the like—in order to keep pay relativities reasonably under control (13). The attempts to ensure the pay primacy of the most senior civil servants have led to some tension, especially in relation to chief executives of state-sponsored bodies whose field of reference is often the private, rather than the public sector, and this has contributed to a noticeable drift of senior staffs from these bodies.

Public servants in the geographical or functional areas have full rights so far as engaging in politics is concerned. Should they be elected to parliament they must take leave without pay. Civil servants may not engage in political activity; subordinate staff may, however, be elected to local bodies but not to either house of parliament. There is a widespread acceptance within the civil service of the desirability of maintaining the separation of politics and administration.

Overall there is considerable scope for more dynamic public personnel policies, primarily in the interest of developing human resources in public bodies. For example, there is an educational problem. By the standards of other countries a relatively low proportion of the most senior officers have had third-level education—most have been recruited after the second level. There has been in Ireland, as in other countries, a substantial educational revolution, and a very large proportion of bright young people nowadays get third-level education. The public service has been slow to adapt itself to this shift. One of the effects is that the public servants at the higher levels now tend to be, on average, rather less well educated than those who staff, for example, the higher levels of the bigger organizations in the private sector. The Irish secondary education system, for all its advantages, has a notably authoritarian bias. This has discouraged the speculative mind and has reinforced the native bent towards the practical and the unintellectual approach. Moreover, until fairly recently secondary education laid great emphasis on the classics and tended to neglect modern languages, science and technology. This formation left a very strong mark on its products in the public service. A good deal has been done to facilitate those public servants who wish to improve their education and to give them access to various forms of training, but substantial problems remain. Again, the staff associations within the public service are exceptionally strong and have been able to strike very hard bargains about recruitment and promotion procedures. These procedures on the whole have tended to militate against a bracing or stimulating climate within many organizations.

There is, therefore, a long agenda for personnel management in the Irish public service.

POLICIES

One of the driving forces making for Irish independence was the belief that the country had been badly, or at least inadequately, governed. However, when Independence was achieved it was not clear what, apart from the conventional virtues of respect for law, hard work, economy and prudence, would in fact make for good government. These were the days before Keynes wrote that seminal essay, *The End of Laisser Faire*, before governments had realized that an overriding purpose of government was to bring about national development. But, given that increasing realization, what policies were needed to bring this about?

The basic development problem in Ireland was lack of enterprise and consequently jobs, and the basic indicator of good or bad government was the level of involuntary emigration. For the first decade after Independence the virtues of careful, honest, economical government were not sufficient to stimulate enterprise. In a typically pragmatic and non-ideological way the lack of private enterprise was to an increasing degree supplied by State enterprise, especially in the technological sphere, and in the development of such natural resources as were then known to exist in the country. For the next decade an active program of industrial protection was also engaged in. This led to the founding of many "infant industries" and some stimulus to enterprise; but there remained a big shortfall. For the decade after World War II there was a vogue for what used to be called social Keynesianism, in the hope that public expenditure on desirable social objects—such as housing, hospitals, etc.—would have a multiplier effect on enterprise. This proved to have unfortunate consequences for economic growth and for the balance of payments and, in consequence, on such enterprise as had been manifesting itself. During all this time heavy emigration continued, reaching a peak in the crisis of the mid-1950s, a crisis that was not only economic but, more seriously, was also one of morale and of political purpose.

Eventually from the late 1950s, as younger civil servants and some others much influenced by Keynes and alert to the implications of European integration began to move into more influential posts, there began a concern for positive, indicative planning and a disenchantment with protectionism and isolationism. The main instrument of planning proved to be the orientation of public capital investment towards economic growth. This had the desired effect and economic development took off. This was supplemented by a policy of importing industrial enterprise, leading to significant economic growth, exports and employment. This growth, in turn, provided the resources to develop social services—income maintenance, education and health. The sense of administrative purpose spread to the political field and, from the late 1950s to about 1970, there was a partnership of strong, confident leadership in both politics and administration, each contributing to the other. This brought about a period of good, active government. Emigration stopped and was succeeded by the return of many of the emigrants of the 1950s. The population began to rise rapidly, the first sustained rise for well over a century. If this were to be the criterion—as was commonly accepted—it looked as if, at long last, Ireland was being successfully governed (14).

However, during the 1970s and early 1980s this momentum was lost as, both politically and administratively, leadership began to fail. Part of the difficulties arose from the troubles in Northern Ireland, dating from 1968-69, and their political, security and economic overspills; part arose from the severe strains imposed on politicians and administrators from a small country by membership of the European Community from 1973; and much by the series of recessions in the subsequent years. But, just as administrative creativity had been at the heart of the revival at the end of the 1950s so, in the late 1970s, administrative decline contributed substantially to the loss of credibility of Irish government.

One can discern in some other societies a sort of reciprocal responsibility as between the political and administrative systems for the quality of government—if one partner is in decline the other puts on a special spurt; but the experience of the past generation in Ireland shows both partners rising and falling together, each contributing to the rise and each contributing to the fall. The recent decline can be illustrated by the failures of three major politico—administrative techniques—economic and social planning, budgeting, and public capital investment.

Economic and social *planning*, which had been such a useful administrative tool in the 1960s, was dropped, briefly revived in the 1970s in a spirit of "irrational optimism" (15), then dropped again, to stage a nominal revival in 1984.

As to public expenditure, the *budget* is in large deficit and has been for a long time. Fifty years of self-discipline was abandoned in 1972, since when the budget has not been balanced and public debt has rapidly expanded.

The careful scrutiny of *capital investment* and the establishment of clear orders of priority gave way to unrestrained spending. For a number of years we vied with Japan at the top of the OECD tables for proportion of GNP invested on capital account, but managed to secure poor returns in terms of both economic growth *and* quality of public services. Yet these were the years in which new techniques of financial appraisal—the programming, planning, budgeting system, cost benefit analysis, and the rest—were being disseminated. Their usefulness may have been oversold, but their effective use might have prevented some waste of resources (16). The disarray of the public finances in recent years has led to concern for better methods of financial control (17). Progress has been made, but major problems remain.

The central analysis of the Devlin Report of 1969 was that the policy formulation process was not working effectively in Irish public administration. Hence the proposals to revive and improve the planning process on the macro level, to use departmental planning as a stimulus to departmental policy formulation, and to encourage the use of planning and financial techniques to this end. Some departments came to be equipped with planning units and with finance units, but, in terms of policy formulation, with indifferent success.

IMPLEMENTATION

There is a good deal of unhappiness at the quality of public management. Public bodies are huge information processing agencies, but much of the information revolution has still to affect them. We have seen some of the problems that arise in relation to personnel management, and the scant regard paid to the techniques of capital appraisal. There have been some staggering cost overruns. There are persistent complaints about the inadequacies of communications between public bodies. The system of central taxation is in a process of breaking down, and that of local taxation has largely done so. The attempt to manage the problems of the eighties with the methods of the forties and the fifties has largely failed; at the level of the special, management can often be very good; but at the level of general management there has too often been failure to cope with the increasing problems posed by size and complexity. Congestion of government from overload is a common modern disease. The importance of its diagnosis, much less its treatment, and the associated management problems have not with us been grasped. In 1973 a Department of the Public Service was established to act as a focus for structural, policy and management reform in the public service, but it has had little effect. Indeed, it has itself proved a significant part of the general problem. As against all this there have been striking, isolated successes. The Industrial Development Authority has been regarded internationally as a leader in its field and it has had much success in importing enterprise and in getting established new industrial technologies. The result has been very remarkable industrial growth especially in the new technologies and a quite phenomenal increase in exports on which Ireland, as a small open economy, so greatly depends. This has not solely been the work of the Industrial Development Authority—other bodies such as the Export Board, the Shannon Free Airport Development Company, and so on, have made significant contributions. These illustrate the practical advantage of single-purpose administrative bodies with clear mandates operating with significant degrees of autonomy.

CLIENTELE

The small size of the country, and perhaps something in the temperament of the people, tend to keep matters on a human, not too bureaucratic scale. Nonetheless, there are deep-seated problems of bureaucracy. Perhaps the most surprising feature revealed by our chart is the lack of any system of administrative institutions for the redress of grievances. There is nothing in Ireland that would remotely resemble the *Conseil d'Etat.* So far as other systems for the redress of grievances are concerned, Ireland lags far behind other common law countries such as the United Kingdom and the United States. There are a number of administrative tribunals, usually as adjuncts to the relevant departments, but they are *ad hoc* and unsystematized, and have laid themselves open to occasional criticism.

Perhaps too much reliance is laid on the informal, the ready access to ministers, and the willingness of parliamentarians to sort out problems of redress. The enormous volume of the representations made to public representatives gives an idea of the scale of the problem. An Ombudsman Act was passed in 1980 and an ombudsman was eventually appointed in 1984. He receives complaints directly from the public. His remit covers the civil service, local government, the health boards, and the two state-sponsored bodies for posts and for telecommunications that left the civil service in 1984. In 1985 he received close to 5,000 complaints of which he upheld, or assisted with, rather more than half (18). In all of this the approach is, as usual, special; so far as the administrative system is concerned the big *general* issues of citizens' rights, protection, redress and participation continue to be avoided.

We have now very limited institutions for local democracy, probably fewer than those of any other small democracy in Europe, and they have limited functions and discretion. In consequence there is not much provision for the rising tide of interest in participation in government in Ireland.

The systems of communication between government and people are not well developed and, on the whole, communication is very bad over the main range of public business. There is no access to current documents, except, occasionally, through the courts. Even to historical documents there is inadequate access. For example, in relation to Anglo-Irish and Irish-U.S. issues historians have too often to rely on British or United States official sources, being denied access to Irish ones of comparable date. A more enlightened information policy has often been promised but has not appeared. Also, there is little administrative concern for simplification of schemes and forms, so that clients are unnecessarily bewildered. Finally, there is only slowly mounting concern at the lack of adequate means to cope with the new technological assaults on the privacy of the citizen.

These failures have led to tension between administration and people. The people seem to have a totally disproportionate distrust of the administration which, whatever its failings, is honestly trying to serve them. In consequence, the administration itself develops a defensive and distrustful attitude to the people. This has been allowed, through neglect, to grow into a major problem of Irish public administration.

The decline in the quality and the authority of government has contributed to the aggressiveness of interest groups over a wide area of operation. Insofar as they represent taxpayers they have prevented attempts to close the budget deficit by increasing taxation. Insofar as they are defensive they have prevented the steps necessary to cut current spending. Insofar as they have mounted raids on the community as a whole—here public service unions have raided with the best—they have been notably successful and have further undermined the authority of government. These are games that can perhaps be played and tolerated in times of relative affluence, but the severe stringencies of the 1980s have provoked signs that government resistance to such activities will get a degree of public support.

What emerges is, of course, that the health of the democratic system also needs care, maintenance and some degree of development. Because democracy in Ireland has such deep roots, it tends to be taken for granted; but like everything else, it needs to be modernized, to be kept abreast of a society undergoing an unprecedented rate of change.

REVIEW

A system is closed, that is, becomes systematic, by a regular process of review—of how effectively resources have been used, of performance against objectives, and of the realism of future plans and projects. By this means the fruits of experience are steadily fed back into the system for improved performance. This process of review can be exogenous—conducted by some outside body; or endogenous—conducted within the system; or both. One can think of exogenous review as being either specific or conducted at regular intervals; and of endogenous review as being periodic and continuous.

The periodic exogenous review of Irish administration is the annual financial audit. For the civil service this is conducted on the British model by an officer of parliament, the Comptroller and Auditor-General, reporting to a parliamentary committee, the Public Accounts Committee, which scrutinizes the accounts as reported on and examines witnesses. The accounts of local authorities and health boards are examined by local government auditors, civil servants who report to the relevant authorities and boards. Those of the state-sponsored bodies are examined either by the Comptroller and Auditor-General or by commercial auditors who report to the boards of directors. These audits—except those of trading bodies—are primarily concerned with legality and regularity and, regular procedures having long since been established, now are of limited value.

In recent times a number of other parliamentary committees have been established, notably the Committee on State-Sponsored Bodies, first set up in 1978, concerned to review the accounts and reports of nearly all the "commercial" state-sponsored bodies. This has done useful work especially in the sphere of public information and shows promise of doing more; but it is too soon to say how far it can contribute to countering the serious decline in the quality of performance of many of these bodies. A Committee on Public Expenditure was established in 1983 but has yet to show its paces. The parliamentary question system has largely broken down from being overloaded with trivial matters of administration. Generally speaking, parliamentary review where it has taken place at all has not had any significant effects; for example, control of projected expenditure, either on capital or on current account, has tended to be formal, not real.

Less systematic, but much more forceful has been the judicial review of procedures, legality and constitutional implications of administrative acts.

Of the specific reviews, the Brennan Report of 1936 had little of substance to propose (19). More extensive was the report of the Devlin Group of 1969 (20). This body found plenty to recommend, chiefly the need to gear the higher civil service for the appraisal and review of policy and to recognize the logic of the growth and relative success of the state-sponsored bodies by hiving off executive work to bodies modeled on them. However, of its major recommendations only that for a Department of the Public Service was accepted and implemented. Only during 1982–85 had the Department the whole time attention of a cabinet minister. A 1985 White Paper (21) on civil service reform had little impact, apart from a decisive advance in promotion procedures for higher posts.

There have been individual reviews from time to time, especially when major problems cropped up in special areas. A notable example was the Dargan Report of 1979 on the telephone and postal services and the administrative impediments to good performance (22). This led to decisive action to set up these two services as statesponsored bodies. Two major and long-standing state-sponsored bodies, the national Electricity Supply Board and the national transport organization (Coras Iompair Eireann), have been subjected to several outside inquiries, one of which was to lead to some restructuring of the latter. Following widespread protests at the growing failure of the taxation system, a Commission on Taxation sat 1980 to 1985 and produced five radical reports, far too radical for a nerveless Government (23).

An important exogenous review mechanism has been the National Economic and Social Council, drawn from representatives of farmers, employers, trade unions, the civil service, and some others. In twelve years from 1974 this Council has published 83 reports on various operations of the administration; but with occasional exceptions— notably about the updating of industrial development policy—without much apparent effect on public policy-making. Generally one can say that, so far and for many years past, exogenous review has made little contribution to the development of the administration.

At the heart of the matter is the continuous and regular practice of endogenous review. The partial adoption of the Devlin proposals for finance and planning units went some way to institutionalize this, but the results have been disappointing. The Department of Local Government (now Environment) insisted on keeping to itself the question of the reform of local government while presiding over its disintegration during the 1970s and 1980s. In the 1970s it published a number of wholly inadequate documents on local structures and finances, none translated into action. Further proposals in 1985 promised some action, of which the most important seemed to be a commitment to some degree of devolution to local authorities of central government functions; but by the end of 1986 nothing noteworthy had happened (24).

CONCLUSION

In 1974, concluding on a theme closely related to that of this chapter, I wrote (25):

> When all is said and done, and the items on both sides added up, there is a substantial balance to credit. Ireland has a system of public administration that is basically sound, is remarkably devoted, diligent, and honest. The failings—that is to say the intellectual failings—that we have been touching on are now being transcended, at least in some degree. One can see many improvements that might be made. Nonetheless, I think one might say that, by comparison with a number of countries, we have not too much reason to be displeased with our system.
>
> One views the future of Irish public administration in a truly native mood of wary optimism.

Alas for optimism, wary or otherwise! The intellectual failings have been far from being transcended. Looking back one can see that the unresolved problems of structures, of policy formulation and management springing from and exacerbating those failings had by 1974 already taken firm root. The balance to credit has been much reduced.

Government, that is the cooperative effort of politics and administration, is in the last analysis about taking decisions, not least in relation to the machinery through which it conducts its business. It is not that the problems of that machinery have not been identified. It is not that many solutions, good or bad, to those problems have not been proposed. It is not that there is not significant public concern about those problems. What has been lacking has been the act of decision emerging from a sense of professional urgency as problems continue to grow in number and intensity.

In the mid 1980s it seemed that the issue of institutional development might once more be on the agenda. The Government published a three year plan (26) promising parliamentary reform, some reforms of public enterprise, a strengthening of civil service management, reform of the financial administration, and local government reform. Some small beginnings have been made. But of action commensurate with the scale of the problems there was, by the end of 1986, no sign.

REFERENCES

1. The best general introduction is B. Chubb, *The Government and Politics of Ireland* (London: Longmans, 2nd edn. 1982). This has an extensive bibliography. See also B. Chubb, *Source Book of Irish Government* (Dublin: IPA, revised edn. 1983). An annual directory to all bodies of the public service is *Administration Yearbook and Diary* (Dublin: IPA). IPA means Institute of Public Administration.
2. The standard modern history is F. S. L. Lyons, *Ireland since the Famine* (London: Fontana/Collins, 2nd edn. 1973).
3. R. B. McDowell, *The Irish Administration 1801–1914* (London: Routledge and Kegan Paul, 1964).
4. The standard work is J. M. Kelly, *The Irish Constitution* (Dublin: Irish Jurist, 1980).

5. A factual description is J. McG. Smyth, *The Houses of the Oireachtas* (Dublin: IPA, 4th edn. 1979).

6. See T. J. Barrington, *The Irish Administrative System* (Dublin: IPA, 1980, 1981).

7. P. C. Humphreys, *Public Service Employment, An Examination of Strategies in Ireland and Other European Countries* (Dublin: IPA, 1983), Ch. 3.

8. S. Dooney, *The Irish Civil Service* (Dublin: IPA, 1976).

9. Devlin Report—Public Services Organisation Review Group, 1966–69, *Report* (Dublin: Stationery Office, 1969), Ch. 13.

10. There is no recent or comprehensive picture of the state-sponsored sector but see G. FitzGerald, *State-Sponsored Bodies* (Dublin, IPA, 2nd edn., 1963), and T. J. Barrington, "Public Enterprise in Ireland," *Annals of Public and Co-operative Economy* (Liege) 56 (July–Sept., 1985).

11. Joint Committee on State-Sponsored Bodies. *Irish Shipping 1985* (Dublin, Pl.3091).

12. The standard account is D. Roche, *Local Government* (Dublin, IPA, 1982).

13. Review Body on Higher Remuneration in the Public Sector, *Reports* (Dublin: Stationery Office, continuing).

14. Two useful accounts of this period are J. A. Murphy, *Ireland in the Twentieth Century* (Dublin: Gill & Macmillan, 1975), and J. J. Lee (ed.), *Ireland 1945–70* (Dublin: Gill & Macmillan, 1979).

15. T. K. Whitaker, *Interests*, (Dublin, IPA, 1983).

16. See, *passim*, F. Litton (ed.), *Unequal Achievement—The Irish Experience 1957–82* (Dublin: IPA, 1982) for a wide ranging discussion of these issues.

17. E.g., the official publication, *A Better Way to Plan the Nation's Finances* (Dublin: Stationery Office, 1981).

18. R. M. Stout: *Administrative Law in Ireland*, (Dublin: IPA, 1986); *Annual Report of the Ombudsman, Ireland 1985* (Dublin: Stationery Office, Pl. 3748).

19. Brennan Report—Commission of Enquiry into the Civil Service 1932–35, *Report* (Dublin: Stationery Office, 1936).

20. See n. 9.

21. *Serving the Country Better* (Dublin: Stationery Office, 1985, Pl. 3262).

22. Dargan Report—Posts & Telegraphs Review Group 1978–9, *Report 1979* (Dublin: Stationery Office, 1979).

23. Commission on Taxation, *Reports*: 1. Direct Taxation, Pl.617, 1982; 2. Incentives, Pl.1755, 1984; 3. Indirect Taxation, Pl.2136, 1984; 4. Special Taxation, Pl.2917, 1985; 5. Tax Administration, Pl.3142, 1985. (Dublin: Stationery Office).

24. Department of Environment, *The Reform of Local Government, Policy Statement*, 1985. See also Munitir na Tire: *Towards a New Democracy?* (Dublin: IPA, 1985).

25. T. J. Barrington: "Some Characteristics of Irish Public Administration", *Administration* (Dublin) 22 (Autumn 1974), 233.

26. *Building on Reality 1985–1987* (Dublin: Stationery Office, 1984, Pl.2648), Ch. 3.

12

Switzerland

ULRICH KLÖTI
University of Zurich, Zurich, Switzerland

THE ENVIRONMENT

Functions, structures, and processes in the Swiss administrative system cannot be discussed without taking into account the general conditions of Swiss politics.

Geographically, Switzerland is a relatively small country (6.4 million inhabitants on 41.3 km^2) in a mountainous region in the heart of Europe. Transit traffic and tourism therefore have had a long tradition. Although there are no mineral resources or raw materials besides water, the Swiss economy has managed to produce one of the highest gross national products per capita (39.500 sFr. in 1985) in the world. Efficiency is considered an important value.

Culturally, Switzerland is marked by two important crosscutting cleavages. German (spoken by 65 per cent of inhabitants in 1980 as their mother tongue), French (18.4 per cent), and Italian (9.8 per cent) are the official languages of the federal administration (1). All bills and laws have to be published in the three versions. The first Constitution of 1948 can be understood as the conciliatory solution of a civil war between the two main religious denominations. Today religion is no longer a salient issue among Catholics (47.6 per cent of inhabitants in 1980) or Protestants (44.3 per cent) (2).

The basic institutional and political order is marked by a number of characteristics. These remain of great importance whether they are praised as unique and reliable or whether they are criticized as obsolete and unable to meet the necessities of our time.

First, Switzerland is a *confederation*. On each of the three levels, federal, cantonal, and communal, authorities can decide more or less autonomously on certain matters. According to the Swiss constitution, the 26 cantons (states) exercise all rights not explicitly entrusted to the federal power (3). The cantons, in addition, are responsible for most of the implementation of federal laws. At the same time they participate in the policy-making process at the federal level. The cantons have to be consulted prior to the enactment of most legislation. These are considered important reasons for the slow and late development of federal government and administration.

Second, the provisions of *direct democracy* affect all stages of the political decision-making process. Amendments to the constitution and revisions thereof are subject to a mandatory referendum. New and revised articles of the Constitution enter into force only if they have been adopted by a majority of the Swiss citizens and a majority of the cantons (4). Federal laws, generally binding federal decrees, and important international treaties face the possibility of an optional referendum. They must be submitted to the people for approval or rejection if 50,000 Swiss citizens entitled to vote or eight cantons so demand (5). These two instruments give the pre-parliamentary procedures a particular weight. The federal government and the bureaucracy have to seek a prior consensus among interest groups in order to avoid a failure of bills in the popular vote. We shall show below how the federal administration manages and influences this bargaining process. The popular initiative has different implications. It consists in the request of 100,000 Swiss citizens entitled to vote, aiming at the introduction, the repeal or the modification of specified articles of the federal constitution (6). This right is to be viewed as the voter possibility of asking new political questions and of exerting pressure on established forces in government and administration.

Third, Switzerland has a *non-parliamentary system* of government. The executive is not based on a majority in parliament as it is in the British model. The Federal Council (government) is elected by the Federal Assembly (two chambers of parliament) for a four-year term. The "supreme executive and governing authority" can be overthrown only after each renewal of the lower house (National Council). This provision partly explains the relatively strong position of the Federal Council compared with the two chambers of the Federal Assembly which, in addition, are still not fully developed as a professional parliament. The decision-making capacity of the government is further emphasized by its small size. Since 1884 the Swiss Federal Council has consisted of no more and no less than seven members. The president of the executive body changes every year. The seven members govern collectively on a basis of "equality among colleagues." This system of collegiality has the effect that, if a consensus cannot be reached, the Council is unable to issue general instructions. The administration profits from this circumstance.

The combined factors of federalism, direct democracy and non-parliamentary, "collegial" government result in a system which cannot be easily compared with other countries. The uniqueness of the institutional arrangement affects the system of administration in many ways.

STRUCTURE

Central Government Organization

The basic structure of central government has never been changed. Since 1848 the constitution has constantly fixed at seven the number of ministries, which are called *departments* (7).

Most other countries have more ministers. And in most other systems, the creation, the dissolution, and the restructuring of ministries is government routine. In Switzerland, the question of enlarging the cabinet was debated on several occasions. Twice, in 1900 and in 1942, there was a public vote about it. In each case the Federal Council was successful in keeping government and the number of ministries small.

Looking closer at the ministries, it becomes evident that there were some innovations nevertheless. Several of their names were changed. The "Political Department" became the "Department of Foreign Affairs," the "Railway Department" changed into the "Department of Transport and Energy," and the "Department of Finance and Customs" lost the last part of its name. But the "Department of Interior," the "Military Department," the "Department of Justice and Police" and the "Department of Public Economy" have not altered their names.

Names do not tell the whole story. The seven ministries have grown considerably. As Table 1 (8) and Fig. 1 (9) show, the number of offices directly subordinated to the federal councillors has reached 72. Part of this development is due to the Military Department being reorganized by distributing classical tasks among more offices. New offices were created in the Department of Interior (physical planning, protection of environment, education and sciences) and in the Department of Public Economy (economic development, housing). These offices could only be devised after an article for each one was introduced in the constitution giving the federal government the competence to act in the field.

Reforms

Organization and structures are very rigid in Switzerland. Hence administrative reforms are even more difficult to realize here than elsewhere. In the mid-sixties, after the so-called "Mirage affair," when several political and administrative mistakes were made as the Military Department ordered a series of Mirage combat planes, a wide reform debate was started (10). In two reports (11) by expert commissions, and in the message of the Federal Council containing proposals for parliament, the following points were discussed.

> The *size* of the Federal Council was not to be changed for numerous reasons. A large government would make it impossible to maintain the system of "collegiality." This system allows for a better distribution of power; no single person (president or prime minister) can rule alone. This makes proportional representation possible. Interests of parties, regions, linguistic and religious groups can be represented in government more evenly. Through the four largest parties, 80 per cent of the electorate are represented in government. Two federal councillors at least have been representatives of the linguistic minorities. Not more than one member of government may be elected from one canton at the same time. In addition, the collegial body acquires better knowledge and more experience. Its smallness facilitates coordination and guarantees continuity and stability.

> In order to relieve the federal councillors from their heavy administrative burden, it was proposed to introduce the institution of *state secretaries*. The result of this discussion was modest. Two directors of important federal offices (foreign affairs and trade) now hold the title of state secretary which offers them a better position in international negotiations. On the other hand, their title does not change their function or rank within Swiss administration.

> *Staffs* were another device proposed to support the directory level of government. As a result, each department was equipped with a coordinating secretariat. More important: the Federal Chancellery was upgraded. From an office which dealt with administrative routine and translations only, it developed into a modern staff agency which organizes the decision-making process of government. The Chancellor can be considered an eighth member of the Federal Council although he does not have the right to vote.

Table 1   Switzerland: Offices and Personnel in Federal Departments

Department (Ministry)	Personnel			Offices		
	1930	1950	1987[e]	1928	1959	1984[c]
Foreign Affairs[a]	506	1521	1769	1	4	5
Interior	734	1489	7341	7	12	15
Justice and Police	200	495	1352	6	6	9
Military[b]	2553	10225	14791	15	11	22
Finance[f]	3355	5586	6115	7	8	8
Public Economy	200	1399	1791	6	6	8
Transport and Energy[d]	109	209	519	3	6	5
Chancellery and Courts	112	190	437	–	–	–
Total	7769	21114	34115	45	53	72
PTT	21385	28943	58121			
Federal Railways	34305	36896	37391			
Federal armament factories	2131	4773	4900			
Total	65590	91726	134527			

[a] Diplomats included.
[b] Without armament factories.
[c] According to "Staatskalender der Eidgenossenschaft" (*Federal Yearbook*). Secretaries-general not counted.
[d] Post, Telephone, Telegraph (PTT) and Federal Railways (SBB) not included.
[e] Budget of 1987.
[f] Administration of Alcohol and Customs included.

Two other measures with the aim of narrowing the span of control were discussed. A new *hierarchical level* between the department and the office was proposed for two of the civilian departments. However, this solution of the so-called "group," which was rather successful in the Military Department, was not adopted in the other ministries. The second measure proposed by the expert reports, was a new assignment for twelve offices. At the end of a long process, finally four offices changed from one department to another (military insurance, sports, road construction, administration of grain).

Originally, parliament had the right to organize and reorganize the federal administration. In order to obtain more flexibility, it was proposed that this right be given to the Federal Council. However, parliament kept the right to create new offices and to define their tasks. In the case of reassignment of offices, parliament can now veto the proposals of the Government. Stability is valued more highly than flexibility.

It is safe to conclude that the long process of reforming the federal administration has not reached its goals of rationalizing government and of improving the working conditions for the federal councillors.

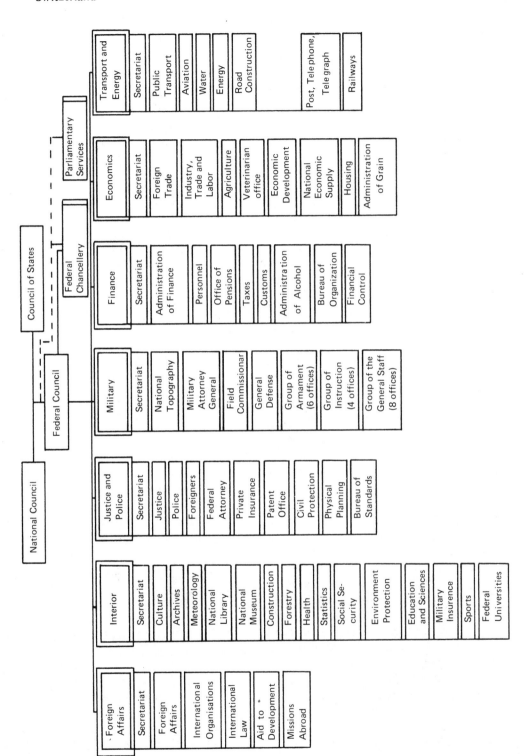

Figure 1   Offices in Federal Departments.

Decentralization

Politically and legally, Switzerland has followed a centralizing trend like most federations. The constitution lists more and more tasks and rights entrusted to the federal power. The cantons kept their full autonomy in a limited number of policy areas only. The most important ones are primary education, churches, health (hospitals particularly), taxes, and organization of their own political system within the limits of the federal constitution.

Administratively, however, the Swiss system has remained highly decentralized. Most of the federal legislation is implemented by the cantons. Besides customs and defense, there are no policy fields in which the federal government has its own executing administration. It is worth noting particularly that there is no federal police corps. The federal police bureau deals with policy formulation only. It does not apply regulations.

In many cases federal law is implemented by the *communes* (local governments), although, according to constitutional law, the federal government does not communicate with the communes directly without contacting the cantons first. Nevertheless, local government is very important. Communes can levy their own income taxes within a frame set by cantonal law. This leaves a considerable autonomy to local government. Cities as well as small communities are still in a good position to solve problems like running schools, fire brigades, civil protection, local physical planning and transportation, water and energy supply etc. on their own.

Two indicators in Table 2 (12) illustrate the growing importance of the lower levels in the Swiss federal system. For the last forty years, expenditures of the federal government have diminished relatively. In 1946, immediately after the second World War, the federal government spent more than half of the total expenditures of all three levels. In 1980, its share was less than one third. Furthermore, about 25 per cent of the federal budget is transferred annually to the cantons and communes as subsidies or revenue sharing. Financially, cantons and communes have been in a better position, at least for the last ten-year period, than the federal government.

The same development can be shown regarding personnel. In 1910, almost half of the public servants were employed by the federal government. By 1980, this share had dropped to about 30 per cent. The fastest growth has taken place in the administrations of the communes, particularly in the big cities.

The structure and functioning of the 26 cantonal administrative systems cannot be described in any detail. Four generalizations can be made. First of all, the administrations of the cantons vary dramatically in size. The smallest canton (Appenzell Inner Rhodes) has fewer inhabitants than the larger cantons have public servants. Second, cantonal administrations have developed autonomously, have grown their own traditions and are organized in different ways. There are from five (Aargau) to nine (Berne) ministries. The Political composition of the Government differs according to the political strength of parties. Third, due to their different geographic, economic and financial situation, the cantons have to deal with different problems. Whereas in some mountainous regions, cantons have to invest much of their resources in the development of tourism, some urban cantons are more preoccupied by the problems of traffic, higher education, youth and economic development. As Switzerland is small, the urban centers of the large cantons serve as economic, social and cultural centers for some other cantons. Fourth, as a result of differences in size, resources,

Table 2   Switzerland: Federal Government's Share of Expenditures and Employees

	1910[a]	1930[a]	1946[b]	1950	1960	1970	1980
Federal expenditures as percentage of total expenditures of federal, cantonal and communal levels			51	38	35	32	31
Federal employees as percentage of total of federal, cantonal and communal employees	47	41		41	39	35	30

[a]No statistics available for communal expenditures.
[b]No statistics available for non-federal employees.

organization, and socio-economic situation, public services are delivered unequally in the various cantons.

PERSONNEL

Status of Public Servants

In most modern societies, public servants have a special legal status. On one side, they are offered particular rights and privileges. On the other side, they have certain duties. In Switzerland, the special regulations for public servants are kept at a strict minimum. Therefore, working for a public service is not much different from working for a private enterprise. For employees who are hired on the basis of ordinary contracts, there is no important legal difference at all. Officials enjoy some minor privileges.

Swiss officials are appointed for four years. They cannot obtain tenure, but their risk of losing their job is small. Reappointment is routine. Only about thirty federal officials were not reappointed on the last occasion (less than 0.1 per cent). Even the highest civil servants stay in office when the political head of a department, the federal councillor, changes. They almost have to commit crimes in order to be dismissed. Incompetence is no reason for not being reappointed. Although the security of Swiss civil servants is better than for private employees, they have more duties of loyalty to their superiors.

The most important of these is that they have no right to strike. Their rights of co-decision and participation are also limited.

Salaries in the public service are comparable to those in private enterprise, although they have not always developed at the same rate. During the crisis of the thirties, the public sector lowered them less than did the private sector. In the fifties, it is assumed that civil servants were paid less than employees in private business, as seems to be the case in the USA at least at the upper levels. The compensation for a smaller income was job security. During the boom of the sixties, the public service had some difficulties in recruiting qualified personnel, so salaries were raised, sometimes even above the level of private business. Today, it is hard to say whether the private or the public sector pays more attractive salaries. It depends on the profession, on the hierarchical rank and on the branch of the private sector with which the comparison is made.

Every type of occupation is listed and ranked in a "classification of offices" (*Aemterklassifikation*). Every position is linked with a class of salary. Table 3 shows the hierarchy with some examples of positions and professions and with the maximum salary. This maximum is reached after eight to nine years of service. A young academic with a university degree usually starts in class 7 and rises to class 3 during his or her career before obtaining a leading position as a chief of a section. The so-called "over-class" (*Ueberklasse*) is subdivided into six groups. The highest class, with a maximum of about sFr. 200,000, was reached by only about a dozen persons in 1985.

The classification of offices is not always flexible enough. If new professions with a shortage of qualified labor—e.g., computer specialists—are not adequately ranked, it is difficult for the administration to recruit the personnel. Special treatments are not possible. Efficiency bonuses are unknown at least in the federal administration. As a rule, on the lower levels the public sector is relatively attractive, whereas in the director ranks the private sector seems to pay much higher salaries.

The hierarchical structure has changed drastically. In 1952, 59 per cent of the personnel occupied positions in the classes 21 and lower. Today less than one third belongs to this group. At the upper end there has been considerable growth. In 1955 there were 56 positions in the over-class (13). Now there are more than 400.

Salaries are adapted to inflation almost automatically at the end of every year. In 1985, Swiss federal servants still worked 44 hours a week. A reduction of the weekly working hours to 42 was introduced in 1986. A vacation of four weeks, and of five weeks after the age of 50, is the rule.

Salaries, working hours and vacations of the federal administration are about Swiss average. Any improvement of the working conditions of federal public servants usually has to be followed by the cantons, cities, and finally by private business as well. The federal administration is the pace-maker on the Swiss labor market.

Discussions in parliament on labor legislation for the public sector are closely followed by trade-unions as well as by employers' organizations. Federal personnel are organized in different unions. The Association of Public Servants (*Verband des Personals öffentlicher Dienste*/VPOD) is linked with the main trade union and with the social-democratic party. The Association of Federal Personnel (*Bundespersonalverband*) is not related to a particular party, but defends liberal policies. The Christian unions have a smaller section for personnel in federal administration as well. Finally, there is an Association of Higher Civil Servants in federal administration, defending the interests of officials in class 3 and above.

Recruitment and Career

The Swiss administrative system is relatively open. For most positions in the public service, no formal qualifications are required. It is still possible, although it is the rare exception, to become a director of an office without having an academic education. There are no schools or preparation courses for the different categories of personnel. A National School of Administration like the *Ecole Nationale d'Administration* (ENA) in France has never existed. In Switzerland, young people learn a profession without deciding in advance whether they are going to work for the private or

Table 3 Switzerland: Classes of Salary 1986

Classes	Example	Maximum p.a. sFr.
Over-class	Director of office	ca. 200,000
1,a	Vice-director	119,906
1	Chief of division	109,050
2	Chief of section	99,575
3	Assistant to chief of section	90,126
4–7	Scientific personnel	82,008
11	Bookkeeper	58,789
12	Architect	56,735
13	Craftsman	54,743
15	Social worker	50,784
17–19	Secretary, typist	46,800
21	Driver	39,691
24	Copyist	37,141

for the public sector. Whenever a post is vacant, an invitation to apply has to be published. Competition is open. Everyone who fulfills the professional requirements can apply. No examinations have to be passed.

There are exceptions to these rules. The career of diplomats is strongly regulated. After taking an entrance examination future diplomats spend two years as trainees in different services. If they pass a second examination, they follow a hierarchical scale. After several steps which are taken every four or five years, they usually become ambassadors at the age of 45 to 55. A similar career regulation exists for army instructors.

In the other branches of the public service, careers are similar to the ones in the private sector. In 1969, when the only study of careers in the Swiss federal administration was undertaken (14), 106 out of 332 higher civil servants (diplomats not counted) worked for more than one office in the course of their career. Only 22 came from the private sector. On lower levels of the administration, horizontal mobility seems to be more important. It has grown substantially over the years.

Representation

Openness of competition for most posts in federal offices is guaranteed because of the political need for equal representation of the numerous minorities in Switzerland. Most important are the linguistic groups.

Table 4 (15) shows that linguistic groups are represented proportionally to their demographic importance. Two exceptions must be mentioned. In the entire federal bureaucracy, French is underrepresented. And, politically more important, among directors and their substitutes, German predominates. Italian and Romansh, the third

Table 4 Switzerland: Linguistic Groups in Federal Administration (percentage)

Mother tongue	Total administration (1972)	Second class and higher (1979)	Directors and their substitutes (1979)	Swiss[a] citizenry (1980)
German	76.5	73.6	78.8	73.5
French	15.4	20.9	19.0	20.1
Italian	5.2	3.5	2.2	4.5
Romansh	0.8	0.6	–	0.9
Other	2.1	1.4	–	1.(
Total	100	100	100	100
N	38,653	2,153	184	

[a]Percentages for citizens are different from those of the entire population.

and fourth national languages, are the losers, whereas French is represented almost correctly. The German over-representation is particularly felt in the departments of Economy and Finance. The French-speaking have maintained their strong position in Foreign Affairs. Language problems have become more salient in recent years, mainly because of the growing importance of the welfare state which regulates more social fields than fifty years ago. As most of the drafts (about 90 per cent!) for new bills are conceptualized and first written in German, the linguistic minorities have the impression that they are ruled by a majority whose way of thinking is still quite different. And it is probably true that the German mentality dominates legislation in Switzerland.

The other traditional political cleavage in Switzerland has lost much of its significance in federal administration. Catholics are still slightly underrepresented among the higher civil servants. But religion is no longer an important factor in most political problem areas.

The most salient issue at the moment is the proportional representation of political parties in the higher civil service. Since 1959 the Federal Council has been a great coalition of the four largest parties in the country. The Liberals (*Freisinnigdemokratische Partei*: FDP), the Christian-Democrats (*Christlichdemokratische Partei*: CVP), the Social-Democrats (*Sozialdemokratische Partei*: SPS) each could claim two seats, and the People's party (*Schweizerische Volkspartei*: SVP) one seat, according to their electoral strength. This distribution of seats is called the "magic formula" (Zauberformel). The same proportionality is not found in the higher civil service. Urio found that almost half of 111 high officials whom he interviewed in 1980 were members of or closely related to the Liberal party, which governed alone until 1881 and which had a majority until the second world war. The Christian Democrats, who have had at least two seats on the Council since 1919, were still under-represented a few years ago. They have recovered in recent years, however. The Social Democrats, who entered government in 1943 only, still are in a marginal position in the higher civil service. According to Urio, they occupy only five of the 111 posts (16).

Women are even more under-represented in the higher ranks of the federal administration. It was only in 1973 that the first woman reached an over-class position. In

1984 three women were directors or vice-directors of federal offices. In 1978 only, 1.6 per cent of the personnel in class 4 or higher were women. Not much has changed since 1971 when women got their right to vote on the federal level. It will be many years before women have a fair chance to rise to the top of the federal administration.

DECISION-MAKING

Government Decisions

The decision-making process in the Swiss federal system of government and administration is guided by three principles. Article 103 of the federal constitution states that

decisions are to be taken by the Federal Council as a body (principle of collegiality);

the affairs of the Federal Council are to be distributed among its members according to departments (principle of departments); and

federal legislation may authorize the departments or their offices to settle certain matters directly (principle of delegation).

The system of departments has been explained in the section on organization and structure. Delegation is possible within the legal framework (for policy implementation and the application of norms and rules). When Swiss federal departments or offices make their decisions while executing laws, this is not much different from the similar activity in most other administrations.

More interesting is the process of *policy formulation* in a collegial body. The decisions of the Federal Council are preceded by an extensive two-stage procedure. First, a consultation on the level of offices takes place. Second, the departments engage in a "procedure of co-reports" (*Mitberichtsverfahren*).

Whenever an office which is in charge of preparing a new bill wants to make a proposal to the responsible head of department, it has to consult all other offices inside and outside its own department which are possibly affected. In every case, the office of justice gives its advice on legal questions and the administration of finance is consulted because of possible consequences in expenditures and personnel. The Federal Chancellery reviews the language used and judges the comprehensibility of a new bill. More important is coordination between offices with conflicting goals and viewpoints. Of course, not all points in dispute can be solved at this stage. This consultation procedure takes about two months.

The second step, the "procedure of co-reports," is more formalized. It must be carried out before the Federal Council can make a decision. It starts with a head of a department submitting a proposal for circulation. The Federal Chancellery, which organizes the procedure, sends the proposal to all departments, inviting those particularly interested in the matter to write a report. Any department can raise objections to the proposal or express consent. Through the Chancellery, every department is informed about the points of view of all others. Then the submitting department has to defend its proposal or to accept objections. Its written opinion is again distributed to all other departments. A second or even a third round can take place before the proposal is discussed and decided upon in session by the Federal Council.

The written procedures of consultation allow for a meticulous exchange of arguments between the offices and departments concerned. They are a useful preparation for the Government's meetings, which are relieved from discussions of minor points. Though they have this advantage, they may lead the federal councillors to highly departmental points of view. Councillors are not compelled to study the matters of departments other than their own. And if they do, they often check only whether a proposal contains points which could be against the interests of their own department. The result is negative coordination. Common goals are not necessarily pursued. Planning and the pursuit of global perspectives become difficult if not impossible, and the collegial body is weakened.

The Federal Administration in the Political System

The federal administration has a very strong position in the Swiss political system. This may seem surprising with regard to *implementation*, which is the affair of the cantons for most legislation. In spite of this delegation, the Confederation maintains a supervision over the administrative acts of the cantons. In many cases the implementation of federal laws by the cantons is accompanied by heavy subsidies. This gives the federal administration a means to impose sanctions upon the cantons for insufficient implementation. The small cantons with little resources depend on the federal offices because they need the know-how of the central administration in order to implement federal legislation satisfactorily.

Federal administrators can influence *policy-making* in many ways, as well. Processes of decision-making can be initiated by different actors. The popular initiative was mentioned above. However, only in a very few exceptionai cases has this instrument been used to initiate a new policy-making process. In the classic theory, parliament initiates new legislation. In practice, however, less than half of the legislative activity can be traced.to motions or proposals of members of parliament. More important is the initiative of the federal administration itself.

In any case, every move towards new legislation is handled by the responsible federal office first. The administration can then decide whether there will be a policy-making process at all and when it will be started. The first preparatory step usually consists of the analysis of the problem. At this stage, the administration is responsible for the inquiries and for the selection of the specialists who will give their advice. The department appoints these experts to a commission and fixes the tasks of the commission and the time when it has to report. In more than 60 per cent of the cases, the administration controls the work of the expert commissions by supplying the secretariat. Also, almost one third of the members of expert commissions are federal civil servants.

After the group of experts has finished its preparatory work, a procedure of consultation with the main interest groups, the cantons and the political parties takes place. The interpretation and evaluation of the results of this procedure is again in the hands of federal administrators. By giving different weights to certain arguments, they can influence the decision-making process considerably. This is even more important because they alone control the next step: they write the official proposal and the accompanying reports addressed to the Federal Assembly.

The administration has possibilities of influencing legislation even at the parliamentary stage. The head of the responsible department and its top officials play an important role when the committees of the two chambers discuss the proposals. The Swiss non-professional, part-time parliament depends heavily on the expertise of federal administrators.

Of course, the federal bureaucracy cannot legislate without the approval of the Federal Council and parliament, and hence without taking into account the political, social, and economic forces of the country. However, it is institutionally in a very good position for mediating between the different interests and can bring in and defend its own conceptions in many instances.

Control

Looking at the constitutional arrangements alone, one might expect that the federal administration is under no parliamentary control. The Federal Assembly cannot overthrow the Government. Federal councillors remain in office for ten years on the average. There are no secretaries of state. Officials even in top positions do not leave when a federal councillor retires. Parliament seems to have no means of controlling the administration effectively.

This impression is not correct: After the "Mirage affair," the Federal Assembly was equipped with quite efficient instruments of control. Two standing committees do a great part of the work. The Committee on Finance not only checks budgets and accounts, but with the help of a small delegation and a professional secretariat examines the financial transactions of the federal administration. The other commission investigates the non-financial conduct of administrative business. Every year, two or three offices fall under special scrutiny.

Parliament is only in charge of a general supervision of federal administration. It is the Federal Council, being the supreme executive and directing authority, which is responsible for a close control of the activities of officials and employees of the federal administration. Besides a typical hierarchical organization, there are several special agencies which guarantee control of administrative acts. (Administration of Finance, Bureau of Organization, Justice, etc.). Politically the Federal Council cannot delegate responsibility. An ombudsman is not yet institutionalized in federal administration. Though there is a plan to introduce this new citizen's advocate, it has not yet been carried out partly for financial reasons. As most of the federal legislation is implemented by the cantons and as the communes solve many problems autonomously, citizens have little direct contact with federal administrators. Therefore, no urgent need for an ombudsman is felt on the federal level. The city and the canton of Zurich have had ombudsmen for some years.

Finally, it should be noted that a federal administrative and disciplinary appeal jurisdiction is well developed. Complaints against instructions issued by the federal administration can be raised with the Federal Council. The Administrative Section of the Federal Court adjudicates administrative litigations and disciplinary cases without further appeal. The Federal Court itself deals with a small part but a growing number of complaints. It is also the last stage of appeal against orders issued by the governments and administrations of cantons.

A COMPARATIVE PERSPECTIVE

In a comparative perspective, five characteristics distinguish the Swiss federal administrative system.

1. The federal administration is *small*. Decentralization is one reason. Implementation of federal legislation is delegated to the cantons and communes. Efficiency may be another reason. Even if civil servants of cantons and communes are included, the public sector is smaller than in most other developed democracies.
2. The federal administration is *structurally rigid*. The number of ministries and the main principles of organization are fixed by the constitution. Reorganizing and reassigning offices to departments is difficult and can be done only with the consent of parliament.
3. The federal administration is characterized by great *stability*. Structural innovations are the exception. The party composition of the Government has not changed since 1959. Federal councillors average more than ten years in office. Top civil servants even outlive them. The result may be insufficient flexibility in policy-making.
4. The federal administration is *effective* and *efficient* in implementation. Personnel are highly qualified, well trained and generously paid. Their performance is constantly compared with that of counter parts in private enterprise. Detailed control has been developed into a very powerful instrument. Working hours are long and strikes have never occurred.
5. The federal administrative system is *responsive*. Federalism and administrative decentralization bring offices closer to the public. Proportional representation of the main traditional political minorities makes them feel that they are administered legitimately by their own people.

Rigidity, structural conservatism and inflexibility—they are the price which has to be paid for efficiency, effectiveness and responsiveness.

REFERENCES

1. *Statistisches Jahrbuch der Schweiz 1983* (Swiss Statistical Yearbook 1983) Basel: Birkhäuser, 1983, p. 37.
2. *Statistical Yearbook, op. cit.*, p. 41.
3. *Constitution of the Swiss Confederation*, article 3.
4. *Constitution*, article 123.
5. *Constitution*, article 89.
6. *Constitution*, article 121.
7. *Constitution*, article 95.
8. Germann, Raimund, in: Klöti, Ulrich (Ed.), *Handbuch Politisches System der Schweiz*, (Manual of the Swiss Political System) vol. 2, Bern: Haupt, 1984, p. 56.
9. *Eidgenössischer Staatskalender 84/85* (Federal Yearbook) Bern, 1984.
10. Urio, Paolo, *L'affaire des mirages* (The Mirage Affair), Genève: Médecine et hygiène, 1972.
11. *Expertenbericht über Verbesserungen in der Regierungstätigkeit und Verwaltungsführung des Bundesrates* (Report on improvements of the Federal Council's activities of government and directing administration), Hongler-Bericht, Bern, 1967; *Bericht und Gesetzesentwurf der Expertenkommission für die Totalrevision des Bundesgesetzes über die Organisation der Bundesverwaltung* (Report and Proposal of the Commission of Experts about the Total Revision of the Federal Law on the Organization of the Federal Administration), Huber-Bericht, Bern, 1971.
12. Nüssli, Kurt, "Zentralisierung—Tatsache oder Fiktion?" (Centralization—Reality or Fiction?) in: *Schweizerisches Jahrbuch für Politische Wissenschaft*, 23/1983, p. 45–64.

Durrer, Hans: *Die Entwicklung des Personalbestandes im öffentlichen Dienst der Schweiz 1910-1960* (The Development of Personnel in the Swiss Public Service), Zürich: Keller, 1967.

13. Klöti, Ulrich, *Die Chefbeamten der schweizerischen Bundesverwaltung* (Higher Civil Servants of the Swiss Federal Administration), Berne: Francke, 1972.

14. Klöti, Ulrich, *op. cit.*

15. *Rapport du Conseil fédéral sur sa gestion en 1980* (Report of the Federal Council on its Management in 1980), p. 234 f.

16. Urio, Paolo, *Le rôle politique de l'administration publique* (The Political Role of Public Administration) Lausanne: Loisirs et Pédagogie, 1984.

REFERENCES IN ENGLISH

Baylis, T. A., "Collegial Leadership in Advanced Industrial Societies: The Relevance of the Swiss Experience," *Polity* 13, (1980), 33–56.

Boeschenstein, H., "Bern," in D. C. Rowat, ed., *The Government of Federal Capitals.* Toronto: University of Toronto Press, 1973, 285–94.

Codding, George Arthur, *The Federal Government of Switzerland.* Boston: Houghton Mifflin, 1961.

Friedrich, Carl J., and Taylor Cole. *Responsible Bureaucracy: A Study of the Swiss Civil Service.* Cambridge, Mass.: Harvard Univ. Press, 1932.

Huber, Hans., *How Switzerland is Governed.* Zurich: Schweizer Spiegel, 1968.

Hughes, C., *Switzerland.* London and Tonbridge: Benn, 1975.

Hughes, C. J., *The Parliament of Switzerland.* London: Cassel, 1962.

Kerr, H. H., *Switzerland: Social Cleavages and Partisan Conflict.* London and Beverly Hills: Sage, 1974.

Luck, J. M., ed., *Modern Switzerland.* Palo Alto, California: Society for the Promotion of Science and Scholarship, 1978.

McRae, K. D., *Conflict and Compromise in Multilingual Societies: Switzerland.* Waterloo: Wilfrid Laurier University Press, 1982.

McRae, Kenneth D., *Switzerland: Example of Cultural Coexistence.* Toronto: Canadian Institute of International Affairs, 1964.

Meylan, Jean, "Switzerland," in Donald C. Rowat, ed., *International Handbook on Local Government Reorganization* (Westport, Conn.: Greenwood Press, 1980), 72–84.

Schmid, C. L., *Conflict and Consensus in Switzerland.* Berkeley: University of California Press, 1981.

Steiner, J., *Amicable Agreement versus Majority Rule: Conflict Resolution in Switzerland.* Chapel Hill: University of North Carolina Press, 1974.

13

Austria

HEINZ SCHÄFFER
Institute of Constitutional and Administrative Law, University of Salzburg, Salzburg, Austria

HISTORY AND ENVIRONMENT OF ADMINISTRATIVE SYSTEM

Austria nowadays is a small country which has inherited its administrative structure and the style of its administration in general from the notedly good administration of the old Austro-Hungarian monarchy (Habsburg empire). The shrinking of the administration to the proportions of a small country, the development of a real federalism in this small country and especially the challenges of the modern welfare state are the main problems and tendencies in the modern Austrian administration.

Historical and Environmental Influences

Austria, situated in the core of central Europe, is a small federal state of 83,850 km^2 and approximately seven million inhabitants. It got its present boundaries after the dismembering of the Austro-Hungarian monarchy and once again after World War II (by the Vienna State Treaty 1955). From the natural preconditions it is mostly characterized by alpine regions. Economically it has recovered as a developed industrial state. Politically it has a permanent neutral status and plays an active political role between the western and eastern block systems.

As to the most important historical influences, one has to point out the steadiness of the organizational structures and behavioral attitudes of the Austrian administration. Only the most remarkable points of administrative history (1) can be mentioned: the official style of formulating and recording (registering) administrative files has been mostly influenced by the reforms of Emperor Maximilian (16th century) and Empress Maria Theresia (18th century). The period of Empress Maria Theresia and Emperor Joseph II can be characterized as a period of centralization, a grand design of rationally constructed administrative organization and a unified administrative hierarchy throughout all crown lands. Moreover, two basic concepts of the Austrian administration can be traced back to the spirit of enlightenment in the era of Joseph II: (a) that it is the function of the public administration to care for the well-being of its citizens like a good father by stabilizing public order and by undertaking necessary reforms and (b) that administration requires a special ethical standard of the public service personnel.

The modern administrative structure was introduced after the 1848 revolution (together with the constitutional responsibility of government towards the monarch). Since then Austrian administrative organization has been characterized by a ministerial (departmental) system. The district administrative authorities (*Bezirksverwaltungsbehörden*) were installed as the lowest level of "general" state administration throughout all crown lands. Further main features were the granting of self-government to the local communities and the beginnings of a non-territorial self-administration (chambers of commerce). In the following era industrialism and political liberalism were the causes of the development of a very elaborate administrative law. The basic idea of the "rule of law" was realized in the 19th century for large parts of the administration by the enacting of numerous laws and by the protection of individual rights by an administrative court. In the 20th century the world wars and economic crises were the reasons for the development of an administratively directed economy and the completion of a large-scale system of social security. The codification of administrative procedures in 1925 became a model for numerous other European countries.

Constitutional and Political Framework

Since 1918 Austria has been a republic, and since 1920 a federal state. The federal parliament is bicameral, formed by a lower house (*Nationalrat*) and an "upper house" (*Bundesrat*), of which the latter ordinarily is only entitled to a suspensive veto. In the beginning the federal constitution provided a strictly parliamentary system, as the federal government was elected by the lower house. Since 1929 the system also contains features of a presidential system, as the federal president (directly elected by the people) appoints the federal government. Nevertheless, the system can be characterized as parliamentary, because the federal government requires the lower houses confidence and can be removed by a vote of censure. After 1945 Austria returned to the constitutional situation of the so-called First Republic. Remarkable stability after World War II can be explained by a relatively stable spectrum of political parties (a conservative Austrian People's Party, a social democratic Socialist Party and a smaller Liberal Party), and a special political style and climate of cooperation. This cooperation has been cultivated for a long time during the period of the "Grand Coalition" (2) and in the framework of the so-called "Social Partnership," i.e. the cooperation of the great chambers and interest groups with each other and with the public administration.

Unusual Features of the System

1. An Administrative State *Par Excellence*

Austria can be called an administrative state *par excellence*. Its public administration not only forms a part of the political system but has become a dominant feature of the civic culture, penetrating all spheres of life by regulating, ordering, financing, subsidizing, promoting and planning activities. In its style Austrian administration still combines some traditions of the preconstitutional authoritarian state with the modern welfare state. The situation can be best characterized by an often quoted aperçu of Metternich: "Austria is not governed but administered . . . ."

2. The Concept of Legality

According to article 18 of the federal constitution all executive/administrative actions must be based on legislative acts. This constitutional principle has become a key for

Austrian public administration not only because of its wording, but even more because of the interpretation that it receives in constitutional life. It is a fundamental basis for the spirit and work of Austrian public administration that every administrative action must be precisely regulated by statute law in such a way that it is clear which administrative authority may act in a certain case, according to which determined procedural provisions, and must come to determined results on the basis of law. The principle is valid for all administrative authorities and is guaranteed additionally by administrative and juridical review procedures as well as by provisions for the liability of federal and state offices and officers. Austrian public administration does not differ from others in the sense that the rule of law is a constitutional principle, but by the fact that this principle is applied more strictly and seriously and thought to be more fundamental than in other administrations. According to this interpretation, law not only sets limits to administrative action but it is thought to be an indispensable pre-condition for every administrative action. Thus, according to the Austrian constitutional concept the division between legislation and administration is the following: all important questions, especially the response to and engineering of social change have to be decided as a political function by democratic legislation, whereas administration in principle is a dependent apparatus for execution, not entitled to make policy on its own.

In recent years it has become clear that the rule of law, as understood in Austrian public administration, has not only the positive effect in many fields that administrative activity can be foreseen and controlled, but also negative effects. The requirement of legal regulation has led to an inflationary production ("flood of norms"), which could even paralyze the concept of legality (3).

The legal normalization of administrative acts has been pushed ahead very intensively especially in the sphere of the classical sovereign (i.e. authoritative) administration (*Hoheitsverwaltung*), but on the other hand it has led to an opposite tendency. Whereas by a progressive legal determination discretionary powers have been nearly removed, perhaps inevitably certain new discretionary margins have been created by the use of indefinite legal terms (e.g. relating to "a price justified by political economy") or vague guidelines for administrative decisions (if they are "in the interest of the economy," "appropriate," or needed for promptness, simplicity and economy of costs, etc.), and also by reference to non-legal standards (e.g. "as the technical standards require"), or by ordering legal regulations to be implemented through administrative planning activities.

Moreover, blind confidence in regulations can in many cases lead to a strictly legal interpretation without consideration of the purpose of the regulation. Sticking to regulations tends to release superior organs and the general public from responsibility. The scholarly community and the public have become aware of these problems and are now warning not to continue over-regulation.

3. Atypical Federalism

The Austrian system deviates in some respects from the classical model of federalism. As to the division of powers, there is not only a political preponderance of the federation (*Bund*) over the states or provinces (*Länder*), but also a peculiar and highly complicated constitutional arrangement—even compared to Switzerland and Western Germany. This can be explained by the following reasons.

The constitution distinguishes between legislative and executive powers and distributes both types, independently of each other, the consequence being that the administrative realm of the federal or state governments does not always follow from the corresponding legislative realm.

Though certain federal administrative matters are charged to federal offices, the greater part—according to a constitutional provision—must be administered by the state governments on the district and state level. State authorities thus fulfill federal administrative tasks—so-called "indirect federal administration" (*mittelbare Bundesverwaltung*). In these matters federal ministries are only competent in administrative review, if a special legal clause provides so, as well as for planning, coordination and issuing orders and decrees of federal scope.

This system was established when the imperial and provincial administrations of the former Austro-Hungarian monarchy were merged into one administration at the state level (1920 and 1925). Certainly the system shows the features of an "administrative federalism;" but one must not underestimate the benefits of this simple administrative structure as well as the state administration's closer relation to the people and the possibilities to take into consideration state and regional interests.

Further anomalies of Austrian federalism are the following. The judiciary is an exclusively federal matter, and there are no state courts for historical reasons. More peculiar and more important, the distribution of powers between the federation and the states refers only to the field of sovereign (governmental) action of the administrative authorities (*Hoheitsverwaltung*); it is not binding for the so-called private economy administration (*Privatwirtschaftsverwaltung*), i.e. if the federation or the states as legal entities participate in economic affairs on the basis of private and commercial law. This form of administrative action, moreover, is not bound by the strict principle of legal pre-determination. Accordingly some important fields of economic and administrative life are either weakly or not at all legally determined (e.g. subvention matters and matters of placing orders), and are left to the "private" initiative of the state or federal governments. The effect is that both levels can take even concurring initiatives (e.g. in subsidizing public housing or weak industries or supporting regions).

Another anomaly is the lack of financial provisions in the federal constitution. The distribution of powers does not include the right of taxation. These questions are regulated in a special constitutional law (*Finanz-Verfassungsgesetz 1948*) (4).

In principle the federal, state and local governments must finance their own activities. The states can get federal support for activities, but they have to bear even those costs which are caused by fulfilling federal tasks within the framework of the "indirect federal administration." The distribution of taxation powers is not decided upon directly in the constitutional law, but is left to a special federal law concerning the distribution of financial burdens and the competences concerning the different types of taxes (finance equalization law). Although the states are left the right to find new sources of taxation, most of the taxes have already been "invented" and distributed in favor of the federation. The finance equalization law is negotiated between the federation and the states for a period of five years, but can be modified unilaterally by the federal legislator. On the whole, the financial side of Austrian federalism shows clearly unitarian features.

4. Maintenance of Continuity and Expertise

Austria's political history of the 20th century was shattered by several radical changes. Leaving out especially the German occupation of Austria, the well-trained bureaucracy was able to provide continuity and administrative stability. This was possible only because the concept of "servant to the state" was so strong that the change from monarchy to party democracy and to different political regimes could take place without severe problems on the administrative level. Also, the fact that Austria recovered after both world wars is largely due to its good administration.

Bureaucracy is an indispensable expert for policy formation in the political process. This can be seen clearly from the circumstance that more than 80 per cent of all federal bills originate in the ministries (5). Besides having this eminent role in law drafting, where all professional views and outside expertise (e.g. from interest groups) are integrated, bureaucracy even supports the legislature directly by civil servants acting as committee experts, counsels and secretaries.

5. The Influence of Interest Groups

Finally, a special feature of Austrian administration is the integration of interest groups and chambers into the administrative and political system. Some tasks are delegated from the public administration to the self-administering chambers (which are legally provided professional self-administration bodies with public law status). For many administrative matters legislation has installed advisory boards (*Beiräte*), in which the interest groups can articulate partly their expert opinion, partly their interests. The federal or state administrative authorities usually orientate their decisions according to the compromises arrived at in such advisory boards. Some important matters which could be regulated administratively (e.g. prices) are normally left to the interest groups, which handle and solve problems by collective agreements in the framework of so-called "social partnership" (6). By guaranteeing the results through a self-discipline of their members, they make state interference unnecessary. In other fields of the partly directed economy (especially the sectors of milk, cattle and cereals), regulations and subsidies are negotiated between the administration and the economic organizations (interest groups and chambers).

STRUCTURE AND MANAGEMENT OF THE SYSTEM

Central Government Organization

Central government organization on the top level shows a duality of heads: on the one hand the federal president, on the other hand the chancellor and the federal ministers. The president is assisted only by a rather small staff of civil servants not belonging to the ministerial service, and in principle he can act only on the proposal of the federal government. The chancellor is a prime minister. In legal terms he is only one of the ministers, albeit "primus inter pares;" but naturally as a political leader he plays an important role, as he proposes the list of ministers to the president and can even propose the recall of a minister.

The federal administration is structured according to the typical European ministerial-departmental system. The cabinet is a political forum and coordinates the activities of all ministeries. As a collegial authority, the federal government is competent only in a few cases. Acting as a—unanimous—board is especially necessary for voting a draft bill. Besides that, the whole administration is divided among ministries. The structure of the ministerial system has become more and more differentiated in the last decade; nowadays there are thirteen ministries (7): 1. chancellory; 2. ministry for foreign affairs; 3. for economic affairs; 4. for labor and social affairs; 5. of finance;

6. of interior; 7. of justice; 8. of defense; 9. for agriculture and forestry; 10. for environment, youth and family; 11. for education, arts and sports; 12. of public economy and transport; 13. for science and research.

The federal ministers regularly are politicians, seldom non-political experts. They are equal in rank and directly accountable to parliament. Sometimes they are supported by state secretaries or deputy ministers (*Staatssekretäre*); these second highest federal officers belong also to the leading political personnel, but constitutionally they are bound to the instructions of their minister and do not have a vote in cabinet.

All other positions are filled by civil servants. The ministries internally are divided into departments (*Sektionen*) and the departments are regularly subdivided into sections (*Abeilungen*) which are usually grouped for several areas and sometimes combined into groups of sections. There is a direct line of instructions from the minister to the department head to the section's head. In addition to the linear structure there may optionally exist special staffs (cabinets of ministers, policy-making groups, research groups or coordination groups). In the direct federal administration there may also exist outside offices on the federal, state or district level, such as the federal tax and police authorities (8), or offices for special purposes (e.g. the new federal office for environmental protection).

Indirect federal administration is carried out on the state level by the governor (*Landeshauptmann*) and on the district level by the district commissioner and his office (*Bezirkshauptmann, Bezirksverwaltungsbehörde*). In this function the state organs are bound by the instructions of the minister and accountable to him. Administrative review is ordinarily possible in two steps: after the exhaustion of administrative appeals, a complaint to the Administrative High Court or to the Constitutional Court is admissible.

State Administration

There are nine states in the federation (Burgenland, Carinthia, Lower and Upper Austria, Salzburg, Styria, Tyrol, Vorarlberg, Vienna). Vienna is at the same time a state and a municipality, and the municipal officers are both municipal and state officers. According to the principles of the federal constitution the state government (*Landesregierung*) is a collegial body which is in charge of all state administrative matters. It consists of a coalition of all political parties in the state parliament, and its decisions are based on majority rule. It is supported by the office of the state administration which is staffed with civil servants and which also carries out the indirect federal administration for the governor. Below the governmental level are the districts of the state administration which in principle are competent for all administrative affairs, though special authorities may exist (e.g. state tax authorities, real estate transaction boards). In state administration, review regularly goes to the government, against whose decision a complaint is possible to the Constitutional Court or to the Administrative High Court.

Decentralized Organization

Spheres without state intervention are the internal affairs of the religious communities and the collective labor relations. As a decentralized and therefore autonomous form of public administration can be mentioned the territorial self-administration by the muncipalities and the non-territorial self-administration by the chambers (professional self-administration), by social insurance bodies (social self-administration) and by the universities (cultural self-administration). In all cases there is an autonomous sphere and a delegated sphere of administration. In the autonomous administration there is no instruction by review to state authorities but only a state's supervision; nevertheless, after the exhaustion of remedies an appeal to the Administrative High Court or to the Constitutional Court is possible.

Municipalities form the lowest level of public administration. In some cases they fulfill tasks of the federation (e.g. income tax matters) or of the state (e.g. citizenship). Most important self-administration competence they are charged with is building permits and zoning plans. The chambers are legally provided interest groups with public law status, e.g. the chambers of trade, labor, and agriculture as well as the chambers for attorneys, notaries, physicians, etc. Social insurance bodies are formally organized as self-administration bodies, but practically they have become mighty bureaucracies of their own beside the state administration. Universities nowadays have a reduced autonomy and are administered for the most part by the federal ministry for science and research.

Another type of decentralized organization is the region. Regions are not self-administering bodies; but regions of different size, sometimes with regional boards, are used as basis for public planning and subsidizing activities at a supra-municipal but sub-state level.

Public Corporations

Nationalization after World War II was the way Austria rescued property assets formerly occupied by Nazi Germany, and introduced the recovery of the war-rotten national economy. Most of the shares of commercial companies are held by some nationalized banks and a federal holding company. As a result Austria has a "mixed economy," with approximately 59 per cent directly or indirectly in the state sector (9), which is an important, but also problematic, instrument to fight unemployment. Moreover, numerous funds and public corporations have been created to steer and to administer public tasks with big financial implications and a long duration, e.g. hydraulic engineering, highway construction, financing of hospitals, etc. Also, in recent years there has been a trend to separate several tasks from public administration into corporations (e.g. the federal salt works, pawn brokery, printing office, publishing house, and postal bank) (10).

Structural Reforms and New Management Techniques

Reforms and new techniques have been adopted in the last decade. Most of the states have modified their structure of local government by creating fewer and bigger, more functional municipalities. In the federal ministries the internal organization has been reformed by new organization plans and new standing orders for filing, recording and registering. Moreover, the sequence of operations has been simplified by means of automation and the use of computers. It has become rather usual for ministries to order research work and use expertise. In some administrative sectors computer-based or -aided systems are used, especially for prognoses in economic and taxation policies.

These reforms, in the beginning, had no immediate influence on the style of leadership. But the top civil servants are nowadays trained in administrative academy institutions and become acquainted with modern management methods. In this connection a more cooperative leadership style and more delegation of tasks are propagated.

PUBLIC SERVICE PERSONNEL

Classes and Numbers of Personnel

The public service personnel fall into two classes. First are civil servants appointed by an authority on the basis of public law provision and whose employment is in principle not terminable. This is the traditional type of so-called "pragmatical" officers (*Beamte*). Second are employees under contract on the basis of special private law provisions (*Vertragsbedienstetengesetz*). This formal distinction is important from a juridical point of view, but practically it has become less and less meaningful, because the status of those classes has become rather similar as to their protection in labor law and by social insurance, and because there is in principle no reservation of functions for the pragmatical officers, the only exception being some top functions in the ministries reserved to these officers.

The federal service is divided into different branches: 1. officers of the "general administration"; 2. judges and district attorneys; 3. university teachers; 4. school teachers; 5. officers for school supervision; 6. police officers; 7. officers of the army; 8. postal employees. All this shows the multiplicity of administrative tasks in the modern state; moreover, the Austrian public service includes occupations and sectors which in other countries often would belong to the private sector (e.g. railroads, public utilities, hospitals and schools of all levels) (11).

Therefore Austria is notorious for its rather large bureaucracies: approximately 290,000 federal, 120,000 state and 70,000 municipal employees, a total of nearly half a million, which seems high in relation to the population and the active labor force (2.9 million). Nevertheless Parkinson's law of steadily expanding bureaucracies does not seem to be verified in Austria's case. The number of public employees was rather stagnant in the 1930s and in the 1950s, and the personnel expenditure has been rather stable at 30 per cent of the yearly federal budget. The secular growth of administrative tasks is reflected only in the personnel statistics of some branches and not in general; expanding sectors were the school and university teachers, the police force, and—especially on the state level—health institutions, whereas the core of public administration, especially the higher civil service, remained stagnant or decreased over the long run.

Recruitment, Promotions, Positions and Pay

In the old monarchy it was usual for officers to start in the provinces, and qualified ones were called to the ministerial service, a tradition which was ended in the federal republic. Nevertheless, the first republic had inherited the well-trained bureaucracy of the old multinational empire, which even guaranteed bureaucratic continuity after World War II. But with the change of generations, at least after World War II, the public service lost its historical background of a privileged group and was gradually transformed into a professional group like others, open to all strata of society, and nowadays recruited from the general labor market.

Although in the beginning of the republic there was the idea of a unified administrative corps, even based on a constitutional clause, this program never could be realized. Especially the states used to staff their offices from the regional labor market, and mobility decreased, because the states offered better salaries than the federation. Uniform rules were not issued, and in 1974 a constitutional law acknowledged the practically separate personnel policies and staff regulations of the federal and state legislatures. Nowadays federal ministries recruit their staffs directly, as there exists no central federal recruitment institution.

Leaving aside the payment conditions, which are very important on the labor market, the structures of the federal and state systems are still similar. In Austria the public service is not based on a position, but on a merit (career) system. There are five groups of careers (A, B, C, D, E), different in payment; for the highest career (A) a university degree is necessary. Within this system the public servant advances biennally in payment and can be promoted to a higher group according to his record and according to administrative directives after a certain period.

The scheme of salaries is negotiated with the public service unions and is afterwards codified to the details in the laws regulating the public service. In general, the differences between the lowest and the highest classes of personnel have been diminished in the last decade. In general public service personnel are paid somewhat lower than personnel in the private sector, owing to their greater social security.

Public Service Unions and Political Rights

As a special type of social partnership, practically all problems and amendments of public service law are negotiated between the federation, the states and the union of municipalities on the one hand and a committee of four public service unions (general/ public service, railroad workers, post and telegraph employees and municipal/civil servants). This is a form of global participation. It must not be mixed up with the representation of the public personnel in federal and state authorities which is based on special public law provisions and gives the personnel a direct participation at the office level, but does not go so far as to install a civil service chamber.

The political rights of public servants are not legally restricted in any respect. But civil servants are expected to guard the secrets of their office and not to comment on the policies of their department, unless they say that this is their private opinion.

THE BUREAUCRACY AND POLICY-MAKING

The Policy-Making and Budgeting Systems

It has become usual that any new government sets up a government program. This not only serves for realizing the political program of a party, but is usually based mainly on a compilation of the bureaucracy's current projects. For the administration steadily observes the needs of the population and the statements of the political forces and tries to keep going a continuous process of reform and adaptation. Leaving aside some fields of politics, in which traditionally the social partnership is active (politics of wages, prices and connected questions of directing the economy and subsidizing agriculture, where the state practically only ratifies the policies of the interest groups), usually the preparation of legislative initiatives and therefore the bulk of the policymaking is in the hands of the central bureaucracy, whose expert knowledge is indispensable. The bureaucracy negotiates with the great interest groups, drafts the laws, and even cares for and supports the legislative process in parliament.

As to the budgeting system, parliament is formally the sovereign over expenditures, public properties and debts. Whereas in the constitutional monarchy the budget vote of parliament was a limitation of the monarchy executive, in a modern democracy the parliamentary vote has no reasonable limit, for the government is practically identical with the majority fraction of parliament. As in many other states, group interests in Austria have heavily burdened the state budget, as has the special policy of deficit spending (Austro-Keynesianism), which has been used for fighting unemployment. But this policy cannot be continued indefinitely and has been criticized in recent times. A special technique to gain more flexibility in budget execution and to avoid political opposition has been the organized "flight from budget," whereby in many cases administrative tasks are managed by an extra-budgetary financing: public corporations or special funds permit long-term financial planning and the raising of capital on the market without charging the current budget, although in the long run this involves a liquidation of debts or at least a liability of the state.

The budget is prepared in the typical classical way, the agencies ask their central offices for the necessary credit, the ministries ask the ministry of finance. The expenditure plan is finalized by the ministry of finance, the staff plan, by the federal chancellor.

The totals of the requests are cut back in negotiation rounds of top civil servants according to budgetary guide-lines of the minister of finance with the political backing of the chancellor. Afterwards the budget is negotiated on the minister's level and voted in cabinet. The budgetary directives are prepared and based on a computer-aided simulation model in the ministry of finance, but also on evaluations and pre-estimations of a small expert bureaucracy of the scientific advisory board of the social partnership groups. Nevertheless, this is in principle the traditional trial-and-error method of preparing the annual budget. It does not include an official mid-term financial planning system, PPBS or a zero-based budgeting system. The result is that the maneuvering room for economic policies has become rather small (maximum 15 per cent) because the greater part of the expenditure is fixed by legal provisions or political necessities (12).

The Top Civil Servants

In Austrian law there does not exist a type of "political" civil servant (as e.g. in Western Germany). Therefore, the top civil servants—head of department in a ministry (*Sektionschef*), head of the office of state administration (*Landesamtsdirektor*)—have to play the role of a liaison officer and interpreter between the leading political personnel and the bureaucracies. If he does his part well, he delegates the tasks "in the line," coordinates the occasional consultative staffs and gives specialized advice and information for political decisions to his minister or deputy minister with a good sense for the politically possible. Sometimes, yet, especially if a top servant cannot fulfill this function to the best, informal structures become more important; advice and information may come then rather from a minister's cabinet or from a civil servant of lower position in the hierarchy, who has the politician's confidence.

As to the education and social background of top civil servants, as has been mentioned already, the older generations of bureaucracy have been replaced by a new generation: this one comes from all strata of society and regards itself mainly as an efficient corps of white collar workers.

At the beginning of the era of the Grand Coalition there was established more or less a quota system in personnel appointments (not only for the top posts!) according to the proportional strength of the two great political camps. The unusual and unique system of the Grand Coalition nearly made the parliamentary system ineffective. The really important political decisions were taken in a small coalition committee, whose decisions were ratified—so to say, rubber-stamped—by parliament. Thus the Grand Coalition was a system of balance between the two big parties, a balance of collaboration as well as one of distrust. It worked mainly on the basis of dividing spheres of influence. In most cases the minister of one party was given a state secretary (deputy minister, *Staatssekretär*) of the other party—not so much as an aide, but as a cross control. Also, party patronage became an integrating factor in the political system. The ministries were filled up with partisans. Top civil servants did not and still do not need to be party members, but from the viewpoint of a minister's party they have to be "reliable" persons.

Even in the following era of one-party governments (since 1966), patronage continued to form a part of the political and bureaucratic system, working on the basis of an informal understanding of the political parties. Respecting legal provisions against political transfers of public employees the patronage methods have become somewhat more subtle: although the party in power is formally free in its decisions, it permits the opposition party to present or nominate candidates for a certain percentage of positions (e.g. a quarter of posts in federal ministries). Therefore, even after fifteen years of Socialist government (since 1970), there is still to be found in the federal civil service a remarkable share of sympathizers of the conservative People's Party.

The top bureaucrats thus have close ties with the political leadership. Also, public employees with political and organizational talent often become parliamentarians. In the course of time the political penetration of the public service has been expanded to nearly all levels, a fact which is regretted and criticized in public. Nevertheless, on the lower levels political affiliation is not a requirement and does not strongly touch the political creed and attitudes of the public employees. The bureaucracy still feels and acts as a loyal executive instrument of the duly elected, democratically legitimate government.

Generalists and Specialists

The Austrian bureaucracy traditionally has been stamped by the legal training of its top ranks and has developed a particular legalistic culture. According to the former legal education, jurists at least up to the 60s, were really versatile. The principle of legality still is valid and regarded as fundamental. But the situation has somewhat altered, as there is no longer a monopoly of the jurists in administration, and jurists have become more specialized in law. The complexity of modern administration requires more and more specialization; particularly on the state level certain technological, medical, cultural, agricultural and other specialized tasks predominate and require appropriate qualification. In the higher federal service legal questions, planning, policy-making, international relations and commerce dominate the work. Personnel policies have taken these developments into account and have opened new positions to social scientists and academically trained persons in diverse disciplines. Highly specialized officers are particularly employed in the federal tax administration.

ADMINISTRATIVE ACCOUNTABILITY

The Role of Parliament and Parties

The administration is accountable to parliament via the political and constitutional responsibilities of highest officers (federal ministers, state governments). Practically these controls in a system of parliamentary government have to rely on the effects of parliamentary work on public opinion, otherwise they are practically ineffective, because the possible sanctions (the strongest being a vote of no confidence and impeachment before the Constitutional Court) would require a majority vote in the lower house of parliament. According to the constitutional doctrine the vote on the budget is also regarded as an instrument of parliamentary control (*ex ante*). For the same reasons this, too, is not really an effective control: the opposition may point out mistakes, problems and possible consequences, but cannot alter the government's policies.

Control of Expenditure

Parliamentary control of expenditure has a long tradition (200 years) in Austrian administration. The court of audit has existed since 1867. In the republic its competence has been steadily extended. On behalf of parliament it controls the entire federal administration, and in addition the administrations of states and of the municipalities with more than 20,000 inhabitants. It also controls the social insurance bodies (since 1948) and state-owned companies, as well as other public corporations, funds and institutions under public control. Recently the states have created additional state audit offices.

The federal court of audit (13) is headed by a president and a vice president, who are elected by parliament (lower house) and whose responsibility is analogous to that of a federal minister. The members of the federal court of audit are public servants under the direction of the president. The office is organized quite similar to a federal ministry. It is independent from government, but bound to instructions and orders it gets from parliament. Its control function is mainly post-audit of the budget execution, but also the authentication of debts in the ledger of indebtments. Its control aims at economy, expediency and correctness of administration. It works particularly on the psychological level, since the administration fears its unveiling of abuses and malfunctions. It is exercised steadily *ex officio*, but special control activities can be ordered by parliament and even demanded by a one-third minority, i.e. in practice by the opposition. The court reports annually to parliament on its control activities, especially on whether the criticized mistakes have been rectified in time or not at all. Its report is discussed in the competent committee and in plenary session.

The Courts and the Ombudsman Board

The ordinary courts are strictly separated from administration. The traditional control of administration is bestowed on two public law courts. The control of constitutionality is exercised by the Constitutional Court (as already by its predecessor being the *Reichsgericht*, which was established in 1867) and the control of legality is exercised by the Administrative High Court (existing since 1876). After the exhaustion of administrative remedies an appeal (complaint) can be addressed to the mentioned courts by the individual against any sovereign (i.e. authoritative) administrative action infringing his rights. Illegal administrative acts are reserved by the respective court, obliging the administrative authorities to render a legal decision or to restore the lawful situation. The Constitutional Court moreover has the function to control even generally binding normative rules meaning that it can abrogate illegal decrees and ordinances. This control system combines the separation of powers (judiciary/administration) with an elaborate judicial review, but it includes only illegal sovereign actions of administrative authorities.

This is why an additional ombudsman-like institution was established in 1977. A collegial board of three independent members, elected by the lower house of the federal parliament, forms the so-called People's Attorneyship (*Volksanwaltschaft*). It may investigate *ex officio* or on an individual's complaint any administrative action, even if carried out in the forms of private law. Seven of the nine states, too, have accepted this control institution for their administration by special clauses of their state constitution (14). The institution has no sanctions, but only makes recommendations and published critiques. Nevertheless, because of its influence on public opinion, this informal control has become very effective.

Public Administration and the Public

Public opinion is an important control factor. It becomes more and more critical and the mass media even intensify this effect. A certain tension, however, exists between the traditional principle of official secrecy as enacted in the federal constitution (1920) and the modern information obligation as enacted in the Federal Ministries Act (1986). At any rate there is no general public access to documents, a situation which certainly will be changed in the near future with special regard to planning activities and ecological problems which always affect and interest a broader public. For a long time Austrian public administration has been heavily influenced by interest groups, partly by interventions and partly via advisory boards, commissions and working groups (more than 200 on the central federal level). In the last decade the public administration has undertaken strong efforts to offer more service and openness to the citizens and to realize administrative reforms step by step.

The main aims have been: 1. a consolidation of the legal texts as well as a reduction of regulations; 2. improvements in the public personnel system; 3. improvements in the organization of the federal administration; and 4. developing the service function of administration. As to the latter, there have been installed specialized inquiry units in the federal ministries which procure information material and blank forms and give information about the competence of the ministry and who is the official in charge. The printed forms have been simplified to some extent. Moreover, the ministries try to inform people of their rights and about the administration's service and activities, especially by means of brochures (15).

CONCLUDING COMMENTS

Administration is a prominent aspect of the modern state. Its bureaucracy guarantees continuity, administrative stability and functional expertise. In Austria, as elsewhere, the administration is inevitably becoming more professionalized. Notwithstanding its transition from bureaucratic organization towards modern service-oriented forms, the administration still preserves some signs of old-Austrian traditions, particularly: 1. a loyal bureaucracy with deep respect for the principle of legality and a rather legalistic culture; 2. a strong consciousness of hierarchy and of the limits of its legal competences; 3. a tradition of cooperation with other administrative agencies and interest groups, which pay partly curb initiatives, but still favors a general climate of mutual understanding and cooperation.

Moreover, Austrian administration is characterized by a complicated federal structure with a rather subtle division of powers between federation and states, to which is added a comparably detailed catalogue of the municipalities' autonomous competences. And in Austrian constitutional and administrative tradition these distributions of power are interpreted rather strictly; in principle, one does not acknowledge the concept of implied powers. Therefore, if new problems require responses which cannot be found within the framework of written competences, the constitution has to be amended or the situation necessitates difficult negotiations between the federation and the states. New complex problems, such as ecological questions, in the beginning often cause a demand for uniform federal regulations. But in recent years the political self-consciousness of the states has grown. They ask the federation for consultations and, if necessary, for a bargain of competences ("cooperative federalism"). In this situation the federation has a constitutional and political preponderance, as the amendment of the federal constitution and the final decision on the distribution of financial resources belongs to the federal government. Therefore, the Austrian administrative system—in comparison with Federal Germany and especially Switzerland—shows some unitarian features. As a result, sometimes the real federal character of Austria has been doubted. Nevertheless one can say that Austria's structure is a federal one and not only that of a decentralized or regionalized unitary state like France or Italy.

In local administration the autonomy is constitutionally guaranteed and based upon a liberal tradition more than a hundred years old. In practice its results are not always the best. Especially in building survey and local planning, exceptions and misuse of power may occur by local administrative officers because of local and personal interests instead of respecting the public interests. Even more important, many of the municipalities have overestimated their economic possibilities in the course of time. The local budgets often are overburdened and indebted by expensive installations (sports facilities, indoor swimming pools, etc.) and by communal enterprises. The supervision by the states, mainly focused on questions of legality, in practice seems too weak. But this is, perhaps, not an Austrian peculiarity, but due to a general phenomenon in Western democracies of the welfare state type: very often there is no effective denial or sufficient obstacle against social demands if economic reasons would require a cutback of public deficit-spending and debt.

The most remarkable differences of the Austrian compared with other administrative systems derive from Austria being not only a state dominated by two strong political parties, but also a "chamber state." The chambers as autonomous bodies of professional self-administration cover nearly all fields of social life. By nominating members to advisory boards they heavily influence a good deal of the public administration on the federal and state level; by giving their expert opinion and advice they influence legislation and are fully integrated into the political process.

REFERENCES

1. For Austrian administrative history see especially Stolz, Otto, *Grundriss der österreichischen Verfassungs- und Verwaltungsgeschichte* (Innsbruck: Tyrolia, 1951) p. 162; Hellbling, Ernst, *Österreichische Verfassungs- und Verwaltungsgeschichte* (Vienna: Springer, 1956), pp. 118 and 287; Link, Christoph, "Die Habsburgischen Erblande, die böhmischen Länder und Salzburg," in: Jeserich—Pohl—von Unruh (eds.), *Deutsche Verwaltungsgeschichte* I, p. 468; Hoke, Rudolf, "Österreich," in: Jeserich—Pohl—von Unruh (eds.), *Deutsche Verwaltungsgeschichte* II (Stuttgart: DVA, 1984), p. 347.

2. Steiner, Kurt, *Politics in Austria* (Boston: Little, Brown and Company, 1972), pp. 168 and 278.

3. As to the phenomenon "flood of norms" see Schäffer, Heinz, "Austria, Quantitative analyses of the sources of law in Austria," in: Schäffer, Heinz—Racz, Attila—Rhode, Barbara (eds.), *Quantitative Analyses of Law. A Comparative Empirical Study. Sources of Law in Eastern and Western Europe* (Budapest: Academiai Kiado, 1988).

4. See Melichar, Erwin, "Die österreichische Finanzverfassung," and Wissgott, Franz Xaver, "Finanzausgleich in Österreich," in: Andreae, Clemens-August, *Handbuch der österreichischen Finanzwirtschaft* (Innsbruck, etc.: Tyrolia, 1970), pp. 13–22 and 59–73; Ruppe, Hans Georg, *Finanzverfassung im Bundesstaat* (Vienna: Jupiter, 1977); Pernthaler, Peter, *Österreichische Finanzverfassung* (Vienna: Braumüller, 1984), especially pp. 119 and 157; Schäffer, Heinz, "Die österreichische Finanzverfassung," in: Weigel, Wolfgang—Leithner, Eckhardt—Windisch, Rupert, *Handbuch der österreichischen Finanzpolitik* (Vienna: Manz, 1986), pp. 87–106.

5. Regularly more than three quarters of the legislative initiatives come from government. See e.g. Wittmann, Heinz, "Regierung und Opposition im parlamentarischen Prozess," in: *Österreichisches Jahrbuch für Politik 1979*, pp. 39 and especially 44.

6. As to the famous "social partnership" see e.g. Knoll, Reinhold—Mayer, Anton, *Österreichische Konsensdemokratie in Theorie und Praxis. Staat, Interessenverbände, Parteien und die politische Wirklichkeit* (Vienna, etc.: Böhlau, 1976).

7. According to the Federal Ministries Act 1973 (*Bundesministeriengesetz*), as recently re-published 1986 and amended 1987. Moreover, according to article 77 paragraph 3 of the federal constitution there have been installed (by decree of the federal president) two additional federal ministers with special tasks within the organizational framework of the chancellory: i.e. for health and public service; for federalism and administrative reform.

8. It should be noted that there are no state police.

9. See Drennig, Manfred, "Vermögensverteilung in Österreich—ihre politische Relevanz," in: Fischer, Heinz (ed.), *Das politische System Österreichs*, 2nd ed. (Vienna: Europaverlag, 1977), p. 481.

10. Löschnak, Franz—Tieber, Herbert, *Vom Amt zum Unternehmen. Bundesbetriebe— öffentlich und selbständig* (Vienna: Schriftenreihe der Gemeinwirtschaft, 1984).

11. For the system of public service in Austria and empirical data see Schäffer, Heinz, "Verwaltungspersonal," in: Wenger, Karl—Brünner, Christian—Oberndorfer, Peter (eds.), *Verwaltungslehre* (Vienna—Cologne: Böhlau, 1983), pp. 181–226.

12. See explanatory notes to the yearly federal budget, federal ministry of finance.

13. Hengstschläger, Johannes, *Der Rechnungshof. Organisation und Funktion der obersten Finanzkontrolle in Österreich* (Berlin: Duncker & Humblot, 1982).

14. The people's attorneyship has not been accepted by the states of Tyrol and Vorarlberg. (In Vorarlberg, since a recent constitutional reform, there exists a separate state people's attorney.) The federal people's attorneyship gives a yearly report to

parliament about its activities. See Rossmann, Harald, "Volksanwaltschaft und Grundrechtsschutz", in: *Österreichische Juristenzeitung 1979*, p. 169 and Rowat, Donald C., *The Ombudsman Plan* (Lanham, London: University Press of America, 1985), pp. 145.
15. See *Verwaltungsreformbericht 1980*. Schriftenreihe zur Verwaltungsreform 3 (Vienna: Bundeskanzleramt, 1980).

REFERENCES IN ENGLISH

Crane, W., *The Legislature of Lower Austria*. London, 1961.

Haller, Herbert, "Vienna," in Donald C. Rowat, ed., *The Government of Federal Capitals* (Toronto: Univ. of Toronto Press, 1973), 181–206.

Kneucker, Raoul F., "Austria: An Administrative State. The Role of Austrian Bureaucracy," in *Österreichische Zeitschrift fur Politikwissenschaft*, 1973, 95–127.

Rickett, Richard, *A Brief Survey of Austrian History*. Vienna: Prachner, 1966.

Rossmann, Harald, "Austria," in Donald C. Rowat, ed., *International Handbook on Local Government Reorganization* (Westport: Greenwood Press, 1980), 255–260.

Shell, K., *The Transformation of Austrian Socialism*. New York, 1962.

Steiner, Kurt, ed., *Modern Austria*. Palo Alto: Sposs Inc., 1982, especially 261–278.

Steiner, Kurt, *Politics in Austria*. Boston: Little, Brown and Company, 1972, especially 373–408.

14
Belgium

ANDRÉ MOLITOR
Catholic University of Louvain, Louvain-la-Neuve, Belgium

THE HISTORICAL ENVIRONMENT

Situated at the crossroads of the countries of Western Europe, Belgium has been a battlefield for them for centuries. It is a land of ancient civilization, urbanized and industrialized since the Middle Ages. In the 19th century, it was a pioneer of the first industrial revolution. With an area comparable to the State of Maryland in the United States (about 30,000 square kilometers), it has a population of nearly ten million.

Some historical information may be useful to explain the origins and the essential features of its administrative system. With the beginning of modern times at the end of the 16th century, the seventeen Provinces of the Netherlands, assembled some decades before under the rule of the Dukes of Burgundy, were split by the religious wars. The northern provinces seceded to form a Republic, which is today the Kingdom of the Netherlands. The southern provinces remained under the rule of the King of Spain and were called the Catholic Low Countries. At the beginning of the 18th century, they passed under the sovereignty of the Emperor of Austria. In this cluster of provinces, each one had its own institutions, but there were between them many similarities, especially important constitutional liberties and the beginning of a parliamentary system. They were also known by the strength of their local self-governments (*communes*). This century saw also, under the Austrian influence, the first tentatives of a centralized bureaucracy. During the French Revolution, the southern provinces were annexed by France and submitted to the Napoleonic *régime*. After the fall of the French Empire, they were reunited with the northern provinces to form the Kingdom of the Netherlands. This interlude lasted only fifteen years. By the Revolution of 1830, the former Catholic Low Countries became the sovereign and independent Kingdom of Belgium. The Constitution of 1831 made of this entity a unitary and decentralized State.

The form of government was a constitutional and parliamentary monarchy, on the model of Great Britain and of the French Orleanist system. Such was the framework for the new Belgian administration. Its organization was a compromise between the Napoleonic model and the traditions of local and provincial autonomy inherited from the *Ancien Régime.*

It is important to take note here of salient features of Belgium which have ruled its public life during the past 150 years. These features explain the major institutional transformations which are on their way today.

Crossroads of Western Europe, Belgium appears also as a meeting-place for all the conflicts and sources of tension which characterize this part of the world. The population of Belgium is made up of 3/5 Dutch-speaking citizens against 2/5 French-speaking ones, plus about 70,000 German-speaking people on the eastern border (1). Although with a majority of Dutch-speaking Flemings, Belgium has for its capital a city—Brussels— of which 80 per cent of the residents are French-speaking. These two regions, Flanders in the north, and Wallony in the south, have known a much contrasted economic and social evolution. Until the first world war, Wallony, having reaped most of the benefits of the industrial revolution, had a privileged situation, while Flanders was predominantly agricultural, socially backward and ruled by a French-speaking *bourgeoisie*. Since then, the situation has reversed. The demographic evolution, the decline of Wallony parallel to the difficulties of its big industry, made of Flanders, in most fields, including the political world, the most dynamic element of the whole.

Another salient feature of Belgium is that ideologies, tracing back to the religious wars and to the enlightenment, have played and still play an important role in the national life, where we find face to face Roman catholic and rationalist conceptions and institutions.

Finally, the Belgian political system is strongly influenced by the presence, together with public or official structures, of well organized *de facto* powers: political parties, trade unions, educational and social institutions, etc. Whether legally recognized or not, or whether integrated into the political system, they play a significant role.

This multiplicity of "bipolar" or "multipolar" factors, a potential source of tensions and conflicts, holds an important place in Belgium's political and administrative life.

From 1830 to 1970: A Unitary and Decentralized State

We said above that the Belgian State born in 1830 was *unitary* and *decentralized*. Its *unitary* form is manifest in the organization of the central administrative structure. This structure takes its inspiration in the Napoleonic model, which influenced many among the countries occupied by France in the first years of the 19th century. The principal feature of this model is the division of activities into ministerial departments. It is also necessary to mention the growing importance, since the end of the last war, of the centralized administrative services, sometimes called in U.S. administrative literature the *central machinery of government*. This feature seems to be a result of the return to collegial government, and also of the necessity to coordinate the activities of a continuously expanding public service.

From the end of the 19th century until today we have seen, beside the ministries, the birth of an impressive number of governmental agencies (more than a hundred), many of which are similar to the British public corporations. These organizations are submitted to the supervision of the government, but they are otherwise autonomous and have their own organs of decision and management. They exist in many fields of action, but especially in the financial and social ones. Some of them, because of their power, have been compared to "great vassals" of the state.

The local authorities also play an important role in the governmental structure. The word *decentralization* used for them is historically inadequate. Indeed, they have

inherited a legacy of *self-government*, but are submitted now to the supervision of the
State. The local authorities in Belgium are the *provinces* and the *communes* (municipalities). When Belgium was annexed to revolutionary France, the nine Belgian provinces took the place of the feudal structures of the *Ancien Régime*. Until 1970
(see below) they were the only intermediary body between the central power and the
communes. Their role is limited, but surely not negligible in some parts of the collective life. Within the limits of their autonomy, each of them has oriented its activity
towards specific fields in addition to their general and compulsory functions. Their
autonomy is in fact greater than that of the French *départements*. During the major
institutional reforms of which we are going to speak, the suppression of the provinces
was discussed. This is no longer an issue, but it is probable that the functions of the
provinces will be modified and adapted to the new situation.

With respect to the communes, their significant role in the life of the country led
somebody to say that "Belgium is a republic of communes." They embody the
individualism of the Belgian citizens. Their functions are manifold, though often
under supervision of the central government (and now of the regions). Some years
ago, this supervision was strengthened, especially because of the financial difficulties
of many of them. The central power requires in exchange for its financial help a
greater intervention.

We must note a recent and important reform in the organization of the communes.
At the beginning of the present Belgian State, there are more than 3,000. A need was
felt to reduce this great number, just as the Netherlands had done a long time ago, and
also Great Britain. After long studies and lively debates, a law of 1971 required a
fusion of the communes. Their number has been brought down today to a little less
than 600. It is too soon yet to evaluate the results of this reform. Also, a law of
1922 allowed the communes to enter into partnership with other communes for joint
activities in specific fields under intercommunal authorities. The development of such
authorities has been considerable.

Since 1970: Major Institutional Reforms

To complete this historical introduction, it is necessary to speak of the important
institutional reform started in Belgium about twenty years ago, and which is still in
progress. It has already involved two successive revisions of our Constitution, in 1970
and 1980. It has also had decisive results in the field of public administration. The
goal of this reform is to substitute for the unitary structure of the State a regional or
even federal system. The origin of this change lies in the claim for a greater autonomy
of Flanders, and in reaction by Wallony. Originally, and especially since the 19th century, this claim took a linguistic and cultural form in Flanders, expressing itself in a
desire to escape from the rule of the French language in public and economic life. As
this situation was set right by legislation, Flanders also became conscious of its
numeric superiority and of an economic and financial dynamism which went along
with the Walloon decline. Simultaneously, Wallony considered that to counteract this
decline, and to escape from what it calls the domination of the central State by
Flanders, it must get its own powers of decision. This is how, through long and lively
debates, the will grew to put into the framework of a modified central State a sufficient freedom of action for both parts of Belgium. With very specific features in
Belgium, this trend is related to the general current against centralization since the last

war in almost all the countries of Western Europe, including France, federal Germany, Italy and Spain.

In the majority of regional or federal systems, there is only one sort of federated structure for the whole territory. This is not the case in Belgium. The constitutional revision simultaneously gave birth to *communities* (*communautés*) and *regions*. The origin of this lies in the complicated situation of the country, and especially in the existence of populations speaking three different languages and of a capital where the great majority of the inhabitants speak a minority language. The result was the creation of three *communities* (French, Dutch, German) and three *regions*: Flanders, Wallony and Brussels. Communities and regions are to a certain extent overlapping. The communities are concerned with the problems of culture in the broad sense of the word, and the questions called "personalized" (*personnalisées*), i.e. concerning sundry personal rights and interests of the citizens (for example the problems of health). The responsibilities of the regions are mainly economic and social but include also the environment. The central State has kept the functions generally reserved to the national or federal level, together with a significant number of functions in the fields covered by the communities and regions. Each community or region has a legislative assembly and an executive. However, for reasons which would be too long to explain here, the region of Brussels has not yet been organized. It is now managed by the national government.

We would not be justified in calling the new system in its present state a federal one, in the classic sense of the word, as in the United States or the German Federal Republic. It could be more justly compared to the Spanish regionalism, but here also with many differences. The autonomy given to the communities and regions is in some ways broader, especially for legislation. But above all, the system is more complicated because of the coexistence of two different types of new organizations, the communities and the regions. There is no standard model for states that are neither unitary nor centralized. We have just spoken of a "classic" federalism. It is the system described in the texts on political science—nothing more. In fact, each national system has its own features.

The reforms we have briefly outlined call for two comments. First, they are far from finished. The execution of the constitutional reforms of 1970 and 1980 and of the laws which have completed them is still in progress. There is nothing more difficult than to achieve a devolution of functions and responsibilities in a contemporary State whose activities and services cover practically all fields of collective life. Besides, hardly have the reforms been promulgated when voices call for modifications and ask for an extension in the transfer of functions from the national government to the new entities. The process will thus yet go on for some time. Second, it is practically impossible in this process of devolution to divide the political from the administrative level. Thus, the idea of a *politico-administrative system* seems to be pertinent and useful for the analysis.

STRUCTURE OF THE SYSTEM

These introductory remarks were necessary to give a general idea of the political and administrative institutions in Belgium. In the following pages, we will limit ourselves, with some exceptions, to organization and management at the national level. And we will speak only of the centralized services of the State. We will leave aside the public corporations. However, we must not forget that these organizations carry out tasks in very wide fields. But they do not take part directly in policy-making.

The centralized services of the State have a double structure, *vertical*, with the ministries, and *horizontal*, with a number of services forming what we called above the central machinery of government.

Vertical Structures

The ministries (*départements*) go back to the ideas of the French Revolution and of Napoleon. Each of them is responsible for one of the major functions of the State. We now have fifteen ministries. There is no necessary identity between the number of ministers and the number of ministries. We can have in the Government ministers *without portfolio*. They do not have responsibility of a ministry, but of some special mission. It may also happen that the same minister is in charge of two ministries, but this is not frequent. Since the constitutional reforms of 1970 the position of Secretary of State was created. The state secretaries are second-class ministers. Their constitutional situation is somewhat different from that of a minister. They are assistants to a minister and in charge of a part of his functions.

The internal structure of the ministries is similar to what we find in other Western European countries, having originated in the bureaucratic model of Max Weber and Napoleon. At the head of the bureaucratic pyramid we always find a permanent under-secretary (*secrétaire général*) just as in Great Britain or in federal Germany (but not in France, where it is exceptional). The ministry is divided into main services, called *administration* or *direction générale*, which are sub-divided into less important units. Beyond this cluster of central services, most ministries also have field services (*services extérieurs*).

Horizontal Structures

The central machinery includes a number of services with varied functions, but also with one common feature. In different ways, these services help the functioning of the whole governmental or administrative system. This is the case, for example, with the services working for the Cabinet (*Secrétariat du Conseil des Ministres*) or for the Prime Minister (*Services du Premier Ministre*). It is also the case with the services which coordinate the activities of different ministries (e.g. *Services de Programmation de la Politique Scientifique–Bureau du Plan*). We also find there some services working for all the ministries (e.g. the Permanent Secretariat for Recruitment, equivalent to the British Civil Service Commission). We cannot list here all of these organizations. For their internal management, they are under either the Prime Minister or a minister in charge of a "vertical" ministry.

We must stress the increasing importance of the horizontal services since the end of the last war. This can be easily explained. The growing scope of State intervention requires more and more coordination of policies. This in turn requires the intervention of special services. But beside the growth, there is also the complexity. The majority of political and administrative questions require the intervention of more than one minister or ministry. This has resulted in a return to collegial action, and the creation of a growing number of ministerial committees for the budget, investments, public works, foreign affairs, etc. The main one is the Ministerial Committee for Economic and Social Coordination. All these committees are the central point of decision-making for matters in which different departments are involved. Here also the compromises are reached which require the consent of all the parties of the coalition. Just as for the Cabinet, these committees need a secretariat and auxiliary services to prepare and follow up their decisions.

Impact of Communities and Regions on Central Services

In execution of the recent institutional reforms, the communities and the regions have naturally created administrative structures. Into these structures were integrated the services or parts of services which were in charge of the corresponding functions in the national administration. Generally these services were transferred with their personnel. Special measures have been taken to safeguard the interests of these civil servants. The personnel of the community or regional services are under the same statute as the State civil servants.

The institutional reforms have had an impact not only on the ministries but also on other State agencies to the extent that their missions now depend on the communities or the regions. The result is a process of transfer, division of services, etc., similar to the one we have just mentioned for the ministries.

These important transformations are far from ended. They also have an impact on the structure of the central ministries, which sometimes lose important functions. This is the case, for example, with the Ministry of Interior (or Home Office) and the Ministry of Public Health. The result should be a reduction in the number of the ministries. The problem is under study, and a decision may be taken soon.

Management Techniques

Just a word about the introduction of new management techniques. In the field of *budgeting*, the old idea, going back to the 19th century, of budgets structured by the administrative nature of expenses, was replaced after the last war by an economic classification related to national income accounting. Studies were pursued on the introduction of foreign techniques, especially the American PPBS. In spite of very far-searching experiments, it was not implemented because of the lack of interest of the politicians. Of course, it must be added that meanwhile the United States itself has not succeeded in fully implementing this system. Nevertheless, the preparation of the budgets and their execution are influenced by a growing rationalization, which is very efficient in some departments, for example Defense.

In another field, the tradition of economic liberalism in our country has for a long time checked the techniques of public planning. A period of very flexible economic programming (1959-1970), was followed by a law of 1970 which created the Planning Bureau (*Bureau du Plan*). The Plan is voted for five years by the Parliament. Its prescriptions are compulsory for the public services and for the contracts between the State and private enterprises. It is only "indicative" for the other activities of the private sector. But the procedure for elaboration and execution of the Plan is so cumbersome that the Plan, in fact, is very ineffectual. The Planning Bureau remains a remarkable technical service, but its principal role today is that of an economic and social expert for the Government.

With regard to management *tools*, as distinguished from *techniques*, we have new developments in the use of computers, and in office automation (*bureautique*). Computers were of course introduced many years ago into Belgian administration. They are used with a variable intensity and efficacy. The great problem for the public services is to realize the fullest output of this tool, and also to elaborate a general policy, global *and* decentralized, for the best use of it. The problems of personnel are also rather difficult in this field, because of the competition with private enterprise in an expanding sector.

PUBLIC PERSONNEL

The Career System

We will limit our study here to public personnel at the national level. The public servants of provinces and local authorities have their own statutes. The central government, however, prescribes a number of uniform rules for them, especially in the matter of compensation.

Belgium has adopted the career system for its public personnel. There are, however, a certain number of temporary employees recruited for a particular job and for a limited duration. They are subject to rules somewhat similar to those of workers in private enterprises. With regard to the career personnel, statutory rules determine their relations with the State: designation, rights and duties, promotion, salary, social security, etc. Their system of pensions is fixed by law.

The permanent civil servants are divided into four classes or levels. Each of them corresponds, for admission into the services, to a level of education, from class 1 (university degree) to class 4 (primary school). They are recruited at a single point for each level by competitive examinations organized by the Permanent Secretariat for Recruitment, with every guarantee of fairness. The officials of the lower levels can, however, have access to the higher ones through examinations, similar to the qualifications required from the outsiders. The outsiders, after the competitive examinations, must pass through a period of probation before being admitted to the career service. They will afterwards get promotion to another grade, either by getting a new post, or exceptionally in the same job.

Promotion inside the same level depends on merit, with a system of evaluation by the chiefs. Seniority also plays a role in the lower grades. For the top grades of class 1, choice by the Minister or by the Cabinet is the rule. In fact, political considerations are decisive. We will speak later about them.

Mobility inside the administration, i.e. the possibility for an official to switch from one service or department to another, exists in principle and has recently been more encouraged. In fact, however, it is not frequent. This is a result of the very limited character of professional mobility on the whole in Belgium. In the higher posts, it is more developed, but it cannot be compared to that in France or even Great Britain (see below).

Salary

The system of remuneration is related to the career system. For each type of function singled out in the ministries, we have a scale of salary with a minimum, a maximum and periodical (generally biennal) raises. The beginner gets the minimum salary in the scale of his function. In case of promotion, he will go according to established rules to the scale corresponding to his new grade.

The whole system is submitted to very complicated rules, as in many other countries. The salary—in principle—varies automatically with the cost of living. In fact, because of budgetary restrictions, these variations are now limited. Beside the monthly salary, civil servants get a "holiday premium" and another one at the end of the year. Save in very exceptional cases, one does not find examples of compensation similar to the more or less occult *indemnités* which exist in France, and which very substantially increase the salary of the higher and middle levels. Civil servants also get sundry social benefits: family allowances, health insurance (to which they must contribute), leave with salary in case of illness and/or invalidity, etc.

A word should be said about the salaries of the public personnel as compared with salaries in the private sector. In the first years of a career, and for non-specialized jobs, the salary is similar to that in private enterprise. But after a few years, with equal qualification, the civil servants are out-distanced by the private sector. For the top level, the difference is considerable. It is true that they enjoy for themselves, their widows and their orphans a more favorable system of pensions. But recent decisions have reduced substantially these advantages for the higher civil servants. It seems that this privileged system of pensions will gradually disappear. Finally, the tax system, very heavy in Belgium, plays a role in cutting down the net salaries of the higher civil servants.

Public Services Unions

The affiliation of civil servants with public service unions, and the regulations governing such bodies, were fixed at the end of the last war by statutes which have since been modified a few times. The proportion of the civil servants who are members of these unions is considerable: about 65 per cent of the total (2). It is comparable to the situation in the private sector. The regulations provide for such matters as the official recognition of the unions by the government, the procedure of negotiations, and the fields of competence—all the problems pertaining to the individual and collective interests of civil servants.

We have three great unions of civil servants, which correspond to the traditional, ideological and political currents in Belgium, catholic, socialist, and liberal (in the British rather than in the American meaning of the word). They have been able to obtain from the government a *de facto* monopoly over the negotiations, which conclude as collective agreements. When such agreements are not reached, the unions may proclaim a strike. The striking of civil servants is not officially recognized as a right, but it is not punished. If a strike fails, the government will take unilateral decisions. The economic and budgetary situation and the "austerity program" have helped recently to create difficult differences between the Cabinet and the unions.

Political Rights

Like other Belgian citizens, the civil servants naturally have the right to vote without any restriction. The voicing of their own political opinions comes under the general rules concerning the duty of reserve required of all public servants. These rules especially apply to political matters. This excludes, for instance, the oral or written appreciation or censure of governmental policy. However, the rules must be interpreted. For example, within limits of course, papers written under a pseudonym are permitted, as in France. Some public service unions fight for a total freedom in the voicing of opinions in every field. This of course is not accepted. Indeed, such a freedom is also limited in fact, if not in law, in the private sector. Nevertheless, the old image of the "mute civil servant" no longer corresponds to reality.

As for the right to be elected to public office, a distinction must be made. The civil servants can be elected to the councils of communes. They may even occupy positions of leadership, such as mayor (*bourgmestre*), at least in the less important communes. But for the Parliament (House of Representatives and Senate), civil servants elected as members must resign. This seldom happens because of the professional risk it involves, and the very restricted professional mobility in Belgium. We do not have, as in France and other countries, a system of political leave for the civil servants. Proposals have been introduced in Parliament, but so far without success.

In concluding this section on public personnel, it may be useful to give some indication of the number of civil servants. For some years, the Belgian and international press have often quoted *con amore* the figure of more than 800,000 "fonctionnaires" in Belgium as the symbol of an excessive bureaucracy. This includes not only the civil servants themselves, but the armed forces, the judges, and the teachers of official and private schools: in other words, all the persons paid from public funds. The total of only the civil servants of the State, the public corporations, and the regional, provincial and local authorities was, on 30 June 1985, 457,547 persons, which is still very numerous. We know how difficult and even hazardous the international comparison of statistics in such a field can be. Globally, however, the rather summary observation made by some observers can be admitted: Belgian bureaucrats are too numerous and underpaid. The cause of their excessive number is principally the multiplication of institutions and administrative levels.

POLICY-MAKING AND BUDGETING

In Belgium as in other countries, policy-making is subjected to the interplay of contending forces. It takes place within the constitutional framework and legally depends on the political organs officially in charge: Parliament and Government. In fact, it also depends on the intervention of what have been called in our country the informal or *de facto* powers (*les pouvoirs de fait*). A number among these (political parties, trade unions, employer's associations, ideological and financial forces, various lobbies, etc.) have been progressively and in different ways integrated into the institutional process. According to their own interests, they will of course not hesitate to act simultaneously *outside* this process. In this way, Belgium has been, at least for half a century, a land of permanent debate. One of the present problems is the difficulty of continuing this debate in a normal way. It goes on, first, inside the Government. Since the end of the first world war, with only rare exceptions, we have had coalition Governments. Besides, in these Governments, Flanders and Wallony must be equally represented. The preparation and the execution of policies are thus subject to a continuous debate in the Council of Ministers between representatives of the various political parties.

This goes on whether the policy relates to the revision of the Constitution or the purchase of jeeps for the Armed Forces. The debate begins with the formation of the Government, when they must frame their general policy in the form of a Declaration presented to the Parliament. It will go on during the whole life of the ministerial team, accompanied by the formal or informal interventions of the *de facto* powers. Decisions arise out of a process of bargaining among the *de facto* powers and within the governmental structures—the administration, ministerial *cabinets*, advisory councils, ministerial committees, and the Cabinet.

The preparation and the execution of budgets follows the same path. The budgetary proposals for the next year are drafted by each department according to the general principles laid out by the Government and with respect to the programs in progress and to the new policy decisions. The general principles are based on economic, financial and social forecasts in which the Planning Bureau plays an important role. Inspectors of finance, seconded to the ministries by the Budget Administration, supervise the whole procedure very closely. The ministerial Budget Committee and the Council of Ministers finally determine the amount of the expenses and of the revenues.

Role of the Higher Civil Servants

Except in some departments like Foreign Affairs and Finance, the role of senior officials has been progressively reduced. Among the causes of this reduction, we stress the impact of coalition governments. They have considerably increased the place of political parties in public life, with various results.

First, there has been a great development of politicization in the higher civil service. The appointment to functions at the top is related to the political affiliation of the candidates. It leads, inside the governmental coalition, to debates, "package deals," bargaining. The situation is complicated by the fact that officials, once appointed to a job, can keep it until the end of their career, or until another appointment with their own agreement. The system is thus very different, for example, from that in France, where the appointments are also political, but remain within the disposal of the Government, and where the higher civil servants move on the administrative "checker board" according to the will of the President and the ministers. The result of the Belgian system can be a latent fear of the ministers about the loyalty of the higher civil service. Such a fear is very often not justified.

Besides, the Belgian administration is not elitist. We have seen above that the holders of a university degree (except for specialized jobs, e.g., engineers or medical doctors) do not have a monopoly of the higher jobs. Apart from the competitive examinations for entrance, we have no selection system comparable to the French National School of Administration. The higher civil service does not show the sociological coherence deriving from their membership to a privileged class, as was the case (and as it is still now in part) in Great Britain. Finally, the model of the "Grands Corps," so typical of the French administration, is not a general feature of our civil service. We have, indeed, *corps* of civil servants (Engineers of Public Works, *Cour des Comptes* (audit), *Conseil d'Etat*, etc.). But most of them are very specialized and closed bodies. One exception is the *Inspection des Finances*, which has remained since its creation a nursery for top civil servants in many fields.

These factors do not necessarily influence the quality of the higher civil service. But they explain why officials do not show towards the political class the cohesion which we find in other countries. Their recruitment and their social structures do not make of them an elitist group or a cast. They have no close links with the ruling classes of the private sector. They are rather open to external currents, through the mediation of politics and trade unions. But their degree of external mobility is very low. We mean here the mobility between public service and private enterprises. Many social and economic factors, and particularly the career system, play a role in such a situation. The rigidity of the statute for the civil servants also checks this mobility when compared, for example, to the possibility of French civil servants being seconded for a long time in quasi-governmental or even private functions.

The weakness of the higher civil servants before the ministerial power is also a result of the considerable importance in Belgium of the ministerial *cabinets*. The ministerial cabinet is the private staff of a minister. The institution has existed since the beginning of the modern Belgian State. Originally, it was limited to a very small number of collaborators, who helped the minister in his personal activities. But the number of their members and their functions grew progressively. They have developed a tendency to become a sort of delegation of the minister's political party, more than his private staff. And they try to get a monopoly in the decision making, and even to annex some administrative tasks. The high civil servants, thus lose some of their normal functions and are therefore deeply frustrated. However, a number of them occupy key posts in the *cabinets*.

The inflation of these institutions has been for many years, just like in France, a matter for numerous complaints, but vainly and without results. The measures taken to limit the number of their members are not respected. But it is rather curious that, when in Belgium and in France the *cabinets* are strongly censured, we hear in Great Britain, and even within its House of Commons, proposals for an examination of the system, as a means of limiting the excessive power of the civil servants.

Generalists and Specialists

Whether the senior personnel should be generalists or specialists we have always considered to be a "false problem." It originated in the literature on public administration from a study of the British Civil Service, with its clear-cut traditional distinction between administrators and professionals, and the impossibility for the members of this last class to get access to the highest functions of the ministries. This is absolutely not true in Belgium. There exists, of course, in fact a distinction between officials in charge of matters of general administration and those in charge of a technical function which requires a specialized training (engineers, agronomists, M.D., etc.). For the general administrators coming from outside the service, lawyers have often been chosen. But this situation is changing, and cannot be compared with the *Juristenmonopol* often passionately discussed in Germany. For many years the holders of very different university degrees have been recruited for the general functions. As for the higher jobs, there is no exclusivity "on principle." On the contrary, it is quite normal in the departments with technical functions (Public Works, Agriculture, Health, etc.) for these jobs to be given to "professionals" who during their career have progressively acquired an administrative competence outside the strict borders of their previous training. This solution does not perhaps give a sufficient place to the development of the techniques of management. But this raises the whole question of the permanent preparation for the higher jobs: a question to which the powers that be have not yet given an adequate answer. We must, however, point out the initiative taken for almost twenty years by the *Institut Administration-Université*. This foundation, of private origin, has organized, with grants of public money and with the help of our universities, a great number of training and refreshment sessions for the higher personnel of State services and local authorities. But the political world does not seem to show a sufficient interest in such developments, nor in administrative problems generally.

ADMINISTRATIVE ACCOUNTABILITY

Belgian administration, like others, submits to various internal systems of supervision, in the form of inspection services. We will only discuss two of them, the first being the Financial Inspection Service (*Inspection des Finances*). It is an external branch of the Budget Administration. Created in 1938 and recruited through a difficult competitive examination, this highly competent group of inspectors follows the budgetary procedures in all departments. The other supervising body is the Superior Control Committee, dating from 1911 and working under the Prime Minister. It is a sort of internal police of the administration. They investigate all the irregularities in the services, especially—but not exclusively—in the field of public works. They submit their conclusions to the Prime Minister, and also have the right to refer matters to the courts when it is appropriate.

The Parliament, naturally, also supervises the actions of the public services. This it does through questioning each responsible minister during the discussion of the budgets, or by way of oral and written questions and also of *interpellations*. The Parliament has also a constitutional right to hold inquiries, but they are rather unusual. In the case of an inquiry, public servants may be called to appear before a parliamentary commission.

The financial supervision of the use of the budgetary funds allocated by Parliament is entrusted to the Court of Accounts (*Cour des Comptes*). This jurisdiction is totally independent from the executive. It is subject to Parliament only, which appoints its members and it regularly sends to Parliament a report on its activities. It is also a court with jurisdiction over the accountants of the State. The Court mainly supervises the *lawfulness*, not the wisdom of expenses. Some years ago, it began to investigate this latter field, like the French *Cour des Comptes*.

The civil and penal responsibility of civil servants is a concern of the ordinary courts, which have elaborated an important jurisprudence, especially about the notions of tort.

Quite a number of administrative tribunals have been created over the years. Most of them have specific functions. Belgium took much time to organize a tribunal with a general competence, the Council of State, which dates only from 1946. On the whole but with some appreciable differences, its functions may be compared to those of the French institution with the same name. It has a double mission. First, it is the great law expert of the government, and gives advice on draft laws and regulations. Besides, it is the principal administrative court. It has power to cancel regulations and individual decisions of the administrative authorities if they are contrary to a law, or if these authorities have exceeded or diverted their powers. It can also in some cases grant compensation for exceptional damage suffered by a citizen because of an administrative decision. The role of the Council of State has progressively increased, and it has now taken an important place in the national life.

There is no institution in Belgium which could be compared to the Nordic ombudsman or to the comparable organizations which we find in other countries: Austria, France, Great Britain, Spain, etc. A number of proposals coming from members of Parliament have been submitted to the Houses to realize such a reform, but without success yet. The same remark must be made about the efforts to give to the public services more "transparency." We refer for example to the Swedish and more recent laws in other developed countries such as Denmark, Canada, France and the United States, which give the public a right of access to administrative documents. Nothing similar can be found in Belgium. In everyday life, the administrative practice, with laudable exceptions, remains true to the tradition of secrecy. However, for some years there has been a definite trend towards a more direct and more effective participation of the citizens in the administrative process. Likewise, specific laws prescribe the publicity of administrative acts and projects and the right of the citizens to be heard, for certain fields of administration.

CONCLUSION

In every industrialized society, the administration is today being subjected to a severe test. This is also the case, of course, in developing countries, but for other reasons, and their own problems lie outside the present study. The advanced industrial societies face an evolution whose rapid rhythm is in contrast with the *tempo* of administrative procedures. We believe that it is one of the major difficulties faced by the public services. Others are the unprecedented extension of the State's services, and the extraordinary development of technology. These factors exist in Belgium as much as elsewhere. For our country, we must add to them the specific problems we discussed in the historical introduction: linguistic duality, a different economic evolution in the north and the south, institutional reforms, specific features of decision-making, etc.

Let us also add, for Belgium as for other countries, the general economic and financial depression. Having enjoyed a hitherto unknown prosperity from approximately 1960 to 1973, Belgium is now confronted with the absolute necessity of reducing its standard of living, and of accepting a severe cure of austerity in the public and private sectors. The public services must accept a revision of their methods, with the double objective of more efficiency and lower budgets. We have already pointed out some of the past shortcomings of our administrative system. But it is fair to say that the public service contributed in a very positive way to the recovery of the country during the quarter of a century which followed the end of last war. This comes from its realism, to which we must add its effective proximity to the citizen. Today, however, we need an extraordinary effort of modernization of techniques and methods, and also a permanent adaptation of the personnel to the new situation.

Two facts make such a task more difficult in our country. First is the already-mentioned lack of interest of the political class in administrative matters. This lack of interest is, with brilliant historical exceptions, one of its permanent features. Second is the traditional distrust by the citizens of the State, from which, on the other hand, they do not hesitate to ask more and more benefits. This distrust is a result of the individualism of the Belgians, and also of the fact that during the *Ancien Régime* the central power was in the hands of rulers living in Madrid or in Vienna, or—worse—was held by British, French, Dutch or German occupation armies. Of course, this has not contributed to a flowering of civic feelings.

Finally, the administration suffers from the uncertainty which results from a long and slow process of institutional reforms. The transfer of functions and services, the new distribution of the power to decide, and the organization of the new levels of authority are not yet well spelled out and known, and there is a risk of new changes in future. This situation must seriously influence the mentality and the attitude of public servants. Such a crisis must of course be solved, but it needs the cooperation of all those who care for the commonweal. In this respect, we can state one positive symptom. The economic *entrepreneurs* have always pleaded, in Belgium as elsewhere, for a limitation of State intervention. This attitude generally went together with a real ignorance of the problems of public administration, including the need for highly qualified public personnel, especially in the higher posts. This is now changing. The desire to see public authorities reduce their intervention continues. But the importance of an administration of high quality seems more and more to be felt in these circles. If this feeling grows and is conveyed to the political circles, we may hope that the politicians will be more mindful of what is today in our country a major problem, on which may well depend the future of the national community and of its constituent parts.

REFERENCES

1. Belgium also has about 800,000 immigrants, principally of Mediterranean origin, not to speak of the foreigners at work in the various international organizations located in the country: the European Community, NATO, etc.
2. This figure, dating from 1973, is the most recent one available. It covers all the public services, including railways, schools, etc. It is probable that for the ministries the ratio would be less.

MAIN REFERENCES

André Molitor, *L'Administration de la Belgique.* Brussels: Institut belge de Science politique et Centre de Recherche et d'Information socio-politiques, 1975, 448 pp.

Belgica 1945–1975, in *Res Publica* (the Belgian Journal of Political Science), Vol. XXV, no. 4, 1983. Articles by different authors, especially André Molitor, "L'évolution de l'Administration belge depuis 1945", 661–686.

ADDITIONAL REFERENCES IN ENGLISH

The reader will find an important bibliography on Belgium at the end of the collection of essays edited by Arend Lijphart, *Conflict and Coexistence in Belgium: The Dyanmics of a Culturally Divided Society* (Berkeley: Institute of International Studies, University of California, 1981). Among the books and essays quoted in this bibliography, we recommend especially:

Dabin, Paul, "Community Friction in Belgium: 1830–1980," in *Resolving Nationality Conflicts: The Role of Public Opinion Research*, W. Phillips Davison and Leon Gordenker (eds.), (New York: Praeger, 1980).

Fox, Renée C., "Why Belgium?" *European Journal of Sociology* 19, 2 (1978), 205–28.

Frognier, André-Paul, "Paeties and Cleavages in the Belgian Parliament," *Legislative Studies Quarterly* 3, 1 (February 1978), 109–31.

Lorwin, Val R., "Belgium: Conflict and Compromise," in *Consociational Democracy: Political Accommodation in Segmented Societies*, Kenneth D. McRae (ed.), (Toronto: McClelland and Stewart, 1974).

Lorwin, Val R., "Segmented Pluralism: Ideological Cleavages and Political Cohesion in the Smaller European Democracies," *Comparative Politics* 3, 2 (January 1971), 141–75.

Lorwin, Val R., "Labor Organizations and Politics in Belgium and France," in *National Labor Movements in the Postwar World*, Everett M. Kassalow (ed.), (Evanston, Ill.: Northwestern University Press, 1963).

Mabille, Xavier, and Val R. Lorwin, "Belgium," in *Political Parties in the European Community*, Stanley Henig (ed.), (London: Allen and Unwin, 1979).

Senelle, Robert, *The Reform of the Belgian State*. Memo from Belgium, No. 179. Brussels: Ministry of Foreign Affairs, External Trade and Co-operation in Development, 1978.

Senelle, Robert, *The Reform of the Belgian State*. Memo from Belgium, Nos. 315 and 319. Brussels: Ministry of Foreign Affairs, External Trade and Co-operation in Development, 1979.

Zolberg, Aristide R., "Belgium," in *Crisis of Political Development in Europe and the United States*, Raymond Grew (ed.), (Princeton, N.J.: Princeton University Press, 1978).

Zolberg, Aristide R., "The Making of Flemings and Walloons: Belgium, 1830–1914," *Journal of Interdisciplinary History* 5, 2 (Fall 1974), 170–225.

Zolberg, Aristide R., "Transformation of Linguistic Ideologies: The Belgian Case," in *Multilingual Political Systems: Problems and Solutions*, Jean-Guy Savard and Richard Vigneault (eds.), (Québec: Laval University Press, 1975).

Zolberg, Aristide R., "Splitting the Difference: Federalization without Federalism in Belgium," in *Ethnic Conflict in the Western World*, Milton J. Esman (ed.), (Ithaca, N.Y.: Cornell University Press, 1977).

ADDITIONAL REFERENCES

Huggett, F. E., *Modern Belgium*. London: Pall Mall, 1969.

Jorion, E., "Belgium," in Donald C. Rowat (ed.), *Administrative Secrecy in Developed Countries* (N.Y.: Columbia University Press, 1979), 127–154.

Moulin, Leo, "The Politicization of Administration in Belgium," in Mattei Dogan (ed.), *The Mandarins of Western Europe* (N.Y.: John Wiley, 1975), 163–186.

Senelle, Robert, *The Reform of the Belgian State, Vol. 3: Regional Structures in Terms of the Laws Passed on 8 and 8 August 1980*. Brussels: Ministry of Foreign Affairs, External Trade and Cooperation in Development. Memo from Belgium—Views and Surveys, No. 189, 1980.

Stassen, Jacques, "Belgium," in Donald C. Rowat (ed.), *International Handbook on Local Government Reorganization* (Westport, Conn.: Greenwood Press, 1980), 97–110.

Weil, G. L., *The Benelux Nations: The Politics of Small-Country Democracies*. London: Holt, Rinehart and Winston, 1971.

15

The Netherlands

JAN KOOIMAN
Erasmus University, Rotterdam, The Netherlands

JAAP BREUNESE
Ministry of Home Affairs, The Hague, The Netherlands

CONSTITUTIONAL AND POLITICAL FRAMEWORK

The administrative system of the Netherlands has of course been heavily influenced by the constitutional and political framework. The main body of the Dutch constitution dates from 1848. This constitution was a completely new law, establishing political freedom and democracy in the Netherlands for the first time. Never has there been any question of curtailing the rights it confers on the people. After twenty years of work, a revision of the constitution was completed in 1983. An important difference from the constitution of 1848 is that, besides classical rights such as provision for civil liberties guaranteeing freedom of religion, press and assembly, it includes social rights such as the right to work and housing.

Under the constitution the Crown is inviolable, the ministers being responsible to both Houses of Parliament. The Lower House (*Tweede Kamer*) is invested with four rights: amendment, inquiry, interpellation and inquiry, enabling it to fulfill its legislative functions and to keep a check on the government. The Upper House (*Eerste Kamer*) is invested with three of the four above rights, not having the right of amendment, being able merely to vote for or against a bill in its entirety. Consequently, only when it has very serious objections does the Upper House vote against a bill.

The Dutch political system has certain key features, similar in certain respects to other systems but also cumulatively having a special character. These features must be seen in the historical context of both pluralism and accommodationism. First, the Dutch political system has always been a highly pluralized society from its earliest days, with extreme territorial dispersion of authority until 1795, after which it became a much more centralized state but with continuing geographical diversity. In the nineteenth and twentieth centuries its pluralism has become more a function of religion and class than of locality or region. But the need for developing rules and procedures for negotiating among competing interests has always been paramount. Second, the slow process by which the Dutch state was centralized and developed into its present unitary form saw the emergence of particular political practices and institutions designed to achieve a central governmental authority that could make acceptable decisions while recognizing and respecting the conflicting demands of intensely involved, rival groups.

The Dutch parliamentary system is the typical example of a multi-party situation. Partly because of the strict system of proportional representation, it is difficult for a party to receive a majority on its own. This means that governments are based on coalitions. The usual coalition parties are the christian democrats, who have participated in some form in all coalition governments since 1918. The other partners change, although since the second world war the christian democrats have formed more coalitions with the liberal-conservatives than with the socialists.

In the Dutch multi-party system, cabinet formation serves as the medium in which political power relations are materialized. Although often there is a "winner" during the elections, it is not always the winning party that forms the government. It may turn out that matters of political substance are so defined between the parties that a certain coalition, although "logical" as an outcome of the elections cannot be formed. In the Netherlands cabinet formation takes a long time. Endless negotiations not only are needed to establish agreements and disagreements, but also serve to diminish certain electoral successes and losses: a winner may have to work with a loser.

Once a coalition is formed and a cabinet sworn in, almost invariably based on a parliamentary majority, different forms of relations between the cabinet and its supporting parliamentary groups may be practiced. According to the constitution a combination of parliamentary membership and membership in the cabinet is not allowed. This means a certain "distance" between the cabinet and parliament, even its supportive side. Degrees of support will vary. In practice the cabinet will be able to live as long as the party-groups which have formed it go on supporting it. Although four years is the constitutional period for a cabinet, not many have made their full term. Between 1946 and 1984 the country saw seventeen cabinets, the average being somewhat more than two years.

The role of parliament has been relatively subordinate to the cabinet once it is formed. Parliament has certain rights, powers, and resources in its relationship to the cabinet, but generally the initiative comes from government (i.e. the cabinet). There is general recognition that the government dominates the political agenda, has the responsibility for presenting the major policy proposals, decides on what information is to be disseminated, and usually prevails on legislation in its disagreements with parliament. Parliament does perform important functions of scrutiny of proposed laws, debating their content and thereby securing publicity for the different positions, querying ministers over administrative matters, and occasionally forcing the cabinet to reverse or withdraw proposed legislation. The role of the M.P. as the representative of political interest groups and sectors has become more important, as has his role in maintaining contact with, and developing support from, the public (1).

CENTRAL GOVERNMENT ORGANIZATION

The main features of the organization of the Dutch government services date back a good 130 years. It is a strongly bureaucratized system with considerable emphasis on formal rules and regulations, a hierarchical structure and a division of responsibilities within and between the authorities on the different levels.

The national administration, which has a workforce of about 160,000 civil servants, consists of fourteen ministries. At the beginning of this century there were eight: four with a task externally oriented, four having to do with internal governance. This expansion reflects the much broader scope of governmental activities in this century. The growth has been gradual, with two highpoints: during the depression in the thirties and after the second world war. In recent years there has been for the first time in decades serious discussion that the central administration is too big and that the number of ministries for a country the size of the Netherlands is a maximum. Shifts of task areas between ministries more often stem from political needs during cabinet formations than "rational" combinations of task areas. Where the coalition "numbers game" has to result in a certain ratio between participating parties, it often occurs that task areas are "created" to fulfill the wishes of one of the coalition members.

Ministers are, with their state secretaries, politically responsible for all acts of their ministries to parliament. When there is an unresolvable political conflict with parliament the minister has to go. However, it has become political practice that such conflicts will be part of cabinet politics. This means that the cabinet as such puts its life at stake. Then almost always parliament gives way: parties do not want the responsibility for a cabinet crisis when there are problems with only one minister. It is uncommon in the Netherlands for the prime minister to change his cabinet during his term; coalition bargaining usually prevents this.

The administrative responsibility for a ministry lies with the highest civil servant, the secretary general. This official is also the first advisor of the political leadership, he serves as the highest coordinator of ministerial activities, and he manages the political policy of the minister and the state secretaries. All the ministries are divided into directorates general (varying from three to five per ministry), these again into directorates, and so on. The directors general and the directors form together with the secretary general the administrative leadership of the ministry.

DECENTRALIZED GOVERNMENTAL ORGANIZATION

The Netherlands can be characterized as a "decentralized unitary state." The gist of the philosophy behind this is that the public interest must be promoted at as low a level as possible and as effective administration permits. According to this view, the central government should only take on the promotion of an interest if lower authorities cannot cope with it all or cannot do it effectively.

Provinces

The Kingdom of the Netherlands is divided into twelve provinces, with the number of inhabitants ranging from about 3,000,000 (South-Holland) to 200,000 (Flevoland). The provinces have a twofold task. First, they promote their own provincial interest, either acting on their own initiative, or by order of higher authorities. Secondly, they play the part of intermediary between central government and municipalities and have a supervising function with regard to municipalities. Whereas provincial tasks used to be restricted to health service, planning and maintenance of roads and canals, this responsibility has been greatly extended in recent years. Provinces have acquired important tasks in the fields of physical planning, pollution control, cultural development (by means of state grants) and recreation. Economic matters may also be an object of provincial care, but here it is the gathering of relevant data and stimulation of certain developments rather then being actually engaged in these matters.

The second important responsibility of the provinces lies in their function of intermediary between municipalities and central government. This is brought out clearly by the way in which—sometimes preventively, sometimes repressively—the provinces exercise supervision of municipal policy. Particularly in financial affairs this supervision is extensive: the municipal estimates for instance must be submitted to the provincial executive for approval. But also in other matters provincial approval is required, such as with municipal physical allocation plans.

Another means by which—although indirectly—supervision is exercised is the power of the provincial executives to settle certain disputes between citizens and municipal authorities. It is, for instance, possible to appeal to a provincial executive if a municipality refuses to provide relief to those requiring it. They reach a decision which may be appealed to the Crown (in effect, the cabinet). Besides testing the lawfulness of municipal decisions, the provincial executive may also consider their suitability. Therefore this task is entrusted to a governing body, and we may for the same reason consider this form of administrative appeal as another means of supervision of municipal policy. We should add, though, that some authors say that the settlement of disputes should be withdrawn from the provincial executive because of its political composition, which makes it unfit for this purpose.

In many other fields the province has tasks as well, but they are limited to stimulation, coordination and supervision. An important expedient is the provincial grant, which consequently plays a part in many fields of government care, especially in cultural affairs, recreation and social welfare.

The provinces are under the supervision of the Crown. This is partly preventive control, e.g. in those cases in which the Crown's approval is required such as the budget. The Crown also has the power to take repressive measures in that decisions of provincial authorities can be annulled by the Crown in case they are considered to violate the law or to be opposed to the public interest.

Municipalities

The smallest administrative units in the Netherlands are the municipalities, about 700 in number. The municipalities have the responsibility to promote municipal interests either on their own initiative or by order of higher authorities. Here too the interference of the government in the social structure of society has greatly increased in recent years. This applies especially to education, social security, welfare work, housing and pollution control.

The municipality's tasks are not static. It has been shown that many tasks can be performed with greater efficiency when done on a larger scale than the municipalities can provide. Hence there has been a tendency to shift these tasks to regional administrative units, but the municipalities have retained the tasks that require direct contact with the citizens—civil registration, licenses, social provisions and the like.

For the municipalities the State has an appropriation fund into which a certain percentage of government taxes is deposited. The distribution among the various municipalities is complicated and hence is a subject of continual disputes.

For municipalities of more than 100,000 inhabitants, certain financial decisions do not require approval by the province. Evidently it was thought that large municipalities had sufficient specialized manpower to make this preventive control unnecessary. In view of the enormous budgetary deficits of especially the large municipalities, this must have been wishful thinking.

Revision of the Local Government Act of 1851

The existing Dutch Local Government Act dates from 1851. The idea behind that Act was that the local authorities were to have maximum autonomy. Since that time the development has gone from a decentralized unitary state in the direction of a centralized unitary state. Because of this development the position of local government has become rather weak. The sixties brought a wave and a call for a more democratic government. The Dutch government appointed a commission to revise the Act of 1851. In 1980 the commission finished it task, and in February 1986 the government submitted a bill to the lower House. The main element of the bill is to reduce the very extended regulations allowing preventive and repressive control over local government by the national and provincial governments.

Polder-Districts

A particular branch of decentralized authority should be mentioned, namely the polder- (or riverboard) districts. These are governmental bodies that are organized territorially and are only responsible for the promotion of some interests in the field of water control. They date back to the earliest times of our history and are administrated by the whole body of landowners in a district. The province, in this case the Provincial Executive, is entitled to set up, dissolve and supervise the "polder-board" districts.

Changes in the Relations between Government Levels

In the Dutch situation there are four main topics which dominate the discussion on administrative reorganization: 1. decentralization of national government tasks, 2. provincial regrouping, 3. local government regrouping, and 4. cooperation between local authorities (2).

1. Decentralization

   In the last decades the Netherlands have become a rather centralized country through the many tasks and competencies which the national government has attracted, with insufficient attention given to whether the national government is the right level for them. As a result, the national government is overburdened and its democratic, efficient and effective functioning is at stake. Some decentralization efforts undertaken have succeeded, but others are continuously delayed. The political effort for decentralization is rather weak. Decentralization is more an ideology than a reality.

2. Provincial Regrouping

   Dutch provinces are different from provinces, departments or districts in other European countries in that they have nothing to do with regional government.

The efforts since 1975 to upgrade the position of the provinces have almost failed. The plans to create "new style" provinces (25–40 in number), which would solve the regional and national problems, are over. There does not seem to be sufficient political courage to change the stalemate in this area.

The role of the provinces in connection with the cooperation between local authorities has been given much attention. In the law a province can oblige a local authority to take part in cooperation. If cooperation between local authorities is to really mean something, this role of the provinces is not necessary.

3. Local Government Regrouping

Since 1850 the number of local authorities has been reduced from 1,209 to about 750. Some regrouping is still in progress. Local government regrouping is an integral part of the reorganization of Dutch government. The new Constitution makes it possible that for border corrections the normal procedure does not have to be followed but that the national government or even the provinces can do this. Local government regrouping will go on in spite of all the criticism. It seems to be the easiest way to reorganize government. In a memorandum to parliament, the Minister of the Interior stated that the time required to effect a regrouping has to be reduced from 8–10 years to about 5 years, and that a minimum number of 10,000 inhabitants is necessary to fulfill local tasks now and in the future. The main criticisms are that there are hardly any criteria for regrouping and that there is no clear plan for the reorganization of government at large.

4. Cooperation between Local Authorities

Local government cooperation has become one of the most important problems of the Dutch governmental system since 1945. After the second world war, there was a growing need for local authorities to cooperate with each other. In 1951 the Law for Communal Regulations made it possible for local authorities to cooperate, but for every task a separate regulation had to be made. Since that time more than 1,500 regulations have been made.

A number of regional authorities have been formed as well. But before they could become a kind of fourth governmental level, the politicians at the national level decided, in a revised edition of the law of 1951, that in a small country like the Netherlands there was no need for a fourth level of government. And to under-line this viewpoint they withdrew the financial support for the regional authorities. In their view regional cooperation has to be paid for by the participating local authorities. Through this revision the national government wants to ensure that the cooperation of local authorities will be limited to local affairs. For a number of regional authorities this will mean their disappearance.

Public Corporations

Public corporations differ from other public bodies in the sense that they are managed on the basis of profit making, or at least paying their own way. In principle their activities could be carried out by private firms. In the Netherlands energy, railways, water supply and the communication sector are government owned or controlled. Here we can distinguish two forms: one in which the legal status is public. This applies to the Post, Telephone and Telegraph (PTT) authority, and to some smaller units like the State Printing Office and the Mint. The second form has a private legal status: ownership belongs to the government either on the national, provincial or local level. Examples are the railways, the Royal Dutch Airlines and almost all public utilities. Privatization of public corporations is under discussion. Serious efforts to implement this are being made, especially in the communication sector.

THE CIVIL SERVICE

The Position of the Civil Servant

The special legal status of civil servants in the Netherlands follows from two factors:

1. The particular character of the civil servants' position because of the special place and function of government in society;
2. The fact that in public administration, long before in trade and industry, a set of conditions of employment had developed.

The position of the civil servants has a so-called "status character." This means that changes in the legal position of civil servants are applicable for those already in government service. This in contrast with labor agreements which can not be changed unilaterally; that is to say, they have a "contract" character.

The labor contract of a civil servant is not per individual but is under the rule of general regulations. Therefore there is in an appointment not much room for negotiations. Civil servants are appointed in a particular rank, connected with a particular function. The rights and duties connected with the function are fixed in advance. Dismissal is regulated in a exhaustive way. The salary is connected with the rank and the salary increase is regulated. Pensions are calculated by means of a specified number of objective criteria, of which the number of years as a civil servant and the final salary are parts.

The one-sided settlement of the labor conditions of civil servants has been criticized and discussed for a long time, especially the prohibition against strikes embodied in the criminal law after the "railroad strike" of 1903. Set against this prohibition there had been the need to offer a satisfactory regulation of labor conditions. To get this the Labor Act forsees an organized deliberation between representatives of government and representatives of the unions of civil servants. Because of the status character of the labor agreement the general conditions are drawn up by the Crown, sometimes against the wishes of the civil service unions.

In 1970 the government appointed a commission to examine the question of whether a right to strike for civil servants can be reconciled with the character of civil service labor relations. The commission suspended its activities when in 1973 the government declared that the civil servants' right to strike had to be honored. In 1980 the strike prohibition was eliminated but a right to strike was not specifically granted. However, judges in court had already recognized the right to strike and strike actions in principle. The recognition of the principle of the right to strike is necessary because in 1980 the Dutch government signed the European Social Charter, though that Charter gives the possibility to limit the right to strike to protect the public order, national health or in certain other circumstances.

The labor unions are, against the background of the one-sidedness of the labor agreement, advocates of a controversial regulation that would include the possibility of arbitration over all conflicts. An arbitration regulation, however, can have serious consequences for the treasury and for the social-economic policy in general if there is a judgement in favor of the unions. Here we have to do with a constitutional problem. It is parliament that gives the room to the Minister of Home Affairs, who is in charge of government personnel, to negotiate. But if conflicts can be settled by arbitration, then the sovereignty of parliament is at stake.

Top Civil Servants

Patterns in the source of recruitment and social background of the top civil servants at the national level have both stable and dynamic elements in them. A longitudinal study shows that from 1961 to 1981 the source of recruitment was very stable, in the sense of the administrative background (3). In 1961, 35 per cent of those at the top had been recruited from their own departmental unit; by 1981 this had grown to 47 per cent. The second main source of recruitment is the rest of the department: in 1966, 36 per cent in 1981, 28 per cent. All in all external recruitment comes as the third source, between 25 per cent and 30 per cent. Somewhat more dynamic is the time spent in one's job: internal mobility shows that most top civil servants are highly experienced from a substantive point of view: from 1961 to 1981, from one quarter to more than half of them stayed less than five years in their present position. This—as far as one can see—has primarily to do with the growth of governmental agencies, which means that the top also broadens.

Stable again is their age: most recruitment to top positions happens through the twenty years after the age of 44; only 20 per cent of the top positions are taken by people younger than that age. Somewhat dynamic are the disciplinary backgrounds of top civil servants in the departments. From 1961 to 1981 the role of jurists declined from 38 per cent to 18 per cent; while the proportion of economists grew from 7 per cent in 1961 to 21 per cent in 1981. Other social science grew also, but at a low level: from 2 per cent to 6 per cent in 20 years. Technical and other exact sciences as a background have been stable: 33 per cent in 1961 and 36 per cent in 1981. Non-academic and other backgrounds were very stable: 20 per cent through all twenty of these years.

THE POLICY PROCESS

The World of the Administrative Units

In the policy process the government services discharge various functions such as policy preparation, policy implementation, supervision of policy implementation, the management of policy preparation, supervision and implementation, and the provision of the required legal and other instruments (4). The civil servants responsible for this work serve in highly specialized units and it is they, in fact, who make and carry out policy in most policy areas. Each working unit has its own policy area, defined according to objective, product or clientele group. The emphasis lies on specialization and vertical communication. Every unit does its own work which is monitored from hierarchically higher levels.

There is usually little or no built-in organizational capacity for harmonizing policy. To do this a work unit would require a coordinating section or project organization and these are very seldom met with. The head of a unit is generally the only coordinating factor within and between work units and it is difficult to determine how effective this coordination is.

All units have dealings with some section of society. They operate at all levels in a fairly close network of relations with social organizations which represent the interests of various sectors of the population (employees, the disabled, farmers, etc.) or a specific interest that concerns the whole population (e.g. the quality of consumer goods or the environment). Contact is established in many different ways and may be formalized in advisory committees, interministerial committees (on which social organizations are often represented), consultative and participatory bodies, or unofficial in small and relatively closed circles of personal contacts and informal discussion. Typical of relations between certain sections of the government services and social organizations is that in fairly small circles of influential experts drawn from these two sectors (and from the political parties and local and regional authorities), groups of anything from 10 to 20 people, lines of policy are determined in close, intensive consultation. The big social organizations (for example those of the employers and trade unions) draw more or less the same dividing lines as the government services. This facilitates harmonization between the policy areas but also strengthens the somewhat isolated policy development in each separate area.

Which subjects are tackled by the government services and for which do they show a preference? Before answering this question we must distinguish between the maintenance and amendment of existing policy on the one hand and the development of new policies on the other. Policy-making officials are usually fully occupied with existing policy and its gradual amendment and development. It is seldom that the government services themselves initiate new policy (the development of a new policy area or a radical change in an existing one). Ideas on new policies usually emanate from a small number of social organizations and from the political parties whose influence is mostly confined to the main points of a required development but may include priority of treatment as well. The actual form and content of the policy is largely determined by the civil servants concerned, who are more knowledgeable and have more time at their disposal than the organizations and parties.

There is persistent tension between existing policy and proposed innovations. The highly specialized work units are difficult to direct from above and to guide into other tracks. The existing organization lacks flexibility and is extremely difficult to change, since the responsibilities of the units and the civil servants are more or less firmly established. The culture of the organization and the status of the civil servants constitute obstacles to major changes. Given this situation, the pressure from outside must be really strong before new policy can be discussed. This pressure, which is exerted by social organizations and political parties, must be passed on by the ministers to the heads of the government services, and the directors-general in turn channel it to the work units. The directors-general and directors, in particular, contain and filter these signals from society.

All the actual work, such as research, the preparation of proposals, and the organization and reporting of meetings, is carried out by the work units concerned. There is usually one unit that "pulls the cart." The procedure is generally very informal:

One or more senior civil servants responsible for policy are assigned to prepare
   proposals;

A form of vertical and horizontal discussion is agreed upon;

A deadline is set, which is often the only form of pressure the ministers can exert
   to get new policies discussed.

The units evince a strong tendency to operate within their own departments and to
postpone consultation with others until a departmental viewpoint has been formulated.
Only then do serious negotiations take place with other work units and representatives
of social organizations.

This procedure is not strictly controlled and policy preparation is mostly carried
on with only very occasional intervention from outside. Regulation is a question of
"mutual understanding" and is conducted "in the spirit of political and administrative
management." The upper echelons make the necessary amendments at the end of the
procedure when the proposals have been worked out, and check whether the work has
been harmonized with that of other work units before submitting the proposals to
the ministers for their decision.

The World of Integration

The world that is concerned with the integration of government policy presents a
bleak picture. There are many interrelationship patterns (representing a network of
organizational units) but the management of the network as a whole is undermined by
the independence of its component parts. The centers of gravity of policy preparation
are situated in the separate departments and units. Here we think of the council of
ministers, the prime minister, the government program, the subcouncils, coordinating
ministers and generalizing advisory bodies.

The *Standing Order of the Council of Ministers* (1979) lays down that the council
shall deliberate and decide on general government policy and shall promote unity
therein. The text of the new constitution, in which mention is made for the first time
of a council of ministers, likewise refers to the promotion of unity in government
policy. General government policy includes agreements between the political parties
forming a government, the government program and other common policy principles.

Of great importance to the functioning of the council is the relationship between
the collective and the individual aspects of ministerial responsibility. They are certainly not completely divorced from each other: every policy activity of an individual
minister is also part of government policy as a whole for which the ministers are jointly
responsible, and vice versa. But to what extent does collective responsibility over-
shadow individual responsibility? This is a controversial issue. However, within the council the principle of good-fellowship predominates. Not only is a vote seldom taken but
decisions are seldom forced through against the will of any one of the ministers who
may not be in accord with the rest.

The council of ministers has little integrating effect for a number of reasons. The
constitution lays down the principle of ministerial equality, so all ministers have an
equal right to demand their share of the agenda. On the administrative side, all
ministers have their individual legal powers which the council of ministers cannot alter.
A political factor is that ministers, knowing that they have only a short time in which
to "score," have little inclination to give priority to matters which lose much of their

attraction because they are complicated or carry political risks. The poor monitoring of the agenda is one organizational defect among many, despite minor improvements that are being made. It is for these reasons that the cabinet cuts a poor figure as the center or stimulator of an integrating political and administrative movement.

Official recognition of the office of prime minister was accorded only after the second world war, and although it has gradually gained in prominence, the prime minister is still spoken of as "primus inter pares." The prime minister has a number of powers, laid down in the standing order of the council of ministers and elsewhere, enabling him to discharge his duties and responsibilities. They include the chairmanship of the council and the subcouncils, and the final say in drawing up the agenda. He is served in this by the Ministry of General Affairs, which, though it has been expanded somewhat in recent years, is still small compared with the other ministries.

The length of time it takes to form a government due to the stubborn struggle between political parties hoping to participate in the coalition, on the question of the government program, justifies the belief that this program must be an important element in any government's policy. It is true that the attitude of the different parties to the program varies quite considerably (the socialists usually attach more importance to it than can be expected) and that political signposts will be planted on the most important areas of policy. The failure of the government's program to achieve the significance it should have can be attributed to factors both outside and within the cabinet. A government program of course reflects the situation at a given point of time. Circumstances change rapidly so that elements on which the program is based, such as economic forecasts, may no longer tally. On the other hand, the enormous amount of political energy spent on thrashing out a program justifies the expectation that its guidelines remain valid even under changed circumstances. One of the major shortcomings of the cabinet itself is that it fails to check the progress made in implementing the program.

Linking the Two Worlds: Relations between Politicians and Senior Civil Servants

The two worlds discussed in the foregoing are linked at the management level of the ministries where both are represented in the organizational structure and in the processes that take place there. Insofar as the management level constitutes a "separate" world, the fact that it serves to link the other two worlds can be seen as its most important function. The management level of a ministry consists of the minister, the state secretary, the secretary general, the directors general and their deputies. Supportive units such as the information department, the office of the secretary general, the senior civil servants of the financial, economic, personnel and organization units and central legislative and policy-analytical units can also be accounted as management level to a greater or lesser degree.

The duties of the secretary general are adviser to the minister, coordinator of policy and manager of the department. The degree to which he coordinates sometimes causes friction, the management role varies from one department to another, and little is known about the role of adviser to the minister since it is not one that is played in public. Many secretaries general have divided their duties and delegated the management side to a deputy, thus creating the impression that management is inferior to policy coordination. Policy coordination itself raises other problems, sometimes deep-felt and long-drawn-out, since it is in this field that the secretary general soon finds himself trespassing on the territory of his directors general.

Within a ministry politicians and senior civil servants frequently meet in consultation. Such consultation may be broadly based or confined to a small group, formal or informal, periodic or sporadic. The object of these various forms of consultation is seldom clear. The exchange of information, combined with elements of policy-framing, decision-making, and policy implementation are mixed together at one and the same meeting, so that not all the participants are meaningfully occupied. The result is loss of time and unnecessary overloading. Under these circumstances it is scarcely surprising that coherent policy for a ministry as a whole, evincing a firm grasp of political affairs, is virtually non-existent. Some ministries even insist on regarding internal cohesion as artificial; officials have closer working relationships outside the ministry than within it.

Only in very special cases is there some form of policy plan or detailed program for the whole ministry from which policy intentions can be derived or against which they can be checked. The explanatory memorandum on the budget is in practice little more than a summary of activities, a glorified progress report. Matters of long-term consequence presented in a structured form are very seldom discussed in any detail, nor are "brain-storming" techniques used.

Policy Analysis

The introduction of policy analysis in the Netherlands in the seventies was induced to a large extent by the early enthusiasm about the planning, programming and budgeting system (PPBS) in those years in the United States and in other countries. The minister of Finance in 1971 established an interdepartmental commission to guide and stimulate policy analysis in central government. The commission, composed of top-level civil servants from various ministries and chaired by the director general of the budget developed a number of methods and techniques, especially with respect to *ex ante* evaluation. Training programs and seminars were organized and ministries performed a substantial number of policy analytical studies.

In this respect the commission had a useful function in bringing different types of policy analytical methods and techniques to the attention of an administrative and scholarly public. However, a generally directed project to create a comprehensive deductively developed "objectives structure" for all departments collapsed. This was one of the reasons that the commission was abolished in 1983. In its place a more "service oriented" structure has been established, with the understanding that the actual policy analytical performance is a decentralized responsibility of departments themselves.

Somewhat along the same line, rather ambitious efforts by the National Association of Local Communities to stimulate and guide local communities in the area of policy analysis, e.g. the promotion of integrated policy models for local government, gave some impetus to a critical look at amny conventional ways of local policy making. All in all these efforts have become more modest and redirected towards introducing new techniques into local administration, such as computers (6).

The Role of the Bureaucracy

There is some concern that the bureaucracy has recently become a "fourth power." Its historical role was subordinate, nonpolitical, and advisory in the policy process. In the early history of the United Provinces there was no central bureaucracy, and later it remained of modest size until the early twentieth century. In Dutch nineteenth-century history, one looks in vain for a salient role of the bureaucracy. Other observers have also noted the strict hierarchical structure of the bureaucracy, the loyalty of civil servants to the ministry in which they serve, the capacity of the civil servant to work effectively with any minister regardless of his political persuasion, the relative independence of the bureaucracy from parliament in the performance of administrative tasks, and the development of close social and personal ties among civil servants.

This picture of a rather exclusive, politically neutral, nonactivist bureaucracy is not shared today by all observers. And in actuality one gets the impression from what little research has been done that the role of the top bureaucrat is more complex, less simplistically administrative, and thus more controversial. While formally the rules of behavior for top civil servants remain the same, observance of civil servants in reality has led to statements about their policy role, and concern about their power as having become too great and not subject to proper controls. Some fear that the bureaucratic apparatus has become both separate and independent. Others argue that the bureaucracy is not a bloc, that it reflects internal differences. It is pointed out also that the policy role of civil servants varies greatly by sectors of policy, in some ministries being very restricted while in others having more latitude. Nonetheless, the view emerges more and more that the Dutch higher civil servant is not merely a reticent technician who takes a back seat in the policy process.

This view is supported by a recent study. The classical view of bureaucracy, exemplified in Max Weber's writings, can be operationalized in three elements of the bureaucrat's role: technical knowledge and expertise, hierarchical status of the bureaucrat, and policy analysis style, in which he conceives of problems and solutions as technical ones. When the attitudes of senior Dutch officials are measured against these three criteria, only 5 percent of these officials are of the "pure" Weberian type, that is, they fulfill all the requirements for the type. On the other hand, 40 percent of them have none of the attitudes or orientations that would be expected of Weberian civil servants. If emphasis on either hierarchical loyalty or technical expertise is alone used, the Weberians constitute 53 percent; if loyalty alone is used, it is 37 percent; if belief in the superiority of technical approaches is used only 25 percent are Weberians. Whatever requisites one wishes to apply, it is clear that in utilizing all three types of variables Dutch senior civil servants tend to be non-Weberian in their total perspectives.

ADMINISTRATIVE RESPONSIVENESS

Tasks of Parliament

The controlling tasks of parliament are severely hampered by a lack of real sanctions. In fact in situations of conflict with the cabinet, parliament is rather powerless. "Motions of distrust" are, for reasons mentioned earlier, rare incidents. Because of the uncertainty in the life cycle of sitting cabinets it becomes attractive to concentrate control activities on "popular" items; in this process pressure groups play an important role. There exists a tight bond between social organizations and governmental branches. A minister can waive criticisms quite easily with the argument that this or that measure has been extensively discussed with social partners, or that such deliberations will still take place. A next major hindrance to effective control by parliament is the inter-weaving of subjects of policy across boundaries of ministeries. Not only is it some-times difficult to ascertain which minister carries primary responsibility, also the organization of parliamentary work in specialized committees makes a broad control almost impossible. It is in this way comprehensible that MP's have doubts about the effectiveness of their traditional "weapons" against the government in their controlling tasks. Of the three tasks—controlling the cabinet, influence on the budget and control over the bureaucracy—the last one is considered to be the least important, but also the most effective.

Budget Control

In a democratic system control of the budget lies primarily in the hands of elected bodies such as parliament, provincial or local councils. They ensure that incomes and expenses of public bodies as agreed with the executive are collected and spent in the proper manner. The question is how this control is exercised, because in practice in the Netherlands political sanctions are seldom applied in budgetary control matters. This is partly due to the lack of interest of parliament in such things and partly because of the difficulty of applying political sanctions in coalition politics.

In the Netherlands the General Accountings Council is the body which has the task of the direct financial control of budgetary matters on behalf of parliament. It reports annually to parliament, presenting detailed information necessary to form an opinion on the lawfulness and efficiency of the money spent. Judgements on the effectiveness of expenditures are scarce, because of the difficulties in setting objective standards. However the council itself explores possibilities in this area more than it used to. The council is an independent body. The members are appointed by the Crown, based on a nomination in the Second Chamber. The council organizes its own work and selects the parts of the budget it wants to scrutinize independently. To carry out its tasks it has unlimited access to all materials necessary. All civil servants are by law required to give the information requested. The only limitation is that control of provincial and local budgets is not within the competence of the council.

The National Ombudsman

On January 1st, 1982, a national ombudsman came into operation and the Dutch ombudsman started his job. The reason for the interest in such an institution is mainly the growing activities of government, and the growing fear that individuals may be dealt with unfairly or arbitrarily by the bureaucracy. The ombudsman is appointed by parliament, and his main tasks are: a) to receive and investigate complaints from the public and to give an opinion on the behavior of branches of the central govern-ment or the national police force towards the complainer; b) to give an opinion when there is a complaint against a decree against which there is no legal appeal available; c) to report to parliament annually. He is not an integrated part of the administration of justice, but can be seen as a supplementary protection of justice to cover the gaps in the system of judicial protection.

Access to Information

The Administrative Publicity Act has a rather long history. During the mid-fifties the press was already discussing a right to information, to enable journalists to follow the actions of the government critically. In those days politicians regarded publicity in administration as a means to increase the participation of citizens in the governmental process. The idea that a bureaucracy operating publicly may be easier to control, also played a part.

In 1968 the cabinet created a committee to consider the limits on governmental information. At the instigation of parliament the committee also worked out a right to governmental information for citizens. When its report appeared in 1970, the committee added a preliminary design of an Administrative Publicity Act. Most reactions to this design were positive. The committee's strong plea for the principle of publicity being the rule and secrecy the exception, was much appreciated, and in 1975 the cabinet succeeded in introducing such an Act in parliament.

Significant for the Act is its "compromise" character, a compromise with two appearances. In the first place the Act is a combination of a publicity and an information act. Apart from the enforceable right to ask for governmental information (which has been restricted by several exceptive clauses), the Act imposes on government the duty to give information: government must provide information of its own account "whenever good and democratic administration requires it." However, sanctions are not incorporated in the Act for whenever this duty is not performed. The compromise character manifests itself in another way, too. The Explanatory Statement and the Preamble of the Act turn out to be very publicity-minded. But the clauses of implementation enable a very restricted attitude towards those who ask for information. Whatever the government professes abstractly and in words, it is not obliged to put into practice.

Four consecutive cabinets of different political composition have worked on this Act. In May 1980 it was finally put into operation. However, an evaluation in 1984 shows that it hardly plays a significant part in the publicity policy of the different authorities. Insofar as public authorities changed their policies after May 1980, those changes had primarily a symbolic meaning. Considering the conclusions of the evaluation, one sees the paradoxical picture of an Act which, when first introduced, caused a lot of commotion due to its supposedly revolutionary contents, but which, ten years later, after its implementation, hardly causes any effect.

CONCLUDING REMARKS

Deeply based in its historical developments (cultural, social and political), public administration in the Netherlands has been—and to some extent still is—of a dispersed nature. Even in the 19th and the beginning of this century, unlike many of its neighbors, the country did not have a central administrative apparatus to speak of. Although the French occupation in the Napoleontic period prepared the country for a public administrative system with a national character, and later Prussian bureaucratic experiences somewhat influenced the way in which an administrative apparatus was set up, it was not until after the second world war that "The Hague" was administratively anything like Berlin, Paris or even Brussels in their respective countries. In the Netherlands the "State" never had the same connotations as in most of the surrounding countries (7).

A second main characteristic, somewhat in line with the preceding one, has to do with structural and cultural aspects of the (party-)political arrangements in the country. For many reasons—also historically based—politicy authority has been diffuse: a cabinet often based on fragile compromises between coalition partners, a government consisting of ministers individually responsible to parliament, a prime minister who is more a primus-inter-pares than a strong leader, a parliament with strong ties to well established social groups, government-parliament relations based on the socalled "dualistic" principle (each having its own responsibility). All of these factors have contributed to a central public administrative system of a diffuse nature. In organizational terms one would say: more an interorganizational network weakly steered from a top which in itself also has more the character of a network than a unit. Such elements will be present in other Western European administrative systems, but in their combination in the Netherlands they seem to be of a more outstanding and singular character.

The Netherlands does not have anything like a general bureaucratic elite: experiences, attitudes and careers are predominantly departmentally oriented. Related to this are the facts that traditionally (although changes are seemingly taking place) the civil service has been politically neutral, more policy advising than policy managing, strongly policy sector oriented and rather competitive interdepartmentally. The greater complexity of social problems and governmental tasks becomes a source for the need of coordination in often complicated interdepartmental battles.

In the same context one can sketch the national, provincial and local relations in the country as being somewhat precarious. On the one hand, the lower authorities in the system have constitutionally based autonomous tasks and powers; on the other hand, all kinds of factors contribute to an increasing influence of ministries on the day-to-day functioning of these bodies. Formal and informal powers are used to keep regional and local authorities as much as possible in line with what the national authorities (political and administrative) think is best. No fundamental reorganization has taken place in these arrangements for almost a century, although the scope of problems and tasks has changed completely. In many respects, then, the administrative system of the Netherlands has neither a typical decentralized nor a unitary character: it is not only on the national level but also in its central-local relationships a system characterized by a complex of interorganizational networks with horizontal and vertical links, and with political and administrative dimensions.

REFERENCES

1. J. Kooiman, *Over de Kamer gesproken* (Parliament in Discussion), 's-Gravenhage, 1976.
2. J. N. Breunese, "Bestuurlijke reorganisatie: een spel zonder grenzen" (Reorganization of the relations between central, regional and local administration), *Acta Politica*, 79/4, 82/3 and 83/4.
3. U. Rosenthal, "De mandarijnen van de rijksdienst" (Mandarins at the national level of public administration), *Bestuurswetenschappen* 5/83.
4. Commissie Hoofdstructuur Rujksdienst, *Elk kent de laan die derwaart gaat* (Committee on the General Structure of Government Services, main report), 's-Gravenhage, 1980. See also J. van Putten (ed.), *Haagse Machten* (Powers at the national level), 's-Gravenhage 1980.

5. From material given by the Ministry of Finance.
6. S. J. Eldersveld, J. Kooiman, T. van der Tak, *Elite Images of Dutch Politics*, Ann Arbor/The Hague, 1981, ch. 4.
7. H. Daalder, "Sturing, het primaat van politiek en de bureaucratische cultuur in Nederland" (relation between political dominance and bureaucratic culture) in: M. A. P. Bovens, et al., *Het schip van de staat*, Zwolle 1985, pp. 197–206.

REFERENCES IN ENGLISH

Abert, James Goodyear, *Economic Policy and Planning in the Netherlands 1950–1965.* New Haven: Yale Univ. Press, 1969.

Bours, A., "Proposals for the Netherlands," in Donald C. Rowat, ed., *International Handbook on Local Government Reorganization* (Westport, Conn.: Greenwood Press, 1980), 165–173.

Daalder, H., "The Netherlands," in R. A. Dahl, ed., *Political Oppositions in Western Democracies.* New Haven, 1966.

Daalder, H., "Consociationalism, Center and Periphery in the Netherlands," in P. Torsvik, ed., *Mobilization, Center-Periphery Structures and Nation-Building.* Bergen (Norway), 1981.

Diamond, J., "The New Orthodoxy in Budgetary Planning: A Critical Review of the Dutch Experience," *Public Finance* 32 (1977), 56–76.

Eldersveld, Samuel, Sonja Hubée-Boonzaaijer, and Jan Kooiman, "Elite Perceptions of the Political Process in the Netherlands," in Mattei Dogan, ed., *The Mandarins of Western Europe* (N.Y.: Halsted, 1975), 129–61.

Eldersveld, S. J., J. Kooiman, and T. van der Tak, *Elite Images of Dutch Politics.* Ann Arbor and The Hague, 1981.

Huggett, F. E., *The Modern Netherlands.* N.Y.: Praeger, 1971.

16

Spain

MIGUEL BELTRÁN
Autonomous University of Madrid, Madrid, Spain

THE HISTORY OF THE ADMINISTRATIVE SYSTEM

A Napoleonic System

Modern Spain's system of public administration gradually took shape during the course of the nineteenth century in a process fraught with difficulties. The century began with the War of Independence (1808-1814) which prevented Napoleon's domination of the peninsula and put an end to the reign of Jose I, brother of the emperor. In this war, the Spanish and the English fought against the French, and in 1814 Fernando VII was put back on the throne, which in practice meant a return to the absolutist *Ancien Régime*, and the collapse of the liberal revolution begun shortly before the Constitution of 1812, known as the "Constitution of Cadiz."

This conflict between absolutism and liberalism lasted throughout the entire nineteenth century, provoking a series of civil wars, the "Carlist Wars," in which liberalism eventually was the winner. The process of Spain's political modernization is, therefore, slow and difficult, in all likelihood because of the weakness of her bourgeoisie, which was incapable of dominating the social and political forces of the *Ancien Régime*. The liberals, moreover, were almost always divided between an extremely conservative party (the *partido moderado*) and a radical one (the *partido progresista*), the leaders of which were often military men, who did not hesitate to make use of the *coup d'Etat* in the form of the *pronunciamiento* (in which a prestigious general illegally takes over leadership of the government, normally in a peaceable manner and without it meaning that the Army as such has taken power).

The nineteenth century is also the period in which Spain lost her empire. The vast American territories gained their independence at the beginning of the century, and the last colonies (Cuba, Puerto Rico, the Philippines) were lost in the war with the United States in 1898. While other European countries were building their colonial empires, Spain was dismantling hers, and thus emerged the Latin American countries of today. It is obvious that, from the point of view of the economy, the loss of the empire severely limited Spain's prospects, just when it was in the process of becoming a modern country. That there were problems with the economy is apparent in the low level of industrialization achieved by Spain in the nineteenth century. At the time of World War I, Spain was still predominantly an agricultural country, and only in the second half of the twentieth century would it become a developed, industrialized country.

It is in this prolonged period of economic and political difficulties that the modern Spanish public administration system took shape. Paradoxically, and although the War of Independence was waged against French domination, the modern system of public administration in Spain is a Napoleonic one, perhaps the most Napoleonic one on the entire continent with the exception of that of France. In the opinion of Brian Chapman, Alejandro Olivan's *De la administración pública con relación a España*, published in 1843, is the clearest and most systematic statement of the Napoleonic model of public administration (1).

This model involves several things. In the first place, centralization: there are no autonomous administrative systems, and even local administrations have very little self-government; the administrative hierarchy follows the model of the military hierarchy, which means that the chain of command stretches from the central government all the way to the most remote parts of the land. In the second place, the Napoleonic model implies a set of legal codes with a comprehensive body of regulations and rules of conduct, which severely limits administrative discretionary powers and gives the actions of state agencies a quasi-judicial meaning. In the third place, the liberal principle of equality before the law does away with exceptional cases and special privileges, and brings about an increasing uniformity in the conduct of the administration and in the delivery of public services. Finally, public employees in the Napoleonic system of administration are not co-opted but appointed after successfully passing objective merit examinations; the selection of public employees is based, therefore, on a democratic principle: access to the French *Grands Corps*, created or reformed by Napoleon, was by the merit system, opening the way to a real professional career in public administration.

Not all of these features were present at the emergence and formation of the Spanish system of public administration in the nineteenth century. The administration was, of course, centralist, especially in a country in which political unity was relatively weak, and in one that experienced, during the First Republic (1873), an explosion of federalism and of local independentist movements (the phenomenon of the "cantones" or small regions that declared themselves independent and sovereign). The codification of statutes and the issuing of regulations were also widely developed in Spain, especially in the latter part of the nineteenth century, thoroughly regulating public activities and citizens' rights. Equality before the law was introduced in a more erratic manner: the War of Independence brought about a profound democratization in the military profession, which led the Army to favor liberalism for most of the century; by contrast, in the civilian administration the use of the merit system in recruiting public employees never entirely took effect, and the spoils system, based on a relationship with the party in power, predominated. As a result, the notion of a professional career in public service was an extremely vague one throughout the century.

Consolidation of the Administration

The political and economic problems referred to earlier hindered the speedy consolidation of the modern system of public administration in Spain, in spite of the fact that certain elements of a rational system appeared very early. An important example is the introduction of a national budget, which dates from 1814 (although it was little more than a defense budget, due to the situation the country was in at the time). But the precocity of the idea of an annual budget prepared by the executive branch and submitted to Parliament for approval contrasts sadly with the erratic fortunes of the budgets themselves—well into the second half of the century. In many years budgets would not be drawn up, nor would Parliament discuss the revenues and expenditures detailed in them; it would simply extend the budget from the preceding year.

Also appearing very early in Spain was the decision to abandon the spoils system and to replace it with the merit system and a dependable professional career in the civil service for public employees. In 1852 Prime Minister Bravo Murillo published a decree to this effect, but perhaps the measure was premature (one must remember than in England the date of the Northcote-Trevelyan Report is 1855, and that the Pendleton Act was not approved in the United States until 1883). In fact it wasn't put into effect until 1918. In the nineteenth century a significant number of public employees would lose their jobs with each change of party in power, and their places would be taken by those who had lost them in the preceding change. As far as we know, the spoils system had no ideological basis in Spain, be it that of the Jacksonian concept of democracy, or that of membership in a political party, but rather it was a phenomenon similar to the practice of patronage in Great Britain.

Another important factor of political and administrative modernization was the clear separation of administrative and judicial powers, which took place in 1834 with the definitive abolition of the old "Councils" of the *Ancien Régime* (which combined both kinds of powers), and the creation of a Supreme Court separate from the executive branch. Also in the same year, the structure of the ministries or government departments, consisting of a government minister, an undersecretary and several head offices, was established, and a territorial redistribution of the nation was carried out, resulting in the creation of fifty provinces, drawn up on the basis of an equal mixture of historical and rational criteria.

Just before the middle of the century, and with regard to local government, an intense political struggle took place between those who thought of mayors principally as representatives of the central government, even to the extent of being appointed by the King (this is the position of the conservative Moderate Party), and those who were in favor of local autonomy and self-government (the position of the radical Progressive Party). In 1845 a Municipal Administration Act was approved which granted the central government the power to appoint mayors, with the proviso that the appointee must be one of the town councillors elected by the townspeople; under this compromise, mayors ended up being more important as local representatives of the central government than as local authorities.

It has already been mentioned that in 1918 the spoils system disappeared in Spain and a real professional career for public employees was established. Public employees in Spain are subject to a statutory system, not a contractual one, in which merit is the criterion for appointment, and seniority (the number of years of service) the criterion for promotion through a gradual acquisition of personal status; the criterion of *rank in the man* based on seniority was in force from 1918 to 1964.

In the nineteenth century public employees were organized into various corps or divisions, which were divided, in each ministry, into a technical staff and an auxiliary staff, and somewhat apart from these, in rapidly increasing numbers, a great many corps regulated by special laws which came to be known as "Special Corps." Presently about 200 corps of public employees exist in the national central administration, each one consisting of a series of homogeneously classified positions which are filled by an identical process of selection.

In the decade of the 1920's, under the dictatorship of General Primo de Rivera, public administration in Spain witnessed an interesting new development: the creation of many semi-independent agencies and state-owned enterprises, each with financing of its own separate from the national budget, but subject to the authority of the government and also to control by Parliament and by the General Accounting Court. Organizations of this kind were to become very important in the subsequent development of the Spanish state.

For its part, the Constitution of the Second Republic (1931) acknowledged for the first time in recent Spanish history the possibility of the existence of regions or autonomous territories, governed by their own statutes. Cataluña obtained its Statute of Autonomy in 1932, Galicia in 1936, and shortly thereafter, the Basque Country. It will be remembered that under Franco regional autonomy was abolished, but it has reappeared with the return to a democratic regime, and has become one of the most important features of the political and administrative structure in Spain today.

Public Administration under Franco

When Franco's side won the civil war in 1939, the democratic institutions established during the Second Republic, and even those that had existed since the Restoration of the Monarchy in the Constitution of 1876, were thoroughly dismantled. In imitation of fascism and national socialism, Franco established a one-party system in Spain in which everything revolved around his personal power. Unlike what happened in Italy and Germany, however, the ideology under Franco was not concerned with modernization nor was it "revolutionary." Rather, it was actually an old-style reactionary oligarchical dictatorship. Moreover, the defeat of the fascist powers in the Second World War forced the Franco government to limit or disguise any resemblance it might have to such regimes, and as a result, as early as the 1950's the regime in Spain cannot be described as a totalitarian one, but rather as an authoritarian one, as Linz does (2).

Under Franco, the most interesting aspect of the system of public administration is the importance that public employees assumed as a recruitment pool for the political class. Indeed, since neither political parties nor democratic institutions existed under Franco, the recruitment of political appointees was carried out on a massive scale among public officials, preferably, of course, among the ideologically conservative or the simply pragmatic. So, in the Franco regime, it was not so much the case that power was in the hands of the public officials as such, but rather that the appointments of cabinet ministers, undersecretaries, and agency heads often fell to professional public employees, of whom little more was demanded than technical competency and passive loyalty to the regime.

Similarly, the lack of a class of professional politicians meant a significant presence of public officials in the Franco "parliament": their presence was compatible with their professional position in the administration or with their performance of political duties in the executive branch, and in the "parliament" they were in direct contact with the representatives of the most important interest groups (agricultural, industrial, commercial, financial, religious, professional) that enjoyed institutional representation there.

Another important characteristic of public administration under Franco was the significant degree of self-government achieved by many of the corps of public employees. Since there was no possibility, within the law, of public employees forming a union, nor of establishing a system for representing their professional concerns to the administration, nor of negotiating their working conditions, the corps of public employees took it upon themselves to advance and defend the collective interests of their members. Thus appeared the phenomenon of corporativism in the form of self-government and particularism. The corps of public employees were authentic pressure groups confronting the government, succeeding in many cases in controlling the amount of their salaries by means of the establishment of charges and fees—technically illegal—for the concession of permits, licenses, tax collections, fines, etc. And the government tolerated it all because in this way it avoided otherwise necessary pay raises for public employees, whose salaries had been seriously undermined by inflation (3).

One of the most important stages in the evolution of the Franco regime and in the transformation of Spanish society came into existence in 1957, when a plan for the stabilization and liberalization of the Spanish economy was introduced under the advisement of the International Bank for Reconstruction and Development. This plan was followed in 1964 by a Plan for Economic Development. The consequences of these new economic policies are well-known: in the decade of the 1960's the Spanish economy underwent an extraordinary period of development; the levels of industrialization and urbanization and the standard of living showed spectacular gains; the Spanish economy was integrated into the international economy to a very high degree; tourism, the emigration of Spanish workers to European countries, and foreign investment in Spain all reached very high levels. In this atmosphere of modernization and economic development—one that would raise Spain in the early 1970's to tenth place among the industrial powers of the world—an important reform of the public administration system was gradually taking place over the course of several years. Although thwarted in its objectives to a large degree, the reform meant a significant overhauling of the system, carried out with the dual objective of increasing efficiency and rationalizing administrative activity. This reform involved the adoption of basic management techniques, and its essentially pragmatic orientation represented an attempt to sidestep the problems facing an antiquated authoritarian regime which was finding it hard to adjust to the demands of a modern, developed society.

Public Administration under the Democratic Regime

Following the death of General Franco at the end of 1975, the transition to democracy took place in Spain. It began with the immediate dismantling of the former regime's institutions (the Political Reform Act of 1976) and continued with the general elections of 1977. The newly elected parliament approved the Constitution of 1978, at which point Spain joined the ranks of the democratic nations. New elections were held in 1979 which were won, as before, by the reformist Democratic Center Party, headed by President Suarez. Finally, in 1982 elections were held for the third time in democratic Spain and this time the majority of the votes were won by the moderately leftist Socialist Party, led by President Gonzalez. The transition in Spain from Franco to democracy is considered a model for peaceful political change, although it has not been completely free of violence and uncertainty (persistent terrorism; the threat of military involution, quickly suppressed). In any case, the inherent risks involved in such a process have been overcome thanks to the co-operation of the political parties (all of which were interested in the restoration and the consolidation of democracy in Spain); to the influence of the King (whose democratic tendencies have made many Spaniards forget their former republicanism); to the moderation and pragmatism of all Spaniards; and to the identification with the democratic regime shown by a professionalized civil service.

The civil service has not undergone significant changes during the period of transition from Franco to democracy. The non-violent, consensual nature of the process allowed the public administration system to remain outside the political arena, as a purely operational and professional sphere, ready to serve the government that came to power in each election, no matter which party won. For the same reason, there were no purges or political vendettas, although in some of the most sensitive areas (such as the police or prison officials) the public officials most identified with Franco in the past faded discreetly into the background. Even some of those who had been career public officials in agencies specifically created by Franco (such as the official labor unions and the official party itself) were given purely professional technical positions in the national administration since, in practice, they had merely been carrying out bureaucratic tasks in their former posts.

There is however an area in which the period of transition produced a significant change in the civil service. Public employees were granted the freedom to form unions, and their right to strike was recognized. Today Spanish public employees join unions freely, official channels through which union and administration representatives can negotiate working conditions now exist, and the government negotiates such matters in compliance with Agreement 151 of the I.L.O., ratified by the Spanish government.

Taken as a whole, the Spanish public administration system has undergone one very important change in the period of transition from Franco to democracy: the creation of the autonomous communities has destroyed the old political and administrative centralism, and there has appeared instead another level of decision making and public activity on a regional basis. The change has been so great that the present political and administrative system in Spain today can be described as quasi-federal.

After the elections of 1982, the newly-elected Socialist government revealed that it intended to carry out a reform of the administrative system which, up to the present time, has not progressed beyond the introduction of several concrete reform measures for the civil service, which are stipulated for the most part in the Civil Service Reform Measures Act (*Ley de Medidas para la Reforma de la Funcion Pública*) of 1984: to a certain extent the number of existing corps or divisions of public employees has been reduced, and recruiting practices have been standardized; the transfer of public employees from one branch of the public administration system to another has been made possible, administrative-type contracts to perform extra, seasonal, or special work for public employees who are not career officials are no longer permitted, the age of retirement has been cut to 65 years, the system of remuneration has been modified, etc. Because such a short time has passed since the implementation of these measures, it is impossible to fully evaluate their impact as yet, although some important questions have already emerged.

The implementation of the reform introduces a factor of uncertainty into the civil service, because it is directed toward weakening the professional corps, but without setting up any alternative system in its place. Job provision is carried out through public announcement of vacancies, but appointments are made freely among suitable candidates and, of course, free nomination also means free removal. Job classification is more apparent than real: job descriptions are not sufficiently clear cut, and not infrequently vacant positions are filled with civil servants initially recruited for very different jobs in the same or other public agencies. There is the possibility as well of the jobs not being occupied by civil servants but by workers hired on a labor contractual basis.

An administrative career in the proper sense does not exist at the present time. Freshly recruited civil servants can be appointed to positions at a high level of hierarchy and responsibility, whereas civil servants of great experience may be relegated to positions of secondary importance.

A rather widely extended critique of the present situation of the Spanish civil service holds that the socialist administration is practicing a sort of spoils system, limited, it is true, to civil servants, but systematically favoring the appointment of socialist sympathizers. This politicization of the civil service would represent a step back in contrast with the tendency towards professionalism which characterized the Spanish public administration in the period prior to the general elections won in 1982 by the Socialist Party. A new and more discretionary system of pay and allowances, recently introduced, may mean a further step in the current trend toward deprofessionalization of the Spanish civil service.

THE STRUCTURE OF THE SYSTEM

The Different Parts of the System: Central, Autonomous and Institutional

The system of public administration in Spain is divided into four different levels or spheres: the central administration of the country as a whole, the administrations of the regional autonomous communities, the administration at the local level (the administration of provinces, and of cities and towns) and the institutional administration (or the administration of semi-independent agencies and of state-owned enterprises).

The government and the central administration of the country make up the nucleus of the Spanish administrative organization. In Spain the word "government" means the same as "council of cabinet ministers." The government controls the central administrative system of the country, which is presently divided into fifteen different ministries or departments, through which the semi-independent agencies and the state-owned enterprises are managed. The government and the central administration have jurisdiction over the whole country.

The Council of Ministers is made up of the president of the government, who presides over it, the vice-president (or vice-presidents), and the cabinet ministers. The government controls the civil and military branches of the administrative system and can divide itself up into committees (five at present), in which a few ministers, together with the president, meet to deal with a specific area (for example, foreign policy, the environment).

Each department is headed by a minister, who may be assisted by a politically appointed state secretary with special and more limited powers. Subordinate to the minister is the undersecretary (or undersecretaries, because there can be several), who is the administrative head of the department. The undersecretaries play an important role through the General Commission of Undersecretaries, which prepares the topics that subsequently are to be debated and decided on by the Council of Ministers.

At the level immediately below that of the undersecretaries are the directors general, each one of whom is responsible for a specific area within his department. At the same level of hierarchy as the director general there is, in each department, a General Technical Office: this is a staff agency that advises the minister and draws up the policy programs of the department after the necessary studies.

The ministers, state secretaries, undersecretaries, directors general, and general technical secretaries are all political appointees designated freely by the party in power: the president of the government designates his ministers, and the latter designate their undersecretaries and directors general. The ministers and state secretaries can have a limited number of personal advisors, also freely designated. Civil service posts which must be filled by career public officials begin at the assistant director level; normally each director general has several assistant directors.

The national administration extends its operations throughout the country by means of civil governors and provincial offices or local branches of government departments, both of which operate at the provincial level. In Spain there are fifty provinces, which are administrative divisions or districts of the country. The highest authority in each province is the civil governor, who is the representative of the government in the province; he is also responsible for the co-ordination and smooth functioning of the provincial offices, or local branches of the different government departments.

As far as the administrative system of the regional autonomous communities is concerned, the Constitution of 1978 specifies the conditions under which a given geographic area can be granted the right to self-government, in accordance with the constitutional principle of the right to regional autonomy. At present, the entire territory of Spain is divided into seventeen autonomous communities. The Constitution has provoked an authentic redistribution of power, in accordance with the principle of non-interference on the part of the central government in the affairs of the self-governing bodies, and in the subjection of the latter to judicial control. In accordance with the Constitution, the statutes creating the autonomous communities include functions reserved to them that are performed totally independently of the national administration, as well as functions that are shared with the national administration. Activities in relation to the reserved functions are subject to review by the courts, but not by the central administration.

The autonomous communities have legislative powers and political and executive capabilities in areas granted to them in their statutes. Unlike what happens in the regional system in Italy in the case of reserved functions, an autonomous community in Spain can legislate directly, without previous authorization by national law. The autonomy that the autonomous communities enjoy is, then, a real political autonomy, which makes it possible to speak of a quasi-federal structure of government in Spain. In the process of the formation of the autonomous communities, the state has transferred to them the functions (reserved and shared) included in their respective statutes, in accordance with the Constitution. With the functions, of course, they also transferred the personnel and material resources necessary for carrying out public activities.

Most of the resources at the disposal of the autonomous administrations come from the national government.

Each autonomous community has a legislative assembly (elected by universal suffrage, and with proportional representation) and a government council (which carries out executive functions and is responsible to the assembly) and a president, elected by the assembly from among its members, who direct the government council. In each autonomous community there is a representative of the central government, whose duties include directing the agencies of the national administration located in the autonomous community and co-ordinating the activities of the national and autonomous systems.

The Constitution also provides for self-government for the 8,000 municipalities and fifty provinces that, taken together, make up the local administration. Spain is divided into 8,000 townships, each one containing a city or a town, which is governed by a municipal government. This municipal government is made up of a number of town councilmen, which varies according to the number of inhabitants. The councilmen are elected by universal suffrage on a proportional basis, and they elect, in turn, a mayor from among their members. The townships can join together in groups or associations for the delivery of services held in common, and this allows them to undertake construction projects that would otherwise be difficult.

The fifty provinces have provincial governments, the members of which are elected by the town councilmen from all the municipal governments in the province. They in turn elect their president from among themselves. The provincial governments carry out activities for the benefit of the population of the provinces and of the municipalities located in their territory, and they coordinate the system of local administration with the autonomous and central systems.

Finally, the so-called institutional administration is made up of public agencies that have no particular territorial limits and that are more or less autonomous, although they may be directly or indirectly dependent on an executive department of the government, may be funded entirely or in part by the national budget, and may be subject to regulation by Parliament and the General Accounting Court. The public agencies that constitute the Institutional administration can be of two kinds: semi-independent agencies and state-owned enterprises. The semi-independent agencies are regulated by public law, and are part of the national administration although they are not identified with the central administrative system. The state-owned enterprises, on the other hand, are subject to private law and have the form of a private company whose capital is, all or in part, public property. These publicly-owned private companies carry out the industrial activity of the State, public transportation, the central banking system, etc.

A Quasi-Federal Political System: Decentralization and Autonomy

The delegation of powers under the Spanish Constitution comes close to being a federal state in concept. The cities, provinces, and autonomous communities do not operate by virtue of a decision by Parliament nor by the national government, but by virtue of an inalienable right that is recognized and protected by the Constitution. The autonomy that characterizes the different levels of the Spanish system of public administration under the present democratic regime has meant a significant transfer of functions and of resources which, during the period of Franquist centralism (more precisely, during the entire history of the system of public administration in modern Spain), were in the hands of the central administration of the country. With respect to these functions the decision-making process no longer belongs to the central administration of the country but to the autonomous and local systems.

The nature of the autonomy enjoyed by the seventeen autonomous communities is not the same as that enjoyed by the fifty provinces or the 8,000 townships. The communities have legislative powers (as do, for example, the states in the United States), which means that they have the highest degree of political autonomy. By contrast, the provinces and townships do not have the power to legislate, although they can enact ordinances and regulations, subject to prevailing law. The Constitution specifies in detail the powers and functions of the autonomous communities, establishing which powers are reserved to them, which must be shared with the state, and which are reserved to the state; by contrast, the Constitution does not specify the functions of the provinces and townships, which are enacted in statutes that complement and complete the Constitution in this respect.

THE CIVIL SERVICE

The Size and Structure of the Civil Service

Spain is a country with a total population of about 40 million inhabitants, and with a labor force of about 13 million. The total number of those employed by the combined public administration systems is estimated at one and one-half million, which means that about 12 percent of the labor force in Spain works in one branch or another of public administration (4). The level of public employment is noticeably lower, relatively speaking, than in other comparable countries (or, in other words, the public sector of the economy is smaller in Spain): indeed, for the years 1980–1982, employment in the public sector, including the state-owned enterprises, reached 38.2 per cent of total employment in Sweden, 31.4 per cent in the United Kingdom, 24.4 per cent in Italy, 32.6 per cent in France, 18.3 per cent in the United States, and only 12.3 per cent in Spain (5).

The data in Table 1 merely constitute an estimate: there is no official document in Spain that describes completely and in detail the entire group of people working for the public administration system. As a result, it is sometimes said, even by government sources, that the number of public servants is unknown. This is true if one wants an exact figure, but it is also true that the above data, all of which comes from official sources, constitute a reasonably close estimate.

It is necessary to highlight several things in relation to the above data. Perhaps one of the most interesting things is the relatively low number of employees at the local administrative level, especially as compared with what is customary in other European countries. In an earlier study dealing with this matter (6), which revealed that Spain has the lowest proportion of public employees at the local level in all of Europe, the phenomenon was explained as being a result of the high degree of administrative centralism in Spain. Indeed, throughout the history of the Spanish public administration system, as has been seen, the national administration has constantly limited or hampered local self-government. Things have changed since the Constitution of 1978, however, which gives rise to the hope that, in the future, administration at the local level will become a larger part of the Spanish system of public administration.

Table 1   Employment in Spain's Public Sector

1. Central and Autonomous Administrations[a]		
Education[b]	257,000	
Police[b]	128,000	
Other	221,000	
Total	606,000	606,000
2. Local Administration		
Municipal Governments	160,000	
Provincial Governments	44,000	
Total	204,000	204,000
3. Institutional Administration		
Semi-Independent Agencies	178,000	
Social Security and Public Health	248,000	
State-Owned Enterprises		
Central Banking System	31,000	
Oil, Tobacco and Telephone Companies	72,000	
Railroads	79,000	
Companies with 50 Per cent or More State Ownership	151,000	
Total	759,000	759,000
TOTAL		1,569,000

[a]Employment in the central administration and in the autonomic administrations is grouped together because the process of transferring personnel and material resources is not yet complete for many of the autonomous communities.

[b]Employment in education and law enforcement are noted separately in order to show the degree to which they dominate the total.

Sources: Direccion General de la Funcion Publica, "Datos sobre el empleo en el sector publico español," I, II and III, in *Documentacion Administrativa*, numbers 166, 167 and 168, Madrid, 1975; Direccion General de la Funcion Publica, *Datos sobre funcion publica*, mimeograph, Madrid 1981; and Ministerio de Hacienda, *El presupuesto para 1982*, Madrid 1982.

Also notable is the fact that there are 333,000 people working for state-owned enterprises in Spain (central banking system; oil, tobacco and telephone companies; railroads; and companies with a majority ownership by the state). The reason for the large size of this group of workers in the public sector of the economy lies in the industrial policy followed, for the most part, by the governments in power from 1940–1965, which created and developed a National Industrial Institute to promote industrialization and to share in its financing. In Spain, an important part of basic, heavy industry was established by the National Industrial Institute, and this explains the relatively high number of people working for state-owned enterprises.

Another important group of public employees is the one that works for social security and public health systems, almost a quarter of a million people. One must keep in mind that Spain has instituted a comprehensive system of social security covering almost the entire population, in which medical and hospital services absorb most of the employees indicated above. Education also has a quarter of a million people in its ranks at all levels, from elementary school through the university. Health and education are two of the activities typical of the Welfare State, and in Spain a great effort has been made, and is still being made, to fulfill the needs of the population in both areas in the most efficient way possible. There is also a significant supply of private medical services and educational institutions (many of the latter being subsidized with public funds).

Regulation of the Civil Service

Some of the people in the Spanish public administration system are public officials and some are public workers. The officials have a statutory relationship with the administration rather than a contractual one: they are selected by means of merit examinations, and subsequently they are appointed as officials, their duties and rights being regulated by the laws in force at the time. The workers, on the other hand, have a contractual relationship with the administration much the same as the one that industrial or service workers have with private enterprises. Most of the civil servants in the central and autonomous administrations are officials, that is to say, they are subject to a statutory relationship with the administration they serve. By contrast, most of those who work for the Institutional administration, and more precisely for the state-owned enterprises, are workers: their relationship with the administration is based on a labor contract similar to that of the rest of the country's workers. For their part, the local administrations have many civil servants who are public officials but also many who are workers with a labor contract.

We will not discuss here whether public employees who work under a labor contract should be considered civil servants. But it is clear that in the continental European tradition (with some exceptions), a civil servant is, typically, the public official, that is, the person who has a statutory and not a contractual relationship to the administration. For this reason we will refer exclusively to the latter as we describe how the civil service is regulated.

The basic element in its regulation is the National Civil Service Act (*Ley de Funcionarios Civiles del Estado*), which establishes how one attains the status of public official and how one loses it, what the rights and duties of a public official are, and how the civil service is organized and administered. As already mentioned, there have been several Civil Service Acts in Spain: the one in 1852, which established the foundations of the modern civil service, the one in 1918 which consolidated the civil service system, and the one in 1964, still partially in effect today, which modernized it. In 1984 Parliament approved a reform measures Act (*Ley de Medidas para la Reforma de la Función Pública*) which modifies the 1964 Act.

The civil service is divided into corps, patterned after the old French model, and all public officials belong to one or another of them. A corps is a group of civil servants who have been selected according to a specified procedure, who have the same professional background, and who hold posts with similar functions. In the central administration there are presently around 200 of these corps, which are very important from the standpoint of how the civil service is regulated under law, and for the day-to-day functioning of the administrative system.

Indeed, the existence of corps of public officials has meant that the civil service is regulated not only by the Civil Service Act but also, in the case of almost all the corps, by a specific set of regulations that apply the general provisions of the Act to the particular case of the civil service workers of the corps involved. Traditionally, therefore, the regulations have differed widely from one branch to another, and consequently there has been a wide range of selection practices and a significant degree of organizational fragmentation. The large number of regulations has always made public personnel policy and management difficult in Spain.

From the point of view of the day-to-day functioning of the administrative system, the corps system has brought with it the danger of a certain amount of self-regulation, each corps trying to gain all the independence from the civil service authorities that it could, and competing with the other corps for privileges of all kinds. Historically, the corps of public officials have shown a tendency to divide into distinct particularistic factions in defense of the interest of their members and in search of a power base. This has permitted them to make decisions on the number of public officials there should be, how often merit examinations should be given for the selection of new members, the kind and character of such examinations, the duties and rights of their members, and sometimes even what their level of compensation should be, which positions should be restricted exclusively to members of the corps, what functions should be performed in each one, and what their relative position should be in relation to the public officials in another corps.

This corporativist tendency was particularly strong during the Franquist era, especially during the period before the Act of 1964. Since no structure existed for the representation or protection of the professional interests of public officials, the only channel for such protection was that of the Corps themselves. Moreover, for a long time there was no central authority in the civil service. Instead there were a great many central personnel offices which were not very well coordinated.

We have, then, the paradox that a civil service system that is quite rational as an organizational model, has yielded over the course of its history a series of disfunctions that are very characteristic of the Spanish system and that can be summarized in two words: fragmentation and factionalism. However, the idea that the corps system is bad and should be abolished is an exceedingly simplistic and superficial one: it is one of the basic structural features of the public administration system in Spain, especially of the administration at the national level, and its disfunctions can and ought to be corrected with a rational and efficient personnel policy.

Besides the corps system, two other basic structural elements of the Spanish civil service system should be mentioned: academic degree levels and the general scale of levels of difficulty and of the hierarchy.

Similar to what happens in other European public administration systems, in Spain public officials are classified according to the academic degree they hold. In order to be admitted into a corps of public officials, there is a definite academic degree requirement, which means that all of the civil servants in a given corps have fulfilled a minimum academic requirement, and they hold positions that are rated at a corresponding level. The academic qualifications required in Spanish civil service encompass the following levels:

Level 10: University Degree
Level 8: Technical School Degree
Level 6: High School Degree
Level 4: Junior High School Diploma
Level 3: Elementary School Diploma

Furthermore, all civil service jobs are rated on a scale according to their level of difficulty and to their position within the hierarchy. The scale has 30 steps and the highest one (step 30) is the one that corresponds to the position of Assistant Director-General, that is, the highest ranking position in the administrative hierarchy of the professional civil service.

In summary, all civil servants in Spain belong to a corps, and they are classified according to the academic qualifications required by that corps (a classification that determines in part their salary level); and at the same time, all civil servants occupy positions which are classified according to their degree of difficulty and their level within the hierarchy (which also partially determines their salary level).

SUPERVISION OF THE ADMINISTRATIVE SYSTEM

Parliamentary Oversight of the Administration

The basic authority over the administrative system is the law, and Parliament plays an important role here (both the national Parliament, for the central administration, and the legislative assemblies of the regional autonomous communities, for their respective administrations). But it is necessary to distinguish between parliamentary supervision of political acts of the government and supervision of the administration.

It is Parliament's job to supervise the political acts of the government using two principal methods: the motion of censure (introduced by the opposition party), and the question of confidence (introduced by the party in power). But these methods are too general to use in dealing with the specific questions that arise in the day-to-day activities of the public administration system. For parliamentary control over these matters, there are interpellations and parliamentary inquiries, and, on another level, Investigating Committees.

The difference between interpellations and inquiries is that interpellations must deal with the aims and objectives involved in carrying out matters of general policy, while inquiries must deal with questions of a specific nature. Both interpellations and inquiries can be directed to the government as such or to any of the cabinet ministers.

The Investigating Committees are an extraordinary means of oversight, since they are used only in cases of serious irregularities of significant public importance. These committees do not try to settle legal matters, and their findings are not a substitute for a decision in court; their purpose is, rather, to investigate serious cases of administrative negligence or irresponsibility. As a result, the oversight exercised by the Investigating Committees does not deal with acts by the government as such.

The General Accounting Court

This court, which is accountable to Parliament, is charged with overseeing the accounts and the management of the financial affairs of the State and of the public sector of the economy in general. Its internal operations are divided into two sections: the first involves supervision or oversight, the second one to conduct court-like trials dealing with the accounting of public revenues.

The function of supervision or oversight involves making sure that, in the conduct of the public sector, the principles of lawfulness, efficiency and thrift are adhered to. To do this, the Court examines the nation's accounts and those of the autonomous communities, also checking on the implementation of the budget, the contracts signed by the national government, and the state of public assets of all kinds. The results of this oversight activity are stated in a white paper or report that the General Accounting Court must submit annually to Parliament. The Court's oversight powers are not restricted to matters of financial legalities, but also include questions about efficiency of public operations. This gives rise to the possibility of suggesting measures to the administration to improve management.

The Defender of the People (Ombudsman)

The office of Defender of the People was created by the Spanish Constitution along the lines of the ombudsman in other countries. The Defender not only investigates complaints against abuses by government officials or agencies involving failure to act, negligence, or untimeliness, but also acts as a defender of the constitutional rights of Spaniards. As such he can appeal to the Constitutional Court. He is appointed for five years by Parliament, with a necessary three-fifths majority vote in favor of the proposed candidate in each of the two Houses. The incompatibilities established for the office are perhaps the most rigorous of those established by Spanish law: he cannot be a member of any political party of labor union, association or foundation, nor can he perform other activities in the public or private sector.

The jurisdiction of the Defender of the People covers all levels of government, which means that he has the authority to investigate complaints against administrations of the autonomous communities as well. In the statutes of some of them, nonetheless, there are provisions for the creation of an ombudsman of their own. In these cases, the ombudsmen must coordinate their activities with the one at the national level (who can, in turn, request their cooperation).

Typically, the activities of the Defender of the People are directed at the administrative system. The process begins with the arrival of a complaint, in writing, at his office. The complaint can be filed by anyone, including minors, the mentally handicapped, and people serving time in prison, for example. The Defender undertakes an informal investigation of the department or agency involved, whose authorities and employees are required to cooperate with him. Based on the results of his investigation, though he cannot change administrative actions, he can publicize abuses by the administration and report them to Parliament. He can also offer suggestions about the criteria on which administrative actions are based and even about the advisability of changing rules and regulations currently in force.

Judicial Authority over the Administration

The Spanish Constitution provides that the courts of justice have jurisdiction over the administration's rule-making power and over the legality of administrative acts. This authority is exercised by courts that specialize in the areas of appeals against final decisions of the administration. The process begins with a complaint against a regulation imposed by the administration or against an act it committed. But before calling on the courts to rule on the legality of the conduct in question, the interested party must have filed a complaint with the administration itself, and only when the response of the latter proves unsatisfactory, can he appeal that decision before the courts.

This judicial authority over the legality of administrative acts, both in the case of a regulation imposed and in that of an act committed, is only applicable to operations governed by administrative law. Complaints of any other kind against the administrative system—for example, those of a civil nature or those related to labor disputes—are presented before the regular courts, not those that deal with appeals against decisions of the administration. The power of judicial review on appeal over the legality of the administration's regulations is an important tool since it is the only control that exists in Spain over the administration's rule-making powers, even though the Spanish system fully recognizes the government's power to make regulations in the course of implementing legislation.

Finally, the Constitutional Court, whose purpose is to make sure that constitutional provisions are complied with, has jurisdiction only over the constitutionality of laws, not over the regulations issued by the administration (the ordinary courts have jurisdiction over these, as we have seen). What the Constitutional Court does do, however, is protect the rights of private citizens against acts committed by government officials or agencies by means of an appeal to obtain protection against the violations of the fundamental rights and liberties enjoyed by Spaniards under their Constitution. In order to bring this kind of appeal before the Constitutional Court, it is necessary to have brought a complaint before the ordinary courts, without having received satisfaction.

ACKNOWLEDGMENT

The author gratefully acknowledges the assistance of José M. Garcia Madaria, Professor of Public Administration, Universidad Complutense de Madrid, in the preparation of various parts of this chapter, and of Nancy Lopez Aranguran, Professor of Spanish Language and Literature, Mankato State University, in the English translation of this chapter.

REFERENCES

1. Brian Chapman, *The Profession of Government* (London: George Allen and Unwin, 1959), p. 29.

2. Juan J. Linz, "An Authoritarian Regime: Spain," in E. Allardt and S. Rokkan, eds., *Mass Politics: Studies in Political Sociology* (New York: Free Press, 1970).

3. Eduardo Garcia de Enterria, *La Administración española* (Madrid: Instituto de Estudios Politicos, 1964), pp. 201–220. Alejandro Nieto, *La retribución de los funcionarios en España* (Madrid: Revista de Occidente, 1967).

4. Juan Junquera, "La burocracia en la Europa de los nueve," in *Papeles de Economía Española*, 2 (1980). Mariano Baena, *Estructura de la función publica y burocracia en España* (Oñati: Instituto Vasco de Administracion Pública, 1984).

5. John P. Martin, "Public Sector Employment Trends in Western Industrialized Economies," in *Public Finance and Public Employment,* Proceedings of the 36th Congress of the International Institute of Public Finance (Detroit: Wayne State University Press, 1982). Richard Rose, ed., *Public Employment in Western Nations* (Cambridge: Cambridge University Press, 1985), p. 6.

6. Juan Junquera, *op. cit.*, pp. 175 and 180.

ANNOTATED REFERENCES IN ENGLISH

The classic study of Brian Chapman, *The Profession of Government: The Public Service in Europe* (London: Allen and Unwin, 1959), contains references to Spain, many of which are still of interest. In preparation for the Plan for Economic Development of 1964, the International Bank for Reconstruction and Development published a report, *The Economic Development of Spain* (Baltimore: John Hopkins Press, 1963), which contains information about some features of Spanish public administration at that time.

A complete picture of the condition of the Spanish civil service around 1970, after the adoption of the reforms of 1964, is found in the article by Alberto Gutierrez Reñón, "The Spanish Public Service," in *Revue Internationale des Sciences Administratives* (Brussels, 1969). There is an interesting article by Kenneth M. Medhurst, "The Political Presence of the Spanish Bureaucracy," in *Government and Opposition* (London: Spring, 1969), but even more interesting is his book, *Government in Spain: The Executive at Work* (Oxford: Pergamon, 1973), which offers an overview of the government machinery in the Franco regime, discussing its nature and origin, and describing the structure and operation of the cabinet, the civil service, the government departments, local administration, and oversight of the administration.

The book by Charles W. Anderson on *The Political Economy of Modern Spain: Policy-Making in an Authoritarian System* (Madison: University of Wisconsin Press, 1970) deals with the implementation of Spanish economic policy between 1957 and 1967, with special attention to the Stabilization Plan (with which the liberalization of the economy was initiated) and the Plan for Economic and Social Development. The book by Richard Gunther, *Public Policy in a No-Party State: Spanish Planning and Budgeting in the Twilight of the Franquist Era* (Berkeley: University of California Press, 1980), deals mostly with budget policy, with public spending, and with public investment during the late 1960's and the early 1970's, with special attention to their instrumentation and administration.

There are many well-known studies in English that deal with the democratic system established in Spain in 1975, and with the process of political transition from authoritarianism to democracy. Although none of the studies focusses exclusively on the system of public administration, many of them offer analyses of the new political and constitutional framework of which it is a part. See, for example, David S. Bell, ed., *Democratic Politics in Spain* (London: Pinter, 1983), esp. Pierre Subra de Bieusses, "Constitutional Norms and Central Administration."

ANNOTATED REFERENCES IN SPANISH*

Although in Spain the public administration system has received most attention from jurists, contributions from the social sciences permit the following basic bibliography to be selected.

On the recent history of the Spanish public administration system, one can consult several books which offer good syntheses: Eduardo Garcia de Enterria, *La Administración española* (Madrid: Instituto de Estudios Politicos, 1964); Alejandro Nieto, *La retribucion de los funcionarios en España* (Madrid: Editorial de la Revista de Occidente, 1967); Mariano Baena del Alcazar, *Curso de Ciencia de la Administración* (Madrid: Tecnos, 1985); and José M. Garcia Madaria, *Estructura de la Administracion Central (1808-1931)* (Madrid: Instituto Nacional de Administracion Publica, 1982). One can also consult three articles by Alejandro Nieto which were published under the title, "De la República a la Democracia: la Administración española del franquismo," in *Civitas. Revista Española de Derecho Administrativo* in 1976 (number 11), 1977 (number 15) and 1978 (number 18).

On the size and structure of the civil service, the two most recent and most interesting studies are the book by Juan Junquera, *La función pública en la "Europa de los Doce"* (Madrid: Instituto Nacional de Administración Pública, 1986), and the book by Mariano Baena del Alcazar *Estructura de la función pública y burocracia en España* (Oñati: Instituto Vasco de Administración Pública, 1984). In 1966 Alberto Gutiérrez Reñón published an important article, "Estructura de la burocracia española: notas para su estudio," in *Revista Española de la Opinión Pública*, number 3, which is still useful to consult.

A fundamental article on the civil service corps is the one by Andrés de la Oliva and Alberto Gutiérrez Reñón "Los Cuerpos de funcionarios," published in the collectively authored book *Sociologia de la Administración pública española* (Madrid: Centro de Estudios Sociales, 1968). A good evolutionary approach in Alejandro Nieto, "Afirmacion, apogeo, decadencia y crisis de los Cuerpos de funcionarios," in the collectively authored book *Estudios sobre la burocracia española* (Madrid: Instituto de Estudios Politicos, 1974).

On the bureaucratic elite, studied in a survey, see the book by Miguel Beltrán *La élite burocrática española* (Barcelona: Ariel, 1977); other studies of interest on the relationship among the bureaucratic elite, politics and the financial world, are in number 522 of the journal *Información Comercial Española*, Madrid 1977, a monograph devoted to the topic "La burocracia en España."

An analysis of the attitudes and opinions of public officials towards the current reformation of the Spanish public administration system is the book by Miguel Beltrán *Los funcionarios ante la reforma de la Administración* (Madrid: Centro de Investigaciones Sociologicas y Siglo XXI, 1985).

Editor's Note: Since there are so few up-to-date references in English, Professor Beltrán has kindly prepared this annotation on materials in Spanish.

17

France

YVES MÉNY
University of Paris II, Paris, France

HISTORY AND ENVIRONMENT

France's monarchical heritage and the innovations of 1789, synthesized under Napoleon, determined in large part the character and conduct of French administration for more than a century. This continuity was further ensured by an "administrative law" governing the administration inspired and implemented by the Council of State—the guardian and guarantor of the basic values of a centralized and hierarchical administration—according to uniform, egalitarian and universal criteria (1). However, as we shall see, this ideal conception of the French administration has never been perfectly realized.

The complexity of the French administrative system has increased in line with the growth of state economic intervention. The tradition of "Colbertism," of state intervention in the economy, has been continuously maintained in France, even during periods of economic liberalism (between 1830 and 1848 and under the Second Empire). To the administrative sector as such there has been added, in successive waves, a public economic sector which, since the nationalizations of 1981, now accounts for a quarter of the French workforce. The change has not only been quantitative: the administration is more than ever at the center of economic activity whether controlled by the state or managed by the private sector.

To these factors deriving from the history of the State can be added those which derive from the constitutional and political framework. Although the Constitution of 1958 considerably strengthened the powers of the executive (2), it mentions the administration only fleetingly. Given the influence of the Council of State in the drafting of the Constitution, this would appear surprising were it not for the fact that this has been the case of nearly all of the French constitutions. Implicity or explicitly, the Constitution of 1958 refers to the state administration only four times (arts. 13, 20, 21, 34).

From these scarce elements, two fundamental principles are derived. The first is that of the subordination of the administration to the government. Article 20 specifies that "the government determines and conducts the politics of the nation" and emphasizes that the administration is at its disposal. The power of nomination accorded to the President and the Prime Minister are a clear expression of this subordination, especially with regard to those appointments "at their discretion." The second principle concerns, paradoxically, the independence of public officials from political power. In providing legislative protection for public servants, the Constitution continues the tradition established by the Preamble to the 1946 Constitution, giving the basis for the general statutes of the civil service (3). The principle of the independence of the administration has three facets: it protects civil servants from political interference; it ensures them a minimum of decision-making autonomy; and it ensures an administrative continuity above and beyond the short-term evolution of the political system.

However, both the principle of subordination and that of independence have been subject, in practice, to important qualification. It could be assumed, for example, that the stability of executive power enhances its control of the administration. In fact, the government of the Fifth Republic has never been able to ensure a strict control of civil servants, who have benefitted from strong legislative and judicial protection and from powerful trade unions (unlike the private sector, the public sector is heavily unionized in France). In addition, the principles of subordination and independence have been submerged by a merging in practice of politics and administration "at the heights of the State" (4). For instance, the number of deputies to emerge from the civil service has continued to grow: they accounted for 172 of the total 491 in 1978 and for almost half of the assembly elected in 1981. Also, since the beginning of the Fifth Republic, there has been a tradition of conferring ministerial portfolios on non-elected civil servants who eventually launch themselves upon a political career (5). It is striking to note that the nine prime ministers of the Fifth Republic between 1958 and 1984 have all been recruited from the senior levels of the civil service. Finally, the entry of bureaucrats into the political world is particularly marked in that twilight zone between the administration and politics, the ministerial secretariats (*cabinets*). Increasingly, their senior civil servants have encroached upon domains of activity traditionally reserved for the regular administrative departments. Hence the conflicts and delays illustrated particularly well by the work of Ezra Suleiman (6).

STRUCTURE AND MANAGEMENT

The French administrative system is reputed to be the archetype of the centralized Nation-State, and it has often served as a model for the construction of hierarchical administrations, centralized under government control and organized according to a "rational" and uniform conception of the State. However, this is an ideal-type impression rather than a realistic analysis. A more critical examination reveals a much more complex situation. Under the nominal authority of the central administration, the field services of the State, the local administrations and the many *ad hoc* administrative institutions enjoy a large margin of maneuver and a considerable capacity for independent action (7).

The Central Administration

Although the government and the Prime Minister are formally responsible for the management of the administration, the 1958 Constitution (contrary to that of 1946) confers supreme administrative power on the President of the Republic, who signs all edicts and decrees in the Council of Ministers and is responsible for appointments at the highest levels of the State. This administrative dualism has not led to serious conflicts, however, and in general has functioned well, essentially for political reasons. Since 1958, there have never been any fundamental clashes between the President of the Republic and his Prime Minister, the representative of the parliamentary majority (8). Nevertheless, certain problems have been created by the coexistence of two powerful centers of initiative and coordination, the Office of the President (the Elysée) and the Office of the Prime Minister (Matignon).

The Services of the Elysée and Matignon

Although the presidency of the Republic is not itself an administration in the strict sense of the term, the head of state is assisted by personal advisers in the preparation of important dossiers. Apart from the President's general secretary, who is responsible for information and coordination, the Presidents of the Fifth Republic have been assisted by a secretariat (*cabinet*) of around twenty senior political advisors who cover the most important areas of administrative and political life, the division of tasks corresponding to that between ministries: economic, financial, educational, foreign affairs, etc. In each sector for which they are responsible, these assistants must keep the President informed, assist in decision-making, and, in certain cases, ensure that presidential orders are properly executed. These advisers are not well known to the public (except for notable exceptions where the advisers are better known than the ministers in charge). They exert a varying degree of influence, depending on their personal relationship with the President (common experiences, political positions and activities) and especially on the degree of interest taken by the President in any particular dossier or sector (9). It is well known that these *éminences grises* are often more influential and powerful than the ministers themselves.

The lightweight character of the President's entourage prevents his advisers from becoming involved in administrative management or from substituting themselves for any one of the numerous groups and committees which surround the Prime Minister. However, this does not prevent conflicts and disruptions, particularly when the advisers of the Elysée and those of the Matignon and of specialized ministries disagree on policies to be pursued or appointments to be made. These occur most frequently in the public industrial or banking sectors.

The Prime Minister is assisted by a *cabinet* which is somewhat smaller than that of the President. Apart from fulfilling an advisory and coordinating role, it often stands in for the Prime Minister in presiding over numerous committees. Its members are delegated prime ministerial powers of decision and can deal with problems requiring the intervention of the Prime Minister, notably in arbitrating between ministries whose interests or points of view are at odds. The Prime Minister is also assisted by the General Secretariat of the Government which is responsible for "arranging interministerial meetings, ranging from the Council of Ministers to the meetings of high-ranking civil servants at the Matignon; for arranging contacts between the executive and legislative branches of government and, finally, for following all procedures which require the Prime Minister's intervention: the formulation of legislation, the preparation and signing of decrees, etc." (10). Finally, several important administrative institutions are attached to the Prime Minister: the General Secretary for National Defense, the

General Commissioner of the Plan, and the General Secretary of the Interministerial Committee on European Economic Cooperation (S.G.C.I.). The latter is particularly important because it takes and implements decisions pertaining to the European Economic Community. This centralization regarding Community affairs has definitely strengthened the position of French negotiators in Brussels.

The Ministries

The structure of the ministries is, in contrast, much more flexible. The number of ministries and the distribution of tasks among them have been determined both by structural factors (increasing State intervention in all areas) and by particular circumstances, such as the distribution of portfolios among parties, or political differences within the government. A ministry can be created or dissolved by simple command and the prerogatives of each department are fixed by decree in the Council of Ministers following approval from the Council of State.

Each ministry is divided between its central services and its external field services which are responsible for implementing policy. Among the central services is the minister's secretariat (*cabinet*), composed of civil servants selected for their abilities and political proximity to the minister (in general, a dozen official plus numerous "unofficial" members). The main part of the ministry is divided into *directions*, some of which are responsible for carrying out ministerial tasks, while others are responsible for managing the ministry. The minister formulates and implements his policies mainly through circulars and directives. Their use compensates for the minister's lack of statutory powers which, for reasons of coordination and collective ministerial responsibility, are monopolized by the President and the Prime Minister.

The ministries also include three other subsidiary institutions, the importance and prestige of which vary according to the "weight" of the ministry and to the role acquired by the corps in its service. First there are the *corps d'inspection* which are connected directly to the minister. They are responsible for keeping him informed of the ministry's affairs and for ensuring that ministerial policy is properly executed and that its activities are consistent. Examples are the Inspectors of the Armed Forces and the Inspectors of Education. The most well known and powerful *corps d'inspection* is that of the Ministry of Finance, whose influence extends well beyond that of the Ministry itself, even into the private sector and politics (V. Giscard d'Estaing, M. Rocard and L. Fabius are all members of this corps, for example). One in every two Inspectors of Finance is on secondment elsewhere!

The advisory committees (*conseils consultatifs*) are another feature of the French administrative system. While it has a reputation—which is often justified—for being authoritarian, the administration is often described as a *polysynodie*, a régime of multiple committees. The administration seeks to take all interests into account, but it has been unable to avoid two shortcomings: the often clandestine character of relations between the administration and interest groups, and a tendency to select its negotiating partners from among those groups least opposed to its policies.

Finally, there are numerous public institutions or offices which, although legally autonomous, are placed under the supervision of the ministries. The degree of supervision depends not only on the status of the institution and the nature of its activities (those involved in economic affairs often enjoying the greatest autonomy), but also, according to the attitude of the incumbent minister, who can exercise a degree of discretion in applying administrative rules. Among these institutions, some of the most important are: the National Centre for Scientific Research, the National Institute for Health and Medical Research, the *grandes écoles* (for which the Ministry of Education or various technical ministries are responsible), and the museums under the Ministry of Culture.

The Field Services

While the central services are few in number but highly influential in decision-making, the field services account for the three million State servants in France and play a considerable role in the implementation of government policies. The role of the field services has long been neglected due to the prestige attached to the activities and posts of the central administration. However, in recent years their importance has been reassessed by a number of studies which have revealed the significance of the implementation phase of the policy process. The field services of the ministries are generally organized at the level of the French *département* (district) which, since the French Revolution, has been the strongest of the local administrative units. Since the 1960s, there has been a general shift to the higher regional level, but this level of decision-making often remains weaker than that of the *département*, since it is concerned more with planning and coordination than with administrative management. The financial and human resources of the administration are therefore concentrated largely at the level of the 95 départements.

The field services can be divided into two major categories: those specialized services connected to the central services of each ministry; and those with general responsibilities under the direct authority of the prefect in the region or *département*, or of the mayor at the level of local government (the *service d'Etat-civil*, for example). In certain cases, specialized services at the level of the *département*, play a role not only in implementing State policy but also in conceiving and executing the policies of decentralized local authorities. Quite often there is an intermingling of State and local services (13), either because State and local authority personnel work in the same service areas—regardless of the Cartesian rationality often attributed to the French administration—or because the State services work on behalf of the local authorities. Thus the district health authority (*direction départementale de l'action sanitaire et sociale* includes civil servants both from the State and from the local authorities. Similarly, the district planning authority (*direction départementale de l'equipement*) is responsible for the investment programes and town planning of most of the 36,000 French *communes* (local governments), with the exception of the large towns. The communal jigsaw is therefore pieced together and coordinated by the services of the State. In other cases, administrative management assumes a quasi-corporatist form, as, for example, in that of agriculture where the district agricultural authority (*direction départementale de l'agriculture*) implements ministerial policy jointly with the professional and trade associations of the sector. Nothing can be done without, or in opposition to, these organizations.

The field services with general responsibilities are placed under the authority of the prefect (14) of the region or the department, or under that of the sub-prefect at the level of the sub-department (*arrondissement*). Since the 1982 reform, prefects have become Commissioners of the Republic and are no longer both government representatives and executives of the regional and *département* assemblies. Henceforth they have become simply State representatives responsible for coordinating the field services of all ministries. At their particular level they perform a role similar to that of the Prime Minister with regard to his ministers. In order to do so, they depend on the field service heads to keep them informed and they monitor communications from and to the ministries. They are also equally the chairmen, in law, of the administrative committees in their area and are responsible for assessing the performance of the service heads. They are also responsible for the preparation and implementation of the economic plan, for the distribution of public investments and for public works programmes at the regional and *département* levels. But despite the large panoply of powers placed at their disposal, in particular by the reforms of 1964, 1970, 1972 and 1982, they have had great difficulty in asserting their authority over the field services, especially the oldest and most powerful, such as agriculture and public works (15). Furthermore, entire ministries—and not the least important—escape their supervision: education, the armed forces and the postal services, the three largest ministries.

However, although deprived of some of their powers since the 1982–1983 reform, the Commissioners of the Republic are still the mainspring of administrative action in the provinces. They are assisted by a *cabinet* composed of young and often dynamic senior officials, which is aided in turn by a General Secretary on behalf of the subprefects of the *arrondissements*. Since the Commissioner is the sole representative of all of the ministries, he is responsible for maintaining order, making contracts and for public expenditure. He is therefore in a position to exert pressure on the heads of the field services. Finally, although he no longer exercises any control over the assemblies of the *départements* and *communes*, he remains the *de facto* adviser consulted by mayors, in particular those from the smallest communes.

Noting that he is obliged to remain loyal to the government and is unable to join a trade union or to strike, we can conclude that the Commissioner provides the government with one of its most effective means of administrative control and policy implementation.

The Decentralization of 1981–83

A set of reforms instituted between 1981 and 1983 gave more power to the authorities of local government and changed the relationship between them and the State's field services. This reform movement was set apart from earlier attempts at reform (16) by a determined will to succeed, and was largely pragmatic in nature. The principal measures were (17):

> the transfer of the powers of the regional and *département* executives from the prefects to the chairmen of the regional and *département* councils;
> the prefect (now commissioner), has become simply a representative of the State, responsible for coordinating the field services;
> prefectoral supervision of the *communes* and *départements* (which had largely become fictitious) has been removed and replaced by the jurisdictional control of the regional administrative tribunals and the financial control of the new *chambres régionales des comptes*;
> local authority personnel have been awarded a new statute, analogous to that of civil servants;
> the regional assemblies will (from 1986 on) be elected by universal suffrage;

Corsica and overseas regions have been awarded specific statutes;

the responsibilities of local authorities have been redefined and extended, assigning
   local management to the *communes*, social services to the *départements*, and
   responsibility for economic development to the regions.

Beyond this basic design it seems that a "marble cake model" is replacing a "layer
cake model." This means that decision-making processes are becoming more complex,
even more cumbersome, but also more democratic. The reform of the local financial
system, however, has been disappointing, and financial transfers from the State cannot
be considered as an adequate substitute.

The Instruments of Administrative Action

The administration intervenes in many areas and its intervention takes many different
legal forms. In fact, the government and the administration are quite pragmatic and
use any means available, often using certain instruments for purposes other than those
for which they were originally intended. For instance, the administration often uses
legal forms of action originally designed for civil society such as for commercial associations. Thus there is an extra spectrum of administrative actions which extends from
the use of the instruments of private law to those peculiar to public law.

A form frequently used for administrative intervention is that of the *contract*. By
way of *concessions*, a public institution (State or local authority) makes an individual
responsible for a public service and imposes certain obligations in return for the
resources required for providing this service (tax collection, monopoly, guarantee of
financial aid in the case of price fixing, compulsory purchase, etc.). Numerous public
services are provided according to this technique, especially in urban areas: distribution of water, urban transport, heating, roads, theaters, etc. When the administration
takes responsibility for a service itself, the technique employed is that of State control
(*la régie*), i.e., purely administrative control. The administration also uses the simple
technique of the *association* (reserved in principle for private individuals), due to the
ease of creation and managerial flexibility of this type of institution and to avoid the
bureaucratic and financial inertia of administrative structures. But the *Cour des
Comptes* has condemned the use of this technique during the past twenty years and
has always maintained—not always with success—that the administration should use
those procedures with which it is legally provided.

The administration can also delegate important tasks to private institutions which
often become bureaucratized and eventually identify themselves with the administration. This is the case, for example, of the social security offices, which have an
important role and which manage considerable sums of money as mutual benefit
insurance societies.

The *Sociétés d'Economie mixte* provide another example of the hybrid character of
certain administrative institutions. Formally private, in principle they ally private with
public capital. But more often than not, most of the capital comes from the public
sector. These companies have been responsible for large-scale public projects (hydraulic
development of the Rhône, highways, etc.) and have played a fundamental role in
urban development since the 1950s. There are around 800 local *Sociétés d'Economie
mixte*, and they are often subsidiaries of the SCET (*Société centrale pour l'équipement
du territoire*), itself a subsidiary of the *Caisse des dépôts et consignations*, the State

institution which accumulates public funds and lends them at low rates of interest, mostly to local authorities. Most new town suburbs and urban infrastructures are developed by these companies.

Etablissements publics form the largest and most heteogeneous group of administrative institutions. Some organize private interests (Chambers of Commerce, agriculture and trade), allowing the latter to take advantage of tax resources and to carry out public investments (airports, industrial zones, roads). Others control local private institutions. Still others are powerful banking and financial institutions, economic, scientific or cultural agencies, or, at the local level, museums, hospitals, institutions for inter-communal cooperation, new towns, or low-rent housing agencies.

In the 1970s, the Council of State attempted in a report to order and classify these different types, but found the only workable distinction to be that which separates administrative ones (called EPAs) from industrial and commercial ones (called EPICs). In theory the distinction would allow each of these categories to be provided with statutes, financial rules and controls adapted to its particular needs. However, the term "industrial and commercial" is often attributed to administrative activities to provide them with greater independence and flexibility of management. While all EPA personnel are civil servants, only the director and the accountant of the EPICs are. EPAs can engage in public purchasing and are subject to the laws of the public sector while EPICs, at least in principle, do not benefit from such public sector prerogatives and are restricted to the normal techniques of the market.

In sum, the importance of the public establishments resides in the flexibility they allow the administration. The price, however, is a proliferation of institutions, which often jealously guard their privileges and prerogatives.

PUBLIC SERVICE PERSONNEL

Since the second world war, each important political rupture (1946, 1958, 1981) has been accompanied by reforms of significance for the development of the civil service. Their governing idea is to apply a uniform set of rights and obligations to all civil servants, at least at the level of general principles (forms of recruitment and promotion, civil liberties, etc.). In fact, the general statute of the civil service contains provision for special dispensations, allowing certain clauses to be adjusted for particular personnel with the approval of the High Council of the Civil Service. In consequence there are many special statutes (more than 850!) providing dispensation from the general statute, notably concerning civil liberties. In return for concessions of a financial type, personnel responsible for certain tasks have their rights of strike and unionization restricted: police, prison wardens, prefects, etc.

The Categories of Personnel

The civil service is highly heterogeneous despite the general rules which govern it. There are three broad categories of personnel: State officials, local authority officials, and personnel outside the civil service as such who work for the central or local authorities.

The first group, the State civil servants, are the most important in every respect. Numerically, because they number more than two million, nearly half of whom belong to the education system (teachers and administrators), and a further 350,000 of whom are attached to the armed services. But also hierarchically: traditionally in France, tasks of decision-making are more highly valued than those of implementation. The division of labor between the State and local authorities has long been based on this cleavage. Therefore there is a greater concentration of bureaucrats of senior grade in the service of the central State than in that of the local authorities. Thus, grades B and A, reserved for those with the *baccalauréat* or with a teaching diploma, account for 60 per cent of those attached to the State civil service, while only 8 per cent of those at the local authority level have the same qualifications. Highly qualified personnel are over-represented in the State civil service not only in comparison with the local level but also with respect to French society as a whole, in which, in 1975, only 15 per cent of the working population had the *baccalauréat*. Within the State civil service, soldiers, magistrates, parliamentary officials, and external secret service agents (DGSE) have independent statutes, and other special statutes containing dispensations from the general rules have proliferated since 1958.

The second group, also rather disparate, includes local authority officials, mainly from the *départements* and *communes* ahd their *établissements publics*, the regions having been allowed their own public officials only since 1982. This group have increased in number to a little more than 700,000. Until now, the local civil service has been inferior in both numerical and statutory terms, communal officials (about 600,000) being the only ones benefitting from a legislative statute, while departmental officials (100,000) were governed by a statute decided by each departmental council. But 35 per cent of communal officials, 60 per cent of departmental officials and 60 per cent of those attached to local housing offices were not governed by any public statute. To the local authority personnel should be added hospital staff (about 700,000), housing staff (40,000), and officials of the city of Paris (56,000) who have their own statutes.

Until 1983 local civil servants did not enjoy guarantees regarding either recruitment (the discretionary power of the mayors being very large) or career, and their incomes were well below those of State officials at similar professional levels. In 1983 a new statute, creating a "territorial public service" aligned the statute for local authority officials with that for State officials, and allowed for professional mobility between the two groups.

The third group is comprised of non-civil servants recruited by contract for limited periods without guarantee of continued employment and often at a low level of income. In 1981, 461,681 such non-civil servants recruited by the State or local authorities were given public service status by the Socialist government, thus putting a previously unfair and conflictual state of affairs in order, but also preventing a renewal of recruitment and ratifying *a posteriori* appointments often made according to questionable criteria.

The structure of the civil service—at least for those governed by statute—is based on a number of diverse categories within which the position of officials is strictly identical with regard to rights and obligations. At present the concept of *corps*—that is, of a group of officials with the same statute and eligible for the same grade—is the basic principle of administrative organization. The *corps* are themselves based on a hierarchy of tasks and include a number of grades which correspond to different positions with specific responsibilities and salary. The grades are themselves divided into levels or classes, which allow career promotion within a grade and eventually from one grade to the next. Finally, the corps are divided into categories A, B, C and D:

A—management and decision
B—implementation
C—specialized tasks
D—simple tasks.

These distinctions are particularly important in determining conditions of recruitment (diplomas, type of examination) and salary. Lastly, administrative law and practice distinguish between the *position*, which denotes a financial category, and the *grade*. This allows a change of grade without a change of position, or the suppression of a position without firing the official.

Recruitment and Promotion

Recruitment to the civil service is carried out according to qualifications or examinations, but the latter is the most important. The preference given to examinations can be explained by the importance of the principle of equality in France. The interpretation of this principle is essentially legal, the equality sought being strictly formal: the impersonal and general character of the rules and procedures seems to be the best guarantee of equality, as well as of impartiality and objectivity.

Within this impersonal and general framework, one can detect a number of mitigations of these rules which would otherwise be too rigid. Equality is not conceived in a universal sense, but rather in terms of various categories. It is possible, for example, to organize examinations in certain sections of the administration reserved for men or for women; to fix quotas on the number of external candidates (students) and internal candidates (officials seeking promotion); to guarantee positions to the handicapped or to old prisoners of war. Within this rigid system there are therefore certain types of "quotas." But more often than not, candidates for examination are only subject to conditions of qualification or age. Examinations for categories A, B, C, D are based on an academic model and are highly theoretical. There is virtually no link between the abilities tested in the exam and the capabilities expected from the future public servant. This lack of relevance reaches absurd proportions in the case of the exam for the National School of Administration (ENA), which provides access to the senior levels of the administration as well as to the public industrial and banking sectors.

The principle of recruitment by examination is so deeply anchored in the system of administrative values and practice that it has tended to spread to domains where previously it did not exist: thus the new statute for local civil servants adopted in 1983 extends recruitment by examination and restricts considerably the discretionary power of the mayors. Similarly, internal promotion within each administrative category and between categories tends to occur increasingly through internal examinations. It is the possibility of internal promotion (and the narrow salary difference between categories) that makes the system of stratification by categories A, B, C, D more tolerable. Ten to fifteen per cent of positions are set aside for internal promotion, and in recent years ENA has recruited an equal number of students by external examination (open to students) and by internal examination (reserved for civil servants with more than five years of service). Despite the cumbersome nature of this system (both for civil servants themselves and for the administration), it compensates for the present system of promotion based on seniority and selection. The system of promotion by seniority prevents any arbitrary choice on the part of civil service chiefs and is approved of particularly by the trade unions. The system of promotion by selection is based on the estimation of subordinates by their superiors, notably through administrative points. In fact, the allocation of points for performance is conditioned more or less completely by administrative practice and the margin of maneuver for superiors is almost non-existent. Unless they commit a gross misdemeanor, public officials consider that they have the "right" to the points normally awarded to their colleagues at that stage in their career. Promotion by selection has therefore become another form of promotion by seniority (18).

Rights of Civil Servants

The modes of recruitment, promotion and organization of administrative services ensure an effective protection of civil servants not only against political interference, but equally against their superiors in the hierarchy. One reason why the civil service remains so attractive, despite salaries lower than in the private sector, is because it guarantees not only security of employment but also the freedom to enjoy civil liberties.

With the exception of certain *corps* which are submitted to special statutes (the police or prison staff), all public officials enjoy the right to strike. In certain instances, this right is restricted, although not in a heavily constraining manner. For example, since 1963, the civil service unions must deliver notice of a strike five days in advance. The law also requires that a minimum service be provided, if necessary by requisitioning certain of those on strike. For example, primary or secondary school teachers can strike, but headmasters must organize a means of catering for the children; the television can refuse to transmit programs but it must transmit at the very minimum a film and a news bulletin.

The same balance is sought with regard to the freedom of expression. The civil servant enjoys the same rights as other French citizens on the sole condition that the expression of his opinions or his actions do not depart from the "reserve" expected of someone in his position. This "obligation of reserve" is applied in various ways, however. Senior civil servants (prefects, diplomats, administrative chiefs) have an obligation of "loyalty" but obligations are minimal for civil servants involved in trade union or political activities. In fact, the existing system is very liberal, so liberal that the most virulent criticisms of government policy come from the civil service and the latter has become the most important source for the recruitment of politicians: one-third of French members of parliament (including both houses) now come from the administration, and their number is also growing at the local level at the expense of other social categories. In addition, the administration has been very generous towards civil servants who perform trade union or political functions; numerous national leaders of political parties or trade unions have a full time position at the same time as being paid by the administration. These "privileges" are available regardless of party or trade union and constitute a sort of "gentleman's agreement" that no one can challenge.

These legal guarantees, which are further strengthened in practice, attest to the liberalism of an administration open to all, despite various attempts made in the 1950s to prevent access to its senior levels by candidates suspected of membership in the Communist Party. These attempts were prevented by the Council of State which, in a 1954 decision, forbade any discrimination on political grounds. It is not surprising, therefore, that unionism in the civil service should have developed to such an extent since there has never really been any obstacle to it. The highest union density in France is found in the civil service (90 per cent of teachers, two-thirds of postal workers, for example). The civil service unions are usually attached to the large union federations—the CGT (*Confédération Générale de Travail*), which is close to the communist party; the CFDT (*Confédération Française démocratique du travail*), which is close to the socialist party; and the moderate union, the FO (*Force ouvrière*). Teachers are unionized by the powerful FEN (*Fédération de l'Education Nationale*), and certain independent unions, especially in the transport sector (SNCF, métro, Air Force) are extremely powerful and less interested in political issues than in defending their own sectional interests (19).

THE BUREAUCRACY AND POLICY-MAKING

It has been calculated that between 1971 and 1983, 1,033 laws and measures were adopted and 16,682 decrees issued for applying them. During the same period, the ministries published 71,458 orders, 3,550 "decisions," 126,516 notices, and 500 circulars. This does not take into account the thousands of internal circulars which were not published. Such a mass of general decisions gives an impressive quantitative idea of the scale of administrative activity and of the importance of its role in the life of the country.

The strength of the administration derives first of all from the weakness of countervailing forces. Citizens exert only a minimal influence over an administration which has gradually transformed itself from a "service for the public" into a "public service." Its purpose and activities are sometimes as much for the benefit of the organization as they are for its clients. Also, the judiciary has a close rapport with the administration due to a common educational background and a shared values system regarding administrative jurisdiction and administrative practice. Finally, both constitutionally and in reality, parliament has only a subsidiary role.

Relation to Parliament and to Local Government

The Fifth Republic has given the executive and the administration a considerable role. Even in domains falling under its jurisdiction, the parliament has in practice lost the initiative: 90 per cent of laws passed come from the government, and all legislation proposed by the government must be reviewed by the Council of State, whose advice is generally followed. Of course, parliament does have powers of amendment which it uses increasingly often. The two chambers sometimes voice their criticism, proposing to reduce symbolically such and such a category of expenditure, but there are no real means of evaluating the activities of the administration. On the few occasions that parliament has undertaken a detailed analysis of a public service (for example radio-television), there has been little result of consequence.

The weakness of parliament is the result of several factors. First is the absence of links and channels of communication between parliament and the administration. The latter considers that parliament has no right to give it orders or directives, and the executive vigorously defends this position. Moreover, parliament does not possess (or not yet) the services which would allow it an equivalent level of expertise. Apart from certain members of parliament whose previous professional experience allows them to confront the administration on its own terms, politicians have generally accepted the propositions of the administration without question.

The importance of the administration in shaping and controlling the State budget should also be noted. Here again parliament must be content with making minor modifications and symbolic criticism. The budgets of each ministry emerge from parliamentary debate more or less unaltered.

The role of the State administration is equally determinant at the local level. Throughout the 19th century and until the 1950s neither those elected to the local councils nor the central government have wanted to create a local civil service capable of challenging the role of the State administration. It has only been with the urban and economic development of the post-war period that the most dynamic local élites have sought to provide themselves with an independent means of formulating and implementing their policies. Despite these attempts, local administrative personnel are inferior in terms both of numbers and expertise. Above all, local authorities lack the expertise of senior personnel and most of the 36,000 French communes will never have the technical and financial resources for obtaining it.

However, there has been a growing determination of the most dynamic local politicians to free themselves from the supervision of the technical services of the State. Large towns have created a local public service with more and more of the resources required for elaborating and implementing their policies; and certain *départements* have created technical agencies, independently of the State, to assist the smaller communes.

The Administrative Elite

The latter example illustrates the most important characteristic of the French administrative élite: its capacity for adaptation, a quality which Pareto and Mosca saw as critical for the survival of an élite. The commissioners of the Republic are the descendants of the prefects who, in turn, were the successors of the intendants of the *Ancien Régime*; the Council of State has its origins in the Council of the King and the powerful *Corps des Ponts et Chausées* has evolved from the creation of examinations for bridge engineers by Louis XV in the mid-18th century. This capacity for maintaining control over the affairs of State can be explained in large part by the organization of the bureaucracy at the summit and by its modes of recruitment and training.

The strength of the *grandes écoles* resides in their role as "selecting machines." A strict entry exam, an even more demanding one when leaving, and the small number of the "elect" are more important than the teaching or qualifications gained. The research of Ezra Suleiman has shown that former students held no illusions as to the nature of their training: they consider themselves "generalists" rather than specialists. But far from drawing negative conclusions from their experience, they point out that this general education has prepared them for adaptation to all types of situation. Moreover, the *grandes écoles* have instilled in their students the spirit of competition, aggression, and mobility more often found in the private sector.

At least at the highest levels (400–500 positions) the careers of civil servants progress in the same conditions of competition and mobility. The students who, when leaving their *grande école*, have been able to gain a place in the most famous corps of the administration (the *grands corps*), that is the *Conseil d'Etat*, the *Cour des Comptes*, the *Inspection des Finances* (and to a lesser degree the *Corps Prefectoral* and the *Corps diplomatique*), or in the prestigious technical corps (*Corps des Ponts, Corps des Mines*), know that their career prospects depend on their capacity for moving—thanks to the procedure of secondment—within different administrative, political and even economic circles. These lateral moves have as their ultimate goal progression towards the summits of State: a *maître des requêtes* (master of petitions) in the Council of State accepts a position in a ministerial *cabinet* for a brief period which will allow him, if the opportunity arises, subsequently to obtain a managerial post in a ministerial service or *établissement public*, the chair of a prestigious committee, or membership on the staff of a public company. Essential stepping stones to these dazzling careers (hence the term "*jeunes loups de l'ENA*") are the ministerial *cabinets*. They allow a certain pragmatic arbitration between the spoils system, tied to the presidentialization of the régime, and the neutrality of the civil service guaranteed by the statutes of 1946 and 1959 (20).

This community of men and values constitutes an informal interorganizational network which facilitates the exercise of power and allows bureaucratic rigidities to be avoided. But this equally means that, in the event of a political change such as that of 1981, it is more difficult to find other men or other forces to support the political transition. The socialist experience has revealed that changes cannot occur against the wishes or without the cooperation of the senior civil service.

The price paid for this system is equally high at the social level: all studies of the senior civil service in the last twenty years show that there has been hardly any democratization of recruitment: senior civil servants are usually the sons of senior civil servants, of company directors, of doctors and lawyers. They come from the Parisian region and are educated, before entering ENA, at the *Institut d'Etudes Politiques de Paris* or certain prestigious Parisian schools prior to attending the *Ecole Polytechnique*. The *grands corps* provide further privileges and fight hard to maintain them and to pass them down. This situation is even more outrageous given that the public sphere or domain of state control goes well beyond the administration as such. The senior civil service not only has an administrative monopoly but has also colonized the political sphere, the public economic sector (and even the private sector) and, through secondment, the banks and the media.

ADMINISTRATIVE ACCOUNTABILITY

As has been suggested above, constitutional and legislative guarantees, the high degree of unionization and the jurisprudence of the Council of State combine to ensure public officials a particularly effective system of protection. Can one go further and say that they are "irresponsible" and not at all accountable for their actions? In reality, things are more complex. To begin with, several levels of the administration must be distinguished. First, a line must be drawn between the senior civil service and the rest of the administration. As far as the lower levels of the civil service are concerned, the responsibility of public officials has rarely been challenged due both to the subordinate character of their functions and to strong trade union protection.

What of the responsibility of senior civil servants? Are they truly accountable? Clearly not, if one considers that the Court of Budgetary and Financial Discipline has sentenced fewer than thirty public officials for irregularities in the management of public funds since its creation in 1947. Clearly not, if the results of parliamentary enquiries are examined or of administrative enquiries into major scandals, such as that of the *abattoirs de la Villette*. Such enquiries become useless before they are completed. They often conclude that it is impossible to attribute blame to particular individuals within a complex, confused decision-making process where no one in particular seems to have taken the principal decisions.

In contrast, it can be maintained that the senior civil service is responsible to the executive, judging by certain sudden transfers or certain "suspensions from duties" (a statutory position in which the official is temporarily without appointment). However, "responsibility" is hardly an accurate way of describing this form of sanction. It bears greater resemblance to a disgrace of a monarchical type: if occasionally a prefect or the director of a public company is sacked for incompetence, in most cases such officials are ousted for obscure reasons suggesting the condemnation "of the prince" and the need to find a scapegoat for government errors.

Control by the Executive and Parliament

If public officials are not personally accountable, is the administration itself accountable for its actions to the executive, parliament and the public? The executive has a number of ways of keeping itself informed and of ensuring that the administration properly executes its decisions while respecting the laws and rules in force. First, each sector of the administration is "monitored" by administrative or technical control agencies which undertake periodical inspections and enquiries. Of course, the objectives of these enquiries are legal and formal rather than detailed analyses of management or results, but the *Inspections* are nevertheless an important means of administrative control, respected by most sections of the civil service. However, the reports of the *Inspections* are reserved for the ministers, and errors, misdemeanors (and sometimes even crimes) remain unknown to the public, Parliament and the judiciary. This treatment of problems "within the family" can be effective but it is hardly democratic and does not sufficiently allow external influence to correct lapses in behavior.

Only the annual report of the Court of Accounts (*Cour des Comptes*), which is largely reproduced by the press, allows the public some understanding of the administrative and budgetary problems of managing public services. However, the assiduous reader of this austere document cannot help being struck by the extremely legalistic rather than public-oriented tones of the report and by the formality of ministerial replies which invariably justify their policies and "protect" their services after having made certain concessions to the Court. A comment once made with regard to the jurisdictional control of the Council of State can equally be applied to the report of the Court: "It makes the State more wary for the future than it redresses the mistakes of the past" (21).

As has been shown, despite the rather military tones in which the Constitution states that the "administration is placed at the disposal of the government," the latter's powers of control are in reality relatively limited. It is so ill-equipped for correcting bureaucratic inertia that its only recourse is to create new structures, rather than reforming the old ones, in the hope that they will be more dynamic, at least for a time. Under these circumstances it is rather surprising that the administration does not suffer from more ills and corruption than it does.

Parliamentary accountability on the part of the administration is not provided for in the Constitution. Furthermore, the executive has always been fiercely opposed to any encroachment by parliament on what it considers its exclusive domain. In the event of a scandal or a major conflict, the only solution available to parliament is to call for the resignation of the minister concerned or to overthrow the government. And it is clear that in a system dominated by a majority party or coalition, this recourse is hardly ever taken. However, parliament does have some means of influencing the administration at its disposal, but these are often based on individual initiative rather than collective action. Members of parliament can play a mediating role between the administration and the public, intervening to speed up the processing of a particular dossier, to overcome bureaucratic obstacles, to claim for a less rigid interpretation, etc. Each member of parliament makes several thousand such interventions during his term of office. It is an element of humanity and flexibility in an otherwise rigidly uniform system. This system of interventions does not, however, produce systematic dispensations, although this does occasionally occur, because the administration knows how to protect itself and to distinguish between what amounts to an overmechanistic application of the rules and what could become a latent form of clientelism. In addition, the relations between the citizen, the member of parliament and the administration have become a vital source of information for politicians, who use written and oral questions and even legislation to propose changes to the rules, structure and behavior of the administration.

The office of mediator (the French ombudsman)—created in 1973—acts in the same spirit. Although this new institution is inspired by its Swedish counterpart, it does have a number of specific features which allow it to deal with the French administration. In fact, the existence of a long-standing tradition of administration jurisdiction which protects the public against arbitrary administrative acts prevented a full adoption of the Swedish model. Furthermore, many politicians were not favorable to an institution which would have competed with them on their own terrain of mediation. Thus the office of mediator was created on condition that it did not interfere in or attempt to substitute itself for the administrative courts. Also, the public must contact the mediator through a member of parliament (who, if he considers it necessary, can intervene in the affair himself). Thus the mediator has found himself at the center of a large number of complaints against the administration—3,500 in 1977 and more than 8,000 in 1983. The mediator not only rules on individual cases but tries through his annual report or through specific processes to suggest reforms which would prevent the most frequent faults recurring in administrative affairs. While the mediator's role has not been negligible during the last ten years, it must be said that he has faced some difficulty in carving himself a place in a political-administrative system accustomed to dealing with problems either politically (through members of parliament) or legally (through the administrative courts).

Control by the Administrative Courts

France has an ancient and solid tradition of protecting the public against the excesses of the administration through the Council of State and the administrative tribunals. Since the creation of the latter in 1953 as a means of unburdening the Council of State which had a 7–8 year backlog of claims to be processed, the public has enjoyed greater access to the administrative courts. The twenty-three metropolitan administrative tribunals are the courts of the first instance for all litigation involving the public and the administration, except in the case of claims against the decisions of the national authorities (ministerial decrees and measures, for example). All proceedings must be brought against an explicit decision of the administration within four months. Beyond this period it is no longer possible to request the cancellation of the decision. However, in the case of a subsequent individual measure, it is always possible to raise the *exception d'illégalité* of the principal measure, which prevents in practice the latter from being implemented. The administrative tribunals have been submerged by claims, a problem worsened still further by the suppression of prefectoral supervision and by the strengthening of the power of the courts.

The considerable delays with which rulings are made explains in part why administrative jurisprudence has a greater impact on future administrative affairs than it does on current situations. Very often, the litigant receives only a vain response to a problem whose consequences cannot be repaired: he obtains the cancellation of a building permit after the building has already been built (and it will not be removed!), or the cancellation of an administrative examination five years after it took place and which in any case had been put in order retroactively by legislation, etc. This situation does not have only negative consequences however: the administration pays close heed to decisions taken by the Council of State and these become veritable guidelines for public officials; second, in the cases where the real outcomes of litigation are minimal or non-existent, the Council is keen to ensure that the rules are better applied in the future; third, this "policy making" role of the courts has encouraged claims from groups, associations, and unions whose concerns are long-term and less specific.

Apart from the cancellation of decisions (*contrôle de légalité*), the public can also obtain compensation for harm caused by administrative decisions or behavior. However, not only are proceedings of this type subject to long delays (several years) but the compensation awarded by the courts is often minimal if not derisory. For example, the courts have long refused to give compensation for moral wrongs. This attitude can be explained in large part by the background, training and ideas common to both the judiciary and the senior civil service. Although they are not part of the administration itself, the judges are hardly foreign to it and this explains their "understanding"–which is often excessive–with regard to the interests of the State. Thus there are no prospects of a revolution at the Palais Royal (the seat of the Council of State), but only of a progressive evolution conditioned by the policies of the administration and by the pressures of public opinion.

Moreover, the courts are often rather insensitive to the claims of the administered, and further intervention on the part of the legislator is required to free administrative jurisprudence from its conservatism and restrictions. It is parliament rather than the Council of State which has extended the obligation of the administration to justify its decisions (law of 11 July 1979), and which has enlarged the opportunity for the public to gain access to administrative documents (law of 17 July 1978). Thus the legislator has been more progressive in this domain, given the still predominant character of the administrative culture: a regal altitude ill-disposed to justifying its actions to a public which it is supposed to serve.

CONCLUSION

The French administration is thus characterized by a hierarchical and rigid structure, with uniform rules, universal solutions to problems and a degree of equality which borders on egalitarianism. Its mode of operation, the inertia of its procedures and the stratification and resistance to change of the civil service seem to justify the Crozerian analysis of the French system as the "stalled society."

However, this bureaucratic machinery has produced its own antidotes. From beneath the rule of equality, uniformity and universality, has emerged the exception, the dispensation, adaptation, and sometimes even preferential favors. Behind the appearance of inertia there lies a process of change, even if it occurs in areas where one would least expect it: since the old structures cannot be reformed, new ones have to be created; since procedures are too complex, they are bypassed by exploiting the least flaw in the system. The French administration, like Janus, has two faces: that of inertia and that of adaptation, that of rigidity and that of flexibility. Paradoxically, from the excessive dogmatism which dominates the philosophy of the administration has emerged an almost cynical pragmatism which allows a rule to be made without any conviction that it will be applied, which declares certain practices to be forbidden while turning a blind eye to their persistence, and which proclaims a principle while arranging for its violation. The absence of illusions on the part of administrators has its parallel among the administered: they detest the State but ceaselessly demand its intervention; they demand general rules but contrive to disobey them; they call for equality but pursue the cultivation of privilege. Thus any juridical and formal analysis of the administration is bound to be mistaken.

The administrative system adapts as well as can be expected to changing circumstances. But there is a heavy price to be paid: in avoiding a direct confrontation with problems, decisions and processes must follow tortuous paths which, although often leading to the results required, must overcome considerable hurdles on the way. Relations between bureaucrats and the public are often appalling and characterized by a mutual hatred which only the impotence of those confronting one another can justify; the irritation of the citizen, who finds himself lost in the administrative maze, is matched by the frustration of the public official, who is the prisoner of the rules he must apply. The French administrative system may be an "admirable" machine, but it functions only with the benefit of continuous repairs.

REFERENCES

1. Charles E. Freedeman, *The Conseil d'Etat in Modern France* (New York, 1961).
2. Jack Hayward, *Governing France: The One and Indivisible Republic* (London—Weidenfeld and Nicolson, 1983).
3. Roger Gregoire, *The French Civil Service* (London, 1954).
4. Pierre Birnbaum, *The Heights of the State* (Chicago: University of Chicago Press, 1983).
5. Francis De Baecque and Jean-Louis Quermonne (eds.), *Administration et politique sous la Ve République* (Paris, Presses de la FNSP, 1982).
6. Ezra N. Suleiman, *Politics, Power and Bureaucracy in France* (Princeton University Press, 1974).
7. Pierre Gremion, *Le pouvoir périphérique* (Paris, Ed. Du Seuil, 1976).
8. Richard Rose and Ezra N. Suleiman (eds.), *Presidents and Prime Ministers* (Washington, American Enterprise Institute, 1980).
9. Samy Cohen, *Les conseillers du président* (Paris, PUF, 1980).
10. Francis De Baecque, *Qui gouverne la France?* (Paris, PUF, 1976), p. 115.

11. Jean-Claude Thoenig, *L'ère des technocrates* (Paris: les éditions d'organisation, 1973).

12. Ezra N. Suleiman, *Elites in French Society – The Politics of Survival* (Princeton University Press, 1978).

13. Yves Mény, "Permanence and Change: The Relations between Government and Local Authorities in France", *Policy and Government* (Cambridge) No. 1, 1983.

14. Howard Machin, *The Prefect in French Public Administration* (London, Croom Helm, 1977).

15. Catherine Gremion, *Profession: décideurs – Pouvoir des hauts fonctionnaires et réforme de l'Etat* (Paris, Gauthier-Villars, 1979).

16. Yves Mény, *Centralisation et décentralisation dans le débat politique français* (Paris, LGDJ, 1974) and Jacques Lagroye and Vincent Wright (eds.), *Local Government in Britain and France* (London, Allen and Unwin, 1979).

17. Yves Mény, "Decentralisation in Socialist France," *West European Politics*, vol. 7, No. 1 (1984), pp. 65–79.

18. François Dupuy et Jean-Claude Thoenig, *Sociologie de l'Administration française* (Paris, A. Colin, 1983).

19. See J. Hayward, *op. cit.*, pp. 132–155, and Vincent Wright, *The Government and Politics of France* (London, Hutchinson, 1983), pp. 84–107.

20. Jean-Luc Bodiguel, "A French Style Spoils System?", *Public Administration* Vol. 61 (1983), pp. 295–300.

21. Gérard Belorgey, *Le gouvernement et l'administration de la France* (Paris, A. Colin, 1967), p. 189.

REFERENCES IN ENGLISH

Abraham, Henry Julian, *The Judicial Process: An Introductory Analysis of the Courts of the United States, England, and France.* New York: Oxford University Press, 1962.

Anderson, Malcolm, *Government in France: An Introduction to the Executive Power.* Oxford, N.Y.: Pergamon, 1970, ch. 1.

Ashford, Douglas E., *British Dogmatism and French Pragmatism.* London: Allen and Unwin, 1982.

Ashford, Douglas E., *Policy and Politics in France.* Philadelphia: Temple University Press, 1982.

Avril, Pierre, *Politics in France.* Baltimore: Penguin, 1969.

Birnbaum, Pierre, *The Heights of Power: An Essay on the Power Elite in France.* Chicago: University of Chicago Press, 1977.

Blondel, Jean, *The Government of France.* London: Methuen, 2nd 1974.

Brown, L. N., and J. F. Garner, *French Administrative Law.* London: Butterworths, 1967.

Cerny, Philip G., and Martin A. Schain, *Socialism, the State and Public Policy in France.* London: Pinter, 1985.

Crozier, Michel, *The Bureaucratic Phenomenon: An Examination of Bureaucracy in Modern Organizations and its Cultural Setting in France.* Chicago: University of Chicago Press, 1964.

Diamond, Alfred, "The French Administrative System," in W. J. Siffin, ed., *Toward the Comparative Study of Public Administration* (Bloomington, Ind.: Indiana Univ. Press, 1962).

Dogan, Mattei, "How to Become a Cabinet Minister in France," *Comparative Politics* 12 (1979), 1–25.

Ecole Nationale d'Administration, *Recruitment and Training for the Higher Civil Service in France*. Paris, 1956.

Ehrmann, Henry, *Politics in France*. Boston: Little, Brown, 1976.

Frears, J. R., *France in the Giscard Presidency*. London: Allen & Unwin, 1981.

Grégoire, Roger, *The French Civil Service*. Brussels: International Institute of Admin. Sciences, 1964.

Hayward, J., *The One and Indivisible French Republic*. London: Weidenfeld and Nicolson, 1973.

Howorth, Jolyon, and P. G. Cerney, *Elites in France*. London: Pinter, 1981.

Keating, Michael, "Decentralisation in Mitterand's France," *Public Admin.* 61 (1983).

Langrod, Georges, *Some Current Problems of Administration in France Today*. San Juan, Puerto Rico: School of Public Administration, University of Puerto Rico, 1961.

Lord, Guy, *The French Budgetary Process*. Berkeley: University of California Press, 1973.

Machin, Howard, *The Prefect in French Public Administration*. London: Croom Helm, 1978.

Meynaud, Jean, *Technocracy*. London: Faber, 1965.

McArthur and Scott, *Industrial Planning in France*. Cambridge: Harvard University Press, 1969.

Nicholas, Barry, "Loi, Reglement and Judicial Review in the Fifth Republic," *Public Law* (1970), 251–276.

Ridley, Frederick F., *The French Prefectoral System*. London: HMSO, 1973. Research Paper for Commission on the Constitution.

Ridley, Frederick F., and J. Blondel, *Public Administration in France*. London: Routledge, 2nd 1969.

Robson, William A., ed., *The Civil Service in Britain and France*. London: Hogarth, 1956.

Rohkam, William, *Studies in French Administrative Law*. Urbana: University of Illinois, 1947.

Sharp, W. R., *The French Civil Service—Bureaucracy in Transition*. New York, Macmillan, 1931.

Suleiman, Ezra N., *Elites in French Society: The Politics of Survival*. Princeton, N.J.: Princeton University Press, 1978.

Suleiman, Ezra N., *Politics, Power and Bureaucracy in France: The Administrative Elite*. Princeton: Princeton University Press, 1974.

Williams, Philip M., and Martin Harrison, *Politics and Society in de Gaulle's Republic*. Garden City, N.Y.: Doubleday, 1972.

Wright, Vincent, *The Government and Politics of France*. New York, N.Y.: Holmes and Meier, 3rd 1983.

18

Italy

SABINO CASSESE
University of Rome, Rome, Italy

ENVIRONMENT AND HISTORY

A Case of Delayed Development

In the period following the second world war, Italy became one of the major industrialized countries. During the same period, a public education system developed in the country, offering free education to young people until the age of thirteen. A national health service, guaranteeing free medical and hospital care for all, as well as a pension scheme, which ensured old-age pensions even for those who had not contributed to the scheme, so long as their income fell below an established minimum, were also developed. In addition, the public industrial sector (today accounting for approximately 25 to 30 per cent of the Italian economy) and the tax system grew to finance increasing public expenditures. In a few years the number of tax-payers increased from 5 to 20 million.

The Italian administrative system is in singular contrast to the development described above: antiquated structure, poorly paid personnel that works the bare minimum, complicated procedures, and prolonged delays. Even the briefest contact with Italian administration leads to the conclusion that the services rendered to the public are poor and the administrative machinery is extremely ineffective. While the Italian economy and society have developed, the administrative system has lagged behind.

What are the reasons for this delayed development in Italian public administration? The causes are usually attributed to the *constitutional position of the administration*, because it is subject to the law and government ministers. Thus it is pointed out that the Constitution of 1948 provides for the organization of administration to be regulated by law. Only the law, for example, may establish a ministry. On this basis, Parliament has produced a plethora of laws, reaching the point of even detailing the functioning of public administration. A further contribution along these lines has been made, first by the Council of State and then by criminal court judges. The Council of State (and later the Regional Administrative Tribunals, founded in 1971) has extended its control on the conformity of administration to the law, forcing the administration to act within the narrow confines of the law. Criminal court judges, from

1971, have multiplied their legal action against public officials, increasing preoccupation with respect for the law and the pettifoggery of bureaucrats.

This is the basis for the fairly widespread opinion that the origin of Italian administrative malaise is that the administration is conceived and conceives itself as having the single objective of enforcing laws. The Italian bureaucrat's prevalently legal training and passive attitude of mere executor reflect this opinion. According to this view, the bureaucrat is thus a good example of the Weberian public official.

Such an explanation, however, is not convincing. Weber himself realized that the bureaucracy often represented something completely different from legal rational domination because it attempts to increase its own power and defend its own private interests. Today it is even more evident with the importance that administrative systems have acquired and the interests they must protect. This is also true of Italy, where bureaucrats, far from being robots guided by laws promulgated by Parliament, represent interests and negotiate. The image of an "executive" administration appears to have its origins in legal tradition.

Another current explanation for the delayed development of Italian administration is its politicization. The Constitution of 1948 (Art. 95) provides that the administration is subject to the body politic: at the head of each ministry there is a minister-member of the Council of Ministers, who is responsible for the activity of the ministry. It is said that this juxtaposition results in the politicization of public administration so that it serves special interests (those of the party to which the minister belongs), rather than the general interest. However, the recruitment of public officials is carried out primarily by means of open competition, and thus politicization may exist only at the top since incumbents at the highest grades are appointed by the government. Nor can it be claimed that such a vast body may be influenced from above so profoundly.

The Social Position of the Administration

The main causes for the delayed development are to be found not in the administration's constitutional position (its relationship with the law and with the government), but rather in *its social position*. To explain this, the origins of Italian administration must be briefly examined.

The administrative apparatus was formed, after 1861, with the annexation to Piedmont of the pre-unity states (Lombardy-Veneto, Tuscany, Pontifical State, Kingdom of the Two Sicilies). The first bureaucratic nucleus was formed by the Piedmontese. For approximately forty years they maintained a strong influence on administration, partly as a result of the absence of strong administrative traditions in the other states. It was referred to as the "Piedmontization" of Italian administration.

At the beginning of the century, the higher echelons were still half composed of persons from the North, with the other half coming from Central and Southern Italy. This situation changed radically during the first thirty years of the century: in the 1930s, half of the higher civil servants came from the South, 30 per cent from Central Italy, and only 20 per cent from the North. This tendency towards "Southernizing" became more noticeable after the 1930s. Today, higher civil servants of southern origin constitute 70 per cent of the total, whereas the North accounts for only approximately 10 per cent (1).

This shifting of influence from the North to the South would simply be an interesting example of the low level of geographical distribution in Italian administration, if the two parts of Italy were equally developed. However, this is not the case. The North is industrialized, but the South has been until recently prevalently agricultural, and is still underdeveloped. This dualism of areas of unequal development results in few candidates for civil service positions in the North since they are attracted by the higher salaries that they can earn in private business. In the South, on the other hand, jobs are scarce, and there is a great demand for employment in public administration.

This assault on public administration by an army of ants from the South produces several consequences. In the first place, because most of the personnel originates from one area, which until a few years ago had a strong peasant mentality, there is an absence of the industrial type of productive mentality. In the second place, personnel from the South, where inequities characteristic of underdevelopment are most noticeable, are motivated by a need for justice and equal treatment. This accounts for the continuous demands for precise guarantees both of status and career development, as well as activity, in the exercise of employees' functions. Southern civil servants know that they have no other alternative on the job market and that they can only rely on the government. Perhaps this is precisely the reason why they want to protect themselves.

Preindustrial culture and a fixation for guarantees in turn act as a brake, causing further reactions. One in particular is the "flight from the State," namely the establishment of public agencies outside the departmental organizations, brought into being to circumvent the inflexibility of the administrative system. This phenomenon began as early as the second decade of the century and developed during the 1930s when a great number of public agencies were created, where higher salaries were paid, not only to attract the best trained personnel but also to attract personnel from the North. However, with the passing of time it has become evident that a network of rules and controls has formed even around public agencies, resulting in time-consuming battles to shake off the network and in tedious interadministrative tensions.

Thus delayed development of Italian administration has been caused by the "Southernization" of the public personnel (particularly in the higher grades). Italian public administration, it may be said, is insufficiently developed because that is how the South is, and administration is a reflection of the South. The "administrative problem" is a consequence of the "Southern problem."

The legalism of Italian public administration is used to weave a network of rules that protect the public personnel. Moreover, it is helpful in order to find one's way through the labyrinth created by such rules. Finally, public employees use the legalism to their own advantage: it is no accident that one of the best known mottoes in administration is that "rules are *enforced* for enemies and *interpreted* for friends."

Politicization should be interpreted in a different way as well. In actual fact, political backing is always sought by civil servants. This does not however mean party support can be expected from them. On the contrary, civil servants complain about politicization since they aspire to complete autonomy. For example, the very few appointments of general directors of ministries made by the Council of Ministers, selecting persons external to the administration, although they are perfectly legitimate, have been the cause of scandal. Appointments to the higher grades, based on criteria different from seniority, also provoke negative reactions.

On the other hand, "clientelism" and favoritism are inherent in bureaucracy itself, which manages "increases in staff" accordingly. Since the "Southern problem" has not been solved in any other way, this is an attempt to pay off the South, giving it a free rein for access to civil service jobs.

Our conclusion, then, is that the asymmetry and inequity in Italy's economic, social and administrative development can be attributed to its history and geography, not to an executive concept of administration, or its connection with politics.

STRUCTURE AND MANAGEMENT

Size of Administration

Employees in all public administrations, including central and local public enterprises, total over 4½ million in Italy, and amount to approximately 10 per cent of the population and 25 per cent of the workforce. From this point of view, Italian administration is not smaller than that of other countries. If, however, only civil servants are taken into account, calculated in line with the criteria of national accounting used by the OECD (Organization for Economic Cooperation and Development), their percentage of the total workforce amounts to only 12 per cent in Italy, compared with 14 per cent in Germany and France, 19 per cent in the United States, and 22 per cent in the United Kingdom (2).

The distribution of public employees by type of administration is shown below in rounded figures (3):

Ministries (central and local personnel, including teachers)	1,600,000
National public agencies (social security and others)	150,000
National health service	600,000
National public enterprises (railway, electricity, telephones, etc.)	570,000
Companies with state participation	700,000
Regions, provinces, municipalities	700,000
Local public agencies	100,000
Local public enterprises	150,000
	4,570,000

This tabulation illustrates the size of the various components in the administrative system. It can be seen that the central ministries, with 1,600,000 employees, have more than double the employees in the decentralized authorities (regions, provinces, municipalities). However, the National Health Service depends on the regions and municipalities to a great extent. Thus the difference between the central and local authorities diminishes. Also, the size of national public agencies is greater than local public agencies by only one third. The greatest gap can be seen between national public enterprises and companies with state participation on one side, and local public enterprises on the other: those on a national level are more than eight times the size of the local ones.

One also notices that when the employees of ministries and those of regions, municipalities and provinces are added up and compared with the employees of other bodies, the two groups are more or less the same size (2.3 million). It may thus be said that the quasi-governmental sector (public agencies and public enterprises) has grown, both at the center and locally, to the point of reaching the same size as the original bodies (ministries and local authorities).

The structure of Italian public administration was relatively simple for the first fifty years of the country's history as a unified nation (1861–1910). The dominant form was the ministry, with its own central and local organization. It is true that there were local authorities, namely provinces and municipalities, but they were controlled by the ministries.

This situation had already begun to change during the first decade of the century, in particular with government management of the railways, for which a State body was founded, which was partially autonomous and thus called an autonomous state agency. Later, during the second and third decades of the century, further changes took place with the institution of public agencies and private companies with state participation. These components in the administrative system then developed almost to the point of clashing with the original ministerial organization.

The situation also changed locally; this, however, occurred later, after the 1940s. Provinces and municipalities acquired greater independence from the central government, and in 1970 the regions were founded, to which many former central functions were transferred. Even later, mixed types of organization developed.

Following is an overview of the principal characteristics of the different types of organization, both central and local, as well as those bodies defined as mixed.

Ministries

Ministries are unitary apparatuses, organized mainly by sector, extending from the center and to the local level, and placed under the guidance of a minister-member of government. Their task is usually to maintain liaison between the center and the periphery.

Today there are twenty ministries. Four are the traditional ones: Foreign Affairs, Defence, Interior and Justice. There are now eight economic ministries: Finance, Treasury, Budget and Economic Planning, Agriculture and Forestry, Industry, Commerce and Small Industry, Labour and Social Security, Foreign Trade and State Participation. There are also four ministries for general services: Public Works, Transport, Merchant Marine, and Post and Telecommunications. Lastly, there are four ministries for cultural and social activities: Education, Health, Tourism and Entertainment, and Culture and Environment.

To these apparatuses must be added the Presidency of the Council of Ministers, the Civil Service Department, the Office of the Ministry for Scientific and Technological Research, the Ministry for the South, and the recently-created Ministry for Ecology (ministries without portfolio). A minister is assisted by a cabinet (made up of the head of the cabinet, a legislative office, and a press office), and a ministry is usually divided into departments, then further subdivided into divisions.

The ministries, however, are not all equal. In the first place, they differ in size. Over a million employees (most of whom are teachers) work for the Ministry of

Education. The Interior and Finance Ministries have approximately 100,000 employees each. There are, however, ministries with a staff of only 500 (such as the Ministry of State Participation and that of Budget and Economic Planning). Secondly, half of the ministries have local field organizations (often more than one and sometimes, as in the case of Finance, as many as there are departments in the ministry), whereas others have only central offices, such as the Ministry for Foreign Trade and the Ministry of State Participation, whose function is simply that of directing the holding corporations. Thirdly, whereas usually the powers of the minister extend only as far as the scope of his ministry, in some cases the minister has broader powers. The Minister of the Budget and Economic Planning, for example, since he is also Chairman of the Interministerial Committee for Economic Planning, has powers that go beyond his ministry.

Autonomous Administrations

Autonomous administrations and agencies are midway between ministries and public agencies. Although they are a part of the ministries, they have their own board of directors (presided over by the minister) and their own budget (attached to that of the State), as well as accounting and contractual norms that are partially different from those of the State, and "ex post" checking of their final accounts by the State Audit Board. The main autonomous agencies are those responsible for roads (part of the Ministry of Public Works), railways and air traffic control (Ministry of Transport), telecommunications, mail and telephones (Postal Ministry), state monopolies (Ministry of Finance), and intervention in the agricultural market (Agriculture). The structure of autonomous agencies is not uniform. In some, the minister-chairman has greater powers; in others, the general director has the real decision-making power.

Precisely because of its lack of autonomy, the so-called autonomous administration or agency has been suprassed by the public agency; thus it is proposed that the major autonomous administrations and agencies (railways and state monopolies) be transformed into public agencies.

Public Agencies

Public agencies are legal persons separate from the State. Their governing organs consist of a chairman, a board of directors, and a board of auditors. They generally have public aims and are subject to the reference and direction of a ministry, but unlike autonomous bodies they are not considered to be part of the ministry and are not directly headed by the minister.

Some public agencies deliver services, such as the National Social Security Organization (INPS, *Istituto Nazionale per la Previdenza Sociale*), which administers the pension scheme; others are business organizations, such as the National Electric Power Board (ENEL, *Ente Nazionale per l'Energia Elettrica*), which has a monopoly on the production and distribution of electric power. Among the latter are public holding companies, such as the Institute for the Reconstruction of Industry (IRI, *Istituto per la Ricostruzione Industriale*) and the National Hydrocarbon Corporation (ENI, *Ente Nazionale Idrocarburi*).

There are numerous public agencies, estimated by some to be approximately 40,000 in number. They differ from one another not only because of their functions, but also because of their origins. Some of them, in fact, were private corporations which then became public such as some public banks, the Italian Automobile Club (ACI, *Automobile Club d'Italia*), and the Italian National Olympic Committee (CONI, *Comitato Olimpico Nazionale Italiano*). Others, on the contrary, were ministerial organizations whose functions were transferred to public agencies, as mentioned previously, for the purpose of circumventing the enforcement of state accounting norms, ensuring more efficient management, and paying higher salaries to employees. Examples of these are the Central Statistics Institute (ISTAT, *Istituto Centrale di Statistica*) and the Institute for the Control of Private Insurance (ISVAP, *Istituto per la Vigilanza sulle Assicurazioni Private*) whose functions were previously carried out by the Ministries of Agriculture and Industry.

Some of these organizations are complex, such as the Italian and provincial automobile clubs. The provincial clubs are associations to which motorists belong; their decision-making bodies are composed of persons elected by the assembly of the associates. At the same time they are also public agencies. Provincial automobile clubs, in turn, are federated into the Italian Automobile Club, which is thus both a public agency itself and a federation of public agencies.

Since the presence of such a vast quasi-governmental sector is one of the characteristic features of the Italian administrative system, the reasons for its existence need further explanation. First of all, the tendency towards uniformity in government administrative systems must be considered; this meant that when faced with new needs and functions, not easily incorporated into the traditional apparatus, it became necessary to found public agencies. Secondly, public agencies often (but not always) offer a further advantage: the hiring of personnel without following the procedure for open competition. Bearing in mind the fact that the governing bodies of public agencies are usually appointed by the Council of Ministers or by a minister, it is easy to see that having a free hand in hiring lends itself to political patronage. A third factor in the establishment of public agencies is pressure from the personnel. For example, one of the most active movers in the transformation underway of the Italian State Railways into a public agency is the railway workers' union, simply because they are counting on higher salaries after the transformation.

While some public agencies are subject to laws that regulate their aims, governing bodies, relationship between employer and employee and, in general, their activities, other public agencies are regulated only by *ad hoc* norms as regards their organization and sometimes their aims. The rest is regulated by private law. This is true in particular for public agencies that manage an enterprise. The employees of these public agencies do not therefore have either the status or the salary of civil servants but that of employees of a private business. It may thus be said that these public enterprises are half public and half private in the sense that although they are public they enjoy the advantages of private companies.

Companies with State Participation

Another typical feature of the Italian system is the existence of about 2,000 companies with state participation. These are joint stock companies, regulated by the civil code, in which public agencies participate through total ownership, majority ownership or a controlling share of the stock.

Some of these companies were founded by the government itself, as private companies, to explore new activities; for example, in 1926 the government founded the National Italian Oil Company (AGIP, *Azienda Generale Italiana Petroli*). Most of the companies, however, originated in the salvage operation necessitated by the crisis of 1929–1933. During those years, the three largest banks, which held the majority shares of numerous industries, found themselves in a liquidity crisis. The government took over both the banks and the industries owned by them and transferred the holdings to the Institute for the Reconstruction of Industry (IRI, *Istituto per la Ricostruzione Industriale*).

At first companies with state participation were governed by private company law and were a form of mixed economy because, in addition to public shareholders, there were private shareholders as well. But after the crises they went through during the 1970s (such as the increase in oil prices and the chemical and steel industry crises), private shareholders maintained very few shares. Thus the companies have become, for the most part, totally state participation companies.

Companies with state participation carry out productive activities in sectors such as steel, machinery, ship building, broadcasting, petroleum, etc. In some cases, the law calls for the public agency to keep a controlling interest in the company in order to ensure continuity of the public presence, as in the case of the Italian Broadcasting Corporation (RAI, *Radiotelevisione Italiana*). In other cases, the law calls for the holding company to obtain authorization from the Ministry of State Participation when it wishes to transfer shares in an amount that would mean loss of the controlling interest, as in the case of the National Hydrocarbon Corporation (ENI, *Ente Nazionale Idrocarburi*). In most cases, however, the holding company is free to keep or transfer its shares. Thus it may be said that the line between public and private is a flexible one.

Local Structures

In contrast with other administrative systems, such as the German one, where ministries do not have local offices (with the exception of the post office and the railway), in Italy the local offices of ministries and the local authorities (regions, provinces and municipalities) operate in close proximity. Nine of the twenty ministries have their own decentralized offices. Some of them have very complex organizations. As mentioned, often there is not one single local organization for the entire ministry, but as many local organizations as there are departments in the ministry. The local offices are organized at various levels, with their own territorial-regional, provincial-zonal, or municipal boundries. Current opinion is that after the establishment of the regions many of these offices should have been transferred to the regions.

The *Regions*, provided for in the Constitution of 1948, but established only in 1970, are authorities not subject to the central government. They have their own elected regional council with legislative powers, a board with executive and administrative powers, and a president. There are twenty regions, with legislative and administrative powers in sectors such as agriculture, town planning, health and regional public works.

There are only 70,000 employees working for the regions, which however administer a significant portion of public financial resources. Taxation is not the route by which these resources reach the regions; funds are transferred from the state budget. More than 90 per cent of regional income consists of transfers from the State treasury. The majority of such transfers are given to the regions with the obligation to spend them for a specific purpose (for example, to be spent in the agricultural sector, for the benefit of persons with certain prerequisites).

Consequently the regions, on the whole, although autonomous and possessing legislative powers, are strongly conditioned by the central government. In addition, their administration is very weak, so that, at least in this first phase of their existence, they operate as pressure groups and as an instrument to channel social demands (mainly directed towards obtaining further financial resources) from local areas to the center, more than as deliverers of services.

The *Provinces*, numbering 90 and with as many employees as the regions, are intermediate authorities. They have an elected council, with regulatory powers, a board with administrative powers, and a president. Their functions are few, concentrated mainly on assistance, roads, etc. For some time there has been discussion on whether it would be opportune to abolish the provinces. Prevailing opinion is to retain them, transforming the provinces in metropolitan areas into second-level authorities.

The *Municipalities*, of which there are approximately 8,000, have 550,000 employees. They also have an elected council with regulatory responsibilities, and a borad and a mayor with executive and administrative powers. Municipalities have broad, numerous areas of responsibility, ranging from street cleaning and rubbish collection to traffic control and public transport. Like the regions, municipalities have extremely limited power to decide on how resources will be spent. Financed mainly by the State treasury, municipalities may also turn to the Deposit and Loans Bank (*Cassa Depositi e Prestiti*), the largest Italian bank, even though it is not incorporated into the credit system nor subject to the control of the Bank of Italy (*Banca d'Italia*). The Deposit and Loans Bank gathers the savings that are deposited in post offices and finances local authorities (particularly municipalities).

Alongside the regions, provinces and municipalities, a broad local quasi-governmental sector has developed: approximately 4,000 associations of local authorities, 350 mountain communities (also associations of local authorities), 350 municipal public utilities (water, transport, electric power within the municipal area, etc.), 700 local health units (made up of one or more municipalities), etc. Thus it may be said that on a local level there is a repetition of what occurs with the State, that is the establishment of a parallel administration.

Mixed Central-Local Bodies

As mentioned, alongside central and local bodies there are also *mixed* central-local bodies. A first example is the National Health Service, composed of the Ministry of Health, the regions and municipalities. The latter two make up the basic units, called local health units (USL, *Unita' Sanitarie Locali*), and appoint the local administrators. Central administration furnishes the financial resources. All levels of the Health Service are called to participate in the National Health Council (*Consiglio Sanitario Nazionale*).

Along with mixed organizations, such as the health service, which manages a nationwide service, there are other joint, mixed state–region organizations. They constitute a further development of so-called cooperative federalism. Rather than an agreement between two parties, the central power and a region, this is a case of an "association" between the center and all the relevant local organizations.

In Italy this type of "association" is widespread: there are more than 100 such organizations, and there are many reasons for this. In the first place, it must be remembered that the central power has retained control over the "purse-strings," so that the local organization is compelled to come to an agreement with the center. Secondly, this partnership probably also has the function of assuring the presence of the Communist Party in the decision-making process. Although not included in the central government, the Party is represented in many regional governments.

To understand the reason why mixed state–region–local authority organizations have multiplied, one needs to know that in Italy the regions are associated in a National Conference, which has been recognized by the State. The provinces are associated in a Union of Italian Provinces (UPI, *Unione Province Italiane*), and the municipalities in the National Association of Italian Municipalities (ANCI, *Associazione Nazionale Comuni d'Italia*). These three organizations, and particularly the third, have three characteristics: uniting representatives of the majority and opposition parties in the Italian Parliament; constituting powerful lobbies in Parliament, because of the following they have and because they unite representatives of the majority and the opposition; and finally, acting as associations in private law, but being consulted by the Government in the exercise of many public functions (this consultation often being required by law).

Management of the System

The organization described above is composed of a great number of bodies, with many internal subdivisions. The distribution of functions is so irrational that numerous overlaps are produced. Two ministries, for example, are involved with the budget (Ministry of Budget and of the Treasury).

There is the additional complication of numerous and highly inflexible laws. This complication, constituting one of the greatest constraints to management, was caused by many factors. First, a leaning towards the law is implicit in the Constitution of 1948. Second, the plethora of laws (that determine not only the duties and objectives of administrative action, but also the functioning of the administration) is a result of lack of confidence in the administration. Because of frequent delays, for example, the law often sets down the terms within which the administration must take action (nevertheless, even these terms are often not respected). In the third place, many laws are detailed because of the influence brought to bear on their drafting by the largest opposition party, the Communist Party. Excluded from the Government after the second world war (with the exception of two brief periods), the Party makes every effort in Parliament to place as many constraints on administration as possible.

These constraints make management of the administrative system difficult. To make matters more complicated, there are two further handicaps to good administration, namely a *lack of interest on the part of ministers* and *resistance from top-level bureaucrats*. The former is caused by frequent government crises, the general instability of the Council of Ministers and the time and energy that Parliament demands of ministers. Resistance to change from top-level bureaucracy originates in its poor integration into the management of the country, a subject to be dealt with later.

The snail-like pace of Italian administration can therefore be traced to irrational distribution of functions, a plethora of legal hamstrings, lack of interest by ministers, and resistance from top-level bureaucrats. Studies on the subject have revealed a situation often defined as dramatic. To bring an open competition for a post to conclusion for example takes over a year. When a person retires at age sixty-five, it takes at least one year to begin receiving pension payments. It takes much more time for more complex operations, such as the execution of public works. In order to overcome the shortcomings of these procedures, usually minor corrective measures are introduced instead of reorganizing the entire sequence in the procedure. These corrective measures, however, only mitigate some of the more negative effects. For example, people who become pensioners are usually given a temporary pension while the final calculations are being prepared. Paradoxically, the snail's pace in procedures is damaging not only to private citizens but also the civil servants themselves, whose morale is generally rather low.

PERSONNEL

Italian public administration utilizes various types of personnel. On the one hand, there are civil servants, bound to public administration by a true employer-employee relationship and selected, as a rule, by open competition. These will be discussed more fully below. An additional large number of public employees carry out full or part-time public functions because they were elected or appointed by a political authority or by a union. This second group amounts to over half a million persons: 80 ministers and undersecretaries; 41,000 regional, provincial and municipal councillors; about 420,000 on governing boards of national and local public agencies; and about 50,000 other people who are members of councils, boards and commissions with consultative functions (approximately half of whom are union representatives) (4). In some cases these non-professional public employees offer their services free. In most cases, however, they receive an emolument, to which is often added the right to a pension after a certain number of years of service.

As regards career or professional civil servants, their situation varies, depending on whether they are employed by the State or by public agencies. Employees of public agencies are governed by as many different regulations as there are bodies (or categories of them: for example, those governed by Law n. 70 of 1975, known as the law on "para-State" bodies). Some of them have private, non-government status, as do the employees of companies with state participation. The analysis which follows applies only to civil servants employed by the State (the most numerous group). The regulation of other public employees of public agencies cannot be summarized briefly, except to say that it is similar to the state archetype.

State Civil Servants

State employees are divided into various categories: civil servants, teachers, career military personnel, etc. The first category is the subject of this section. It is divided into two large groups, the first of which includes eight functional grade levels, in order of importance and complexity of the work done. To give an overall idea, the third level includes domestic staff, such as ushers; the seventh, university graduates; and the eighth, section chiefs in the basic units of the system.

Above this group is the director level, subdivided into three categories: first director, superior director, general director. As a general rule, the management of a division is handled by a first director, while a general director is at the head of a department.

Recruitment

The recruitment of civil servants is effected by means of public competitive examinations for a limited number of posts. A competition notice is published in the Official Gazette to enable all interested parties to file an application. An applicant must have minimum qualifications, depending on the post (for example, a university degree for entrance at the seventh grade level). There is usually more than one written and oral examination, and examinations vary according to the administration and grade level. Examinations are given in such a way as to ensure an impartial selection and thus avoid political or other interference. Once the examinations have been completed, a graded list is made up of suitable candidates and the top-ranking candidates, according to the number of posts available, are declared the winners and appointed to the posts.

The competitive examination method has undergone numerous modifications which have diminished its scope. At times, for example, internal competitive examinations are held, where applications are limited to people who are already employed in the administration at the immediately lower grade, or a certain number of posts in a public competition are set aside for those already employed. In some cases, those who qualified but were not placed in a post are then appointed one or two years after the competitive examination in order to avoid a new competition.

In addition, often persons are hired without having won an open competition. Normally, this occurs in the following manner. On the basis of *ad hoc* laws, people outside of the administration are hired for a fixed term, for specific tasks. After a certain number of years, under pressure from the unions, laws are adopted to widen the rolls and convert temporary personnel into tenured personnel.

The description above illustrates the method of placement in the functional grade levels (in practice, however, public competitions are held for only three or four of them). For placement at the first director level, there are three different methods. An internal selection from among the officers in the eighth functional grade level fills 40 per cent of the posts available. A further 40 per cent of the posts are filled by means of a competition-course, lasting one year, with a period of on-the-job training in a private company, to which officers of the eighth functional grade level, on the basis of their experience in service, are admitted. The remaining 20 per cent of the posts are filled through a competition also open to applicants outside public administration, providing they have administrative experience.

Conditions of Employment

Once hired, the civil servant is included in the staff roll. This consists of a fixed number of posts, generally established by law, attached to a ministry or office. It is estimated that there are one-thousand staff rolls.

Regulations and rules applying to civil servants are set down in a wide-ranging law, governing rights, duties, discipline, careers, termination from service, etc. However, salaries and working conditions are covered by contract. The law governing the employment of civil servants (*legge quadro sul pubblico impiego*) provides that a representative of the government and the unions, together with representatives of civil servants, stipulate contracts "compartments" or sectors of public administration. Contracts are then approved by the Council of Ministers. Parliament, in turn, passes a law, appropriating the necessary funds.

Negotiations on salary scales and other aspects of service, informally initiated in the 1960s and then gradually recognized and generalized, constitute one of the most important developments in the Italian administrative system since World War II. They have resulted in a limitation to the powers of Parliament over the civil service and a reinforcement of the powers of the Government.

The Italian law follows the French model as regards political rights, which are fully recognized, and apply to joining a political party or a union (granted to the police force as well), running as a candidate for political or local elections, and election to the national Parliament or local councils. In the latter case, the employee is granted leave of absence, and may thus continue to receive part pay, and may have indefinite return rights to his or her post and to a pension.

The career of a civil servant is conditioned, first of all, by the limits imposed by the staff roll: since there is a fixed number of posts, a career may advance vertically only when a post is vacated. Within the eight functional grade levels there are salary increases based on seniority (so-called economic career). To advance from one functional grade level to another the civil servant must participate in open competition. Advancement from one director grade level to the next, instead, occurs through government appointment, which generally follows the criterion of seniority in the civil service.

The description above illustrates the vertical career structure. It must be added, however, that there are very few cases in the central administration of horizontal mobility and career, with movement from one staff roll to another or one ministry to another. This can be accounted for by the inflexible structures as well as the unwillingness of personnel to allow movement from one ministry to another since this would frustrate the career expectations and aspirations of internal ministry personnel, who would see personnel from other ministries promoted above their heads.

On the whole, the salaries of civil servants are lower than those paid in the private sector. However, it must be borne in mind that Italian civil servants have shorter working hours than their colleagues in private business. The civil servant's working day extends from 8:00 to 14:00 hours, from Monday through Saturday, with two afternoons of overtime per week. In actual fact, on the average, the civil servant works no more than three hours per day (as shown by the Formez enquiry), due to late arrivals, long coffee breaks, and early leaving.

Another unusual feature of Italian administration is the so-called leveling of salaries imposed by the unions particularly in the 1970s, so that the ratio between the highest and the lowest salary is now 2 to 1. Nor can it be said that the director levels enjoy fringe benefits or that all directors have access to additional emoluments: these are available only to directors in the financial ministries who are members of councils governing public agencies. This situation of low salary differentiation has been imposed in the name of equality and against what has been called the "salary jungle" in the civil service.

It can thus be seen that the unions play an important role in public administration. Approximately 60 per cent of Italian civil servants are members of a union, while union membership in the private sector amounts to only 51 per cent. By way of comparison, union membership in the public sector is only 55 per cent in Great Britain, 42 per cent in Germany, and 35 per cent in France (5). Union membership has tended to increase over the last few years. The three main unions have become increasingly important: Italian General Federation of Trade Unions (CGIL, *Confedera-zione Generale Italiana del Lavoro*; Communist and Socialist leanings); Federation of Italian Trade Unions (CISL, *Confederazione Italiana Sindacati dei Lavoratori*; Christian Democrat); and Italian Worker's Union (UIL, *Unione Italiana del Lavoro*; Socialist and Republican).

Two distinct tasks are performed by the unions. On the one hand, they negotiate the salaries of civil servants (and in this sense they are in an adversary position *vis-a-vis* the government). On the other, they participate, with their own representatives, in public organisms, such as the councils of the ministries, which are consultative bodies on personnel matters.

On the whole, the personnel in the civil service are badly distributed and badly utilized. Since civil servants are predominantly from Southern Italy and are loathe to relocate, they are allowed to work mainly in the South. On the other hand, there are very few people in the North interested in working in administration. A serious lack of balance is the result of this situation: offices are overstaffed in the South and understaffed in the North. The situation is even more serious where the workload in the offices in the North is heaviest, for example in the tax offices, because of the greater wealth of the North. Thus the supply of personnel is in a ratio opposite to the workload. The personnel are also badly utilized. Personnel administrations (usually a department in each ministry) are so taken up with routine work that they are unable to cope with the problem of motivating civil servants and improving their efficiency.

POLITICS AND TOP-LEVEL ADMINISTRATION

Of approximately 7,000 directors, only about 100 are top-level, placed at the head of departments. It is their responsibility to manage administration.

A close look at this group of top-level administrators reveals that they are not integrated with the political leadership. In the first place, most of them came from the South, twice as many as politicians from the South. Ninety-three per cent of them are over 50 years of age, while only 45 per cent of ministers are over 50 (6). Legal training forms the educational background of the great majority of them. Their careers have been limited to one ministry where, over a period of more than twenty years, they have moved up all the grades in the career path. Notwithstanding the fact that norms facilitate a parliamentary career, very few bureaucrats choose one. Civil servants in Parliament amount to about 4 per cent, while teachers account for slightly over 10 per cent. In France, civil servants amount to 15–20 per cent of Parliament (7). In addition to having different training and being in a different age group, as well as having a separate career, top-level bureaucrats view ministers with suspicion. As a rule, ministers occupy their posts for a short time and often are not even able to come to an understanding with their staff.

The Separation of Politicians and Administrators

On this basis, the relationship between politicians and top-level administrators is one of *separation*. The latter, because of their Southern roots, tend to lend importance to their post and career. They aspire to avoid political interference in that which is vital to them and which they believe is their property. Consequently, they end up being more interested in their need for employment, personnel management, a careful defence of their own post and career prospects than in the need to be productive and furnish services to the community.

Politicians, in turn, must obtain the cooperation of top-level bureaucrats in order to make the administrative machine work. To reach this objective, they use their power to appoint top-level administrators. They use it, however, by declining to use their power of selection, and by appointing (as a general rule) the person with the greatest seniority in the immediately lower grade, thus respecting seniority and the expectations that go along with it.

This exchange enables top-level political power to obtain the cooperation of top-level bureaucracy and enables the latter to be assured that politicians will not interfere in their careers. Top-level bureaucrats trade power for security. The political class trades independence of action for loyalty. This unusual *modus vivendi*, based on the fact that each of the two parties adopts a policy of self-restraint, produces inefficiency and immobility and sets off a vicious circle.

Thus the political class reacts by taking corrective measures through political patronage. First of all, ministers surround themselves with an ever-growing number of staff who work directly for them. In this way, the minister's cabinet has become inflated; it sometimes exceeds 100 people. The cabinet positions itself between the minister and top-level bureaucracy, interpreting the minister's views or passing on their own views (despite Royal Decree Law No. 1100 of 1924, which specifically lays down that cabinets "may not obstruct the normal action of administrative offices, nor act in their stead"). Usually, the chief of cabinet is a state councillor, who, in many cases, follows the minister in his movement from one ministry to another and therefore has a very close, personal relationship with the minister. The Council of State is a body whose functions are judicial and consultative, as in the French model. In the period following the second world war, when the ties between the top-level bureaucracy and ministers were loosened, the Council of State became a seedbed for the minister's immediate staff.

In the second place, the ministers, since they cannot influence the selection and careers of the ministerial bureaucracy, appoint the chairmen and members of the boards of public agencies. It is here that political patronage truly comes into play, with subdivision into "lots" (distribution of posts among the different parties forming government coalitions).

To sum up, two separate top-level groups or systems coexist: one with neutral tendencies, but blocked because it is excluded from the decision-making process and utilized only in an executive function, and the other (ministerial cabinets, chairmen of public corporations, etc.) politicized and substantially foreign to the administrative machinery.

These two coexist in an unstable balance. There are phases during which they compromise, with trade-offs being made between them. For example, a more active and loyal top-level bureaucrat may be appointed to the Council of State by the government. (Though usually such an appointment is won by competition, it may also be made by decision of the Council of Ministers.) There are also phases during which the two parties entrench themselves, reacting in different ways. The top-level bureaucracy intensifies its legalism, enforcing laws to the letter, and in this manner playing a restraining role. The political class, to blunt the edge of this weapon, makes every effort to change the law, but it is usually too late.

In conclusion, the relationship between top-level bureaucracy and the political class in Italy bears no resemblance to either the French elitist model or the U.S. spoils system. The apolitical, neutral attitude of the bureaucracy would bring to mind the British model. There are, however, two features which distinguish it from that model. In the first place, the Italian bureaucracy has neither the salaries nor the social status that permit British higher civil servants to be neutral vis-a-vis the political system. In the second place, the Italian political class uses political patronage freely when legally permissible, namely in the cabinets and in the governing bodies of public agencies.

CONTROL OF PUBLIC ADMINISTRATION

Traditional parliamentary control of administration is extremely ineffective, while the use of new controls, such as the ombudsman, is very limited. However, the control exercised by the State Audit Board and the Council of State remains effective and tends to become more so. To this has been added, in recent times, control by ordinary judicial authority (criminal court judges).

Parliamentary Control

There are three traditional means for Parliament to exercise control (in the broad sense of setting policy and re-examining) over public administration: the law, which furnishes a guide to administrative action; the budget, which allocates the financial resources available to each office; and questions, interpellations and motions, with which information is requested of the government and attention is brought to bear on particular problems.

As mentioned previously, Parliament legislates freely, defining administrative objectives, standards, rules of procedure, etc. However, this copious legislation attempts to regulate administrative services without sufficient knowledge or with inadequate means. The result is that legislation is often not implemented. Lack of or partial implementation of laws is one of the most frequently lamented defects in the Italian administrative system. The responsibility for this state of affairs is sometimes attributed to Parliament, which is accused of promulgating laws blindfolded. At other times, it is attributed to the bureaucracy, because of its inefficiency, tortuous complexity, and pettifoggery. This paper has attempted to offer another, "ecological" explanation of a more general nature, illustrating how Italian bureaucracy is an example of delayed development, has remained cut out of the decision-making process, and in general, from the management of the country. (This does not of course exonerate Parliament from responsibility, since it too often has recourse to laws which are badly drawn up).

The budget is obviously important as a pacesetter for political economy (because of its impact on the economy) and as an administrative pacesetter (because of its allocation of resources among the various offices). Nevertheless, whereas Parliament examines the budget from the political economy outlook (particularly since, with Law no. 468 of 1978, the finance law was introduced, following the French model), it does not even take the administrative outlook into consideration. Thus, in actual fact, the allocation of resources in the system is left to those who prepare the budget (the Budget Office in the Ministry of the Treasury).

As regards questions, interpellations and motions, these are utilized primarily to point out or complain about single cases. Moreover, they produce answers too late, and are not followed up with measures (such as disciplinary sanctions). A related recent development is that an increasing number of laws provide that administrative organizations submit annual (sometimes biannual) reports to Parliament. Now several hundred reports are submitted each year. The majority of them are published in the parliamentary records. Nevertheless, very few members of parliament read them, so that the reports are a dead letter.

The State Audit Board

The control effected by the State Audit Board is carried out in two different ways. The first is a control over the statement of accounts, by means of a judgement preceded by a detailed report. This documented annual report is doubtless the most complete and analytical source of information on Italian administration. Notwithstanding this, though the report is addressed to Parliament, it does not give rise to much comment there.

On the other hand, the preventive control exercised by the State Audit Board is significant. All administrative decisions that involve an expenditure (in practice, however, all administrative decisions), after having been taken by a minister or high-level bureaucrat must, before being promulgated, undergo the close examination of a magistrate of the State Audit Board, who checks its legality. (The Board is a judicial as well as an administrative body, so that its personnel have the status of judges.) The magistrate's examination is almost always meticulous, and may result in a refusal to grant approval of the decision, thus preventing it from becoming effective.

As may be imagined, this control is less meticulous in ministries such as public education, where every day thousands of administrative decisions are made. Moreover, this control is exercised only over ministries (central and local offices). Some public agencies are subject to general control by the Board. The majority of public agencies, however, are not subject to its control.

For some time there have been proposals for the abolition of this control, which was called for by the Constitution of 1948 only for "government measures," and is thus unduly generalized in practice. Paradoxically, those least in favor of its abolition are top-level bureaucrats. They feel more secure under the protection of the Board's control, which involves an examination made by a magistrate, but not in a trial, and constitutes an obstacle to intervention by criminal court judges (although it does not prevent such intervention).

The Council of State

The Council of State has always played an important role in controlling public administration. It performs not only a consultative function (by expressing an obligatory and binding opinion on some measures) but also a judicial function. The latter expanded after the establishment in 1971 of the Regional Administrative Tribunals (TAR, *Tribunali Amministrativi Regionali*), for which the Council of State has become an appeals court.

In the 1970s and 1980s, administrative justice administered by the Council of State and the Regional Administrative Tribunals has undergone a great change. This change consists not only of the creation of twenty judges in place of the single Council of State, but also an increase in the number of cases and decisions. In the 1960s, the

Council of State handled approximately 5,000 cases per year. In the 1980s, the twenty Regional Tribunals are handling approximately 40,000 cases per year (an eightfold increase in ten years). Approximately 40 per cent of these cases involve civil service matters. This helps to confirm the hypothesis above concerning the poor integration between bureaucracy and government.

Criminal Court Judges

Starting in the 1970s, criminal court judges acquired increasing importance. Their interventions as regards public administrators, particularly in the town planning and banking areas, have increased many times, utilizing appropriate provisions in the criminal code. Though no reliable data are yet available for the 1980s, there were twice as many interventions by criminal court judges in the 1970s as there were in the preceding decade. More important, while in the past the sentences pronounced by criminal court judges applied, on the whole, to lower-grade civil servants, starting in the 1970s they applied for the most part to top-level bureaucrats.

The Ombudsman

The office of ombudsman, or defender against bureaucratic injustice, exists in only eight regions (Tuscany, Liguria, Campania, Umbria, Lombardy, Latium, the Marches, Piedmont), and in the Province of Bolzano. Moreover, the ombudsmen's activity is narrow in scope and is limited to regional offices. Whether they may interfere in the functions of municipal offices which carry out functions delegated by the regions is under debate. Regional laws, almost all similar to the original Tuscan law, have set up the ombudsman's area of influence with great prudence, so as not to create interference in the regional decision-making process. An ombudsman may recommend a remedy in cases of undue delay, injustice, etc. Usually, he does not report to the Regional Council. In practice the ombudsman acts as a kind of complaints office, committed to personal cases, mainly involving pensioners and civil servants. There are some new provisions, which cannot as yet be evaluated concretely, in the Piedmontese law of 1981. These grant the ombudsman the prerogative of supervising the merit of administration; require reporting conclusions and comments to the chairman of the Regional Council, so that he or she may inform the Council; and enable the ombudsman to take action not only on request but on his own initiative.

Other Types of Control

As observed, non-juridical means of controlling administration are practically non-existent in Italy. The judicial path appears to be the preferred one. Recently, however, there have been some developments in control through participation. In the largest public services there is now some noticeable, stable participation of representatives of the community. Important examples are: in various types of school councils, there are representatives of the students, their families and local authorities; in central and local decision-making bodies for social security, there are union representatives; and in decision-making bodies in the local health service offices, representatives of local authorities. The majority of these forms of participation are too recent to be fully evaluated.

In Italy, contrary to other European countries such as France, no provisions have yet been adopted to regulate and facilitate public access to administrative documents, nor have standards of administrative ethics been adopted (since the subject has preferably been left to criminal court judges).

CONCLUSIONS

The Italian administrative system, as has been seen, is poorly integrated into the economy and society. Just as Southern Italy is not fully integrated into the national economy, remaining partially underdeveloped, administration, which is influenced by the underdevelopment of the South, is not completely integrated into the political system.

One could say that the constitution, in the course of its transformation, has left out the bureaucracy. During the first fifty years after Italian national unity, top-level bureaucracy was a part of the political class. A large number of bureaucrats sat in Parliament and they were often called to become a part of the government. With the advent of Fascism, its one-party regime and dictatorship, things changed. Bureaucracy was seen with a jaundiced eye by Mussolini and the Fascists. They rarely resorted to purges in order to substitute the old bureaucracy with one loyal to the regime. They were content to isolate it.

After the fall of Fascism and the end of the war, the new top-level politicians, consisting for the most part of people who had lived outside of Italy for two decades, adopted the new constitution (1948), overlooking administrative problems. The importance of the changes which had occurred during twenty years of Fascism eluded them, particularly the isolation of the ministerial bureaucracy and the creation of new bureaucracies in the public agencies. The former remained cut off from the decision-making process. The latter were utilized by the political class even more than by Fascism and Mussolini. In governments composed of five or six party coalitions, political patronage needs are multiplied by five or six.

All of this has resulted in a lack of balance and inefficiency. Subjected by Parliament to frequent accelerations, the administrative machinery does not respond. Attempts by Parliament to make it move faster result in failure or even an increase in administrative inertia. The bureaucracy takes refuge in legalism, which it uses for its own objectives and as a shield. This results in further attempts by the political class to find surrogates in order to maneuver around the administration.

REFERENCES

1. S. Cassese, *Questione amministrativa e questione meridionale* [The Administrative and "Southern" Question] (Milan: Giuffré, 1977), p. 139.
2. OCDE, *Evolution des dépenses publiques* (Paris: OCDE, 1978), *passim*.
3. ISTAT, *Annuario statistico italiano 1984* [Italian Statistical Yearbook 1984] (Rome: ISTAT, 1984), p. 281.
4. S. Cassese, *Il sistema amministativo italiano* (Bologna: Il Mulino, 1983), pp. 112–115.
5. *Ibid.*, p. 120.
6. S. Cassese, "The Higher Civil Servants in Italy," in E. Suleiman, ed., *The Higher Civil Servants* (forthcoming 1985).

7. F. De Baecque, "L'interpénétration des personnels administratifs et politiques," in
    F. De Baecque and J. L. Quermonne, eds., *Administration et politique sous la
    Cinquième République* (Paris: F.N.S.P., 1982), p. 19.

REFERENCES IN ITALIAN

The Italian administrative system is covered in two general works: V. Mortara, *Intro-
duzione alla pubblica amministrazione italiana* (Introduction to Italian Public Administration) (Milan: Angeli, second edition, 1982); and S. Cassese, *Il sistema amministrativo
italiano* (The Italian Administrative System) (Bologna: Il Mulino, 1983). In Mortara's
work, the thesis is expounded, and criticized in the first section of this paper, that the
origin of the Italian "administrative malaise" is merely an executive concept of administration. In the latter work are a broader exposition of the theses expounded in this paper
and a further bibliography. For up-dated information on controls, see S. Cassese, "Contrôle juridictionnel et nouvelles protections en Italie," published in *Annuaire Européen
d'Administration Publique, 1983*, vol VI (Paris: Centre nationale de la recherche
scientifique, 1984), p. 15. The main official enquiry on the Italian central administration
is Formez, *Ricerca sull'organizzazione ed il funzionamento delle amministrazioni centrali
e periferiche dello Stato* (Research on the Organization of the Central and Decentralized
Administration in Italy), 4 vols. (Rome: Formez, 1983).

REFERENCES IN ENGLISH

Main References

In English, the following publications on the subject may be consulted: R. C. Fried,
The Italian Prefects (Yale University Press, 1963); D. Germino and S. Passigli, *The
Government of Contemporary Italy* (Harper and Row, 1968); M. Posner and S. J.
Woolf, *Italian Public Enterprise* (Duckworth, 1967); R. Zariski, *Italy: The Politics of
Uneven Development* (Dryden Press, 1972); P. A. Allum, *Italy: Republic Without
Government?* (Weidenfeld and Nicolson, 1973); D. Hine, "Italy", in F. F. Ridley, ed.,
Government and Administration in Western Europe (Martin Robertson, 1979), p. 156;
S. Cassese, "Is there a Government in Italy? Politics and Administration at the Top,"
in R. Rose and E. Suleiman, eds., *Presidents and Prime Ministers* (American Enterprise
Institute, 1980), p. 171; S. Cassese, "The Higher Civil Service in Italy," in E. Suleiman,
ed., *Bureaucrats and Policy Making* (N.Y.: Holmes & Meier, 1984).

Other References

Adams, J. C., and P. Barile, *The Government of Republican Italy*. N.Y.: Houghton
    Mifflin, 3rd, 1972.
Allen, K., and A. Stevenson, *An Introduction to the Italian Economy*. London:
    Robertson, 1974.
Allum, P., *Italy: Republic without Government*. London: Weidenfeld and Nicolson,
    1973.
Calamandrei, Piero, *Procedure and Democracy*. N.Y.: New York Univ. Press, 1957.
Evans, Robert H., "Italy," in Donald C. Rowat, ed., *International Handbook on Local
    Government Reorganization* (Westport, Conn.: Greenwood Press, 1980).
Passigli, Stefano, "The Ordinary and Special Bureaucracy in Italy," in Mattei Dogan,
    ed., *The Mandarins of Western Europe* (N.Y.: Sage, 1975).

Pignatelli, Andrea Cendali, "Italy: The Development of a late Developing State," in Richard Rose, ed., *Public Employment in Western Nations* (Cambridge: Cambridge University Press, 1985).

Putman, Robert D., "The Political Attitudes of Senior Civil Servants in Britain, Germany and Italy," in Mattei Dogan, ed., *The Mandarins of Western Europe* (N.Y.: Sage, 1975).

Tarrow, Sidney, *Between Center and Periphery: Grassroots Politicians in Italy and France* (New Haven: Yale Univ. Press, 1977).

Zimmerman, Virgil B., "Departmental Personnel Administration in Italy," *Public Personnel Review*, xxiii, 4 (1962).

19

Western Germany

HEINRICH SIEDENTOPF
Post Graduate School of Administrative Sciences, Speyer, Federal Republic of Germany

HISTORY AND ENVIRONMENT

The administrative system of the Federal Republic of Germany is determined on the one hand by a deep-rooted tradition and continuous development and on the other by historical upheavals and an ever-increasing rate of change. The federal structure, with the differently sized states (*Länder*) of unequal political weight, given to the Federal Republic of Germany after the second world war, goes back to the tradition of the territorial states in medieval Germany that were not united until 1871, when Bismarck established the German Empire as a federal state. Similarly, the structure of the federal system laid down in the Basic Law of 1949 which accords the states a much stronger position than did the Weimar constitution, must be understood as a consequence of experiences with the unconstitutional centralist state of the National Socialists.

The Basic Law of 1949 combines the tradition of the German state with the lessons of the past. It was not intended to be a constitution for Germany but a union of the ten western states and Berlin "to give a new order to political life for a transitional period" (Preamble to the Basic Law). The Basic Law purported to be a temporary arrangement coupled with constant appeal to work for and achieve the unity of Germany. That temporary arrangement has proved to be stable and flexible for over 35 years in terms of both government and administration; it has created unity in the state without sacrificing the characteristic features and traditions of the constituent states. The Federal Republic of Germany thus meets the requirements of a modern industrial and social state without renouncing the history and individuality of its constituent states.

The state administration in Germany has likewise been molded by continuity and change. Even under the absolute monarchy, the state was shaped not only by the monarch and the army but also by the administration; a professional, academically educated civil service evolved which was characterized by a common sense of duty. The cameralistics of the day developed into a practical science of governmental administration in the 17th and 18th centuries that was not only able to define the claims of

absolutist government but also the subjects' right to welfare. The transition from
absolutism to the constitutional state of the 19th century was sustained and demanded
by a highly qualified and open-minded administration, not only in Prussia but also in
the southern German states of Bavaria, Wuerttemberg and Baden. By that time, the
promotion of agriculture, business, mining and transport had already become public
responsibilities, which the state administered with the aid of professionally trained
officials who, as a rule, were higher civil servants from the bourgeoisie. That administration promoted economic and social development. In his *Verwaltungslehre* (*The
Study of Administration*), Lorenz von Stein united all governmental action, combining
the social mission of domestic administration with the task of a constitutional state to
ensure that all of its citizens enjoy equality under the law.

From the middle of the 19th century, under the influence of liberalism and constitutionalism, there developed alongside this science of government the particular
German state based on the rule of law. Administrative action with regard to individuals
was now seen primarily as the application of the law. The bourgeois constitutional
state required that the branches of government be separated and that administration
be carried out on the basis of laws. Administration was restricted to the execution of
laws. State administration and adjudication were strictly separated. The protection
of citizens against administrative decisions that encroached upon their rights was an
aim pursued not only through the subjection of the administrative system to the rule
of law but also through the establishment of separate administrative courts (1863 in
Baden and 1872 in Prussia). The development of a systematic science of administrative law and education of future civil servants in the legal sciences are in keeping with
this goal. Since that time, the majority of higher civil servants in the German administration have had legal training. The principle of the state based on the rule of law is
most clearly exemplified in Article 19 (4) of the Basic Law, which lays down that
recourse to the courts, in general the administrative and the constitutional courts,
shall be open to any person whose rights are violated by public authority.

This brief historical survey provides an indication of the main principles of public
administration in the Federal Republic of Germany, which remain valid today.

Constitutionality of the Administration

The administration is bound by the constitution and by administrative legislation, and
in particular by the basic rights stipulated in the first part of the Basic Law, which
confers personal rights upon the individual. The administration is subject to the rule
of law and is required to afford the individual, through specialized courts, the legal
protection due to him under the Basic Law. This applies not only to the classical
responsibility of the state to enforce the law, but also to its responsibility to ensure
the subsistence of the population and to provide through the state a wide range of
services on a large scale. Over the last decade, the principle of the rule of law has
meant that the administrative apparatus has become subject to an increasingly complex
network of provisions ranging from laws and ordinances to administrative regulations.
This network of rules is supplemented by a large number of individual decisions taken
by administrative and constitutional courts, which, by establishing precedents, have an
ever greater impact on administrative action. This increasing network of judicial control has limited the decision-making scope of the administration by defining principles
that were originally open to interpretation, such as the weighing of interests, propor-
tionate action of reasonableness (1).

In view of the new administrative functions that must be fulfilled in a modern state, the principle of legal control of state action has reached its limits. The multitude of provisions, the mass of standards often hamper administrative action to an intolerable extent. An administration planning for the future cannot merely react to the fixed substance of a legal provision but must take its decisions in consideration of a great many social, economic and political factors. Where planning is concerned, administrative decisions affect many people, with highly varied consequences. At the same time, more and more people are claiming the right to participate in administrative decision-making at an early stage, and the right to legal protection against such decisions once they have been taken. The civil service is increasingly avoiding the rigid forms of law enforcement and is taking informal administrative action whereby arrangements are made with the population.

The Tiered Administration

The division of the Federal Republic of Germany into the Federal Republic and its constituent states, as well as the important role given to local self-government, are part of a system of checks and balances within the overall structure of state administration. Federalism and the tiered system of local self-government not only mirror historical development since the times of the territorial states but also reflect the polycentric structure caused by the main centers of population being scattered throughout the territory of the Federal Republic. This divides political authority and public responsibilities and prescribes a civil service organizational structure that permits an overall system of political administration with a graded and diversified distribution of functions at the middle and lower levels of administration. This facilitates the performance of administrative duties in situ and relieves the central government of a good many political conflicts. The federal structure promotes development and innovation at its various levels.

However, the desire for an equally high quality of life in all areas of the federal state and the increased mobility of modern society have given rise to a process of standardization which has culminated for the time being in the "cooperative federalism" provided for in the Basic Law. By making full use of its legislative powers, the central level has attained legal and financial control over the constituent states. The Federal Republic has established clear predominance in matters of legislation through the enactment of concurrent and skeleton legislation. However, the states contribute to the legislative process at federal level through the Bundesrat, the council of constituent states. Since 1969 the Basic Law has contained provisions on joint tasks, which are a manifestation of cooperative federalism; the assumption of a major share of financing has enabled the center to influence matters that originally lay within the purview of the states.

The dangers that joint financing poses to the independence and political weight of the states have become obvious in recent years. Particularly at a time when budget resources are scarce, and in order to emphasize their own political identity, the Federal Republic and most states now seek clearer separation of their tasks and financing responsibilities again. Communes and associations of communes are fighting for similar objectives, namely to obtain greater decision-making scope and to be allowed to allocate their own resources for their own tasks. The federal system has turned out to be a flexible organizational structure; however, the distribution and redistribution of powers need to be reviewed continually in the light of the constitution.

The Professionalism of the Administration

The professional civil service has a firm tradition in Germany, and although it underwent several upheavals with no less than four different political systems prevailing during the 20th century, it was never truly destroyed. In Article 33 (5), the Basic Law requires the legislature to pay due regard to the "traditional principles of the professional civil service" and thus to uphold a traditional set of fundamental structural principles. In addition, it is a permanent responsibility of government to develop the public service and the system of service regulations in such a way that the administration can fulfill the responsibilities and exercise the powers of a modern state. The term "public service" (*öffentlicher Dienst*) is a broader term than civil service (*Beamtentum*) as not all people in public employ have the status of official. The historical division of the personnel of the public service into officials (*Beamte*), employees (*Angestellte*) and workers (*Arbeiter*) has been retained.

The public service regulations were reformed in 1973. Like any public service reform, this reform had to reconcile varying objectives and conditions, namely the effectiveness of the public service, its legal and economic independence, its efficiency and motivation as well as the legitimate interests of the civil servants. With its 4.5 million employees (approximately 20 per cent of the working population), the combined central, state and local public service is also a major employer, an important financial and economic factor. Interest groups and organized lobbies make specific changes in this field particularly difficult.

The central, state and local public services are governed by a close-knit fabric of regulations that are intended to preserve their quality and independence. However, the impartial performance of duties despite changes of government may be impaired if recruitment and promotion are influenced by party political considerations. Patronage in the appointments system or the penetration of the administrative machinery by party politics, discernible at all levels of administration, cannot be kept within reasonable bounds by legal regulations alone; this must primarily be done by the public servants themselves, through firm belief in themselves and adequate self-imposed standards. This is particularly important at a time when the public administration is having to play an increasingly significant part in designing social policy, when changes of government are part and parcel of a functioning democracy, and when the public service is exposed to strong public criticism (2).

Public administration in the Federal Republic of Germany is bound up with a change in the responsibilities of the state. During the 20th century, these responsibilities have changed not only in terms of quantity but above all in terms of quality. It is not sufficient to invoke tradition and established principles in order to fulfill these responsibilities. New demands are made on the civil service by the population, which expects more and better administrative services and seeks greater participation in administrative decision-making. New demands also result from the creative responsibilities of the administration in the face of social, technical and communication problems. Last but not least, the involvement of the national administration in international matters, for example in regulations and decisions of the European Community, is also a source of new demands.

The aim of the following section is to examine the ways in which the German public administration tries to meet this challenge.

STRUCTURE AND MANAGEMENT OF THE SYSTEM

When viewed from outside, state and administration in the Federal Republic of Germany seem multi-tiered and confusing. There are indeed numerous levels of administration. The importance of the central administration of the Federal Republic, to judge by the number of authorities and their staff, appears limited. Important public services, such as education from primary schools to universities, numerous welfare facilities and hospitals, fall under the responsibility of the states or of the communes and associations of communes. However, the central government in Bonn is responsible for legislating in important areas that affect national interests. In these areas, the actions of the state and local authorities are bound by the laws, ordinances and regulations enacted in Bonn.

The Basic Law governs the legal and political order in the Federal Republic, the external structures of state and administration. The major elements of the Federal Republic's organizational structure are:

> federalism, comprising the central level and the constituent states with their own sovereignty and their right to participate in federal legislation;
>
> the two tiers of local self-government, namely the communes and the associations of communes, or counties (*Kreise*), each entitled to regulate the affairs of the local community on its own.

Accordingly, the civil service organization is divided into three main levels, which are organized horizontally in principle and are independent of each other: the Federal, state and communal administrations. The accompanying chart (Fig. 1) shows their structure and relationship.

Central Government Organization

According to the Basic Law, the primary function of central government is to legislate, while most of the administrative work devolves upon the states. For this reason, the Federal Republic may take administrative action only where it has a constitutional right to do so. Even Federal laws are in principle executed by the states as matters of their own concern (Article 83 of the Basic Law). Nevertheless, the Federal civil service (332,000 civil servants in 1983) has grown constantly and has developed additional forms of indirect federal administration.

The supreme Federal authorities are at the top of the administrative hierarchy in the Federal Republic, first and foremost the Federal President as the head of state, with the Office of the Federal President, and administrations of the Bundestag (Federal Parliament), and the Bundesrat (Council of Constituent States). The Federal Government consists of the Federal Chancellor and the Federal Ministries. As instruments of government, the Federal Chancellor has at his disposal the Federal Chancellery and the Press and Information Office of the Federal Government. At present, there are 16 Federal Ministries, which are also designated as supreme federal authorities.

The Basic Law contains a binding definition of those areas of responsibility in which the Federal Republic is entitled to execute laws through its own administrative authorities and hence to establish its own administrative substructure at an intermediate or local level. Examples of this are: the Foreign Service, with its embassies, consulates-general and consulates; the Federal Revenue Administration, with Regional Finance

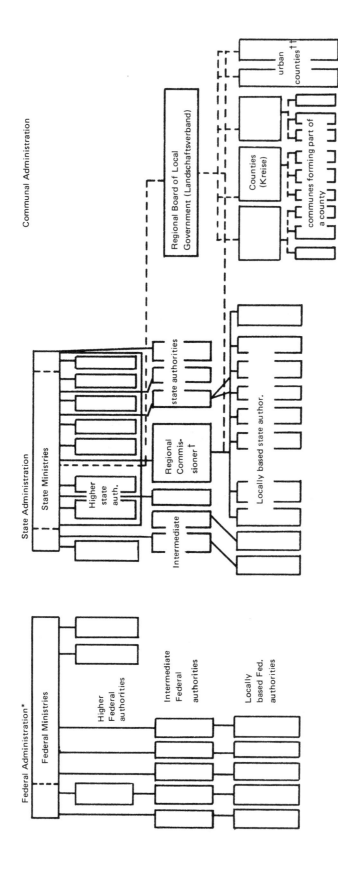

Figure 1 The administrative structure of the Federal Republic of Germany.

*Federal PTT Administration, Federal Railways, Customs, Foreign Service, and Armed Forces Administration.

†Cities constituting a county.

††German "Regierungspräsident".

Offices at an intermediate level and with the local tax and customs offices at the lower level: the German Federal Armed Forces administration; and, with their own particular forms of organization, the Federal PTT Administration and the Federal Railways. In some cases the Ministries control higher-level Federal authorities which fulfill specific administrative functions for the entire country, such as the Federal Statistical Office, the Federal Criminal Investigation Agency, and the Federal Health Office. Moreover, there are Federal administrative functions that, as far as they are not executed by the states, are fulfilled by authorities undertaking indirect federal administration and organized as corporate bodies with legal status; for instance, social insurance duties are undertaken by the Federal Social Insurance Office for Salaried Employees and labor exchange functions are fulfilled by the Federal Labour Office. These administrative authorities have very specialized responsibilities and do not invalidate the statement that the majority of administrative functions in the Federal Republic of Germany are fulfilled by the states and the communes. The states have nearly six times and the communes have nearly four times the number of civil servants employed by the Federal Republic:

federal public service	0.33 million
states public service	1.89 million
local public service	1.18 million

The number of civil servants, however, is only a limited indicator of the importance of the Federal government. The instruments with which it can guide the actions of the states and communes are laws and finances. About three quarters of all Federal legislation is addressed directly to the states and local governments and must be implemented by them. As far as public spending is concerned, however, Federal responsibilities for social security and defense mean that Federal expenditure is about the same as that of the states.

State Administration

Although the states all have essentially the same responsibilities, their public administration systems are organized very differently. This results primarily from their historical traditions, but it applies even to North Rhine-Westphalia and Rhineland-Palatinate, which did not assume their present shape until after the second world war, when they were formed out of formerly independent parts. It follows from the federal principle underlying the Basic Law that the design of their administrative organizations was left to the states themselves. Also the differences in the geographical sizes of the various states affect their internal administrative organization, for instance the number of tiers of state and communal administration. There are obvious differences in particular between larger and smaller states. Finally, the administrative organizations of the city-states, Berlin, Bremen and Hamburg, show some special characteristics. Table 1 shows the nature and numbers of administrative districts and local authorities within each state.

The larger states (for instance, Baden-Württemberg, Bavaria and North Rhine-Westphalia) have a three-tier administrative hierarchy:

Table 1   Administrative Districts and Local Authorities, by States, As of 1 January 1985.

State	Administrative Districts (administered by intermediate Länder authority)	Counties			Communes[a]		
		Total	Urban Counties	Rural Counties	Total of all Communes	Communes belonging to an administrative union of local authority	Administrative Unions of Local Authorities[b]
Schleswig-Holstein	–	15	4	11	1,131	1,026	119
Hamburg	–	1	1	–	1	–	–
Lower Saxony	4	47	9	38	1,031	744	142
Bremen	–	2	2	–	2	–	–
North Rhine-Westphalia	5	54	23	31	395	–	–
Hesse	3	26	5	21	427	–	–
Rhineland-Palatinate	3	36	12	24	2,303	2,253	163
Baden-Württemberg	4	44	9	35	1,111	922	272
Bavaria	7	96	25	71	2,051	1,083	345
Saarland	–	6	–	6	52	–	–
Berlin (West)	–	1	1	–	1	–	–
FEDERAL TERRITORY	26	328	91	237	8,506	6,028	1,041

[a]Including inhabited areas not belonging to a commune.
[b]In Schleswig-Holstein *Amt* or *Kirchspielslandgemeinde*; in Lower Saxony *Samtgemeinde*; in Rhineland-Palatinate *Verbandsgemeinde*; and in Baden-Württemberg and Bavaria *Verwaltungsgemeinschaft*.

The supreme state authorities are the state ministries, which fulfill both governmental and administrative functions; these are supplemented by high state authorities which undertake specific administrative tasks for the whole state without an administrative substructure of their own.

The intermediate state authorities are responsible for an administrative district within the state (*Regierungsbezirk*), and they unite all public functions to be fulfilled at that level of administration under one authority, the office of the Regional Commissioner (*Regierungspräsident*) unless specific independent administrative bodies, such as the school or forestry boards, are the competent authority; these district governments, which are comparable to the French prefecture system before the decentralization of 1983, have become the most important level of state administration, since they ensure that administrative functions in all fields of responsibility are fulfilled in uniform way while at the same time they act as the government's supervisory authority over the local administrations.

The lower state authorities are either specific state administration authorities at the local level, such as road authorities, health offices or veterinary offices, or they are the communal authorities of that geographical level, i.e. counties and cities not forming part of a county, which exercise governmental functions on behalf of the state; where this is the case, either state administration divisions are incorporated into the local authority, or the head of the local authority also functions as an authority within the state administrative hierarchy.

The smaller states have no intermediate authorities. The city-states combine state administration with local government and try to assign as many responsibilities as possible to their urban districts, thereby making administrative action as citizen-oriented as possible.

Decentralized Organization

In the Federal Republic of Germany, a substantial share of public responsibilities is fulfilled by the communes and associations of communes. These entities also bear considerable responsibility for implementing Federal and state legislation. Of the 4.5 million civil servants, no less than 1.2 million are employed by communes and associations of communes. These have a long tradition as self-government bodies with legal status and their own administrative and fiscal jurisdiction, sovereignty and the right to enact by-laws. They have local, directly elected representative bodies, namely the municipal and county councils. Local self-government is understood as the development of democracy from the grass roots upward, enabling the individual to participate in local decision-making, and as a form of decentralization, a tiered division of state power.

Local self-government is realized within the framework of national laws. Today it is restricted by a multitude of national legal provisions, by the dependence of the communes and counties on the allocation of funds by the central authorities, and also by the fact that the local organizations of the national political parties are bringing more and more influence to bear on communal decision-making. Through the active participation of elected citizens, local self-government nevertheless continues to be an important element of democracy at the local level, and it helps to guarantee that public functions are exercised for the public good.

The communes and associations of communes deal primarily with administration at the local level, the communes being responsible in particular for purely local matters, such as the construction and maintenance of streets and sewage systems, for cultural and social amenities, nursery schools, and sports and recreation facilities. The associations of communes have wider responsibilities, such as the construction of certain roads within their county, hospitals, vocational colleges and secondary schools.

The organization of communes and associations of communes in the various states shows some noticeable differences, which result from their respective histories. Despite varying designations, however, their common features outweigh these differences. The communes are the principal units of local administration. Under the law on local government, villages with a few hundred inhabitants and cities with over a million inhabitants are both termed communes (*Gemeinden*). Larger communes bear the designation town (*Stadt*), a designation that has no bearing on their constitutional status. What does matter is whether a commune is *kreisangehörig* or whether it is *kreisfrei*, i.e. whether it is incorporated administratively in a county or is large enough to be independent of it? The limit is set at about 100,000 inhabitants.

Essentially, the communes must fulfill two sets of responsibilities: First, there are the self-government functions which they either fulfill voluntarily—i.e. the commune decides freely whether and how it wishes to undertake them—or which are compulsory, meaning that central government legislation obliges the communes to assume such responsibilities (such as the establishment and maintenance of schools, protection against fire).

In the exercise of their self-government functions, the communes are only subject to state supervision as regards the lawfulness of their decisions but not as regards their expediency. Second, the communes, and in particular cities constituting counties, act as national administrative authorities when they fulfill national administrative functions (for example passport matters and registration of residents) and are thereby integrated into the national administrative hierarchy. Accordingly, in such matters the local administrations are under the professional authority of the superior organs of the central government.

The counties form part of the system of local self-government. They have to assume responsibilities that would be beyond the capabilities of communes. They are territorial authorities covering the communes of all states, excluding the city-states. The counties, too, have to fulfill both self-government functions and the functions assigned to them by the central government. As far as the self-government functions of communes and counties are concerned, the principle of subsidiarity is applied, i.e. wherever possible, tasks are entrusted to the smaller unit. The higher level of self-government only undertakes public functions that relate to the whole territory administered by it and that are beyond the capabilities of the lower level (special schools, theatres, etc.).

Such an outline of the various Federal, state and communal levels of administration must not create the impression that the various tasks are carried out in isolation. The very fact that one level is responsible for making laws and the other for implementing them means that the two levels are inherently linked. Reporting and authorization requirements ensure frequent feedback between administrative levels. Nevertheless, there is always a danger that the executive level might be required to implement unrealistic regulations or be subject to excessive control. Deregulation is currently being pursued with great vigor with a view to giving each level of administration the scope for action and decision-making it needs. Cooperative federalism has developed procedures aimed at preventing complete separation of the various administrative levels These efforts are part of the continuous extensive endeavors to adapt the tiered and sophisticated administrative structure in the Federal Republic of Germany by means of administrative reforms to meet the changing requirements of a modern industrial state.

New Management Techniques

The administrative system in Western Germany is characterized not only by its organizational division into horizontal levels of administration, namely the Federal Republic, the states and the communes, but also by political and administrative interrelations and links between these levels. In those fields where the Federal Republic enjoys the right of exclusive legislation (Article 73 of the Basic Law) or of concurrent legislation (Article 74 of the Basic Law), this very legislation is a source of considerable control over administrative action in such fields. This control is supplemented by the enactment of general administrative regulations by the Federal level. The code of fiscal law and its reforms demonstrate further areas of interdependence between the Federal Republic and the states: under the 1969 reform of fiscal law, the major taxes, the shared taxes whose political significance and revenue are very considerable, such as corporation tax, income and sales tax, are apportioned *pro rata* between the center and the states; the distribution of revenue from other taxes is agreed upon in consultation among those concerned. Some taxes, for example income taxes, are shared with the communes as well.

The preponderance of the Federal Republic and its financial resources, as well as the unequal strength of the states, has meant that, despite the division of responsibility among the administrative levels, the central government has been increasing its financial contribution to state projects on the grounds that the projects in question are in the national interest. Cooperative federalism has outgrown the division of responsibility provided for in the constitution. The joint tasks referred to in the Basic Law since the 1969 reform (Article 91a: expansion, improvement of the regional economic structures, improvement of the agrarian structure and of coast preservation) provided retrospective legitimization for Federal participation in some areas of cooperation. The Federal Republic and the states work together to produce a planning framework, with the former contributing 50 per cent of the cost of fulfilling these state responsibilities. Similarly, Article 104a of the Basic Law enables the Federal Republic to acquire a stake in investments made by the states by providing financial aid, for instance in the spheres of publicly assisted housing, urban redevelopment, local public transport or the construction of hospitals.

Such joint tasks, joint administration and joint financing have been labeled as political entanglement in a federal state (3), and criticized for blurring the dividing lines between areas of responsibility within the federal system and for causing decisions to be taken by joint committees of specialized bureaucrats instead of by the politically legitimized and responsible bodies. Meanwhile, the states themselves have also noticed that their cooperation with Bonn could cost them their political independence. This applies even where the party affiliation of the state government is in harmony with that of the Federal government. In the last few years, increased efforts have been made to phase out joint financing and overlapping responsibilities between the Federal Republic and the states and to establish clearer dividing lines.

The Federal Republic and the states are trying to achieve more continuity in carrying out and financing their tasks and to integrate these into medium-term planning schemes. But in reality, government action continues to be dominated by expenditure ceilings and budget allocations. Drawing up a budget often becomes a dialogue between the Minister of Finance and his fellow minsiters; rarely is it the result of a careful ordering of priorities or the outcome of an overall government strategy aimed at specific goals. This ultimately means that the existing distribution of responsibilities is upheld and that the allocations for every individual budgetary item are increased.

The integrated programming strategies pursued by the various departments have not yet caught on. In Germany, the ministries enjoy a high degree of political independence within the machinery of government. The political responsibility of a Minister for his ministry and for the fulfillment of its responsibilities is embodied constitutionally in the departmental principle of government organization. In addition, the Head of Government is responsible for laying down government policy guidelines, while the settlement of disputes is a matter for the cabinet. However, within coalition governments in particular, the independence of the component parts of the cabinet tends to prevail.

The administration tries to counteract the continual extension of public responsibilities and the constant growth in the web of regulations, on the one hand by means of deregulation and on the other by reviewing critically its terms of reference. Deregulation means the systematic streamlining, reduction and simplification of legal provisions. With the aid of standardized test questions, superfluous and duplicated provisions are checked by administrative, governmental and parliamentary bodies. Practical tests are conducted with a view to estimating the practicality and the real effects of provisions before they are enacted. If necessary, a provision is initially applied only in a certain region or is restricted to particular areas of activity. The effects of legal provisions are analyzed, and the duration of their validity is limited from the outset. At the present time, such deregulation is practiced at both Federal and state levels. It does not result in a sweeping administrative reform but in a systematic and continual simplification of administration in the interest of the government, the people and the administrative system.

Similarly, a critical review of the terms of reference means a systematic examination of existing or newly assigned functions as to whether they need to be fulfilled by the public administration and in what way they should be fulfilled. In this context, the idea of privatizing public functions, of returning administrative responsibilities to the society has been mooted; its aim is not only to save public resources, but also to extend the freedom of action enjoyed by the individual and to reduce his dependence upon state services. Notwithstanding the passionate ideological debate on this subject, this strategy has achieved demonstrable successes at both central and communal levels.

One area in which administrative reform has achieved an impressive degree of success is the territorial and functional adaptation of administration in all states to the requirements of modern professional administration that took place during the years 1964–1974. The territories of the central and communal units of administration underwent extensive redistribution on the basis of verifiable criteria, a redistribution that was reviewed by the constitutional courts. Reorganization of the states which had originally been intended as well, was dropped because of the political resistance of the states, which had grown stronger and acquired their own identities. The reasons for that reorganization of administrative units, in particular of communes and counties, was that their responsibilities had increased in both quantity and cost, that rural areas sought infrastructural facilities equivalent to those enjoyed in the towns, and there was a need for more specialized administrative staff. The existing units of administration had developed over the course of time and were not tailored to the fulfillment of new administrative functions.

With some differences among the states, the reform was begun in 1964. First of all, the geographical limits of the administrative units were redrawn. The deciding factors in that process were the principle of central places of various levels and the economically optimum size of administrative units (in terms of inhabitants and area). The reform included communal and national administrative units. Through a great deal of decentralization and deconcentration, many administrative duties that had hitherto been fulfilled by the next higher level of administration could now be assigned to the newly defined units.

In spite of discussions on many details of that reform, its underlying principles and its results are largely uncontested today. The sheer reduction of the number of administrative units is itself an impressive success. But the real result lies in the improved quality and efficiency of the services rendered by these new administrative units. The reduction in the number of units between 1966 and 1980 is shown in the following table (4):

Administrative Level	1966	1980
States	11 states	11 states
Administrative Districts	33 such districts (*Regierungsbezirke*)	25 such districts (*Regierungsbezirke*)
Counties	425 rural counties, and 141 urban counties (*kreisfreie Städte*)	236 rural counties, and 88 urban counties (*kreisfreie Städte*)
Communes	24,444 communes incorporated administratively into a county, the smallest ones in North Rhine-Westphalia, Schleswig-Holstein, Saarland and parts of Rhineland-Palatinate being united in administrative unions of local authorities (*Ämter*)	3,436 local units of administration = 2,390 standard communes incorporated administratively into a county, and 1,046 administrative unions of local authorities with professional administration (*Ämter, Samtgemeinden, Verbandsgemeinden, Verwaltungsgemeinschaften*) comprising 6,135 single communes

The whole territory of the Federal Republic of Germany is covered with a network of administrative authorities of various levels, belonging partly to the central state administration and partly to the system of local self-government. Many public functions that, in other countries, are undertaken by legally and organizationally independent bodies (swimming baths, theaters, utilities, transport) are fulfilled within the traditional administrative organization. At the same time, there are public duties that are undertaken by self-administering organizations subject to government supervision (Chambers of Industry and Commerce, social insurance institutions). But alongside there are other public services that are offered by private bodies in which central government or the communes have a stake (gas and electricity companies). The state has a responsibility to supervise the provision of such vital services but seeks to emphasize, through the legal status of such companies, that its aim is a private-enterprise approach. For that reason, these utilities, important though they may be, are not regarded as part of the public administration system.

PUBLIC SERVICE PERSONNEL

The quality of public administration at the Federal, state and commune levels depends on the efficiency of the public servants and on their morale. This professionalism of the public service in the Federal Republic of Germany is uncontested, although much public criticism is leveled at individual aspects of it. The traditions of, and changes in, Germany's public administration are reflected particularly well in its civil service. Especially the civil service has repeatedly been the object of reforms, not all of which, however, proved enforceable.

The tradition of the professional civil service goes back to the 18th century, when the sovereign's servant became a public servant; the bond of personal ties to the sovereign was removed and replaced by the civil servant's commitment to the public good. This change soon became the basis of the professional civil service's conception of itself, which encapsulated a number of political, ethical and professional postulates. A particular civil servants' ethos gave rise to the emergence of the civil servants as persons with special rights and obligations, as a separate social group with a specific identity. In his actions, the civil servant embodies the common good, the idea of objective justice and order which must be safeguarded and defended, under political leadership, even against the government, parliament and the political parties.

This historical tradition is illustrated in the definition of the civil service set forth by the Federal Constitutional Court saying that the professional civil service is an institution which, on the basis of specialized knowledge, professional work and loyal fulfillment of duty, is intended to ensure stable administration and thus to act as a balancing factor vis-à-vis the political forces that shape public life. Nothing, not even the changes of political system during the 20th century has altered this orientation in any fundamental way. The Basic Law has therefore drawn upon this tradition. In Article 33 (4), it obliges the state to entrust the permanent exercise of its authority as a rule to members of the public service "whose status, service and loyalty are governed by public law." In paragraph 5 of the same Article, the Basic Law obliges the legislature to regulate "the law of the public service with due regard to the traditional principles of the professional civil service."

Nevertheless, the professional civil service has had to endure upheavals and dislocations since the beginning of the 20th century. The monopoly position in the civil service that was enjoyed by the *Beamte*, the established civil servants, has been undermined by a growing number of nonestablished salaried and wage-earning employees in the civil service; although these were originally employed for temporary work, they now also serve in permanent functions under employment contracts drawn up on the basis of private law on a different pay-scale to the *Beamte*. A further concroachment has to be seen in the phenomenon characterized as patronage in the appointments system or as party politicization of the bureaucracy. This is related to the increasing importance of the political parties and to the extension of public responsibilities in a modern industrial and social state. There are a growing number of civil service officers who do not regard the duty of the civil service as consisting solely in the enforcement of laws and regulations but see it as including creative action in the field of social policy. Party political considerations also play a part in determining the recruitment and promotion of civil servants. The other aspect of this party political influence on the professional civil service is the entry of civil servants into the Federal and state parliaments. When up to 50 per cent of the members of these parliaments are established civil servants temporarily released from office, the questions must be asked whether the parliaments are still convincing representatives of all major sections of society.

The Classes of Personnel

In 1983, about 4,539,000 persons, approximately 20 per cent of the active population were employed in the public service. Of these 4.5 million public servants, 332,000 are employed by the Federal government, 1,890,000 by the states, and 1,180,000 by communes and associations of communes. Also, 1.1 million public servants are employed by the German Federal Railways, the German PTT (Post, Telephone and Telegraph) Administration and institutions indirectly attached to the public service, such as the Social Insurance Administration (5).

Regarding the growth of the civil service, there has been contradictory criticism. In the early 1970s, when the civil service was extended to cover new fields of responsibility that required large numbers of staff (education, security, social affairs), the resultant criticism led to substantial cuts in some areas. During the late 1970s, the civil service had to take on extra staff so as to exert an influence on the labor market, which was plagued by high unemployment. The scarcity of public budgetary resources during the mid-1980s has again led to an employment freeze and to drastic cuts in the personnel budgets. Since so many administrative levels are affected, and since personnel policy, by tradition, has always been greatly decentralized, it is often hard to ensure that a common and stable approach to the control of staff figures and costs is being pursued in the civil service.

The distinction between *Beamte* (46%), on the one hand, and salaried employees (*Angestellte*, 28%) and wage-earners (*Arbeiter*, 26%), on the other, is based not so much on differences in their functions as on differences in their legal status. The status, service and loyalty of the *Beamte* are governed by public law and are therefore determined by the legislature. The relationship between other salaried or wage-earning employees and their employers is governed by private law and is thus defined generally in collective agreements. The terms of service of the *Beamte* are based on the principle that they are pursuing a career, whereas the other two classes are contracted to perform a specific task or function. Their terms of service do not begin to provide the sort of job security enjoyed by the *Beamte* for a long time; only on the completion of 15 years' service do they receive full protection from dismissal.

Recruitment, Promotions, Positions and Pay

A number of traditional principles apply to the *Beamte*, which are above all intended
to guarantee their legal and economic independence. The established civil servants are
linked with their employer for life. They undertake to place their entire working
capacity at their employer's disposal. In turn, the employer commits himself to
ensure their subsistence and to pay pensions to them in accordance with the applicable
laws. At the age of 65, the established civil servant is legally obliged to retire; as a
rule, he receives retirement pay amounting to up to 75 per cent of his service pay.
This lifetime principle is in line with the principle that an established civil servant is
pursuing a career during his time of service. There are several career levels within the
civil service departments; a *Beamter* starts with an appropriate initial post and can
then be promoted in accordance with his performance, his years of service and the
posts established under the budget. There are specific regulations governing the entry
of civil servants into a career as a *Beamter*: they must have certain educational qualifications and have successfully completed a fixed term of preparatory service. In the
German civil service law, there are four different categories of grade:

Category	Education	Preparatory Service	Share in %
einfacher Dienst (lower grades)	successful completion of education at a non-selective secondary school	at least 6 months	15%
mittlerer Dienst (clerical grades)	successful completion of intermediate secondary school or non-selective secondary school plus apprenticeship	generally 2 years	28%
gehobener Dienst (higher or executive grades)	advanced-technical-college or university entrance qualification	3 years	47%
höherer Dienst (senior or administrative)	university degree	at least 2 years	10%

As the civil servant's career level depends on the qualifications he has obtained in
the public education system, the individual careers may appear very exclusive. But
civil servants can rise from a lower category to a higher one if they pass certain internal
civil service examinations. Further exceptions to the rigid principle of career-pursuit
within a particular range of grades may be made with the consent of special staffing
committees.

The system of career categories and its limits have given rise to immobility in the
civil service, which has been criticized repeatedly; one reason for this criticism is that
the system relates to a system of public education which is changing continuously. A
demand was made for greater opportunities, promotion and competition. In 1985 a
committee for the development of new management structures in government administration suggested in particular that appointment to key positions carry a time limit, so

that, on the completion of the appointment periods, new decisions must be taken on whether the civil servants in question are to continue in their key posts.

Public Service Unions

Civil servants are involved in decision-making by the legislature or the civil service management in two clearly separated areas. The civil service unions participate in determining the legal and financial terms and conditions applying to the entire civil service; the staff representatives of an authority take part in specific individual decisions on staff matters within that authority. Details of the scope and the legal effects of participation in these decision-making processes are set forth in laws. The unions and staff representatives participate very actively in these areas.

Since the legal relations of salaried and wage-earning civil servants are determined in collective agreements negotiated between the public employers (Federal Republic, states, local authorities) and the trade unions, participation is particularly active in this field. Terms of service cannot be specified without the trade unions' consent. The system of free collective bargaining also implies that salaried and wage-earning civil servants may take industrial action against their public employer and go on strike. It is not unusual for negotiations on collective wage agreements to be accompanied by strike threats or strikes. Since the terms of service for established civil servants are defined by law, it is only logical that such law does not concede the right to go on strike to established civil servants, whose legal realtionship to their employer is one of special service and loyalty. However, the trade unions are allowed to contribute in an advisory capacity to legislation governing established civil servants; given the weight of the trade unions, such contributions can have substantial effects on legislation.

Staff representative bodies are formed in an authority to represent all the employees of that authority. These bodies do not represent the unions but the employees. In the staff council, the size of which depends on the number of employees in the service of an authority, the *Beamte*, the *Angestellte* and the *Arbeiter* are represented separately. The law distinguishes between two forms of staff council involvement in the decision-making of an authority, namely co-determination and participation; co-determination means that a decision can only be taken with the consent of the staff council, if necessary after conciliation or decision-making at a higher level, and participation means that the staff representatives must be consulted in advance but cannot prevent a decision. All major staffing decisions, such as recruitment, promotion or transfer, are subject to co-determination. In recent years, the scope of co-determination has been extended substantially. The staff representatives are trained by the unions for their functions and are partly released from service duties. The scope of decision-making enjoyed by heads of authorities in staff matters has thus been restricted substantially.

Political Rights of Public Servants

The Basic Law defines the relationship between established civil servants and their employer, the state, as "the special relationship of service and loyalty to the state"; that relationship comprises above all a number of obligations, which are balanced, however, by the state's duty to ensure the welfare of its officials. The obligations as well as the rights of established civil servants are defined in great detail in Federal and state laws, supported by a large number of precedents from the constitutional and administrative courts. The obligations of an established civil servant also include his duty to safeguard the common good in performing his duties and to fulfill his public tasks legitimately and impartially. Article 130 of the Weimar Constitution enacted that civil servants were servants of the entire body politic, not of one party.

Established civil servants enjoy all political rights and may be active in politics, for instance as members of a party. Many members of the parliaments are established civil servants who have been released from office for the term of their political mandate and are entitled to return to office after the termination of the mandate. However, when expressing their political opinion, even while off-duty, the form and content of their utterances must be such as befit their office. A particularly contested issue continues to be whether and in what way political extremists are to be barred from entry into the civil service. In view of the civil servant's obligation to be loyal towards the state, the laws governing established civil servants require them to serve the free and democratic, constitutional and social order of this state and to dissociate themselves from groups and endeavors whose aim is to attack, combat and slander this state, its constitutional organs and the existing constitutional order.

THE BUREAUCRACY AND POLICY-MAKING

To Max Weber, the bureaucracy, with its concentration of expert knowledge and factual information, is the proper instrument for the durable and technically efficient exercise of legal authority, an instrument in the hands of politicians and government. The character of the administration as a neutral instrument is being increasingly questioned both in its empirical validity and in its usefulness as a norm. On the one hand, the administration possesses the expert knowledge, factual information and physical resources to fulfill public duties responsibly and professionally and needs scope to take responsibility and act on its own. On the other hand, there is the danger that the administration will become independent and use such free scope to further its own interests and objectives. This trend towards independence is attributed to the increasing complexity and technical character of administrative decisions but, equally, it always indicates a lack of political control over the administration.

Political direction and control of the administration is carried out by means of laws and ordinances that govern administrative action, as well as through the budgetary rights of parliament. Only by formulating its political objectives precisely can the government direct administrative planning and administrative action. The training and selection of civil servants for key administrative posts determine not only the quality of administration but also its political direction and control.

The Role of Top Civil Servants

In Western Germany's public administration, the coexistence of political leadership and departmental continuity is most distinct in the highest echelons of a ministry. A balance between these two objectives is attained by designating some positions as *politische Beamte* posts, which are filled by established civil servants with political status (state secretaries and directors general); although these office-holders are established civil servants, they must enjoy the government's permanent political confidence. They may be replaced and temporarily retired at any time without any reason being given. The list of such positions is laid down by law. Persons serving in these positions must possess the general qualifications for an established civil servant. The appointment

of these *politische Beamte* constitutes an acknowledgement that these positions of
power within a ministry require a political orientation to the government program.
This is done with the express aim of safeguarding the political neutrality of the civil
servants in subordinated positions within the administrative hierarchy.

Public administration in Western Germany distinguishes very clearly between the
ministries which are responsible, in Bonn and in the states, for the development of
political programs and the preparation of laws on the one side and executive administration in the subordinated authorities on the other. Due to its participation in the
preparation of policies, the departmental administration has considerable opportunities
to exert influence, not only at the supreme level of a ministry but above all at the
specialized base, in the divisions responsible for a specific field of policy. These divisions observe developments in their sector and are in constant contact with the relevant lobbies and with the competent parliamentary committees. They forecast political
problems, formulate alternative ways of action and draft laws. It is only a selection of
filtered information and alternatives, which may have been subject to a process of
interdepartmental harmonization, that arrives at the top of a ministry or even in the
cabinet.

These customary mechanisms of departmental administration, demonstrated empirically in numerous individual studies, underline the political role of civil servants
in the ministries. The political function extends far beyond the circle of *politische
Beamte.* Today, most civil servants in the ministries are conscious of the fact that, by
submitting proposals for action in their spheres of responsibility to the political
leaders, they are fulfilling a political function (6). This consciousness of fulfilling a
political function must be distinguished clearly from party-political orientation of, and
party-political influence on, civil servants in top positions.

Politicization, Education and Social Background

Western Germany's civil service is subject to an extensive network of provisions and
objective procedures and to the staff representatives' participation in most staffing
decisions. The *politische Beamte* are clear evidence that party-political considerations
are taken into account when officials are appointed to certain positions. The influence
wielded by the political parties with regard to decisions on the recruitment or promotion of civil servants, however, has come to extend far beyond this group. But party
affiliation is a decisive factor only as regards the selection of these *politische Beamte*
and not for other administrative positions. The term "party-book administration" (7)
is an inapplicable generalization based on the upper echelons alone, a characterization
that does not apply to the other administrative posts. One can prove this by analyzing
the percentage of outsiders in the administration, i.e. of those who did not attain their
positions through the pursuit of a service career. In 1980, 25.3 per cent of top
politische Beamte posts in the Federal administration were held by outsiders; but outsiders accounted for only 12 per cent of the heads of directorate and only seven per
cent of the heads of division, the two hierarchical levels directly below the *politische
Beamte.*

Staff for top positions are selected not only on the basis of party political criteria,
but also on the basis of the breadth of professional experience they have gained in
other Federal, state and local administrations or outside of public administration, in
business or in associations. This is essential, given the increasingly close contacts that

government and administration maintain with these sectors, their dependence on co-operation with them and the great lack of mobility of key staff between, for instance, business and public administration in Western Germany. In the administration and among the general public, the political civil servant without party affiliation is still recognized as symbolizing a long professional tradition. Although most state secretaries are members of a political party, only every second division chief is, while no less than 70 per cent of the *Beamte* of the next rank down declare that they are not affiliated to a party (8).

There is no contradiction between this neutrality in party politics and the awareness that a civil servant holding a top position is active politically. The traditional bureaucrat, the stereotype from Max Weber's ideal bureaucracy, has largely been replaced in the past 15 years, above all in the top positions in the Federal and state administrations, by the political civil servant who is aware of the political implications and realities of his work, who acknowledges their legitimacy, and who takes them into account in his dealings with political leaders, parliament and interest groups.

Top-level civil servants generally come from the middle or upper-middle class of society. A similar situation applies in other professions. Compared with the business sector, a key position in public administration guarantees a sure and steady income and the subsistence of one's family, but the level of income in the civil service is far surpassed by the learned professions, such as medicine and law, and even further surpassed by managers in the private sector. Contrary to practice in Anglo-Saxon countries, and in keeping with the tradition of continental Europe, the position and role of lawyers in the German civil service are central ones; they form the general, interior administrative service. This accords with the traditions of a constitutional state and with the duties of the ministries, namely to formulate political programs in the form of laws and regulations in accordance with the constitution and with the existing legal provisions and codes.

The study of law at the universities is not oriented specifically to an administrative profession, but it does impart the ability to think clearly and with a view to taking decisions. Moreover, two and a half years of post-graduate training take the junior lawyer into very diverse professional fields which also equip him to serve in public administration. This can explain why the lawyers are still managing to hold their position in the public administration, and in particular in key positions, against economists and social scientists.

ADMINISTRATIVE ACCOUNTABILITY

Article 20 (3) of the Basic Law lays down that the executive shall be bound "by law and justice." Legal control of the administration is therefore of particular importance in the traditionally liberal and constitutional state of the Federal Republic. Every individual is entitled to have any administrative decision affecting him re-examined by court. In addition, legal control is exercised in the form of legal supervision of local government bodies and separate administrative units by central organs. Internally, the individual authorities are subject to administrative control by their own superiors and, within the administrative hierarchy, by the immediately superior authority. The control of administration from outside has its own structures and organs: parliament and the political parties, the audit offices and public opinion, which is very critical towards public administration. The control of public administration is becoming increasingly necessary in view of its growing importance as a market factor and of the trend towards greater independence within it.

Role of Parliament and Parties

Phenomena inherent in a modern state have led to general weakening of the Federal and state parliaments *vis-à-vis* the administration. The parliaments bring their influence to bear only on completely formulated political programs. Their own support services are but a weak instrument with which to counteract the concentrated expertise of the administration. Above all, they are hardly able to develop their own options or to review in detail the execution of political programs. In Western Germany, as in other countries, most legislative initiatives originate from the technically competent executive. Moreover, the preceding process of harmonizing such initiatives with the lobbies concerned further reduces the scope for political action by the parliament, which in any case is divided into a governing majority and an opposition. The parliaments and the political parties tend to involve themselves in details of execution by the administration, for instance through questions in parliament or through direct intervention by members of parliament, instead of becoming involved at an early enough stage in the formulation of political programs. As a result, the administration is subject to intervention on individual issues rather than to overall control.

However, the parliaments and the political parties also avail themselves of opportunities to mobilize "counterexpertise" to arrange hearings with those affected, with interest groups and experts, or to have the programs examined. The parliaments have established specific committees whose purpose is to forecast and determine in advance the effects of their legislation, to analyze such effects after a certain period of time and also to develop their own proposals regarding the updating of laws. Above all, the parliaments are asking to be involved in the planning activities at the Federal and state levels at a very early stage, so that they can influence the shape of such plans.

About fifteen years ago, groups outside of the parliaments and parties began to articulate their resistance to the administration's dominance in the formulation and execution of policies. These groups include the numerous citizens' action committees which demanded that they be involved in specific administrative projects (road construction, provision of public utilities, school policy). The parliamentary democracy of the established political parties was reproached for inadequately representing local and individual interests and for being insufficient capable of making the administration respond to its demands. Since then, these action committees, though often short-lived, have acquired substantial influence on public administration, even if that influence is confined to isolated current issues. They have found formal recognition in the right to institute a group action against the administration; this allows them to assert their general interests in some policy fields, such as environmental protection, even in a court of law.

The Courts and the Ombudsman

The administrative courts developed out of the liberal constitutional tradition of the 19th century, with the duty to guarantee the legal protection of the individual against any infringements of his rights through administrative action or decisions. This was in accord with the fact that measures taken by the administration were usually directed against individual citizens. In the present-day social and industrial state, however, action taken by the state (such as authorization of industrial plants, local building plans, business promotion) generally affects a large number of people. Legal protection has evolved into collective legal protection of large groups with similar interests. The administrative courts are increasingly called upon to conciliate between conflicting interests. In this way, the courts themselves created conciliation and social justice within the framework of the law. More than in other countries, the administrative and constitutional courts in Western Germany help to settle political and administrative conflicts. The people accept court decisions more easily than decisions taken by the administration. Between an ever more comprehensive network of legal provisions enacted by the legislature on the one hand and ever closer control by the administrative and constitutional courts on the other hand, the scope of the administration to take decisions has been more and more restricted. A balance among the three branches of government is no longer ensured. For this reason, it has been proposed that the legislature undergo deregulation and that controls by the courts be limited. The strength of the administrative judicature in all the states and at Federal level has not so far made an ombudsman appear necessary. The citizens enjoy sufficient legal protection against the administration. There are ombudsmen for particular fields, namely the Federal Data Protection Commissioner and the Commissioner for the Armed Forces.

CONCLUDING COMMENTS

Western Germany's public administration is based on its traditions and adapts itself to new challenges. It safeguards constitutionality, continuity and efficiency in the performance of public functions. In doing so, it can rely on civil servants who, by their education and selection, ensure high quality and professionalism. Over 50 per cent of all civil servants consider their work a particular obligation towards the general public. The administration is very closely directed and controlled by means of law and regulations. This is part of the principle of the rule of law and a reaction to a system in which unjustice prevailed.

At the same time, Western Germany's administration is tending to move towards independence from political leadership in its specialist fields, and to extend its terms of reference by itself; its civil servants tend to behave bureaucratically, and its administrative machinery tends to be incomprehensible to the individual. The great number and the relative autonomy of the administrative levels and specific administrative services intensify this impression. Nevertheless, the administration is a surprisingly adaptable and responsive instrument. The civil servants know that, through their work, they are rendering a service to the public and to society.

REFERENCES

1. Nevil Johnson, "Law as the Articulation of the State in Western Germany: A German Tradition Seen from a British Perspective," *West European Politics* 1978, p. 188 ff.
2. Renate Mayntz, "German Federal Bureaucrats: A Functional Elite between Politics and Administration," in: Ezra N. Suleiman, editor, *Bureaucrats and Policy Making—a Comparative Overview*, New York 1984, p. 174 ff.

3. K. Hanf and Fritz Scharpf, editors, *Interorganizational Policy Making*, London 1978.
4. Further details in: Heinrich Siedentopf, "Die Reformen der kommunalen Gebiets-körperschaften und Regionen in der Bundesrepublik Deutschland, in Österreich und in der Schweiz" (Reforms of local government units and regions in the Federal Republic of Germany, Austria and Switzerland) in: Franz Zehetner, ed., *Reform der Kommunen und Regionen in Europa*, Linz 1982, pp. 15–65.
5. These figures are from: Statistisches Bundesamt, *Personal des öffentlichen Dienstes 1983* (Public Service in 1983), Stuttgart 1985, p. 232.
6. Renate Mayntz and Fritz W. Scharpf, *Policy Making in the German Federal Bureaucracy*, Amsterdam 1975.
7. Kenneth Dyson, "The West German 'Party-Book' Administration," in: *Public Administration Bulletin*, December 1977, p. 3 ff.
8. Renate Mayntz, see note 2, p. 191.

REFERENCES IN ENGLISH

Administration and Administrative Sciences in the Federal Republic of Germany, International Review of Administrative Sciences 2 (1983).

Arndt, Hans J., *West Germany Politics of New Planning*, 1966.

Brecht, Arnold, *The Art and Technique of Administration in German Ministries*, Cambridge, Mass.: Harvard U.P., 1940.

Chaput de Saintonge, R. A. A., *Public Administration in West Germany*. London: Weidenfeld and Nicholson, 1961.

Conradt, D. P., *The German Polity*. London: Longman, 1978.

Denton, G., *et al. Economic Planning and Policies in Britain, France and Germany*. London: Allen & Unwin, 1968.

Dorwart, R. H., *The Administrative Reforms of Frederick William I of Prussia*. Cambridge: Harvard U.P., 1953.

Dunsire, Kenneth, "The West German 'Party-Book' Administration: An Evaluation," *Public Administration Bulletin* 25 (1977), 3ff.

Dyson, K. H. F., "Improving Policy-Making in Bonn: Why the Central Planners Failed," *Journal of Management Studies* (May 1975).

Dyson, K. H. F., *Party, State and Bureaucracy in West Germany*. Los Angeles: Sage, 1977.

Dyson, Kenneth, "The German Federal Chancellor's Office," *Political Quarterly* (1974), 364.

Gunlicks, Arthur B., "Administrative Centralisation and Decentralisation in the Policy-Making of Modern Germany," *Review of Politics* 46 (July 1984), 323–345.

Jacob, Herbert, *German Administration Since Bismarck*. New Haven, 1963.

Heidenheimer, A. J., and D. P. Kommers, *The Government of Germany*. N.Y.: Crowell, 4th 1975.

Jacob, Herbert, *German Administration Since Bismarck*. New Haven: Yale Univ. Press, 1963.

Johnson, Nevil, *Government in the Federal Republic of Germany: The Executive at Work*. Toronto: Pergamon, 1973.

König, Klaus, H. J. von Oertzen, and F. Wagener, eds., *Public Administration in the Federal Republic of Germany*. Antwerp: Kluwer-Deventer, 1983.

Mayntz, Renate, and Fritz W. Scharpf, *Policy-Making in the German Federal Bureaucracy*. Amsterdam: Elsevier, 1975.

Mende, R., *Notes on the Political Activities of Civil Servants in Germany*. Frankfurt, 1950.

Muncy, Lysbeth Walker, *The Junker in Prussian Administration Under William II, 1888-1914.* Providence, R.I.: Brown Univ. Press, 1944.

Pakuscher, E. K., "Administrative Law in Germany—Citizen vs. State," *American Journal of Comparative Law* 16 (1968-69), 309-331.

Pinney, Edward L., *Federalism, Bureaucracy, and Party Politics in Western Germany: The Role of the Bundesrat.* Chapel Hill: University of North Carolina Press, 1963.

Scharpf, Fritz W., and Kenneth Hanf, eds., *Interorganizational Policy-Making: Limits to Coordination and Control.* London: Sage, 1978.

Sigrist, H., and H. Roding, "Selection and Training for the German Foreign Service," *Indian Quarterly* (July–Sept. 1956).

Southeimer, K., *The Government and Politics of West Germany.* London: Hutchineson, 1972.

Spahn, P. Bernd, ed., *Principles of Federal Policy Co-ordination in the Federal Republic of Germany.* Canberra: Australian National University, 1978.

Wallich, Henry C., "The American Council of Advisers and the German Sachnerstaendigenrot: A Study in the Economics of Advice," *Quarterly Journal of Economics* 82 (August 1968).

Wolfsperg, Ellsworth, *Efforts Toward Reform of the German Civil Service.* Bonn: Office of the U.S. High Commissioner for Germany, 1952.

20

A Comparative Overview

HEINRICH SIEDENTOPF
Post Graduate School of Administrative Sciences, Speyer, Federal Republic of Germany

DIVERSITY AND UNITY

If you take a look at the map of public administration in continental European countries, you get confused by their diversity and variability. France is known to be the prototype of a centralistic state with the tradition of Napoleon's administration, which could not really be changed by the different Republics. In the center of Western Europe there are situated three confederations—Switzerland, Austria, Federal Republic of Germany—whose types of federalism are totally different. The Federal Republic of Germany is known to be a federation in which the Federal Republic causes an intensive control of development by its legislation and finances, but in which at the same time the federal laws are being executed by the multitudinous administrations of the states and communities. In Switzerland, however, the cantons are sovereign and competent for all tasks that have not expressly been transferred to the federation. Finally, Italy and Spain are unitary states, but they have regions of increasing political strength. This diversity of political and administrative characters seems to make international comparison in Western Europe more difficult, or even totally impossible.

The observer can either ignore this diversity and its causes by concentrating his attention on the parts and types of public administration that correspond with each other—as Woodrow Wilson did in his famous essay *The Study of Public Administration* (1887)—or he can take the diversity as an encouragement to perceive and advance his own national administrative system—as Lorenz von Stein did in his great work *The Study of Administration* (1865).

When he was looking at the governments and administrations of Europe, Woodrow Wilson tried to find regularities and rules of public administration beyond history and beyond the political systems: "The field of administration is a field of business." He just did not want to search for political principles and did not at all want to ask for the constitutional and political reasons of governmental practice in France and Germany: "We can thus scrutinize the anatomy of foreign governments without fear of getting any of their diseases into our veins, dissect alien systems without apprehension of blood poisoning." With these remarks, Wilson steered public administration and comparative public administration for a long period into an orientation in which history,

339

tradition and the political environment of public administration were hardly taken note of: the field of administration is a field of business.

For the Europeans themselves at that time this confusing diversity of politics and administration was not so easy to unravel. The countries of Western Europe were and are entangled too closely. In the 19th century the development of democratic forms of government occurred in a pan-European discussion; political and administrative programs and governmental practices in the neighboring countries became encouragements and examples for the further development of their own country. That applies for the constitutions, the organizations of government and the self-government of the communities. Lorenz von Stein gave his comprehensive work *The Study of Administration* the significant subtitle: "The study of executive authority, its law and its organisation—with a comparison of the state of law in England, France and Germany." In his preface he gave comparative public administration its direction: "Europe is the part of the world where all human things are the same and yet not the same; in this diversity rests the hidden wealth of Europe, the inexhaustible source of its power, for in Europe it is necessary to think of the same in the different, of the different in the same."

Public administration in Europe has often been connected and compared with Max Weber's conceptual features of bureaucracy: the specified model of a classical study of organization with the elements of hierarchical authority, of formal structure, of determination of behavior by written standards and of a professional staff of administration. This ideal typical construction seemed particularly appropriate to Max Weber for making legal use of power. Even though his ideal type was based on the reality and experience of an economically developed and politically centralized nation-state such as Prussia, it should not and could not describe the reality of administration and government in the countries of Western Europe at the beginning of the 20th century.

However, in this European diversity all administrations and governments correspond in two elements of structure that were named by Max Weber: the constitutional obligation of public administration to the law, and the existence of a specially trained, professional public service.

Obligation of Administration to the Law

In all European countries, the obligation of public administration to law and justice is an achievement of Constitutionalism and Liberalism; the constitutional state emerged from the struggle of the bourgeoisie against the absolutist police state. In the middle of the 19th century Robert von Mohl called the constitutional state the "type of new state that restricts its efficiency in the interest of the liberty of its individuals, that issues exact laws and provides courts for the protection of the subjects." The liberal constitutional state tried to hold off state despotism and state intervention from the individual, to restrict state tasks by law and to guarantee its citizens security, personal liberty and protection of ownership by equal treatment and legal protection. The means of this obligation of public administration were the laws issued by the parliament. The obligation of administration to the law, born in the sphere of politics and firmly established in the constitution, had three direct consequences that remain in effect today:

> the formation of a special administrative law, a dogmatic law with strict obligations
> for administration (not as Dicey wrongly said: with privileges for administration);

the establishment of special administrative courts for legal review of administrative action in the light of the constitution and the laws (the first administrative court was established in Germany in 1863); and

the management of administration by specially trained jurists, and the formation of a juridically molded permanent civil service.

The law became the frame and the basis of administrative action. Governmental and administrative programs were issued in the form of statutes. Even when the contents of governmental and administrative action turned from liberal constitutional state action to welfare state action and finally to planning and formulating state action, the legal obligation and the statutory shape were maintained. The legal means of administration formed as legal foundations for intruding on the individual's sphere of rights had to be transformed and completed when the tasks of administration gradually turned into planning, programming and shaping the future.

Even today the tradition of the constitutional obligation of administration results in a steadily rising number of statutes and ordinances. Attempts at deregulation have been only partially able to get this flood of statutes under control. The review of administrative action by the courts increasingly has restricted the scope of administrative decisions and action. In times when the citizens of all West European countries are viewing public administration more and more critically and are more and more becoming aware of their rights, administrative decisions are being increasingly contested before the constitutional and administrative courts. In all countries the administrative courts are overburdened. Often final decisions are pronounced only after several years and often have a binding effect on similar state actions. A liberty, once won in the struggle against the absolutist police state, can now become a barrier to the new social and industrial state.

Permanent Civil Service

Also in the 19th century, a specially trained permanent civil service was forming: the servant of the sovereign became a servant of the state. Even in the "Prussian Common Country Law" of 1794 essential civil service regulations were established: the conditions for appointment and for the execution of office and the protection against arbitrary dismissal. In 1848 the first Ecole Nationale d'Administration was founded in Paris. At the beginning of the 20th century Max Weber stated that "in a modern state the real power lies necessarily and unavoidably in the hands of the permanent civil service."

Unquestionably, with the growth of central administration and the expansion of public tasks the influence of the permanent civil service is increasing. Civil servants get security of employment and an old-age pension that is not to be compared with the private sector. In some countries, their special positions and the coincidence of special rights and duties are creating special social identities and a specific professional ethical code of behavior. For instance in France, the public service is developing an elite of workmanship that feels obliged to serve the nation: "profession:fonctionnaire" (Bloch-Lainé). In some countries there are strained relations between such a permanent civil service and the political leaders, between the continuity and the independence of the civil servants on the one hand and the change of the political leaders which is usual in democracies on the other. The German Constitutional Court expressed this in a classical formulation: the permanent civil service is an "institution, which shall, based on competence, workmanship and loyal performance of duty, guarantee a firm administration and thus be a conciliating factor vis-à-vis the political forces which form the life of the state." In recent years, this opposition between politics and civil service has given way to a mutual entwinement: governments and political parties try to increase their influence by means of their policy of appointing civil servants to leading positions in the ministries, while more and more civil servants start their activities in political parties and parliaments.

In all countries of Western Europe the members of the public service have achieved the right to be in politics, to exercise their political rights and to join unions representing their interests. This ends in another strained relationship between the protection of their interests and their specific duty of loyalty towards the state.

HISTORY AND THE ENVIRONMENT

In their historical development, state and administration are closely entangled with each other: administration participated in the change from a liberal constitutional state to a welfare state, and administration even helped to prepare that change. Administration made the development to increasing state intervention possible by assuming that task. But without state determination of direction and without political force, even the highly efficient French administration of the IVth Republic was not able to carry out needed reforms because of the frequent changes of government. Only the Vth Republic under the constitution of 1958 installed a powerful executive and thus an administrative continuity for putting political programs into action.

Napoleon's conception and practice of public administration, the conception of centralistic state control, became a model for administration not only in France, but also in Belgium and in Spain. Centralistic state control exists not only on the national level but also in the Regions and Departments. Part of the Napoleonic tradition is the system of prefectures, i.e. the combination and coordination of all state measures in one administrative body, in one person, the prefect, who is a representative of the state in the Department as a self-government corporation, and he thus combines a state function with a local function. Only in 1982 was this connection broken by the decentralization laws of President Mitterand. Austrian administration is as well molded by its history, by its task to keep a multi-national state together with an efficient and yet flexible administration. Belgium is not only an example of a uniform and centralistic administration with a Napoleonic tradition. This tradition was not able to overcome great variations of language, religion, and, most of all, differences in economic development. What is more, Belgium is an example of geographically based ethnic groups that have an urge to become independent and to achieve regional autonomy.

When formerly independent parts were assembled in one unified federal state, administration sometimes was an essential factor of unification. The federal states in Europe—Switzerland, Austria and Germany—reveal different degrees of unification and different conceptions of balancing the weights between the federal states and the member states. Also in Italy, the Regions and Provinces derive from the political history of this country before its unification and from the different development standards in North and South Italy, with the understanding of the central government that some regional problems can be perceived and solved better on a subnational level. The central state meets the wishes for a regional participation and share of decision-making by subdividing into regions and thus relieves itself of solving regional problems. In Spain, the seventeen autonomous Regions, which are provided with some legislative powers, are already experiencing to a certain extent a transition from a decentralized unitarian state to a federal state with subnational units which are becoming more and more aware of their political autonomy. In Switzerland, where federalism is based on the historical voluntary union of some cantons, the independence of the cantons is complemented by a distinctive autonomy of the communities and by extensive co-determination rights of the citizens (people's initiative and referendum). The cantons have a comparatively large autonomy in taxes, whereas the federal taxes are definitely enumerated in the Federal Constitution. In Austria and Switzerland, tasks with national interests are assigned to the federal level and the remaining tasks are reserved to the member states, but in several domains the federal legislature can issue skeleton laws that are to be filled out by the member states.

In all three federations this distribution of tasks in not static. During recent years it has been evaluated and altered in many ways. Generally, important tasks have moved up to the federal level and the member states have had to submit to more federal control, which in some cases has been caused by financial participation of the federal government in projects of the member states. "Co-operative federalism" in a "unitarian federal system"—these were the notions for explaining and legitimating such changes. Only since about 1980 have there been new attempts at a distinct separation of levels, and the federal level has been trying to relieve itself by increasing decentraliza-tion and by assigning tasks to the member states.

The present development in the West European countries reveals a slowly advancing convergence. It is true that a centralized state and a federal state are two different types of state organization. But in both there have been changes—different with regard to content and time in the various countries—that lead to an increasing differentiation and distribution of legislative and administrative state authorities and tasks, to a reor-ganization of intergovernmental relations in the federal systems and to a reinforcement of decentralization in centralized systems.

A second common course of development in the West European countries is closely connected with the increase of tasks in the modern state: a differentiation in the forms of state and administrative action and organization. The state is acting no longer only by laws and administrative execution of laws. Political and social programs, economic and technical developments are more and more being put into action by organizations with only a partial-state, quasi-governmental character, by means of sub-ventions and financial incentives. The state is pursuing economic goals also with the help of nationalized public utility enterprises. In the modern state, classical bureau-cracy is only one of many means of intervention. Besides that, there has been develop-ing an almost unsurveyable zone of quasi-governmental organizations that on the one hand are intensifying the effectiveness of state action, but on the other can make democratic control and responsibility more difficult.

STRUCTURE AND MANAGEMENT OF THE SYSTEM

The traditional boundaries of state and local bureaucracy have become vague. It is no longer just the ministries and their subordinate offices that form part of the state administration. Today there are also special agencies of various legal forms that are independent to a large extent. Classical bureaucracy with its legal, budgetary and procedural restrictions frequently turned out to be unable to assume new complex state tasks and fit them into its organizational system. In France such *administrations de mission* have been established outside of the ministries. Because they are flexible in formulating their targets and provided with an adaptable shape of organization, they are able to overcome the restrictions of the ministerial system. These new functional bodies are often charged with economic and technical development and promotion. Tensions and conflicts between them and the traditional departmental administrations are unavoidable. In spite of their importance for putting government politics into action, they have—compared with the departmental administrations—only specialized, partial competences. Now as ever, the main emphasis for formulating and executing governmental programs depends on departmental administration.

The management of government lies in the hands of the head of the government or in the hands of the cabinet. There are two remarkable exceptions to that rule: in France, besides the prime minister, the president claims a part of governmental management, especially in the field of the *domaines reservées*: foreign policy and defense policy. The secretariat of the president, the general secretariat of government, and the personal cabinets of the president and the prime minister as well, are centers of coordination and initiative towards government and the departmental administrations. In the Vth Republic the offices of president and prime minister have been politically homogeneous until recently. The election of March 1986 has caused a new situation the settlement of which still is totally open to question in governmental practice. The Swiss government, however, is characterized by the concordance democracy of this country, by the principle of compromise and agreement between the political parties, and by the proportionally shared participation of many political forces in government. All of the parties take a part in the executive body, and the position of head of government rotates periodically among the members of the government.

For the purpose of governmental management, in all of these countries the heads of government are provided with their own agencies, general secretariats, Office of the Federal Chancellor etc., which have experienced a large increase in functions and personnel during recent years. With a term such as "government secretariat," their tasks are insufficiently described: they start initiatives in the departmental administrations by themselves; on behalf of the head of government they control and coordinate the activities of the departmental administrations; and they supervise the execution of cabinet decisions. While doing so, they follow the guidelines of the governmental program. The interdependency between the different fields of politics requires early coordination; subsequent corrections of insufficient coordination often are no longer possible. This change from negative coordination to positive coordination can only be successful with the help of modern management and of communication technologies. But the politics of government follow their own peculiar rules. In a coalition government, the ministers will not easily be ready to submit to the directions and instructions of the government secretariat. Also, a minister bears political responsibility for his department, and just for that reason he will try to gain popularity within the government by his own initiatives.

Frequently there are further agencies, for example press and information offices, or persons, for example secretaries of state, who are assigned to the head of government or to his agency. They are charged with representing government politics to the public and the mass media, or with keeping in contact with the parliament and the political parties. In some countries, these secretaries of state or parliamentary undersecretaries are at the same time members of the parliament and thus, in addition to the head of government and the ministers, increase the political character of government and the top level of its administration.

Within governmental organizations, departmental administrations have gained in significance in their capacity as administrative agencies specializing in concrete policy fields. The departmental administrations possess expert knowledge and continuity. Usually they have surrounded themselves with a multitude of advisory boards. They often cultivate direct contacts with the competent parliamentary committees as well as with the interest groups concerned with their policies. In this field there has emerged a network of communications and identical interests, which has contributed to making the departmental ministers more independent. This process of becoming independent, of segmentation and fragmentation of departments and departmental administrations, can be observed in many countries. The influence of the departmental administrations on the complex and difficult task of formulating homogeneous governmental policies has steadily increased. Hence it has become all the more necessary to have bodies and procedures for coordination, to interchange personnel among the departments, and to form an interdepartmental group of professional management personnel.

Central and State Government

In unitary states, the departments are provided with subordinate authorities, with field services, which guarantee the execution of departmental policies and laws. Formerly, each department had its own administrative structure and frequently had its own special administrative districts as well—which was also a sign of the independence of the departmental administrations. For that reason, in some of these states, for instance France, a regional level of administration and new authorities had to be established to concentrate and to combine the different field services and to establish administrative districts that were the same for all central departments.

In federal states, the federal laws usually are executed by the member states. Generally, the federal ministries in Switzerland, Austria and Germany are not provided with their own administrative basis such as field services—except the postal services and the railroads. The member states are not free to execute the federal laws as they wish. They are subject to more or less detailed legal prescriptions as well as to federal supervision. However, the member states have their own competences and legislative powers and carry out their own tasks with the help of their own administrations. The different significance of the central and decentralized administrative levels in a unitary state compared with a federal state becomes apparent if one contrasts the numbers of public servants at these levels in France (1983) and Western Germany (1983) (1):

France		Western Germany	
state administration (including field services)	1.77 million	federal administration	0.33 million
		Länder administration	1.89 million
local administration	0.75 million	local administration	1.18 million

In the federal states, the shapes and contents of cooperation between the federal and state levels have undergone decisive changes and have virtually shifted the original constitutional distribution of competence between the federal and state spheres. From the beginning, the distribution of competence was not a distinct and clear separation of the spheres. Soon, the increase and the interdependence of public tasks made manifold cooperation necessary—horizontal cooperation among the states and vertical cooperation between the federal and state levels. At the same time, the cases increased in which the federal government took a financial share in member state tasks, especially in tasks of national interest (such as the foundation and construction of new universities and regional economical development) or maintained the less wealthy states. This was often justified with the goal of leveling out financial and administrative disparities between the federal government and the states. Thus, in all three federations a form of "cooperative federalism" was growing which abolished the distinct separation of the levels and which enabled the federal level to gain influence by way of mixed financing.

In all three countries, this entwinement of levels is being criticized from various angles. It is argued that it is coming about by agreement among the executive authorities and is thus actually eluding the federal and state parliaments. Usually, the only contribution of the parliaments is the ratification of the decisions taken. The influence of the political parties on these decisions is very small. There are no formal procedures for this cooperation, and the flow of information is between the administrations. Normally the decision is a specialist compromise of the lowest common denominator. During recent years, in all three countries these criticisms have led to striving for a shift, and a clear separation of competences, to the advantage of the member states. Hence, a reform of the Austrian federal constitution in 1974 had already signaled an attempt at decentralization. In Switzerland, in 1978 a research committee for redistribution of tasks between the federal government and the cantons produced suggestions for disentangling the responsibilities. The abolition of mixed financing has been the politics of the German federal government since 1983.

Therefore, the unitary and the federal states of Western Europe meet—despite their different starting points—in one request for differentiation and independence of the decision and administration levels in the total state system. Also, the invigoration of local self-government is intended to contribute to this division and differentiation.

Local Government

"The territorial authorities shall govern themselves independently by council meetings within the limits set by law." In this quotation from Article 72 of the constitution of the Vth French Republic, the guarantee of local self-government has been formulated in much the same way as in Article 28 of the German Basic Law. But behind the verbal correspondence of these wordings, two quite different conceptions and ways of practice are hiding. France is known to be a centralistic state with a close-meshed state control of the communes and Departments—at least until the decentralization laws of 1983. The Federal Republic of Germany is a federation with strong, independent member states (Bundesländer) and a strong local self-government in the communes and counties.

In all of the West European countries the communes and counties vary in their degrees of sole responsibility, in the number and the importance of their tasks, in the extent to which their tasks are chosen by themselves or assigned by state, in their financial resources and in their administrative power. But the basic conception of local self-government is the same in all of these countries. It is closely connected to the idea of democracy and of self-determination.

The communes are obliged to attend to the public tasks of the local community independently and with participation of the local citizens. The communes are the local level of democratic state organization. They are the school of democracy where the citizens are supposed to take part in political decisions. Attending to the public tasks of the local community, the local administration will get a better knowledge of local peculiarities, a closer proximity to the local problems and to the citizens, and thus administrative decisions will be more adaptable to the local conditions.

Local self-government does not mean government outside or apart from the state or state administration. It means decision and administration within the limits set by state law in regard to the common public interest. Local self-government is—to a varying degree in the different countries—incorporated into state administration. However much the autonomy of the municipalities had been emphasized formerly, in the modern industrial and social state a coordination in attending to public tasks by municipal and state administration must be guaranteed. Reforms of local self-government in all of the European countries during recent years reveal that a new balance of autonomy and integration must be found. The local reforms in Germany since 1965, in Great Britain since 1972 and in France since 1983 have given evidence of that.

Local self-government is characterized by the competences of the municipality, by the functions which they are fulfilling of their own free will or which were assigned to them by the state. Even a blanket clause in the constitution ("all the affairs of the local community") must be put into more concrete terms only by the legislature. For this distribution and assignment of tasks, it is crucial that in most of the European countries local self-government is split up into two or even three levels: the commune as the local community, the county or the department, and finally the region as a subdivision of the state or country. The distribution of tasks is according to the principle of delegation: the lowest unit is to fulfill those functions for which it is able to take responsibility, with respect to its administrative and financial power and to the proportions of population and space. Functions that can just as efficiently be fulfilled by smaller administrative units, or the fulfilling of which requires a close connection to the local community, are to be reserved to the municipalities. These principles were applied in the territorial and functional reforms of local government in most European countries in the 1960s and 1970s.

For the purpose of attending to their own tasks and to the functions assigned by the state, the communes stand in need of sufficient financial resources. Generally, local taxes and levies are rather slight compared with the state grants to the communes for financing local projects or assigned tasks. Usually the state makes these grants for a special function or project (specific purpose grants) and thus gains substantial influence over the fulfilling of these functions beyond the legal prescriptions. For that reason, some countries are trying out a system of bloc or standard grants, which on the one hand leaves more freedom of decision to the communes and on the other hand limits state liabilities. Furthermore, the grant system gives rise to an equitable distribution of funds among the poor and the rich communes, like the special adjustment funds in France.

In the 18th and 19th century, local self-government used to be honorary administration—voluntary and honorary participation of elected citizens in fulfilling local functions.

Full-time professional administration by civil servants was only beginning at the regional level, for several communes together. But the rapid increase and interdependence of public tasks at different administrative levels unavoidably led to full-time administration in the communes as well and reduced the honorary elements. In most countries there is now a special local public service which, compared with the state public service, has considerably increased during recent years.

Since the municipalities have grown historically, their locations and sizes have not been designed at the drawing board. The less the communes were able to confine themselves to attending to local tasks and the more they were included in state tasks, the more significant became the tensions between historical patterns and the modern setting of tasks. These tensions were to be abolished by structural reforms, especially by new and bigger local self-government units (territorial reform). In some European countries, these structural reforms have been combined with a new distribution of tasks between the state and the communes (functional reform). With their new territorial pattern and new power, the self-government units have acquired more important and more difficult tasks and competences.

In all West European countries, local government has undergone many years of adjustment, adjustment of historical patterns to the demands of modern society, adjustment of mainly autonomous care of the community to acting and deciding in a wider frame, adjustment to increasing legal control by the state legislator, and finally adjustment of an honorary administration to a full-time professional public service. In this context, the danger is that the loss of honorary participation and locally based decisions will alienate the citizens from their communes and that instead of the political dimension, the mere bureaucratic side of local government will be seen and experienced.

PUBLIC SERVICE PERSONNEL

In the West European countries, public service has grown simultaneously with the increase of public tasks. In Western Germany it has doubled from 2.25 million persons in 1959 to 4.5 million in 1983 (2). With that, public service has become an essential factor of the employment market: in Ireland 30%, in Germany 18% of the persons employed. Security of employment, salaries and old-age pensions in the public service have not been without effect on the other fields of the employment market. All of these countries practice the lifetime principle for public servants: after a probationary period or after several years a public servant will get a lifetime appointment until the day he reaches the age limit. Although Switzerland has adopted the principle of term employment, only 0.1 per cent of the persons affected do not have their terms regularly extended.

There is a difference between civil servants on the one hand and public employees and workers on the other: a civil servant is the historical type of public servant who carries specific duties of loyalty and of allegiance towards the state, whose legal status is governed by law and whose right to go on strike may be restricted. In most European countries the civil service is divided into four categories: basic, clerical, executive and higher service—which are based on the level of school or university education. According to these categories, the civil servants in higher positions are entrusted with an appropriate higher degree of responsibility. Within the categories, their vocational development is determined by the career principle, each category including five grades on a rising pay scale. In this context, especially in France, there is a clear distinction between promoting to a higher grade and assigning to higher functions and positions.

The various specialized professional groups, such as physicians, architects, engineers, etc., are combined in corps or classes governed by very heterogeneous prescriptions. This corresponds to a large extent with the difference between generalists and specialists, which the public service of Ireland adopted together with the British system. These specialized corps often reveal a corporative tendency caused by their specific fields of activity, and develop specific conceptions of their duty. They struggle for their own special service regulations, and thus they form strong pressure groups within the public service. This development corresponds with the already-mentioned process of public administration disintegrating and segmenting into specialized departmental administrations. In the Spanish civil service there are 200 such specialist corps. This specialization considerably reduces the personnel mobility among the departmental administrations, and also between the public service and trade and industry.

The constitution of Federal Germany states that every German citizen is given equal access to any public position according to his suitability, ability and qualifications. In France and Belgium, the access to public service is by competition, the "concours." For the management cadre of its public administration, France has provided a special education at the Ecole Nationale d'Administration. This education of the administrative elite is attracting the best and the most capable personnel in the country. Within this group, education produces a great coherence and a common conception of duty, and later on it makes informal contacts easier for the former students of the ENA when they hold leading positions. In the meantime, ENA graduates have occupied not only leading positions in public administration, but also important domains of political and economic life. In all West European countries, special administration schools are contributing to the education and the further education of public service personnel. Usually, the universities do not provide any courses of training which are preparing mainly or solely for public service. Even law studies are simultaneously preparing for other juristic professions such as for lawyer. Additional education at an administration school begins only after one has finished university education.

In all these countries, too, civil servants are free to express their political opinions and to assert their political rights. Restrictions to this are merely the consequences of their special duties of loyalty and of reticency. A large proportion of civil servants have joined unions and associations, which in some countries mainly are struggling for better wages and service conditions, but in other countries are also participating in personnel affairs such as promotions, and in some countries are mainly politically orientated and are affiliated with certain political parties.

At the beginning of the 20th century the civil service was a homogeneous social group with a specific conception of duty and with a specific code of behavior. The increase of public tasks and public servants has almost dissolved this exceptional position and has rather turned in into a mere employee position. The degrees of approximation to this position differ according to the field of duties and the level of position in the administrative hierarchy.

BUREAUCRACY AND POLICY-MAKING

The very nature of bureaucracy reveals its strained relationship with political management: on the one hand is bureaucracy's continuity, its expert knowledge and its obligation to public welfare; on the other hand is the government's party-political bearings and its goal of achieving its programs. Particularly at the management levels of the departmental administrations, both of these principles intermix, but not without conflict. The different countries have found various ways to deal with this strained relationship.

In France, Belgium and Italy, the minister in charge establishes above his departmental administration a group of personal counselors, the "cabinet," who act as the minister's arms and ears. They give political impulses for the department's bills and drafts, and on behalf of the minister they control the final decisions. They are obliged to the minister by personal loyalty, and they lose their position with the minister. In France and Belgium, the members of these *cabinets ministériels* are generally assembled out of different groupings. In France, they are usually selected out of the *Grand Corps*, the *Conseil d'Etat*, the *Inspection des Finances* or the *Cour des Comptes*, and therefore their high qualifications are acknowledged by the departmental administrations. They share the political orientation of the minister, but in addition to this they contribute their highranking civil servants' professional qualities. In Belgium, the *cabinets ministériels* are assembled much more according to party-political points of view. Their members are rather the delegates of the minister's party. Their quality is the contact with the party. In Germany, on the other hand, supreme management positions of the departmental administrations are occupied with "political civil servants" who must have the ministers' confidence. Without statement of reasons, they can be discharged from their functions at any time. Besides them, the ministers have only very few assistants.

These two models try to deal with the fact that at the ministerial level political and administrative tasks are mixing inseparably, while on the other side departmental administration must be kept clear of party-political demands. In most of the West European countries, these "buffers" between politics and administration do not prevent the political parties and the interest groups from exerting influence on the civil service in the appointment of personnel, especially at the higher level. In most countries, except Switzerland and Ireland, there is a considerable degree of party favoritism and politicizing.

In the field of policy-making, the political system and the administrative system meet in a "reciprocal responsibility." Ministerial administration, the top level of the departmental administration, is the source of many governmental initiatives. Here, most of the laws, programs and drafts are prepared. From the very beginning, ministerial administration is incorporated in the process of policy-making. It plans the projects for the ministries and is responsible for technical and political coordination between the ministries. It controls policy implementation, and it prepares policy corrections. It also keeps contact with the concerned interest groups which are its clients. However, the ministerial administrations do not act in a vacuum, and they are not able to force their own conceptions upon government. The parliament and the political parties have acquired their own expert knowledge. Frequently, the expert committees of the parties and of the parliament have a stronger influence on a ministry's programs and bills than the minister. Some parliaments have established their own scientific advisory services, or they make use of hearings to introduce into their decisions expert knowledge and interests from outside of government. Usually, this way of making decisions is being observed attentively by a critical public.

The problem of policy-making today is not that bureaucracy prevails, and not that government makes non-expert decisions. Faced with the complexity and the diversity of government decisions, the problem is rather to make decisions in the sense of co-herent government policy, and to guarantee their implementation without appreciable frictional loss. For these tasks, some governments have established special advisory boards, for instance the Scientific Council for Government Policy in the Netherlands. This reveals that, today, the integration that is necessary for government policy is no longer performed by the traditional governmental and departmental organizations.

ADMINISTRATIVE ACCOUNTABILITY

In the West European countries, the obligation of administration to law and justice is not merely a constitutional program, but a reality. There are manifold political, administrative, legal and financial controls. Administration is acting in the critical eye of the public. The mass media have made a routine of criticizing administration. Administration sees itself as facing citizens who have become more critical and more self-confident, who are successful with their requests by joining together independently from the political parties, and who are making extensive use of the possibilities of judicial relief. In Germany, there has developed the tenet that the constitutional state has turned into a legal action state.

Even the parliament is not only exercising political control, i.e. control of leading political decisions, but it is also exercising administrative control, i.e. control of single administrative decisions. Frequently, the questions raised in parliament are concerned with actual events in administration. The parliamentary committees are reserving to themselves the right to share in individual case decisions when new laws are going to be carried out, for instance when distributing subventions. Moreover, administration finds itself exposed to direct interventions by members of parliament who have taken up citizens' requests or complaints, or who want to have administrative decisions nullified.

Control is also being exercised internally through the administrative hierarchy and by the different levels of administration. In European administrations, many requests for licenses and permits are either withheld or delayed by superior or other authorities. There is a whole series of procedural cooperations and controls among the authorities and of requirements to report to the ministries. In France, the "inspections" procedure is particularly pronounced. Special *Corps d'Inspection* control the subordinate field services. The best known is the *Inspection des Finances* which is entitled to control the entire French administration.

In West European countries the national, state and local audit offices have a long tradition of control, too. Not only do they establish the financial regularity of public expenses and statements of account, but they are also more and more acting preven-tively as an advisory board for administration. This ensues from the knowledge that sometimes discovering mistakes from a long time ago is less important than avoiding future mistakes. The audit offices are taking part in preparing governmental programs or administrative reforms by giving their expert opinions and commentaries. The independence of their personnel and their expert quality are decisive for their influence.

The constitutional tradition of the West European countries and the orientation of administration towards the rules of administrative law have established and confirmed the significance of the administrative courts. By their jurisdiction, not only do they settle individual legal conflicts between citizens and administration, but they also exert an influence on administrative action because of the precedential effect of their judgements. The jurisdiction of the constitutional and administrative courts affects both administrative action and legislation. It is true that in the different countries, the possibilities of reviewing administrative decisions judicially are differently far advanced—apparently most extensive in Germany with a general clause in its constitution. But it can be stated that administrative court control is generally increasing. Judicial control of administration is one part of the continental European conception of the constitutional state, in this respect differing considerably from the Anglo-Saxon conception. But it is now an open question whether the intensity of legislation on the one hand and the extent of administrative court control on the other hand have not attained a degree of perfection which needlessly restricts administration's scope of decision.

In spite of this judicial control, some countries have—after the Scandinavian example—established the institution of the ombudsman, who is not confined to legal control. Among these countries are Austria, France, Ireland, Italy (regionally), the Netherlands, Portugal and Spain, whereas Switzerland and Germany have so far denied the necessity of this institution at the federal level in addition to the administrative courts. In Germany, comparable institutions exist in the domains of military and data protection.

Yet, all these procedures of controlling administration will remain without effect if administration itself will not perform its tasks with professional responsibility and according to an inner code of behavior.

CONCLUDING COMMENTS

The diversity of public administration in the West European countries should not hide things in common in its development. In all countries, administration has been molded by history and tradition. In spite of changes in terms of quantity and quality of administration's tasks and surroundings, it has kept an amazing continuity, even in view of changes in the political system. Yet, it would be wrong to draw the conclusion: "Constitutions will pass away, administration will stay." Actually, during this century, the shapes of organization, of procedures and of decisions in public administration have undergone considerable changes; new forms of information and of communication have been introduced, new procedures of preparing decisions have been adopted, and a new relationship between citizen and administration is being sought. Where administration turned out to be too inflexible, new forms of organization were found outside of administration or in the shadow of administration. Constitutional accountability and professional orientation are still the basis of an administration designed to serve a democratic policy and its citizens.

REFERENCES

1. The figures for France are from: Secretariat d'Etat chargé de la Fonction publique et des Réformes administratives, *La fonction publique en 1983* (The Public Service in 1983) (Paris 1984), p. 219. The figures for Western Germany are from: Statistisches Bundesamt, *Personal des öffentlichen Dienstes 1983* (The Public Service in 1983)

(Stuttgart 1985), p. 13. The figures for both countries do not include the public employees who work for the national railways, the PTT administration and other public institutions indirectly attached to the public service (*établissements public nationaux*).

2. This figure includes the public employees discussed in Reference 1.

IV
OTHER DEVELOPED DEMOCRACIES

21

Israel

YEHEZKEL DROR
The Hebrew University of Jerusalem, Jerusalem, Israel

ISRAEL AS A LABORATORY

Uniqueness of Israel

As well put by T. S. Eliot in *The Cocktail Party*, "all cases are unique and similar one to another." Still, with all its similarities to other Western democracies, Israel is more unique than similar to other polities. Created by an ideology, populated by multi-cultural immigrants, lacking a tradition of statehood and yet very democratic, developed with large enclaves of underdevelopment, shaped by a mixture of traditionalism and modernity, traumatized by a holocaust, ostracized as well as receiving unequaled material and political support, very small but extremely visible, embedded in an unstable geostrategic environment, subjected to pandemic warfare, rapidly changing and still conservative, very cohesive and loaded with disagreements—Israel is a very unusual state, to put it mildly.

If some Cosmic Think Tank were to design a large-scale experiment to study human institutions and social behavior, something quite similar to Israel might be put up. Its basic socio-political structure is similar enough to other western democracies to permit comprehension and study in terms of western culture and western social science concepts, while the unique features of Israel provide much scope for testing of assumptions and stimulation of new conjectures.

Zionist Ideology and Public Administration

To take up an illustration, the consensus in Israel on Zionism as the main *raison d'etat* of Israel and its *raison d'etre* has fargoing implications for the self-image, as well as public image, of the civil service as a partner in Zionist fulfillment, as contrasted with being "obedient servants" of the public as in Western folklore. Most public discourse in Israel on the civil service uses accepted western terminology and discusses it in terms of serving the public. This is also accepted in some of the more conventional parts of Israeli public administration, such as social services. But, senior officials as a whole and civil servants in the more development-oriented parts of the machinery of

government, such as agriculture and industry, and in defense and foreign affairs, have
a strong sense of Zionist mission.

Antinomies between "serving the public" and "advancing the public interest" or
some other professional or ideological commitments are endemic to public administration in all countries. But, the intensity of Zionism as accepted in Israel is much higher
than any concept of "public interest" in other western democracies, resulting in a
sense of mission in large parts of Israeli public administration which is all the more
unique because it is based on a socially widely accepted active ideology.

The above example serves to illustrate the usefulness of looking on Israel as a grand
laboratory. Study of public administration in Israel within its context can contribute
to sharpening comparative perspectives and building up general theory, for instance by:

1. Sensitization to Mission Commitments in Other Countries:

As in all countries large parts of public administration have commitments to various
images of the "public interest" and/or to professional obligations, the Israeli extreme
case serves to sensitize studies elsewhere to the importance of such factors.

2. Adding a Dimension for Comparative Study:

Differences in mission commitment contents and intensities may well serve as a main
dimension for comparative study of public administration, both within one country,
in country-groupings and for cross-cultural research.

3. Pure-Type Construction:

Israeli experiences can serve as a basis for construction of additional pure type designs
of public organizations and public administration as a whole. Thus, "true believer
organizations" serve as a polar alternative to widely accepted images of self-advancing
or/and interest-group-subjugated civil servants and public organizations.

4. General Public Administration Theory Enrichment:

Study of Israeli realities can help in building up a general theory of public administration (and, within a broader context, a general theory of societal command and control) by adding components as illustrated under points 2 and 3 above; as well as by
stimulating broad theories, for instance on relationships between national ideologies
and public organization behavior.

Additional unique features of Israel add to the theoretic and comparative significance of studying its public administration, within a broad governmental and societal
context: Constant defense pressures, tenfold increase of population and radical changes
in its socio-cultural composition within thirty years, intense conflict on the role of
religion, unique social sectors of the Kibbutz type—these are only some of the inherent
characteristics of Israel having important and unusual implication for its public administration. Furthermore, all these and additional facets are very dynamic and turbulent,
with society as a whole undergoing rapid change and facing novel adversities, as illustrated by the Labor party loosing its hegemonial status in 1977 and the economic
crisis. All this adds up to a very unusual nature-provided "social science laboratory"
indeed.

Approach of This Chapter

Despite many studies going on in and on Israel, this nature-given laboratory is very
underutilized. Many significant processes are not studied; and often not enough

attention is given to unique features of Israel. This is the case, *inter alia*, in respect to public administration is Israel: the subject is grossly understudied; also, with distinguished exceptions (such as by Bertram Gross, Gerald Caiden and Ira Sharkansky), writings on Israeli public administration neglect its uniqueness.

To meet such challenges and constraints, this chapter adopts an approach as follows:

Main attention is devoted to features of Israeli public administration which are relatively unique and even "abnormal," with standard characteristics not being presented. Thus, the macro-structure of public administration and the size of the civil service, which are quite similar to those of other developed countries, are not discussed.

Only some of the most important aspects of Israeli public administration have been selected for discussion, the selection depending necessarily on the interests and experiences of the author. No claim is made to present a coherent and systematic analysis of public administration in Israel as a whole.

Treatment is on an aggregate level and concentrates on central government, without considering the large diversity within Israeli public administration.

The chapter as a whole is conjectural. It is based on close observation of public administration in Israel by the author, both from within and from outside, and on processing whatever studies and hard data (usually in Hebrew) are available. Still, this essay belongs to interpretative social science. Other knowledgeable observers may well reach different conjectures and may even disagree with some of the more factual conclusions of this paper.

SOME HISTORIC INFLUENCES

Multiple Origins

Israeli public administration has been influenced by diverse historic backgrounds, all of them combining with Israel-endogenous developments into a quite mosaic picture. These include:

1. Ottoman Administration:

However surprising this may seem, Ottoman influences left traces for many years, especially in some units which continued quite highly developed Ottoman organizations, such as the Land Registry (introduced into the Ottoman Empire by German influences, in turn) and some municipalities. Such influences were associated with the same persons continuing to serve in the same units. With time these Ottoman traces got fainter and have dissipated, in part because no officials from the Ottoman period remained around.

2. British Mandatory Administration:

The British introduced into Mandatory Palestine a number of quite effective administrative entities, such as the court system, customs and police. As the Jewish community in Palestine (known as the "Yishuv") did not duplicate some of these administrative agencies and as some Jews worked in them and assimilated their patterns, these units were taken over by the State of Israel and continue to demonstrate some Mandatory influences. This also is true for formal relationships between central and local government, with the Ministry of the Interior and District Commissioners continuing to enjoy many legal powers over local government, despite radical transformations in the actual balance between central government and local authorities.

3. United Kingdom Regime:

The image of British democracy held sway in Yishuv thinking and served as the model for the Israeli regime after independence. The basic Israeli constitutional structure is one of a United Kingdom-type parliamentary-cabinet system.

It is interesting to ponder why the image of British government so strongly impressed Yishuv thinking. Possible explanations include: lack of experience of most of the founders of Israel with any other democracy; quite a number of Yishuv-influentials spending time in the U.K. and some studying there; indirect diffusion through colonial administration; the individual influence of Chaim Weitzmann; special admiration for Great Britain as granter of the Balfour Declaration; and special liking of lawyers for the British legal system, where they rather than judges and legislators occupy the center of the legal arena.

Whatever mix of such and additional explanations is correct, three facts are clear: One, images of U.K. governance exerted very strong influences on the Israeli regime, including some aspects of public administration such as legal provisions for a politically neutral civil service. Two, adoption of British institutions was selective, thus the U.K. elitistic structure of the civil service, with special attention to recruitment of an administrative class, was rejected in Israel in favor of United States-like recruitment of individual candidates to specific positions on the basis of internal or public tenders. Three, underlying realities of the British regime were not really understood and inadequate adjustments were made to the quite different conditions of Israel. This is well illustrated by the above-mentioned attempt to build up a politically neutral civil service, which posed too rigid barriers to adjustments of public administration to changing political realities. Therefore the 1977 turnabout in governing party produced large differences between formal regulations and actual politically motivated turnover in the civil service.

4. Yishuv Institutions:

The term "state within state" is frequently applied to the Yishuv institutions and rightly so: from the early emergence of modern Zionism a framework of Zionist institutions slowly developed; and within the growing Yishuv a large number of public organizations were set up, integrated under the British Mandate into an autonomous governance system with many features of a state, though without any formal sovereignty. With the establishment of the state, the Yishuv institutions were the natural building stones for the machinery of government, with different degrees of continuity or discontinuity.

Quite a number of very important non-governmental public institutions enjoyed uninterrupted continuity from the Yishuv period into the state, such as the Zionist organizations and the Jewish Agency; and the General Federation of Labor ("Histadrut") and its affiliates, including the main health providing "Kupat Cholim." This is also true for some local authorities, such as Tel Aviv, and for a few central governmental ministries.

More important than direct institutional continuities are cultural and ideological influences stemming from the Yishuv period, determining initial features of Israeli public administration and exerting strong impacts since them. Two illustrations well bring out the importance of such influences:

One, the Zionist fulfillment epic allocated very low prestige to "clerks" who engage in "unproductive" work, while reserving all policymaking to the political levels. Also, the small size and intimate nature of Yishuv organizations inhibited any division of labor between politicians and administrators. Furthermore, the nature of the tasks and their ideological intensity reduced reliance on professional knowledge and technical competence, in favor of total commitment and belief in the apparently impossible. These features, which are related to the nature of Zionism as a revolutionary movement, serve as main explanations for some crucial features of public administration in Israel.

Two, a strong egalitarian ideology opposed the idea of an "administrative elite" with special recruitment and compensation. While Zionism was elitistic in the sense of emphasizing the importance of a fulfilling avant-garde, the "Hallutzim," this did not apply to "technocrats," who were not highly regarded (as contrasted with scholars, who then and now enjoy high prestige, but little policy influence). This helps to explain rejection of the British "administrative class" idea, despite overall admiration and adoption of U.K. governance.

Taken together, these and additional Yishuv traditions explain, *inter alia*, the non-existence of a distinct senior executive strata in Israeli government, which strongly influences all features of public administration and its performance.

Jewish Background

No administrative history of Israel has been written. Still, historic impacts such as those discussed above are quite clear in main directions. Different is the situation concerning the influences on public administration of its Jewish background. Ranging from the fuzzy concept of "national characteristics" to concrete facts such as the professional qualifications of immigrants, this is a complex subject where speculations are often the best that can be offered. Nevertheless, this is a very important matter for understanding some features of public administration (and governance, as well as Israeli society as a whole). It also raises very significant comparative and theoretic issues, up to the controversy about the relative importance of unique historic explanations of social phenomena ("historicism") versus the very idea of social sciences as able to arrive at generalizations of broad validity.

Recognizing such unresolved and perhaps unresolvable issues, some facets of Jewish background influences on Israeli public administration can be preliminarily explored.

1. Absence of State Tradition and Governmental Aristocracies

Whatever may be the genius of the Jewish People, historically it has not been in the art of governance. Survival of the Jewish people and its creativity throughout 2,000 years of dispersal is historically unique, but this is not the kind of experience which builds up skills in governance, as contrasted with spiritual qualities on one hand and survival capacities on the other. Also, while spiritual elites have been central in Jewish traditional culture, no governmental artistocracy evolved.

However clear the above facts are, their implications for public administration in Israel are speculative. Some possible impacts include: Lack of a recruitment base for top-level professional civil servants, with an already mentioned propensity against an elite top executive class; absence of a baseline for division of labor between politicians and civil servants; lack of cohesiveness in the machinery of government and weakness of informal coordination channels based on social interaction among top civil servants;

difficulties in crystallizing and maintaining codes of ethics, beyond simple anti-corruption legislation; and absence of an unified administrative culture.

It is interesting to ponder the question, whether lack of administrative traditions is more of an advantage or disadvantage, especially under conditions of rapid change which require constant adjustments in the machinery of governance. Hypothetically, lack of traditions might be supposed to enable rapid change and effective adjustments to shifting environments. But this is not the case in Israel, which demonstrates both much administrative rigidities and absence of long administrative traditions. This finding leads to the proposition that lack of an administrative tradition does not produce a vacuum which can easily be filled with learning-prone institutions, but rather constitutes a rigid tradition of its own of absence of an administrative culture which hinders adjustment and learning.

2. Ghetto Governance

A debate proceeds among Israeli scholars whether Ghetto experiences and traditions explain significant features of Israeli society and governance, including public administration. In particular, some features of administrative behavior and of relations between administration and society can be speculated about in such terms. For instance, one can surmise that ad-hocism, favoritism ("protekzia" in Hebrew, going back to a German term), and a strong tendency to ignore written rules go back to Ghetto governance traditions. But such features can just as well be explained by the administrative culture in the countries from which most immigrants to Israel came, as well as by Ottoman traditions. Therefore, the influence of Ghetto traditions on public administration in Israel remains a moot question.

3. Immigrants

The importation of high-quality capacities in the form of immigrants ("human capital") is an important component of any attempt to explain some of the amazing successes of Israel. Thus, the development of high-quality medical services in the Yishuv, which constituted an essential basis for the even better medical facilities in Israel, is unimaginable without the immigration of top medical professionals, initially mainly from Germany.

No comparable importation of high-quality public administrators took place, largely because only very few Jews reached high-level administrative positions in the countries from which most of the immigrants originated. The importance of the few Israeli officials who had high-level public administration experience in countries with good machineries of governments, as illustrated later on in respect to the Budget Division, supports the conjecture on the importance of this factor.

CHANGE DYNAMICS

The Riddle of Rigidity Amid Transformations

Public administration in Israel is confronted by radical discontinuities in its bases, such as the population from which it is recruited and its resources and value inputs; in its environment, that is the situations which it has to face; and in its functions, that is the main tasks it has to fulfill. To mention just a few of the many relevant indicators:

since the establishment of the State of Israel in 1948 the population of Israel has increased more than tenfold and radically transformed in composition; the territory of Israel, however calculated, has multiplied; the economy has been transformed in size, structure and technology; the functions of government have increased manifoldly; a number of wars have been fought successfully; and the political system passed through a radical changeover. Given such a multi-dimensional transformation even a relatively conservative public administration could be expected to have changed radically. But this is not the case, change in public administration having been relatively slow and limited.

However highly one estimates the strength of historic influences and traditions, they hardly explain the relative slowness of change in public administration. To explain the conservative dynamics of public administration in Israel stronger and more persistent variables must be called upon.

Two Cases of Radical Innovations

To balance the overall estimation of Israeli public administration as conservative and to gain some insight into the causes of administrative rigidities, the generalized finding of slow change should be contrasted with the following two cases of radical transformation.

1. Israeli Defence Forces

During the first part of the War of Independence, the Israeli military was based on the Yishuv underground Haggana. Only after the military situation became critical and the possibility of defeat looked real were radical changes made, laying the foundations of the modern Israeli Defence Forces. These changes involved politically, organizationally and in terms of personnel very difficult steps, including changes in senior commanders and disbandment of time-honored and high-prestige military formations stemming from the Haggana. Three factors combined to bring about the radical transformation: One, the specter of defeat unless radical changes were made; two, the availability of a feasible alternative, based on British-trained Israeli commanders who fought in the 2nd World War in the so-called "Jewish Brigade"; and three, the determination and strength of David Ben Gurion, who forced the changes on opposing power centers.

Such unique conjunctions of change-supporting variables are unusual. In most domains of public administration no dramatic failures occur, however weak performance may be; usually, no ready alternative conceptions and personnel are available, and strong political support for fargoing administrative reforms are scarce in all countries and nonexisting in Israel. Therefore, it is not surprising that in other domains of public administration adjustments to rapidly changing conditions have usually been slow and inadequate.

The importance of a credible alternative being available should be emphasized. A good illustration is provided by the recent history of the Income Tax Division: Its performance is perceived by all as a failure and strong political will to improve it does exist. But, no good idea is around how to redesign the Income Tax Division so as rapidly to increase tax collection. Therefore, no radical reform is taking place, despite clear failure and strong political support.

2. The Budget Division

The history of the Budget Division in the Ministry of Finance illustrates a quite different dynamic of change. In the pre-state period there existed no units comparable to a government budget division, financial management in the Yishuv following quite different patterns, for political as well as fiscal reasons. Therefore, after the state was established, an increasingly visible vacuum existed. A number of foreign experts submitted proposals for improving financial and economic management, while the Hebrew University, with the help of a distinguished immigrant scholar, prepared very good economists. These factors converged with the accident of a director who had former experience with government administration in The Netherlands (one of the few immigrants with such qualifications, as mentioned before) and an Assistant Minister of Finance with an open mind, resulting in the rapid build-up of an outstanding budgeting division.

The budgeting division operated for a number of years as an island of excellence in a weak machinery of government. Albeit slowly but surely the division itself lost quality, with the weight of professional budgeting losing ground to political-coalition needs and, later on, the budgeting process being eroded by accelerating inflation. This case poses the question of whether and for how long it is possible to maintain an outstanding island of excellence within an overall weak machinery of government, especially when that island is closely connected with main political and administrative processes, as a central budgeting unit is.

For comparison it is interesting to mention that the central Civil Service Commission Office, which too is located in the Ministry of Finance after a short stay in the Prime Minister's Office, never became an island of excellence. It did not benefit from factors inducing rapid change and has remained bound by Yishuv-traditions of non-professional personnel management, as well as heavy political constraints, exacerbated by growing political interventions following changes in the political compositions of governments.

Strong Rigidities

A few additional cases of radical innovation can be identified, such as the establishment and development of the Israeli State Comptroller Office and some episodes in the Ministry of Agriculture. But, as a whole, Israeli public administration is characterized by dynamic conservatism, despite radical transformations in bases, functions and environments. This surprising characteristic can be explained in terms of strong rigidities caused by a number of converging factors. Before looking at some specific rigidity factors in Israel, it should be remembered that all public administrations tend towards conservatism in regard to themselves. Nevertheless, the antinomy in Israel between the high rate of change in bases, environments and functions on one hand, and the internal features of public administration on the other hand, is unusually strong, requiring some explanation beyond general organizational behavior.

The special nature of public administration rigidities in Israel finds one of its expressions in the fact that no serious attempt at public administration reform has been made in Israel since its establishment. This, in contrast with the prevalence of administrative reform attempts in most western democracies, where needs to upgrade administrative performance have resulted at least in some search for comprehensive improvements, even if only seldom successfully implemented. Only in 1986 was a public-professional government commission for reform of the public service set up, which may bring about much-needed changes.

Some of the main rigidity-causing factors in Israeli public administration have already been mentioned, including the strength of "non-administration" traditions and historic conditionings and the scarcity of alternatives, in part because of non-availability of experiences and personnel, as well as the incrementalism and inertia inherent in large organizations. But, the subject is very important both for understanding Israeli public administration and for construction of a general theory of administrative change and governmental adjustments. Therefore, some further exploration of the causes of rigidities in Israeli public administration is in order.

Israel has been characterized during most of its existence by a paradoxical combination between strong feeling of being successful and acute pressing crises. The sense of self-satisfaction up to a feeling of heroic achievements, based on real historic successes, resulted in lack of motivation to improve governmental capacities, while crises demanded all attention leaving no political and mental resources available for administrative reforms.

The effects of a strong sense of achievement are well illustrated by the fate of the one single major reform attempt till 1986. Initiated in 1966–67, as a result of economic difficulties together with the accidental circumstance of some powerful governmental officials being personally interested in improving the machinery of government, the attempt was abandoned following the successes of the Six Day War and its euphoric aftermath. The reasons frankly given to the author added up to a sense of "if we are so successful, why should administration be reformed?".

Quite different a set of change-retarding factors have been political in nature. Up till 1977 one hegemonial party governed Israel. Such continuity in the ruling party, going back into the early Yishuv period, prevented political change from operating as an administrative change inducer, all the more so as most administrative positions were staffed by officials identified with the hegemonial party and its usual coalition partners respectively.

Related is the permanent coalition structure of Israeli governments, with each partner having full control over the ministries allocated to it. Such apportioning of departments, in addition to impairing administrative performance for instance by inhibiting coordination, hinders administrative changes by reducing the power of central agencies to impose reforms on the machinery of government as a whole. If the lack of interest by politicians as a whole in improving public administration, for reasons to be discussed later, is added to the picture, then main features of the political system can be clearly evaluated as retarding administrative reform rather than pushing for it.

Also basically political in nature and going back to Yishuv governance is the strength of trade unions, with ministerial elected committees of employees frequently exercising a veto power over any change proposals. The authority of ministerial labor committees is well reflected in the unusual fact that in Israel very senior officials participate actively in such committees, up to the absurdity of deputy-director-generals serving as representatives of the employees against the government.

Intra-administrative features add to rigidities. Thus, low professionalization of the civil service in terms of administrative disciplines reduces self-induced improvement below the (usually not very high) level of self-improvement of public administration in other countries. The absence of a coherent senior administrative service and the already mentioned weaknesses of the Civil Service Commission Office add to the change-retarding structural features of the civil service itself.

To balance the picture, important latent functions fulfilled by existing administrative realities must be taken into account. Thus, Israeli public administration fulfilled essential social functions in aiding absorption of new immigrants by providing them with employment. "Efficiency drives" therefore missed a main function of overstaffing and consequently failed. Similarly, an attempt to introduce a sophisticated method of job classification backfired because it ignored local conditions, such as trade union strength, leaving a residual scepticism on the very idea of administrative reforms.

Public pressures for administrative reforms are also minor and often misdirected, concentrating on very visible but not really important issues, such as the number of ministries. Because of such public pressures efforts have been made to abolish a few ministries. This served in 1974 as the main preoccupation of a special ministerial committee for improving the efficiency of public administration, though it well knew that other matters were much more important for the quality of the machinery of government.

It is interesting to note that in Israel no strong public pressures are exerted to change some features of public administration which receive much public attention in other democracies. For instance, despite a government committee raising the issue and some feminist groups, no effective pressures to increase the very small number of women in senior governmental positions exist. Similarly, "freedom of information" and "open government" are demands nearly not made in Israel at all. This leads to the broader proposition that administrative improvements are not an important item on the policy agenda, neither within government nor in the public mind. It is easy to explain this fact in terms of the pressing nature of visible predicaments faced by Israel, with the real importance of high-quality public administration for the capacity to handle difficult issues not being recognized.

Accumulating Factors for Change

Despite the continuous strength of such rigidities, some acceleration of change can be observed. In particular, there is a slow but persistent increase in the academic qualifications of civil servants; and turnover of staff has speeded up in some ministries, with the newcomers having quite different characteristics. These changes are not the result of any deliberate attempt to improve public administration, but constitute side effects of political and social transformations. Two of these in particular are important.

1. Transformations in Politics

Since 1977 the Israeli political system has been changing rapidly, with the former hegemonial labor party having lost its position and other parties, in part new ones, gaining power. Despite the legal inhibitions against changing civil servants because of political preferences, in fact ministers can influence appointments a lot. Therefore, with changes in the political opinions and social backgrounds of ministers, staff turnover has accelerated and the profile of the staff has changed. Thus, in departments controlled by religious or ethnic parties, the number of officials with similar opinions and background has multiplied, with associated changes in administrative behavior.

2. Changes in Demographic Composition of Population

Changes in the population at large slowly influenced civil service composition. Thus, more new entrees have an academic education and many civil servants go to universities in line with national tendencies. Also, political changes as mentioned above accelerated entry into government of different population strata, who in turn were instrumental in bringing about the political change.

Such accumulating change factors should be contrasted with the lack of effect of other variables. Thus, while public administration academics have for many years called for administrative reforms, they have had no discernable impact on reality. Similarly, repeated attempts to reduce the number of government employees because of economic difficulties, and in particular to encourage mobility into more "productive" sectors (a motive going back, as already mentioned, to Yishuv views) have uniformly failed, though the rate of growth of the civil service has been reduced. Another possible source of administrative change, namely initiatives from the civil service itself, have been even less important in Israel than in other countries, for already mentioned reasons.

During the last few years a number of potential change-inducing factors are building up. Especially, the worsening economic situation increases demands to cut public expenditures and reduce governmental activities, with some cuts in the civil service. Pressures in this direction by the U.S.A. as an informal condition for increasing aid to Israel also play a role. Obvious failures by crucial administrative units, such as the already mentioned Income Tax Division, and manifest inability of the machinery of government to implemented some main economic steps adopted by the cabinet, such as reducing the budget, add to a growing sense of frustration about the performance of public administration, also among senior politicians and some the young staff introduced by them into top administrative levels. On a broader front, a feeling of growing "incapacity to govern" becomes widespread.

It is too early to tell if and when such factors will bring about efforts at comprehensive administrative reform and if so, whether such efforts will be nominal or real. Much depends on events in more important domains, such as foreign relations and in defense, as well as the economy, which are in part determined by exogenous variables. Accidents of interest by politicians and reform entrepreneurs may also play a role in utilizing such factors for change for initiating a real administrative reform or ignoring them for a long time to come.

Relevant is the history of The Public Commission for Local Government Affairs. Set up in 1976 to prepare reforms in the relations between central and local government regarded by all as long overdue, the Commission submitted its report in 1981. Despite continuous pressures for implementation of at least some of the major proposals and the strength of many salient changes, nearly nothing has happened. This may well auger little effect of other change factors building up in respect to central public administration discussed in this chapter; still, a critical mass of change factors may come about, though its timing and effects cannot be predicted.

POLITICS, POLICY-MAKING AND ADMINISTRATION

Unique Relationships

A major conclusion of a comparative study of administrative reforms in western democracies by the author is that political support constitutes an essential condition for administrative improvements, and that in most cases it is up to senior politicians not only to support, but to initiate and push, meaningful administrative changes.

Therefore, a main key for understanding the growing gap between the characteristics of public administration, its performance and relative non-change, if not stasis and regress, on one hand, and transformations in its bases, environments, and functions, as well as strengthening change factors, on the other hand, is the lack of concern of Israeli politicians with the machinery of government.

Largely, this is a result of the influences of Yishuv traditions, and perhaps of not having had a state and a governing aristocracy, as already mentioned. But additional factors are at work and explain the rather unique relations between politics, policy-making and administration in Israel.

Politicians Monopolize Policy-Making

As a result of the Yishuv tradition, politicians monopolize policy-making, and indeed decision-making as a whole, including on quite minor matters. Politicians work closely with a number of officials (and with special assistants whom they are entitled to appoint). But the civil service, including its higher echelons, while influential in implementation, has no recognized role in policy-making. The situation varies in different ministries, with the military staff being unusual in its influence on important choices. Still, the picture as a whole is one of politicians monopolizing decision-making.

This important feature of Israeli public administration is influenced by some additional factors:

> While Israel is a very complex country, still its small scale in population and territory reduces the number of decisions to be made. Therefore, given the limited span of attention of human beings, the political heads can personally handle a larger percentage of all decisions than is the case in bigger countries. Also, because of the small population and even smaller elites, as well as traditions of informality, ministers personally are approached by interest groups and concerned individuals in many matters, and no hiding behind civil servants is accepted.
>
> Most Israeli politicians have little experience of working with professional staffs, being used to relying on themselves and discussing issues with their political associates. (This is slowly changing, adding with time another possibly important change-inducing factor.)
>
> Professionalization of the civil service is quite weak, though improving with time as mentioned above. The capacity of the civil service to provide compelling opinions on policy issues is limited. Systematic staff work is scarce. There are exceptions, especially in defense as already mentioned, and also in science and technology and in legal matters and, at some periods, in economics. But, as a whole, the civil service is not "policy professional" and, therefore, does not convince politicians on the importance of its possible contributions to policy-making.
>
> Israeli policy-making as a whole is very ideologized and politicized, with ideological stances on one hand and party-political considerations on the other hand outweighing "professional" considerations. This trend has strengthened with the changes in the political system, as illustrated by the growing importance of political debates on some issues.

Politicians Not Interested in Public Administration

Politicians in Israel are not interested in public administration and its improvement. This is a result of such factors as lack of awareness of the potential importance of

high-quality public administration, the monopolization of decision-making by politicians, Yishuv and other historic backgrounds, the personal biographies of most politicians which lack any governmental experiences, and overload with pressing issues. The
lack of public interest in the real problems of public administration in Israel adds to
the non-concern of politicians with reform.

The influence of shifting public interests is well illustrated by the already-mentioned
efforts to reduce the number of ministries. Another interesting illustration is provided by
the history of the Environmental Protection Service. Before the Yom Kippur War, no
pressing security or economic issues overloaded public agendas and increasingly
"quality of the environment" received attention. Diffusion of this idea from other
countries combined with the initiative of some politicians made quality of the environment into a major issue, resulting in administrative innovation in the form of an
Environmental Protection Service in the Prime Minister's Office and consideration by
top politicians of the possibility of a new ministry for environmental affairs.

All this changed after 1973. Security issues became again paramount, followed
later by the peace negotiations, domestic political transformations, economic crises,
etc. These issues displaced environmental concerns from the public policy agenda,
neither the mass media nor senior politicians paying much attention to them any more.
The Environmental Protection Service was moved from the Prime Minister's Office to
the Physical Planning Division in the Ministry of the Interior and downgraded in influence; and the idea of setting up a special ministry on the environment disappeared
from consideration. This occurred despite continuous degradation of the physical
environment and in the face of strenuous efforts of various environmental protection
groups.

Accountability as a Non-Issue

Overload of the public agenda in Israel with critical policy issues, combined with the
low estimation of the role of public administration in policy-making, reduces interest
in "accountability" of the civil service (as contrasted with much attention to the
accountability of politicians). As the civil service is not regarded as very influential in
policy-making, naturally there is no demand to make it accountable. There have been
a few exceptions, when obvious fiascos were caused by inadequate performance by
officials, such as in the case of the Yom Kippur intelligence failure. Such special cases
have been handled on an *ad hoc* basis, for instance by special committees of inquiry,
with sanctions against a few officials. But there is no significant demand for more
accountability by public administration.

This situation may be changing. Another Public Inquiry Committee has been set
up in 1985, to investigate a fiasco concerning maintenance of artificial bank stock
values by manipulation by the banks with the full knowledge, if not support, of
government. As many persons lost a lot of money, publication of a report by the
State Comptroller criticizing many officials and politicians resulted in a demand to
make officials more "accountable" and some steps may perhaps follow the report of
the Public Inquiry Committee, when ready.

Also, in 1985 the Minister of Finance demanded that personal civil and criminal
responsibility be imposed on senior officials if they knowingly expend public funds
beyond the budget allocation, as parts of rather desperate efforts to cut the budget
and implement cabinet decisions consistently ignored by the ministries. This proposal
was greeted with very cynical reactions, all the more so as no responsibility was to be

put on the ministers in charge. Still, some movement in the direction of holding senior officials legally accountable for some acts may result, at least on the nominal level.

The legislature (the Israeli "Knesset") shares in the main this attitude, despite some usually sporadic and short-lasting attention to public administration failures as regularly exposed by the State Comptroller (who reports to the Knesset). This, not because of a Whitehall-like fiction that civil servants are anonymous and ministers responsible for everything, but because civil servants as a group, as distinct from some particular and well-known individual officials, are not regarded as really very important. Lack of authority by the Knesset and its committees to interrogate officials and the legal duty of officials appearing before the legislature and its committees to express only the position of their ministries further strengthen the Knesset's lack of interest in accountability of officials.

In the mass media and in public debate, too, civil servants are seldom regarded as responsible for policies. The civil service is accused of red tape and of being overblown, but politicians are blamed for nearly all decisions.

An interesting exception is provided by the Israeli Broadcasting Authority, where professional staff enjoy much autonomy in shaping programs. As television is increasingly recognized as a main power with many political implications, acute struggles between the overview body of the Broadcasting Authority, which is composed of politicians representing the main parties, and the professional staff have developed. In this case, where professionals have significant and very manifest autonomy, the issue of "accountability" is strongly raised by the politicians and is continuously debated.

No Demand for Open Government

Some special features of Israel, as compared with other western democracies, are reflected in the absence of any significant demands for more open government. While the freedom of newspapers is quite unlimited, with the exception of security affairs, and leakages of supposedly secret documents both by ministers and by civil servants is widespread, there is no demand for opening up governmental files. It is accepted that in Israel much secrecy must be maintained and that security is much more important than any "right to know." This, in addition to the already mentioned overload of public attention agenda by other matters.

This is but one example of the impacts of Israel's security problems on public administration, which is a subject well worth investigation. Just to mention another impact, because of reserve service a substantial proportion of all employees is absent from work all the time. This requires keeping a larger staff than would otherwise be necessary, as well as additional adjustments for extended absence of staff. It should be born in mind that many of the better officials are officers in the reserves.

Public Administration as a Non-Compensator for Weaknesses of Politics

None of the above observations means that individual senior officials do not exert much influence on critical decisions and on the politicians making them. Neither should one underrate the importance of implementation by the civil service as shaping in part governmental performance. Thus, in the domain of internal revenues it is agreed in

Israel that the problem is less one of taxation policy than of tax administration weaknesses. Still, the overall conclusion on the relatively minor role of the civil service in policy-making stands. With the exception of some domains such as defense, public administration does not fulfill autonomous functions in preparation of main policy decisions and does not make significant decisions on its own. As a result, many Israeli policy decisions lack adequate professional bases, even if outstanding individual devotion and capability partly compensate for this weakness. No amount of individual qualities adds up to a public administration which can compensate for weaknesses of politics.

This is becoming an important matter with the movement of the Israeli political system into a period of accelerated change that may well impair its performance. A more professional civil service, with coherent top-level groups and highly qualified "super-bureaucrats" used to working together as counterparts and advisors to their political masters, could somewhat compensate for transition difficulties of the political system, as illustrated by France during the Third Republic. But Israeli public administration is not able to achieve this, even if the politicians would welcome it, which probably they do not.

In other words, the absence of a developed and experienced technocratic layer and "superbureaucrats" in Israeli public administration not only impairs the capacity to govern under normal conditions, but makes it impossible for public administration to compensate for fluctuations in the quality of the political system and its performance.

IS THE QUALITY OF PUBLIC ADMINISTRATION REALLY IMPORTANT?

Overall Finding

Many additional features and problems of Israeli public administration deserve discussion. These include the under-representation of women in higher positions; the role (or non-role) in the civil service of the Arab minority in Israel and related troublesome security issues; special features of administrative behavior in Israel, such as ad hocism as an extreme version of muddling through (but not necessarily incrementalism) and its successes as better fitting Israeli conditions than classical planning; additional influences of Zionist ideology; and reflections in public administration of social cleavages, such as on ideological positions and in matters of religion.

Recognizing the many empty spots in this brief sketch, still a few overall findings seem to emerge:

> Public administration is lagging increasingly behind rapid change in bases, environment and tasks. Indeed, it may well be justified to regard public administration as obsolete in main features, as compared to rapidly changing predicaments.
> Public administration is not making a sufficient contribution to the capacity to govern, including handling of momentous decisions. In particular, it does not supply professional inputs urgently needed for upgrading the quality of policies. Definitely, public administration cannot adequately supplement the political system and cannot compensate for weaknesses in the latter.
> Rigidity continues to characterize public administration. Some signs of loosening up can be discerned, but these only touch upon a few features.

The Effects of Quality

These and other weaknesses pose a riddle when looked at within the context of Israel's tremendous successes in many domains and against heavy odds. Here, a question of crucial theoretic and applied importance is reached: Is the quality of public administration really a main variable in determining national rise or decline? Given a certain minimum level of performance, perhaps other factors are much more important for societal successes than the quality of public administration.

Before pondering this question, a number of merits of Israeli public administration must be taken into account, such as the existence of some outstanding agencies, the absence of large-scale corruption, the ideological commitment, and the fit of particular behavior patterns such as ad hocism to Israeli conditions. Also, the particular division of labor with politicians, combined with the long-surviving stability of the political system and the availability of high-quality politicians, must be remembered. Still, the question persists.

Certainly the Israeli experience cannot be explained in terms of possible unimportance of the state and of public policies, with perhaps market mechanisms handling main issues. In Israel the state is and will continue to be very active, probably more so than in any other democracies, because of nation-building and ideology-realizing functions. Furthermore, Israel is faced by a larger number of momentous future-shaping decisions than most other developed countries, further augmenting the significance of the quality of government.

Therefore, our question on the effects of public administration quality is of major practical importance for Israel. Maybe Israel could succeed in the past despite a relatively weak public administration (leaving aside the speculation that with a better public administration more could have been achieved) because of circumstances which no longer prevail, making improvement of public administration a must for continuous success in the future. If this is the case, Israel must give priority to public administration reforms; while, if public administration quality continues to be a non-critical factor, other facets of the capacity to govern and of societal problem-handling abilities should receive priority.

This problem, even if often in a less acute a form, is also faced by other countries, developed as well as those less developed. Study of Israel can serve to pose such questions and perhaps help in finding parts of the answer. This returns us to our opening theme on Israel as a laboratory worthy of much more investigation, both from a pure-science and comparative perspective and for applied purposes, in addition to being a very interesting and even exciting subject by itself.

REFERENCES IN ENGLISH

Annotated References

There are very few writings in English on public administration in Israel. In Hebrew too studies are very scarce. Up-to-date publications are even scarcer.

An introduction to some of the peculiarities of public administration in Israel is provided by Gerald Caiden, *Israel's Administrative Culture* (Berkeley: Institute of Governmental Studies, 1970). Some historic features, in part still prevalent today, are examined in Benjamin Akzin and Yehezkel Dror, *Israel: High-Pressure Planning* (Syracuse, NY: Syracuse University Press, 1966). An interesting field study is David

Nachmias and David H. Rosenbloom, *Bureaucratic Culture: Citizen and Administration in Israel* (New York: St. Martin's Press, 1978). Fascinating but outdated is Donna Robinson, *Patrons and Saints: A Study of the Career Patterns of Higher Civil Servants in Israel* (Ph.D. thesis, Columbia University, 1970). Also relevant are some parts of R. Bilski *et al.*, eds., *Can Planning Replace Politics? The Israeli Experience* (The Hague: Martinus Nijhoff, 1980); and some parts of Ira Sharkansky, *What Makes Israel Tick: How Domestic Policy-Makers Cope with Constraints* (Chicago: Nelson-Hall, 1985). Also relevant are parts of Eva Etzioni-Halevy, *Bureaucracy and Democracy: A Political Dilemma* (London: Routledge & Kegan Paul, 1983).

Readers further interested in the subject are referred to the references below, which include books dealing with Israeli government as a whole.

Additional References

Bilski, R., *et al.*, eds., *Can Planning Replace Politics? The Israeli Experience.* The Hague: Nijhoff, 1980.

Brecher, M., *The Foreign Policy System of Israel.* London: Oxford, 1972.

DeVine, Donva, "The Modernization of Israeli Administration," *Internat. Journ. of Mid-East Stud.* 5 (1974), 295–313.

Etzioni-Halevy, E., and R. Shapira, *Political Culture in Israel.* N.Y.: Praeger, 1977.

Galnoor, I., *Sterring the Polity: Communication and Politics in Israel.* Beverly Hills: Sage, 1982.

Globerson, A., "A Profile of the Bureaucratic Elite in Israel," *Pub. Personnel Man.* 2, 1, (1973), 9–13.

Luttwak, E., and D. Horowitz, *The Israeli Army.* London: Allen Lane, 1975.

Mahler, Gregory S., *The Knesset.* London: Associated Univ. Presses, 1981.

Paltiel, K. Z., "The Israeli Coalition System," *Government and Opposition* 10 (1975), 397–414.

Peretz, D., *Government and Politics in Israel.* Boulder, Co.: Westview Press, 1979.

Perlmutter, A., *Politics and the Military in Israel 1967–1977.* London: Frank Cass, 1978.

Raphaeli, N., "The Senior Civil Service in Israel," *Pub. Admin.* 48 (1970), 169–78.

Sager, Samuel, *The Parliamentary System of Israel.* Syracuse: Syracuse Univ. Press, 1985.

Sharkansky, I., "How to Cope with the Bureaucracy," *Jerusalem Quar.* 6 (Winter 1978), 80–93.

Tummala, Krishna, ed., *Administrative Systems Abroad.* Lanham, Md.: Univ. Press of Am., 1982, essay on Israel.

22

Japan

KU TASHIRO
International University of Japan, Tokyo, Japan

HISTORICAL PERSPECTIVE

Although the system of separation of powers was introduced immediately after the Meiji Restoration in 1868, the constitutional governmental system in Japan was actually established.by the Meiji Constitution which was enacted in 1889 and enforced in the following year. Under this constitution, public administration based on and in compliance with constitutionalism was introduced in this country. The power structure, however, was not always in line with the ideal of constitutionalism and the principle of administration by law. For example, the Emperor and his administrative agencies could enact orders or regulations without statutory authorization within a set range of administrative authority.

The present Constitution which was enacted in 1947 provided a solid ground of constitutionalism—the cabinet administers the law faithfully and no administrative agency can institute any order or regulation without statutory authority. Administrative agencies, accordingly, carry out administrative actions strictly to execute the laws.

However, the scope of administrative actions had been expanded in order to cope with a variety of emerging administrative demands. As a consequence, the number and functional coverage of administrative organizations had to be increased to deal with increasing demands. For example, the number of bureaus in the headquarters of central government rose so dramatically as to climb from 90 in 1955, the year of economic recovery from war devastation to the level before World War II, to 133 in 1969, when Japanese exports unprecedentedly exceeded the ten billion mark in U.S. dollars. The number of national public employees increased by 33.4 per cent or by approximately 225,000 persons from 674,000 at the end of fiscal year 1957 to 899,000 at the end of fiscal year 1967. The number of advisory councils attached to ministries and agencies likewise increased from 208 in 1956 to as many as 277 nine years later in 1965.

In view of the need to streamline governmental administration for survival in the world arena, administrative reform has been the grand national policy in the last four decades. Prime Minister Yasuhiro Nakasone, who had been one of the strongest supporters and who assumed office in 1982, clearly described his aim of effecting administrative reforms as "the clearance of the remnants of the past and the readiness for change in the future."

CHARACTERISTICS OF JAPANESE PUBLIC ADMINISTRATION

Under the current Constitution, Japanese public administration is structured on the basis of democratic government and respect for fundamental human rights. Outlined below are its main features.

First, the superiority of legislative power is established over that of executive power. The National Diet, which is composed of two houses of elected representatives, can discuss all matters of government, and under the parliamentary system, the cabinet is collectively responsible to the Diet. Second, the structure of government organizations is so uniform that the level of organizational hierarchy can be easily identified by referring only to the title of a specific organization. Third, public personnel administration aims at promotion of democracy and efficiency for the people. Fourth, public finance is regulated by an annual budget which has to be approved by the Diet.

Fifth, the structure of administration is fairly uniform at the same level of autonomous entities. There are one "to" (metropolis Tokyo), two "fu" (Osaka and Kyoto), one "do" (Hokkaido) and 43 ordinary "ken" (prefectures). Under this "to-do-fu-ken" level, there are three different levels of municipalities: "shi" (city), "machi/cho" (town) and "mura/son" (village). The total number of these municipalities was 3,255 as of September 1981.

Finally, the defense administration is an important issue particularly in these years. While the Constitution forbade any armed force, three defense services have been maintained under the tight control of the Diet. The total manpower establishment of the Self-Defense Force was 271,180 as of March 31, 1983.

Structure of Public Administrative Organizations

1. Central Government

Executive power is vested in the cabinet and the primary administrative organs are the Prime Minister's Office and twelve ministries which are headed by the cabinet members. Within the Prime Minister's Office, there are nine independent agencies, for example the Economic Planning Agency and the Defense Agency, which are headed by Ministers of State. Each ministry has one or two Parliamentary Vice-Ministers who are selected among the Diet members. An Administrative Vice-Minister, who is the head of the ministerial career service, is also posted in every ministry. An organization chart of the central government is shown in Fig. 1.

When it is necessary to divide the administrative affairs of a specific ministry or agency geographically, local branch offices are established by law. The largest jurisdictional areas are "regional," which divide the nation into eight or ten regions. "Prefectural" (to-do-fu-ken level) and "municipal" (shi-cho-son level) offices roughly correspond to the local governments' jurisdiction. There were 248 regional offices, 558 prefectural and about 25,000 municipal offices under the central government, as of March 31, 1985.

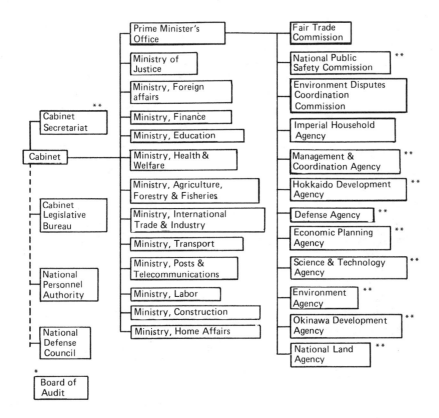

Figure 1 Organization chart of the central government in Japan.

2. Local Governments

Contrary to the old centralized local government system before World War II, the system under the new Constitution is oriented toward decentralization and direct democracy. Local public entities thus have two principal organizations: the assembly as their legislative body and the chief executive officer as their executive.

The local public entities are broadly classified into two types. Ordinary local public entities are general and pervasive ones in terms of organization, functions and other factors, and are commonly found all over the country. "To-do-fu-ken" of the prefectural level and "shi-cho-son" of the municipality level are of this category. Special local public entities are established for special purposes in order to meet special administrative needs of specific areas. The total of special entities was 7,164 as of December 1, 1980.

3. Public Corporations

A public corporation is established by the national government as an instrument for business operations necessary for the state. As of March 31, 1983, Japan had ninety-nine public corporations whose fields of operation range from public works to social welfare. Their total number of employees was 896,529 as of January 1, 1984.

With the slowdown of economic growth and subsequent aggravation of government financial deficits, the national government has been facing various administrative problems of public corporations. It has been the governmental policy, therefore, to control the numbers of corporations and rationalize corporate management. The government has also tried to reduce the membership of every board to directors.

Public Finance

1. Budget of National Government

The national government budget consists of the General Account budget and thirty-eight Special Account budgets. These budgets are submitted along with the budgets of fifteen public corporations to the Diet for approval. The General Account is the basic governmental budget which reflects directly incumbent governmental policies. The total sum of the General Account budget for the fiscal year 1985 amounted to 52,500 billion yen, roughly 20 per cent of expected gross national product for the year.

A Special Account can be established under limited conditions by legislation for enabling the government to carry out specific projects, like postal service, roads improvement, and health and welfare insurance. Each Special Account has its own distinct source of revenue. The budgets of government-affiliated public corporations are wholly financed by the government. Their operations are closely tied to government policies, and their budgets are subject to approval of the Diet. The combined sum of the Special Accounts and the budgets for these government-affiliated corporations for the fiscal year 1985 amounted to 20,858 billion yen.

2. Local Public Finance

Local public finance, together with national finance, plays an important role in the national economy, since the real expenditures of local public entities account for roughly 14 per cent of the gross national expenditures (GNE). Expenditures are about 6-7 per cent of GNE for the central government as far as direct spending is concerned, while the size of total public finance in local entities is approximately the same as that of the central government. This is because of the transfer of about one half of central government expenditures, such as local allocation grants of certain national taxes and central government disbursements, to local public entities. The central government, therefore, spends only about half of its General Account budget as an end consumer, and local public entities disburse nearly twice as much as the central government.

Public Service Personnel

1. Number of Public Service Personnel

Public service personnel can be classified into three major categories: national government service, local public service and the service of public corporations. The breakdown can be shown as follows:

National public personnel (as of March 31, 1982)	1,200,089

Local public service personnel (as of April 1, 1981)	1,705,587 prefectures
	1,462,157 municipalities and others
(Sub total)	3,167,744
Public corporation personnel (as of January 1, 1981)	938,844
Grand total	5,306,677

The total number shows that forty-five public servants serve one thousand Japanese people, and it represents about nine per cent of all employed in Japan.

The number of full time permanent national public personnel, as of March 31, 1982, can be broken down into four groups of services as follows:

Non-industrial service	544,115
General ministries and agencies	364,229
National schools, hospitals and sanatoriums	179,886
Industrial services (Five government enterprises)	354,150
Postal service	312,702
Forest, Printing, Mint and Alcohol Monopoly	41,448
Self-defense forces	271,180
Diet, Courts etc.	30,644
(Total)	1,200,089

2. Legal Framework

The National Public Service Law of 1947 is the basic law for the national civil service system, which assures the people democratic and efficient execution of public administration. However, this law is fully applicable only to the non-industrial "ordinary" service. Industrial services, while the law is basically applicable to them, are given more bargaining rights on salary and other working conditions than the non-industrial service, by their law on industrial relations. The career staffs of the Diet, courts and self-defense forces are regulated by their respective service laws, while the substance is no different from that of the basic law.

The Local Public Service Law of 1950 is similar in concept to the National Law. With regard to public corporations, there is no special service law and instead, like ordinary private companies, the Labor Standard Law of 1947 is applied. However, three major public corporations, Japan Tobacco and Salt Corporation, Japanese National Railways, and Nippon Telegraph and Telephone Public Corporation, had been regulated by special service laws for national government enterprises, but their privatization in 1985 enabled the new "special companies" to handle personnel matters flexibly, like private enterprises.

ADMINISTRATIVE REFORMS SINCE WORLD WAR II

Japan has tried to catch up with the developed countries from the middle of last century. The central government exerted strong leadership with effective guidance, control and surveillance over local governments and the private sector. According to then Minister of State Nakasone, Director General of the Administrative Management Agency in 1982, this machinery "resulted in the compartmentalized and centrally lopsided system of the public administration with various field offices throughout the country for the implementation of administration."

During the period of the accelerated economic growth after World War II, the role of the government expanded rapidly, which subsequently led to the proliferation of bureaucracy. After strenuous effort of postwar reconstruction and industrial development, Japan entered through the period of stable economic growth. Thus the new dimension of the need of administrative reform arose, while no previous administration had failed in tackling administrative reform in its own way. The history of administrative reforms during the period from 1945 to 1985 could best be explained and analyzed in four stages at ten year intervals.

The First Stage (1945-54)

The first half of this stage saw the implementation of administrative reforms under the allied occupation. The enactment of the new (current) Constitution was the stimulus of reorganization and democratization of administrative institutions. Among the new legislation under the Constitution, four important laws should be specified as follows:

1. *The Cabinet Law* of 1947 provided for the structure, authority, and management of the cabinet; the competence of the prime minister and other ministers; the relations with the administrative branches; cabinet orders; and the cabinet's auxiliary organs.

2. *The National Government Organization Law* of 1948 was the law providing the standards for the organization of administrative organs under the control of the cabinet.

3. *The National Public Service Law* of 1947, the basic law on civil service system, aimed at assuring the people democratic and efficient administration of their public affairs.

4. *The Local Autonomy Law* of 1947, contrary to the aim of the previous centralized system, was oriented toward decentralization and contained elements of direct democracy. In addition to this law, a series of related laws like the Public Office Election Law, Local Public Service Law, and Local Finance Law were enacted in order to strengthening local autonomous entities.

After the signing of San Francisco Peace Treaty in 1952, some reforms were made to ameliorate controversial changes introduced during the occupation.

The Second Stage (1955-64)

The expansion of administration was unable to cope with the high rate of economic growth. Administrative machinery was expanded and the public corporations grew in number. While the high economic growth necessitated the expansion of administrative institutions in the public sector, the private sector introduced both technological innovation and rationalization of management. The wide difference between the efficiency of the two sectors was recognized by those concerned, and subsequently in 1962 the First Provisional Commission for Administrative Reform was established in the Prime Minister's Office. The Commission was headed by Kiichiro Sato, one of the most famous bankers, and consisted of six important members mostly from the private sector and a staff of twenty-one experts assisted by seventy researchers. After two years of intensive study, the Commission submitted proposals to the Prime Minister in 1964, the substance of which were as follows:

1. Better coordination among public organizations, especially between the cabinet and ministries;
2. Democratization of administration through strengthening of local autonomy; and
3. Restraining the excessive expansion of public administration without failing to satisfy emerging needs for new services.

The Third Stage (1965–74)

The recommendations of the First Commission were rigorously implemented. Administrative reform efforts were directed at elevating coordination between government organizations and on raising the efficiency and rationality of overall administration. For the improvement of efficiency and inter-ministerial coordination, two new agencies were established: the Environment Agency in 1971, which was given overall responsibilities for the implementation of environmental policies, and the National Land Agency in 1974 for overseeing land utilization.

In order to streamline public administration, a "shock treatment," including an across-the-board abolition of one bureau in each ministry and agency, was introduced in 1968. As many as 131 bureaus of ministerial headquarters were reduced to 114 in the same year. The number largely remained stable thereafter, since a "scrap and build" approach was simultaneously employed.

The enactment of the Act on Total Number of Personnel in Administrative Organs in 1969 was another important cornerstone of administrative reform. The Act stipulated that the total number of national service personnel, exclusive of those in the defense forces and governmental enterprises, could not exceed 506,571, which was the number of established positions for fiscal year 1967. The Act also enabled the cabinet to determine the personnel levels of individual ministries and agencies and therefore the cabinet attained the power to manage governmental manpower in a much more flexible manner. In order to administer this Act, the First National Personnel Reduction Plan was also worked out by the government in the same year. Under the Plan, the government could pool and redistribute personnel from inactive or redundant departments to ones which needed more personnel to meet new administrative demands. The combination of both the Act and the Plan enabled the government to eliminate a total over 10,000 civil service positions in the central government.

The Fourth Stage (1975–85)

The reforms of the third stage resulted in a drastic reduction in governmental organizations. In the headquarters of ministries and agencies, 51 divisions (5 per cent of total numbers then) were either dissolved or incorporated into other divisions in the fiscal years 1978 and 1979. Also, a total of 36 advisory councils were consolidated and/or abolished in 1978, and by this very reform about 1,000 council members were eliminated.

Apart from the staff reduction carried out under the combination of the Act and the Plan, it was also decided that eighteen public corporations should be consolidated or abolished. Approximately 1,000 licensing procedures (about 10 per cent) were streamlined in the period 1981–82. Over a four-year period starting from 1980, a reduction in a quarter of subsidy programs was also decided even if it would affect some 950 subsidy categories.

Furthermore, in order to accommodate the younger generation in national government services to improve administrative efficiency, the National Public Service Retirement Law was enacted in 1981, effective four years later, to stipulate the retirement age, in principle, at sixty instead of the practice under post-war regulations of having no age limit.

A new wave of administrative reforms was triggered by the second oil crisis in 1979. The Second Provisional Commission was thus established in 1981. The Commission aimed at overcoming the difficulties derived from environmental changes in both international and domestic affairs, in particular the accumulation of an enormous international trade surplus and the internal deficit in government finance. The Second Commission, in the process of its review exercises for two years, submitted as many as five consecutive reports.

1. Reform Strategy

While the reform proposals made by the First Commission in 1962 were directed at making administrative procedures more comprehensive, more efficient, and more effective, the Second Commission concentrated its reform efforts on administrative policies and basic governmental systems and organizations. The Commission was fully convinced that the primary goal of this society should be to produce a vigorous culture and a prosperous economy in the world arena. The reform strategy therefore emphasized; (a) further self-help efforts and mutual aids to secure education and welfare, (b) modifying the role of public administration to give the private sector a freer rein, and (c) making a positive contribution to the international community.

2. Spending Cuts

The Commission advocated the reconstruction of central government finance through virile austerity measures. This policy was a major premise of efforts to overhaul public administration. In order to achieve the goal mentioned above, the Commission recommended not to have "big government" which was bloated with social welfare programs and large tax burdens. It was also voiced that financial rehabilitation should be accomplished without any undertaking of new tax measures. If not, the comparatively low rate of tax burden in this country (25.4 per cent of national income as of 1981) would inevitably cause an increase in overall rates. This was expressed very strongly by the Commission in order to avoid the common problem of higher tax rates prevailing in most welfare states in developed democracies. In this connection, the Commission was of the view that the reduction in the amount of government bonds, "special bonds" for making up the deficits in government finance in particular, should be of priority among other reform measures.

3. "Software" Measures

While the First Commission had maintained as its main reform target the "hardware" of government, like administrative organizations and the level of establishments in personnel, the Second Commission paid more attention to "software." Measures aimed at improving the government's relations with the public and securing public trust in the government were proposed. Among these proposals, releasing public information more openly to the public, the rationalization of administrative procedures, and the introduction of an ombudsman system should be noted.

The Commission further recommended that the idea of turning over the management of three major corporations to the private sector should be studied. Before the foundation of these corporations, the businesses of the Japan Tobacco and Salt Public Corporation (TRSPC), the Japanese National Railways (JNR), and the Nippon Telegraph and Telephone Public Corporation were directly run by the government, but soon after the war these corporations were established to promote services to the public under the government's supervision in order to secure harmony between the enterprises' public and business characters. However, the combination of political involvement, intervention by supervisory organs and the laxity in management and discipline in recent years undercut the profitability of these public corporations and threatened to ruin even their public character.

The Commission also recommended that, in adherence to the principle of decentralization of functions between the central and local governments, administrative affairs directly related to local residents should be dealt with as much as possible by the local bodies to which they had to access. With regard to the administration of local governments, the Commission recommendations included two more important items: strict control of the number of local government workers by establishing maximum personnel levels for local public bodies, and holding down excessive salary level of local public employees.

4. Promotion of Reforms

In coincidence with the establishment of the Second Commission, the Headquarters for the Promotion of Administrative Reform was established jointly by the government and the government party (the Liberal Democratic Party) in order to secure coordination of support for the recommendations of the Commission toward implementation. The Headquarters was headed by the Prime Minister and composed of the cabinet members and the executive officers of the government party.

The Second Commission submitted its recommendations as they were formed and the government responded to immediate action in support to them. This led to constant media coverage of reform issues and as a result the interest of the public in administrative reform was kept at high level. Both the Commission and the government then in turn were stimulated to promote further administrative reform.

PROGRESS OF ADMINISTRATIVE REFORMS

The Second Commission for Administrative Reform was dissolved in 1983 after a two-year effort of strenuous reviews. It would be appropriate, however, to summarize the activities of the Commission before delving into the progress of recommended reforms.

The First (Emergency) Report

When the Commission was organized in March 1981, then Prime Minister Zenko Suzuki requested the Commission to submit its first report by the summer of 1981. In response to this request, the Commission did so quickly as of July 10. This was an emergency report by which two specific recommendations were referred for immediate implementation in view of the stringent financial conditions. The first was on the curtailment of expenditures and the reconstruction of government finance. The second was on the streamlining and rationalization of public administration, in which four major areas were specified: governmental administration, public corporations, local public entities, and licensing administration.

The Second Report

The Second Report, which was submitted on February 10, 1982, dealt with the reform of permits and licenses.

The Third (Fundamental) Report

The Third Report, submitted on July 30, 1982, outlined fundamental reform measures in four areas: public administration in general, governmental organization and the function of coordination, public personnel administration, and the redistribution of administrative responsibility between central and local governments and local public finance.

The Fourth Report

The Fourth Report, submitted on February 28, 1983, recommended specifically the establishment of an oversight commission on administrative reform.

The Fifth (Final) Report

The Final Report was submitted on March 14, 1983, before the dissolution of the Commission. This recommended a package of reform programs in eight major fields as follows:

1. Reform of central administrative organizations,
2. Reform of governmental enterprises and public corporations,
3. Reform of national and local relations and local public administration,
4. Rationalization of the system of subsidies to local governments and other entities,
5. Rationalization of the system of permits and licenses,
6. Reform of the public personnel system,
7. Reform of the budget, accounting and public finance systems, and
8. Reform of the system of releasing administrative information to the public, public administrative procedures, etc.

The responsibility for implementing reform recommendations was carried over to the new supervisory body, the Provisional Council for the Promotion of Administrative Reform as recommended by the Fourth Report. Toshio Doko, Honorary Chairman of the Federation of Economic Organizations, was requested to maintain the chairmanship of both the Commission and Council. In addition to this continuity of reform machinery, there was another reform promotion body, the Headquarters for the Promotion of Administrative Reform, jointly established by the government and the Liberal Democratic Party (LDP). In other countries, administrative reform seems to have been carried out when a new president took office or when the opposition party took over. But in Japan, the LDP has been continuously in power for the last three decades and therefore the combination of the Council and the Headquarters was extremely effective in building up support for implementation of the reform recommendations. As of the end of fiscal year 1984 (March 31, 1985), the administrative reform programs implemented pursuant to the recommendations of the Second Commission were as follows.

Reorganization of Administrative Institutions

For the enhancement of management and policy coordination functions in the central government, the Management and Co-ordination Agency was established in July 1984 with the merger of part of the Prime Minister's Office and the Administrative Management Agency. The National Government Organization Law was also amended in order to increase the flexibility of government organization. From July 1984, thanks to the amendment, the creation and reorganization of bureaus and equivalent-level central organizations came to be regulated by cabinet order instead of law, and there was a major reshuffling of twenty internal bureaus and departments in ten ministries and agencies. The amendment stipulated further reorganization, including elimination of divisions of the headquarters of the national government, affecting as many as 150 (10 per cent) of all divisions by 1988.

The local branch offices of the central government could be divided into three different levels, namely regional, prefectural and municipal levels. About 60 per cent of national public servants were employed by these local branches. During fiscal year 1984, forty-four such branch offices were either consolidated, scaled down, or eliminated. In 1985, three more reorganizations were to be made.

Control of Staff Numbers

Following the introduction of the First National Personnel Reduction Plan in 1969, five consecutive Plans were drawn up and the public service was reduced by about 16,000 positions. During the period from 1967 to 1984, some 170,000 positions were eliminated but about 154,000 were added in order to meet the emerging needs of universities, hospitals and sanitaria. The balance of 16,000 was rather small but it did imply the success of the "scrap and build" approach. The Sixth Plan, covering the 1982-1986 period, aims at making a 5 per cent reduction of posts (44,886 from a total of 897,717).

Government Enterprises

Rationalization programs were introduced in four ailing government enterprises as follows:

1. Postal Service
   (a) Expansion of consignment coverage for collection and delivery of mail,
   (b) Promotion of an on-line system for postal savings and insurance, and
   (c) Rationalization of staff deployment.
2. National Forest Service
   (a) Amendment of the existing Improvement Program,
   (b) Improvement of business operations, and
   (c) Rationalization of staff deployment.

3. Printing and Mint
   (a) Improvement of business operations, and
   (b) Rationalization of staff deployment.
4. National Hospitals and Sanatoria
   (a) Within ten years from 1986, consolidation, abolition and transfer of management to other institutions.

Public Corporations

Two major public corporations, Nippon Telegraph and Telephone Corporation (NTT) and Japan Tobacco and Salt Public Corporation (JTSPC), were transformed into special companies effective April 1985. The heavily-indebted corporation, Japanese National Railways (JNR), was to be divided into seven special companies in 1987 with the hope of recovering some twenty-five trillion yen of accumulated deficits.

The reform of other public corporations was also enforced through drastic measures: the merger of four corporations into two in 1984, the merger of four more into two in 1985, and the abolition of two corporations in 1985. Furthermore, the privatization of nineteen corporations was decided upon, twelve by the end of fiscal year 1985. With regard to forty-six corporations, a reduction in the scope of their operations was to be enforced beginning in 1985. Periodical review and standardization of accounting were to be implemented in order to revitalize comprehensively the management of all public corporations.

Administrative Processes

The Diet passed related bills which would eliminate or curtail excessive regulatory measures. Some 191 among 253 cases pointed out by the Commission were deregulated in line with the recommendations. Some 115 out of 496 statistical survey programs were to be either curtailed or rationalized during the 1984–86 period. Also, public accountability and complaint systems like the right of access to administrative information and the ombudsman were to be examined for possible introduction.

National–Local Relations

Fiscal year 1983 witnessed a comprehensive rationalization package, with fifty-five regulatory functions either abolished or transferred to local governments. Furthermore, as many as seventeen administrative involvements of the central government in local government affairs were either abolished or lessened by the end of fiscal year 1984. Rationalization of the system of subsidies to the local governments was also under way, with the main emphasis on consolidation and minimization of personnel costs and petty subsidies.

With regard to the abolition of the system of national government officials working in local government, those who had been engaged in land transport administration returned to national government service. Two more groups, social insurance and employment security, were to be redistributed to either the national or local government services. When the abolition exercise is completed, the "temporary" system introduced in the difficult period of 1947 would finally fade away.

While local governments were urged to have more self-evaluation capacity for the control of their organization and staff numbers, the central government had always regulated them for more economy and efficiency. Measures to rectify excessive salaries and retirement allowances in the local governments had been strenuously enforced. This administrative guidance was extended in line with the Fundamental Principles of Administrative Reform in Local Government, which was approved by the cabinet in January 1985.

Substantive Programs

1. Pensions

In 1984 the government launched the first reform of the Public Employee's Mutual Aid Pension Scheme toward the integration of various pension schemes by 1995.

2. Medical Care

In line with measures to hold down the costs of medical care, both the medical insurance system and the provision of medical services were streamlined by a combination of (a) strengthening the supervisory and audit functions for medical cost control, (b) tightening the check of medical payment claims, and (c) revising price standards for medicines. The controversial system of comprehensive health care for the elderly was finally introduced in 1983.

3. Agriculture

Rationalization of nation-wide usage of paddy field was carried out under the Third Program (1984–86) in order to attain a balanced supply and demand for rice, the staple food of the Japanese. A reduction in the expenditures of the Foodstuff Control System, which was introduced originally during World War II, was given priority in reform. Minimization of price reversion between purchase and supply and a reduction of personnel in the national network of Food Offices were among the major rationalization programs for rice production in Japan.

Reform of Government Finance

Following the Special Act for Administrative Reform of 1981, which incorporated the First Recommendation of the Second Provisional Commission for Administrative Reform, an emergency spending curtailment program was introduced. This program covered seven major items directly relating to thirty-four independent laws and was enforced strictly during the 1982–84 period. Along with this crash program, the so-called "zero-ceiling" on ministerial requests for budget appropriations was enforced so rigorously that the growth of government expenditures was dramatically curtailed as follows:

Fiscal Year 1982	1.8 per cent
Fiscal Year 1983	0.0 per cent
Fiscal Year 1984	−0.1 per cent
Fiscal Year 1985	0.0 per cent

Grants and subsidies provided by the government added up to the enormous amount of about 14 trillion yen in fiscal year 1984, but strenuous efforts for their reduction and rationalization succeeded in saving a net 430 billion yen in the same fiscal year.

Organizations for Administrative Reform

The Second Commission was formed on March 16, 1981, and the Joint Headquarters for the Promotion of Administrative Reform was established as soon as April 7 of the same year, only three weeks later, by the government and government party. This was a good testimony to the serious concern over administrative reform by both politicians and bureaucrats. The creation of the Provisional Council for the Promotion of Administrative Reform, as recommended by the Fourth Report of the Second Commission, was another indication of enthusiasm for reform, and this was done July 1, 1983, only three months after the dissolution of the Second Commission. For the reform of the most controversial public corporation, the Japanese National Railways, the Inspection Commission for the Reconstruction of National Railways was established by the Diet on June 10, 1983.

ANALYSIS OF ADMINISTRATIVE REFORMS

A combination of favorable conditions, internationally and domestically, has enabled Japan to achieve a rapid economic development in the last four decades. However, no such striking performance could have been achieved without the stability of political leadership. Since its creation in 1955, the conservative Liberal Democratic Party (LDP) has been the ruling party thanks to its absolute majority of seats in both houses of the National Diet, the House of Representatives (lower) and the House of Councillors (upper). The LDP therefore has been monopolizing the premiership continuously since 1955, as shown below, because the president of the majority party automatically becomes prime minister under the Constitution.

The Chronicle of LDP Administration

No.	Name of Prime Minister	Period
1	Ichiro Hatoyama[a]	Dec. '54–Dec. '56
2	Tanzan Ishibashi	Dec. '56–Jan. '57
3	Nobusuke Kishi	Jan. '57–Jul. '60
4	Hayato Ikeda	Jul. '60–Nov. '64
5	Eisaku Sato	Nov. '64–Jul. '72
6	Kakuei Tanaka	Jul. '72–Dec. '74
7	Takeo Miki	Dec. '72–Dec. '76
8	Takeo Fukuda	Dec. '76–Dec. '78
9	Masayoshi Ohira	Dec. '78–Jun. '80
10	Zenko Suzuki	Jun. '80–Nov. '82
11	Yasuhiro Nakasone	Nov. '82–Oct. '87 (expected)

[a]Hatoyama became Prime Minister as the President of Japan Democratic Party. The LDP was formed on Dec. 15, 1955 by the merger of the Japan Democratic Party and the Liberal Party.

It was not until December 1983 that the LDP had to form a coalition, formed with the New Liberal Club, a small secessionist group from the LDP which had been one of the opposition parties since its formation in 1976.

Although these LDP administrations were not always coherent in tackling administrative reform, no single administration failed to tackle the subject. Why did conservative prime ministers behave consistently in favor of the idea? The simple answer is that the public had always supported reform plans. Their strong general support enabled the LDP to maintain its long and continuous majority position in the Diet, while the LDP's tactical success in election campaigns should not be disregarded.

How important the support of the public was could be testified by an interesting episode, Prime Minister Zenko Suzuki's unexpected announcement of retirement in 1982. He had been left the chance of the premiership by the sudden death of then Prime Minister Ohira during the election campaign in June 1980. Prime Minister Suzuki, who had enjoyed the reputation of troubleshooter, assumed the office by emphasizing the importance of "wa" (peace and harmony) among LDP members. He had also made such public promises as "termination of heavy reliance on government bonds by 1984" and "reconstruction of government finance without any increase in taxes." However, these promises were gradually proved not likely to be materialized due to a combination of emerging difficulties. Then popular support for him declined dramatically as follows:

December 1981	support	40 per cent
March 1982	support	30 per cent
	nonsupport	49 per cent
September 1982	support	26 per cent
	nonsupport	52 per cent

Even if a factional opposition might occur among the voters of LDP members, he could have gained enough support for his reelection to the LDP presidency, subsequently to the premiership. What actually happened then behind the scenes is not known, but it is clear that the public deserted his camp. They were disappointed by his indecisiveness regarding major pending matters, in particular his reform promises on government finance. He announced his unexpected withdrawal from reelection on October 12, 1982, only four days before the closing date for candidature.

Tripod Support to the LDP

The undefeated LDP has enjoyed an unevenly-shaped tripod support over the last three decades: financial support by financiers and industrialists; popular votes by farmers, fisherman, white-collar workers and junior executives through the "koenkai" (supporters' society); and policy and legislative guidance by the bureaucracy. Each of these three groups has maintained its own stance toward administrative reform.

1. Financiers and Industrialists

Either directly or indirectly through the organizations to which they belonged, both the financiers and industrialists provided funds to politicians and parties. This was the major channel of political funds to the LDP, while the opposition parties received funds from either individuals' donations or the contributions of trade union federations. The financiers and industrialists formed four major national economic organizations: "Keidanren" (The Federation of Economic Organizations), JCCI (The Japan Chamber of Commerce and Industry), "Nikkeiren" (The Japan Federation of Employers' Associations), and "Keizai Doyukai" (The Japan Committee for Economic Development). The leaders of these organizations had been the core of the "zaikai," a group of people who, apart from their identification with specific companies or industries, represented the capitalist position and were considered to be influential with the LDP and often with the prime minister.

The "zaikai" had always been in favor of administrative reform because of its preference for small and cheap government. The most symbolic fact in this context might be the selection of the chairmen of both the First and Second Provisional Commissions for Administrative Reform; Mr. Kiichiro Sato, Chairman of the Board of Directors, Mitsui Bank, for the First Commission; and Mr. Toshio Doko, Honorary Chairman of "Keidanren" and former President of both Ishikawajima-Harima Heavy Industry and Toshiba Inc., for the Second Commission.

2. Farmers, Fishermen, White-Collar Workers and Junior Executives

The constituencies of LDP's Diet members were mostly located in the rural area where primary industry dominated. The white-collar workers and junior executives, though most of them were urban dwellers, supported the LDP or other conservative parties, while the majority of blue-collar workers supported the "progressive" camp including the Socialist and Communist Parties. The "koenkai" of LDP's members was mainly composed of influential persons in the local community. This system functioned comparatively well enough to collect the votes of farmers, fishermen, white-collar workers and junior executives who would honor social traditions and family relations. Thus the popular votes for the LDP had commonly matched or outnumbered those of "progressive" parties.

A byproduct of economic development was middle-class consciousness among the Japanese people. After 1965 government surveys never failed to show people's feeling of belonging to the middle class to be about 90 per cent. This would imply the people's reluctance to see drastic changes, even in public administration, and coincided with their general support to the LDP.

3. The Bureaucracy

The bureaucracy worked closely with both politicians and businessmen in the course of economic development. It served the Diet members in general but especially the ministers who headed the administrative branches. The task of bureaucracy has been not only to execute administrative policies formulated by politicians, but also to collect, process and analyze the data necessary for policy formulation. Furthermore, the bulk of government policies were designed to ensure the health of the national economy, and therefore the bureaucracy had to establish close cooperative relations with both politicians and businessmen in drafting and implementing policies. The bureaucracy has also been the major source of future politicians and business leaders. However, this is applicable to only a small portion of the bureaucracy. The 10,000-odd members of the bureaucratic elite ("kanryo") include 2,500-odd senior administrative officials at the headquarters of ministries and agencies, and their 7,500-odd future successors in lower positions. Their relations with the LDP have been comparatively good, and sometimes senior officials have been named to be among future successors of the LDP's Diet members.

The "kanryo" has occupied most key administrative positions and has been reinforced by as many as 400–odd new recruits every year through the highly competitive open entrance examination at the senior level. Most of these recruits have graduated in law from recognized universities, Tokyo University in particular, and have been recruited and trained primarily by the ministry or agency to which they belonged at the start of their career. They are called the "career class," a core group among the national civil service, and are given a combination of training and development programs, including a wide range of job rotations, inter-ministerial off-the-job training and study abroad. The work they are given usually relates to policy formulation and subsequent coordination. The objective has been to develop administrative generalists.

Accordingly the career group in a specific ministry or agency has been trained as part of the whole career class. The more they become knowledgeable about importan policy areas, the more they are likely to be involved in politics. Thus the career class as a whole has inevitably to maintain close relations with the government party.

National Climate for Administrative Reform

Japan's unique government-business relations helped to explain the astonishing success of its rapid economic growth. There was a unique collaboration between government and business during the period of growth before the first oil crisis. Also, labor-management relations during this period remained in the Japanese cooperative tradition. This climate in the country was referred to by the U.S. State Department as "Japan Inc."

The system of "Japan Inc." demonstrated its effectiveness in both working out and implementing administrative reform plans. One example was the reduction of grants and subsidies provided by the central government. When the First (Emergency) Report of the Second Reform Commission was submitted in July 1981, the total amount of governmental grants and subsidies was as big as thirteen trillion yen for the fiscal year: 36 per cent for social security, 23 per cent for education and science, 21 per cent for public works, and the remaining 20 per cent for miscellaneous purposes. Nearly 80 per cent of this money was allocated to local governments and nearly the same per cent was obligatory as regulated by relevant laws. Accordingly, it was extremely difficult to curtail the funds and programs. However, an across-the-board curtailment and other measures derived from the "Japan Inc." concept helped to reduce grants and subsidies as follows:

Fiscal Year	Amount of Reduction (100 million Yen)	Number of Cases Reduced
1981	1,668	1,329
1982	3,107	2,017
1983	4,007	1,631
1985	7,848	1,239

However, the sweet government-business relations began to sour and become more and more similar to those in other industrialized countries. For example, "zaikai" became not always happy to continue "zero-ceiling" austerity budgets which were deemed imperative by the government. A huge international trade surplus put strong pressure on the Japanese economy, but Prime Minister Nakasone's scenario for amelioration has not produced enough improvement to convince the business interests.

Administrative reform for what? This became another focal point in the process of reform activities. The administrative reforms carried out before the establishment of the Second Reform Commission in 1981 aimed mainly at the improvement of administrative efficiency. The concept of cheap government was the pilot. Advanced technology was also employed. The primary aim of the Second Reform Commission, however, was financial reform. Because of Prime Minister Suzuki's promises to the public in 1980, it was the deteriorated government finance that had to be attacked.

The present difficulty in Japan's public finance stemmed originally from the issuance of the "special bond" in 1975 for filling the financial gap. The total amount of both the "special bond" and the construction bond had been around 10 trillion yen, which was roughly one third of the Annual General Account Budget. The miracle of the quick recovery of the Japanese economy immediately after the first oil crisis may be attributed to this "special bond" issue. However, the cost of the recovery was a huge accumulation of public debts, reaching seventy trillion yen in 1980 when the Second Reform Commission was established. The Commission, therefore, proceeded directly with the reconstruction of public finance.

The financial gap could have been lessened, theoretically, by means of a thorough economization and rationalization of outlays including revisions of the administrative system. Practically, however, it could be adjusted during each year's budget compilation process by spending cuts, by revenue increase measures, or by a combination of these. The Second Reform Commission followed this course of action. As far as the implementation of previous administrative reforms was concerned, an orthodox approach had been effective enough but nowadays agreement on such an approach is not so clear as before. Three new pressures have emerged behind reform: internationalization, requiring a better handling of global responsibilities; the aging Japanese population, making a bigger claim on welfare programs; and individualism, requiring provisions for more diversified tastes and value systems. The expected reform in government finance requires working out effective countermeasures to these difficulties.

CONCLUSION AND PERSPECTIVES

The world has recognized the remarkable collaboration between the government and the "zaikai" that resulted in Japan's administrative reforms. Also, the world has witnessed the creation of a well-managed public service in this country, as evidenced by the following comparative table (Table 1).

While these figures inevitably entail the problem of comparability, particularly the definition of "public servant," the extent of the gap between Japan and the other countries does seem to demonstrate the efficiency of Japanese public administration. One of the reasons for this efficiency has been the devotion of well-trained public servants.

It would be appropriate to refer to the role of officials in governmental decision-making in order to show how they contribute to this efficiency. Actually about

Table 1 Number of Public Servants per 1,000 Population in Japan
and Other Countries[a]

Country	Ordinary Services[b]	Defense Personnel	Total
Japan	42	3	45
U.K.	94	10	104
France	103	8	111
U.S.A.	64	14	78
F.R.G.	64	10	74

[a]Most data by the Management and Coordination Agency of the Japanese
Government as of 1982.
[b]Ordinary services include both national and local services and also employees
of national government enterprises.

70 per cent of the bills submitted to the Diet by the government were originally
drafted by the bureaucrats of ministries and agencies concerned, and the great
majority of them are eventually passed; only a small portion of the remaining 30 per
cent submitted by the members of the Diet are adopted. It has been commonly
stated by many foreign observers, therefore, that the key decisions in the central
government are made by the career bureaucrats rather than the politicians of the Diet
and the cabinet.

This kind of interpretation would have been valid until recent years, or up to
around the mid-1970s. The dominant role of bureaucrats was challenged for the first
time in postwar Japan when the Japanese economy encountered a new dimension of
development. Maturity stagnation in the early 1970s necessitated the introduction of
the ambitious "Remodelling Plan for the Japanese Archipelago" by then Prime Minister
Kakuei Tanaka, which triggered a galloping inflation with an unprecedented price rise
of 30 per cent in 1983. This coincided with the first oil crisis toward the end of the
year. The bureaucrats could not handle the mushrooming of serious issues that ensued,
and this inability caused a decline in the social status of the bureaucracy as well as a
loss of their professional pride. Only political initiatives could lead to final decisions,
on such crucial problems as the "special bond" issue.

In addition to this change in the politician-bureaucrat relationship, another factor to
consider was the influence of the "zaikai" on the reform. The "zaikai" cultivated
stronger self-confidence in their collective bargaining capacity with the government
after overcoming a series of economic difficulties in the first half of the 1970s. One
of the most significant examples of their influence was the privatization of three major
public corporations, as briefly described in the previous section.

Prime Minister Nakasone, whose tenure began in November 1982, has been a major
influence in promoting administrative reforms. This could be the most important
reason why his administration had gained popular acceptance by the public. Administrative reform itself seems to have been accepted favorably by the public. However,
there remains a dilemma in the process of implementing reform measures, because of
the circular relations among the three major groups concerned with Japanese public
administration. Politicians are a stick for the bureaucrats but are rather easily

influenced by the "zaikai." Bureaucrats are not so influenced by the "zaikai" but are rather obedient to politicians. The "zaikai" listen rather cautiously to the views of bureaucrats but they exercise their influence on politicians. This triangular relation does not guarantee that timely decisions can be implemented quickly. It also raises the question of which party among the three will play the leading role in initiating future changes in Japanese public administration.

REFERENCES IN ENGLISH

Administrative Management Agency, *Administrative Management in Japan*. Tokyo: the AMA, 1982.

Administrative Management Agency, *Administrative Reform in Japan*. Tokyo: the AMA, 1982.

Christopher, Robert C., *The Japanese Mind: The Goliath Explained*. Fawcett Columbine, 1983.

Dowdy, Edwin, *Japanese Bureaucracy: Its Development and Modernization*. Melbourne: Cheshire, 1973.

Furuhashi, Genrokuro, "Postwar Administrative Reform Efforts in Japan," paper for Tokyo Roundtable of International Institute of Administrative Sciences, 1982.

Hyoe, Murakami, and Johannes Hirschmeier, eds., *Politics and Economics in Contemporary Japan*. Tokyo: Japan Culture Institute, 1979.

Inoki, Masamichi, "The Civil Bureaucracy," in Robert E. Ward and Dankwart Rustow, eds., *Political Modernization in Japan and Turkey* (Princeton, N.J.: Princeton University Press, 1964), 283–300.

International Review of Administrative Sciences 48, 2 (1982), articles on Japanese public administration, 115–262.

Katzenstein, Peter J., *Between Power and Plenty*. Madison: University of Wisconsin Press, 1978.

Koh, B. C., "Stability and Change in Japan's Higher Civil Service," *Comparative Politics* 11 (1979), 279–297.

Koh, B. C., and Jae-On Kim, "Paths to Advancement in Japanese Bureaucracy," *Comparative Political Studies* 15, 3 (1982), 289–313.

Kubota, Akira, *Higher Civil Servants in Postwar Japan*. Princeton, N.J.: Princeton University Press, 1969.

McMillan, Charles J., *The Japanese Industrial System*. Berlin and N.Y.: Gruyter, 1984.

Pempel, T. J., *Policy and Politics in Japan: Creative Conservatism*. Philadelphia: Temple University Press, 1982.

Tashiro, Ku, "Productivity in Public Administration: Concept and Application in Japan," *Indian Journal of Public Administration* (July–September, 1982).

Tsuji, Kiyoaki, ed., *Public Administration in Japan*. Tokyo: Institute of Administrative Management and University of Tokyo Press, 1984.

Tsurumi, Yoshi, *Japanese Business: A Research Guide with Annotated Bibliography*. N.Y.: Praeger, 1978, esp., bibliog. in Sec. 3.

Ukai, Nobushige, "Japan," in Donald C. Rowat, ed., *International Handbook on Local Government Reorganization* (Westport, Conn.: Greenwood Press, 1980), 248–254.

Ward, Robert E., *Japan's Political System*. Englewood Cliffs, N.J.: Prentice-Hall, 2nd 1978.

Yanaga, Chitoshi, *Big Business in Japanese Politics*. New Haven: Yale University Press, 1968.

23

The United States

FERREL HEADY
University of New Mexico, Albuquerque, New Mexico

ENVIRONMENTAL FACTORS

Historical Influences

The American political system and its administrative subsystem, although in many respects unique in their characteristics, nevertheless bear the imprint of historical forces both foreign and domestic. Born of revolution, incorporating features novel and untried, and bolstered by strong national sentiments of parochialism and isolationism, the governmental framework in the United States is commonly viewed by Americans as a homemade product. This view is prevalent but not accurate. Only through recognition of the historical influences which helped shape American politics and administration can an adequate understanding be achieved, including appreciation of the features which are distinctly American in their origins and in their evolution.

The colonies which became the original thirteen states at the end of the American Revolution were settled mainly by immigrants from the British Isles who regarded themselves as transplanted Englishmen. They were inheritors of the English historical experience, and beyond and behind that, of the Judeo-Christian culture developed over many centuries in Western Europe and the Mediterranean basin. During the century and a half of the colonial period, these Englishmen in the New World gradually formed their own views as to their rights vis-à-vis the British crown and the government in the homeland. Some of these claims, such as the invalidity of taxation without representation and the existence of inalienable human rights not subject to infringement by temporal authority, differed sharply from the notions of contemporary British political officials as to the proper role of colonials in overseas territories. The resulting rupture led to political independence for the former colonies and to a pronounced Anglophobic tendency for several decades, but it did not break the basic reliance on British models as modified during the colonial years in shaping the political institutions of the "first new nation" (1).

In addition, the American founding fathers who wrote the Declaration of Independence, the Articles of Confederation, and the United States Constitution (as well as the *Federalist Papers* which advocated its ratification) brought to their tasks a comprehensive knowledge of and attraction to a variety of historical political experiments and statements of political philosophy which guided them in devising the innovative features which produced an obviously American political edifice on the British foundation. These guides included the republics of the classical period, post-feudal European confederations, and recent or contemporary writing such as Locke's *Two Treatises on Civil Government*, Montesquieu's *Spirit of the Laws*, Rousseau's *Social Contract*, Smith's *Wealth of Nations*, and Paine's *Common Sense*. These and other sources contributed to the amalgam which emerged (2).

Dominant Features of the Political Framework

In the United States as in other countries, the system of public administration must conform to the requirements of the existing political regime, particularly to those political characteristics which are unique or unusual. The American political framework has three dominant features which are different in the sense that they are not commonly found, at least in combination, in the developed democracies examined in this book. These features are *constitutionalism* (a written constitutional document conferring and limiting governmental powers), *federalism* (a division of functions constitutionally between a central government and a number of constituent units in the federal system), and *presidentialism* (a popularly elected chief executive heading the executive branch within a constitutional tripartite separation of powers which also includes legislative and judicial branches). Each of these features has administrative consequences.

1. Constitutionalism

There is remarkably little in the U.S. Constitution which directly affects the pattern of American public administration. The President, as chief executive officer, is assigned a constitutional responsibility that the laws be "faithfully executed." Heads of the major executive departments are appointed by the President (with approval by the Senate, the upper house of the bicameral legislature), and they serve "at the pleasure" of the President, thus giving him wide latitude in top level staffing of the executive branch. Most decisions concerning the structure and management of administrative agencies are made through the regular legislative process jointly by the Congress and the President using his political resources and the constitutionally granted power of the executive veto. Basically, there is no constitutional barrier to change in the administrative system, even as to matters of major importance.

2. Federalism

The constitutional provisions on federalism dealt with governmental powers and functions rather than with details of the administrative machinery for carrying out assigned responsibilities at either the national or the state level. The most crucial choice within the range of options constitutionally available was made early by officials of the national government. During the presidency of George Washington, at the urging of Secretary of the Treasury Alexander Hamilton, a staunch advocate of a strong national government, a far-reaching commitment was made and carried out that the government at the center would create and maintain its own administrative agencies for the execution of national policy, and would not rely on state agencies as instrumentalities for day-by-day operations. This pattern for administration is not mandated by the existence of a federal system, as is illustrated currently by the German Federal Republic, where the central government has a broad array of constitutional powers, but utilizes the constituent federal units (*Laender*) as the primary vehicles for implementation of policies made by the central authorities. This is just one illustration of the variety found among the numerous federal systems now in existence (ranging from British Commonwealth and Western European countries to the U.S.S.R. and numerous Third World nations) both as to bases for constitutional allocation of governmental powers and patterns for administrative action. The long historical experience of the United States with federalism has not produced a standard model for replication.

3. Presidentialism

The President of the United States is one of the most influential chief executives of any contemporary nation, partly because he leads one of the world's superpowers, and partly because of the constitutional scope of the office. Our primary concern is with only one segment of his full array of responsibilities. He is chief of state in the symbolic sense, political party leader, influencer of public opinion, and major participant in the legislative process, as well as being the primary policy implementor during his term as elected head of the executive branch.

The constitutional emphasis is on aspects of the presidency other than the chief administrator role, which receives scant attention in the document itself, as already noted. Nevertheless, creation of the presidential office as part of the separation of powers arrangement initiated a novel method of superintendence over the officialdom responsible for dealing with state administrative affairs. It superseded both the direct obligation of loyalty to the king or emperor which characterized European absolutist monarchies, and the evolving parliamentary system of Great Britain with its prime minister-cabinet approach to conduct of and responsibility for public administration. The President as chief executive became the connecting channel between the public bureaucracy on the one hand and, on the other, the legislative and judicial branches and ultimately the sovereign people. In the contemporary world, the presidential and parliamentary options have evolved as the dominant alternatives in both developed and developing countries with representative forms of government. Presidentialism in the American mode has been widely copied in Latin America and elsewhere in the Third World, although obviously with wide variations in actual practice. The parliamentary system, with the leader of the strongest party as prime minister and a single party or coalition cabinet, has been preferred even more frequently, particularly by the developed democracies covered in this volume. Indeed, among these case studies, only France since 1958 under the Fifth Republic has moved toward presidentialism, but in a form which mixes features of both the presidential and parliamentary systems in such a way that it must be treated as a third option. Hence, presidentialism in the United States warrants special attention for an understanding of how this system impacts on the conduct of public administration, as contrasted to the parliamentary alternative which is represented by more examples.

Modification as a Constant

None of these key features of the American polity has stayed unchanged over two centuries. Each has evolved through time to its present conformation, and future modification is certain. In each instance, only a few examples can be mentioned as to how the political framework has shifted without being fundamentally altered, with the focus on changes which have affected American public administration.

The constitutional base has been revised both formally and informally. Twenty-six amendments have been ratified and added to the original document, the first ten almost immediately and the rest at intervals since. Most have made major changes, some only minor, but very few have directly affected public administration, and then mainly by specifying what could or cound not be legislated.

Much more significant are modifications by interpretation, accomplished primarily through acceptance of the doctrine of judicial review early in the nineteenth century, which made the United States Supreme Court the final arbiter as to the meaning of constitutional language. Changes by court decisions have likewise usually had an indirect rather than direct bearing on the administrative system, but there are a few exceptions such as the determination by the Supreme Court in 1926 that the President was not required to obtain the approval of the Senate to dismiss executive officials who had been appointed initially with Senate confirmation (3).

The balance of power within the federal system has also undergone marked transformations. The long-range trend has been toward a higher degree of ascendancy of the central level of government over the state level, facilitated during the first half of the nineteenth century by judicial construction of the constitution and by the cumulation of problems which led to the Civil War, the outcome of which meant final rejection of doctrines of states rights such as nullification and secession. During the last century this trend has probably also been responsive to governance necessities in an increasingly complex and interdependent world. The outcome is what is commonly referred to as a "marble cake" rather than "layer cake" type of federalism, with an intermingling of central and state government policies and programs in a complicated network of intergovernmental relationships, and with a variety of proposals in recent years for moving toward a "new federalism" which might redress the balance in favor of more reliance on state and local agencies whenever feasible (4). Public administration has had to react to these adjustments in the federal system, initially by rapid expansion of central government agencies and personnel, more recently by placement of greater emphasis on intergovernmental cooperation, and for a prolonged period on increasing professionalization of the public service.

Finally, the presidency as an institution has had its ups and downs as the executive branch has competed against the legislative and judicial branches within the bounds of the constitutional separation of powers. The individual characteristics of particular presidents have clearly had a bearing, with "strong" presidents such as Andrew Jackson or Theodore Roosevelt contrasted to "weak" ones such as Millard Fillmore or Warren Harding, but societal forces have been factors of greater importance in explaining longer term trends. Times of crisis, either domestic or foreign, tend to enhance the presidency. Times of uncertainty or ambivalence (such as the two decades before the Civil War, the post-Civil War reconstruction period, or the uneasy "normalcy" of the 1920s before the Great Depression) diminish it. Perhaps the greatest contrast to date has been between what Woodrow Wilson as a political scientist called "congressional government" in the 1880s, and the so-called "imperial presidency" during the terms of Lyndon B. Johnson and Richard M. Nixon in the late 1960s and early 1970s. As this century draws to a close, the trend lines are unclear, due in part to a reaction against the "imperial presidency" during the same years that Jimmy Carter as a "weak" president was succeeded by Ronald Reagan as a "strong" one.

These term-by-term and cyclical shifts in the presidency have many consequences, primarily in the political and policy arenas, but to a lesser extent in the administrative arena as well. Generally speaking, during the terms of "strong" presidents and during periods in which the presidency as an institution is relatively powerful, presidential direction of and control over the system of public administration will be firmer, more effective, and less successfully resisted. Presidentialism thus has a varying rather than a consistent effect on American public administration in operation.

STRUCTURE AND MANAGEMENT OF THE SYSTEM

Shared Characteristics by Levels

In the American federal system, basic characteristics of the central level of government are found also at the state and local government levels. For example, all of the states have written constitutions incorporating the separation of powers doctrine, and all have as chief executives governors who are counterparts of the President. Local units are legally considered to be creatures of the several states, so they do not have separate constitutions but operate under state constitutional or legislative mandates. They also show more variations in how the executive branch is organized; the most common pattern historically in cities has been to have a mayor directly elected at large as chief executive, but many cities now have an appointed professional city manager or administrative officer and some divide administrative supervisory responsibilities among the elected members of the city council, which is primarily a legislative body. Similar variations occur in counties and other local units.

At the state level, governors as chief executives show a spectrum of constitutional and political powers as compared with the national President. Some have opportunities in the legislative process not available to the President, such as use of the item veto for disapproval of selected provisions in bills passed by the state legislature. In general, however, the office of governor is less potent overall than the presidency in wielding both legal and extra-legal powers at the two levels in the federal system. This discrepancy is most noticeable in the role of the chief executive as manager of administration. Most state governors, for various reasons which cannot be explored here, face a fragmented administrative pattern which restricts their ability to direct the conduct of administration to the extent that the President can do so at the center. Hence, characteristics of autonomy in operation and diffuseness in controls which will be described in more detail for the central government are accentuated at the state level.

The Managerial Role of the Chief Executive

In the United States, the chief executive is also the chief manager of the administrative system. The President's managerial role is only one of many, however, and it tends to be overshadowed by other considerations and obligations. The result is that the presidential system does not match the parliamentary system in providing to the chief executive means for directing and controlling administrative agencies which are available to the prime minister and his ministerial colleagues in the cabinet.

The reasons are partly personal and partly institutional. Presidents are not nominated and elected because of their managerial talents, but for other qualities. Frequently and increasingly, they campaign as critics of the "bureaucracy" and promise to curb its size and excesses if elected, making doubly difficult their later efforts to provide administrative leadership. Their reputations are not made or broken on the basis of their managerial performance, so other activities have priority in the constant competition for attention. Rarely does a president focus consistently and centrally on being chief administrator. His interest is instead partial and sporadic.

Institutionally, the presidency has become increasingly segmented, with administrative activities becoming more compartmentalized and specialized. Commentators choose different ways of describing the administrative aspect within the executive branch, while agreeing that it must coexist with other concerns. Writing in the 1920s, W. F. Willoughby contended that administration should be considered as a fourth branch or function of government, to be distinguished from the executive branch or function. The President in effect holds two offices, according to this view. He is both chief executive and "administrator-in-chief," but his role in the second capacity is due to delegation of power by the legislative branch, which has final authority as to how the administrative branch is organized and operated. The result is a fairly even division of responsibility for the actual conduct of administration between the legislative and executive branches (5). In the 1930s, the President's Committee on Administrative Management, which made recommendations to President Franklin D. Roosevelt, argued that the constitutional principle of separation of powers had contemplated that the executive power should include full responsibility for administration, but that this had been impaired by the creation of a multiplicity of independent agencies which formed a "headless" fourth branch of government. While recognizing existing limitations on the President's role as manager, the goal of this group was to restore the presidency to its rightful place as wielder of full executive power, including responsibility for effective management (6). A prominent contemporary analysis is by Henry J. Merry, who describes the executive-administrative composite as consisting of not one or two but rather three parts—a presidential part centered in the Executive Office of the President, a second part consisting of the rank and file civil service with continuity in office (sometimes referred to as the "permanent government"), and sandwiched in between a third layer with much less continuity made up of political appointees selected by and replaceable by either the President or a department head. The resulting reality, according to Merry, is five-branch rather than three-branch government, when the legislative and judicial branches are included to round out the existing system (7). The common theme in these and other comments is that the managerial role of the President is circumscribed and incomplete.

Managerial Agencies

Over the years, and particularly during the last half century, a group of agencies has been put in place to assist the President in various ways as head of the executive branch. Most of them are located in the Executive Office of the President (EOP), created in 1939. The EOP includes units concerned primarily with policy and public relations matters as well as with administrative management, and it does not contain all of the managerial agencies, so it should not be viewed simply or even primarily as the managerial arm of the President. Within it, for example, are the National Security Council (concerned with security policies), the Office of Policy Development (concerned with domestic policy options) and several units related to more specialized areas such as economic, environmental, trade, and science and technology policies.

The agencies most oriented toward giving advice and assistance to the President on administrative management are the White House Office and the Office of Management and Budget (OMB) within EOP, and the Office of Personnel Management (OPM) outside EOP. The White House Office includes the President's most intimate and trusted lieutenants, who operate in his behalf across the whole array of governmental affairs, from liaison with members of the national legislature to dealing with representatives of the news media. Among these functions in recent years has been channeling of communication between the President and agency heads, and restricting of direct access by them to the President, so that the White House Office has emerged as an intervening mechanism for presidential direction and control of departments and other executive agencies.

Aside from policy directives, the principal means for exerting authority over administrative agencies in any governmental system are through decisions as to organizational structure, budget, and personnel. In the United States, these are joint decisions of the President and the Congress. Presidential participation in the first two types of decisions is facilitated primarily through OMB, and in the last type primarily through OPM. Both of these managerial agencies had predecessors which antedate creation of EOP, and both have been revamped during recent years.

The Bureau of the Budget (BOB), created in 1921, had been given management improvement as well as budgetary responsibilities long before it was renamed Office of Management and Budget (OMB) in 1970 during the Nixon administration to emphasize this aspect of its work, which has dealt both with minor adjustments by executive action and major reorganizations requiring legislative authorization. Presidential reorganization initiatives have usually been mapped out by OMB before presentation to Congress, which has insisted on retaining control through legislation of the creation or abolition of executive departments, but was willing for several decades to allow the President to propose other major changes subject to review by Congress and potential disapproval within a specified period through use of a "legislative veto." In 1983, however, this device was declared invalid by the U.S. Supreme Court as a violation of the constitutional separation of powers between the legislative and executive branches. The effect is likely to be a lessening of presidential influence over structural adjustments affecting administrative management.

On budgetary matters, OMB acts as the President's instrument both for formulation and presentation of the executive budget annually to Congress, and for execution of budgetary decisions after the enactment of appropriation legislation. OMB is thus undoubtedly the most effective tool available to the President for obtaining information about and exercising supervisory controls over administrative agencies, within the discretionary boundaries set jointly by Congress and the President through the legislative process. Presidential efforts, mainly during the Nixon era, to claim a more expansive role by actions such as impoundment of appropriations funded at a level higher than recommended in the executive budget have been rejected in a series of court decisions.

Arrangements for personnel management in American public administration have gone through several historical shifts, as the size of the civil service has grown and as recruitment patterns have changed. Until about 1830, numbers were small and emphasis was on selection of "gentlemen" who were members of the social elite acceptable to the incumbent administration. Then followed a half century of the "spoils system" with civil service jobs parceled out on a patronage basis by chief executives and legis-lators who had been victorious in elections. A civil service reform movement gained impetus after the Civil War, leading eventually to passage of landmark legislation in 1883 which is still the basis for the "merit" approach to selection which replaced the "spoils" approach. The first effective central personnel management agency was established at the same time, in the form of a three-member Civil Service Commission designed to serve as "watchdog of the merit system." It was deliberately insulated from direct presidential control by having its members appointed by the President with Senate confirmation for staggered terms, with no more than two of the three members affiliated with a particular political party.

This arrangement continued until 1978, when the Commission was replaced by the Office of Personnel Management (OPM) headed by a single director responsible to the President. This change provided a presidential instrument for personnel management similar to OMB for organizational and budgetary management. At the same time, some responsibilities of the old Commission, concerned with protection of the rights of civil service employees, were transferred to a new Merit Systems Protection Board less subject to presidential control. Even with these modifications aimed to enhance the President's participation, personnel management continues to be a shared presidential-legislative responsibility, with additional precautions taken here against presidential encroachments beyond those applying to organizational and budgetary matters.

Executive Departments

The process of departmentalization shows remarkable uniformity in a wide variety of countries which differ in many other respects. The normal range in the number of central government ministries or departments is from twelve to twenty, with excep-tions both below and above this range in a few instances. The United States is among a large cluster of countries near the lower end of the range, with about a dozen such major units during recent decades. In 1986 there were thirteen of these "regular" executive departments, the oldest being the departments of State and of Treasury (created in 1789), and the newest the departments of Education and of Health and Human Services (established in 1980 by splitting a larger department in which these functions had been combined). Although the number fluctuates somewhat over time and there are several proposals for departmental additions or abolitions currently under consideration, such changes are relatively difficult under the American presidential system as compared to parliamentary systems such as the British, because passage of a legislative act is required rather than just cabinet action.

These executive departments administer most major governmental programs, and they have similar structural and operating characteristics. Each is headed by a single official (Secretary of State, Secretary of Defense, etc.) appointed by the President and confirmed by the Senate, but removable by the President. The department heads are the core members of the President's cabinet and they rank high in power and prestige. They do not, however, join with the President in constituting a collective executive, so the American cabinet is far different from the cabinet of prime minister and minis-terial colleagues in a parliamentary system. Despite repeated statements by incoming chief executives (including recently both Carter and Reagan) of an intent to rely more on the cabinet for decision-making, cabinet meetings are routinely more form than substance and no President has ever felt bound by a cabinet consensus with which he disagreed. The important relationships between department secretaries and the chief executive are directly with the President or one of his representatives in the White House Office regarding departmental affairs, and not through the cabinet with a focus on government-wide problems and issues.

Although they vary in size from behemoths such as the Department of Defense (with almost 900,000 civilian employees) to a pigmy such as the Department of Education (with slightly over 6,000 employees), the departments are similar in their internal structures. Usually a department has an undersecretary and several assistant secretaries who are in the middle layer already mentioned of political executives with relatively short tenure in office. An assistant secretary for administration or management and a departmental inspector general are now uniformly present also, and they are more likely to be drawn from the ranks of career civil servants. The terminology for program units within a department is not standardized, but the most common designations for successive levels from the top down are bureau, division, and section. The dividing line between political appointees and career civil servants is a wavy one, but beginning at the bureau chief level career officials are more likely than not to be in charge, even though not protected by any tenure claim on the office based on their civil service status.

A few other agencies are like these executive departments except in name. One of the most important and largest is the Veterans Administration, with more employees and higher budget outlays than several of the regular departments. Other examples are the Environmental Protection Agency and the National Aeronautics and Space Administration. There has been no consistent basis for choosing the departmental or some other designation for these agencies, all of which function almost identically in the overall administrative system. Some of the existing departments earlier had non-departmental status, and the fledgling Department of Education faces possible redesignation, as was proposed but not pressed vigorously by President Reagan soon after he took office.

Regulatory Commissions and Government Corporations

These two categories are alike in falling outside the departmental pattern of relationships with the President and Congress, but they differ in how they do relate and why they have been given special treatment.

Beginning in 1887 with creation of the Interstate Commerce Commission, the administrative establishment by now includes a cluster of about a dozen agencies commonly referred to as "independent" regulatory commissions. Their independence is from presidential direction to the extent recognized as proper over regular executive departments and similar agencies, and the rationale is that this is required to prevent political interference in their regulatory control over segments of private sector activity of crucial concern to the general public. The regulatory fields parceled out to these specialized agencies include surface transportation, civil air transport, maritime commerce, operation of securities and financial markets, labor-management relations, transportation and sale of energy sources, and curbing of unfair methods of business competition. In their respective jurisdictions, these regulatory commissions engage in rule-making and administrative adjudication as well as policy implementation, and are thus viewed as wielding "quasi-legislative" and "quasi-judicial" powers. They are in essence "miniature governments" for limited areas of operation.

The standard devices for providing independence are to make these agencies multi-headed rather than single-headed (five to nine is the range in board size), to have members appointed on a bipartisan basis by the President and confirmed by the Senate for terms which overlap and are five years or longer, and to restrict the President's power to remove them to such grounds as "inefficiency, neglect of duty, or malfeasance in office" rather than just disagreement on policy or specific decisions.

The status of these regulatory bodies has long been the subject of debate and many recommendations for change have been proposed. Critics have not only termed them a "headless" fourth branch of government, but have claimed that often they are "captured" by the interests which are supposed to be regulated, and also have pointed out the inconsistency of having some major regulatory functions (such as setting of standards for foods and drugs) lodged within regular executive departments. However, only minor modifications have been made (such as having the President designate the chairperson for most commissions and authorizing that member to supervise the staff of the agency), and no major reforms appear likely. These independent regulatory commissions will continue to be widely regarded as "arms of the Congress" rather than integral parts of the executive branch and will operate outside the usual orbit of presidential controls.

Government corporations have been set up in many countries during recent years for the conduct of a wide variety of "business-type" operations under government auspices. The United States is no exception to this trend, having now established at the national level a plethora of government corporations for diverse purposes. A sampling includes the U.S. Postal Service (formerly organized as an executive department and second only to the Department of Defense among all agencies in number of employees), Amtrak (providing national rail passenger service), the Tennessee Valley Authority (a regional development agency), the Corporation for Public Broadcasting, and numerous corporations engaged in insurance or lending activities. As a group, they enjoy advantages from the corporate form of organization such as being able to acquire or dispose of property and to sue or be sued in their own names. Generally they are headed by a board of directors, but there is no standard pattern for placing them within the executive branch, some being separate units and others being located within an executive department or some other canopy agency. Government corporations tend by their statutory powers and by the nature of their activities to be relatively free from detailed supervision by hierarchical superiors up to and including the President, but this presents less of a challenge to the managerial role of the chief executive than is the case with the independent regulatory commissions, and therefore has not been the subject of as much controversy.

AMERICAN PUBLIC SERVICE PERSONNEL

Criteria for Selection and Advancement

As already indicated, the basis for choosing civil servants in the United States has not remained constant, with the main transition occurring a century ago when the "spoils" system began to give way gradually to the "merit" system. This has meant the substitution of some form of assessment of qualifications to perform assigned duties for the earlier criterion of service to a political party as the primary basis for civil service appointments.

One attitude has persisted throughout, however, and it constitutes the most significant difference between the American and the European approaches to staffing the public service. In western Europe, beginning with the absolutist monarchies of the seventeenth and eighteenth centuries in Prussia and France and continuing in the nation-states of the last two centuries, the emphasis has been on "career" staffing in some form, with individuals customarily entering the service at an early age and remaining throughout their careers until retirement. In the United States, on the other hand, the orientation has been toward shorter-term or "program" staffing. President Andrew Jackson, who best articulated the rationale for a patronage based civil service, justified it on two grounds—that it contributed to the viability of political parties, and that rotation in office could protect against abuses by long-term office holders without adversely affecting performance of duties. The post-Civil War reform movement, although stimulated by the British civil service reforms of the 1850s, differed from them by favoring competitive entrance examinations which would be "practical in character" and related to duties to be performed, rather than designed to select at an early age candidates with promise for distinguished careers in a variety of assignments.

Over the years, this American hesitation about career staffing has persisted, but recent decades have brought renewed debate as to the relative advantages of the two approaches, and limited experimentation has occurred with "career" rather than "program" selection and advancement devices. For example, since the late 1930s successive versions of entrance civil service examinations have been offered for recent university graduates, intended not only for recruitment to entry-level jobs but also for identification of candidates with the most promise for long-range performance in increasingly responsible assignments. Creation of the Senior Executive Service (SES) in 1978, after long consideration, is another illustration. The SES consists of several thousand high-level civil servants with established records of exceptional performance who form an elite corps available for assignment to a variety of administrative posts near the apex of the executive branch. They are selected on the basis of demonstrated competence during their careers rather than their suitability for particular positions. These are significant departures from the short-term or "program" staffing tradition, but they should be viewed as efforts to modify rather than abandon it.

This ambiguity or indecisiveness reflects, according to a perceptive analysis by Herbert Kaufman, a competition among three values all of which have impacted on American personnel selection and advancement practices. These are (1) the quest for strong executive leadership, (2) the desire for a public service that is competent and politically neutral, and (3) the belief in representativeness in governmental institutions (8). The relative priority given to these values has shifted from time to time, with consequent effects on public personnel practices. A drive for stronger executive leadership and for representation from a wider spectrum of society helped explain acceptance of the spoils system during the Jacksonian period. Neutrality and competence were goals sought by advocates of the merit system. More recently, evidence that a competitive civil service had resulted in inadequate representation of women and ethnic minorities in the population led to attacks on "meritocracy" and adoption of "affirmative action" programs to achieve a more representative public service. Similarly, efforts by chief executives to assure a more responsive higher civil service have been directed toward expansion of the middle layer of political appointees at the expense of civil servants recruited by competitive examination. Thus, the interplay of these three deeply held values has had and will continue to have repercussions in public personnel management.

Relating People to Work

All large-scale civil service systems must provide methods for relating people to the work they do and for indicating status in the system. With civilian public employment now totaling about 2.8 million in the central government alone (plus about 13 million in state and local governments), this is obviously a major problem in the United States, and it has been dealt with in a variety of ways. Elsewhere, both historically and currently, by far the most popular approach has been to use "rank" as the basis for determining appropriate work assignments and relative status within the civil service system. The rank held by an individual is crucial rather than the specific duties presently being performed. This has been the choice in most European countries and in their former colonies following independence.

In the United States, on the other hand, the dominant factor has become the position currently held by the individual civil servant, described in terms of its duties and responsibilities. This "position" approach to status was pioneered in the American civil service in the decades following adoption of the merit system. Its purpose was to produce more equity in treatment of employees, particularly with regard to compensation, by striving for "equal pay for equal work." This has led to the evolution of a complex position classification format in the central government civil service which has been widely copied at state and local levels. The focus is on the systematic analysis of particular positions in terms of their duties and responsibilities, with positions which are sufficiently similar then being placed in classes of positions which can be treated alike for purposes of personnel administration. These classes of positions are arrayed in a grid which relates them to one another both horizontally and vertically. The term "grade" is used for the horizontal dimension, referring to classes of positions involving various kinds of work which are at essentially the same level as to difficulty, responsibility, and required qualifications. Vertically, classes of positions are arranged in occupational "series" involving similar kinds of work but at different levels of difficulty. Currently there are eighteen grades in the central civil service system, and over 400 occupational groupings in series which include classes of positions in more than one grade.

This position classification framework offers a basis for compensation equity by having the same range of pay for all classes of positions in a given grade, and it provides ladders of promotion within occupational series from lower to higher positions, even though initial recruitment is normally for a position in a particular class rather than for a lifetime career. It also has disadvantages, however, among them susceptibility to manipulations which distort actual vertical and horizontal relationships, a tendency for classification changes to lag behind changes which have in fact occurred in the assignment of duties and responsibilities to positions, and a somewhat unrealistic assumption that positions can be analyzed abstractly without regard to the personal qualities of different incumbents.

The American public service viewed as a whole utilizes both the "position" and "rank" approaches, partly because in some segments status by rank has never been replaced by installation of position classification, and partly because of recent reforms intended to alleviate some of the operational shortcomings of position classification.

Examples of retention of traditional rank systems are the military services within the Department of Defense and the foreign service within the Department of State. More recently created rank services are the Federal Bureau of Investigation (FBI) within the Department of Justice and the U.S. Public Health Service within the Department of Health and Human Services. A major objective in the establishment of the Senior Executive Service (SES) in 1978 was to replace a large portion of the top three grades based on position classification with an elite corps of high level administrators whose status would be based on rank rather than position held, who would be obligated to move from one assignment to another in response to governmental needs, who would be compensated according to individual performance, and who could be demoted or dismissed if they did not measure up to SES standards. Thus there is considerable variation and experimentation in the American public service as to how individuals are linked to their duties and identified as to their status, despite the prevalence of the "position" approach.

Rights and Restrictions

As compared to their counterparts in many other civil service systems, American civil servants have relatively fewer rights and are subject to relatively more restrictions. This situation is partially due to the absence in the United States of an inherited historical tradition that public officials represent and are closely identified with the monarchy (as in Great Britain or Japan) or the state (as in post-revolutionary France).

Civil servants share with other citizens, of course, such basic constitutional rights as freedom of speech and freedom of religion. Guarantees as to civil service tenure following a probationary period are substantial, but for the central civil service these are not directly protected constitutionally but rest primarily on a statutory base which can be changed by combined legislative and executive action. In earlier years courts tended to view government employment as a privilege rather than a right and have generally declined to intrude on the relationship of government as employer with its employees, but during the last three decades the privilege doctrine has been largely abandoned and replaced by a "substantial interest" doctrine. This recognizes what are still somewhat ill-defined property and liberty rights of individuals to continue as public employees which cannot be abridged without due process procedures protected by the Fourteenth Amendment of the U.S. Constitution (9).

Aside from this shift in constitutional interpretation, the most notable expansion of employee rights has come since the early 1960s with regard to unionization and collective bargaining. For many years national legislation guaranteed that employees in the private sector could organize and join labor unions which could then engage in collective bargaining with and resort to strikes against employers, while the same opportunities were being withheld from public employees in dealing with the government as employer. This policy differential was justified on the basis that government is different, with special emphasis on denial of the strike in public employment. Although employees of the central government have been free since 1912 to join unions which did not assert a right to strike, it was not until a half century later that steps were taken which have now to a limited extent recognized a collective bargaining process in public sector labor-management relations. This has been accomplished both through presidential executive orders and legislation such as the Civil Service Reform Act of 1978. The chief limitations are that the scope of negotiable issues in bargaining is limited to exclude many issues as to pay, fringe benefits, promotions and job security which are negotiable in the private sector, and that a legal right to strike continues to be denied. As a result of these policy changes, there was a dramatic rise in public service unionization, which peaked in the late 1970s and then declined slightly in the early 1980s. Estimates are that unions now represent about 60 percent of central government employees outside the Postal Service (which is highly unionized) but that only about a third of the represented employees actually belong to unions, since membership is not required even if a union is recognized as bargaining agent.

In the American public service, the most significant restrictions on civil servants have to do with their political activities. In many countries even high-ranking civil servants are relatively free to engage in political activities while on duty and can shift to active political life while retaining an option to return later to their service careers, whereas in the United States public policy has been to impose substantial limitations on the exercise of political rights as a condition of public employment. Linked to the objective of ensuring the political neutrality of employees following adoption of the merit system, rules were adopted by the Civil Service Commission in 1907 which assured the right to vote and express political opinions but banned partisan political activity and prohibited active participation in political management or political campaigns. In 1939 Congress adopted legislation (usually referred to as the Hatch Act after its chief sponsor) which continued these restrictions and extended them more generally to officers and employees in the executive branch. The constitutionality of such legislation at both national and state levels has been upheld by the courts, but there was a strong movement during the 1970s for revision of the Hatch Act to expand the political rights of public employees. This reached the stage of a bill being passed by both houses of Congress before it was vetoed by President Gerald Ford. The issue now seems to be quiescent, with no change in the offing which would lessen these restrictions on political activity.

Status and Prestige of the Public Service

Belonging to the American public service does not bring with it the status and prestige often accorded to civil servants in other countries. This is accounted for by a number of characteristics of the environment in which the civil service operates. Historically, private enterprise has had a higher value placed on it than governmental activity, bringing more recognition to private-sector managers in terms of social status and material rewards. American citizens tend to look upon the public bureaucracy with suspicion and distrust, so that they are more intent on trying to make the civil service responsive and subservient than in building up bureaucratic self-esteem. The absence of a career system and the prevalence of movement in and out of the civil service have inhibited the emergence of a cohesive cadre of high-ranking bureaucrats comparable to the administrative class in Great Britain or members of the *grands corps* in France. Advancement within the civil service has commonly been on the basis of competence in a particular professional or technical specialty rather than generalized administrative capability, restricting the range of activity for individual bureaucrats.

The existence of these and other factors producing relatively low status and prestige does not mean that the American public service is unimportant or unappreciated, or that higher civil servants are excluded from the ranks of the elite in American society. What is significant is that the social role of the public service as a whole is less prominent than in many other systems, and that the elite characteristics of the higher civil service are unusual as compared with those elsewhere. The American higher public service is described by James W. Fesler as a "representative, fragmented, open elite" (10). As a consequence of the environment in which it has evolved, the public service in the United States does not enjoy markedly high status or prestige (11), but this seems to be counterbalanced by a closer identification of civil servants with the citizenry as a whole and by a more effective capability for public control over the public service.

BUREAUCRATS AS POLICY-MAKERS

Politics vs. Administration: A Fluctuating Dichotomy

The dividing line between politics or policy-making and administration or policy implementation is a matter of continuing controversy in the United States as it is elsewhere. The result is widespread disagreement as to the proper role of bureaucrats in the formulation of public policy. Despite the prevalence of bureaucratic elite political regimes among contemporary nation-states, there are few defenders of the proposition that bureaucratic officials, either civil or military, should be the principal policy-makers, unresponsive to non-bureaucratic political leadership. On the other hand, almost no observers of the political scene argue that bureaucrats should be or are entirely uninvolved in policy-making or insulated from political processes. This much consensus, excluding the extremes of monopolization and non-participation, still leaves a wide range of possibilities as to the appropriate policy role of the bureaucracy and as to the extent that particular national bureaucracies actually do function as policy-makers. Recent studies focused on European democracies have marshaled considerable evidence that higher-ranking bureaucrats have indeed attained sufficient status as policy-makers to be dubbed "the Western mandarins," but that they nevertheless continue to be subject to effective policy control by extra-bureaucratic political institutions (12).

The United States mirrors the European experience both as to theoretical arguments in the past and current actualities. The relationship between "politics" and "administration" has been a recurring topic ever since public administration became a field of academic interest in the 1880s, with pendulum-like swings over time in the dominant point of view. Woodrow Wilson, Frank Goodnow, and other pioneers emphasized the distinction, wrote in terms of "politics vs. administration," and tended to downplay the role of civil servants in policy-making. These views were in accord with the values of "merit" and "neutrality" in the civil service stressed by the "progressive" movement during the late nineteenth and early twentieth centuries. The period of "scientific management" in both the private and public sectors, which peaked in the 1930s, stressing enhancement of economy and efficiency in management, continued to accept the relationship between politics and administration as one that is dichotomous rather than interlinking.

The years following World War II produced a sharp reversal, reflecting several differing lines of thought which converged in challenging the separation between politics and administration, and concurred in approval of a major role by bureaucrats in policy-making. These forces included skeptics such as Herbert Simon and Dwight Waldo as to the validity of scientific management "principles," analysts such as Paul Appleby who viewed governmental processes as much more complex than a simple division between the making and execution of public policy, and spokesmen for the "new" public administration such as George Frederickson who advocated more activism by administrators of public programs to achieve greater "social equity." Complete abandonment of the politics-administration distinction seemed imminent.

Counter considerations have more recently prevented this from happening. These include renewed recognition that the policy-making role of elected officials and political appointees in a representative democracy is different from that of civil servants, that policy-making by civil servants is appropriate but must be within the boundaries set by politicians, and that opportunities for bureaucratic policy-making diminish by level from higher to middle to lower echelons in the civil service. The current result is retention of the politics-administration differentiation with continuing ambivalence as to exactly what it means. As Dwight Waldo says, "In essence, we can neither live with or without the distinction, realistically separate the two nor find an agreed, proper joining" (13).

Political and Career Officials: An Ambiguous Relationship

In democratic systems, whether parliamentary or presidential, the elected executives must be able to select and place strategically in the upper ranges of administration a sufficient number of political appointees for them to exercise effective policy controls over career bureaucrats. This intermediary layer varies in number and location from one country to another. The American presidential system, as compared with parliamentary systems, has an unusually large number of political appointees distributed over a wide range of higher administrative offices, with indistinct lines between them and career civil servants.

Estimates vary as to the total number of higher positions in the American executive branch, but a conservative number given by James W. Fesler is about 9,000, with 1,500 of them being political and 7,500 non-political (14). This is in sharp contrast to Great Britain, where there are about 4,000 high-level civil servants and no more than one hundred political appointments to be made with a change in party control. In the mixed parliamentary-presidential system of the French Fifth Republic, the comparable figures are more difficult to ascertain, but Fesler has estimated that the maximum number of positions which can be filled by political appointment is below 400, and that there are between 1,500 and 5,000 high level civil servants. These data yield a ratio of political appointees to top civil servants of 1:3.2 for the United States, approximately 1:9 for France, and only 1:40 for Great Britain (15). The spread in these ratios is somewhat misleading, however, because in both France and the United States individuals chosen for political appointment are frequently drawn from the ranks of the higher civil service, whereas this normally does not occur in Great Britain. For example, in France more than one third of the ministers in some recent governments have been civil servants, and civil servants comprise 90 per cent of the members of the small ministerial cabinets which provide advisory and supporting services in each ministry.

In the United States, not only is selection for political positions made from both non-career and career sources, but there is also no clear delineation by function between the political and non-political positions. The result is a confusing comingling of these two categories both as to the backgrounds of the individuals involved and the kinds of activity being carried on. Nevertheless, some general statements can be made as to how these two groupings of officials differ and as to the ambiguous relationship between them.

Political appointees tend to come from more diverse sources, stay in government for much shorter periods of time, and have less previous programmatic or operational familiarity with their areas of responsibility. Drawn primarily from business, law and university posts and to a more limited extent from civil service positions, they are picked mainly because they are viewed as concurring with and committed to carrying out the policy preferences of the current administration. They are unlikely to have prior direct knowledge of the specifics of agency programs or the problems of administering them. Their average tenure (about two years) is so short, and the rate of turnover among them is so high that these political executives as a group have been characterized as participants in "a government of strangers" (16).

Over four times more numerous, the high-ranking officials with civil service status nevertheless have somewhat more homogeneity in background and experience, have made a more substantial career commitment to government service, and are much more likely to have professional training for the programs administered by the agencies to which they are assigned. Most of these officials are now members of the Senior Executive Service (SES), but some are occupants of specialized technical and professional positions without managerial and supervisory responsibilities in "supergrades" 16-18 of the basic classification system, or are members of several small groups authorized outside the regular competitive service. Studies made in the 1970s indicated that on the average such officials had been in the service for more than twenty years, had entered the higher categories in their mid-forties, and were currently in their early fifties. Over 90 percent were college graduates and nearly two-thirds had advanced degrees. Their educational specializations had been heavily in engineering and the physical and biological sciences, followed by the social sciences, public and business administration, and the humanities. They had entered the service at various ages and working levels, with only slightly more than one-third coming in at the beginning level for recent college graduates, almost a third entering at middle grade levels, and a tenth starting directly at "supergrade" levels. Typically, they had "single-agency" careers, with almost half remaining in the same agency from the time they reached middle-grade levels (17). Longer experience with the SES may bring changes, but the pattern in the past has been for these career civil servants to be highly educated in professional specialities, to have made a substantial commitment to civil service employment (although at varying stages in their careers), and to have followed paths of career advancement which are oriented to an agency or specialization.

These differences in background, outlook, and length of governmental experience, combined with vagueness as to their respective areas of responsibility, have resulted in considerable friction and competition between the political and careerist groupings, despite some shared characteristics such as advanced education and professionalism and the relative ease of movement by individuals from one category into the other. Even though attention is being given to ways of achieving smoother cooperation (18), the situation appears to be deteriorating and may be creating a "government of enemies" (19). Clearly relationships between these groups will continue to be a problem.

Participation in Policy-Making by Higher Administrators

In the United States as in other countries, only the administrative officials in a thin layer of about one-half of one percent at the top of the public service have opportunities which provide them with a demonstrably significant policy-making role. Higher American administrators appear to be as much engaged in policy-making as are their counterparts in other developed bureaucracies, but the way in which they participate is different in some notable respects.

Administrative officials who are political appointees belong to a group obviously expected to be engaged in policy-making. Although their number is relatively large and has increased in recent years partly as a means of enhancing presidential control over policy, the results are mixed. As Fesler points out, partisanship as a cohesive force has been replaced by "the politics of policy," which for some political appointees means a commitment to support presidential policies, but for many means "tenacious devotion to particular program areas and particular policies, whether or not they comport with the president's strategic emphases" (20). As a consequence, Fesler concludes that resistance is as likely among political executives as among career executives when there is a course change in presidential policy.

American career officials, when viewed comparatively as policy-makers alongside higher civil servants in most parliamentary systems, tend to be more exposed to public view, more restricted as to the range of their participation, less subject to effective control by their hierarchical superiors, less protected from retribution for linkage with their policy preferences, and freer to move out of the civil service into a more active political role but also less likely to return later to career status.

Some of these features are due to factors which have already been mentioned, but a key explanation is the triangular alliance which is common in mustering support for specific governmental programs. The participants in such a triangle are powerful legislators in one corner, representatives of private interest groups in another, and officials (both political appointees and careerists) from the administrative agency concerned in the third. These "iron triangles" of influentials with shared public policy objectives have been effective in authorizing and then maintaining or expanding governmental programs in various fields. One side effect is that administrative participants become beneficiaries of a political network which is located mainly outside of the executive branch, thus weakening hierarchical restraints and providing opportunities to be publicly identified as policy advocates. In the absence of a practice of anonymity along British lines, the individual administrator moves into public view and either gains or loses, depending on the reactions to his policy position.

In favorable circumstances, opportunities are thus presented for political appointees or career bureaucrats to become prominently identified with a popular program and to wield extraordinary power over policy. Such examples of "public entrepreneurship" have become the object of both public interest and scholarly analysis (21). Two prominent "public entrepreneurs" at the national level have been J. Edgar Hoover, a civilian careerist who was director of the Federal Bureau of Investigation (FBI) in the Department of Justice, and Admiral Hyman G. Rickover, a military careerist who spearheaded the development of nuclear technology in the United States Navy. For decades, each of these men had sufficient legislative and popular support to be virtually immune from direction or interference by incumbent department heads or presidents.

As even these unusual cases illustrate, American higher administrators, however active they may become in policy-making, are restricted rather narrowly as to the range of their participation, and cannot easily shift from one programmatic field to another. They are not generalists of the "mandarin" type found in many European countries with different approaches to recruiting, promoting and assigning higher civil servants. The overall contrast is best summarized by Wallace Sayre, who comments that the American choices have produced "a more internally competitive, a more experimental, a noisier and less coherent, a less powerful bureaucracy within its own governmental system, but a more dynamic one" (22).

ACCOUNTABILITY IN AMERICAN ADMINISTRATION

Multiplicity and Diffuseness as Control Characteristics

The characteristics of arrangements for accountability in American public administration can be summarized by saying that in comparison with many other countries controls over administration in the United States are exerted through an unusually large number of channels with notably diffuse consequences, making evaluation of the overall effectiveness of these arrangements difficult.

This situation reflects both the absence of consensus as to a theory of accountability and the existence of competition for control opportunities among different segments of the American political system.

The tension between bureaucratic and democratic values in American society has led to disagreement as to an appropriate theory of administrative accountability. Bureaucracy requires Weberian characteristics such as hierarchy, specialization, work differentiation, continuity in office, and selection by appointment based on qualifications. Democracy emphasizes qualities such as equality, pluralism, openness of access, rotation in office, and selection by popular election. Widespread acceptance of the necessity for coexistence in modern government of these divergent values and their organizational manifestations has brought with it uncertainties and shifting responses as to how public bureaucracy can be subjected to adequate external democratic controls without impairing administrative performance in carrying out democratically adopted governmental programs.

Because there are differences of opinion as to the proper balance which should be sought, the existing situation leads to a range of judgments as to the adequacy of current accountability arrangements. For example, David Nachmias and David H. Rosenbloom conclude rather pessimistically that "control of public bureaucracies by elective and appointive political authorities is highly problematic," and that "traditional notions about accountability and responsibility to political authorities are largely inappropriate in the modern bureaucratized state" (23). Lewis C. Mainzer makes this more optimistic assessment: "The bureaucracy will be a major participant in our governing process, both in formulating and carrying out policy. But this will be done under controls. The bureaucrats will have no monopoly of power and will not make the major choices of direction for our society" (24). In my own judgment, the United States is among the more successful developed democracies in reconciling the unavoidable tension between bureaucratic competence and political responsibility.

Major Agencies of Accountability

There is less disagreement in cataloguing components of the existing machinery for accountability. The multiple and competing sources of significant controls over public administration can be classified as follows: executive, legislative, judicial, clientele, and electoral. Each of these sources of accountability has a claim for control responsibilities based in part on one or more of the three basic features of the American political system—constitutionalism, federalism, and presidentialism. Each has demonstrated in practice a capability to influence administrative conduct.

The constitutional basis, range and limits of the powers over administration of the elected chief executive and his appointed political associates have already been examined. Accountability through executive hierarchical channels is pervasive and important in the American presidential system, but does not have the sweep and authoritativeness of accountability to the prime minister and cabinet in a parliamentary system. Although it must be ranked as overall most significant, executive supervision over administration is partial and shared.

The legislative branch is the next most potent source of control, because of its constitutional grants of power, which include direct participation in a variety of administrative matters. Congress through legislation must authorize governmental programs, determine the organizational arrangements for implementation, and decide on the amounts and methods for funding. It has wide-ranging investigative and audit powers to insure that administrative performance conforms to legislative intent. Congress has the weapons at its disposal to be the ultimate winner in a prolonged conflict with the chief executive as to the conduct of administration.

Congressional oversight functions have in practice shown serious shortcomings. The quality of administrative operations does not rank high on the priority scale of most legislators, and hence does not receive sustained attention. Administrative oversight is carried out mainly through the mechanism of legislative committees with limited jurisdictions and with members who are likely to be proponents and defenders of the programs under review. As a result, influential legislators are usually inclined to support expansion rather than curtailment or better operation of programs, and often become involved in details of administrative decision-making which should be left to agency officials.

The American judiciary is the most rapidly expanding source of external controls over administration. As in Great Britain, this function resides in the regular court system, rather than in a separate set of administrative courts as is common in continental European nations. The judicial role is enhanced by the well established doctrine that courts in the United States have ultimate authority for constitutional interpretation, and by a more activist stance in recent decades toward intervention in matters which have been dealt with by administrative action.

This expanded role of the courts is too complex for analysis here, but some of its consequences, both advantageous and disadvantageous, can be mentioned. On the positive side, judicial activism can put a stop to administrative abuse of discretion, mandate administrative action when it has been illegally avoided, and protect the rights of underprivileged groups without other means of redress. Negative aspects are that courts are limited to issues raised in particular cases, that litigation is expensive and time consuming, that judges are often ill-equipped by training and experience to decide exactly what should be done when acts taken by administrators have been invalidated, and that judicial intervention often impinges on the representative role of legislators and the application of expertise by administrators. Undoubtedly, courts have emerged recently as more important instrumentalities for administrative accountability than in the past.

Clientele controls over administration are facilitated by the existence of highly organized and well financed interest groups in American society, and by their participation in the "iron triangles" already described for program advocacy in a variety of fields. Agency administrators are likely to be sympathetic rather than antagonistic to spokesmen for their constituencies, but if they are not so disposed they can be subjected to intense pressure by clientele representatives and their legislative allies. As a result, the general impact of clientele forces is toward expansion rather than contraction of governmental programs except in regulatory agencies, and these forces often counteract efforts of higher officials in the executive branch to reduce or reform administrative activity.

The electoral factor in administrative accountability refers to the consequences (usually indirect rather than direct) on the behavior of public administrators of choices made by the electorate at the polls. As a general rule, voters certainly have other things than administrative performance primarily in mind when they choose among candidates for elective office, but bureaucracy and bureaucrats have become favorite targets for successful candidates for the presidency and the legislature from both major parties, with the result that administrative officials are increasingly conscious of being subject to public scrutiny, and are more aware of the possible impact on what they do and how they do it of election victories and defeats.

Public Administration and the Public

No brief unqualified statement is possible as to how the American public relates to American public administrators. The key attribute seems to be ambivalence rather than consistency. If not a "love-hate" relationship, the connection between the general public and the public bureaucracy must at a minimum be viewed as a "dependency-resentment" relationship. It is the product of historical and cultural factors which have fostered distrust of rather than respect for public officials, combined with recognition of the inevitability of vastly expanded governmental programs and appreciation of the quality of services rendered. As a consequence, when the American people express their views about public administration, they "speak in two voices," as Fesler explains (25):

> At the general level they are dissatisfied with the government, with the bureaucracy, and with broad policy directions. At the specific level they express satisfaction with the elected officials they know best, with the bureaucrats they encounter, and with the specific programs in a policy area.

Opinion surveys substantiate this discontinuity in how respondents react to questions on both public policy and public administration issues. They tend to disapprove of government sponsored welfare programs in general, but to approve of specific programs such as food stamps, aid to dependent children, or health care for the poor. They report that citizen encounters with bureaucrats are generally unsatisfactory, but that their own treatment in such encounters has been fair and has resulted in getting problems taken care of. "In other words, most Americans do not let their experience affect their stereotypes; it is apparently much easier to decide that their experiences represent an exception to the rule" (26).

What this seems to mean is that Americans are not really apprehensive about or dissatisfied with public administration and public administrators, but they don't want to admit it. Bureaucratic usurpation or unresponsiveness is less a reality than a complaint voiced to help remind administrators that they are public servants rather than officials of an omnipotent state.

This earlier assessment continues to convey my opinion as to how the American system of public administration relates to the general political system and to the American public after two centuries of nationhood (27):

> The civil service has gradually become more competent in its composition and more professional in its outlook, in response to the demands placed upon government for performance, but the service orientation remains and responsiveness to the political organs of government is universally accepted in theory and largely recognized in practice. The bureaucracy enjoys the benefit of a widespread although somewhat skeptical acceptance of the job it is doing, but it must be prepared to fit into its proper niche in the political system.

REFERENCES

1. Seymour Martin Lipset, *The First New Nation: The United States in Historical and Comparative Perspective* (New York: Basic Books, 1963).
2. Carl B. Swisher, *American Constitutional Development* (Boston: Houghton Mifflin Co., 1943), Chap. 1; Lynton K. Caldwell, "Novus Ordo Seclorum: The Heritage of American Public Administration," *Public Administration Review* 36 (September/October 1976), 476–88; James W. Fesler, ed., *American Public Administration: Patterns of the Past* (Washington, D.C.: The American Society for Public Administration, 1982), 1–27.
3. Myers v. United States, 272 U.S. 52 (1926).
4. For a recent overview, see Deil S. Wright and Harvey L. White, eds., *Federalism and Intergovernmental Relations* (Washington, D.C.: The American Society for Public Administration, 1984).
5. *Principles of Public Administration* (Baltimore, Md.: The Johns Hopkins Press, 1927).
6. *Administrative Management in the Government of the United States* (Washington, D.C.: U.S. Government Printing Office, 1937).
7. *Five-Branch Government: The Full Measure of Constitutional Checks and Balances* (Urbana, Ill.: University of Illinois, 1980).
8. "Administrative Decentralization and Political Power," *Public Administration Review* 29 (January/February, 1969), 3–15.
9. For an excellent up-to-date survey and analysis, refer to Steven W. Hays and T. Zane Reeves, *Personnel Management in the Public Sector* (Boston: Allyn and Bacon, Inc., 1984), 477–82.
10. *Public Administration: Theory and Practice* (Englewood Cliffs, N.J.: Prentice-Hall, Inc., 1980), 126.
11. The most comprehensive study is Franklin P. Kilpatrick, Milton C. Cummings, Jr., and M. Kent Jennings, *The Image of the Federal Service* (Washington, D.C.: The Brookings Institution, 1964). O. Glenn Stahl believes that a similar current survey would show "at least the same degree of low prestige." *Public Personnel Administration*, 8th ed. (New York: Harper & Row, 1983), 22.

12. Refer to Mattei Dogan, ed., *The Mandarins of Western Europe* (New York: John Wiley & Sons, 1975), and Joel D. Aberbach, Robert D. Putnam, and Bert A. Rockman, *Bureaucrats and Politicians in Western Democracies* (Cambridge, Mass.: Harvard University Press, 1981).

13. *The Administrative State*, 2nd ed. (New York: Holmes & Meier Publishers, 1984), Introduction, lv.

14. "Politics, Policy, and Bureaucracy at the Top," *Annals of the American Academy of Political and Social Science* 466 (March 1983), 23–41.

15. *Public Administration: Theory and Practice*, 134.

16. Hugh Heclo, *A Government of Strangers: Executive Politics in Washington* (Washington, D.C.: The Brookings Institution, 1977).

17. These and other characteristics are discussed in more detail by Fesler in *Public Administration: Theory and Practice*, 126–33 and 145–51. The principal sources, in addition to Heclo's *A Government of Strangers*, are U.S. Civil Service Commission (Bureau of Executive Manpower), *Executive Manpower in the Federal Service* (Washington, D.C.: U.S. Government Printing Office, 1972), and U.S. Civil Service Commission (Bureau of Executive Personnel), *Executive Personnel in the Federal Service* (Washington, D.C.: U.S. Government Printing Office, 1978).

18. See, for example, this study sponsored by the National Academy of Public Administration: John W. Macy, Bruce Adams, and J. Jackson Walter, eds., *America's Unelected Government: Appointing the President's Team* (Cambridge, Mass.: Ballinger Publishing Company, 1983).

19. Hugh Heclo, "A Government of Enemies?," *The Bureaucrat* 13 (Fall 1984), 12–14.

20. "Politics, Policy, and Bureaucracy at the Top," 32.

21. Eugene Lewis, *Public Entrepreneurship: Toward a Theory of Bureaucratic Political Power* (Bloomington, Ind.: Indiana University Press, 1980).

22. "Bureaucracies: Some Contrasts in Systems," *Indian Journal of Public Administration* 10, No. 2 (1964), 219–29, at p. 223.

23. *Bureaucratic Government USA* (New York: St. Martin's Press, 1980), 31.

24. *Political Bureaucracy* (Glenview, Ill.: Scott, Foresman and Company, 1973), 120.

25. *Public Administration: Theory and Practice*, 355.

26. Robert L. Kahn and others, "Americans Love Their Bureaucrats," *Psychology Today* 9 (June 1975), 71.

27. *Public Administration: A Comparative Perspective*, 3rd ed., rev. (New York: Marcel Dekker, Inc., 1984), 221.

24
Problems of Cross-National Comparison

JOEL D. ABERBACH
University of California, Los Angeles, California, and The University of Michigan, Ann Arbor, Michigan

BERT A. ROCKMAN
University of Pittsburgh, Pittsburgh, Pennsylvania

The central method of the social sciences is comparison. The more complex the elements of comparison, however, the more profound the challenges to attaining conceptual consistency in analysis. Cross-national comparison of the complex organized systems that we call public administration presents us with one of these formidable challenges. Comparison in this regard is formidable because (1) public administration is complex organization, and complex organization, by definition, resists singular or simple characterization, and (2) the political environments in which public administrative systems exist are also complex and polymorphic.

Thus, the main focus of this chapter is to explore some of the central methodological and conceptual ambiguities relating to the comparative analysis of public administration and administrative systems, particularly those relevant to the relationship between national bureaucracies, policy-making, and the political environment of public administration. Although the issues we point to are ones that we believe have universal relevance, our principal empirical referents are the administrative systems of the Western (advanced capitalist) states.

In dealing with these problems of comparative analysis, we recognize that we are apt to provoke more questions than provide resolutions—a clear sign in social science that we stand in the middle of a muddle.

THREE METHODOLOGICAL AMBIGUITIES

1. The Parts vs. the Whole

A former American civil servant and present professor of public administration once observed that the only thing U.S. civil servants have in common is the source from which they draw their salary checks (1). While this was intended to be a significant

---

This chapter is a slightly revised and reduced version of a paper by the authors, "Comparative Administration: Methods, Muddles, and Models," in *Administration and Society* (Vol. 19, February 1987), and is published here with permission of the journal.

statement about the American federal executive, it is at least equally a statement about the problem of assessing any "system" of public administration. Looked at closely enough, most system level generalizations begin to vaporize. Students of complex organizations especially have struggled with the notion that complexity itself produces large variations within organizations of norms, skills, perspectives and priorities (2). What is true for a single department, agency, or firm is naturally compounded across the entire administrative organization of the state.

Even when selection or indoctrination processes are designed to produce a relatively homogeneous (or at least communal) set of perspectives among administrative officials, the operational consequences of complexity are pervasive and, by definition, complex. These consequences generate a variety of role-related perspectives and priorities which are summed up in the notorious Miles' Law: "Where you stand depends upon where you sit." Richard Rose notes, more generally, in casting a skeptical eye toward management techniques for reducing complexity and enhancing efficient management, that governments have no single objectives to which they are committed or which at least can be comprehended by any observer. Instead, they are committed to multiple and sometimes conflicting objectives not easily summed up in a simple hierarchical scale of priorities (3).

In dealing with the question of whether the parts of a system are so diverse as to resist a common conceptualization, suppose we employ an analogy from statistics. In doing cross-systems analysis of administration, the problem is whether for any "system" we have a high or low coefficient of variability. If we can characterize systems very well by their central tendency (or average characteristics), we are probably safe in making overall comparisons. Under these circumstances, we would have a low coefficient of variability. On the other hand, if the central tendency is overwhelmed by diversity, then clearly any overall comparison or contrast properly would be suspect. The central problem of cross-systems comparison is how to distinguish the conditions under which there is greater variation across than within systems. Frequently, the situation with which we are confronted is the opposite of this. This opposite situation would be similar to having a high coefficient of variability in which the central tendency (or mean) is low in relation to the dispersion (or standard deviation) around it.

This rather formalized way of stating the problem is helpful to its conceptualization, but it needs some concrete points of reference. Functionalist theories of administrative systems dispose us to look at functional equivalents across political systems. Spending departments, for example, likely would be guided by similar impulses (to advance their programmatic missions) regardless of setting, while expenditure control departments and agencies would tend to be guided by similar imperatives across systems. Elsewhere, we have referred to this distinction as one between "demand" agencies and "supply" agencies (4). Similarly, one might distinguish between routine decisions and high-level decisions. In this regard, an effort that compares relatively low-level and routine decision-making processes in the U.S. and U.S.S.R. tends to find more similarity than difference across these settings (5).

Obviously, there are many potential distinctions employing a functional logic—a logic that weakens the analytic role of national system units, or, for that matter, those defined by capitalism or socialism, or by center or periphery. Consequently, in a multi-nation investigation of bureaucratic and political elites, the authors found the logics of role and ideology (themselves somewhat linked) to be more important than nation for examining differences in perspective. Yet, one national setting (the U.S.) was very important in failing to fit the overall pattern (6). The characteristics of the American case were so startlingly different from those of other nations (all in Western Europe) that we had to search for plausible system level explanations. Still, even in the American case (and also in West Germany and in Sweden), significant differences in attitude and perspective were also demarcated by the administrative unit in which a bureaucrat worked, while greater homogeneity across agencies characterized the cases of Britain, The Netherlands, Italy, and France. Picked at random, in other words, any single bureaucrat in, let us say, Britain was likely to be closer to the relevant population mean than his randomly selected counterpart in the U.S. This, of course, also fits with the British tradition of cultivating generalists able to move from organization to organization without being captured by, or helping to promote, an organization's subculture.

To assume that holistic definitions of the administrative system are useful requires us to move beyond the inevitable functional drives of administrative units likely to pervade any system and into the realm of public culture and of institutions. The culture helps us to see how these drives are expressed, while institutions allow us to see the pathways they follow. Not surprisingly, the more complex these institutional pathways are, the more convoluted the relations between administrators and political elites are likely to be. The United States' system again stands out in this regard both because its institutional pathways are so convoluted and its parts so dominant. In fact, it is most stunningly differentiated from other systems by the extent to which its parts tend to dominate the whole.

2. Organization Theory and the Political Environment

The second methodological complication is that of relating universal characteristics of organizational decision making to variations in the setting of administration. Specifically, the issues here are first, what, if any, connection can be drawn between universal properties of organizational decision making and assumptions of collective organizational coherence and second, what, if any, connection can be drawn between such decisional processes and variability in political contexts? These issues are both very broad and also linked. In duscussing them, we will make heavy use of a particular, but highly influential, body of organizational decision-making theory wedded to tenets of cognitive psychology and to limits of individual and, hence, organizational attentiveness.

As March and Olsen argue, assumptions about the purposive behavior of states or their agencies rest upon the basic conception that institutions are able to attain a sufficient level of coherence to be thought purposeful (7). In an effort to cast doubt upon these assumptions, Graham Allison argued that insofar as they related to U.S. decision-making during the October 1962 episode involving reaction to the installation of Soviet missiles in Cuba, such assumptions might be more misleading than edifying (8).

Leaning heavily on the work of Herbert Simon, James March, and Richard Cyert (9), Allison emphasizes limits to collective rationality and stresses instead both the limited cognitive boundaries of organizational actors and the divergent goals and intentions of these actors which, in turn, often were based on the missions and doctrines of the organizations they represented. Thus formulated, information and attention are organized through organizational routines and procedures that "economize" problem-solving efforts. Such routines and procedures both limit and define the picture that organizational actors will see; accordingly, they also tend to define the nature of the problem they see. The second assumption partially derives from the first. Partly because different organizational actors have different vantage points, organizations are conflictual. Organizations are the sum of their routines plus the preferences of dominant political coalitions within them. Coalitions are often fluid, however, and thus settlements about preferences are rarely conclusive. Organizational conflicts are the norm, and they are typically quasi-resolved rather than decisively concluded.

The flow of information to various actors is also critical to these decisional processes. From this perspective, decision makers react to environmental stimuli in ways that are inhibited by constraints stemming from temporal limits, available precedents for behavior, and the flow of others' agendas (10). Decisions are thus continuous rather than discrete. Indeed, from this perspective, while there are decisional premises, there is no "the decision" (11). There are, however, choice opportunities.

Although not directly stated, the emphasis given by Allison in the case of the Cuban missile episode is that the characteristics of the organizational decision processes noted above dominate any notion of strategic rationality that assumes a coherent overall common purpose. Similarly unstated but seemingly implied is the notion that decisional processes in the Soviet Union (the other major protagonist in the episode) were likely to be more similar to those in the U.S. than different.

The basic point here, however, is not to dwell on the case but rather to assess whether the key theoretical building blocks underlying analysis of the case are ones that inevitably lead us to the conclusion that if decisional processes are universally similar, the value of contrasting organizational systems cannot be very great. In other words, are political environmental differences at all relevant to decision-making processes?

This is no simple issue to resolve, but let us review the two key elements underlying the theory and consider each in turn: first, the assumption of bounded rationality, i.e., limited attentiveness and cognitive horizons, and second, the assumption of organizational conflict and fluidity, i.e., coalitions and choice opportunities.

The bounded rationality notion is premised on the need to make shortcuts in calculating decisions. If we had the wits to optimize, in Herbert Simon's phrase, we would, but since (it is argued) we don't, we accept satisfactory rather than optimal resolutions. Complex organizations by limiting jurisdictions and specializing functions simplify the calculating rules for organizational actors so that they respond to salient organizational routines and priorities (expressed in the famous aphorism "where you stand depends upon where you sit") in order to reduce the costs of choice. Yet, if the acceptance of "satisfactory" as a criterion is universal (assuming this theoretical premise to be correct), the comparative question becomes what constitutes satisfactory and why? While this question indeed can be posed at each of three levels of variability—across individuals, across organizations, and across administrative systems—we consider for now the last one, across systems. In this regard, it is interesting to note various forms of "coping" behavior across systems where the standards and norms of satisfactory responses differ considerably. Fred Riggs, for example, writes that administrative formalism is likely to be a coping device of administrators when there is little agreement about the goals of the state and little guidance for their behavior (12). Similar patterns of ritualistic formalism are found by Scott in Malaysia (13). On the other hand, where there is substantial agreement at least as to how government should relate to the citizenry, administrators even when restricted by statutory inhibitions may find a satisfactory solution to consist minimally of showing informal attention and the appearance of a sympathetic ear (14). In brief, even if there is a universal tendency toward the acceptable rather than the optimal, it is likely that there are important differences in decision premises and that these lead to different behaviors across administrative systems. In other words, what constitutes an acceptable solution is susceptible to variation, which is likely to derive to a considerable extent from the political culture of a society and its norms of public behavior.

The mix of ingredients constituting the decisional premises is subject, consequently, to variation among individuals, administrative agencies, and societies. Across individuals, personal values are a part of these decisional premises in spite of the classic doctrine minimizing the influence of personal values in administrative behavior. At the level of organizations and of societies, we can talk about norms and cultures as part of the mix of ingredients influencing decisions. That fact makes comparison worthwhile because it suggests to us that however similarly decision-making processes may be characterized, the range of likely decisions and the options available in the decisional repertoire are exogenous to the actual decision-making processes. Thus, a nearly ten-fold difference between British and Italian bureaucrats in their stated acceptance of the interplay of political actors and of political considerations in administrative activity clearly demarcates a strong effect on the repertoires of behavior likely to be engaged in by British and Italian civil servants even though *how* they actually go about making decisions may not fundamentally differ (15).

The second premise that organizations are largely arenas for conflict (an assumption that runs deeply counter to classic Weberian notions) implies naturally enough that "bureaucratic politics" is a pervasive phenomenon. We agree that it is. Yet, cross-national analysis is especially useful for discerning not whether conflict exists or not since it nearly everywhere does, but for discerning the forms it takes and the channels available for its expression. In this regard, it is likely that the more channels and outlets available to influence decisions, the greater the opportunities to appeal, and the greater the opportunities to appeal, the more visible and overt bureaucratic politics and organizational conflict will be. Evidence comparing the American system (with its numerous channels for influencing decisions deriving especially from the independence of the legislative body and its own complex organization) to other less convoluted systems indicates how extensive such appeals can be in the American system (16). The general point here is that if organizational conflict is a norm, the forms that conflict can take and the outlets available for its expression affect how it will take place and the manner in which it will be conducted. There is, in this regard, powerful evidence that the structure of political and governmental institutions affects how conflict will be played out, and to which audiences efforts to exercise influence will be directed. That, of course, is a compelling reason to try to compare administrative systems (17).

3. Units of Analysis—Structures, Actors, and Actions

The three analytic building blocks of comparative administration are structures (organizations), actors (executives and various species of bureaucratic officialdom), and actions (behaviors). Of these, the first two—structures and actors—are the more tangible and somewhat easier to get a handle on, though not without complication when nuanced comparisons are called for.

Simple inferences drawn from the comparative analysis of structures are usually the safest. Richard Rose's effort, for example, to infer the priorities of governments by tracing historically when particular sets of ministries came into being exemplifies this approach. Rose finds priorities essentially chronologically organized around state-defining activities (external relations, defense, finance, justice), then development activities (agriculture, transportation, industry, etc.), and finally individual rights (social service ministries) (18).

More nuanced comparisons, however, also get more complicated. What Treasury does in Britain, for example, is shared across two agencies in the U.S., Treasury and the Office of Management and Budget, and two ministries in West Germany, Economics and Finance. Moreover, as governmental workloads tax available organizational machinery, they require more coordination and monitoring, and some important structures become essentially *ad hoc*, interdepartmental, or instruments of the central decision makers. While these structures are often very important, they also may be inconstant. In any event, one of the truly perplexing decisions facing any student of comparative administration is whether to compare and contrast structural units or seek to obtain functional equivalencies across administrative systems.

Comparing executive actors across systems, even when done in a relatively straight-forward way, requires delicate judgment. This, in part, is because personnel systems often differ dramatically. Our engagement in a multi-nation study of senior civil servants led us into debates about equivalencies of administrators across systems. The anomalous American case saturates politically appointed executives throughout the bureaucracy to a far greater degree than the other (all Western European) countries involved in our study. Thus, strictly to compare senior civil servants would have led to clear functional non-comparabilities in that the Americans would be in less powerful positions. On the other hand, rough functional comparability could mean that we were comparing a different breed of official altogether (19). Fortunately, while the politically appointed officials in the U.S. did show significant differences from the senior civil servants (in their political preferences, for example), they were remarkably similar to each other on the matters in which key cross-national differences turned up (for example, in their role conceptions).

Ultimately, the connection between organizational structures and personnel must be examined. Organizational roles are a basic point of comparison across administrative systems. We need to know, therefore, how roles are organized and whether comparable roles exist across systems. The role of program analyst, for instance, is one that abounds throughout the U.S. federal bureaucracy but is a less visible role (even if similar functions are necessarily performed) in Britain or West Germany or Japan. Essentially, the comparative analysis of bureaucratic actors must analyze both cross-role differences within each system *and* cross-system differences between similar roles.

Although the comparison of structures and actors is often complex, it is the third component, action or behavior, that is especially elusive in comparative analysis. Partly this is so because action involves decisions, and it may be that, as we discussed above, the process of organizational decision making, whatever the content of the decisions, looks fairly similar everywhere. Undoubtedly, it is also so because organizational activity involves the making of policy, and the making of policy is especially difficult to characterize. Gary Freeman notes, for example, that French policy-making has been described as both reactive, short term, and piecemeal and also active, rational, and impositional (20). It is suggested that the latter style (active, rational, impositional) characterizes the normative bent of French elites at the policy-making summit whereas the former style (reactive, short term, piecemeal) characterizes the actual (unsuccessful from the standpoint of the guiding norms) process of policy-making. For a good many reasons, of course, including those put forth by organizational decision theory, the reactive, short-term, piecemeal style is likely to occur in practice, and the main variation may be not in the "action" but in the norms of the leading actors. This last point is also of special interest to comparisons of the actors across systems because comparing the actors suggests that there may be more variation in policy norms than in actual policy processes.

To sum up, the comparative analysis of administrative systems is inherently a difficult undertaking. This is so not only because so many possible confounding sources of variation must be controlled, but because there also are fundamental and by no means resolved linkage problems between the dynamics of decision-making processes and the more stable elements of actors and structures, between these processes and the norms and values that might guide them, and between efforts to characterize whole systems and variability across the organizational sectors that constitute these systems.

In the following section of this chapter, we turn from these methodological ambiguities in comparative administrative analysis to a set of conceptual ambiguities that deal with (1) the relationship between bureaucracy and politics; (2) centralization and coordination; and (3) identifying systems of bargaining and mediation.

THREE CONCEPTUAL AMBIGUITIES

1. Bureaucracies, Bureaucrats, and Politics

In classic conception, politics and bureaucracy are antinomies. The former involves commitment to partisan causes, to passion, and to serving parochial interest; the latter involves impartiality, impersonalism, and universalistic efficiency. The traits of politics, in this classic conception, are the province purely of politicians and of the political universe, whereas those associated with bureaucracy fall within the province of the caste of professional administrators, and belong to the separate world of management.

Obviously, these conceptions prove to be far too simple, and the strict bifurcation of politics and administration came to be scrutinized with considerable skepticism. Despite this, it is not always clear what one means by politics when it is observed that politics exists in the world of public administration. How, in characterizing administrative systems, behaviors, and actors, is the concept of "politics" used? What is meant by it?

The answer is several things depending upon context. In the context of administration, the concept has many faces, not all relevant to the same level of analysis. We now proceed to discuss these varied notions of "politics" in the context of public administration.

i. Politics as Influence-Directed Behavior

In its simplest manifestation, politics is the process of seeking to gain influence over decisions. As we noted earlier, the processes of influence-seeking and coalition construction within organizations imply the prevalence of internal conflict and are at odds with the Weberian conceptions of the unity of command and of rational or purposive organization. The fact that politics as influence-seeking and Weber's notions are logically conflicting does not mean, however, that they are mutually exclusive; they may, for instance, occur at different levels within an organization or any other collective entity. While organizational politics, in the basic sense of influence-seeking, is itself a constant, it varies in form depending on the instrumentalities and channels available for exercising influence—depending, in other words, on the organization of institutional authority and the operative norms of institutions. Thus, multiple channels for making appeals will produce a more active and visible form of organizational politics. Alternatively, the more concentrated the channels of appeal, the more constrained and subtle will be the style through which influence-seeking is promoted. The issue, therefore, is not whether organizational politics occurs or not but, rather, the size of the stage on which it is played and, relatedly, the number of actors involved in the play.

ii. Politics as Salience

The assumption here is that of the many activities with which central decision makers could be involved, they can deal only with a very few. Presumably, the very few that activate their attention are of central importance by virtue of the fact that central decision makers allocate attention to them. We might call these priority matters. Whether priorities are part of central decision makers' agendas or mostly reacted to is relatively unimportant to this notion. Since many things can be reacted to and only a few are, it is the few that are that we assume have political salience. Unwillingness to delegate is a signal of importance to the decision maker.

At any time, of course, a decisional mix has many of the characteristics that Cohen, March, and Olsen describe as a "garbage can" (21). Yet, some patterns of activity compel the attention of top leadership more than others. Cronin's study of the American cabinet, for example, distinguishes between an outer cabinet whose members rarely meet one on one directly with the president, and an inner cabinet whose members are more or less constantly accessible to the president (22). The inner cabinet that Cronin portrays corresponds closely, indeed almost exactly, to the state defining departments characterized by Richard Rose. In Britain as well, Rose finds a pattern similar to that which Cronin discovers in the U.S. (23).

Salient matters are inherently unstable ones, relatively unaffected by statutory specification and administrative routine. They behave like "active" rather than "stable" or "inert" elements in the physical world. If they are important to political decision makers in that they require responses from them, they must, perforce, be politically important. Many activities of the peripheral (or outer ministries) are routinized through both statutory and administrative law and are often surrounded by a dense thicket of clientele interests. They are the "stable" (in some cases "inert") elements and though they can be subjected to change, this tends to require unusual and concentrated effort from the top leadership. Priorities at the top, however, are likely to be determined not by what is stable, but by what is inherently unstable or problematic. How leaders handle these salient matters (or more importantly are perceived as handling them) often determines their political fortunes.

iii. Politics as Peripheral Policy

An alternative conception of politics in the context of administration relates to party constituencies and clientele interests. In this view, the matters that must engage the attention of top leadership are ones of high policy, not of politics. The routines of politics, the programs that please party and interest clients, are those delegated to the "outer" departments—the ones laden with laws and "lobbyists." A study of politically appointed officials in the U.S., for example, noted that party politicians were more likely to be appointed to these "clientele-centered" departments than to the state-defining ones (24). The tendency also of central policy review exercises to devolve into particularistic defenses of prevailing programs, a notable tendency in the second Wilson government in Britain, results from a need to accommodate key party constituencies.

It is possible, of course, for top leadership to turn peripheral concerns into primary ones—to make the disruption of prevailing subgovernmental coalitions a primary goal. Such has happened in both the U.S. and Britain, and it appears that both the Reagan and Thatcher governments have had some success in their efforts to undermine reigning sub-governments by introducing new actors into the decision process, eliminating or de-emphasizing old ones, and generally centralizing decisions. In a very rough analogue, it might be argued that similar efforts were undertaken in the U.S.S.R. during the Andropov leadership and, perhaps, now in the Gorbachev period.

iv. Politics as Attitude

Moving now to the administrative actors, we can detect yet another form in which the concept of "politics" is applied in administration. This is politics as attitude, a notion implying that there are differences between bureaucrats in the same system and also possibly differences between systems based on differences in bureaucratic attitudes.

The notion of politics as attitude derives from the classic distinction of administration and politics. Presumably, apolitical bureaucrats correspond to that end of the distinction in which bureaucrats are merely the neutral executors of law. Of course, the sharp distinction of classical theory bears little correspondence to the complex realities in which politics and administration share a niche. The extent to which bureaucracies respond to complex forms of accountability and also the extent to which their legitimacy is granted, may each depend on the extent to which bureaucrats themselves accept the routines of politics as a natural part of their environment—an environment jointly inhabited by politics and administration, and by politicians, political interests, and bureaucrats. These concerns led Putnam to evaluate the tolerances of administrators for political pluralism, initially across national settings and then among bureaucrats with technocratic and non-technocratic backgrounds (25). Putnam, and later Aberbach, Putnam & Rockman, found strong cross-national differences in individual bureaucrats' tolerances for the processes of pluralistic politics (26). In reference, therefore, to the broad distinction between political bureaucrats and classical bureaucrats, this attitudinal conception of politics implies that "politically minded" bureaucrats will be more active in the administrative process and, accordingly, may enhance responsiveness, though in more complex forms than the original distinction between administration and politics could formulate.

It turns out that bureaucrats with attitudes more generally tolerant of politics not only are more likely to be strategically located nearer the centers of power in their organizations but also are more likely to be linked to organizational centers of power (an indicator of activism) when their strategic location in the organization is held constant. The organizational "movers and shakers" can be identified rather well by their attitudes regarding politics (27).

It appears to be the case, in short, that at the individual level, holding attitudes favorable to politics has real consequences for behavior. What all of this means at the collective level, however, is less conclusive, mainly because system level concepts of bureaucratic accountability are more open-ended and subject to debate. Complex concepts of accountability, however, that take into consideration responsiveness to multiple interests are likely to be compatible with widespread attitudinal acceptance of the legitimacy of politics.

Partisanship is another set of political attitudes of interest in an administrative system. Generally speaking, within the public bureaucracies of Western multi-party systems, partisan-based attitudes are relatively weak (28). It is often the case, however, that partisan attitudes are deeply held, yet concealed in the form of anti-partisanship. Empirically, this phenomenon has tended to be associated with bureaucrats sympathetic to conservative parties when confronted with governments promoting considerable social change and political regeneration (29). The advent of the Socialist-Liberal coalition in West Germany in the 1969 elections soon brought about charges by senior officials of too much party influence on administration even though there has been ample evidence that political considerations have long influenced state administration and the selection of administrative elites under conservative governments (30).

In fact, there are really two separate notions of partisanship. One is the party-relatedness of political attitudes; the second is the matter of party saturation of the bureaucracy which may exist under the auspices of ostensible anti-partisanship. This second meaning is dealt with under the next category of politics. As to the first, our basic empirical finding for Western democracies is that party is not nearly so strong a honing signal for bureaucrats, even when they admit a party affiliation or tendency, as it is for politicians (31). The exception to this ironically occurs in the United States where partisanship overall tends to be less strong. This exception in the U.S. contributes to the criticism by the executive political leadership that the bureaucracy is an independent and undisciplined source of policymaking (32).

Although bureaucratic politicalness in the sense of tolerance for the inherent messiness of pluralist politics may logically edge over into heightened partisanship in attitudes, there is no direct evidence that it does. The British case here is instructive in that British civil servants have a very high tolerance for pluralistic politics but relative to British politicians a very low tendency toward partisan salience in attitude (33).

v. Politics as Politicization

Perhaps the most obvious way that bureaucracy is said to be political is when it is politicized. Politicization of the bureaucracy is normally thought to occur when the bureaucracy loses its independence to propose alternative choices and, especially, its ability to exercise discretionary choice in the context of rendering impartial and universalistic judgments within the context of prevailing laws. Bureaucracy also is thought to have become politicized when administrative officials are required to meet litmus tests of loyalty to the governing authorities. Often this means showing correct political party standing (the other form of partisanship discussed above). More often it means a proper level of enthusiasm for the political ideas endorsed by the top political leadership.

Another way in which the term politicization is employed has been put forth by Ronge (34). Politicization, in this usage, means the inevitable performance by bureaucrats of roles that once were thought to be exclusively the province of politicians—the nurturing of interest constituencies, for example, or the mediation of various interest groups in formulating and, especially, implementing policy. This concept of politicization is not included under our definition of the term as employed in this section but is evidence of the growing grey area between an idealized or classic politics of electoral struggle and mass mobilization, on the one hand, and an idealized administration of non-political management and technical decision-making, on the other. The politics of governing is politics beneath the headlines, and it is more or less inevitable that, since it is the bureaucracy that provides concrete expression to policy, it also is the bureaucracy that becomes a site for managing the politics of policy implementation.

Returning to the original notion of politicization as an effort to concentrate political control and to politically saturate the bureaucracy so that it will respond in Pavlovian form to its masters, one obvious form of politicization is the use of patronage to pay off political supporters and/or to instill a high degree of doctrinaire loyalty. The control of personnel is essential to most other efforts to achieve administrative compliance. Since the creation of a civil service system is designed to prohibit overt forms of patronage, patronage appointment often takes more subtle forms.

Among Western states, patronage is probably least subtle and most pervasive in the United States where the bureaucracy itself is a relatively new idea and where the pattern of appointing political supporters to top administrative jobs has been a long-standing one. In the American system, the notion of the civil service traditionally has been a limited one. Except for general list positions in the new Senior Executive Service (SES), civil service positions formally are designated as ones not involving policy-making. Even elite general list career positions in the U.S. federal government usually begin at least three levels removed from the heads of departments, a condition that does not obtain in other Western states. Beyond this, there are other mechanisms that a presidential administration with a will to keep the professional bureaucracy on a tight leash can deploy. In recent times, that will has grown markedly.

In Western Europe, the formal distinction between the civil service and a layer of political overseers in departments does not exist. At least on the continent, however, changes in governments tend to bring changes in the very top civil service stratum, and the more politically sensitive the position, the more prudent the selection. In Britain, the tendency of the Thatcher government has been to keep a special eye out for those wedded to Mrs. Thatcher's precepts about the role and size of the state, and especially her devotion to the role of entrepreneurship. While such appointments are made from within the civil service, they are designed to select politically sympathetic personnel, and so represent clear efforts to achieve political control.

Over time, there is a tendency for governments, if they are in power long enough, to try to remold the bureaucracy to their image. Until the grasp of Christian Democracy over Italian governments began to weaken in the 1960s, the Italian bureaucracy mirrored faithfully the party that molded it. The enemies of Christian

Democracy were regularly denied effective access to represent their claims within the bureaucracy while the party's allies were granted special privilege (35).

Similarly, the greater the change a new government wishes to make during its term of office, the more pressure it is likely to exert on the bureaucracy to comply with its directions (36). Often, a party or party coalition that has been out of power over a lengthy period of time (or perhaps never in power), if given the mandate to rule, naturally enough will seek to produce great change. Under the circumstances, it is likely to face a bureaucracy which, if not recalcitrant, is at the very least not habituated to a new government's directions and assumptions. In other words, where the bureaucracy has been molded around the preferences and assumptions of a prior political order or regime, the new government will want to reconfigure the bureaucracy toward its preferences and assumptions. Not very surprisingly, the newly dispossessed will claim that the bureaucracy is being politicized. So claimed the French Right and Center after the election of the Socialist government; so claimed the CDU/CSU and its administrative officials in the aftermath of the Social-Liberal coalition of 1969; so claim the partisans of expansionary social and development programs in the U.S. in the midst of the Reagan efforts to shrink the scope and activities of the state, activities supported, indeed often promoted, by a bureaucracy whose beginnings largely dated to the New Deal burst of state expansionist activity in the 1930s, and whose assumptions continue to be marked by those preferences. Politicization, it turns out, often lies in the eye of the beholder.

Nevertheless, it is possible to point to circumstances where politicization did not take place in spite of conditions that might have promoted its occurrence. The long rule of the Social Democrats in Sweden, for example, potentially accorded them significant opportunities to alter a largely conservative bureaucracy more to their liking. A political culture predicated upon consensus and problem-solving, however, led to a relationship between governments and civil servants built upon trust and a shared commitment to solving public problems more than on policy agreement *per se.*

vi. Politics as Civil Service Curbing

A variant of the politicization path is to disregard the civil service as much as possible by providing clear-cut political direction. The simpler these directions (and the simpler the goals to be pursued), the more likely that the discretionary space of civil servants can be reduced. While it is virtually impossible in the context of modern government to cut civil servants out of implementing activities, their role as consultants and advisers can be sharply curtailed by any government or administration bent on pursuing simple, if often radical, objectives. Under such conditions, even discretion in implementing activities can be severely restricted.

Clear and simple directives when impressed from above and persistently monitored are the stuff of classic scientific management. In this scenario, civil servants are reduced to "managers" in the most technically limited meaning of the term. Such a state of affairs apparently conforms with the jointly held vision of Mr. Reagan and Mrs. Thatcher as to how governing should proceed—simply crafted rules guided by a "political" commisariat, conceived, of course, in somewhat different terms in each country. This strategy seems especially appropriate for a political leadership wishing to diminish the role of government rather than one wishing to employ government as a programmatic tool for social engineering. However, it is plausible to imagine that a strategy of civil service curbing can be undertaken by a political leadership that wishes to maintain a more expansive set of services, the primary suppliers of which would come from competitive private or para-governmental sources. Here, the role of the state would be to maintain supervision over an allegedly more efficient market-oriented delivery system. Such a government would still be one of simple rules, and it is a model that in the United States has found increasing favor among "neo-liberals" within the Democratic party.

vii. Politics as Assimilation

Another way in which politics is defined within the context of administration is through the administrative pathway into politics. The convergence of bureaucracy and political recruitment is very substantial in several advanced capitalist states, notably Japan, France, and West Germany among the larger states. In France, Dogan points out, a well worn route to cabinet ministerial positions is through the grands corps (37). Similar processes are found in Japan and West Germany where membership in the civil service elite can be a springboard into the political elite. In some ways, these systems may be described as bureaucratized polities although they could just as readily be described as political bureaucracies—arenas where individuals of considerable competence and even more considerable connections may be selected for potential political leadership posts as, for example, was Helmut Schmidt in West Germany.

Usually in such systems the parliamentary body contains a substantial number of civil servants granted leave. Many ministers and other political officials have been (or are) senior civil servants. The percentage of civil servants in the West German Bundestag, for instance, is usually over 30 per cent, and the percentage is even higher within the Bundesrat. In France, Birnbaum shows that in the 1970s about 38 per cent of cabinet ministers and secretaries of state had been senior civil servants (38).

The general point about these systems is that the bureaucracy is perhaps the most pivotal institution leading to political eliteness. In Japan and France, the bureaucracy also provides a springboard to the business elite as well (39).

viii. Politics as Overlapping Worlds

While the notion of a bureaucratic-politics assimilation is usually perceived as leading to bureaucratic domination of the polity, the notion of overlapping worlds that emerges from the U.S. experience is one that emphasizes a political style in the bureaucracy (40). The overlapping character of American politics derives from a combination of macro-systemic features, institutionally and culturally. The independence of the legislative body, as previously remarked, provides ample opportunities for bureaucrats to influence decisions at a variety of points. It attunes U.S. bureaucrats to operate as much, indeed more, within the context of legislative as executive routines. It attunes them equally to operate as often, if not more, from the perspectives of key legislators' interests, especially because of the power of congressional work groups, committees and especially subcommittees. So, the institutional and unique features of the American system provide inducements for bureaucrats to think and behave along lines not far removed from the hurly-burly of U.S. legislative politics, notwithstanding that important differences do exist between the two sets of elites.

Management as a scientific activity (or at least as a theorized art) was applied to the management of private enterprise and developed before there was much bureaucratization of the American state. Consequently, the distinction between administration (as management) and politics was drawn most sharply in the U.S., helping to account for the relative scarcity of civil servants at the top of U.S. administrative hierarchies. Since in the American view civil servants were supposed to be essentially neutral technicians rather than involved in making policy, it is understandable from this doctrine that civil servants are not the partners of the governing authorities but entirely, in theory, their obedient underlings. Removed as they are from the very top layers of authority in the U.S. executive system, exercising influence upward is more complicated than exercising it outward to the legislature—an option that exists in no other setting to the magnitude that it does in the U.S. Hence, the worlds of legislative politicians and of senior civil servants in the U.S. system are said to be overlapping not only by the pattern of behavior that emerges but also because of the shared perspectives that tend to develop. While these perspectives tend to be politician-dominant, they also do travel in the opposite direction. For example, U.S. legislative politicians tend to a greater degree than their peers in Western Europe to focus on technical aspects of policymaking, a vintage bureaucratic characteristic (41).

The methodological ambiguity of relating broad system generalizations to the diversity of micro-phenomena is naturally relevant here. Not all U.S. bureaucrats, for example, exhibit the political mentality discussed above. Officials with programs to promote or protect are apt to be different from those who are not in a position to nurture outside political support (foreign service officers) or from those whose organizational mission resists that idea (Treasury officers, for example, or officials whose responsibilities are to bring about budgetary discipline or efficient allocations of resources).

These necessary cautions aside, however, a general contrast between politics as bureaucratic assimilation, i.e., the bureaucratic pathway to politics, and politics as overlapping worlds, i.e., the shared perspective, is that the former portrays a potential (or realization) of the dominance of the civil service elite since the civil service is a gateway to both political and economic power (42). The main fear is that strategic power is dominated by a small group which, if not always cohesive in policy, is almost always cohesive about how policy should be made. Politics as overlapping worlds, on the other hand, is not burdened by fears of elite concentration and cohesion, but precisely the reverse—of the inability to achieve strategic direction in the face of a countless array of tacit political alliances between subsets of bureaucratic and political actors. If the fear pertaining to the "assimilation" model is the suppression of politics by the dominance of a bureaucratically-originated strategic elite, the concern relevant to the "overlapping" model is with achieving policy discipline amidst a diffusion of micro-political relations.

In sum, the concept of politics when applied or related to bureaucracy takes on numerous meanings and often has different implications. Inconsistent usage of the concept abounds. We have here, however, not tried to point to a singular way in which the concept should be applied, but rather to point to numerous (and no doubt not all) ways in which it has been applied.

2. Centralization, Planning and Coordination

The Weberian formulation of bureaucratic organization leaves no doubt that above all it is a command organization. When combined with the features of limited jurisdictions, differentiated roles, specialization, and memory, unity of command makes bureaucratic organization, in the Weberian view, the most technically proficient organizational type. Thus, the concepts of hierarchical command and coordination allow for coherent planning. On this presumption (or delusion), modern governmental organization is rationalized.

Empirical studies, however, often reveal not how well governments plan, but more often how plans turn to dust (43); not how well they coordinate, but how episodically and reluctantly they do. Nor is it often demonstrated how formal centralization promotes unity of command, but more often how that is avoided (44). In a theoretical way, these issues are discussed at some length by Lindblom in his well-regarded book, *Politics and Markets* (45).

In spite of the limited capacity to achieve coordination, especially when one moves from a given organizational unit to the full expanse of governmental organizations, efforts to achieve greater coordination appear to have grown rather than diminished. Colin Campbell's careful study of central agencies in three Anglo polities, Canada, the United States, and Britain, indicates the extent to which these coordinating and monitoring mechanisms have sprouted and how they have functioned (46). Derlien and Müller also note the dramatic growth in the office of the Federal Chancellery in West Germany as a consequence of the need to provide central steering and control organs over the social policy reforms and the new foreign policy initiatives begun after the Socialist-Liberal government was formed in 1969 (47). Whatever the level of actual success, the evidence is that central governments are undertaking a larger policy monitoring and coordinating role. The obvious reason is that government is involved in more programs and activities. It has sprouted more tentacles over time with no greater controlling capacity. Consequently, whether a government is interested in better results for its expenditures or whether it simply wants to spend less, control and coordination from the center are viewed as increasingly essential by the actors at the center.

The terms centralization and its opposite, decentralization, are ones that come naturally to scholars of policymaking and of administrative organization. Centralization implies, in the Weberian framework, a capacity to achieve planning and coordination which in modern usage implies policy success because it also implies coherence. Yet, the concept of centralization is often ambiguous in use. An important reason for this is that the concept is at least two-dimensional.

One dimension is territorial and has to do with the relations between various governmental and organizational jurisdictions; the other is institutional and has to do with the relative concentration or diffusion of authority within a given jurisdiction. Christopher Leman's study of welfare reform policies in Canada and the U.S. nicely illustrates this difference (48). Both Canada and the U.S. have relatively decentralized systems of federal government. In Canada, however, the decisional structures at each level are less convoluted and diffuse than they are in the United States. Consequently, Canadian federal and provincial elites were better able to bargain and to be sheltered from public pressures (which in both countries were dubious of reform) than in the U.S. where far more actors were involved at both the state and federal levels.

In examining the British and French experiences with central-local relations, however, Ashford draws somewhat different conclusions (49). In this case, both systems are territorially highly centralized, but British decisional structures, in this conception, are more austere. Ashford's rich argumentation defies neat summarization, but essentially British dogmatism, in his view, stems from the hallowed role given to the concept of party government and parliamentary supremacy which provides little bargaining and adjustment room. French pragmatism, on the other hand, resulted from the discretionary adjustments made by the bureaucracy in Paris, the prefects, and the dual local-national roles played by a number of French politicians who simultaneously hold local and national office. In Ashford's view, the richness of the French decisional complex produced more accepted and effective policy implementation than in Britain because it resulted from numerous adjustments and bargains.

Insofar as modern pluralistic states are concerned, there is considerable debate about the importance or necessity of centralization in either of its dimensions for effective policy-making. To a considerable degree, whether explicitly or implicitly, the extent to which effective policy-making is defined as a coherently energized and comprehensive product has much to do with one's penchant for increasing centralization, especially the concentration of power resources. To the extent that such a definition is held, the modern pluralistic state is apt to be viewed as the captive of a myriad of particular interests and thus paralyzed from dealing with broad and non-incremental problems (50). Conversely, the conceptual apparatus of "bounded rationality" coincides intellectually with the notions of mutual adjustment and bargaining (51). From this perspective, "big" decisions are likely to cause great error. Not surprisingly, this perspective coincides with an emphasis on policy-making as an iterative process that is disturbed from time to time by new stimuli, actors, events, and opportunities. The concept of a strong state (implied centralization along both the territorial and concentration dimensions) may not correspond to notions of effective policymaking (52). In a casual but provocative comment, Ashford observed that "perhaps weak states make strong policies" (53). The implication is that concentrated and centralized authority leads to imposition of authority, which leads to inability to adjust and bargain, which leads to delegitimation, which then leads to large error. Alternatively, one can infer that diffusion of resources engenders bargaining and adjustment, which leads to legitimacy based on acceptance. In starkest form, the values of coherence vs. consent are sharply brought into play.

No doubt, all of this simplifies too much. However, it is rare, at least among Western observers, for any to think their countries have much capacity to generate coherent direction. The play of interests seems bewildering as the totality of bureaucratic organizations pursues multiple and conflicting objectives, propped up by multiple and conflicting political support groups. Authority to harness these various objectives together is not readily found. This is why the growth of central machinery and, above all, the growth in its importance in Western governments has been so impressive. If the purpose of trying to achieve centralization, however, is to gain coherence in policy, structures may be less important ultimately than shared norms about reaching agreements and about policy goals. As Olsen argues in the case of Norway, "Consultation and anticipated reactions are more important forms of coordination than command" (54).

In sum, the language of centralization, planning, and coordination assumes hierarchically arranged goals around a monolithic preference structure. Centralization is presumed to be the most effective means for goal achievement, though the concept of centralization, as we have argued, is not unidimensional. The extent to which

centralization is perceived to be a mechanism for engendering coordination is itself a
litmus test of the extent to which effectiveness is defined in terms of a monolithic
hierarchy of goals (the plan). Alternatively, the extent to which the norms of elites
are organized around a complex set of adjustments and accommodations of diverse
preferences may influence the actual operation of coordinative processes more deeply
than constructing organizational structures to force monolithic hierarchy.

3. Bargaining, Mediation, and Subgovernments

Complex processes of coordination involve bargaining relationships, whether the bargains are arrived at around a cabinet table or between a supplier and a buyer on a
black market. It belabors the point to suggest that processes of governing which are
not the result of clear hierarchical command are the result of bargaining. That is to
say, nearly all of governing is bargaining—an interpretation that coincides readily with
the conception of organizations as arenas of conflict.

However, to say this is as yet to say little. For the crucial question seems to be,
not does bargaining exist, but where are bargains made? Where, in other words, are
the key sites for reaching agreements, and who are the key actors?

Much of the literature on policy-making suggests that the answers to these questions
depend on the types of policies under consideration rather than on sweeping macro-
level judgments (55). No single policy system or characteristic set of bargaining relationships is likely to exist. Rather, a given policy sector is likely to be characterized
by a fairly distinct pattern of relationships. Indeed, one effort to characterize policy
sectors in the U.S. uses the pattern of participants as a way of differentiating sectors
(56). Obviously, we are back to the problem of the whole and its parts.

However policies are eventually characterized, bureaucracy is the edifice through
which they are institutionalized. The beneficiaries of policies and the groups that are
closely affected take a continuing interest in them long after the dramatic elements of
legislative enactments have disappeared. They are the program constituents. This
connection between program constituencies, usually taking the form of interest groups,
and relevant administrative units typically is referred to as a subgovernment. The
phenomenon of subgovernments is widely regarded as a pervasive one in contemporary
pluralist systems. They occur because of the tendency of bureaucrats to deal almost
exclusively with organized interests directly affected and expressing continuing concern
with decisions made by the administrative unit. At Whitehall, in the words of Lord
Armstrong, for example, "there is now certainly somewhere . . . a little unit of
people whose job it is to acquaint themselves with what is happening in each industry
and, as far as they can, watch over its interests" (57).

Their persistence is due to numerous factors. Among these are the inattentiveness
or inconstancy of attention on the part of the top leadership, the agreement of the
leadership with the purposes and administration of the programs, and an unwillingness
or inability on the part of the leadership to disturb important political constituencies
with a stake in the programs (opportunity costs). Governments often do not wish to
disturb the prevailing subgovernments, or at least not many of them. No political system and certainly no political leader can stand to be sucked up in constant controversy and turmoil. This is why the *status quo* is always advantaged. Well enough,
even if not good enough, is often acceptable because of the opportunity costs involved
in changing existing subgovernmental structures and relations.

Yet, important structural differences across systems exist that potentially affect the relative solidity of the protective shell around extant subgovernments. While opportunity costs to challenging subgovernments are always large, a large number of bargaining arenas and complex authority structures provide special advantages to the *status quo.* The role of a cabinet (or some functional equivalent) as a point of aggregation is structurally important, even if conflict avoidance or brokering is the norm, when governments are confronted with choices that offend important interest groups. For if agreements can be arrived at among parties represented in the cabinet, the affected interests will run out of bargaining space. Not so in the U.S., however. There independent decision makers abound, not only institutionally in Congress but also in the judicial system. It is possible, but more difficult, to run out of bargaining space in the American system because of the multitude of sites within which clientele groups can seek to protect their interests.

Despite the prevalence of subgovernments in all pluralist systems, the U.S. is said to be subsystem dominant (58). In large part, this is because the system lacks an effective cabinet or party system as central points of aggregation and system-wide bargaining. In Western Europe, interest groups typically are fewer but more widely representative (i.e., peak associations are more powerful). There, if accommodations are arrived at within the governing coalition and in the cabinet, subgovernments may be induced to provide inter-sectoral support for the government by a payoff in the form of greater sectoral autonomy under normal conditions. This is particularly true of the Scandinavian model. The American system, however, provides more incentives for narrowly focused interest groups than for peak associations because the congressional work group structure is highly suited to this form of interest aggregation. So, while the American system features a great deal of cross-institutional bargaining between the bureaucracy and the legislature, these bargains are frequently implicit and do not often travel to the top. Bargaining in the U.S. system is almost never system wide. Despite its prevalence in the U.S. system, bargaining is intensively subsystemic, and it is very rarely conducted to provide support for system wide initiatives. More than any other reason, this is why the American system is characterized as subsystem dominant.

CONCLUSION

This chapter explores three methodological and three conceptual ambiguities in the comparative study of public administration. It should be clear that the comparative analysis of administrative systems is a difficult undertaking. This is so for a formidable set of methodological reasons beyond even the many possible confounding sources of variation that must be controlled before we can be confident of any explanation: 1) there are fundamental linkage problems between the parts of the administrative system, usually the focus of inquiry, and the administrative system as a whole, usually the object of theoretical inference; 2) it is difficult to relate the universal characteristics of organizational decision making to variations in the setting of administration (political and administrative context); and 3) the linkage problems between the three analytical building blocks of comparative administration—structures (organizations), actors (officials), and actions (behaviors)—are formidable.

In addition to the methodological ambiguities in comparative administrative analysis, we must deal with a difficult set of conceptual ambiguities: 1) the links between bureaucracies, bureaucrats, and politics are complex, and the concept of politics when applied or related to bureaucracy takes on numerous meanings and often has different implications; 2) the language of centralization, planning, and coordination assumes hierarchically arranged goals around a monolithic preference structure, assumptions rarely if ever met; and 3) it is difficult to define levels of bargaining and mediation across political systems and to define their relation to semiautonomous domains of influence within governments (subgovernments).

Having said all this, it is tempting to abandon the comparative study of administration. But that would not solve the problems discussed in this chapter. They are inherent in any study of administration, whether comparative or focused on a single country or even a single agency. Comparative study pushes them to the fore, however, and propels us to a level of conceptual and methodological self-consciousness and clarity rarely found in non-comparative studies of public administration. As the examples drawn from our own comparative study of bureaucrats and politicians in Western democracies demonstrate, the U.S. administrative system is best understood in a comparative context. The same, of course, is true for the other systems. The conceptual and methodological ambiguities examined are most apparent in an explicitly comparative study; they thereby stimulate clarity and understanding. We not only understand our own systems better when we compare, we gain a better understanding of the methods, concepts, and theories we employ.

The muddle of comparative administrative study may well be a hell, but one whose suggested motto is: "Abandon hope all ye who do *not* enter here!"

ACKNOWLEDGMENT

Professor Aberbach acknowledges with thanks support for this project from the Faculty Assistance Fund of the College of Literature, Science and the Arts at the University of Michigan. Professor Rockman expresses his gratitude to the University of Pittsburgh's Center for International Studies for its considerable support on behalf of this project.

REFERENCES

1. Harold Seidman, *Politics, Position, and Power: The Dynamics of Federal Organization*, 3rd ed. (New York: Oxford University Press, 1980).
2. See, for instance, Herbert A. Simon, *Administrative Behavior*, 3rd ed. (New York: The Free Press, 1976), esp. Chapters 10 and 15.
3. Richard Rose, *Managing Presidential Objectives* (New York: The Free Press, 1976).
4. Joel D. Aberbach and Bert A. Rockman, "Political and Bureaucratic Roles in Public Service Reorganization," Paper prepared for Inaugural Conference of the IPSA Working Group on the Structure and Organization of Government, Manchester, England, November 15–18, 1984.
5. Andrew S. MacFarland, *Power and Leadership in Pluralist Systems* (Stanford, California: Stanford University Press, 1969), esp. pp. 53–69.
6. Joel D. Aberbach, Robert D. Putnam, and Bert A. Rockman, *Bureaucrats and Politicians in Western Democracies* (Cambridge, Massachusetts: Harvard University Press, 1981).
7. James G. March and Johan P. Olsen, "The New Institutionalism: Organizational Factors in Political Life," *American Political Science Review*, 78 (September 1984): 734–749.

8. Graham T. Allison, "Conceptual Models and the Cuban Missile Crisis," *American Political Science Review*, 63 (September 1969): 699–718.

9. Inter alia, Simon, *Administrative Behavior*; James G. March and Herbert A. Simon, *Organizations* (New York: John Wiley, 1958); and Richard M. Cyert and James G. March, *A Behavioral Theory of the Firm* (Englewood-Cliffs, New Jersey: Prentice-Hall, 1963).

10. See, James G. March and Johna P. Olsen, *Ambiguity and Choice in Organizations* (Bergen, Norway: Universitetsforlaget, 1972).

11. In Herbert Simon's language: "Since decisions can become, and usually do become, premises in other decisions . . . there isn't any 'the decision'." See Herbert A. Simon, " 'The Decision-Making Schema': A Reply," *Public Administration Review*, 18 (Winter 1958), p. 62.

12. Fred W. Riggs, *Administration in Developing Countries: The Theory of Prismatic Society* (Boston: Houghton-Mifflin, 1964), p. 183.

13. James C. Scott, *Political Ideology in Malaysia: Reality and the Beliefs of an Elite* (New Haven: Yale University Press, 1968).

14. Charles T. Goodsell, "Looking Once Again at Human Service Bureaucracy," *Journal of Politics*, 43 (August 1981), p. 777.

15. Aberbach, Putnam, and Rockman, *Bureaucrats and Politicians*, p. 220.

16. Aberbach, et al., *Bureaucrats and Politicians*, pp. 228–237.

17. See Joel D. Aberbach and Bert A. Rockman, *The Administrative State in Industrialized Democracies* (Washington, D.C.: American Political Science Association, 1985), and Aberbach and Rockman, "Bureaucratic and Political Roles."

18. Richard Rose, "On the Priorities of Government: A Developmental Analysis of Public Policies," *European Journal of Political Research*, 4 (1976): 247–289.

19. For further discussion of these issues, see Aberbach, et al., *Bureaucrats and Politicians*, Chapter 2.

20. Gary P. Freeman, "National Styles and Policy Sectors: Explaining Structured Variation," Paper prepared for presentation at the World Congress of the International Political Science Association, Paris, France, July 15–20, 1985.

21. Michael D. Cohen, James G. March, and Johan P. Olsen, "A Garbage Can Model of Organizational Choice," *Administrative Science Quarterly*, 17 (March 1972): 1–25.

22. Thomas E. Cronin, *The State of the Presidency*, 2nd ed. (Boston: Little, Brown, 1980), esp. pp. 274–290.

23. Richard Rose, "British Government—The Job at the Top," in Richard Rose and Ezra N. Suleiman (eds.), *Presidents and Prime Ministers* (Washington: American Enterprise Institute, 1980), pp. 1–49.

24. Dean E. Mann with Jameson W. Doig, *The Assistant Secretaries: Problems and Processes of Appointment* (Washington: The Brookings Institution, 1965).

25. Robert D. Putnam, "The Political Attitudes of Senior Civil Servants in Western Europe: A Preliminary Report," *British Journal of Political Science*, 3 (July 1973): 257–290, and Robert D. Putnam, "Elite Transformation in Advanced Industrial Societies: An Empirical Assessment of the Theory of Technocracy," *Comparative Political Studies*, 10 (October 1977): 383–412.

26. Putnam, "The Political Attitudes of Senior Civil Servants," and Aberbach, *et al.*, *Bureaucrats and Politicians*, p. 220.

27. Aberbach, *et al.*, *Bureaucrats and Politicians*, pp. 224–227.

28. *Ibid.*, esp. Chapter 5.

29. As Putnam notes in this regard, "This myth [of non-partisanship] . . . served as an ideological defense for a conservative bureaucracy against an intrusive political environment." Putnam, "The Political Attitudes of Senior Civil Servants," p. 284.

30. See, especially, Hans-Ulrich Derlien, "Zur einstweiligen Quieszierung politischer Beamter des Bundes, 1949–1983" ["On the Temporary Quiescence of Federal Political Executives, 1949–1983"], Universitat Bamberg, Verwaltungswissenschaftliche Beitrage, No. 16, 1984; more generally, on the political selection of senior civil service officials, see F. F. Ridley, "Career Service: A Comparative Perspective on Civil Service Promotion," *Public Administration*, 61 (Summer 1983): 179–196.

31. Aberbach, *et al., Bureaucrats and Politicians*, pp. 155–164.

32. This is especially true under recent Republican administrations that view the bureaucracy, not altogether incorrectly, to be a bastion of Democratic sentiment. See Joel D. Aberbach and Bert A. Rockman, "Clashing Beliefs within the Executive Branch: The Nixon Administration Bureaucracy," *American Political Science Review* 70 (June 1976): 456–468.

33. Indeed, of the 7 national samples analyzed by Aberbach, Putnam, Rockman and their associates, the British samples were marked by the strongest party-based attitudinal differences among politicians and very weak party differences among bureaucrats.

34. Volker Ronge, "The Politicization of Administration in Advanced Capitalist Societies," *Political Studies*, 22 (March 1974): 86–93.

35. For example, see Joseph LaPalombara, *Interest Groups in Italian Politics* (Princeton, New Jersey: Princeton University Press, 1964).

36. See Seymour Martin Lipset, *Agrarian Socialism*, revised edition (Berkeley: University of California Press, 1971), Chapter 12 ("Bureaucracy and Social Change").

37. Mattei Dogan, "How to Become A Cabinet Minister in France," *Comparative Politics*, 12 (October 1979): 1–25.

38. Pierre Birnbaum, *The Heights of Power: An Essay on the Power Elite in France* (Chicago: University of Chicago Press, 1982), pp. 51–55.

39. B. C. Koh, "Stability and Change in Japan's Higher Civil Service," *Comparative Politics*, 11 (April 1979): 279–297, and Ezra N. Suleiman, *Elites in French Society: The Politics of Survival*," (Princeton, New Jersey: Princeton University Press, 1978).

40. See Aberbach, *et al., Bureaucrats and Politicians*, Chapter 4, and Joel D. Aberbach and Bert A. Rockman, "The Overlapping Worlds of American Federal Executives and Congressmen," *British Journal of Political Science*, 7 (January 1977): 23–47.

41. Aberbach, *et al., Bureaucrats and Politicians*, Chapters 4 and 8.

42. For this view, see Birnbaum, *The Heights of Power*, and Suleiman, *Elites in French Society*.

43. See Charles L. Schultze, *The Politics and Economics of Public Spending* (Washington: The Brookings Institution, 1969), Alice M. Rivlin, *Systematic Thinking for Social Action* (Washington: The Brookings Institution, 1971), and Jack Hayward and Olga A. Narkiewicz (eds.), *Planning in Europe* (London: Croom Helm, 1978).

44. For examples, see Rose, *Managing Presidential Objectives*, and Rose and Suleiman, *Presidents and Prime Ministers*.

45. Charles E. Lindblom, *Politics and Markets* (New York: Basic Books, 1977).

46. Colin Campbell, *Governments Under Stress: Political Executives and Key Bureaucrats in Washington, London, and Ottawa* (Toronto: University of Toronto Press, 1983).

47. Hans-Ulrich Derlien and Hans Peter Muller, "Das Wachstum der Ministerialburokratie: Fuhrungspositionen der Bundesministerien 1949–1983" ["The Growth of the Ministerial Bureaucracy: Leadership Positions in the Federal Ministries 1949–1983"], *Verwaltungsrundschau*, (February 1985), esp. pp. 55–56.

48. Christopher Leman, *The Collapse of Welfare Reform: Political Institutions, Policy, and the Poor in Canada and the United States* (Cambridge, Massachusetts: M.I.T. Press, 1980).

49. Douglas E. Ashford, *British Dogmatism and French Pragmatism: Central-Local Policymaking in the Welfare State* (Winchester, Massachusetts: Allen and Unwin, 1982).

50. For instance, in the American context, see Lloyd N. Cutler, "To Form a Government," *Foreign Affairs*, 59 (Fall 1980): 126–143. In the West German context, see Fritz W. Scharpf, Bernd Reissert, and Fritz Schnabel, "Policy Effectiveness and Conflict Avoidance in Intergovernmental Policy Formation," Discussion Paper Series, International Institute of Management, Wissenschaftzentrum, Berlin (December 1977).

51. See David Braybrooke and Charles E. Lindblom, *A Strategy of Decision: Policy Evaluation as a Social Process* (New York: The Free Press, 1963).

52. For example, as criticisms of the centralization paradigm, see Vincent Ostrom, *The Intellectual Crisis in American Public Administration* (University, Alabama: University of Alabama Press, 1973), and Roger Benjamin, *The Limits of Politics: Collective Goods and Political Change in Postindustrial Societies* (Chicago: University of Chicago Press, 1980), esp. Chapter 9.

53. An oral statement made to one of the authors by Professor Ashford.

54. Johan P. Olsen, *Organized Democracy: Political Institutions in a Welfare State—The Case of Norway* (Bergen: Universitetsforlaget, 1983), p. 116.

55. For a theoretical typology, see Theodore J. Lowi, "Four Systems of Policy, Politics, and Choice," *Public Administration Review*, 32 (July/August 1972): 298–310.

56. See Randall B. Ripley and Grace A. Franklin, *Congress, the Bureaucracy, and Public Policy* (Homewood, Illinois: The Dorsey Press, 3rd, 1984).

57. As quoted in A. Grant Jordan, "Iron Triangles, Wooly Corporatism and Elastic Nets: Images of the Policy Process," *Journal of Public Policy*, 1 (February 1981), pp. 118–119.

58. See Richard Rose, "Government Against Sub-governments: A European Perspective on Washington," in Rose and Suleiman, *Presidents and Prime Ministers*, pp. 284–347.

25

Comparisons and Trends

DONALD C. ROWAT
Carleton University, Ottawa, Ontario, Canada

One of the best available indicators of the importance of public bureaucracy in a country is the number of public employees. Fortunately, a recent study for the International Monetary Fund has produced comparable figures for all of our developed countries except Israel, and for a considerable number of developing countries. This makes it possible not only to compare the developed democracies but also to detect some general differences between them and the developing countries. From this source I have compiled Table 1, which shows government employees as a percentage of population for nineteen of our developed democracies and also for nine reasonably representative developing countries. It also shows the percentages separately for the central government, state and local governments, and public enterprises. Unfortunately, this breakdown was not available for four of our nineteen countries: Finland, France, Spain and Switzerland.

SOME BASIC COMPARISONS

One of the basic facts that Table 1 reveals is that public bureaucracy is much more pervasive in the developed democracies. The number of public employees ranges around ten per cent of the population in the developed democracies, whereas in our selection of developing countries it only ranges around four per cent. Among the developed democracies Japan has by far the lowest proportion, at 4.4 per cent. Yet the proportion in all of our developing countries is below that of Japan except for Argentina and Egypt, and the percentages for these two are below those for all of the other developed democracies except the Netherlands. This indicates that a big public sector is characteristic of the developed democracies.

On the other hand, Table 1 also reveals that in most of the developed democracies a majority of public employees work for state and local governments, whereas the

---

The last part of this essay is a revised and reduced version of a paper by the author, based on the essays in this book, prepared for the 1985 meeting of the International Political Science Association and published in the *International Review of Administrative Sciences* 3 (1985), pp. 189–198.

Table 1 Public Employees as a Percentage of Population in the Developed Democracies and Selected Developing Countries.

Country	Year	Central Government	State and Local	General Government	Non-financial Enterprises	Public Sector
Developed Democracies:						
Australia	1980	2.07	7.77	9.83	1.14	10.97
Austria	1979	3.85	4.25	8.06	–	–
Belgium	1980	4.88	1.87	6.75	2.01	8.77
Canada	1981	1.49	4.73	6.22	1.58	7.80
Denmark	1981	2.57	8.78	11.35	1.18	12.53
Finland	1979	–	–	8.11	–	–
France	1980	–	–	5.73	–	–
Germany, F.R.	1980	1.30	4.76	6.06	1.64	7.70
Ireland	1978	2.30	2.21	4.50	2.21	6.71
Italy	1980	2.97	2.12	5.34	0.77	6.11
Japan	1980	1.04	2.73	3.75	0.69	4.44
Netherlands	1980	2.50	2.96	5.46	0.33	5.79
New Zealand	1981	6.86	1.52	8.38	1.96	10.35

Norway	1979	3.19	5.60	8.80	—	—
Spain	1979	—	—	4.00	—	—
Sweden	1979	2.55	12.12	14.66	1.64	16.31
Switzerland	1979	—	—	4.76	—	—
United Kingdom	1980	4.16	5.41	9.57	3.64	13.21
United States	1981	1.87	5.91	7.77	0.29	8.07
Developing Countries						
Argentina	1981	2.12	2.60	4.72	1.16	5.88
Egypt	1979	1.40	2.61	4.00	1.40	5.41
India	1977	0.67	1.14	1.81	0.59	2.39
Kenya	1980	2.10	0.24	2.23	0.61	2.84
Korea	1981	2.66	0.42	3.08	0.58	3.65
Liberia	1982	2.41	—	2.41	0.31	2.73
Philippines	1979	1.71	0.35	2.06	2.29	4.35
Tanzania	1978	1.43	—	1.43	0.98	2.41
Zambia	1980	2.47	0.08	2.60	2.13	4.73

Source: Compiled from Peter S. Heller and A. A. Tait, *Government Employment and Pay: Some International Comparisons* (Washington, D.C.: International Monetary Fund, 1983), Table 21, p. 41.

reverse is true in our developing countries. Among the nineteen developed democracies, the only countries that had more employees working for the central government at the beginning of the 1980's were Belgium, Ireland, Italy and New Zealand, while most of our developing countries are highly centralized. The only ones having a majority working for state and local government were Argentina, Egypt and India. Two of our developing countries, Liberia and Tanzania, had no employees at all at the state or local level. These differences indicate that, though the public sector is large in the developed democracies, the public services tend to be much more decentralized than in the developing countries.

Yet there are wide differences among the developed democracies themselves. The number of public employees in relation to population ranges all the way from 4.4 per cent in Japan to 16.3 per cent in Sweden—nearly four times Japan's percentage. The percentage is low in the Netherlands and Italy, and high in the United Kingdom, Denmark and New Zealand. The countries in which the percentage is high are the ones in which the welfare state and public ownership have advanced the furthest. Yet it will be observed from Table 1 that public enterprises are also popular in the developing countries, though in most cases their employees make up well under one per cent of the population, compared with over one per cent for most developed democracies. The U.K. had the highest proportion of all in 1980, with 3.6 per cent. Other developed democracies with a relatively high percentage in public enterprises were Ireland (2.2 per cent), Belgium (2.0 per cent) and New Zealand (2.0 per cent). Ones with a low percentage were the United States and the Netherlands, each with 0.3 per cent. It should be noted, however, that information on public enterprises is missing for six of the nineteen, including France and Spain.

In studies such as the one we have been using, such information is often incomplete and does not distinguish clearly enough between employees of ministerial departments and non-departmental agencies. There are many types of these agencies in addition to public enterprises, and countries vary in the extent to which they count and report on them as part of the central government. Partly for this reason Professor Richard Rose and his associates at the University of Strathclyde conducted an elaborate statistical study of public employment in six of the largest democracies, in order to produce complete statistics on a comparable basis. The countries covered were Britain, France, Italy, Sweden, West Germany and the United States. The resulting analysis for each country was recently published as a book, entitled *Public Employment in Western Nations*.

Professor Rose's comparative overview, with its accompanying statistical tables, reveals some interesting information about the growth, size and nature of the bureaucracies in the developed democracies that formerly had been only dimly perceived. It shows that the bureaucracies in these countries have grown during the post-war period more than had been assumed, but that most of this growth has occurred in the non-departmental agencies and at the local and regional levels of government. In other words, along with the rapid growth there has been an accompanying hiving off and decentralization of the bureaucracies. Since the study included countries as different in their ideological orientation as Sweden and the United States, it is likely that the main trends Professor Rose and his associates have identified apply to all of the developed democracies. I have therefore compiled tables based on their statistical information which illustrate these trends in summary form.

Growth and Size of the Bureaucracies

Table 2 shows public employment as a percentage of the workforce in the six countries, in both 1951 and 1981. It reveals that between 1951 and 1981 there was a rapid relative growth in public employment in most of these countries. In Sweden and Italy public employment as a percentage of the workforce more than doubled, while in France and Germany it nearly doubled. This rapid growth may be attributed mainly to the expansion of social services, such as health, education and welfare, and to the increase in public enterprises. The slowest growth was in Britain and the U.S., where the increase in the percentage was only 5.0 and 1.3, respectively. The slow growth in Britain is due probably to the high level public employment had already reached by 1951, while that in the U.S. is mainly explained by the minimal relative growth of its social services and public enterprises.

Table 2 also gives a good indication of the increased importance of the public services in the economies of the developed democracies. By 1981 public employment represented between one-quarter and one-third of the total workforce in most of these six countries. But the proportion varied considerably from country to country. Sweden was highest at 38 per cent, followed by France and Britain at 33 and 31 per cent. As might be expected in a country with few social services and public enterprises, the U.S.A. was by far the lowest, at 18 per cent, less than half Sweden's percentage.

Another way of looking at the extent of the state's role in the economy of the developed Western countries is to compare the total number of people dependent upon the state for their income. Professor Rose and his associates did this for the six countries by adding to public employees the number of unemployed people receiving income maintenance payments from the state. The resulting totals are impressive because, as Professor Rose has noted, "In every major Western nation, *the government gives an income to more people who are not working than to public employees*" (1). As a result, in five of the six countries 50 per cent or more of income recipients

Table 2   The Growth in Public Employment, as a Percentage of the Workforce, in Six Western Countries, 1951–1981.

	1951	1981	Change
Britain	26.6	31.4	5.0
France	17.5	32.6	15.2
Germany	14.4	25.8	11.4
Italy	11.4	24.4	13.0
Sweden	15.2	38.2	23.0
U.S.A.	17.0	18.3	1.3

Source: Richard Rose, *et al., Public Employment in Western Nations* (Cambridge: Cambridge University Press, 1985), p. 11, Table I.3.

receive their income from the state. Again, the highest percentage is in Sweden, with 58 per cent, but Britain and France are close behind, with 56 and 55 per cent. Even the U.S.A. is surprisingly high, with about 42 per cent (2).

Decentralization of Bureaucratic Structures

The most revealing table, in my view, is Table 3, showing public employment by type of government organization. It gives the percentages of public employees working for the central ministerial departments, the non-departmental agencies, and the lower levels of government in 1980. When we speak of the state, or the bureaucracy or the public service, we tend to think only of the central ministerial departments. Yet this table shows that by far the largest proportion of public employees in our six countries do not work in the ministerial departments, but either for non-departmental agencies or for local or regional governments. This is true even of unitary countries such as Britain and Sweden. Hence there seems to have been an important trend in recent years toward a decentralization of bureaucracy in the developed democracies. Local and regional governments may be regarded as "vertical" decentralization, and non-departmental agencies as "horizontal" decentralization.

The only countries that still had a relatively high proportion of their public employees working for the ministerial departments in 1980 were France and Italy, with 45 and 37 per cent. The U.S.A. and Sweden had the next highest numbers (22 and 19 per cent), while Britain and West Germany had less than 15 per cent. Since Britain is a unitary country, its low percentage is rather surprising. In West Germany, most federal services are administered by the state governments, with state employees acting as agents for the center.

Horizontal Decentralization

One of the main reasons for these generally low percentages for ministerial departments is that in all of the developed democracies there has been a lush growth of what we

Table 3 Public Employment by Type of Government Organization, as a Percentage of Total Public Employment in 1980, in Six Western Countries.

	Central Ministries	Non-Departmental Agencies	Local and Regional Governments
Britain	14	47	39
France	45	32	23
Germany	13	46	41
Italy	37	50	13
Sweden	19	27	54
U.S.A.	22	8	70

Source: Compiled from Richard Rose, *et al., op. cit.,* p. 25, Table I.9. The figures for non-departmental agencies may include some trading enterprises that are owned by local and regional governments.

have called the Non-Departmental Agencies (NODAs). These bodies perform a wide variety of functions and are of many types, such as public corporations, regulatory bodies, quasi-judicial tribunals and advisory bodies, but their main characteristic is that they enjoy a substantial degree of independence from the executive government. Another characteristic of NODAs is that they are nearly always headed by a collegial board or commission, rather than by a single minister (or secretary in the U.S.) as head of a department. Often there are so many, in such a variety, that exact counts of their number vary. In Canada there are over 400 at the federal level alone, and in Australia there are over 250 at that level. In Britain there are over 1,500, not counting the nationalized industries, and in Italy the number of public agencies, including those at the local and regional levels of government, is estimated to be as high as 40,000 (3).

Generally speaking, NODAs appear to be a device for escaping from the rigidities of departmental bureaucracy, especially in a centralized or unitary political system. This may be a reason for their large numbers in Italy and Britain, where they accounted for about 50 per cent of all public employment in 1980, though in West Germany they accounted for almost as high a proportion, 46 per cent. By far the lowest proportion was in the U.S.A., where they accounted for only eight per cent. This is primarily because there are so few large public corporations in the U.S.A. In France, however, the employees of NODAs account for 32 per cent of public employment and in Sweden 27 per cent.

Vertical Decentralization

During the post-war period there has also been a remarkable decentralization of the bureaucracies of the Western democracies to local or regional governments. Table 4 illustrates this by showing the percentage of public employment attributable to local and regional governments for the six countries in 1980 compared with 1950. Of course federations, by their very nature, have a high proportion of their public employees working for state and local governments. Table 4 reveals that this proportion was

Table 4 Public Employment by Local and Regional Governments, as a Percentage of Total Public Employment in 1950 and 1980, in Six Western Countries.

	1950	1980	Change
Britain	24	39	15
France	14	23	9
Germany	38	41	3
Italy	12	13	1
Sweden	29	54	25
U.S.A.	42	70	28

Source: Compiled from Richard Rose, *et al., op. cit.,* p. 25, Table I.9. The figures exclude trading enterprises owned by local or regional governments.

already high in 1950 for the two federations: the U.S.A. and West Germany. In these two countries about 40 per cent of all public employees worked for state or local governments in 1950. But the proportions were also high for some unitary countries such as Britain and Sweden, which had already created systems of relatively autonomous local governments with important functions and their own personnel. In these two countries, about one-quarter of all public employees already worked for local or regional governments in 1950.

Since 1950 there has been an impressive growth in the number of employees working for local and regional governments in both federal and unitary countries. Among our six countries, the biggest growth has occurred in the U.S.A., where state and local employment rose from 42 to 70 per cent of all public employment by 1980. But the most remarkable change has occurred among the unitary countries. Sweden, for instance, has reorganized its system of local governments and has delegated functions to them to such an extent that over half of all public employees now work for local and regional governments, and less than 20 per cent for the central departments (with the remainder working for non-departmental agencies). The proportion in Britain is also impressive, where in 1980 nearly 40 per cent of all public employment was local or regional. This growth in Britain was partly due to the creation of a new system of second-tier metropolitan governments throughout the country in 1972. However, these governments were later abolished by the Thatcher government, thus going against the decentralist trend. Opponents of the Thatcher government have accused it of abolishing them because a majority of Labour candidates were elected to their councils.

Perhaps the most impressive degree of vertical decentralization has occurred in France, which formerly had, and may still have, the most highly centralized bureaucracy in the Western world. Between 1950 and 1980 the number of public employees working for local and regional governments rose from 14 to 23 per cent of all public employees. Since 1980 this proportion has no doubt increased, because the socialist Mitterand government implemented a far-reaching program of decentralization, which involved transferring powers from the centrally appointed governors (or prefects) of the districts and regions to the elected district and regional councils, and increasing the powers of the local governments.

Several other West European countries have also implemented programs of vertical decentralization, so much so that it became the title of a recent book on the subject, entitled *Decentralist Trends in Western Democracies* (4). An earlier example was Italy, where the provision in its post-war constitution for regional governments was finally implemented beginning in 1970, after many years of delay. But by 1980 the proportion of public employees working directly for local or regional governments in Italy was still only 13 per cent. This low percentage may be partly because half of Italy's public employees now work for public corporations or other non-departmental agencies, some of which are attached to local or regional governments but not counted as part of their employees.

Another example is Belgium, which for the past twenty years has been engaged in a process of constitutional decentralization resembling federalism. This has involved the creation of three regional governments and three cultural communities, one for each of the Flemish and Walloon areas, and one for the Brussels area, which has a mixture of the two cultures. More recently, autonomy has been granted to some of the regions in Spain. Other unitary countries in Western Europe have consolidated their local governments, thus increasing their size and enabling them to take on additional responsibilities and public employees.

Public Service Unions

One indicator of the power of the bureaucracy in society is the role of public service personnel as an interest group pursuing their own aims and interests. A good measure of this is the extent to which public employees are unionized. Professor Rose and his associates were also able to produce comparable information on this. Table 5 shows the percentage of unionized employees in both the public and private sectors for their six countries.

One interesting part of the picture it reveals is that in the big Western democracies the public sector is much more highly unionized than the private sector, except for the U.S.A., where only 22 per cent of public employees are unionized, compared with 23 per cent in the private sector. The greatest difference is in Britain, where 75 per cent of public employees are unionized, compared with only 40 per cent in the private sector. The next biggest difference is in West Germany, where 58 per cent of the public sector is unionized, compared with only 29 per cent for the private sector. In France the proportion of unionized employees is surprisingly low in both sectors, being 35 per cent in the public sector and a mere 16 per cent in the private sector, considerably lower than the 23 per cent for the private sector in the U.S.A. The proportion in Sweden, on the other hand, is surprisingly high—82 per cent in the private sector and 89 per cent in the public sector.

It should also be observed that the percentages for both the public and private sectors vary greatly from one country to another. The percentage of the public sector that is unionized ranges all the way from 89 per cent in Sweden to 22 per cent in the U.S.A. This means that the power of public employees to act collectively varies greatly from one country to another. But it should be noted that this power also depends on the extent to which the public service unions within a country can act in unison. They are often divided along organizational or occupational lines, and in Canada and Western Europe they may also be divided along religious or ideological

Table 5 Percentage of Employees Who Are Unionized in the Public and Private Sectors in Six Western Countries.

	Public Sector	Private Sector	Difference
Britain (1974)	75	40	35
France (1980)	35	16	19
Germany (1980)	58	29	29
Italy (1976)	42	35	7
Sweden (1980)	89	82	7
U.S.A. (1980)	22	23	−1

Source: Richard Rose, *et al., op. cit.*, p. 40, Table I.16.

lines, noteworthy examples being France and Italy. If they are completely fragmented, as they are likely to be where they are dealing with separate central, state and local governments and independent public enterprises, they will not be able to act as a unit. In this way, the recent vertical and horizontal decentralization of government has tended to reduce the power of the bureaucracy.

THE IMPACT OF RECENT TRENDS

Many people believe that one of the most serious problems facing modern democracy is the great influence that appointed officials have in the making of policy. A comparative survey of public administration in the developed democracies reveals a number of recent changes and trends that will have a significant impact on this policy-making role of senior officials. These are: (1) political decentralization, (2) increasing political control over non-departmental agencies, (3) measures to improve the responsiveness of bureaucracy, (4) increasing control over the bureaucracy through what has been called the New Administrative Law, (5) increasing control of policy-making by the political executive, and (6) increasing participation in policy-making by the legislature. Let us review each of these in turn.

Political Decentralization

The centralization of political power inevitably increases the policy role of senior officials because the political ministers at the center do not have time to deal with all of the local policy problems and must delegate decision-making powers to appointed officials. Conversely, the decentralization of political power, as in a federal state, has the reverse effect of greatly reducing the control and the influence of senior officials over local policy matters by substituting instead locally elected policy-making executives and legislatures or councils. This is particularly true of the three federations in which there is a clear-cut constitutional division between the administrative services of the two levels of government—Australia, Canada and the United States. But it is almost equally true of the other three federations among the developed democracies—Austria, Switzerland and Western Germany. Hence the impact of the senior bureaucracy upon policy-making is automatically much less in federal countries because there is no single bureaucratic elite to exert its influence. The creation of strong, relatively autonomous local and regional governments in unitary countries has had much the same impact, because much of the policy-making power these governments have assumed was formerly held by senior officials, such as the French prefects. Also, the local authorities have built up the expertise of their public services to the point where it can rival or replace that of the central bureaucracy.

Non-Departmental Agencies

The growth of NODAs with independent decision-making powers has similarly reduced the power of central officials. The problem with NODAs, however, is that they are almost universally headed by appointed rather than elected officials. School boards in North America are among the few examples where such bodies are made up of elected representatives. Our statistics show that in several large Western countries nearly half of all public employees are thus not directly accountable to elected bodies. If they are independent of the political executive, to whom are they accountable? The more independent they are, seemingly, the less accountable they become. One way of helping to ensure that their decisions are in line with the policies that the political executive is trying to pursue, is for the executive to appoint members to the boards of NODAs who are sympathetic with those policies. And a way of ensuring this is to appoint persons who are supporters of the political party or coalition in power. The new Mulroney government in Canada, for instance, systematically replaced board members, as they finished their periods of tenure, with supporters of the Conservative party. New governments in many other developed democracies do likewise. It seems that, after political patronage was eliminated in the central bureaucracies of the developed democracies, it gradually reappeared—albeit in a more exalted form—through rewarding party supporters with appointments to the boards of the multiplying NODAs. This was probably one of the reasons for the growing popularity of NODAs. The use of positions on their boards as a device for rewarding the party faithful has now developed to such a degree that it may justifiably be dubbed the New Political Patronage.

By creating NODAs, governments created a new problem of bureaucratic independence, which they have only partly remedied by gaining some control over NODAs through making partisan appointments. While observers are now worried about the implications of the New Political Patronage, they are still concerned about the independent power of the NODAs to make policy without sufficient accountability to the government, parliament and the public. Discussions are now taking place and action is being taken in several of the developed democracies to make the NODAs more accountable through new legislation giving the executive more control of their policies and parliament more scrutiny of their activities. Legislation such as this for the main public corporations was adopted in Canada in 1984, empowering the cabinet to review their budgets and plans and to give them general policy directives, and providing for the Auditor General to give them an efficiency audit in behalf of parliament. A proposal now being discussed is whether the cabinet should not also have the power to issue policy directives to the boards of regulatory bodies.

Measures to Improve Responsiveness

Several measures have been taken recently to improve the responsiveness of central bureaucracies to the public. Studies in many of the developed democracies have shown that the senior level of the bureaucracy is unrepresentative of the main interest groups in society, and indeed in some cases comes mainly from very restricted groups in society. Studies of the father's occupation of senior officials in a number of countries have shown that they came disproportionately from among the sons of civil servants and businessmen, and in Britain they are mainly the graduates of "Oxbridge" (Oxford and Cambridge). The extreme example may be France, where the graduates of certain schools, especially the National School of Administration, form a cohesive elite who have spread into many of the top positions not only in the central bureaucracy but also in the NODAs, business and politics. Senior officials usually form part of the cabinet and large numbers are elected to the legislature. It is significant that most of the French prime ministers since the war have been recruited from the senior levels of the civil service.

Australia and New Zealand seem to have been the only exceptions, where a large proportion of senior officials have been recruited from the sons of non-skilled and skilled workers, in proportions much closer to those of the working population. This was partly because of the long-standing policy in these countries of recruiting public servants at a low educational level and promoting them from within. In recent years, however, as the essays on these countries reveal, a change of policy has permitted the lateral entry of university graduates and others at a higher level, so that the social composition of the bureaucratic elite is changing in the direction of the other developed democracies and is becoming less representative of the general population.

The main argument for representativeness is that a bureaucratic elite which is not representative of the major interest groups in society will propose and implement policies that do not fully incorporate the interests of the under-represented population. The extreme example may be Italy, where, as Professor Cassese points out, the senior bureaucracy is mainly from the economically stagnant south and grossly under-represents the attitudes and interests of the dynamic north. This helps to explain the inertia and self-protective stance of the Italian bureaucracy. Another extreme example of under-representation in all of the developed democracies is that of women. As our essays show, the bureaucratic elite in developed democracies invariably contains a minuscule number of women.

In recent years, however, a number of countries have adopted "affirmative action" or "equal opportunity" programs of recruitment to improve the representation of women and minority groups. Canada may have led the way with its program for increasing the representation of French Canadians in the federal bureaucracy, and succeeded in increasing the proportion of francophones to almost exactly their proportion of the Canadian population (27 per cent). However, their proportion of the senior management level was still only about 20 per cent in 1983, while that for women was only about 6 per cent. The federal government followed up its program for francophones with an affirmative action program to increase the recruitment and promotion of women and visible minorities such as the handicapped and blacks. Countries that have recently instituted similar programs are Australia, New Zealand and the U.S., while some European countries have such programs for women. It will be some years before these programs have much effect at the top level. Opponents of such programs argue that they are "the thin edge of the wedge"—that they interfere with selection and promotion on the basis of pure merit by introducing the principle of favoritism, and that this runs the danger of gradually reintroducing nepotism, patronage and partisanship.

Another measure designed to improve the responsiveness of the bureaucracy has been the introduction of the office of ombudsman. This office now exists at the national level in thirteen of the twenty developed democracies, and at the state level in all six of the federations, although Australia is the only one that has it in all of the states as well as at the national level. Its primary purposes are to investigate complaints against administrative action and to recommend remedies and administrative improvements.

A more recent development is the adoption of access laws, providing for the public's right of access to administrative documents. Such laws now exist in ten of the twenty developed democracies: the four Nordic countries, Australia, Canada, France, Netherlands, New Zealand and the United States. They are also being adopted at the state (or provincial) level in Australia, Canada, and the United States. These laws reduce the excessive secrecy of the bureaucracy and provide additional information to the public, thus increasing the public's knowledge of policy matters and administrative decisions in relation to that of the senior officials, for whom knowledge is power.

The New Administrative Law

Recent changes in the supervision and control of administrative procedure have been so extensive, particularly in the developed Commonwealth countries, that they have been dubbed the New Administrative Law. For many years, of course, the European democracies have had administrative courts, which have developed a special administrative law, and in recent years many of them have adopted special laws on administrative procedure. But even these countries have adopted a number of new reform measures which are part of what French scholars have called "the third generation of human rights." This has included reforming and expanding the administrative courts, which have experienced a virtual explosion of cases in recent years. In Italy, for instance, the number of cases has jumped in the past decade from about 5,000 to 40,000 per year. France adopted a law in 1979 requiring administrative authorities to give reasons for their decisions. Also, France and several other European countries have recently passed laws providing for the protection of personal data and for a citizen's right of access to and correction of personal files held by the government. Similar privacy laws have also been adopted at the national level in the Commonwealth countries and the United States.

While the United States adopted a law on administrative procedure as early as 1946, the New Administrative Law movement has probably gone furthest in Australia, where a new administrative appeals tribunal, a new federal court, and a new administrative review council have been created to hear administrative appeals and review the decision-making procedures of administrative bodies. In Canada the institution of a new federal court and privacy law in 1977, the adoption of a Charter of Rights in its revised constitution of 1981, and the approval of access laws by the federal and Quebec governments in 1982 may be considered part of the New Administrative Law. The adoption of the ombudsman institution is also part of this movement, as is the creation of anti-discrimination commissions at the state level in the United States and at the provincial and federal levels in Canada.

These measures related to the New Administrative Law are more concerned with the decision-making than the policy-making powers of senior officials, but are relevant where decisions are important enough to be considered policy decisions. The recent adoption of a federal law in the United States requiring the meetings of regulatory and other collegial bodies to be open to the public is similarly relevant. There has also been a move in this direction in Canada, as well as the adoption of the practice by some regulatory bodies of issuing draft regulations to affected interest groups for criticism and possible revision before their final adoption.

Executive Control of Policy-Making

There has also been a trend toward increased control of policy-making by political executives. This includes such developments as the adoption of the PPB (Planning, Programming and Budgeting) and ZBB (Zero-Based Budgeting) systems, and the development in Commonwealth countries of a senior cabinet committee on policy priorities. These are designed to give the political executive a clearer choice among policy objectives. It also includes the issuing of ethical guidelines for senior officials, as well as the creation of policy advising bodies outside the departmental bureaucracy, such as the Economic and Science Councils in Canada, and the increased use of study commissions and task forces containing members from outside the public service and often including members of parliament.

The secrecy of the policy-making process in parliamentary systems, however, still inhibits the cabinet from consulting sufficiently with outside interest groups before measures are formally presented to parliament. Some European countries such as Denmark, Sweden and Switzerland, in contrast with the developed Commonwealth countries, have instituted the practice of publishing draft legislation and sending it to all interested groups for criticism and possible revision long before it is presented to parliament.

More notable than these developments, however, has been the recent trend in parliamentary systems to increase political input into policy-making by increasing the number of politicized policy advisors and the degree of politicalization of the top of the bureaucracy—a move in the direction of the American system of changing the top level with each change of the executive. In most of the European democracies the prime minister and his ministers have their own secretariats to which they appoint senior officials of their choice as a source of policy advice. These secretariats are outside the regular departmental hierarchy, and have been growing in size. The senior bureaucrats of Western Europe tend to be more politicized than those of the developed Commonwealth countries. As a result, it is usually possible for a new prime minister and his ministers to choose for their political secretariats senior advisors from the public service who are sympathetic with their political orientation. After a government has been in power for a long time, however, it may be difficult for its successor to find sympathizers within the public service to appoint to its secretariats, so it may have to appoint more from outside. For instance, this appears to have been the case with the changeover to a socialist government in France. In Belgium, though some key officials are still appointed from the bureaucracy, the secretariats are so politicized that they have become a sort of delegation from the minister's political party, and have taken over much of the senior bureaucracy's function of policy advice. Thus, in the European countries the number of senior advisors in ministerial secretariats who are appointed from outside the bureaucracy seems to be growing.

The most remarkable change in ministerial secretariats has occurred in the Commonwealth countries, however. Formerly a minister's staff would typically consist of only one or two secretaries and a relatively junior executive assistant, and the prime minister's staff not much more than this. Recent years have seen an impressive growth of these staffs both in numbers and seniority. Prime ministers' offices have grown from a handful of personal assistants to a huge staff of senior advisors who were key party workers and now give political advice in particular policy areas. Under Prime Minister Mulroney, for instance, the staff of the Prime Minister's Office in Canada has jumped from 90 to 120. The Mulroney government has also instituted a new senior political officer for each minister called "chief of staff." The staff of the ministerial secretariats are nearly always appointed from outside the public service and the senior officers are well connected within the party in power for providing political and policy advice. Australia has a similar system with now about 80 senior advisors to ministers, while the U.K. has about 100 senior officers appointed on a political basis. These politically appointed advisors are an important new source of alternative policy advice coming from outside the bureaucracy.

Though the tradition of politically neutral career officials at the top is strong in the parliamentary countries, especially the Commonwealth ones, recent years have seen some inroads on this tradition. In the Commonwealth countries, except for New Zealand, the public service commissions have lost some of their personnel powers to bodies under the direct control of the executive, such as the treasury department in the United Kingdom and the treasury board (a committee of the cabinet) in Canada. This has facilitated more intervention by the prime minister and his or her cabinet in the appointment of the permanent heads of departments and other key officials. In some cases a few key officials have even been appointed from outside the public service.

The European countries vary considerably in the extent to which the top level of the bureaucracy is politicized. The most extreme cases appear to be Austria and Belgium, where strong coalition parties have forced an agreement on the sharing of the top bureaucratic posts. But Finland and West Germany are other cases in which a large number of top posts are partisan appointments. Under an article of the West German constitution certain posts had already been marked out as "political," the incumbent changing with the government, but in practice the number has grown considerably beyond this. Similarly in several other countries, where a party or coalition has been in power for a long time, the top level of the bureaucracy has gradually been replaced by officials sympathetic with the government, through its ultimate control over promotions. After this party or coalition changes, a similar gradual change in the composition of the top level occurs. For instance, the pioneering survey of bureaucrats and politicians in Western democracies by Aberbach, Putnam and Rockman in the early 1970's revealed that a high proportion of the senior officials in the Swedish ministries favored the Social Democratic party, which had been in power for many years (5). In West Germany, where the Christian Democratic party had been in power for many years and a high proportion of senior officials had favored that party, the coming to power of the Social Democratic-Liberal coalition in 1969 brought in a considerable number of leftist senior officials through lateral entry to key posts. With the changeover to a socialist government in France, a similar change took place in the top layer of France's bureaucracy, or at least in key policy posts.

The import of all of these changes in the parliamentary countries is that there is an ever-growing number of senior officials who are appointed for their political views, and who change with a change in government. This new group of political officials, whom Aberbach, Putnam and Rockman identify as "hybrids", we shall call the New Political Bureaucrats.

What are some of the implications of the rise of the New Political Bureaucrats? In the U.S. most of the top layer of the bureaucracy is composed of officials of this type, because each new president replaces senior officials with party supporters. We may therefore look to U.S. experience for some hints. Unfortunately Aberbach, Putnam and Rockman did not separate the political and career officials for purposes of study. This is understandable for the European countries because the number of political bureaucrats is still small and because the dividing line is not as clear, since often officials who are appointed on a political basis do not change with a change in government.

The indications of their survey are that the political officials in the U.S. are in background and educational qualifications not very different from the career officials (6). The main differences seems to be their political orientation and the fact that they owe their jobs to their political masters.

Regarding the significance of the New Political Bureaucrats for the role of the bureaucracy in policy-making, we may advance an interesting argument: where top officials are appointed for their political orientation by political masters for a short term, their power is weaker than that of officials who are independently appointed and hold permanent tenure. Hence, we may say that as their number grows, the power of the bureaucracy will decline. In his book, *The Mandarins of Western Europe*, Professor Mattei Dogan has generalized this argument regarding the incompatibility between the politicization and the power of top officials (7):

> The top grades of public administration can be highly politicized only where powerful and well-organized political parties control the totality of the political system, including the administrative hierarchy. In this case, the mandarins are, by necessity, more influenced than influential since political leaders keep as much power as possible for themselves. We can thus formulate the following generalization: in those countries where top civil servants are strongly politicized, in the sense of partisanship, they cannot play a truly essential role in decision-making processes.

We may conclude, then, that the impact of the rise of the New Political Bureaucrats in parliamentary countries will be to weaken the influence of the bureaucracy on policy-making. It is significant that in the U.S., where the number of political bureaucrats is the greatest, the role of the legislature in policy-making is the strongest. As Aberbach, Putnam and Rockman point out, neither in Europe nor the United States do political appointments to the top posts necessarily represent party patronage of the cruder sort (8):

> Rather, they reflect for the most part the understandable efforts of political leaders to ensure that their closest bureaucratic collaborators are broadly sympathetic to the political and ideological orientations of the government in power. Such mechanisms can mitigate the threat of purely bureaucratic predominance in policy-making.

Parliament and Policy-Making

Finally, there has been a trend in the parliamentary countries toward increased participation by parliament in policy-making and toward increased supervision of the policy-making activities of the bureaucracy, in particular those of the NODAs since they are not directly supervised by the political executive. For instance, in Canada a joint committee of both houses of parliament now monitors executive regulations, and a special committee to monitor the activities of public enterprises has been created in the Australian federal and state legislatures. Also, committees of parliament are being provided with their own research staffs, and in reviewing bills often hold hearings and receive briefs from interest groups, on the basis of which they propose amendments to the bills. The strongest move in this direction appears to be the reformed committee system in the Australian senate. It is now not uncommon for committees of parliament to call senior officials before them to give evidence and answer questions, and in New Zealand they even appear before party caucuses for questioning.

A related change is a gradual improvement in the educational level and competence of ministers and MPs, accompanying the general rise in the educational level of the population, so that they are able to compete in expertise and technical knowledge on more equal terms with the senior officials. It is now common for the "shadow cabinets" of the opposition parties to become specialists in various policy areas. The net effect of all this is to improve parliament's supervision of the appointed bodies and senior officials and thus to increase their accountability.

CONCLUSIONS

In taking an overview of these changes and trends, we should recall that they do not apply as fully to the United States, partly because the problem of too much bureaucratic influence was never as serious there and partly because this problem was tackled earlier there. The United States has never had a system like that of most parliamentary countries in which the legislature is dominated by the executive, which in turn is secretly advised by a permanent senior bureaucracy that does not adequately represent the main political interests in society. The independent power of the Congress has enabled it to have alternative sources of policy advice, thus reducing bureaucratic influence on policy-making.

In any case, the net effects of all these changes on the policy-making role of the bureaucracy, especially in the parliamentary countries, are likely to be as follows:

1. The influence of senior officials will more nearly represent the interests of society;
2. The bureaucracy will be supervised and controlled more closely;
3. The most drastic change will be to reduce the influence of the bureaucracy by increasing the political input into policy-making.

What will be the impact of the recent rise of neo-conservatism in the Western world on the trends we have identified? In recent years there has been a marked swing in favor of conservative governments in a number of the developed democracies, such as Canada, Britain, France and the United States. The supporters of neo-conservatism favor the deregulation of business, the privatization of public corporations, and a reduction in government spending and programs, and hence in the size of the bureaucracy. They also favor greater centralization and more control by the executive over non-departmental agencies and local and regional governments. Policies based on these views will run counter to the trends of growth and decentralization that have so far been characteristic of the post-war period.

Privatization and restraint will certainly reduce, possibly in some cases even reverse, the relative growth of the bureaucracies. But direct cutbacks in the public services will be opposed by public service employees and their unions, and may result in a higher proportion becoming unionized, especially in countries where this proportion is low, such as the U.S.A., France and Italy. On the other hand, fear of unemployment may inhibit unionization. Privatization and deregulation, whose aim is to abolish as many public corporations and regulatory bodies as possible, are certainly draconian ways of solving the problem of accountability for non-departmental agencies. Their abolition would also slow or halt the growth of horizontal decentralization. However, because most public corporations were created for a public purpose and therefore cannot operate at a profit, few of them will find private buyers, and the remainder will continue as public corporations. Similarly, it will not be easy to dispense with any regulatory bodies, which were created to control the excesses of private enterprise. Nevertheless, executive and parliamentary controls over the non-departmental agencies are likely to be tightened.

The New Conservatism will have a similar dampening effect on vertical decentralization. However, the abolition of the metropolitan governments in Britain by the Thatcher government is probably an extreme case. Other neo-conservative governments, including the new Chirac government in France, are unlikely to be able to reverse the reforms implemented by previous governments or to stem the strong decentralist trend that has been in evidence since the end of the second world war.

Hence my prediction for the Western democracies is that the proportion of public employees working for independent agencies and the lower levels of government will probably continue to increase, though at a reduced rate. This means that in the Western world horizontal and vertical decentralization will continue, and bureaucracies will thus become more fragmented and less powerful. Since the bureaucracies in the six federations of the Western world are already fragmented, this trend will be particularly significant for the unitary democracies.

REFERENCES

1. Rose, Richard, *et al., Public Employment in Western Nations* (Cambridge: Cambridge University Press, 1985), p. 44. Emphasis his.
2. *Ibid.*, Table I.17, p. 43.
3. The illustrative figures given here were taken from the country essays in this book.
4. Sharpe, L. J., ed. (Beverly Hills: Sage, 1979).
5. *Bureaucrats and Politicians in Western Democracies* (Cambridge: Harvard University Press, 1981), p. 167.
6. *Ibid.*
7. Mattei Dogen, ed., *The Mandarins of Western Europe* (Beverly Hills: Sage, 1975), pp. 13–14.
8. *Op. cit.*, p. 249.

Bibliography of Cross-National Comparisons

There is so little genuinely comparative literature on public administration in the developed democracies that the editor believes he has here collected references to most of the significant cross-national comparisons that have been published in English. The bibliography is divided into two sections: general comparisons and theoretical works, and comparisons of specialized fields or aspects of public administration. For the convenience of readers, short annotations have been added to many of the comprehensive comparisons, especially to show which countries are included. Also, the Library of Congress catalog number is given at the end of each entry, since this number is the same in most libraries.

A. GENERAL AND THEORETICAL

Aberbach, Joel D., R. D. Putnam and B. A. Rockman. *Bureaucrats and Politicians in Western Democracies.* Cambridge, Harvard University Press, 1981. Britain, Netherlands, Sweden, West Germany, Italy, U.S. JN94.A69E92.

Almond, Gabriel A., and Sidney Verba. *The Civic Culture.* Boston and Toronto, Little, Brown, 1965. Compares Germany, Italy, Britain, U.S. and Mexico. Relevant sections. JA74.A4 1965.

Armstrong, J. A. "Sources of administrative behavior: some Soviet and Western European comparisons," *Amer. Pol. Sci. Rev.* 59 (September 1965), pp. 643–655. JA1.A6.

Armstrong, J. A. *The European Administrative Elite.* Princeton: Princeton University Press, 1973. Britain, France, Germany and Russia from the 17th century. JF1411.A73.

Arora, Ramesh K. *Comparative Public Administration: An Ecological Approach.* New Delhi, Associated, 1972. JF1411.A75.

Barker, Sir Ernest. *The Development of Public Services in Western Europe, 1660-1930.* London, Oxford University Press, 1944. Esp. Ch. I. JF1341.B3.

Berger, Suzanne, ed. *Organizing Interests in Western Europe.* Cambridge, Cambridge Univ. Press, 1981. JN94.A792P76.

Caiden, Gerald E. *Administrative Reform.* Chicago, Aldine, 1969. JF1351.C33 1969.

Campbell, Colin. *Governments Under Stress: Bureaucrats and Political Leaders in Washington, London and Ottawa.* Toronto, Univ. of Toronto Press, 1983. JF1525.D4C35.

Chapman, Brian. *The Profession of Government: The Public Service in Europe.*
London, Allen & Unwin, 1959. Compares eleven countries. JF1351.C4.

Chilcote, Ronald H. "Public policy and administration in comparative perspective,"
in Howard J. Wiarda, ed., *New Directions in Comparative Politics.* Boulder,
Westview Press, 1985. JF51.N49.

Cocks, Paul. "Rethinking the organization weapon: the soviet system in a systems
age," *World Politics* 32 (January 1980), 228-57. D839.W57.

Comparative Administrative Theory Conference, P. Le Breton, ed. *Comparative
Administrative Theory.* Seattle, University of Washington Press, 1968. HD31.C615
1966.

Crozier, Michel. *The Bureaucratic Phenomenon.* Compares France with Britain,
pp. 213-313, and with U.S., pp. 231-236. HD33.C72.

Dahl, Robert A. *Political Oppositions in Western Democracies.* New Haven, Yale Univ.
Press, 1966. JF2051.D3.

Debbasch, Charles, ed. *La politique de choix des fonctionnaires dans les pays
européens.* Paris, editions du Centre national de la Recherche scientifique, 1981.
Essays on 14 countries. JN94.A69A66.

Diamant, A. "European models of bureaucracy and development," *Internat. Rev.
Adm. Sci.* XXXII, 4 (1966), 309-20. JA1.16.

Dogan, Mattei, ed. *The Mandarins of Western Europe: The Political Role of Top
Civil Servants.* Beverly Hills, Sage, 1975. Covers eleven countries. JN94.A69E94.

Eisenstadt, S. N. *The Political Systems of Empires.* New York, Free Press of Glencoe;
London, Collier-Macmillan, 1963. The bureaucratic aspects of empires.
JA71.E38 1963.

Etzioni-Helevy, Eva. *Bureaucracy and Democracy: A Political Dilemma.* London,
Routledge and Kegan Paul, 1983. Part II, Chs. 11 and 12 on bureaucracy and
party politics and electoral manipulation in Australia, Belgium, Britain, Israel,
Italy, France and U.S. JF1411.E89.

Ferkiss, Victor C. "The coexistent universes of comparative administration," *Journal
of Comparative Administration* 1, 2 (Aug. 1969), 177-189. JA1.J57.

Farazmand, Ali, ed. *Handbook of Comparative and Development Public Administration.* New York, Marcel Dekker, forthcoming.

Finer, Herman. *The Theory and Practice of Modern Government.* London, Methuen,
1962 (Part six on the civil service in Britain, U.S., France, Germany). JF51.F52
1962.

Flora, Peter, and A. J. Heidenheimer, eds. *The Development of Welfare States in
Europe and America.* New Brunswick, N.J., Transaction Books, 1981.
HN17.5.D48.

Fougère, Louis, comp. *Civil Service Systems.* Brussels, International Institute of
Administrative Sciences, 1969. On U.S., Latin America, West Germany, France,
Britain and socialist states. JF1351.F6813 1969.

Gladden, E. N. *A History of Public Administration,* Vol. two: *From the Eleventh
Century to the Present Day.* London, Cass, 1972. JF1351.G525.

Gregoire, R. "The civil service in Western Europe," *Public Personnel Review* 17,
No. 4 (1956), pp. 288-94. JK671.P85.

Hayward, Jack, and Michael Watson, eds. *Planning, Politics and Public Policy: The
British, French and Italian Experience.* London, Cambridge Univ. Press, 1975.
HC256.P53.

Heady, Ferrel. "Comparative administration: a sojourner's outlook," *Public Admin.
Review* 38, 4 (July/Aug. 78), pp. 358-365. JK1.P85.

Heady, Ferrel. *Public Administration: A Comparative Perspective.* New York, Dekker,
3rd 1984. JF1351.H4 1984.

Heady, Ferrel, and S. L. Stokes, eds. *Papers in Comparative Public Administration.*
Ann Arbor, Institute of Public Administration, University of Michigan, 1962.
JF1321.H4.

Heaphey, James. "Comparative public administration: comments on current characteristics," *Public Administration Review* 28, 3 (June 1968), 242–249. JK1.P85.

Heidenheimer, Arnold J., *et al. Comparative Public Policy: The Politics of Social
Change in Europe and America.* N.Y., St. Martin's, 1975. On the influence of
prevailing ideas. HN65.H4.

Huddleston, Mark W. *Comparative Public Administration: An Annotated Bibliography.*
N.Y., Garland, 1983. REF. JF1351 BIBL. H83.

Ilchman, W. F. *Comparative Public Administration and "Conventional Wisdom".*
Beverly Hills, Sage, 1971. Against theorizing for theory's sake. JF1411.I53.

Indiana, University of, Dept. of Government. *Toward the Comparative Study of
Public Administration.* Bloomington, 1957. JF1321.I48.

International Political Science Association. *Conference on Comparative Public Administration with Special Reference to Bureaucracy.* Paris, 1953. JF1321.I49.

Jackson, R. H. "An analysis of the comparative public administration movement,"
Canadian Public Administration IX (March 1966), 108–29. JL1.C35.

Kingdom, T. D. *Improvement of Organization and Management in Public Administration: A Comparative Study.* 3rd ed. 1960. JF1351.K5 1960.

Leemans, Arne F., and A. Dunsire, *The Public's Servants: Checks on Public Servants
in European Countries.* Helsinki, Finnpublishers Oy, 1981. JF1621.P82.

Max, F. M. "An inventory of administrative studies in Europe," *Pub. Ad. Rev.*
(July–Aug. 1969). JK1.P85.

Meyer, Poul. *Administrative Organization: A Comparative Study of the Organization
of Public Administration.* London, Stevens, 1957. JF1351.M4.

Meyer, Poul. "The development of public administration in the Scandinavian countries
since 1945," *International Review of Administrative Sciences* XXVI, no. 2
(1960), pp. 135–146. JA1.I6.

Meyers, François, ed. (sous la direction de). *La politisation de l'administration. The
Politicization of Public Administration.* Bruxelles, Int. Inst. of Admin. Sciences,
1985. Includes Belgium, Canada, France, Greece, Netherlands, Sweden, Switzerland,
U.K. and W. Germany.

Michigan, University of, Institute of Public Administration. *Comparative Public Administration. A Selected Annotated Bibliography.* Ed. Ferrel Heady and Sybil L.
Stokes. Ann Arbor, 1960. JF1351.M53 1960.

Miewald, Robert D. *The Bureaucratic State: An Annotated Bibliography.* N.Y.,
Garland, 1984. Section on comparative. REF. JF1351 BIBL. M53.

Miles, Arnold P. *Issues and Problems in the Administrative Organization of National
Governments.* Brussels, International Institute of Administrative Sciences, 1959.
Pamphlet.

Milne, R. S. "Comparisons and models in public administration," *Political Studies* 10
(Feb. 1962), 1–14. JA1.P63.

Modeen, Tore, ed. *Recruiting for High Offices in the Central Administration.* Tampere,
Dept. of Admin. Sciences, Univ. of Tampere, 1983. Italy (in French), Sweden,
Austria, Netherlands, France (French), U.K., W. Germany (French), Belgium
(French), and Finland. JN94.A69E97.

Molitor, André. *The University Teaching of Social Sciences: Public Administration.*
Paris, UNESCO, 1959. Esp. Chaps. 1, 2. UN9 ES73 59U57.

Morstein Marx, M. F. *The Administrative State.* Chicago, University of Chicago Press,
1957. JF1351.M59.

Neustadt, Richard E. "White House and Whitehall," *The Public Interest* 2 (Winter 1966), 55–69. H1.P9. Reprinted in Francis E. Rourke, ed., *Bureaucratic Power in National Politics* (Boston, Little, Brown, 2nd ed. 1972), pp. 164–179, JK421.B86 1972, and in Richard Rose, ed., *Policy-Making in Britain* (London: Macmillan, 1969), JN318.R6 1969.

Page, Edward C. *Political Authority and Bureaucratic Power—A Comparative Analysis.* Sussex, Wheatsheaf, 1985. Britain, France, W. Germany, U.S. JF1501.P34.

Pekonen, Ryosti. "Policy-making and the relationship between politics and bureaucracy," *International Rev. of Admin. Sciences* L1,3 (1985), pp. 207–220. JA1.I6.

Peters, B. Guy. *The Politics of Bureaucracy: A Comparative Perspective.* New York, Longman, 2nd 1984. JF1501.P43 1984.

Pittsburgh, University of, Administrative Science Centre. *Comparative Studies in Administration.* Pittsburgh, University of Pittsburgh Press, 1959. HD30.P5.

Price, W. "Education and the civil service in Europe," *Western Political Quarterly* 10 (December, 1957), pp. 817–32. Britain, France, Germany and U.S. JA1.W4.

Putnam, Robert D. "Elite transformation in advanced industrial societies," *Compar. Pol. Stud.* 10 (Oct. 1977), 383–412. Compares France, Germany and Italy. JA1.C6.

Putnam, Robert D. "The political attitudes of senior civil servants in Western Europe: A preliminary report," *British Journal of Political Science* 3 (July 1973), pp. 257–290. Britain, Germany and Italy. JA8.B7.

Raphaeli, Nimrod. *Readings in Comparative Public Administration.* Boston, Allyn & Bacon, 1967. JF1351.R3.

Richardson, Jeremy John, ed. *Policy Styles in Western Europe.* Winchester, Mass., Allen & Unwin, 1982. Essays on W. Germany, Norway, Britain, France, Sweden and Netherlands. Conclusion sees common trends as: 1) departmental pluralism, 2) unconventional participation, 3) crowded policy communities and overloaded governments. JN94.A91P64.

Ridley, Frederick F. "Career service: a comparative perspective on civil service promotion," *Public Admin.* 61 (Summer 1983), pp. 179–196. JA8.P8.

Ridley, Frederick F., ed. *Specialists and Generalists: A Comparative Study.* London, Allen & Unwin, 1968. On Britain, France, Australia, W. Germany, Sweden, U.S. JF1351.R47 1968.

Ridley, Frederick F., ed. *Government and Administration in Western Europe.* Oxford, Martin Robertson, 1979. Britain, France, Germany, Italy, Belgium, Netherlands. JN94.A5G68.

Riggs, F. W. *The Ecology of Public Administration.* London, Asia Publishing, 1961. U.S., Thailand and Philippines. JF1351.R5.

Riggs, F. W. "The Ecology and context of public administration: a comparative perspective," *Public Administration Review* 40,2 (March/April 1980), 107–115. JK1.P85.

Robson, W. A. *The Civil Service in Britain and France.* London, Hogarth, 1956. JN425.R62.

Ronge, V., "The politicization of administration in advanced capitalist societies," *Political Studies* 22 (March 1974), pp. 86–93. JA1.P63.

Rose, Richard, and Ezra N. Suleiman, eds. *Presidents and Prime Ministers.* Washington, American Enterprise Institute for Public Policy Research, 1980. JF51.P68.

Rothman, Stanley. *European Society and Politics.* Indianapolis, Bobbs-Merrill, 1970. Ch. 22. Britain, France, Germany, U.S.S.R. JF51.R56.

Rowat, Donald C. "Bureaucracy and policy-making in developed democracies: the decline of bureaucratic influence," *Internat. Rev. of Admin. Sciences* L1, 3 (1985), 189–198. JA1.I6.

Sayre, W. S. "Bureaucracies: some contrasts in systems," *Indian Journal of Public Administration* 10, p. 219. Compares Britain and the U.S. JQ201.I55. Reprinted in N. Raphaeli, *Readings in Comparative Public Administration* (Boston: Allyn and Bacon, 1967), pp. 341–354. JF1351.R3.

Self, Peter. *Administrative Theories and Politics.* London, Allen & Unwin, 1972. Britain, France, U.S. JF1351.S44.

Schwartz, Donald V. "Decisionmaking, administrative decentralization and feedback mechanisms: comparisons of Soviet and Western models," *Studies in Comparative Communism* 7 (Spring–summer 1974), 146–183. HX1.C7172.

Sharma, M. P. *Public Administration in Theory and Practice.* Allahabad, Kitab Mahal, 5th 1967. On India, Britain and U.S. JF1351.S47.

Shonfield, Andrew. *Modern Capitalism: The Changing Balance of Public and Private Power.* London, Oxford University Press, 1965. Esp. Part II on planning and IV on control over admin. Britain, France, Italy, Austria, Switzerland. HC59.S45.

Self, Peter. *Administrative Theories and Politics.* London, Allen & Unwin, 1972. Compares Britain, France and U.S. JF1351.S44.

Sisson, C. H. *The Spirit of British Administration and Some European Comparisons.* London, Faber, 1959. JF1351.S54.

Slesinger, J. A. *A Model for the Comparative Study of Public Bureaucracies.* Ann Arbor, University of Michigan, 1957. Pamphlet. JK5801.M5 N.23.

Smith, Bruce L. R., ed. *The Higher Civil Service in Europe and Canada: Lessons for the United States.* Washington, Brookings, 1984. Essays on Britain, Canada, France, U.S. and W. Germany. JN94.A69E93.

Smith, T. Alexander. *The Comparative Policy Process.* Santa Barbara, Calif., ABC-Clio, 1975. Case studies from Britain, U.S., Canada, West Germany, France. JF51.S545.

Sproule-Jones, M. H. *Public Choice and Federalism in Australia and Canada.* Canberra, Australian National University, 1975. Has some comparison of public administration. JQ4020.S8573.

Strauss, Erich. *The Ruling Servants; Bureaucracy in Russia, France—and Britain?* London, Allen & Unwin, 1961. JF1351.S86.

Subramaniam, V. "British administrative institutions: paradoxes of acceptance, adaptation and rejection," *Round Table* (June 1983). DA10.R6.

Subramaniam, V. "The higher bureaucracy and policy-making in the Anglo-Saxon commonwealth," *Internat. Rev. of Admin. Sciences* L1, 3 (1985), 199–206. JA1.I6.

Subramaniam, V. *Transplanted Indo-British Administration.* New Delhi, Ashish, 1977. Especially Ch. 1 on contrast of Afro-Asian and Anglo-Saxon Commonwealth. JF1351.S87.

Suleiman, Ezra N., ed. *Bureaucrats and Policy Making: A Comparative Overview.* New York, Holmes and Meier, 1984. U.S., Italy, Japan, France, Britain, West Germany, Norway and Chile. JF1601.B87.

Tarrow, Sidney, P. J. Katzenstein, and L. Graziano, eds. *Territorial Politics in Industrial Nations.* N.Y., Praeger, 1978. JS113.T47.

Taylor, Charles Lewis, ed. *Why Governments Grow: Measuring Public Sector Size.* Beverly Hills, Sage, 1983. Essays on Netherlands, U.K., U.S.S.R., and E. Europe. HJ2005.W37.

Tummala, Krishna, ed. *Administrative Systems Abroad.* Lanham, Md., University Press of America, 2nd 1984. Israel, U.S.S.R., nine developing countries and Latin America. JF1351.A28 1984.

Urban, Michael E. "Bureaucracy, contradiction, and ideology in two societies," *Administration and Society* 10 (May 1978), 49–85. JA1.J572.

Waldo, Dwight, ed. "Comparative and development administration: a symposium,"
    Public Administration Review 36, 6 (Nov.–Dec. 1976), 615–654. Essays by
    Loveman, Bendon, Tapia-Videla, Springer, Jun and Riggs. JK1.P85.
Waldo, Dwight. *Comparative Public Administration.* Chicago, Compar. Admin. Group,
    Amer. Soc. for Public Admin., 1964. JF1351.W31.
Watts, Ronald L. *Administration in Federal Systems.* London, Hutchinson, 1970.
    Federal-state relations, with lessons for Nigeria. JC355.W37.
White, Leonard D., *et al. Civil Service Abroad: Great Britain, Canada, France,
    Germany.* N.Y., McGraw-Hill, 1935. JF1341.C5.
Wilson, V. Seymour. "The relationship between scientific management and personnel
    policy in North American administrative systems," *Pub. Admin.* (London) (Sum.
    1973), pp. 193–205. JA8.P8.

B. SPECIALIZED COMPARISONS

Arora, R. S. *Administration of Government Industries.* Delhi, Indian Inst. of Pub.
    Admin., 1969. U.S., U.K. and India. HD3850.A73.
Ashby, Eric. *Universities: British, Indian, African.* London, Weidenfeld and Nicolson,
    1966. LB2321.A82.
Ashford, Douglas E. *British Dogmatism and French Pragmatism: Central-Local
    Policymaking in the Welfare State.* Winchester, Mass., Allen & Unwin, 1982.
    JS113.A82.
Atkinson, Michael M., and William D. Coleman. "Bureaucrats and politicians in
    Canada: an examination of the political administration model," *Comparative
    Political Studies* 18, 1 (April 1985), 58–80. Compares with Britain and U.S.
    JA1.C6.
Blondel, Jean. *The Organization of Governments: A Comparative Analysis of
    Governmental Structures.* London, Sage, 1982. JF51.B5815.
Buck, A. E. *The Budget in Governments of Today.* New York, Macmillan, 1934.
    The first comprehensive comparison. HJ2043.B9.
Burn, Barbara B., *et al. Higher Education in Nine Countries.* N.Y., McGraw-Hill,
    1971. France, Britain, Canada, Australia, W. Germany, Sweden, Japan, Soviet
    Union, India; has an annotated bibliography. LB2322.B85.
Caiden, Gerald E., and H. Siedentopf, eds. *Strategies for Administrative Reform.*
    Lexington, Heath, 1982. Has chapters on Asia, Australia, Bangladesh, Germany,
    France, Italy, Netherlands, U.S. JF1525.073S85.
Caiden, Gerald E., ed. *International Handbook of the Ombudsman.* Westport, Green-
    wood Press, 1983. Two vols. JF1525.045I55.
Canada, Task Force on Government Information. *Report: To Know and Be Known.*
    Vol. ii, comparison of systems, pp. 34–40; Ottawa, Queen's Printer, 1969.
    JL86.P8A3 2v.
Canadian Institute on Public Affairs. *Economic Planning in a Democratic Society.*
    Toronto, University of Toronto Press, 1963. HD82.C35.
Castberg, Frede. *Freedom of Speech in the West: A Comparative Study of Public
    Law in France, the United States, and Germany.* New York, Oceana, 1960.
    JC591.C38.
Coombes, David, ed. *The Power of the Purse: A Symposium on the Role of European
    Parliaments in Budgetary Decisions.* London, Allen & Unwin, 1972. Essays by 14
    experts on 6 countries. HJ2094.P68 1972.
Corbett, D. C. "Canadian examples, Australian adaptations," in O. P. Dwivedi, ed.
    The Administrative State in Canada. Toronto, University of Toronto Press, 1982.
    Comparison of civil services. JL651982.A45.

Corbett, D. C. *Politics and the Airlines.* Toronto, University of Toronto Press, 1965. On Australia, Britain, Canada, India, U.S. HE9780.C6.

Daalder, Hans, and E. A. Shils, eds., *Universities, Politicians and Bureaucrats: Europe and the United States.* Cambridge, Cambirdge Univ. Press, 1982. Essays on 12 countries. LC177.2.U54.

Dawson, Helen J. "Relations between farm organizations and the civil service in Canada and Great Britain," *Canadian Public Administration* X, 4 (Dec. 1967), 450–470. JL1.C35.

Denton, G., *et al. Economic Planning and Policies in Britain, France and Germany.* London, Allen & Unwin, 1968. HC256.5.D37 1968.

Economic Council of Canada. *Eighth Annual Review.* Ottawa: Queen's Printer, 1971. Comparison of PPBS in Canada and U.S. Doc. Div. CA1 EC 21-71A08.

Einaudi, Mario, M. Bye, and E. Rossi. *Nationalization in France and Italy.* Ithaca, Cornell University Press, 1955. HD4168.E3.

Flexner, Abraham. *Universities, American, English, German.* New York, Oxford University Press, 1930. LA183.F6.

Frank, Thomas M., and E. Weisband, eds. *Secrecy and Foreign Policy.* New York, Oxford University Press, 1974. On U.S., Britain and Canada. KF5753.F73.

Freeman, Gary P. "National styles and policy sectors: explaining structured variation," paper for Congress of International Political Science Association, Paris, 1985.

Freund, Ernst. *Administrative Powers Over Persons and Property: A Comparative Survey.* Chicago, University of Chicago Press, 1928. K3400.F74.

Friedmann, Wolfgang G. *The Public Corporation: A Comparative Symposium.* Toronto, Carswell, 1954. HD3850.F7.

Friedmann, Wolfgang G., and J. F. Garner. *Government Enterprise: A Comparative Study.* London, Stevens, 1970. K1366.G68.

Galeotti, Serio. *The Judicial Control of Public Authorities in England and in Italy: A Comparative Study.* London, Stevens, 1954. KJF.G34J83.

Galnoor, Itzhak, ed. *Government Secrecy in Democracies.* New York, Harper and Row, 1977. On U.S. and 7 other countries. JF1525.S4G72.

Gélinas, André, ed. *Public Enterprise and the Public Interest: Proceedings of an International Seminar.* Toronto, Institute of Public Administration of Canada, 1978. Canada, Australia, U.S., W. Germany, Italy, Sweden. HD4007.P94.

Gellhorn, Walter. *Ombudsmen and Others: Citizens' Protectors in Nine Countries.* Cambridge, Harvard University Press, 1966. JC578.G35.

Goodin, Robert E. "Rational politicians and rational bureaucrats in Washington and Whitehall," *Public Administration* (1982), 23–41. JA8.P8.

Hamson, C. J. *Executive Discretion and Judicial Control: An Aspect of the French Conseil d'état.* London, Stevens, 1954. KJV4385.H34.

Hanf, Kenneth, and F. W. Scharpf, eds. *Interorganizational Policy Making: Limits to Coordination and Central Control.* Beverly Hills, Calif., Sage, 1978. U.S., W. Germany, France, Denmark, Holland, Sweden. JF1525.D4I57.

Hanson, A. H., ed. *Public Enterprise: A Study of Its Organisation and Management in Various Countries.* Brussels, International Institute of Administrative Sciences, 1954. Canada, Australia, France, Germany, Norway, Sweden, Belgium, Greece. HD3850.H3.

Harris, Richard L., and R. H. Kearney. "A brief comparison of the public services of Canada and Ceylon," *Philippine Journal of Public Administration* (1966). JA26.P5.

Hayes, C. J. *Report on the Public Service Commissions of British Commonwealth Countries.* London, Civil Service Commission, 1955. HD2768.G74H3.

Hayward, Jack, and Olga A. Narkiewicz, eds. *Planning in Europe.* London, Croom Helm, 1978. HC240.P573.

Heidenheimer, Arnold J., ed. *Political Corruption*: *Readings in Comparative Analysis*. New York, Holt Rinehardt, 1970. JF1525.E8H42 1970.

Heller, Peter S., and Alan A. Tait. *Government Employment and Pay*: *Some International Comparisons*. Washington, International Monetary Fund, Occasional Paper 24, 1983. Covers 57 countries. UN9MF 1-83P24.

Heper, Metin, *et al.* "The role of bureaucracy and regime types: a comparative study of Turkish and South Korean higher civil servants," *Administration and Society* 12,2 (Aug. 1980), 137–157. JA1.J572.

Hofstra, Hendrik J. *New Techniques of Budget Preparation and Management*. Brussels, International Institute of Administrative Sciences, 1965. Surveys numerous countries. HJ2005.H64.

Indian Journal of Public Administration, special issue: *Secrecy in Government*, XXV, 4 (October–December 1979). Recent changes in developed democracies. JQ201.I55.

International Political Science Association, and Henry Walter Ehrmann, *Interest Groups on Four Continents*. Pittsburgh, University Press, 1958. JF529.I5.

Inter-parliamentary Union. *Parliaments, a Comparative Study on the Structure and Functioning of Representative Institutions in 41 Countries*. London, Cassell, 1962. (Part on control of the executive). DOC.ZZ IPU 62P11.

Kernaghan, Kenneth, and O. P. Dwivedi, eds. *Ethics in the Public Service*: *Comparative Perspectives*. Brussels, Internat. Inst. of Admin. Sciences, 1983. Canada, Ghana, U.K. and Japan.

Kersell, John E. *Parliamentary Supervision of Delegated Legislation*: *The U.K., Australia, New Zealand and Canada*. London, Stevens, 1960. JF423.K4.

Knight, Kenneth W., and K. W. Wiltshire. *Formulating Government Budgets*: *Aspects of Australian and North American Experience*. St. Lucia, Queensland Univ. Press, 1977. HJ2052.K65.

Kruisinga, H. J. *The Balance Between Centralization and Decentralization in Managerial Control*. Leiden, Stenfert-Kroese, 1954. HD31.K7.

Kuruvilla, P. K. *A Comparative Study of Recruitment and Training of Higher Federal Civil Servants in Canada and India*. Ottawa, Carleton Univ. Ph.D. thesis, 1969.

Leman, Christopher. *The Collapse of Welfare Reform*: *Political Institutions, Policy, and the Poor in Canada and the United States*. Cambridge, Mass., M.I.T. Press, 1980. HV91.L38.

Levine, Robert A., *et al.*, eds. *Evaluation Research and Practice*: *Comparative Perspectives*. Beverley Hills, Calif., Sage, 1981. Essay by Levine covers 9 countries. AZ191.A43 1979.

Mathur, R. N. "Legislative control of delegated legislation: Survey," *Indian Journal of Political Science* (Jan.–Mar. 1960), pp. 25–37. U.S., U.K., N. Ireland, Irish Republic, Australia, New Zealand, India. JA26.I525.

McCrensky, Edward. *Scientific Manpower in Europe*. London, New York, Pergamon Press, 1958. Q127.E8M2.

McLean, J. E., ed. *The Public Service and University Education*. Princeton, Princeton University Press, 1949. JK421.M325.

Musolf, Lloyd D. "Mixed enterprise in a developmental perspective: France, Italy and Japan," *Jour. Compar. Admin.* 3, 2 (Aug. 1971), 131–168. Has a bibliography. JA1.J57.

Nedjati, Z. M., and J. E. Trice. *English and Continental Systems of Administrative Law*. Amsterdam, North Holland, 1978.

"New techniques in government budgeting," *Public Administration* (London) 48, 3 (Autumn 1970). Articles on Canada, Britain, France and Germany. JA8.P8.

Normanton, E. L. *The Accountability and Audit of Governments*. Manchester, M. Univ. Press; New York, Praeger, 1966. HJ199N6. Surveys 11 countries. HJ199.N6.

OECD. *Employment in the Public Sector*. Paris, OECD, 1982. Compares the OECD countries. ZZ EC 82E53.

Robson, W. A. "The missing dimension of government," *Political Quarterly* 42, 3 (July, September 1971), pp. 233–246. On regions, esp. in Britain and France. JA8.P72.

Rose, Richard, ed. *Public Employment in Western Nations*. Cambridge, Cambridge Univ. Press, 1985. Britain, France, Germany, Italy, Sweden, U.S. JF1601.P86.

Rose, Richard, ed. *The Dynamics of Public Policy: A Comparative Analysis*. London, Sage, 1976. Cases from U.K., W. Germany, Sweden, Austria, Ireland, Canada. H61.D96.

Rose, Richard, and B. Guy Peters. *Can Government Go Bankrupt?* N.Y.: Basic Books, 1978. U.S.A., Britain, France, Germany, Italy, Sweden. HJ141.R64.

Rowat, Donald C., ed. *Administrative Secrecy in Developed Countries*. New York, Columbia University Press, and London, Macmillan, 1979. Chs. on 12 countries. K3560.S413.

Rowat, Donald C., ed. *Bureaucracy in Developed Democracies: Comparative Essays*. Ottawa, Dept. of Political Science, Carleton Univ., 1986. JF1351.B87.

Rowat, Donald C., ed. *Global Comparisons in Public Administration*. Ottawa, Dept. of Political Science, Carleton Univ., 2nd 1984. JF1351.G56 1984.

Rowat, Donald C., ed. *The Government of Federal Capitals*. Toronto, University of Toronto Press, 1973. Chs. on 17 capitals. JF1900.R69.

Rowat, Donald C., ed. *International Handbook on Local Government Reorganization*. Westport, Greenwood Press, 1980. Covers many developed and developing countries. JS67.148.

Rowat, Donald C., ed. *The Ombudsman: Citizen's Defender*. Toronto, University of Toronto Press, 2nd 1968. JC578.R6 1968.

Rowat, Donald C., ed. *The Ombudsman Plan: The Worldwide Spread of an Idea*. Lanham, Md., Univ. Press of America, 2nd rev. ed. 1985. JF1525.04R68 1985.

Rowat, Donald C., ed. *Public Access to Government Documents: A Comparative Perspective*. Toronto, Ontario Commission on Freedom of Information and Individual Privacy, 1979. DOC.CA2ONAJ 811-78P03.

Schaffer, Heinz, *et al.*, eds. *Quantitative Analyses of Law: A Comparative Empirical Study*. Budapest, Academiai Kiado, 1986. Sources of law in Eastern and Western Europe.

Schwartz, Bernard. *French Administrative Law and the Common-Law World*. New York, New York University Press, 1954. KJV4669.S38.

Scott, James C. *Comparative Political Corruption*. Englewood Cliffs, Prentice-Hall, 1972. Early England, U.S., Thailand, Ghana, India. JF1081.S35.

Seabury, Paul. *Universities in the Western World*. N.Y., Free Press, 1975. LB2331.4. U54.

Sharkansky, Ira. *Wither the State? Politics and Public Enterprise in Three Countries*. Chatham, N.J.: Chatham, 1979. Australia, Israel and U.S. HD3850.S45.

Sharpe, L. J., ed. *Decentralist Trends in Western Democracies*. London, Sage, 1979. JS113.D42.

Skeoch, L. A., and I. Trakhtenberg. *Economic Planning: The Relevance of West European Experience for Canada*. Montreal, Canadian Trade Committee, 1963. On Sweden and France. HC115.S62.

Smith, Brian C. *Field Administration, An Aspect of Decentralisation*. London, Routledge, and N.Y., Humanities, 1967. Britain, Burma and Nigeria. JS113.S6 1967.

Smith, M. H. "Thoughts on a British conseil d'état," *Public Administration* (Spring 1967). JA8.P8.

Snow, Sir C. P. *Science and Government*. Cambridge, Mass., Harvard University Press, 1961. Compares Britain, U.S. and Russia. Q127.G4S62.

Stacey, Frank A. *Ombudsmen Compared*. Oxford, Clarendon, 1978. JF1525.O45S83.

Street, Harry. *Governmental Liability: A Comparative Study*. Cambridge, Eng., Cambridge University Press, 1953. K967.S87.

Subramaniam, V. "Graduates in the public services: a comparative study of attitudes," *Public Admin*. 32 (1957), 373–. On India, Australia and New Zealand. JA8.P8.

Taylor, Charles Lewis, ed. *Why Governments Grow: Measuring Public Sector Size*. Beverly Hills, Sage, 1983. Netherlands, U.K., U.S.S.R., East Europe, and statistics on other advanced countries. HJ2005.W37.

Toren, Martin. "The influence of political culture on public administration in Britain and France." Ottawa, Carleton Univ. M.A. essay, 1969.

United Nations, Dept. of Economic Affairs. *Budgetary Structure and Classification of Government Accounts*. 1951. Italy, Sweden, U.S., U.S.S.R. DOC.ST/ECA/8.

United Nations. *Government Accounting and Budget Execution*. 1952. France, Netherlands, Sweden, U.S. DOC.UN/ST/ECA/1-6.

Walsh, Annmarie Hauck. *The Public's Business: The Politics and Practices of Government Corporations*. Cambridge, MIT Press, 1978. HD3887.W34.

Waterston, Albert. *Development Planning: Lessons of Experience*. Baltimore, Johns Hopkins Press, 1965. HD82.W28.

Wildavsky, Aaron B. *Budgeting: A Comparative Theory of Budgetary Processes*. Boston, Little, Brown, 1975. HJ2009.W54.

William, R. H., ed. *Planning in Europe*. London, Allen & Unwin, 1984. Covers the 10 members of the EEC. HT169.E85P58.

Wraith, Ronald, and E. Simpkins. *Corruption in Developing Countries*. London, Allen & Unwin, 1963. Compares Nigeria and earlier Britain. JQ1876.W7.

Wright, Vincent, and Y. Meny, eds. *Centre-Periphery Relations in Western Europe*. London, Allen & Unwin, 1985. JN94.A38S827.

Author Index

Authors contributing to this volume are followed by the page range of their chapter.

Aberbach, Joel D., 419–440, 21, 47, 156, 417, 427, 437, 438, 439, 455
Abert, James Goodyear, 253
Abraham, Henry J., 291
Adams, Bruce, 417
Adams, J. C., 312
Adie, Robert, F., 99
Akzin, Benjamin, 372
Albrow, Martin, 88, 97
Alcazar, Mariano Baena del, 271
Allardt, E., 168, 270
Allart, E., 168
Allen, K., 312
Alley, R. M., 21, 22
Allison, Graham, 421, 438
Allum, P. A., 312
Anderson, Charles W., 271
Anderson, Malcolm, 291
Anderson, Paul, 153
Anderson, Stanley V., 156
Andreae, Clemens, 219
Andren, Nils, 156
Andrew, C., 64
Anton, Thomas J., 156
Appleby, Paul, 409
Armstrong, John, 97
Armstrong, Lord, 435
Arndt, Hans J., 337
Arnesen, B., 168
Arter, D., 168
Ashford, Douglas E., 291, 433, 434, 440

Aucoin, P., 63
Ausabel, David P., 3, 20
Avril, Pierre, 291

Barile, P., 312
Barker, Ernest, 88, 97
Barrington, T. J., 171–188, 188
Baylis, T. A., 203
Bell, David S., 271
Belorgey, Gérard, 291
Beltrán, Miguel, 257–272, 272
Benjamin, R., 440
Bentham, Jeremy, 89
Bernt, Jan F., 116
Berthold, T. M., 21, 22
Bieusses, Pierre Subra de, 271
Birch, A. H., 84
Birnbaum, Pierre, 290, 291, 431, 439
Blondel, Jean, 291
Boag, P. W., 16, 21
Board, Joseph B., 156
Bodiguel, Jean-Luc, 291
Boeschenstein, H., 203
Bogason, Peter, 133–145
Boston, Jonathan, 22
Bottomore, T. B., 13
Bours, A., 253
Bovens, M. A. P., 253
Braybrooke, David, 440

Subject Index